The Longman Handbook of World History since 1914

The Longman Handbook of World History since 1914

Chris Cook and John Stevenson

Longman

London and New York

Longman Group UK Limited,
Longman House, Burnt Mill, Harlow,
Essex CM20 2JE, England
and Associated Companies throughout the world.

Published in the United States of America
by Longman Inc., New York

First published 1991

British Library Cataloguing in Publication Data
Cook, Chris *1945–*
  The Longman handbook of world history since 1914.
  1. World, 1900
  I. Title II. Stevenson, John *1946–*
909.82

ISBN 0-582-48588-6 CSD
ISBN 0-582-48589-4 PPR

Library of Congress Cataloging in Publication Data
Cook, Chris, 1945–
  The Longman handbook of world history since 1914 / Chris Cook and
John Stevenson.
    p. cm. – (Longman handbook to history)
  Includes bibliographical references.
  ISBN 0-582-48588-6 (U.S.). – ISBN 0-582-48589-4 (pbk.: U.S.)
  1. History, Modern – 20th century – Handbooks, manuals, etc.
I. Stevenson, John, 1946– . II. Title. III. Series.
D421.C64 1991
909.82 – dc20
89-77970
CIP

Set in Linotron 202 9/10 pt Universe

Produced by Longman Singapore Publishers (Pte) Ltd.
Printed in Singapore

Contents

viii

List of maps

Preface and acknowledgements

This handbook attempts to provide a convenient reference work for both teachers and students of modern world history from 1914 to the present day. It is a much condensed work, bringing together chronological, statistical and tabular information which is not to be found elsewhere within the confines of a single volume. The handbook covers not only political and diplomatic events but also the broader fields of social and economic history. It includes biographies of important individuals, a glossary of commonly used historical terms, and a topic bibliography. No book of this type can be entirely comprehensive, nor is it intended to substitute for textbooks and more detailed reading, but we have attempted to include those facts and figures which we believe are most useful for understanding courses in contemporary world history. The coverage of the volume ranges in time from the outbreak of the First World War to the end of the 1980s. It is hoped that the volume has included essential material on all the major themes of world history. The authors would, however, welcome constructive ideas and suggestions for future editions of this book.

Both authors would like to acknowledge the considerable help and advice in the preparation of this book of Harry Harmer and Ted Cater. For secretarial help, we are indebted as ever to the long labours of Linda Hollingworth. Finally, thanks to all those who have helped us at Longman.

The publishers would like to acknowledge the following for permission to use copyright material: Weidenfeld and Nicolson, London for the use of tables from C. J. Argyle, *Japan at War, 1937–45*, 1976; G.P. Putnam & Sons, New York and R. Goralski for the use of a table from R. Goralski, *World War II Almanac, 1931–1945*, 1981.

Chris Cook

John Stevenson   1 May 1990

In memory of
John Michael Cook
(1930–1990)

Section I
Political history

Political events
Europe

The First World War

1914 June 28   Francis Ferdinand assassinated in Sarajevo.
July 28   Austria-Hungary declares war on Serbia.
Aug. 1   Germany declares war on Russia.
Aug. 2   Germany invades Luxembourg.
    British fleet mobilized.
Aug. 3   Germany declares war on France.
Aug. 4   Germany invades Belgium;
    Britain and Belgium declare war on Germany.
Aug. 5   Turkey closes Dardanelles.
Aug. 5–12   Germans seize Liege.
Aug. 6   Austria declares war on Russia.
Aug. 7   British troops arrive in France.
Aug. 10   Austrians invade Russian Poland.
Aug. 10–20   Austrian advance on Serbia halted at Battle of the Jadar.
Aug. 12   Britain and France declare war on Austria.
Aug. 14–24   French suffer defeats in Lorraine, the Ardennes and on the Sambre;
    British retreat from Mons.
Aug. 17–20   Russians invade East Prussia and Galicia.
Aug. 20   Germans occupy Brussels.
Aug. 22   Hindenburg becomes German Commander in East Prussia.
Aug. 26–28   Germans cross the Meuse.
Aug. 26–29   Russians defeated at Tannenberg.
Sept. 5–9   Battle of the Marne.
Sept. 5–11   Austrians defeated in the Battle of Rawa Ruska.
Sept. 8–16   Serbs halt second Austrian invasion.
Sept. 10–14   Russians forced to retreat from East Prussia following Battle of the Masurian Lakes.
Sept. 14   Falkenhayn replaces Moltke as German Commander-in-Chief.
Sept. 14–18   Allied offensive fails at first Battle of the Aisne.
Sept. 27   Russians invade Hungary.
Sept. 28–Nov. 1   Austro-German offensive in east checked, leading to withdrawal from Poland.
Sept.–Oct.   'Race for the Sea': series of outflanking manoeuvres towards the Channel fails.
Oct. 9   Germans take Antwerp.

Manpower and casualties of major combatants, 1914–18

	Standing armies and trained reserves	Total mobilized	Killed or died of wounds
Austria–Hungary	3,000,000	7,800,000	1,200,000
British Empire	975,000	8,904,000	908,000
France	4,017,000	8,410,000	1,363,000
Germany	4,500,000	11,000,000	1,774,000
Italy	1,251,000	5,615,000	460,000
Russia	5,971,000	12,000,000	1,700,000
Turkey	210,000	2,850,000	325,000
United States	309,208	3,200,000	50,300

Peace treaties after World War I

The Treaty of Versailles, 28 June 1919

1. Germany surrendered territory:
   (a) Alsace-Lorraine to France.
   (b) Eupen-Malmédy to Belgium (following plebiscite in 1920).
   (c) Northern Schleswig to Denmark (following plebiscite in 1920).
   (d) Pozania and West Prussia to Poland, Upper Silesia to Poland (following plebiscite in 1921).
   (e) Saar put under League of Nations control for 15 years and mining interests under French control (returned to Germany following 1935 plebiscite).
   (f) Danzig (Gdansk) put under League of Nations control.
   (g) Memel placed under Allied control, then transferred to Lithuania.
   (h) German colonies become mandated territories of the League of Nations: German East Africa (to Britain); German South-West Africa (to South Africa); Cameroons and Togoland (to Britain and France); German Samoa (to New Zealand); German New Guinea (to Australia); Marshall Islands and Pacific Islands north of the Equator (to Japan).
2. Germany lost concessions and trading rights in China, Egypt and Middle East.
3. Demilitarization of the Rhineland and Heligoland.
4. German army limited to 100,000 men, denied U-boats and airforce.
5. Army of occupation on west bank of the Rhine and bridgeheads at Cologne, Coblenz and Mainz from January 1920.
6. Germany accepts 'war guilt' clause.
7. Germany agreed to pay reparations and accepted responsibility for war damage.
8. The Treaty of Brest-Litovsk declared void; Germany required to evacuate Baltic States and other occupied territory.
9. The Covenant of the League of Nations written into the Treaty.

The Treaty of Saint-Germain, 10 September 1919

1. The Austro-Hungarian Empire was effectively dissolved:
   (a) Austria and Hungary to become separate states with total loss of control over other former parts of the Austro-Hungarian Empire.
   (b) New state of Czechoslovakia created.
   (c) New state of Yugoslavia set up.
   (d) Galicia ceded to Poland.
   (e) Transylvania ceded to Romania.
   (f) South Tyrol, Trentino and Istria ceded to Italy.
   (g) Plebiscite to define boundary with Austria in southern Carinthia.
2. Austria forbidden to unite with Germany without League of Nations approval.
3. Austrian army limited to 30,000 men.

Oct. 12–Nov. 11   First Battle of Ypres: Germans fail to reach Channel ports; Allied counter-attack fails.

Oct. 16   'Race for the Sea' concluded by Battle of the Yser.

Nov. 1   Hindenburg becomes German Commander-in-Chief on Eastern Front.

Nov. 2   Russians renew advance on East Prussia.
Britain declares North Sea a war-zone and begins blockade of Germany.

Nov. 5–Dec. 15   Serbs repel third Austrian invasion.

Nov. 11–Nov. 24   Russians retreat after Battle of Lódź.

Nov. 14   Turkey proclaims Holy War.

Dec. 2   Austrians take Belgrade.

1915 Jan. 8–15   French attack halted by Germans at Battle of Soissons.

Jan. 23   German and Austrian armies launch offensive in Carpathians.

Feb. 7–21   Germans encircle Russian Tenth Army at Battle of Masuria; Austrian attack in Carpathians collapses.

Feb. 11   British air-raid on Ostend and Zeebrugge.

Feb. 18   Germany commences submarine warfare against merchant vessels.

Feb. 19–Mar. 18   British Navy fails to force the Dardanelles Straits.

Mar. 10–13   British advance checked at Battle of Neuve-Chapelle.

Mar. 14–15   Battle of Saint-Eloi.

Mar. 19–20   Germans mount raid on Yarmouth and King's Lynn.

Mar. 31   Zeppelin raids on southern English counties begin.

Apr. 22–May 25   Second Battle of Ypres: Germans employ poison-gas for the first time.

Apr. 25   Allied forces land on Gallipoli Peninsula.

May 2–4   Russian line between Gorlice and Tarnow broken by German-Austrian offensive, forcing Russians to retreat.

May 4   Italy leaves the Triple Alliance.

May 7   *Lusitania* sunk.

May 9–June 18   Second Battle of Artois.

May 15–25   Battle of Festubert.

May 23   Italy enters war on Allied side and declares war on Germany and Austria.

June 1   German air raid on London.

June 20–July 14   German offensive in the Argonne fails.

July 16–18   Russians defeated in Battle of Krasnotav.

Aug. 4–5   Germans enter Warsaw.

Aug. 6–21   Allied attacks in Dardanelles fail.

Sept. 18   Germany limits submarine attacks in view of American hostility.

Sept. 25–Nov. 6   Allied offensives at Loos and in Champagne.

Sept. 28   British enter Kut el Amara after defeating Turks.

Oct. 5   Allied forces land in Salonika.

Oct. 7   Serbian army collapses in face of joint

German-Austrian-Bulgarian offensive, and is evacuated to Corfu.

Dec. 3   Joffre becomes French Commander-in-Chief.
Dec. 7   Turkish forces lay siege to British at Kut el Amara.
Dec. 19   Haig replaces French as British Commander-in-Chief.
Dec. 20   Allied forces evacuated from Anzac and Suvla Bay in Dardanelles (completed 9 Jan 1916).

1916 Feb, 21–Dec. 18 Battle of Verdun results in 550,000 French and 450,000 German casualties.
Mar. 15   Admiral von Tirpitz resigns.
Apr. 29   British surrender at Kut el Amara.
May 15–June 17   Austrians defeat Italians at Asiago but withdraw to strengthen Eastern front.
May 24   Britain introduces conscription.
May 31–June 1   Battle of Jutland.
June 4–Sept. 20   Massive Russian offensive south of Pripet Marshes results in heavy casualties on both sides.
June 5   Arab revolt against Turkish rule begins.
June 6   *HMS Hampshire* sunk: Lord Kitchener drowns.
June 10   Russians cross Dniester.
June 21   Turks begin offensive against Persia.
July 1–Nov. 18   Allied offensive at Battle of the Somme fails to achieve major breakthrough; results in 420,000 British 195,000 French and 400,000 German casualties.
Aug. 26   Italy declares war on Germany.
Aug. 27   Romania enters war and commences invasion of Transylvania.
Aug. 29   Hindenburg becomes German Chief of General Staff.
Sept. 10–Nov. 19   Allied forces launch offensive in Salonika.
Sept. 15   British use tanks for first time during Battle of the Somme.
Oct. 24–Dec. 18   French launch successful counter-attacks at Verdun.
Dec. 3   Nivelle succeeds Joffre as French Commander-in-Chief.
Dec. 6   Bucharest captured; Russians and Romanians forced to retreat.
Dec. 7   Lloyd George forms Coalition government in Britain.
Dec. 12   Central Powers make peace offer.
Dec. 13   British begin offensive in Mesopotamia.
Dec. 30   Allies reject peace offer made by Central Powers.

1917 Jan. 31   Germans announce resumption of unrestricted submarine warfare.
Feb. 23–Apr. 5   Expecting an Allied offensive, Germans withdraw to Hindenburg Line.
Feb. 25   British recapture Kut el Amara.
Mar. 11   British enter Baghdad.
Mar. 12   Revolution in Russia leads to abdication of Tsar Nicholas II.
Mar. 16–19   Germans take stand along Siegfried Line.

Mar. 26–27   British fail to capture Gaza.
Apr. 4   British launch offensive in Artois.
Apr. 6   USA declares war on Germany.
Apr. 9   French begin offensive in Champagne.
Apr. 9–May 3   Canadians take Vimy Ridge during Battle of Arras.
Apr. 16–May 9   French offensive fails at second Battle of the
              Aisne.
Apr. 17–19   British attack fails in second Battle of Gaza.
June 7–8   British capture Messines Ridge.
June 15   Pétain becomes French Commander-in-Chief.
June 20   Outbreak of mutinies in French Army.
June 25   US troops land in France.
July 31–Nov. 6   Third Battle of Ypres results in eventual capture
              of Passchendaele.
Sept. 20   British resume offensive near Ypres.
Oct. 24–Nov. 12   Italians forced to retreat after Battle of
              Caporetto.
Oct. 31–Nov. 7   Turks forced to withdraw following third Battle
              of Gaza.
Nov. 2   Germans retreat behind Aisne-Oise and Ailette
              Canals.
Nov. 4   British forces reach Italian front.
Nov. 6   British take Passchendaele.
Nov. 7   Bolshevik Revolution in Russia.
Nov. 17   Clemenceau becomes French Premier.
Nov. 20–Dec. 3   First mass use of tanks at Battle of Cambrai
              leads to temporary Allied breach of Hindenburg Line.
Dec. 2   Fighting ceases on Russian front.
Dec. 3   Austro-German campaign in Italy suspended.
Dec. 7   USA declares war on Austria-Hungary.
Dec. 9   Romania signs armistice.
              Allenby enters Jerusalem.

1918 Jan. 8   President Wilson issues his Fourteen Points for
              ending the conflict.
Feb. 18   Fighting resumes between Russia and Germany.
Mar. 3   Bolsheviks accept German peace terms at
              Brest-Litovsk.
Mar. 21–Apr. 4   Germans launch offensive on the Somme.
Apr. 9–29   Germans launch offensive on the Lys.
Apr. 14   Foch becomes supreme commander of Allied forces
              in France.
Apr. 22–23   British raid on Zeebrugge.
May 7   Romania concludes Treaty of Bucharest with Central
              Powers.
May 27–June 6   Germans launch offensive on the Aisne.
June 9–13   Germans launch Noyon-Montidier offensive.
June 15–24   Italians repulse Austrian attack across the Piave.
July 13   Final Turkish offensive in Palestine.
July 15–17   Germans launch final (Champagne-Marne) offensive.
July 18–Aug. 6   Allied forces launch Aisne-Marne offensive,
              leading to reduction of Marne salient.

Aug. 8–Sept. 3   Amiens salient is reduced.

Sept. 3   German armies commence retreat to Hindenburg Line.

Sept. 14   Allied armies begin offensive against Bulgarians.

Sept. 19   Turkish army defeated in Battle of Megiddo.

Sept. 25   Bulgaria requests armistice.

Sept. 26   Foch launches final offensive, breaching Hindenburg Line on 27 Sept.

Sept. 29   Bulgaria concludes armistice.

Oct. 1   French forces take St Quentin.
               British forces enter Damascus.

Oct. 3   Prince Max of Baden becomes German Chancellor.

Oct. 9–10   British take Cambrai and Le Cateau.

Oct. 14   USA demands cessation of submarine warfare.

Oct. 17   British reach Ostend.

Oct. 20   Submarine warfare abandoned by Germany.

Oct. 24–Nov. 4   Italians defeat Austrians at Vittorio Veneto.

Oct. 31   Armistice with Turkey comes into force.

Nov. 3   Austria agrees to Allied peace terms.
               Mutiny in German High Seas fleet.

Nov. 4   Armistice concluded on Italian front.
               Germans withdraw to Antwerp-Meuse line.

Nov. 9   Revolution in Berlin leads to proclamation of Republic.

Nov. 10   William II flees to Holland; Emperor Charles of Austria abdicates.

Nov. 11   Armistice concluded on Western Front.

Nov. 21   German High Seas fleet surrenders to British.

4. Reparations required for war damage.
5. Covenant of League of Nations written into the Treaty.

The Treaty of the Trianon, 4 June 1920

1. Hungary accepted break-up of Austro-Hungarian Empire and surrender of territory to Romania, Czechoslovakia, Yugoslavia, Poland, Italy and the new Austrian republic.
2. Hungarian army limited to 35,000 men.
3. Hungary required to pay reparations.
4. Covenant of the League of Nations written into the Treaty.

The Treaty of Sèvres, 10 August 1920 (*never ratified by Turkey*)

1. Turkish Empire lost territory:
   (a) Cyprus to Britain.
   (b) Rhodes, the Dodecanese, and Adalia ceded to Italy.
   (c) Part of European Turkey to Bulgaria.
   (d) Eastern Thrace to Greece; Greek claims to Chios and other islands recognized; Greece allowed to occupy Smyrna for five years until a plebiscite held.
   (e) Hejaz and Arabia become independent.
   (f) League of Nations mandates over Syria (to France); Palestine, Iraq and Transjordan (to Britain).
2. The Straits placed under international control.
3. Turkey occupied by British, French and Italian troops.
4. The Covenant of the League of Nations was written into the Treaty.

The Treaty of Neuilly, 27 November 1919

1. Bulgaria lost territory:
   (a) Territory along Bulgaria's western boundary ceded to Yugoslavia.
   (b) Part of western Thrace ceded to Greece.
2. Bulgaria gained territory from European Turkey.
3. Bulgarian army limited to 20,000 men.
4. Bulgaria made liable for reparations.
5. The Covenant of the League of Nations written into the Treaty.

Treaty of Lausanne, 24 July 1923

1. Turkey surrendered its claims to territories of the Ottoman Empire occupied by non-Turks, effectively surrendering the Arab lands.
2. The Turks retained Constantinople and Eastern Thrace in Europe; both sides of Greek-Turkish border demilitarized.
3. Turkey takes Smyrna from Greece but surrenders all the Aegean Islands except Imbros and Tenedos which return to Turkey.

4. Turkey recognizes the annexation of Cyprus by Britain and of the Dodecanese by Italy.
5. Turkey left free of foreign troops.
6. The Straits were declared to be demilitarized (in July 1936 by the Montreux Convention Turkey was allowed to refortify the Straits).
7. No restrictions were placed on Turkey's armed forces and no reparations required.

The Russian Revolution and Stalin's Russia 1914–1941

1914	Aug. 1	Germany declares war on Russia.
	Aug. 26	Russia defeated at Battle of Tannenberg.
	Sept. 3–12	Russians force Austrians from Galicia.
	Sept. 5	Russia suffers severe losses at battle of the Masurian Lakes.
1915	May	Austro-German offensive in Galicia defeats Russians.
	July	Further Austro-German offensive leads to over a million Russian casualties by the autumn.
	Aug. 1	Duma meets to consider the way the war is being conducted.
	Aug. 22	Six parties in the Duma form the Progressive Bloc and demand a responsible ministry.
	Sep. 6	Tsar assumes supreme command of the armed forces.
	Sept. 8	Reform programme put before council of ministers by Progressive Bloc.
	Sept. 15	Tsar rejects offer of resignation by his ministers to make way for a more popular administration.
	Sept. 16	Tsar prorogues Duma.
1916	Feb. 15	Duma meets; Goremykin replaced as Prime Minister by Sturmer.
	June-Oct.	Brusilov offensive gains territory but fails to achieve decisive victory and costs over a million casualties.
	Sept.-Oct.	Wave of strikes in Russia; sporadic mutinies of soldiers at the front.
	Oct.	Survey of manpower resources reveals that after February 1917 the Russian army would begin to decline in numbers.
1917	Feb. 27	Duma meets.
	Mar. 7	Tsar leaves Petrograd for army GHQ; beginnings of large-scale demonstrations in the capital.
	Mar. 8	Queues at bakeries and crowds continue to demonstrate against the regime.
	Mar. 9	Police fire on crowds.
	Mar. 10	Strikes break out and soldiers join with the people; the Tsar orders suppression of the trouble.
	Mar. 11	Police fire at demonstrators, but more soldiers join the protesters. Tsar prorogues Duma.
	Mar. 12	Formation of Committee of State Duma to replace Tsarist government. Formation of Petrograd Soviet of Workers' and Soldiers' Deputies.
	Mar. 13	Soviet news sheet *Izvestya* calls on people to take affairs into their own hands.
	Mar. 14	Appointment of Ministers of the Provisional

	Government. 'Army Order No. 1' issued by Petrograd Soviet puts armed forces under its authority and urges rank and file to elect representatives to the Soviet.
Mar. 15	Tsar abdicates in favour of his brother, Grand Duke Michael, at the same time confirming the new ministry and asking the country to support it. Duke Michael chose not to accept the throne unless he was bid to do so by the Assembly.
	The Provisional Government forbids the use of force against rioting peasants.
Mar. 16	Constituent Assembly meets; abdication of Grand Duke Michael.
Apr. 11	All-Russian Conference of Soviets overwhelmingly votes to continue war in spite of Bolshevik opposition.
Apr. 16	Lenin arrives back in Petrograd.
May 3–5	Bolshevik-organised demonstrations by garrison in Petrograd against the Ministers Guchkov and Milyukov. Kornilov resigns command of forces in Petrograd and Milyukov and Guchkov resign from the government.
May 18	Kerensky helps to reorganize Provisional Government.
June 18	Start of renewed offensive on southern front.
June 26	Soldiers at front refuse to obey orders. Kornilov insists on offensive being called off and is appointed commander-in-chief.
July 2	Start of northern offensive backed by Kerensky, Minister of War. Germans and Austrians drive Russians back after early successes.
July 12	Provisional Government restores capital punishment and courts martial.
July 16–18	Bolsheviks organize demonstrations by sailors and Red Guards but the unrest is put down by loyal troops.
July 18	Fearing arrest, Lenin flees to Finland.
July 20	Lvov and Kadet ministers resign.
July 21	Formation of new Government with Kerensky as Prime Minister.
Aug. 3	Kerensky resigns. Party leaders give him a free hand to form new government.
Aug. 25–28	Kerensky holds Moscow State Conference to settle differences with Kornilov, but fails to reach agreement.
Sept. 3	Riga falls to Germans.
Sept. 8	Troops begin to move against Petrograd and Kerensky denounces Kornilov 'plot' against the government. Collapse of movement, followed by arrest of Kornilov and fellow generals.
Sept. 19	Bolshevik majority in Moscow Soviet.
Oct. 6	Trotsky becomes Chairman of Petrograd Soviet.
Oct. 23	Decision by Bolshevik Central Committee to organize

	an armed rising.
Oct. 25	Formation of Military Revolutionary Committee by Bolsheviks.
Nov. 1	Provisional government tries to remove units from the Petrograd garrison, but Bolsheviks prevent this.
Nov. 2	Parliament refuses to give Kerensky powers to suppress the Bolsheviks.
Nov. 6	Bolsheviks organize headquarters in Peter and Paul fortress and move on strategic points. Lenin takes command.
Nov. 7	Bolsheviks seize power in Petrograd, taking key installations and services. The Winter Palace cut off and ministers of provisional government arrested. Kerensky flees. Lenin announces the transfer of power to the Military Revolutionary Committee and the victory of the socialist revolution.
Nov. 8	Lenin makes the Decree on Peace, an appeal for a just peace without annexations and indemnities, and the Decree on Land, affirming that all land is the property of the people. A Bolshevik government is formed.
Nov. 13	Counter-offensive by Kerensky against Petrograd fails.
Nov. 15	Bolsheviks establish power in Moscow.
Dec. 1	Left-wing social revolutionaries enter government after agreement with Bolsheviks.
Dec. 2	Escape of Kornilov and fellow generals from prison in Bykhov.
Dec. 3	Bolsheviks occupy Supreme Headquarters at Mogilev.
Dec. 17	Russia and Germany agree a ceasefire and start negotiations for a peace treaty in Brest-Litovsk (22nd).
Dec. 20	Establishment of the *Cheka*, the secret political police of post-revolutionary Russia.
1918 Jan. 18	Opening of Constituent Assembly.
Jan. 19	Constituent Assembly dispersed.
Feb. 1–14	Introduction of the Gregorian calendar.
Feb. 9	Central Council of the Ukraine concludes separate peace with Central Powers, having declared its independence.
Feb. 10	Brest-Litovsk negotiations broken off after Germae ultimatum.
Feb. 18	Germany resumes hostilities in the Ukraine.
Feb. 24	Soviet Government decides to accept Germany peace ultimatum.
Mar. 2	Germans occupy Kiev.
Mar. 3	Russians sign Treaty of Brest-Litovsk, giving up large areas of pre-Revolutionary Russia (see p. 255). German troops continue to advance into central Russia and the Crimea.

Mar. 12	Soviet Government moves from Petrograd to Moscow.
Mar. 13	Trotsky appointed Peoples' Commissar of War.
Apr. 5	Allied ships and troops arrive in Murmansk.
Apr. 13	Kornilov killed fighting with anti-Bolshevik 'Volunteer army'.
	Bolsheviks mount drive against anarchists and other deviant elements.
	Germans take Odessa.
Apr. 14	Germans and Finns occupy Helsinki.
Apr. 29	Germans set up puppet Ukrainian government.
May	Georgia, Armenia, and Azerbaijan declare independence.
May 8	Germans occupy Rostov.
May 14	Czech Legion (ex-prisoners recruited into service against the Central Powers) clash with Soviets at Chelyabinsk on their way to Vladivostok.
May 25	Revolt of Czech Legion who seize eastern part of Trans-Siberian Railway.
May 29	Partial conscription introduced for Red Army.
June 23	Allied reinforcements arrive in Murmansk.
July 16	Execution of Imperial family at Ekaterinburg.
Aug. 2	Establishment of anti-Bolshevik Government at Archangel, followed by landing of more Allied troops.
Aug. 6	White forces take Kazan.
Aug. 14	Allied forces land at Baku. British, Japanese and American forces land at Vladivostok.
Sept. 10	Bolsheviks take Kazan.
Sept. 13	Allied forces leave Baku.
Sept. 23	'White' forces set up Directorate as All Russian Provisional Government.
Oct. 9	Directorate fixes capital at Omsk.
Nov. 13	Following armistice between Allies and Germany, the Soviet Government denounces the Brest-Litovsk Treaty.
Nov. 18	Directorate suppressed at Omsk. Kolchak assumes supreme power.
Dec. 14	Collapse of Skoropadsky regime in the Ukraine.
Dec. 17	French land in Odessa.
1919 Jan. 3	Red Army takes Riga and Kharkov.
Feb. 6	Red Army occupies Kiev.
Feb. 15	Denikin assumes supreme command of White forces in south-east Russia.
Mar. 2–7	First Congress of Communist International in Moscow. Creation of Politburo and Communist International.
Mar. 13	Spring offensive by Kolchak.
Mar. 21	Allies decide to withdraw forces from Russia.
Apr. 5	British and Indian troops leave Transcaspia.
Apr. 8	French evacuate Odessa.

Apr. 10	Soviet troops enter Crimea.
May 19	Denikin begins offensive against Bolsheviks.
June 4	Kolchak defeated in centre and south, but Denikin continues advance, capturing Kharkov by end of month.
July 15	Red Army takes Chelyabinsk.
Aug. 23	Denikin takes Odessa.
Aug. 31	Denikin occupies Kiev.
Sept. 19	Allies evacuate Archangel.
Sept. 28	Yudenich reaches suburbs of Petrograd.
Oct. 14–20	Denikin takes Orel, but is forced to retreat; general retreat of White armies.
Nov. 14	Defeat of Yudenich by Red Army and occupation of Omsk.
Dec. 12	Red Army occupies Kharkov.
Dec. 16	Red Army occupies Kiev.

1920	Jan. 4	Abdication of Kolchak as Supreme Ruler.
	Jan. 8	Red Army takes Rostov.
	Jan. 15	Czechs hand Kolchak over to revolutionaries in control of Irkutsk.
	Feb. 7	Execution of Kolchak.
	Feb 19	Northern government at Archangel collapses.
	Apr. 4	Denikin succeeded by Wrangel.
	Apr. 24	Outbreak of Russo-Polish War. Poles invade the Ukraine.
	May 6	Polish forces take Kiev.
	June 12	Red Army retakes Kiev.
	July 11	Russian counter-attack takes Minsk and Vilna (14th).
	July 20	Second Congress of Communist International.
	Aug. 17	Russian forces almost reach Warsaw, but are beaten back by Polish counter-offensive.
	Sept. 21	Start of Russo-Polish peace negotiations.
	Oct. 12	Russo-Polish provisional peace treaty.
	Oct. 25	Red Army offensive against Wrangel.
	Nov. 2	Wrangel forced to retreat to the Crimea.
	Nov. 11–14	Defeat and evacuation of Wrangel's forces in the Crimea.

1921	Feb.	Strikes in Petrograd. Red Army invades Georgia.
	Mar. 1	Beginnings of revolt of Kronstadt sailors.
	Mar. 5	Trotsky delivers ultimatum to sailors.
	Mar. 16–17	Bombardment and assault of Kronstadt.
	Mar. 18	Kronstadt Rising crushed. Treaty of Riga defines Russo-Polish frontier. 10th Party Congress; Lenin introduces New Economic Policy (N.E.P.), allowing peasants to keep their surplus grain for disposal on the open market.
	Apr.	Beginnings of famine in the Volga regions.
	Aug.	Famine relief agreements signed with America and the Red Cross.

1922	Mar.–Apr.	11th Party Congress. Stalin becomes General Secretary. Lenin forced to convalesce after operation

		to remove two bullets, the result of Kaplan's attempted assassination in 1918.
	Apr. 16	Treaty of Rapallo with Germany establishes close economic and military co-operation.
	May 26	Lenin has stroke.
	Oct. 2	Lenin returns to Moscow.
	Dec.	Lenin's second stroke.
	Dec. 23–26	Lenin dictates the *Letter to the Congress*.
	Dec. 30	Formation of Union of Soviet Socialist Republics, federating Russia, the Ukraine, White Russia and Transcaucasia.
1923	Jan. 4	Lenin adds codicil to the *Letter*, warning of Stalin's ambitions.
	Mar.	Lenin's third stroke.
	Apr.	12th Party Congress.
	July	Constitution of USSR published.
1924	Jan. 21	Death of Lenin.
	Feb. 1	Great Britain recognizes Soviet Union.
	Feb. 3	Rykov elected prime minister.
	May 23	13th Party Conference opens. Zinoviev demands Trotsky's recantation of belief in 'Permanent Revolution'.
1925	Jan. 16	Trotsky dismissed as War Commissar.
	Jan. 21	Japan recognizes Soviet Union.
	April	14th Party Conference adopts 'socialism in one country'.
1926	Oct. 19	Trotsky and Kamenev expelled from Politburo.
1927	May 26	Britain temporarily severs relations with Soviet Union because of continued Bolshevik propaganda.
	Nov.	Trotskyists organize political demonstrations and Trotsky expelled from Party.
	Dec.	15th Party Conference condemns all deviations from party line and resolves upon the collectivization of agriculture. Stalin emerges as dominant voice.
1928	Jan.	Trotsky banished to provinces.
	Spring	Serious grain procurement crisis.
	Sept.	Bukharin publishes opposition articles in *Pravda* in support of peasants.
	Oct. 1	Beginning of First Five-Year Plan, aimed at developing heavy industries.
	Nov.	Bukharin and Tomsky exiled to Turkey.
1929	Jan.	Trotsky exiled to Turkey.
	Autumn	Start of forced collectivization and dekulakization.
	Nov. 17	Bukharin and other 'rightists' expelled from Party.
1930	Jan.	Quickening of tempo of collectivization; resistance harshly dealt with by force and deportation. Widespread disorder and destruction in rural areas.
	Mar.	Stalin publishes *Dizzy with Success*, calling for slowing down of collectivization.

	Nov.	Trial of so-called 'Industrial Party' for
	Dec.	alleged conspiracy within the State Planning Commission, Gosplan.
1931	Mar.	Trial of Mensheviks.
	July	Harvest failure as a result of chaos of collectivization.
1932	Apr.	Central Committee resolves reform of literary and artistic organizations.
		Beginnings of famine in Ukraine and other parts of Russia.
	Dec.	Introduction of internal passport.
1933	Nov.	Second Five-Year Plan inaugurated. USA recognizes the Soviet Government.
1934	Jan.	17th Party Conference.
	July	GPU (former *Cheka*) reorganised as NKVD.
	Sept.	USSR joins League of Nations.
	Dec.	Assassination of leading Bolshevik Kirov by Nikolayev leads Central Executive Committee to issue a directive ordering summary trial and execution of 'terrorists' without appeal.
	Dec. 28–29	Nikolayev and 13 'accomplices' tried in secret and executed.
1935	Jan.	Zinoviev, Kamenev and 17 others tried in secret for 'moral responsibility' for Kirov's assassination and sentenced to imprisonment. Widespread arrests of 'oppositionists'.
	Feb.	Statute regulating collective farms promulgated. Commission appointed to draw up a new constitution.
	June	Draft constitution presented to Central Committee for approval.
	Aug.	'Stakhanovite' programme launched to encourage industrial production.
	Sept.	Reintroduction of ranks in Red Army.
	Dec.	Central Committee declares that the purge is complete.
1936	Jan.	Renewed purge of party members.
	Aug. 19–24	Trial and execution of Zinoviev, Kamenev and other members of the 'Trotskyite-Zinovievite Counter-Revolutionary Bloc' for alleged plotting against the leadership. Tomsky commits suicide following accusations made at their trial.
	Sept. 25	Yagoda dismissed as head of NKVD and replaced by Yezhov.
	Dec. 5	Eighth Congress of Soviets approves the new constitution.
1937	Jan.	Trial of Radek, Pyatakov and 15 others for alleged conspiracy with Trotsky and foreign powers to overthrow the Soviet system. Four are imprisoned, the rest shot.

Mar.	Bukharin, Rykov and Yagoda expelled from the Party.
June	Tukhachevsky, Chief of the General Staff, and other senior officers tried in secret for plotting with Germany and executed. Widespread purge of the armed forces begins, removing over 400 senior officers.

1938 Mar. 2–13 Third Five-Year Plan inaugurated.
Trial of Bukharin, Rykov, Krestinsky, Rakovsky, Yagoda, and other leading party and NKVD members for terrorism, sabotage, treason and espionage.

Mar. 28	Stalin offers support to Czechoslovakia if attacked.
Mar. 29	Russia offers to assist Czechoslovakia if Romania and Poland will allow the passage of Russian troops across their territory; both refuse.
Dec.	Beria succeeds Yezhov as head of NKVD.

1939 Mar.   18th Party Congress.

Apr. 18	USSR proposes defence alliance with Great Britain and France. Offer not taken up by the western allies.
May 3	Molotov replaces Litvinov as commissar of foreign affairs in the USSR.
Aug. 12	Anglo-French mission to USSR begins talks in Moscow.
Aug. 18	Germany makes commercial agreement with USSR.
Aug. 22	Ribbentrop, German Foreign Minister, arrives in Moscow.
Aug. 23	Nazi-Soviet Pact signed. A non-aggression pact, it also contains secret clauses on the partition of Poland and allocation of Finland, Latvia, Estonia and Bessarabia to Soviet sphere of influence.
Aug. 31	Supreme Soviet ratifies German non-aggression pact.
Sept. 17	Red Army invades eastern Poland.
Sept. 22	Red Army occupies Lvov.
Sept. 28	Secret accord with Germany transfers Lithuania to Soviet sphere of influence.
Sept. 29	Estonia, Latvia, and Lithuania conclude treaties with
Oct. 10	USSR allowing Soviet military bases in their territory.
Oct. 12	Talks in Moscow between Finland and USSR. Stalin presents his territorial demands.
Nov. 9	Finns reject Soviet demands.
Nov. 29	USSR breaks off diplomatic relations with Finland.
Nov. 30	Russians bomb Helsinki and Red Army crosses Finnish frontier.
Dec.	Finnish forces inflict heavy defeats on Russia in the south and east.

1940 Feb. 1–12 Major Russian offensive on Karelian isthmus.

Mar. 12	Treaty of Moscow concludes war. Finns cede ten per cent of their territory, including the Karelian isthmus and territory in the north-east.
June 15–17	Soviet troops occupy Lithuania, Latvia, and Estonia.

	June 28	Soviet troops occupy Bessarabia and north-eastern Bukovina.
	July 21	Lithuania, Latvia, and Estonia 'request' incorporation into USSR
	Nov. 17	USSR demands control of Bulgaria and withdrawal of German troops from Finland before joining Tripartite Pact of Germany, Italy and Japan.
	Dec. 18	Hitler issues directive for Operation Barbarossa, the invasion of Russia.
1941	Apr. 13	Non-aggression Pact signed with Japan.
	June 22	Germany invades USSR.
	June 29	State Defence Committee formed.
	July 3	Stalin broadcasts to the people.
	July 12	Anglo-Soviet mutual assistance agreement signed.
	July 15	Fall of Smolensk.
	Aug. 7	Stalin becomes Supreme Commander of the Soviet Armed Forces.
	Sept. 8	Kiev captured.
	Oct. 2	German offensive against Moscow opens.
	Oct. 19	Declaration of state of siege in Moscow. Stalin remains in city, though thousands are evacuated or flee in panic.
	Nov. 27	German forces come within twenty miles of Moscow.
	Dec. 5	Russian counter-offensive in Moscow sector. Hitler abandons Moscow offensive for winter.

Germany 1918–1939

1918 Jan. 8   President Wilson outlines his 'Fourteen Points'.

Mar. 3   Treaty of Brest-Litovsk with Russia. Only Independent Socialists in the Reichstag vote against it.

Mar. 21   Ludendorff begins 'St Michael' offensive on the Western Front.

Mar. 26   After initial success, the first German offensive comes to a halt within 75 miles of Paris.

Apr. 9   Renewed German offensive in Flanders.

May 27   Germans reach the Marne.

July 18   Allied counter-attack begins.

Aug. 8   'The Black Day of the German Army' (Ludendorff) as German forces break under fresh allied offensive.

Sept. 11   Allies break through the Hindenburg line.

Sept. 28   Ludendorff concedes that military victory is impossible.

Sept. 30   Chancellor von Herling resigns in the face of proposals to transform Germany into a democracy.

Oct. 1   Ludendorff asks parliament to make peace.

Oct. 3   Prince Max of Baden appointed Chancellor and asks the USA for an armistice on the basis of the 'Fourteen Points'.

Oct. 12   Germany and Austria-Hungary agree to Wilson's terms that they withdraw from occupied territory, but hesitate over demands for a democratic, civilian government.

Oct. 20   Germany suspends submarine warfare.

Oct. 21   German sailors at Wilhelmshaven mutiny.

Oct. 23   Wilson refuses to make peace with an autocratic regime in Germany.

Oct. 26   Ludendorff is forced to resign. The Reichstag makes the Chancellor dependent on parliament and military appointments are to be countersigned by the Minister of War.

Oct. 29   Kaiser leaves Berlin for army headquarters at Spa.

Nov. 2   Scheidemann, one of the majority Socialist leaders, writes to Prince Max requesting the Kaiser's abdication.

Nov. 3   German Grand Fleet mutinies at Kiel. Sailors set up their own workers' and sailors' councils, mainly for redress of grievances.

Nov. 7   Bavaria is proclaimed a republic and a socialist government is set up in Munich. In Berlin, the majority Socialist Party executive threatens to withdraw support from the Government unless the Kaiser abdicates.

Nov. 9   General Strike in Berlin. The Kaiser flees to Holland. Prince Max resigns and hands office to Ebert.

	Scheidemann proclaims a Republic from the Reichstag building and Ebert forms a socialist-dominated government. Ebert makes pact with Groener, with the army assuring its support in return for suppression of Bolshevism.
Nov. 11	German representatives sign armistice with Allies at Compiegne.
Nov. 22	Agreement reached for transitional government until a National Constituent Assembly meets.
Dec. 20	Workers' and soldiers' delegates in Berlin demand nationalization of major industries.
Dec. 30	German Communist Party (KPD) founded by Spartacists and other groups. They decide to boycott the elections for the National Constituent Assembly and stage a rising in Berlin.
1919 Jan. 5–11	Spartacist revolt in Berlin put down by Ebert-Noske government using 'Free Corps' (*Freikorps*) of ex-soldiers.
Jan. 15	Rosa Luxemburg and Karl Liebknecht, leaders of the Spartacists, are arrested and murdered by Free Corps.
Jan. 19	National Constituent Assembly elected on basis of proportional representation but fails to give any party an outright majority.
Feb. 8	National Constituent Assembly meets at Weimar.
Feb. 11	Ebert becomes President of Weimar Republic, following the formation of coalition of majority socialists and the centre and democratic parties under Scheidemann.
Feb. 13	Scheidemann forms a Cabinet.
Feb. 21	Assassination of the Premier of the Bavarian Republic, Kurt Eisner, by right-wingers.
Apr.	Bavarian Republic overthrown by Federal German forces.
June 29	Treaty of Versailles signed (see p. 255).
1920 Mar. 13–17	Kapp Putsch, Freikorps officers attempt to make Wolfgang Kapp Chancellor of the Reich in pro-monarchist *coup d'etat* in Berlin. Although troops refuse to fire on the Freikorps and the Government is forced to flee Berlin, a general strike frustrates the putsch.
Apr.	Hitler's German Workers' Party changes its name to the National Socialist German Workers' Party (Nazis).
1921 Aug. 29	Assassination of Matthias Erzberger, leader of Centre Party, by right-wing officers.
1922 Apr. 16	Treaty of Rapallo provides for economic and military co-operation between Germany and Russia.
June 24	Assassination of Walter Rathenau, Foreign Secretary, by right-wing nationalists.
1923 Jan. 11	Non-payment of reparations leads to French and

	Belgian troops occupying the Ruhr. Germany adopts passive resistance to the occupation.
Aug. 12	Stresemann becomes Chancellor.
Sept.–Nov.	Massive inflation in Germany. Interest rates raised to 90% (15th September) but by October German mark trading at rate of 10,000 million to the £.
Sept. 26	Passive resistance in Ruhr ends. A state of military emergency is declared.
Oct. 22	Bavarian troops take an oath of allegiance to right-wing regime in Bavaria. Communist revolt in Hamburg put down and left-wing governments deposed in Saxony and Thuringia.
Nov. 8–9	Unsuccessful 'Beer Hall' putsch in Munich led by Hitler and Ludendorff. Hitler captured.
Nov. 20	German currency stabilized by establishment of the *Rentenmark*, valued at one billion old marks.
Nov. 23	Stresemann becomes foreign minister.

1924	Apr. 1	Hitler sentenced to five years' imprisonment for part in Munich putsch (but released in December).
	Apr. 9	Dawes Plan provides a modified settlement of the reparations issue.
	May 4	In Reichstag elections, Nationalists and Communists gain many seats from the moderate parties.
	Dec. 7	In further elections, Nationalists and Communists lose seats to Socialists.
	Dec. 15	Beginning of Cabinet crisis in Germany.

1925	Jan. 15	Hans Luther, an independant, succeeds Wilhelm Marx of the Centre as Chancellor, with Stresemann as Foreign Minister.
	Feb. 28	Death of President Ebert.
	Apr. 26	Hindenburg elected President.
	July 7	French troops begin to leave Rhineland.
	Oct. 16	Locarno Pact guarantees Franco-German and Belgian-German frontiers and the demilitarization of the Rhineland.

1926	May 17	Marx takes over from Luther as Chancellor.
	Sept. 8	Germany admitted to the League of Nations.

1927	May 13	'Black Friday' with collapse of economic system.
	Sept. 16	Hindenburg, while dedicating the Tannenburg memorial, repudiates Article 231 of the Versailles Treaty, the 'War Guilt' clause.

1928	May 20	Social Democrats win victory at elections, mainly at the expense of the Nationalists.
	June 28	Hermann Muller, a socialist, is appointed Chancellor, following resignation of Marx's ministry on the 13th.

| 1929 | Feb. 6 | Germany accepts Kellogg-Briand Pact, outlawing war and providing for the pacific settlements of disputes. |

June 7	Publication of Young Plan for rescheduling German reparation payments in the form of annuities over 59 years, amounting to a quarter of the sum demanded in 1921.
July 9	Nationalists and Nazis form a National Committee to fight the Young Plan with Hugenberg as chairman and Hitler a leading member.
Oct. 3	Death of Stresemann.
Oct. 29	Wall Street crash and cessation of American loans to Europe.
Dec. 29	National referendum accepts Young Plan, frustrating Nationalist hopes.

1930 Mar.	Young Plan approved by Reichstag and signed by Hindenburg.
Mar. 17	Muller's socialist cabinet resigns in Germany.
Mar. 30	Heinrich Bruning, of the Centre, forms a minority coalition of the Right.
May 17	Young Plan reparations come into force.
June 30	Last Allied troops leave Rhineland.
July 16	Hindenburg authorizes German budget by decree, when Reichstag fails to pass it.
Sept. 14	In Reichstag elections, Hitler and the Nazi Party emerge as a major party with 107 seats, second only to the Socialists with 143 seats.
Oct.	Rohm becomes leader of SA or 'Brownshirts'.

| 1931 July | Worsening economic crisis in Germany. Unemployment reaches over 4.25 million. Bankruptcy of German Danatbank (13th) leads to closure of all banks until 5th August. |
| Oct. 11 | Hitler forms an alliance at Hartzburg with the Nationalists led by Hugenberg – the Hartzburg Front. |

1932 Jan. 7	Bruning declares that Germany cannot and will not resume reparations payments.
Mar. 13	In presidential elections Hindenburg receives 18 million votes against Hitler's 11 million, and a communist's 5 million. With failure to achieve an overall majority, a new election is called for 10 April.
Apr. 10	Hindenburg re-elected President with an absolute majority of 19 million against Hitler's 13 million and communist 3 million.
Apr. 14	Bruning unsuccessfully attempts to disband the SA and SS. (q.q.v.)
Apr. 24	Nazis achieve successes in local elections.
May 30	When Hindenburg withdraws support for disbanding the SA and SS, Bruning resigns.
June 1	Franz von Papen forms a ministry, with von Schleicher as Minister of Defence and von Neurath as Foreign Minister.
June 16	Ban on SA and SS, in operation since April, is lifted.
July 31	In Reichstag elections Nazis win 230 seats and

become largest party, producing a stalemate since neither they nor the Socialists (133 seats) will enter a coalition.

Aug. 13   Hindenburg asks Hitler to serve as vice-chancellor under von Papen, but he refuses.

Sept. 12   Von Papen dissolves the Reichstag.

Sept. 14   Germany leaves League of Nations disarmament conference.

Nov. 6   New elections fail to resolve the stalemate, with the Communists only gaining a few seats from the Nazis.

Nov. 17   Von Papen forced to resign by Schleicher; Hitler rejects Chancellorship.

Dec. 2–4   Schleicher becomes Chancellor and forms a ministry, attempting to conciliate the Centre and Left.

1933 Jan. 28   Schleicher's ministry is unable to secure a majority in the Reichstag and resigns.

Jan. 30   Hindenburg accepts a Cabinet with Hitler as Chancellor, von Papen as Vice-Chancellor and Nationalists in other posts.

Feb. 27   Reichstag fire blamed on Communists and made pretext for suspension of civil liberties and freedom of press.

Mar. 5   The Nazis make gains in elections, winning 288 seats, but fail to secure overall majority.

Mar. 13   Goebbels becomes minister of propaganda and 'enlightenment'. Pius XI praises Hitler's anti-communism.

Mar. 17   Schacht becomes President of the Reichsbank.

Mar. 23   Hitler obtains Enabling Law with the support of the Centre Party, granting him dictatorial powers for four years.

Mar. 30   German bishops withdraw opposition to Nazis.

Apr. 1   National boycott of all Jewish businesses and professions.

Apr. 7   Civil Service law permits removal of Jews and other opponents.

July 5   Centre Party disbands.

July 8   Concordat signed between Nazi Germany and Holy See.

July 14   The Nazi Party is formally declared the only political party in Germany: all others are suppressed.

July 20   Concordat ratified.

Sept.   Ludwig Muller, leader of minority 'German Christians', becomes 'Bishop of the Reich'

1934 Mar. 21   'Battle for Work' begins.

May   German Protestants at Barman synod express disapproval of close complicity of Muller and 'German Christians' with Nazis.

June 14   Hitler visits Mussolini in Italy.

June 20   Hindenburg demands dissolution of SA.

June 30	'Night of the Long Knives'. Nazis liquidate thousands of opponents within and outside the Party. Over 170 leading Nazis lose their lives including Rohm, leader of the SA, and Strasser, leader of Berlin Nazis. General von Schleicher also a victim.
Aug. 2	Death of President Hindenburg. Hitler assumes Presidency, but retains title *Der Führer*. Army swears oath of allegience. Schacht becomes Minister of Economics.
Oct. 24	German Labour Front founded, a Nazi organization to replace trade unions.

1935 Jan. 13	Saar plebiscite favours rejoining Germany.
Mar. 16	Germany repudiates disarmament clauses in Treaty of Versailles, restores conscription and announces expansion of the peace-time army to over half a million men.
June 18	By the Anglo-German Naval Agreement Germany agrees that her naval tonnage shall not exceed a third of that of the Royal Navy.
Sept. 15	Nuremberg laws prohibit marriage and sexual intercourse between Jews and German nationals.

1936 Mar. 7	German troops reoccupy the demilitarized Rhineland in violation of the Treaty of Versailles.
Aug.	Olympic Games in Berlin turned into an advertisement for Nazi Germany.
Aug. 24	Germany adopts two-year compulsory military service.
Oct. 19	Hitler announces four-year plan under Goering as economic overlord.
Nov. 1	Rome-Berlin Axis proclaimed.
Nov. 18	Germany and Italy recognize the Franco Government.

| 1937 Dec. | Schacht resigns as Minister of Economics. Leading members of the Protestant opposition arrested, including Pastor Niemoller. |

1938 Feb. 4	Hitler appoints Joachim von Ribbentrop Foreign Minister. Fritsch is relieved of his duties as Commander-in-Chief of the army. Hitler takes over personal control of the armed forces. The War Ministry is abolished and the OKW (High Command of the Armed Forces) is set up.
Mar. 11	The Anschluss: German troops enter Austria which is declared part of the Reich (13th).
Apr. 23	Germans in the Sudetenland (Czechoslovakia) demand autonomy.
Aug. 18	Beck resigns as Chief of the Army General Staff.
Aug. 21	Germany mobilizes over Czech crisis.
Sept. 30	Munich agreement gives Sudetenland to Germany.
Nov. 9–10	Anti-Jewish pogrom, the *Kristallnacht*.

| 1939 Jan. 21 | Schacht dismissed from presidency of Reichsbank. |

Mar. 15   German troops occupy remaining part of
           Czechoslovakia.
Aug. 23   Nazi-Soviet Pact signed.
Sept. 1   Germany invades Poland.
Sept. 3   Great Britain and France declare war on Germany.

France 1918–1944

1918	Jan. 14	Cailloux, former Premier, arrested for treason.
	Mar. 21	German offensive brings them within 75 miles of Paris. Paris bombarded by long-range guns.
	Mar. 26	Foch assumes united command of armies on Western Front.
	Apr. 27	Renewed German offensive captures Rheims.
	July 15–Aug. 4	Second battle of the Marne halts German offensive.
	July 22	Allies cross the Marne.
	Sept. 4	Germans retreat to Siegfried Line.
	Oct. 30	Allies sign armistice with Turkey.
	Nov. 1	Anglo-French forces occupy Constantinople.
	Nov. 3	Allies sign armistice with Austro-Hungary.
	Nov. 11	Allies sign armistice with Germany at Compiègne.
1919	June 28	Versailles Treaty signed.
	Nov.	Victory of right-wing 'Bloc National' in elections to the Assembly.
1920	Jan. 17	Deschanel elected President of France. Resignation of Clemenceau; Millerand forms ministry.
	May. 16	Joan of Arc canonized.
	Sept. 7	Franco-Belgian military convention.
	Dec. 23	Millerand becomes French President.
	Dec. 29	French socialists at Tours agree to join Moscow International; formation of French Communist Party.
1921	Jan. 16	Briand becomes Prime Minister.
	Jan. 24–29	Paris conference agrees reparations for France.
	Feb. 19	Franco-Polish alliance.
1922	Jan. 15	Poincaré becomes Prime Minister and Foreign Minister.
	Dec. 9–11	International conference in London considers Germany's request for a reparations moratorium.
1923	Jan. 11	Franco-Belgian occupation of the Ruhr in retaliation for non-payment of reparations; passive resistance by German workers.
1924	Apr. 16	Germany accepts Dawes Plan on reparations and agreement reached that France should withdraw from the Ruhr.
	May	Cartel des Gauches wins victory at the elections.
	June 10	Millerand resigns as President. Doumergue elected President (13th); Herriot becomes Prime Minister (15th).
1925	Apr. 10	Painlevé becomes French Prime Minister.
	July 20	French begin evacuation of Ruhr.
	Dec. 1	Locarno Treaties guaranteeing Franco-German and Belgian-German frontiers signed.
1926	Jan. 31	First part of the Rhineland evacuated.

	May 26	Rebel Abd-el-Krim in Morocco submits to France.
	July 15	Briand resigns over financial crisis; Poincaré becomes premier of French National Union ministry. Measures taken to stabilize the franc.
1927	Nov. 11	Treaty of friendship between France and Yugoslavia.
1928	Apr. 22–29	Left-wing parties win victory at elections.
	June 24	Devaluation of the franc. Decision to build Maginot Line; military service reduced to one year.
	Aug. 27	France and 64 other states sign the Kellogg-Briand Pact, outlawing war and providing for peaceful settlement of international disputes.
1929	July 27	Poincaré resigns as Prime Minister and is succeeded by Briand.
	Sept. 5	Briand proposes a European federal union.
1930	May 17	Young Plan for reduced German reparations comes into force. Briand produces memorandum on united states of Europe.
	June 30	Last section of Rhineland evacuated.
1931	Jan. 27	Laval becomes French Premier.
	May 13	Doumer elected French President.
	June 20	Hoover Plan for moratorium of one year for reparations and war debts in view of world economic crisis.
1932	Feb. 21	Tardieu ministry formed.
	May 1	Cartel des Gauches successful in elections.
	May 6	President Doumer assassinated; succeeded by Lebrun (10th).
	June 4	Herriot ministry formed.
	Dec. 18	Paul-Boncour ministry formed.
1933	Jan. 31	Daladier ministry formed (until October 1933).
	Dec.	Flight of Stavisky brings about scandal of financial corruption amongst politicians.
1934	Jan. 30	Daladier second ministry formed, after brief ministries by Sarraut and Chautemps.
	Feb. 6–7	Rioting in Paris. Police kill 14 right-wing demonstrators.
	Feb. 7	Daladier resigns and Doumergue forms National Union ministry of centre and moderate parties (8th).
	Feb. 12	French CGT calls General Strike. Demonstrations in defence of the Republic.
	Mar. 16	The French complete suppression of rebel Berber tribes in Morocco.
	Oct. 9	Barthou, Foreign Minister, and King Alexander of Yugoslavia assassinated at Marseilles.
1935	Mar. 7	Saar basin restored to Germany following plebiscite (13th January).
	Apr. 11–14	Stresa Conference of Britain, France and Italy to discuss alliance.

	May 2	Franco-Russian treaty of mutual assistance.
	July 14	Mass demonstrations throughout France demanding democracy and the dissolution of right-wing Leagues.
	July 27	French government granted emergency financial powers.
	Nov. 3	Socialist groups merge as Socialist and Republican Union under Léon Blum; later forming with Radical Socialists and Communists a Popular Front.
1936	Jan.	Popular Front agrees common programme.
	May 3	Popular Front wins major success in elections with 387 seats to 231 for other parties.
	June 4	Blum forms Popular Front government.
	June 17	Decrees 40-hour week, collective labour agreements, and paid holidays.
	Sept.	Widespread strikes in French industry.
	Oct. 2	Franc devalued.
	Nov. 18	In spite of protests from the Left, Blum proposes non-intervention in the Spanish Civil War.
1937	Jan.	Blum slows down social reform programme.
	Feb. 27	French Chamber passes defence plan; Schneider-Creusot factory nationalized and Maginot Line extended.
	June 21	Chamber rejects Blum's programme of financial reforms. Blum resigns, replaced by the radical Chautemps.
1938	Mar. 13	Blum forms second Popular Front government, but Senate rejects financial reforms.
	Apr. 10	Blum resigns, replaced by Daladier.
	Sept. 29	France signs Munich agreement.
	Nov. 9	France recognizes Italian conquest of Abyssinia.
1939	Feb. 27	France recognizes Franco's government in Spain; Pétain sent as first ambassador.
	Mar. 17	Daladier granted powers to speed rearmament.
	Mar. 31	France and Britain guarantee support for Poland.
	Apr. 13	France and Britain guarantee independence of Romania and Greece.
	Aug. 26–31	Negotiations by Daladier and Chamberlain with Hitler fail.
	Sept. 3	Britain and France declare war on Germany.
	Sept. 4	Franco-Polish agreement.
	Sept. 26	Daladier dissolves French Communist Party.
	Sept. 30	British Expeditionary Force sent to France.
	Nov. 3	Roosevelt allows France to purchase US arms on 'cash and carry' basis, amending Neutrality Act of May 1937.
1940	Mar. 21	Reynaud succeeds Daladier as Premier.
	May 10	German attack on Holland, Belgium and Luxembourg.
	May 12	German panzer forces cross into France.

	May 14	German forces cross the Meuse.
	May 19	General Weygand takes command of the French army from General Gamelin.
	May 20	German forces reach Channel, cutting off Allied armies in the north.
	May 29	British begin evacuation from Dunkirk.
	June 10	Italy declares war on France.
	June 14	Germans enter Paris.
	June 16	Reynaud resigns, replaced by Pétain.
	June 18	De Gaulle, from London, calls for continued resistance.
	June 22	French sign armistice with Germany at Compiègne.
	June 23	British government supports London-based French National Committee, 'Free French', headed by de Gaulle and breaks off relations with Pétain government.
	June 24	Armistice signed with Italy.
	July 1	French government moves to Vichy.
	July 3	British attack on French fleet at Mers-el-Kebir.
	July 5	Vichy regime breaks off relations with Britain.
	July 10	National Assembly votes full powers to Petain as 'Head of the French State', ending Third Republic.
	Oct. 22–24	Laval, followed by Pétain, holds discussions with Hitler at Montoire.
	Dec. 13	Laval dismissed. Replaced by Darlan.
1941	Apr. 18	Vichy government withdraws from League of Nations.
	May	Darlan offers French air bases in Syria to the Germans.
	June 6	Allied invasion of Syria.
	June 30	Vichy government breaks off relations with Russia.
1942	Apr. 18	Laval returns to head government.
	Nov. 11	German troops occupy Vichy France.
	Nov. 27	French fleet scuttled at Toulon.
1944	June 6	Allied landings in Normandy.
	August 25	Paris is liberated.
	Oct. 23	De Gaulle's provisional government recognized by Allies.

Spain: the Civil War and its background 1923–1939

1923	Dec. 14	Primo de Rivera assumes Spanish dictatorship, supported by military and middle classes and with acquiescence of King, Alfonso XIII.
1930	Dec. 28	The King accepts the resignation of Primo de Rivera, following Spain's deteriorating economic condition and failure to achieve progress towards constitutional government.
1931	Apr. 14	King Alfonso XIII abdicates. Spain becomes a constitutional republic.
	May 10	Left-wing Republican, Azāna, becomes Premier.
	Oct. 20	'Protection of the Republic' Law passed in Spain.
	Dec. 9	Spanish Republican Constitution introduced; Zamora elected President.
1933	Jan. 2–12	Rising of anarchists and syndicalists in Barcelona.
	Nov. 19	Spanish Right wins elections to the Cortes. Foundation of *Falango Espanola* by José Antonio Primo de Rivera (son of the dictator).
1934	Jan. 14	Catalan elections won by the Left.
	Oct. 4	Right forms a Ministry; followed by socialist rising in Asturias and Catalan separatist revolt in Barcelona. Moroccan troops used to suppress risings with great ferocity.
1936	Feb. 16	Popular Front wins elections; Azāna elected President and re-establishes 1931 constitution. Amnesty granted to rebels of 1934; growing clashes between Left and Right with assassinations and attacks on church property.
	Apr. 20	Cortes dismiss President Zamora.
	May 10	Azāna elected Spanish President, although large numbers of voters boycott the elections.
	July 17–18	Outbreak of Spanish Civil War with rising of the army in Morocco under General Franco; revolt spreads to mainland led by General Mola.
	July 19	Rebels reject offer of a cease-fire and the formation of an all-party national government. Republican Giral government formed and orders arming of revolutionary organizations.
	July 20–31	Republican forces seize the Montana barracks in Madrid and secure Catalonia, the Basque country and much of the south. The rebels, or Nationalists, overrun Morocco, parts of southern Spain and much of the north.
	July 26	Léon Blum declares that France cannot intervene on behalf of the Republic. Communist Comintern decides to raise international force of volunteers – the International Brigades – for service in Spain.

	Hitler offers aircraft and supplies to the Nationalists, as does Mussolini.
Aug. 6	France and Britain submit draft 'non-intervention' agreement to the European powers.
Aug. 19	Britain imposes embargo on arms to Spain.
Aug. 21	Italy accepts non-intervention, but makes exceptions for 'volunteers' and financial support.
Aug. 23	Germany accepts non-intervention, as does the Soviet Union, although both continue to supply advisers and other support.
Sept. 4	Formation of Largo Caballero government in Madrid, composed of republicans, socialists and communists.
Sept. 27	Nationalists capture Toledo.
Oct. 1	Nationalists appoint Franco Generalissimo and head of state.
Oct. 22	Most of Spanish gold reserves shipped to the Soviet Union. Russian advisers supervise reorganization of Republican army and appoint political commissars.
Nov.	Nationalist forces advance on Madrid. Air-raids on Madrid and Republican forces by German Condor Legion. First International Brigades go into action and assist in repelling nationalist advance. Republican government moves to Valencia.
Nov. 18	Germany and Italy recognize Franco government.
Dec. 16	Protocol signed in London by major powers agreeing non-intervention in Spain.
1937 Feb. 8	Malaga falls to Nationalists.
Mar. 3–12	Republican government orders disarming of workers' and anarchist militias in Catalonia following clashes between them and the communists.
Mar. 20–23	Battle of Guadalajara. Republicans defeat Italian forces advancing on Madrid.
Apr. 19	Franco orders unification of the Nationalist movement, fusing the Falange and other political bodies into a single political body, and para-military groups into a militia responsible to the army.
Apr. 26	German Condor Legion destroys village of Guernica in Basque country.
Apr. 30–May 6	Street fighting in Barcelona between workers' militias and republican-communists.
May 15	Largo Caballero resigns in opposition to communist call for greater control and suppression of rival groups.
May 17	Negrin government formed with backing of Comintern to pursue victory by means of communist control of the republican forces.
June 18	Anarchist militia (POUM) dissolved and leaders arrested; anti-Stalinist leader, Nin, executed.
June 19	Nationalists capture Basque capital of Bilbao.
July 5–28	Failure of Republican offensive at Brunete to restore position in north.

Sept. 10–14	Following attacks on shipping by Italian submarines and aircraft, Nyon Conference of nine European powers agrees to patrol the Mediterranean and sink submarines attacking non-Spanish ships. Italy and Germany do not attend, but sinkings cease.
Oct. 17	Largo Caballero denounces repressive policies of Negrin government.
Oct. 20–22	Franco's forces complete reduction of north-west with capture of Gijon and Oviedo.
Oct. 31	Republican government moves to Barcelona.
Dec. 15–26	Republican forces go over to the offensive at Teruel to avert threat to Madrid.
1938 Feb. 5–22	Nationalists launch counter-offensive at Teruel; recaptured (23rd). Nationalist offensive in Aragon.
Mar.	Nationalists begin advance from Aragon to the Mediterranean with aim of cutting Republican territory in half, and achieve rapid early success.
Apr. 15	Nationalist forces reach Mediterranean at Vinaroz, cutting off Catalonia from the rest of Republican Spain.
Apr.–May	Opening of French frontier permits some resupply of Republican forces. 200,000 new conscripts called up and organized on flanks of the Nationalist corridor.
July–Aug.	Last Republican offensive on the Ebro forces Franco to suspend attack on Valencia.
Aug.	Basque and Catalan separatist ministers resign from Negrin ministry.
Nov. 15	Last Republican forces driven out of Ebro bridgehead.
Dec.	Nationalists begin offensive against Catalonia.
1939 Jan. 26	Fall of Barcelona to Nationalist forces.
Feb. 7	President Azāna goes into exile in France (resigns on 24th).
Feb. 9	End of resistance in Catalonia by Republican forces; over 200,000 cross French frontier and are disarmed. Negrin makes last attempt to obtain a negotiated peace without reprisals.
Feb. 26	Negrin tries to organize last stand of Republic at Cartagena naval base.
Mar. 4	Negrin appoints communist military leaders to key defence positions.
Mar. 5–12	Military commander in Madrid, Casado, leads rebellion against Negrin government on account of its communist domination and sets up a National Defence Council. On Comintern instructions, communists attempt to defeat the rebellion, but are themselves defeated by non-communist elements. Negrin flees to France.
Mar. 23	Casado sends emissaries to Nationalist capital in Burgos to negotiate peace terms. Franco demands surrender of Republican Air Force by 25 March and rest of armed forces by 27 March.

Mar. 25	Franco breaks off negotiations because his terms are not met.
Mar. 27	Last meeting of National Defence Council.
Mar. 28	Nationalist forces enter Madrid.
Apr. 1	General Franco announces end to the Civil War.

Italy 1919–1945

1919	Mar. 23	Foundation of the first *Fascio di Combattimento* by Mussolini in Milan.
	Aug. 25	Italian forces evacuate Fiume.
	Sept. 2	Universal suffrage and proportional representation introduced.
	Sept. 12	D'Annunzio, Italian nationalist and irredentist seizes Fiume.
	Nov. 11	The Pope lifts the prohibition against Catholics participating in political life.
	Nov. 16	Socialists and Catholics receive strong support in the elections; fascists gain only a fraction of the vote.
1920	June 9	Giolitti takes over as Prime Minister from Nitti.
	Aug. 31–Sept.	Widespread strikes and lockouts in engineering, metal and steel industries.
	Nov. 12	Treaty of Rapallo settles disputes between Italy and Yugoslavia. Fiume to be an independent state.
	Nov. 21	Fascists fire on crowd in Bologna during Mayor's inauguration.
	Dec. 1	D'Annunzio declares war on Italy.
	Dec. 24–25	Clashes between Italian troops and Fiuman troops. *Andrea Doria* shells the royal palace.
	Dec. 31	D'Annunzio makes peace with Italy.
1921	Jan. 5	D'Annunzio leaves Fiume.
	Feb. 27	Communists and Fascists clash in Florence.
	May 15	Liberals and Democrats successful at the elections.
	June 26	Giolitti cabinet falls, replaced by Bonomi.
1922	Feb. 9	Bonomi government resigns.
	Feb. 25	Facta heads new government.
	May	Fascist takeover in Bologna.
	Aug. 3–4	Fascist takeover in Milan.
	Oct. 24	Mussolini calls on Facta to resign and for the formation of a fascist cabinet. Facta refuses.
	Oct. 28	Fascist 'March on Rome'.
	Oct. 30	Mussolini arrives in Rome and organizes victory march.
	Oct. 31	Mussolini forms cabinet.
	Nov. 25	Mussolini is granted temporary dictatorial powers to institute reforms.
1923	Jan. 14	King Victor Emmanuel authorizes voluntary fascist militia.
	July 21	Electoral law passed, guaranteeing two-thirds of the seats in the Chamber to the majority party.
1924	Jan. 27	Treaty with Yugoslavia recognizes Fiume as Italian, but cedes surrounding area to Yugoslavia.
	Apr. 6	Fascists obtain almost two-thirds of votes in election amidst widespread use of violence and intimidation.

	May 30	Matteotti launches attack on the Fascist government.
	June 10	Matteotti is abducted and murdered. Non-fascists resign from Chambers and condemn violence.
	July	Press censorship introduced.
1925	Oct. 2	Palazzo Vidoni pact between 'industrialists' association (Confindustria) and the fascist syndicates.
	Dec. 24	Mussolini's dictatorial powers increased. Press censorship tightened, secret non-fascist organizations banned, and widespread arrests.
1926	Jan. 31	Government decrees given the power of law.
	Apr. 3	Right to strike abolished: collective contracts reserved to the fascist syndicate.
	Apr. 7	Mussolini wounded in assassination attempt.
	Nov. 25	Law for defence of the state; creation of a special tribunal for political crimes; death penalty introduced for plotting against royal family or head of state.
1927	Dec. 21	Exchange rate fixed at 'quota 90' (92.45 lira to £1).
1929	Feb. 11	Lateran Treaties with Papacy creating the Vatican City as a sovereign independent state (see p. 437).
1933	Jan. 23	Creation of IRI, organisation for Italian industry on corporatist lines.
1934	Jan. 17	Mussolini signs the Rome Protocols with Austria and Hungary.
	June 14	Meeting of Hitler and Mussolini at Venice.
	July	Mussolini sends troops to the Austrian frontier following Hitler's attempted coup.
	Nov. 10	Council of Corporations inaugurated at Rome.
1935	Oct. 3	Italy begins invasion of Ethiopia (Abyssinia).
1936	May 5	Italian forces occupy Addis Ababa.
	Oct. 24	Rome-Berlin Axis formed.
1938	July 14	Publication of *Manifesto della Razza* – first anti-Semitic measures.
1939	Jan. 19	Creation of the *Camera del Fascie delle Corporazioni,* replacing parliament.
	Apr. 7	Italy invades Albania.
	May 22	Pact of Steel signed between Hitler and Mussolini.
1940	June 10	Mussolini declares war and invades France. First air attacks on Malta.
	Aug. 3	Italy invades British Somaliland.
	Sept. 13	Italian forces invade Egypt.
	Oct. 28	Italy invades Greece.
	Nov. 11–12	Destruction of large part of Italian fleet at Taranto by British aircraft.
	Dec. 9	British offensive in North Africa routs the army of Graziani.
1941	Mar. 24	Italians defeated in British Somaliland.

Mar. 27–28	Italian fleet defeated at Cape Matapan.
Apr. 6	British enter Addis Ababa.
May 16	Capitulation of Italian forces under the Duke of Aosta in Italian East Africa.
Dec. 11	Italy declares war on United States.

| 1942 June | Allied convoys resupply Malta. |
| Nov. 4 | British break through Axis line at El Alamein. |

1943 May	Surrender of Axis forces in North Africa.
July 10	Allied invasion of Sicily.
July 25	Grand Council of Fascism votes Mussolini out of power. Badoglio takes over the Italian government.
Aug. 17	Sicily finally conquered by the Allies.
Sept. 8	Italian surrender announced. Nazis take over power in Italy.
Sept. 9	Salerno landing by US 5th Army.
Sept. 12	Skorzeny rescues Mussolini.
Sept. 23	Mussolini announces creation of fascist social republic of Salò.

1944 Jan. 22	Anzio landing by US 5th Army; German counter-attack stalls advance.
Mar. 15	Allies bomb Monte Cassino.
Mar. 17	Monte Cassino falls.
June 4	Rome falls.

| 1945 Apr. 28 | Mussolini executed by partisans at Dongo. |

International background to the Second World War

1933 Jan. 30   Hitler becomes Chancellor of Germany.

Mar. 16   Britain's plan for disarmament fails as Germany insists on exclusion of the S.A. (paramilitary 'Brownshirts').

Mar. 19   Mussolini proposes pact between Britain, France, Italy and Germany, signed as the Rome Pact.

Mar. 27   Japan announces intention to leave League of Nations.

July 15   Rome Pact binds Britain, France, Germany and Italy to the League Covenant, the Locarno Treaties, and the Kellogg-Briand Pact.

Oct. 14   Germany leaves disarmament conference and League of Nations.

1934 June 14–15   Hitler meets Mussolini for the first time, in Venice.

July 25   Austrian Chancellor Dollfuss murdered in Nazi coup.

July 30   Kurt Schuschnigg becomes new Austrian Chancellor.

Dec. 5   Italian and Ethiopian troops clash at Wal Wal inside Ethiopia.

1935 Feb. 1   Anglo-German conference on German rearmament; Italy sends troops to East Africa.

Mar. 15   Hitler repudiates the military restrictions on Germany imposed by the Treaty of Versailles, restores conscription and announces that the peace-time army strength is to be raised to half a million men. Germany announces the existence of the Luftwaffe.

Apr. 11–14   Britain, France and Italy confer at Stresa to establish a common front against Germany.

May 2   France and the Soviet Union sign a treaty of five years' mutual assistance.

May 16   Czechoslovakia and Soviet Union sign mutual assistance pact.

May 19   Pro-Nazi Sudeten Party makes gains in Czechoslovak elections.

June 18   Anglo-German Naval Agreement. Germany undertakes that her navy shall not exceed a third of the tonnage of the Royal Navy.

June 27   League of Nations attempts to defuse the Wal Wal shows strong support for the League.

Sept. 3   League of Nations attempts to defuse the Walwal Oasis incident by stating that neither country was to blame as possession was unclear.

Oct. 2   Italian forces invade Ethiopia.

Oct. 7   League of Nations declares Italy the aggressor in Ethiopia and votes sanctions.

Oct. 19   League of Nations sanctions against Italy come into force.

Dec. 9	Hoare-Laval Pact, lenient to Italy, is met by hostile public reaction in Britain and France.
Dec. 13	Beneš succeeds Masaryk as President of Czechoslovakia.
1936 Feb. 16	Popular Front wins a majority in the Spanish elections.
Mar. 3	Britain increases defence expenditure, principally on the air force.
Mar. 8	German troops reoccupy the demilitarized Rhineland in violation of the Treaty of Versailles.
May 5	Italians take Addis Ababa; Emperor Haile Selassie flees. Italy annexes Ethiopia (9th).
July 11	Austro-German convention acknowledges Austrian independence.
July 18	Spanish Army revolt under Emilio Mola and Francisco Franco begins Spanish Civil War.
Aug. 24	Germany introduces compulsory conscription.
Sept. 9	Conference held in London on non-intervention in Spanish Civil War.
Oct. 1	Franco appointed 'Chief of the Spanish State' by the nationalist rebels.
Oct. 14	Belgium renounces its military pact with France in order to ensure its liberty of action in the face of German reoccupation of the Rhineland.
Oct. 19	Germany begins four-year economic plan to develop its economic base for war.
Nov. 1	Mussolini proclaims Rome-Berlin Axis.
Nov. 18	Germany and Italy recognize Franco's government.
Nov. 24	Germany and Japan sign Anti-Comintern Pact.
Dec. 16	Protocol signed in London for non-intervention in Spain.
1937 Jan. 2	Mussolini signs agreement with Britain ensuring the safety of shipping in the Mediterranean.
Jan. 15	Amnesty granted for Austrian Nazis.
Feb. 27	France extends Maginot Line.
Mar. 18	Defeat of Italian push on Madrid.
Apr. 27	Basque town of Guernica destroyed by German Condor Legion.
June 18	Spanish nationalist forces take Bilbao.
June 23	Germany and Italy withdraw from non-intervention committee.
July 7	'China incident'; outbreak of Sino–Japanese War (see p. 279).
July 17	Naval agreements between Britain and Germany, and Britain and Soviet Union.
Sept. 10–14	At Nyon Conference, nine nations adopt system of patrol in Mediterranean to protect shipping.
Oct. 13	Germany guarantees inviolability of Belgium.
Oct. 17	Riots in Sudeten area of Czechoslovakia.
Oct. 21	Franco's forces complete conquest of Basque country.
Nov. 5	Hitler informs his Generals in the Hossbach

	memorandum that Austria and Czechoslovakia will be annexed as the first stage in *Lebensraum* for Germany.
Nov. 6	Italy joins Anti-Comintern Pact.
Nov. 8	Japanese take Shanghai.
Nov. 17–21	Lord Halifax (Lord President of the Council) accepts unofficial invitation to visit Germany, where he has inconclusive discussions with Hitler about a European settlement.
Nov. 29	Sudeten Germans secede from Czech Parliament following a ban on their meetings.
Dec. 11	Italy leaves the League of Nations.
Dec. 12	American patrol boat sunk on Yangste river in China by Japanese aircarft.
Dec. 13	Japanese take Nanking.
1938 Feb. 4	Von Ribbentrop becomes German Foreign Minister.
Feb. 12	At Berchtesgaden Hitler forces the Austrian Chancellor Schuschnigg to accept a Protocol promising the release of Nazis in Austria, accepting a pro-Nazi (Seyss-Inquart) as Minister of the Interior and virtually attaching the Austrian army to that of Germany, subject to the consent of Austrian President Miklas.
Feb. 16	Amnesty for Nazis proclaimed in Austria; Seyss-Inquart becomes Minister of the Interior.
Feb. 20	In a speech to the Reichstag Hitler proclaims the need to protect the ten million Germans on the frontiers of the Reich.
Mar. 6	President Miklas of Austria accepts Schuschnigg's proposal of a plebiscite on the future independence of Austria. Announced on 9 March, voting was to take place on the 13th.
Mar. 10	Hitler mobilizes for immediate invasion of Austria.
Mar. 11	Schuschnigg accepts Hitler's ultimatum demanding that the plebiscite not be held.
Mar. 12	German army marches into Austria.
Mar. 13	Austria is declared part of Hitler's Reich.
Mar. 28	Hitler encourages German minority in Czechoslovakia to make such demands as will break up the state.
Apr. 16	In Anglo-Italian pact Britain recognizes Italian sovereignty in Ethiopia in return for withdrawal of Italian troops from Spain.
Apr. 24	Germans in Sudetenland demand full autonomy.
Apr. 29	Britain reluctantly joins France in diplomatic action on behalf of the Czech government.
May 9	Russia promises to assist Czechoslovakia in the event of a German attack if Poland and Romania will permit the passage of Russian troops. Both, however, refuse.
May 18–21	German troop movements reported on Czech

	border; Czech government calls up reservists (20th); and partial mobilization (21st).
May 22	Britain warns Germany of dangers of military action, but makes it clear to France that she is not in favour of military action herself.
Aug. 3	Walter Runciman visits Prague on mediation mission between Czechs and Sudeten Germans.
Aug. 11	Under British and French pressure, the Czech Prime Minister Beneš opens negotiations with the Sudeten Germans.
Aug. 12	Germany begins to mobilize.
Sept. 4	Henlein, leader of the Sudeten Germans, rejects Beneš's offer of full autonomy and breaks off relations with the Czech government (7th).
Sept. 7	France calls up reservists.
Sept. 11	Poland and Romania again refuse to allow the passage of Russian troops to assist Czechoslovakia.
Sept. 12	Hitler demands that Czechs accept German claims.
Sept. 13	Unrest in Sudetenland put down by Czech troops.
Sept. 15	Chamberlain visits Hitler at Berchtesgaden. Hitler states his determination to annex the Sudetenland on the principle of self-determination.
Sept. 18	Britain and France decide to persuade the Czechs to hand over territory in areas where over half of the population is German.
Sept. 20–21	Germany completes invasion plans. The Czech government initially rejects the Anglo-French proposals, but accepts them on the 21st.
Sept. 22	Chamberlain meets Hitler at Godesberg. Hitler demands immediate occupation of the Sudetenland and announces 28 September for the invasion. The Czech cabinet resigns.
Sept. 23	Czechoslovakia mobilizes; Russia promises to support France in the event of her aiding the Czechs.
Sept. 25	France and Britain threaten Hitler with force unless he negotiates.
Sept. 26	Partial mobilization in France.
Sept. 27	The Royal Navy is mobilized.
Sept. 28	Hitler delays invasion for 24 hours pending a four-power conference at Munich.
Sept. 29	At the Munich conference Chamberlain, Daladier, Hitler and Mussolini agree to transfer the Sudetenland to Germany, while guaranteeing the remaining Czech frontiers.
Sept. 30	Hitler and Chamberlain sign the 'peace in our time' communiqué.
Oct. 1	Czechs cede Teschen to Poland. Germany begins occupation of the Sudetenland.
Oct. 5	Beneš resigns.
Oct. 6–8	Slovakia and Ruthenia are granted autonomy.
Oct. 25	Libya is declared to be part of Italy.
Dec. 1	British prepare for conscription.

Dec. 6	Franco-German pact on inviolability of existing frontiers.
Dec. 17	Italy denounces 1935 agreement with France.
Dec. 23	Franco begins final offensive against last Republican stronghold in Catalonia.
1939 Jan. 10	Chamberlain and Halifax visit Rome for discussions with Mussolini.
Jan. 26	Franco's forces take Barcelona.
Feb. 27	Britain and France recognize Franco's government.
Mar. 14	At Hitler's prompting, the Slovak leader Tito proclaims a breakaway 'Slovak Free State'.
Mar. 15	German troops march into Prague and occupy Bohemia and Moravia.
Mar. 28	Hitler denounces 1934 non-aggression pact with Poland. Spanish Civil War ends with surrender of Madrid.
Mar. 31	Britain and France promise aid to Poland in the event of a threat to Polish independence.
Apr. 7	Italy invades Albania. Spain joins the Anti-Comintern Pact.
Apr. 13	Britain and France guarantee the independence of Greece and Romania.
Apr. 15	The United States requests assurances from Hitler and Mussolini that they will not attack 31 named states.
Apr. 16–18	The Soviet Union proposes a defensive alliance with Britain and France, but the offer is not accepted.
Apr. 27	Britain introduces conscription. Hitler denounces the 1935 Anglo-German naval agreement.
Apr. 28	Hitler rejects Roosevelt's peace proposals.
May 22	Hitler and Mussolini sign a ten-year political and military alliance – the 'Pact of Steel'.
Aug. 11	Anglo-French mission to the Soviet Union begins talks in Moscow.
Aug. 18	Germany and the Soviet Union sign a commercial agreement.
Aug. 23	Germany and the Soviet Union sign non-aggression pact, with secret clauses on the partition of Poland. Chamberlain warns Hitler that Britain will stand by Poland, but accepts the need for a settlement of the Danzig question. Hitler states that Germany's interest in Danzig and the Corridor must be satisfied. The Poles refuse to enter negotiations with the Germans. Hitler brings forward his preparations to invade Poland to the 26th (from 1 September).
Aug. 25	Anglo-Polish mutual assistance pact signed in London. Hitler makes a 'last offer' on Poland and postpones his attack until 1 September.
Aug. 28–31	Britain and France urge direct negotiations between Germans and Poles, but the Poles refuse.

Aug. 31	Hitler orders attack on Poland.
Sept. 1	German forces invade Poland and annex Danzig. Britain and France demand withdrawal of German troops.
Sept. 2	Britain decides on ultimatum to Germany.
Sept. 3	Britain and France declare war on Germany.

The Second World War

1939 Sept. 1   Germany invades Poland and annexes Danzig.
     Sept. 2   Great Britain introduces National Service Bill calling
                up men aged between 18 and 41.
     Sept. 3   Britain and France declare war on Germany.
     Sept. 7   Germans overrun western Poland.
     Sept. 17   Soviet Union invades eastern Poland.
     Sept. 19   Polish government leaves Warsaw.
     Sept. 28   Fall of Warsaw.
     Sept. 30   Germany and Soviet Union settle partition of
                Poland. Last of British Expeditionary Force (BEF)
                arrives in France.
     Oct. 6   Peace moves by Hitler rejected by Britain and
                France; opening of Auschwitz concentration camp
                symbolises systematic elimination of opponents of
                Nazis.
     Oct. 8   Western Poland incorporated into the Reich.
     Nov. 3   United States allows Britain and France to purchase
                arms in USA on a 'cash and carry' basis.
     Nov. 30   Soviet Union invades Finland.
     Dec. 13   German battleship *Graf Spee* forced to scuttle itself
                off Montevideo after Battle of the River Plate.

1940 Mar. 12   Finland signs peace treaty with Soviet Union ceding
                territory on the Karelian Isthmus and in
                north-eastern Finland.
     Apr. 9   Germany invades Norway and Denmark.
     Apr. 14   British forces land in Norway.
     May 2   Evacuation of British forces from Norway.
     May 10   Resignation of Chamberlain as British prime
                minister, replaced by Winston Churchill.
     May 14   Dutch army surrenders after bombing of Rotterdam.
     May 28   Belgium capitulates.
     May 29–June 3   Over 300,000 British and Allied troops
                evacuated from Dunkirk.
     June–Sept. Battle of Britain.
     June 10   Italy declares war on Britain and France.
     June 14   Germans enter Paris. French government moves to
                Bordeaux.
     June 16   France declines offer of union with Britain. Marshal
                Pétain replaces Paul Reynaud as head of French
                administration.
     June 17–June 23   Russians occupy Baltic states.
     June 22   France concludes armistice with Germany.
     June 24   France signs armistice with Italy.
     June 27   Russia invades Romania.
     July 3   Britain sinks French fleet at Oran.
     Aug. 5   Britain signs agreement with Polish government in
                exile in London and with Free French under de
                Gaulle (7th).
     Aug. 23   Beginning of 'Blitz' on Britain.

Oct. 7	Germany seizes Romanian oilfields.
Oct. 12	Hitler cancels Operation Sealion for the invasion of Britain.
Oct. 28	Italy invades Greece. Britain offers help.
Nov. 11	Major elements of Italian fleet sunk at Taranto, Sicily.
Dec. 9–15	Italian forces defeated at Sidi Barrani in North Africa.
1941 Jan. 6	F. D. Roosevelt sends Lend-Lease Bill to Congress.
Jan.–Feb.	Further Italian reverses in North Africa.
Feb. 6	German troops under Rommel sent to assist Italians in North Africa.
Mar. 11	Lend-Lease Bill passes Congress. See p. 437.
Apr. 6	German ultimatum to Greece and Yugoslavia. Britain diverts troops from North Africa to Greece.
Apr. 7	Rommel launches offensive in North Africa.
Apr. 11	Blitz on Coventry.
Apr. 13	Stalin signs neutrality pact with Japan.
Apr. 17	Yugoslavia signs capitulation after Italian and German attack.
Apr. 22–28	British forces evacuated from Greece.
May 10	Rudolf Hess flies to Scotland and is imprisoned.
May 27	*Bismarck* sunk by Royal Navy.
May 20–31	Germans capture Crete.
June 22	Germans launch invasion of Russia, Operation Barbarossa. Finnish forces attack on Karelian Isthmus.
July 6	Russians abandon eastern Poland and Baltic States; systematic extermination of Jews (the "Final Solution") begun by Nazis.
July 12	Britain and Russia sign agreement for mutual assistance in Moscow.
July 16	Germans take Smolensk.
Aug. 11	Churchill and Roosevelt sign the Atlantic Charter.
Sept. 8	Germans lay siege to Leningrad.
Sept. 19	Germans take Kiev.
Sept. 30–Oct. 2	Germans begin drive on Moscow.
Oct. 16	Russian government leaves Moscow but Stalin stays.
Oct. 30	German attacks reach within 60 miles of Moscow.
Nov. 15	Renewed German offensive takes advance elements within 20 miles of Moscow.
Nov. 20–28	German forces take Rostov but retreat.
Dec. 5	Germans go onto defensive on Moscow front as Russians launch counter-offensive.
Dec. 7	Japanese bomb Pearl Harbour, Hawaii and British Malaya.
Dec. 8	Britain and the USA declare war on Japan.
Dec. 11	Germany and Italy declare war on USA.
1942 Jan. 2	Britain, United States, Soviet Union and 23 other nations sign Washington Pact not to make separate peace treaties with their enemies.
Feb. 1	Pro-Nazi Quisling becomes premier of Norway.
Feb. 6	Roosevelt and Churchill appoint Combined Chiefs of Staff.

Feb. 11	German battleships make Channel 'dash' from Brest to Germany.
Feb. 15	Surrender of Singapore to Japanese.
Mar. 10	Rangoon falls to Japanese.
Mar. 28	RAF destroys much of Lübeck, first major demonstration of area bombing.
May 12–17	Russian offensive on Kharkov front defeated.
May 26	Signing of Anglo-Soviet treaty for closer co-operation.
May 29	Soviet Union and United States extend lend-lease agreement.
May 30	First British 1,000-bomber raid on Cologne.
June 6	Germans wipe out village of Lidice in Czechoslovakia in retaliation for assassination of Gestapo leader Heydrich.
June 10	German offensive in the Ukraine.
June 21	Fall of Tobruk after Rommel's advance in North Africa. Eighth Army retreats to El Alamein.
June 25	Dwight Eisenhower appointed Commander-in-Chief of US forces in Europe.
July 2	Fall of Sevastopol.
July 28	Germans take Rostov and northern Caucasus in drive to take Baku oilfields. Zhukov takes over command of southern armies.
Aug. 14	Raid on Dieppe by British and Canadians ends in failure.
Sept. 5	Germans enter Stalingrad.
Nov. 11–12	Vichy France occupied.
Nov. 19–20	Russians began counter-attack at Stalingrad, cutting off von Paulus's troops.
Nov. 27	French navy scuttled in Toulon.
Dec. 29	Final failure of effort by German forces to relieve von Paulus.
1943 Jan. 2	German withdrawal from Caucasus begins.
Jan. 14–24	Churchill and Roosevelt at Casablanca Conference, declare that they will only accept 'Unconditional Surrender'.
Jan. 31	Von Paulus surrenders at Stalingrad.
Feb. 2	Last German forces surrender at Stalingrad.
Feb. 8	Russian offensive takes Kursk.
Feb. 14	Russians capture Rostov.
Feb. 16	Russians take Kharkov.
Mar. 15	Russians forced out of Kharkov.
Apr. 20	Massacre of Jews in Warsaw ghetto.
Apr. 26	Discovery of the Katyn massacre and demand by Polish government in London for investigation by the Red Cross. Stalin breaks off diplomatic relations with Poles in London.
May 12	Axis armies in Tunisia surrender.
May 17	RAF bombs Ruhr dams, causing widespread destruction.

June 4	French Committee of National Liberation formed under General Charles de Gaulle.
July 4	General Sikorski killed in an aircrash.
July 5	Germans launch an offensive on Kursk salient, Operation Citadel.
July 10	Allied landings in Sicily.
July 12	Russian counter-offensive against Orel Salient causes Germans to halt Kursk offensive.
July 26	Mussolini forced to resign. King Victor Emmanuel asks Marshal Badoglio to form a government. Secret armistice signed with Allies.
Aug. 4	Russians take Orel.
Aug. 23	Russians take Kharkov.
Sept. 3	Allied landings in Italy; Italy surrenders unconditionally.
Sept. 25	Russians take Smolensk.
Oct. 13	Italy declares war on the Soviet Union.
Nov. 2	Moscow declaration of Allied foreign ministers on international security.
Nov. 6	Russians take Kiev.
Nov. 28–Dec. 1	Churchill, Roosevelt and Stalin meet at Tehran.
Dec. 20	Britain and USA agree to support Tito's partisans.
Dec. 26	*Scharnhorst* sunk in Barents Sea by British ships.
1944 Jan. 22	Allied landing at Anzio in attempt to by-pass German forces blocking the road to Rome.
Jan. 27	Relief of Leningrad.
Feb. 15	Bombing of Monte Cassino by Allies fails to dislodge German defenders.
Mar. 18	Fall of Monte Cassino to Allied forces.
Apr. 2	Russians enter Romania.
June 2	Fall of Rome to Americans.
June 6	'D-Day' landings in Normandy.
June 13	V-I 'Flying Bomb', campaign opened on Britain.
July 1	Monetary and financial conference at Bretton Woods, New Hampshire, lays foundation for post-war economic settlement.
July 9	Fall of Caen to Allied troops.
July 20	Failure of 'July Plot' to assassinate Hitler.
July 26	Soviet Union recognizes the Lublin Committee of Polish Liberation in Moscow as the legitimate authority for Liberated Poland.
Aug. 1	Rising of Home Army in Warsaw. American armies begin breakout from Normandy bridgehead at Avranches.
Aug. 11	Allied landings in Southern France.
Aug. 13–20	German forces destroyed in Falaise Pocket in France.
Aug. 25	De Gaulle and Allied troops enter Paris.
Aug. 30	Russians enter Bucharest.
Sept. 4	Cease-fire between Soviet Union and Finland. Armistice signed on 19th.
Sept. 5	Brussels liberated by Allied troops.

	Sept. 8	V-2 rockets begin landing in Britain.
	Sept. 17	Arnhem airborne landings in Allied attempt to seize vital river crossings for advance into northern Germany.
	Oct. 3	Final suppression of Warsaw rising by German forces.
	Oct. 14	British troops liberate Athens.
	Oct. 20	Belgrade liberated by Russians and Yugoslav partisans.
	Oct. 23	De Gaulle's administration recognized by the Allies as provisional government of France.
	Dec. 3	Rioting in Athens and British police action sparks off communist insurrection.
	Dec. 16	Germans begin Ardennes offensive, the 'Battle of the Bulge'.
	Dec. 31	Regency installed in Greece by British.
1945	Jan. 3	Allied counter-attack begins in Ardennes.
	Jan. 11	Truce declared in Greek Civil War.
	Jan. 17	Russians take Warsaw.
	Feb. 4–11	Yalta Conference. Churchill, Roosevelt and Stalin plan for Germany's unconditional surrender, the settlement of Poland, and the United Nations Conference at San Francisco.
	Feb. 12	Amnesty granted to Greek Communists.
	Feb. 13	Fall of Budapest to Russians.
	Mar. 23	American armies cross Rhine at Remagen.
	Mar. 28	End of V-Rocket offensive against Britain.
	Apr. 3	Beneš appoints a National Front Government in Czechoslovakia.
	Apr. 20	Russians reach Berlin.
	Apr. 25	Renner becomes Chancellor of provisional Austrian government.
	Apr. 26	Russian and American forces link up at Torgau.
	Apr. 28	Mussolini killed by partisans.
	Apr. 30	Hitler commits suicide in Berlin. Dönitz is appointed successor.
	May 1	German army in Italy surrenders.
	May 2	Berlin surrenders to Russians.
	May 3	British take Rangoon in Burma.
	May 7	General Jodl makes unconditional surrender of all German forces to Eisenhower.
	May 8	Victory in Europe, 'VE' day. Von Keitel surrenders to Zhukov near Berlin.
	May 9	Russians take Prague.
	May 14	Democratic Republic of Austria established.
	June 5	Allied Control Commission assumes control in Germany, which is divided into four occupation zones.
	June 22	Americans complete capture of Okinawa, campaign declared ended on 2 July.
	July 12–15	Japan seeks Russian mediation to end war.

1,000-bomber raid on Tokyo; ten Japanese cities devastated by air attacks.

Aug. 6   Atomic bomb dropped on Hiroshima.

Aug. 8   USSR declares war on Japan.

Aug. 9   Atomic bomb dropped on Nagasaki; Russian troops enter northern Korea and Manchuria.

Aug. 14   Japan surrenders.

Mobilization and casualties: World War II (all theatres)

	Strength of armed forces	Military killed and missing	Military wounded	Civilian[1] dead
Australia	680,000	29,395	39,803	
Austria	800,000	380,000	350,117	145,000
Britain	4,683,000	271,311[2]	277,077	95,297
Canada	780,000	39,319	53,174	
Finland	250,000	79,047	50,000	35,000
France	5,000,000 (est)	205,000	390,000	173,000
Germany	9,200,000	3,300,000	2,893,000	800,000
Greece	150,000	16,357	49,933	155,300
Hungary	350,000	147,435	89,313	280,000
India	2,393,891	36,092	64,354	79,489
Italy	4,500,000	279,820	120,000	93,000
Japan	6,095,000	1,380,429	295,247	933,000
Netherlands	500,000	13,700	2,860	236,300
New Zealand	157,000	12,162	19,314	
Poland	1,000,000	320,000	530,000	6,028,000
Romania	600,000	300,000	219,822	465,000
South Africa	140,000	8,681	14,363	
USSR	20,000,000	13,600,000[3]	5,000,000	7,720,000
USA	16,353,659	292,131	671,278	5,662
Yugoslavia	3,741,000	305,000	425,000	1,355,000

[1] Includes Jews killed by the Nazis.
[2] 19,753 POWs died in captivity.
[3] Includes POWs who were killed or died in captivity.

The Holocaust: Jews killed in Europe 1941–1945

	Jewish population in 1941	Estimated number of Jews killed by country
Austria	70,000	60,000
Belgium	85,000	28,000
Bulgaria	48,000	40,000
Czechoslovakia	81,000	60,000
Denmark	6,000	100
France	300,000	65,000
Germany	250,000	180,000
Greece	67,000	60,000
Holland	140,000	104,000
Hungary	710,000	200,000
Italy	120,000	9,000
Poland	3,000,000	2,600,000
Romania	1,000,000	750,000
USSR[1]	2,740,000	924,000
Yugoslavia	70,000	58,000

[1] Includes Baltic States

The Cold War and Eastern Europe 1942–1989

1942 May 26   Twenty-year Anglo-Soviet treaty signed, but without any territorial agreement for post-war Europe.

June–Aug.   Stalin steps up demands for opening of 'second front' to relieve pressure on Russia.

July   British suspension of convoys to Russia because of losses causes Stalin to accuse allies of lack of genuine support.

1943 Jan. 14–24   Churchill and Roosevelt agree to insist on the 'unconditional surrender' of Germany.
The decision to mount an invasion of Italy, agreed by the Allied commanders, led to bitter recriminations from Stalin, who saw it as bad faith on the part of the Western powers.

Aug.   Stalin objects to not being consulted about the surrender of Italy and demands a say in the Italian settlement.

Oct.   Three-power foreign ministers' conference in Moscow agrees upon an advisory council for Italy and makes broad plans for a world security organization.

Nov. 28–Dec. 1   Meeting of 'Big Three' (Churchill, Roosevelt, and Stalin) at Tehran, the first conference attended by Stalin. As well as discussing arrangements for the Allied landings in Europe and a renewed Soviet offensive against Germany, the main lines of a territorial settlement in Eastern Europe were agreed, including the Polish frontiers. No agreement was reached about the future of Germany, although there was discussion of the dismemberment of Germany.

1944 Aug. 21–Oct. 9   Dumbarton Oaks Conference draws up broad framework of the United Nations.

Sept. 11–17   Churchill and Roosevelt meet at Quebec and move towards acceptance of Morgenthau Plan for the destruction of German industry and the conversion of Germany into a pastoralised state.

Oct. 9–10   Churchill and Stalin meet in Moscow and decide on 'spheres of influence'. Romania and Bulgaria are ceded predominantly to Russian influence, Greece to Britain, and Yugoslavia and Hungary equally between Russia and Great Britain.

Dec. 3   Attempted Communist insurrection in Athens.

1945 Jan. 11   Communists in Greece seek truce.

Feb. 4–11   Meeting at Yalta between Churchill, Roosevelt and Stalin decides upon four occupation zones in Germany, the prosecution of war criminals, and prepares Allied Control Commission to run Germany on the basis of 'complete disarmament, demilitarization and dismemberment'. Removals of national wealth from Germany were to be permitted within two years of the end of the war and reparations were tentatively agreed. Agreement reached that the Provisional government already functioning in Poland, i.e. the communist Lublin-based group, with the addition of other groups including the London Poles, be the government. A three-power commission based in Moscow would supervise the setting up of the new regime. The Provisional Government was pledged to hold free and unfettered elections as soon as possible. Declaration on Liberated Europe signed by the three powers to allow European states to 'create democratic conditions of their own choice'.

Feb. 12	Greek Communists granted amnesty and lay down arms.
April	Members of non-communist delegation to the three-power commission in Moscow arrested. Russians conclude a treaty of alliance with the Lublin administration in Poland.
July 5	Great Britain and United States recognize Provisional Government of National Unity in Poland.
July 17–Aug. 1	Stalin, Truman, Churchill (after 25th, Attlee) meet at Potsdam and finalize four-power agreement on administration of Germany and the territorial adjustments in Eastern Europe. The Oder-Neisse line is to mark the new boundary between Germany and Poland. Although Germany is to be divided into zones, it is to be treated as a single economic unit. Germans living in Poland, Hungary and Czechoslovakia are to be sent to Germany.
Oct. 28	Provisional Czech National Assembly meets, representing communist and non-communist parties.
Nov.	Tito elected President of Yugoslavia.
1946 Mar. 6	Churchill makes 'Iron Curtain' speech at Fulton, Missouri: 'From Stettin in the Baltic to Trieste in the Adriatic, an Iron Curtain has descended upon the Continent.'
May 26	At Czech elections, communists win 38% of the vote and set up a single party 'National Front' government.
May	Fighting breaks out in Northern Greece, marking renewal of civil war between monarchist forces, assisted by Britain, and communist guerrillas, backed by Albania, Bulgaria and Yugoslavia.
1947 Feb. 21	The British inform the Americans that they cannot afford to keep troops in Greece because of their domestic economic difficulties and intend to withdraw them by the end of March.

Feb. 27	Dean Acheson privately expounds the 'Truman Doctrine' of economic and military aid to nations in danger of communist take-over.
Mar. 12	In message to Congress, President Truman outlines the Truman Doctrine 'to support free peoples who are resisting attempted subjugation by armed minorities or by outside pressures', effectively committing the United States to intervene against communist or communist-backed movements in Europe and elsewhere.
Apr. 22	Truman Doctrine passed by Congress.
Apr. 24	Council of Foreign Ministers in Moscow ends without formal peace treaties for Germany and Austria.
May 22	US Congress passes Bill for $250 million of aid for Greece and Turkey.
June 5	George Marshall, American Secretary of State, calls for a European recovery programme supported by American aid.
June 12–June 15	Non-communist nations of Europe set up Committee of European Economic Co-operation to draft European Recovery Programme.
Aug.	First American aid arrives in Greece, followed by military 'advisers' to assist in the Civil War against the communists.
1948 Feb. 25	Czech President Beneš accepts a communist-dominated government.
Mar. 10	Czech Foreign Minister, Jan Masaryk, found dead in suspicious circumstances.
Mar. 14–31	Congress passes the Foreign Assistance Act, the Marshall Plan. $5,300 million of 'Marshall Aid' is initially allocated for European recovery.
Mar. 17	Belgium, France, Luxembourg, the Netherlands and Great Britain sign a treaty setting up the Brussels Treaty Organization for mutual military assistance.
Mar. 20	Russian representative walks out of Allied Control Commission, over plans for unified German currency.
Mar. 30	Russians impose restrictions on traffic between Western zones and Berlin.
April	Paris Treaty sets up Organization for European Economic Co-operation to receive Marshall Aid.
May 30	No opposition parties are allowed to stand at Czech elections and electors called on to vote for a single list of National Front candidates.
June 7	Beneš resigns as President of Czechoslovakia; succeeded by Gottwald.
June 24	Russians impose a complete blockade of traffic into Berlin. Berlin airlift begins (25th).
June	Yugoslavia expelled from Comintern, effectively putting it outside direct Soviet control.
Sept. 5	Head of Polish Communist Party, Gomulka, forced to resign.

	Nov. 30	Russians set up separate municipal government for East Berlin.
1949	Jan. 25	Comecon, Communist economic co-operation organization, set up.
	Apr. 4	Creation of NATO. North Atlantic Treaty signed by members of Brussels Treaty Organization, with Canada, Denmark, Iceland, Italy, Norway, Portugal and the United States. It pledges mutual military assistance.
	May 4	Representatives of four occupation powers in Germany come to an agreement for ending of Berlin blockade.
	May 15	Communists take power in Hungary on the basis of a single-list election for the 'Peoples Front', replacing the communist-dominated coalition which had been elected in 1947.
	May 12	Berlin blockade lifted.
	May	Federal Republic of Germany (West Germany) comes into existence.
	June	Purge of Albanian Communist Party.
	Sept. 30	End of Berlin airlift.
	Oct. 16	Greek communists cease fighting.
	Oct.	German Democratic Republic (East Germany) comes into existence.
	Nov.	Russian Marshal takes command of Polish army.
	Dec. 1949–Jan. 1950	Purge of Bulgarian Communist Party; 92,000 expelled.
1950	May 28	Pro-Stalinist Hoxha confirmed in power in single-list elections in Albania.
	May–June	Last non-communists expelled from Hungarian government.
	July	Romanian Communist Party admits to expulsion of almost 200,000 members in past two years.
	Sept.	United States proposes German re-armament.
1951	Sept.	First Soviet atomic bomb exploded.
1952	Feb. 18	Greece and Turkey join NATO.
	May 27	Belgium, France, Italy, Luxembourg, the Netherlands, and West Germany sign mutual defence treaty for proposed creation of a European Defence Community.
1953	Mar. 5	Death of Stalin. Khrushchev confirmed as First Secretary of the Communist Party (September).
	June	Risings in East Germany suppressed.
1954	May 5	Italy and West Germany enter Brussels Treaty Organization.
1955	May 9	West Germany admitted to NATO.
	May 14	Warsaw Pact formed.
1956	Feb.	At Russian Twentieth Party Congress Khrushchev attacks abuses of Stalin era in 'Secret Speech'.

June	Suppression of workers' riots in Poznan, Poland; Gomulka becomes First Secretary of Polish United Workers' Party (October).
Oct. –Nov.	General strike and street demonstrations in Budapest. Russians intervene, depose Imre Nagy and crush the rising. Kadar becomes the First Secretary of the Hungarian Communist Party and Premier. Thousands of Hungarian refugees flee to the West.
1958 Feb.	Khrushchev replaces Bulganin as Prime Minister.
1961 Apr.	First manned Soviet space flight. Arrests of dissident writers.
July	Anti-clerical legislation in Russia, restricting role of the clergy in parish councils.
Aug.	Berlin Wall constructed to prevent flight from East to West Berlin.
Oct.	Twenty-second Party Congress; new Party programme and further 'de-Stalinization', including the removal of Stalin's body from Red Square mausoleum.
1962 Oct.	Cuban missile crisis after Soviet Union attempts to set up ballistic missile bases in Cuba. Imposition of naval 'quarantine' by the United States forces the Soviet Union to back down in the face of the threat of nuclear war. A major diplomatic triumph for the will and resolve of President John F. Kennedy.
Nov.	Publication of Solzhenitsyn's *A Day in the Life of Ivan Denisovitch* marks first public recognition of the conditions in Soviet labour camps.
1963 Mar.	Khrushchev warns Writers' Union of 'bourgeois influences'.
Aug. 5	Partial Test Ban Treaty signed in Moscow, banning nuclear weapon tests in the atmosphere, outer space, and under water (in force from October).
1964 Oct.	Brezhnev replaces Khrushchev as First Secretary.
1965 Mar.	Central Committee of the Soviet Union makes a number of agricultural reforms.
Sept.	Central Committee approves further set of economic reforms.
1966 Feb.	Trial of leading 'dissidents', Sinyavsky and Daniel, who are sentenced to periods of imprisonment.
1967 June	Arab-Israeli 'Six-Day' War leads to acute tension between United States and Soviet Union.
1968 Jan.	Soviet dissidents Ginsburg and Galanskov tried and imprisoned. Dubcek becomes First Secretary of Czechoslovak Communist Party and process of liberalization begins – 'Socialism with a human face'

– including decentralization of economic planning and more open contacts with the West.

July 1	Non-proliferation treaty signed in London, Moscow and Washington.
Aug.	The Soviet Union and other Warsaw Pact forces invade Czechoslovakia and end the 'Prague Spring'. The Czech leaders are forced to agree in Moscow to the re-imposition of censorship, return to centralized planning, and the abandonment of closer links with the West. Husak takes over Party Secretaryship from Dubcek (Jan. 1969).
1969 Mar.	Dubcek demoted and sent as ambassador to Turkey; he is eventually expelled from the Party and given menial work.
Oct.	Czechoslovakia repudiates its condemnation of the Warsaw Pact invasion and consents to the stationing of Russian troops.
1970 Dec.	Widespread rioting in Poland over food prices and economic conditions; Gierek replaces Gomulka as First Secretary of Polish United Workers' Party.
1971 Feb.	Mass Jewish demonstration at Supreme Soviet building. Jewish emigration to Israel increases.
1972 Jan.	Seizure of documents and leading intellectuals in the Ukraine.
May 26	President Nixon visits Moscow. Strategic Arms Limitation Treaty (SALT 1) signed between United States and Soviet Union on limitation of anti-ballistic missile systems (in force from October) and interim agreement on limitation of strategic offensive arms.
May	Disturbances in Lithuania.
1973 Apr.	Andropov and Gromyko join Politburo.
1974 Feb.	Solzhenitsyn deported from Soviet Union.
1975 Aug.	Helsinki agreement on European Security and Co-operation provides for 'Human Rights'.
Oct.	Soviet physicist and dissident Andre Sakharov awarded Nobel Peace Prize.
1976 June	Strikes and sabotage in Poland in opposition to attempted price rises which were temporarily withdrawn, although unrest is severely put down.
1977 Jan.	Dissident civil rights group 'Charter 77' formed in Prague.
June	Brezhnev replaces Podgorny as President of the Soviet Union.
1978 July	Trial of Scharansky.
1979 June	Visit of Polish Pope John Paul II to Poland helps to arouse strong national feeling.

Dec.	Soviet invasion of Afghanistan. The United States imposes a grain embargo on Russia. Large commemorative services held in Poland for those killed in the disturbances of 1970.
1980 Jan.	Sakharov sentenced to internal exile in Gorky.
Mar. –Apr.	Dissident groups in Poland advocate boycott of official Parliamentary elections on 23 March, and mass commemorative service for Polish officers killed at Katyn in April 1940 leads to arrests.
July	Olympic Games in Moscow boycotted by the United States.
July–Sept.	Widespread strikes amongst Polish workers at Gdansk (Danzig) and elsewhere as a result of rise in meat prices. In August, Gdansk workers publish demands calling for free trade unions. Soviet Union begins jamming of Western broadcasts. Resignation of Babinch as Prime Minister (24 August) and of Gierek as First Secretary of the Polish United Workers Party (6 September); replaced by Pinkowski and Kania. Gierek's departure followed by the signing of the Gdansk agreement with Lech Walesa, the leader of the Gdansk 'inter-factory committee'. This recognised the new Solidarity unions, granted a wage agreement and promised a 40-hour week, permitted the broadcast of church services on Sunday, relaxed the censorship laws, promised to re-examine the new meat scales, and review the case of imprisoned dissidents. National Confederation of Independent Trade Unions, 'Solidarity', formed under leadership of Lech Walesa (8 September) attracts an estimated 10 million members. 'Rural Solidarity' claims an estimated half a million farmers.
Dec.	Death of Russian Prime Minister Kosygin.
1981 Jan.	Walesa visits Pope in Rome.
Feb.	General Jaruzelski replaces Pinkowski as Prime Minister of Poland.
Dec.	After visiting Moscow, General Jaruzelski declares martial law in Poland. The leading members of Solidarity are arrested and the organization banned.
1982 Nov.	Death of Brezhnev. Andropov beomes First Secretary of the Communist Party of the Soviet Union.
1984 Feb.	Death of Andropov, Chernenko becomes First Secretary of the Communist Party of the Soviet Union.
1985 March	Death of Chernenko. Gorbachev becomes First Secretary of the Communist Party of the Soviet Union. Announces programme of *Glasnost* and *Perestroika*.

July	Gorbachev replaces four members of politburo with his own supporters, veteran Foreign Minister, Gromyko, moved to Presidency and replaced by Gorbachev supporter Shevardnadze.
1986 Jan.	Gorbachev continues process of removing the personnel of the Brezhnev era from Central and Regional government.
Sept.	Solidarity announce intention of working within the existing system.
1987 June	Karoly Grosz, an economic liberal, becomes Prime Minister in Hungary.
July	Protests by Crimean Tartars in Moscow permitted to take place.
Aug.	Protests in the Baltic States demanding greater autonomy and an end to 'Russification'.
Nov.	Polish Government hold referendum for programme of radical reform; Solidarity calls for boycott and the proposals are rejected. Radical Boris Yeltsin dismissed as head of Moscow Party for outspoken criticisms of conservatives.
Dec.	President Reagan and General Secretary Gorbachev sign Intermediate Nuclear Forces Treaty in Washington; a major breakthrough in East-West arms negotiations.
Dec. 17	Gustav Husak resigns party leadership in Czechoslovakia; succeeded by another conservative, Milos Jakes.
1988 Jan.	Gorbachev calls for acceleration of drive to democratization; calls special party Congress in the summer. Major reform of Soviet Constitution sets up a Supreme Soviet consisting of two chambers to meet in almost continuous session, the members selected by a Congress of People's Deputies representing national areas, social organizations and constituencies. Hungarian government announces end of price controls.
Feb.	Serious ethnic riots in Naborno-Karabakh region of Azerbaijan.
Mar.–Aug.	Wave of strikes and unrest in Poland; Solidarity demands talks with Government.
May	Russian agreement to withdraw all troops from Afghanistan by February 1989. In Hungary, Kadar relegated to post of Party President; Grosz becomes Party Secretary and Prime Minister; purge of conservatives in Central Committee and Politburo.
Dec.	Polish Government accepts 'round table' talks with Solidarity. Gorbachev announces unilateral force reductions of 500,000 troops and 10,000 tanks.

1989 Jan.   Law on Association in Hungary allows political
               parties to be formed; new draft constitution (Mar.)
               drops reference to leading role for Communist Party.

Feb. 6   Solidarity and Polish Government open talks on
               future of Poland.

Mar.–Apr.   Solidarity accepts terms for participation in
               elections; Government agrees to admit opposition to
               the lower house of parliament (*sejm*); a freely
               elected Senate, and create office of President.
               Solidarity legalized.

June   First free parliamentary elections in Poland since
               Second World War; Solidarity obtains landslide
               victory in seats it is allowed to contest. Hungarian
               Government recognizes Imre Nagy, leader of 1956
               rising, and permits his reburial with full honours.

July   General Jarulzelski elected President of Poland by
               one-vote margin. General Kiszczak appointed Prime
               Minister but fails to form a government and resigns;
               Solidarity activist Tadeusz Mazowiecki becomes
               Prime Minister heading first non-communist
               government.

Sept.   Hungary opens border with Austria allowing flight of
               thousands of East Germans to the West.

Oct.   Erich Honecker replaced as President by Egon Krenz
               in East Germany (18th) following flight of East
               Germans to the west and mass demonstrations in
               East German cities organised by New Forum
               opposition group. Krenz meets opposition group
               (26th); travel restrictions discussed.

Nov.   East German Council of Ministers resigns en masse
               following huge demonstrations in East Berlin and
               other cities. New Forum opposition legalized and
               Politburo resigns (7–8th). Berlin Wall opened and
               travel restrictions lifted on East German citizens
               (9th). Reformer, Hans Modrow, President (13th).
               President Todor Zhivkov of Bulgaria resigns (10th).
               Entire Czech Politburo resigns (24th) following mass
               demonstrations in Prague by Civic Forum opposition
               group.

Dec.   Malta summit between President Bush and President
               Gorbachev; declare the Cold War 'at an end' (4th).
               Resignation of Czech Prime Minister, Adamec,
               forced by further mass demonstrations and General
               Strike. Communist monopoly of power ended and
               joint interim government formed with members of
               Civic Forum. (7th–9th).
               Resignation of Egon Krenz as Communist leader in
               East Germany (8th). Preparations for free elections
               begin.
               Thousands reported killed in anti-Ceausescu
               demonstrations in Romanian city of Timisoara (19th).
               Bulgaria declares will hold free elections (19th).
               Brandenburg Gate opened between East and West

Berlin as symbolic act of reconciliation between the two Germanies (22nd).
Mass demonstrations in Bucharest and other Romanian cities. After initial attempts to disperse them, the army joins the crowds and Ceausescu and his wife flee. (22nd). Heavy fighting between pro-Ceausescu forces and the army leaves several hundred killed and wounded in Bucharest and other Romanian cities; Ceausescu and his wife arrested and executed by Military Tribunal (25th). Free elections announced for April 1990; Ion Iliescu becomes President (26th).
Vaclav Havel, former dissident and political prisoner, unanimously elected President of Czechoslovakia (29th); Alexander Dubcek earlier elected Chairman (Speaker) of Czech Parliament (28th).

1990 Jan.	Czechoslovakia calls for abolition of Comecon.
Feb.	First steps to German reunification with establishment of commission on single currency (13th). Victory of *Sajudis* (Lithuanian nationalist movement) in general election. First Soviet troop withdrawals from Czechoslovakia (26th).
Mar.	Lithuanian declaration of independence (11th); Gorbachev pronounces declaration 'illegal and invalid' (13th); Soviet troops seize Lithuanian Party headquarters (27th); Estonia pledges restoration of independence (30th).
Apr.	Oil supplies to Lithuania cut by Moscow (18th).
May	'Consultation with the people' promised by Gorbachev on future of the economy (23rd), followed by panic buying in shops; renewed violence in Armenia; Yeltsin successfully challenges for Presidency of Russian Federation.
July	Economic union of East and West Germany.

Western Europe since 1945

1945 June 5   Allied Control Commission set up to administer Germany.

July   Churchill voted out as Prime Minister in Britain; Labour Party under Attlee takes power, pledges to introduce a 'welfare state'.

Dec.   De Gasperi becomes Prime Minister of Italy as head of Christian Democrat Party.

1946 Jan.   De Gaulle resigns as President of French Provisional Government after his draft constitution is rejected; he tries to rally right-wing opinion in his non-party, *Rassemblement du People Français (RPF)*.

Mar.   Churchill makes 'Iron Curtain' speech at Fulton, Missouri.

May   King Victor Emmanuel II of Italy abdicates; a referendum votes Italy a Republic.

July   Bread rationing introduced in Britain; more severe rationing than the war because of economic crisis.

Oct.   Fourth Republic established in France.

Dec.   Britain and USA agree economic merger of their zones in Germany.

1947 Mar.   Anglo-French Treaty of Alliance.

June   General Marshall proposes economic aid to rebuild Europe; Paris Conference (July) meets to discuss the 'Marshall Plan'.

1948 Apr.   Organization for European Economic Co-operation (OEEC) set up to receive 17,000 million dollars of Marshall aid from the United States, Member states: Austria, Belgium, Denmark, France, West Germany, Greece, Iceland, Ireland, Italy, Luxembourg, the Netherlands, Norway, Portugal, Spain, Sweden, Switzerland, Turkey and the United Kingdom. Customs Union set up between Belgium, the Netherlands and Luxembourg – 'Benelux'.

1949 May 23   German Federal Republic comes into existence on basis of constitution drafted the previous year with Konrad Adenauer as first Federal Chancellor. Council of Europe set up for 'political co-operation', consisting of the OEEC states apart from Spain and Portugal. Strasbourg becomes head-quarters for a Consultative Assembly.

Aug. 24   North Atlantic Treaty Organisation (NATO) formed including United States, Canada, United Kingdom, Norway, Denmark, Holland, Belgium, France, Italy, Greece and Turkey.

1950   Britain rejects idea of joining a European coal and steel community.

1951 Apr. 18   Paris Treaty between Benelux countries (Belgium,

	Netherlands and Luxembourg), France, Italy and West Germany – 'the Six' – sets up a 'Common Market' in coal and steel. A European Commission is set up as the supreme authority.
Oct.	Fall of Labour Government in Britain; Churchill returns to office. De Gaulle retires from politics.
1952 Oct.	Britain explodes an atomic bomb in Monte Bello islands, off N. W. Australia.
1953	European Court of Human Rights set up in Strasbourg.
1954	Western European Union proposed by the British as a substitute for a single European army.
May	Defeat for French forces at Dien Bien Phu (see p. 282).
Aug.	Death of De Gasperi, Christian Democrat Prime Minister of Italy 1945–1953.
1955 Jan.	Germany joins NATO.
Apr. 5	Resignation of Churchill as British Prime Minister. Anthony Eden takes over. Messina Conference of 'the Six' discusses a full customs union. Britain expresses preference for a larger free trade area of the OEEC countries.
1956 Oct.–Nov.	Anglo-French intervention at Suez (see p. 287).
1957 Jan. 9	Fall of Eden as a consequence of Suez crisis; Harold Macmillan takes over (10th) as Prime Minister.
Mar. 25	Rome Treaties between 'the Six' set up the European Economic Community (EEC) and Euratom.
1958 May	Rioting by French settlers in Algeria leads to French army taking over (13th); De Gaulle voted into power in France after period of chronic political instability (29th) and given power to produce a new constitution.
Oct. 9–28	Death of Pope Pius XII; election of John XXIII.
Dec. 21	De Gaulle elected President of Fifth French Republic.
1959 Nov.	European Free Trade Association (EFTA) set up as a counterweight to the EEC, comprising Austria, Denmark, Norway, Portugal, Sweden, Switzerland and the United Kingdom.
1960 Feb.	France explodes her first atomic device.
1961 Apr. 21	French army revolt begins in Algeria against de Gaulle's plans for Algerian independence.
Aug. 10	United Kingdom, Ireland and Denmark apply for membership of EEC; also Norway (1962).
Aug. 17–18	Berlin Wall erected to halt flood of refugees to West.
1962	EEC agrees Common Agricultural Policy to come into operation in 1964; a system of high guaranteed prices to be paid for out of a common fund;

	beginning of period of agricultural prosperity in rural Europe and huge food surpluses.
Dec.	Britain arranges with USA to adopt Polaris missile system as its nuclear deterrent.

1963 Jan.	De Gaulle vetoes British entry into EEC; Irish, Danish and Norwegian applications suspended.
June 3–21	Death of John XXIII; election of Pope Paul VI.
Aug. 5	France refuses to sign Test Ban Treaty, signalling intention to build up *force de frappe*.
Oct.	Adenauer retires as Chansellor of Germany; succeeded by Dr Ludwig Erhard.

1964 Oct.	Labour, under Harold Wilson, returns to power in Britain after thirteen years of Conservative rule.

1966 Mar.	France withdraws from Military Committee of NATO. Labour government re-elected in Britain.
Nov. 30	Dr Kurt-Georg Kiesinger becomes Chancellor of Germany.

1967 Nov. 27	Further British, Irish, Danish and Norwegian application to join EEC vetoed by de Gaulle.

1968 May	Violent student unrest in Paris and mass strikes against de Gaulle's government.
Sept.	Dr Salazar of Portugal, western Europe's longest surviving dictator, succeeded by Dr Marcello Caetano.

1969 Apr. 28	De Gaulle resigns as President after unfavourable vote in referendum on the constitution; Gaullist Georges Pompidou becomes President.
Aug.	First British troops sent to Northern Ireland (see p. 296).
Oct.	German Social Democrats take power under Willy Brandt; begins policy of *Ostpolitik*, seeking friendly relations with eastern Europe, and encourages enlargement of EEC.

1970 Mar.	Heads of East and West Germany meet for first time.
June 18	Defeat of Labour Government in Britain, Edward Heath, a committed European, leads Conservative government.
Nov. 9	Death of de Gaulle.

1971 Oct. 28	British Parliament votes in favour of application to join the Common Market.

1972 Mar. 24	Britain imposes direct rule in Northern Ireland.
Apr.	Defection from German coalition leads to early election in November.
Sept. 5	Arab terrorists kill Israeli athletes at Munich Olympics.
Nov.	Brandt's government returned to power with SPD as largest party in Bundestag.

1973	Jan	Britain, Denmark and Ireland join EEC; Norway does not, following unfavourable referendum vote.
	May	Britain in dispute with Iceland over fishing rights – 'Cod War'.
	June 22	West and East Germany join the United Nations.
	Dec.	Conservative Prime Minister Heath declares state of emergency as a result of miners' strike.
1974	Feb. 28	Heath defeated in general election; Labour government in Britain under Wilson.
	Apr. 2	Death of Georges Pompidou; Giscard d'Estaing becomes President (May).
	Apr. 25	Military junta deposes Portuguese government, ending dictatorship and colonial wars.
	May	Willy Brandt resigns following security scandal; Helmut Schmidt takes over as Chancellor.
	Sept. 30	General Spinola resigns and replaced by Costa Gomes in Portugal.
	Oct. 10	Labour Party in Britain obtains small majority at general election.
1975	Jan.	British government announces referendum on EEC membership
	Feb. 28	German opposition leader, Peter Lorenz, kidnapped by terrorists.
	Apr. 25	Portugal holds first free elections for 50 years.
	June	Britain votes by two to one in referendum to remain in EEC. Greece, Spain and Portugal apply for membership.
	Nov. 20	Death of Franco; King Juan Carlos I succeeds to the throne (27th).
	Dec.	Terrorist attacks by Indonesian immigrants in the Netherlands.
1976	Apr. 5	James Callaghan becomes Prime Minister of Britain following resignation of Harold Wilson.
	Sept. 19	Social Democratic Party in Sweden defeated for first time in 44 years.
1977	June 15	First general election in Spain for 40 years. Señor Suarez's Democratic Centre Party wins power.
	Sept. 5	German terrorists kill Dr Hans-Martin Schleyer, head of West German Employers' Federation.
1978	Mar. 16	Aldo Moro, former prime minister of Italy, kidnapped in Rome by Italian terrorists; found dead (9 May).
	Aug. 6–26	Death of Pope Paul VI; election of John Paul I.
	Sept. 28– Oct. 16	Death of Pope John Paul I; election of John Paul II, former Cardinal Karol Wojtyla, first non-Italian Pope for 400 years.
	Dec. 27	First democratic government in Spain.
	Dec.–Apr.	'Winter of Discontent' in Britain with widespread strikes against Labour government's wage policy.

1979	May 3	Conservatives under Margaret Thatcher take power following general election in Britain. European Monetary System (EMS) introduced with common European Currency Unit (ECU) linking the exchange rates of the individual countries.
	June	First direct elections to the European Parliament.
1980	Apr. 30– May 5	Iranian embassy in London seized by terrorists. and stormed by British specialist anti-terrorist forces, the SAS.
	Aug. 2	Terrorist bomb explodes at Bologna railway station killing 76 people.
	Oct. 5	German coalition of SPD and Free Democrats retains power in elections.
	Dec. 4	Prime Minister of Portugal, Dr da Carneiro, killed in air crash.
1981	Jan. 1	Greece becomes member of EEC.
	Feb. 23	Attempted coup in Spain led by Lt.-Col. Trejero Molina; leaders arrested.
	Mar. 26	Social Democratic Party formed in Britain by breakaway of four senior figures from Labour Party.
	May 10	François Mitterrand, leader of socialists, becomes President of France in place of Giscard d'Estaing.
	May 13	Pope John Paul II shot and injured by Turkish terrorist.
	July	Rioting in several inner city areas of Britain.
	Nov.	Sensational by-election successes of British SDP/Liberal Alliance leads to predictions of Alliance victory if an election called.
1982	April	Britain sends Task Force to recapture Falkland Islands from Argentina (see p. 303).
	May 30	Spain joins NATO.
	June 15	Argentine forces on Falklands surrender.
	Sept. 19	Social Democrats return to power in Sweden.
	Oct.	Felipe Gonzales leads socialists to victory in Spanish elections. Helmut Kohl of Christian Democrats becomes Chancellor of Germany following breakup of governing coalition.
1983	March	Crisis economic package in France and Cabinet re-shuffle.
	Mar. 6	Helmut Kohl wins a substantial electoral victory; Green Party passes 5 per cent threshhold for seats in the Bundestag.
	June 9	Mrs Thatcher returned for second term of office in Britain. Labour Party and Alliance split the opposition vote.
1984	Mar. 9	Beginning of 12-month miners' strike in Britain.
	Apr. 20	Britain confirms intention to leave Hong Kong in 1997 when the lease from China expires.
	July 19	French communists withdraw support from Mitterrand.

	Sept. 4	Herr Honecker, East German premier, cancels trip to West Germany because of Soviet opposition.
	Oct.	IRA bomb explosion at Grand Hotel, Brighton, narrowly misses killing Mrs Thatcher.
1985	Nov.	Anglo-Irish agreement signed between Mrs Thatcher and Dr Fitzgerald, the Irish premier, giving Irish government a consultative role in Northern Irish affairs.
	Dec.	Single European Act agreed at Luxembourg Summit.
1986	Jan. 1	Spain and Portugal join the Common Market.
	Jan.	Two cabinet ministers resign in Britain over 'Westland Affair'.
	Mar. 12	Referendum in Spain favours continued membership of NATO.
	Mar.	General election in France gives socialists largest number of seats, but neo-Gaullist Jacques Chirac forms government; beginning of period of 'cohabitation' between socialist President Mitterrand and conservative Chirac.
	June 22	Gonzales and socialists returned to power in Spanish elections.
1987	Jan. 25	Helmut Kohl's government confirmed in office at elections.
	June 11	Mrs Thatcher wins an unprecedented third term as Prime Minister of Britain.
1988	Apr.–May	Mitterrand defeats Chirac in French Presidential elections.
	June 5–12	Mitterrand calls elections for National Assembly but fails to achieve the expected overall majority.
	Sept. 20	Mrs Thatcher's 'Bruges Speech' attacks EEC attempts to introduce socialism by the back door.
1989	June	European elections witness rise in Green votes throughout Europe. Socialist bloc increases substantially in European Parliament.

The Middle East

The Middle East since 1914

1914   Outbreak of the First World War; Turkey joins the Central
       Powers (see p. 2).
       Egypt becomes a British Protectorate.
       British force sent to Mesopotamia to safeguard the Persian
       oil-fields.

1915   British advance on Baghdad, but fall back on Kut (Nov.) and
       besieged by Turks.

1916   Sykes-Picot agreement between Britain and France divides the
       Middle Eastern provinces of the Turkish Empire – Syria,
       Lebanon, Palestine and Iraq – between the two powers.
       Fall of Kut.

1917   Balfour Declaration on a Jewish homeland in the Middle East
       (for Palestine see p. 75).
       General Allenby takes Jerusalem (Dec.); growing success of
       'Arab Revolt' led by T. E. Lawrence and Amir Feisal.

1918   British take Amman and Damascus; French naval forces take
       Beirut. British forces free Iraq from Turkish rule (Sept.–Oct.).
       War in Middle East officially ends (31 Oct.).
       Wilson's Fourteen Points propose 'self-determination';
       Anglo-French agreement promises independence to peoples
       'oppressed by the Turks'.
       Egyptians call for a delegation (a *Wafd*) at Versailles.

1919   Vice President of Egyptian legislative council, Saad Pasha
       Zaghlul, arrested and deported; Wafdist revolt by students in
       Cairo put down by force and over a thousand killed (Mar.).
       Zaghlul released and attends peace conference at Versailles;
       President Wilson recognizes the British Protectorate (Apr.).
       Milner Commission on Egypt set up (Oct.).
       King Feisal proclaimed King of Syria (Mar.).

1920   Great Britain given League of Nations' mandates over
       Palestine, Transjordan and Iraq; France given mandates over
       Syria and Lebanon (Apr.).
       King Feisal expelled from Syria by French (July).
       Iraqi National Government set up, transferring government
       from military to civil rule (Nov.).
       Breakdown of talks between Milner and Wafd leader, Zaghlul.
       Soviet forces occupy northern Iran.

1921   Cairo Conference invites Feisal to become King of Iraq (Mar.);
       confirmed by plebiscite (Jun.).
       Following Wafdist demonstrations, Zaghlul deported (Dec.).

Further protest strikes and demonstrations (Dec.-Mar.).
Reza Shah Pahlavi leads coup in Persia (Iran); Soviet troops leave.

1922   Egyptian protectorate ended and Egypt declared independent but with Britain retaining her imperial communications via the Suez Canal, the defence of Egypt and the Sudan, and the protection of foreign interests and minorities (Feb.).
Sultan Faud becomes King of Egypt and Zaghlul released (Mar.); Constitutional Committee set up to draft constitution (Apr.).
Anglo-Iraqi treaty signed accepting implementation of mandate. Palestine west of Jordan River becomes part of British mandate for Palestine; eastern area becomes part of Transjordan.

1923   Overwhelming election victory for the Wafd in general election (Sept.).
Reza Shah Pahlavi becomes Prime Minister of Iran.

1924   Zaghlul becomes Prime Minister of Egypt (Jan.).
Resigns following assassination of Sir Lee Stack, British Commander-in-Chief (Nov.).
General Sarrail becomes High Commissioner of Syria; outbreak of Druze rebellion.
Constituent Assembly of Iraq meets for first time (Mar.); ratifies 1922 Treaty.
British troops withdraw from Iran.
Hussein Ibn Ali, King of Hejaz, driven from his kingdom by Ibn Saud.

1925   Wafdists gain majority in new general elections in Egypt, Zaghlul prevented from becoming Premier by High Commissioner, Lord Lloyd.
Reza Shah Pahlavi overthrows last of the Qajar dynasty and establishes his own as Shahs of Iran.

1926   Final suppression of Druze revolt in Syria.

1927   Death of Zaghlul; Mustafa al-Nahhas succeeds as leader of Wafd.

1930   Last Anglo-Iraqi treaty signed relinquishing British control apart from retention of two air bases (Jun.).

1932   Iraq joins League of Nations (Oct.).
Saudi Arabia Kingdom created by Ibn Saud.

1935   League of Nations awards Iraq control over Shatt-al-Arab water-way.

1936   Anglo-Egyptian Treaty; proposals for Franco-Syrian treaty agreed but not ratified.
Discovery of oil in Saudi Arabia.

1938   Saudi Arabian oil production begins.

1939   French forces in Syria and Lebanon reinforced.
Outbreak of Second World War (see pp. 42–3).

1940   British defeat Italian forces operating from Libya.

1941   British and Free French forces occupy Syria and Lebanon.
        German troops sent to assist Italians in North Africa (Feb.).
        Reza Shah Pahlavi deposed by British in Iran for pro-German
        sympathies and replaced by his son, Mohammed.
        British and Soviet troops occupy Iran for duration of war.

1942   German and Italian forces drive British back to El Alamein
        (June).
        British victory at El Alamein and pursuit of German and Italian
        forces across Libya into Tunisia (Oct.-May).

1943   Axis armies in Tunis surrender (May).
        Independent Lebanese state established.

1944   Free French concede Syrian independence.

1945   Formation of the Arab League by Egypt and five other Arab
        states in March (see p. 247).
        Fighting in Syria over delay in implementing French withdrawal.

1946   Syria becomes fully independent of the French.
        Abdullah Ibn Hussein becomes King of Jordan.

1948   State of Israel established.

1948-9 Arab-Israeli War (see p. 282).
        Jordan seizes West Bank and part of Jerusalem; Egypt takes
        Gaza.

1949   Britain recognizes Mohammed Idris al-Senussi as emir of Libya.

1950   Jordan annexes the West Bank of Palestine.

1951   Military government in Syria.
        Idris becomes King of Libya as an independent state.
        Iran nationalizes oil-fields and refineries, including giant
        Abadan complex.

1952   Anti-British riots in Egypt.

1953   Overthrow of the Egyptian monarchy; Egypt becomes a
        Republic and one-party state; disbanding of the Wafd and other
        groupings.

1954   Civilian rule returns to Syria.

1956   Gamal Abdel Nasser elected President of Egypt; nationalization
        of the Suez Canal and Suez invasion by Anglo-French and
        Israeli forces (see p. 287).

1958   Anti-Western insurrection in Lebanon put down with assistance
        of US marines.
        Military coup in Iraq, which is declared a Republic.

1961   Syria joins Egypt to form United Arab Republic (UAR).
        Break-up of United Arab Republic.
        Kuwait becomes an independent state; Iraq's claim to the
        territory resisted with the aid of British troops.

1963   *Coup d'état* brings radical Ba'ath Party to power in Syria as a
        socialist military government.

1964   Palestine Liberation Organization (PLO) founded by Yasser Arafat in Jordan.

1967   'Six-Day' War between Israel and Arab States (see p. 295).

1968   Coup in Iraq led by Saddam Hussein and Ba'ath Party.

1969   King Idris of Libya overthrown by military coup; Revolutionary Command Council led by Qadhafi proclaims a Republic, institutes Koranic law, a welfare system, and economic development programme. Colonel Nimeiri seizes power in the Sudan.

1970   Death of Nasser; Anwar Sadat becomes President of Egypt. Palestine Liberation Organization moves headquarters to Beirut. General Assad seizes power in Syria.

1973   Qadhafi takes control of foreign-held oil interests in Libya. 'Yom Kippur' War (see p. 298). Arab oil boycott against the West.

1975   Outbreak of fighting in Beirut.

1976   Syrian troops enter Lebanon.

1977   President Sadat visits Israel in major gesture of reconciliation. Short war between Egypt and Libya.

1979   Overthrow of the Shah's regime in Iran. Ayatollah Khomeini returns from exile in France to Iran and becomes head of government. Beginning of institution of Islamic fundamentalist regime in Iran and elimination of opponents. Soviet Union invades Afghanistan and installs Babrak Karmal as head of new government; beginning of Mujaheddin resistance, partly influenced by Islamic fundamentalism. Saddam Hussein becomes President of Iraq and begins purge of rivals and of Iraqi Shi-ite community. Riots by Iranian fundamentalists in Mecca.

1980   Iran revives claim to Shatt-al-Arab waterway; Iraq bombs Iranian targets and launches land assault on Iran beginning Iran-Iraq War (see p. 303).

1981   President Sadat assassinated by Islamic fundamentalists. Islamic Commission fails to end Iran-Iraq War.

1982   Temporary cease-fire by Iraq fails to end the war (June). Israeli troops invade Lebanon (see p. 77); PLO evacuated from Lebanon.

1983   Major Iranian offensive recaptures much of territory seized by Iraq.

1984   Iran-Iraq War escalates into attacks on Iran's Kharg Island oil installations by Iraqis and Iranian attacks on foreign ships entering the Persian Gulf en route to Iraq and Kuwait.

1987   'Intifada' begins amongst Palestinians on West Bank and in Gaza see (p. 305).

United States and Britain step up naval activity in the Persian Gulf; Iranian mine-layer seized.

Iraqi warplane accidentally hits American frigate.

Rioting by Iranian pilgrims in Mecca put down.

1988   American warship in Persian Gulf mistakenly shoots down civilian Iranian airliner (July).

UN-sponsored peace accord with Afghanistan, USSR, US and Pakistan for removal of Russian troops from May 1988 to be completed by February 1989. Mujaheddin denounce cease-fire.

PLO declare Palestinian independence and renounce terrorism (see p. 77)

1989   Final removal of Russian troops from Afghanistan completed but fighting continues between Mujaheddin and Marxist Kabul government under Najibullah.

Death of Ayatollah Khomeini; elections lead to his replacement as head of government by Hashami Rafsanjani.

The Atatürk Revolution and the fall of the Ottoman Empire

1914 Turkey declares war on the Allies (Oct).

1915 Dardanelles campaign.
British forces land on the peninsula (Apr.) but can make no headway. Allied evacuation of Gallipoli begins (Dec.).

1916 Arab Revolt begins (June).

1917 Allies recognize Hussein as King of Hejaz (Jan). Baghdad falls to the Allies (March). General Allenby sent to Palestine and captures Jerusalem (Dec.).

1918 Damascus, Beirut and Aleppo are lost as the Turks withdraw from Syria.
Armistice agreement signed at Mudros (Oct.).

1919 Greek forces land at Izmir with Allied approval (May).
Mustafa Kemal (Atatürk) is officially dismissed from his command by the Sultan.
Nationalist Congress meets at Erzurum under Kemal's chairmanship (July).
Nationalist Congress at Sivas promulgates National Pact (Sept).

1920 First Grand National Assembly under Kemal's Presidency meets in Ankara (April). Treaty of Sèvres is signed by the Sultan's government and renounces all claims to non-Turkish territory. Nationalists do not recognize this treaty (Aug.).

1921 Greek successes in Battle of Sakarya River threaten Ankara's security (Aug.).

1922 Nationalists defeat the Greeks and recapture Izmir (Sept.).
Armistice agreement between the Nationalists and the Allies is signed (Oct.).
Kemal abolishes the Sultanate (Nov.).

1923 Treaty of Lausanne replaces Sèvres and guarantees Turkish independence within her own frontiers (July). Kemal proclaims the Republic and becomes President (Oct. 29).

1924 National Assembly abolishes the Caliphate, Ministry of Religious Affairs, religious schools and religious courts (March/April). Constitution is adopted (April).

1925 Kurdish revolt is crushed (April).

1926 Treaty of Ankara between Turkey, Britain and Iraq (June). Plot on Kemal's life is uncovered. Ring leaders are tried and executed (June/July).

1928 Turkey is declared to be a secular state (April). Latin alphabet is introduced (Nov.).

1930 Religious riot at Menemen followed by executions (Dec).

1932   Turkey joins the League of Nations (July).

1934   First Five-Year Plan for industrial development is announced (Jan.).
Law requiring all citizens to adopt family names is passed (June).
Kemal takes the name Atatürk (Nov.). Women are granted the vote and made eligible to stand for election (Dec.).

1937   Autonomy of Hatay (Alexandretta) is agreed between Turkey, France and Syria (Jan.).

1938   Atatürk dies (Nov. 10) and is succeeded by Izmet Inönü.

Palestine: from the Balfour Declaration to 1948

1917 Balfour Declaration is issued, supporting the establishment in Palestine of a national home for the Jewish people (Nov. 2). General Allenby captures Jerusalem (Dec.).

1919 Third migration of Zionist Jews to Palestine – *aliyah* – begins.

1920 League of Nations assigns the mandate of Palestine to Britain (April). Herbert Samuel is appointed as the first High Commissioner.

1921 Serious anti-Jewish riots by Arabs (May). First *moshav* (co-operative village), Nahalal, is founded.

1922 Britain excludes Transjordan from the 'Jewish national home' provisions of the mandate.

1924 Fourth *aliyah* begins (mainly from Poland).

1925 Hebrew University opened on Mt Scopus.

1929 First large-scale attacks by Arabs upon Jews with massacres at Hebron and Safed (Aug.).

1931 Jewish terrorist organization, Irgun Zvai Leumi, is formed.

1933 Fifth *aliyah* begins (mainly from Germany and German-held territory).

1937 Peel Commission recommends the partition of Palestine into Jewish and Arab states (July).

1937–8 Repression of the Arab Revolt in Palestine.

1939 British White Paper limits Jewish immigration and land purchase.

1946 US President, Truman, publicly endorses the demand for the immediate admission of 100,000 Jewish refugees to Palestine. British refuse (April). Irgun blow up the King David Hotel, the British head-quarters; 91 people are killed (July).

1947 Steamer *Exodus* turned away from Palestine with 4,500 Holocaust survivors on board (July). UN General Assembly adopts the plan to partition Palestine (Nov.).

1948 Massacre of Arab villagers at Deir Yassin by Irgun (April). Ben-Gurion proclaims the state of Israel (May 14). Arab armies invade (May 15). UN mediator Count Bernadotte is assassinated in Jerusalem by Jewish terrorists (Sept.).

Arab-Israeli conflict since 1948

1949 Armistice agreements are signed between Israel and Egypt, Lebanon, Jordan and Syria which set Israel's borders until 1967 (Feb.–July). Israel admitted to United Nations. Ben-Gurion elected Prime Minister.

1953 USSR breaks off relations with Israel.

1954 Israeli agents are caught and hanged in Cairo. Increasing *fedayeen* (Arab commando) attacks on Israel.

1955 Ben-Gurion again becomes Prime Minister (Nov.).

1956 Nasser announces nationalization of Suez Canal Company (July). Israel invades Egypt (Oct.). British and French attack the Canal Zone but soon withdraw under super-power pressure (Nov.). United Nations Expeditionary Forces (UNEF) take over Canal Zone.

1957 Israel withdraws from Sinai and Gaza. UNEF stationed there.

1958–9 Fatah founded.

1962 Adolf Eichmann, the Austrian Nazi war criminal, executed in Israel (May).

1964 Palestine Liberation Organization (PLO) formed under Nasserite auspices.

1967 Nasser closes Gulf of Aqaba to Israeli shipping (May). Six-day war gives Israel a total victory over Egypt, Syria and Jordan (June, 5–10). UN Security Council Resolution 242 calls for a complete peace in Middle East. (See p. 295).

1968–9 Re-organization of PLO with Yasser Arafat as chairman.

1969 Golda Meir becomes Prime Minister of Israel.

1970 Sadat succeeds Nasser in Egypt.

1972 Israeli athletes kidnapped at Munich Olympics by al-Fatah.

1973 Yom Kippur War (see p. 298). Egypt and Syria launch a surprise attack on Israel (Oct. 6–25).
Arab-Israeli ceasefire agreement is signed (Nov.).

1976 Menachem Begin, former leader of Irgun, forms a government.

1977 Sadat visits Jerusalem (Nov.).

1978 Israel invades southern Lebanon (March). Camp David summit in USA between Carter, Begin and Sadat (Sept.). Arab summit in Baghdad denounces the Camp David Accords (Nov.).

1979 Egypt and Israel sign peace treaty which ends the state of war which had existed between the two countries since 1948 (March 26). Israel agrees phased withdrawal from Sinai.

1981 Israel annexes the Golan Heights (Dec.).

1982   Israel invades southern Lebanon as far as Beirut (June). PLO evacuate Beirut (Aug.). Massacre of Palestinians in refugee camps in Chatila and Sabra with Israeli complicity, causes outcry in Israel. Begin agrees to full and independent inquiry and sets up Kahan commission (Sept.).

1983   Kahan commission report precipitates government crisis (Feb.). Begin resigns and is succeeded by Shamir (Sept.).

1985   Israel completes the withdrawal from Lebanon. Arafat and King Hussein reach accord on common approach to negotiations, but hijackings frustrate peace process.

1986   King Hussein repudiates PLO as partner in Middle East and closes PLO offices in Jordan.

1987   Arafat unites Palestinian movement at meeting of Palestinian National Council in Algiers (April).
        Beginning of *intifada*, widespread unrest amongst Palestinians in occupied West Bank and Gaza Strip (Dec.).

1988   Jordan renounces role of representing Palestinians at future peace negotiations (June); PLO decares Palestinian independence (Nov.) and acceptance of Security Council Resolutions 242 and 338 recognizing Israeli independence. Arafat renounces terrorism at General Assembly of UN in Geneva.

Africa

The making of modern Africa

1914 *East Africa* Defeat of British forces at Tanga in East Africa by German forces, beginning of protracted guerrilla war in East Africa.

1915 *South West Africa* Defeat of German forces in South West Africa.

1916 *East Africa* General Smuts leads British conquest of East Africa.

1917 *East Africa* German forces from East Africa under Lettow-Vorbeck driven into Mozambique.

1918 *Northern Rhodesia* Lettow-Vorbeck invades Northern Rhodesia but hostilities halted by armistice.
   Africa First Pan-African Congress convened in Paris by W.E.B. du Bois and Blaise Diagne.

1919 *Rhodesia* Rhodesian Native National Congress formed.
   South Africa Strikes organized in the Rand (South Africa).

1920 *West Africa* National Congress of British West Africa formed.
   Kenya/Uganda British East Africa divided into colony of Kenya and Uganda protectorate.

1921 *Morocco* Abd el Krim defeats Spanish army of 11,000 men under General Silvestre in Spanish Morocco at battle of Anual, and assumes title of Emir.

1922 *Morocco* Abd el Krim proclaims 'Rif Republic', is elected President, and sets up an elected Chamber and Council of Ministers.
   Kenya Riots in Kenya over the expulsion of Harry Thuku, leader of the East African Association.

1923 *Africa* Second Pan-African Congress.
   Nigeria Nigerian National Democratic Party founded under Herbert Macaulay.
   Southern Rhodesia Southern Rhodesia becomes a-self-governing colony.

1924 *Morocco* Spanish launch offensive against Rif Republic with army of 100,000 men and air force; Abd el Krim defeats Spanish at battle of Sidi Messaoud. General rising in Spanish Morocco. Peace talks break down when Abd el Krim demands complete Spanish evacuation of Morocco, complete independence and the title of Sultan.

Kenya   Kikuyu Central Association comes into being in Kenya to represent grievances of Kikuyu people.

1925 *Fr. Morocco*   Abd el Krim attacks French-protected Beni Zeroual tribe and comes into conflict with French forces defending French Morocco. French forces under Marshal Lyautey prevent Rif forces from taking Fez and Taza.

1926 *Morocco*   Franco-Spanish military agreement reached to co-ordinate suppression of Rif revolt.
Franco-Spanish forces reduce Rif fortifications and take Targuist, Abd el Krim's headquarters. Abd el Krim surrenders to the French and is exiled to Réunion.

1927 *Africa*   Third Pan-African Congress.

1928 *Kenya*   Jomo Kenyatta becomes general secretary of the Kikuyu Central Association (KCA).
Senegal/Fr. Colonies   Lamine Gueye campaigns for extension of full French citizenship to all its African subjects; forms *Parti Socialiste Senegalais* at Dakar.

1933 *Kenya*   Split in Kenyan KCA when Thuku forms Kikuyu Provincial Association.

1934 *Ethiopia*   Incident at Wal Wal oasis on border between Ethiopia and Italian Somaliland heightens tension between Ethiopia (Abyssinia) and Italy.

1935 *Ethiopia*   Italy invades Ethiopia.

1936 *Ethiopia*   Italian forces occupy Addis Ababa.

1937 *Tunisia*   Rising in Tunisia against French rule.

1940 *Somaliland*   Britain evacuates Somaliland following Italian invasion.
Kenya   Leaders of Kenyan tribal associations detained.

1941 *Ethiopia*   British forces begin to occupy Italian East Africa.

1944 *Fr. Colonies*   Free French hold Brazzaville Conference to discuss future of French possessions in Africa.
Nigeria   Formation of Nigerian NCNC (Aug.); Richards proposals for a Nigerian constitution (Sep.).

1945 *Buganda*   Rioting in Buganda. (later part of Uganda).

Algeria	Nationalist demonstration at Setif in Algeria leads to rioting which is suppressed by French authorities – the 'Setif massacre'.
Nigeria	Nigerian strike.
Africa	Egypt, Liberia, Ethiopia and South Africa join the United Nations as founder members. Fifth Pan-African Congress held in Manchester. Arab League founded in Cairo.

1946 *Gold Coast* Gold Coast Constitution published and becomes first British colony to have an African majority on legislative council (March); Nkrumah attends Fabian Conference at Clacton, England (April).
Nigeria Tour of Nigeria by NCNC leaders.
Algeria *Mouvement pour le Triomphe des Libertés Democratiques* founded by Nessali Hadj in Algeria.
Fr. Colonies French abolish forced labour in the colonies; by Loi-Lamine-Gueye French citizenship extended to all inhabitants of overseas territories. *Fonds d'Investissement pour le Developpement Economique et Social* (FIDES) set up by France for development of the colonies.
Africa *Rassemblement Democratique Africain* (RDA) founded by Bamako Congress.

1947 *Nigeria* New Constitution for Nigeria with African majority on the legislature.
Madagascar Nationalist insurrection in Madagascar.
Gold Coast United Gold Coast Convention founded by Dr J. B. Danquah; Kwame Nkrumah appointed Secretary.
Tanganyika Groundnut scheme begun in Tanganyika.

1948 *Gold Coast* Boycott of European goods in Gold Coast and riots in Accra (Feb.); Watson Report (June).
Cameroon *Union des Populations du Cameroun* (UPC) formed.
Egypt Egyptian war with Israel begins.
South Africa Smuts defeated by Malan in South African election. National Party begins implementation of apartheid policy.
Tunisia Bourguiba returns to Tunis.
Senegal *Bloc Democratique Senegalais* founded.
Zanzibar General Strike in Zanzibar.

1949 *Gold Coast* Convention People's Party (CPP) founded in Gold Coast by Nkrumah (June); British Cabinet accepts Coussey report on Gold Coast (Oct.).
Rhodesia/Nyasaland Victoria Falls Conference in favour of federation of Rhodesia and Nyasaland; African opposition to proposed federation.
Buganda Riots in Buganda.
British Cabinet accepts Coussey report on Gold Coast.

Nigeria	Industrial disturbances and shootings at Enugu colliery and riots in southern Nigeria.
Somalia	United Nations decide that Britain should return Somalia to Italy as a United Nations' trust territory for ten years.
Ivory Coast	Widespread disturbances in Ivory Coast.

1950 *Gold Coast* 'Positive Action' policy in Gold Coast.
South Africa Apartheid laws passed in South Africa.
S.W. Africa International Court rules that South West Africa should remain under United Nations' trusteeship.
Congo *Association des Bakongas* (Abako) formed in Belgian Congo.
Nigeria Action Group formed in Nigeria.
Sierra Leone Sierra Leone People's Party (SLPP) founded by Milton Margai.

1951 *Gold Coast* Gold Coast constitution becomes operative (Jan.); CPP wins General Election in Gold Coast; Nkrumah becomes 'leader of government business' (Feb.).
Nigeria Macpherson constitution enacted in Nigeria.
Rhodesia/Nyasaland Victoria Falls Conference on Central African Federation; British Government accepts idea of a federation of Rhodesia and Nyasaland.
Sierra Leone Elections in Sierra Leone; Milton Margai in office.
Libya Libya becomes an independent kingdom.

1952 *Gold Coast* Kwame Nkrumah becomes Prime Minister of the Gold Coast.
Egypt Army coup in Egypt; committee of 'Free Officers' forces King Farouk to abdicate; General Neguib takes power.
Ethiopia Eritrea federated with Ethiopia.
Kenya Following increased violence in Kikuyuland, 'Mau Mau' Emergency proclaimed.
South Africa All non-whites compelled to carry passes in South Africa; non-white political organizations launch 'passive resistance' campaign against apartheid; leaders arrested.

1953 *South Africa* Emergency powers introduced by the South African government against passive resistance; new racial laws introduced.
Sudan Anglo-Egyptian agreement on the Sudan.
Egypt Egypt becomes a republic; Party of National Liberation under Neguib becomes Egypt's sole political party.
Kenya Jomo Kenyatta and five others convicted of managing 'Mau Mau' in Kenya.
Gold Coast Nkrumah announces 'Motion of Destiny'.
Nigeria Nigerian Constitutional Conference held in London.
Morocco French deport Mohamed V from Morocco.
Rhodesia/Nyasaland Central African Federation of Rhodesia and Nyasaland created.

Tanganyika	Julius Nyerere elected President of Tanganyika African Association.
Morocco	Franco deposes the Sultan of Morocco.

1954 *Egypt*   Colonel Nasser seizes power in Egypt.
    Nigeria   Nigerian Constitutional Conference in Lagos (Jan.). Federal system of government formalized by Lyttleton Constitution (Oct.).
    Gold Coast CPP wins elections in Gold Coast and Britain promises independence.
    Tanganyika Tanganyika African National Union (TANU) formed with Julius Nyerere as President.
    Egypt   Anglo-Egyptian agreement on the evacuation of Suez Canal Zone.
    Algeria   Beginning of Algerian War of Independence (see p. 286).

1955 Africa   Bandung Conference in Indonesia (see p. 417).
    Morocco   Moroccan Army of Liberation attacks French posts in West Algeria (Aug.); King Mohamed V restored to throne by French (Nov.).
    Sudan   Beginning of armed rebellion in South Sudan.

1956 *Sudan*   Sudan becomes an independent Republic.
    Algeria   Violent settler demonstrations in Algiers.
    Fr. Colonies Deferre introduces *loi cadre* providing for local autonomy in Black African territories.
    Morocco/Tunisia France recognizes independence of Morocco and Tunisia.
    Egypt   Nasser nationalizes the Suez Canal (July); Egypt-Israel war and British and French landings at Suez (Nov.).
    Cameroon Civil War in Cameroon.
    Algeria/Nigeria Oil discovered in Algeria and Nigeria.
    Northern Rhodesia State of emergency declared in Northern Rhodesia after miners' strike in the copper-belt.
    Fr. Guinea and Cape Verde African Party for the Independence of Guinea and Cape Verde (PAIGC) founded.
    Angola   Popular Movement for the Liberation of Angola (MPLA) founded.

1957 *Gold Coast/Ghana* Gold Coast becomes independent as Ghana.
    Nigeria   Second London conference on Nigerian constitution; eastern and western regions of Nigeria become self-governing.
    Fr. West Africa Houphouet-Boigny President of Grand Council of French West Africa.
    Sierra Leone SLPP wins general election in Sierra Leone.
    Tunisia   Bey of Tunis deposed; Tunisia becomes a republic.
    Africa   Afro-Asian Solidarity Conference in Cairo.

1958 *Tunisia*   French military raids into Tunisia.
    Togo   Togo becomes independent.

Nyasaland   Dr Hastings Banda returns to Nyasaland.
Fr. Colonies   General de Gaulle advocates a federation with internal autonomy for French overseas territories as the French Community; at Brazzaville he announces independence for French Africa.
Algeria   Algerian provisional government set up in Cairo.
Guinea   Guinea becomes independent with Sekou Touré as President; all other French African territories remain within French Community.
Sudan   Military coup led by General Abboud overthrows Sudanese government.

1959 *Nyasaland*   State of Emergency declared in Nyasaland; Dr Banda imprisoned.
Libya   Oil discovered in Libya.
Nigeria   Northern Region of Nigeria becomes self-governing.
Africa   Saniquellé meeting of Presidents Nkrumah, Tubman and Toure to plan union of free African states.
Congo   Riots in Belgian Congo.
Fr. Colonies   Senegal and Sudan demand independence and bring about the end of the French Community.

1960 *Africa*   Harold Macmillan's 'wind of change' speech in Cape Town.
French atomic device exploded in the Sahara.
South Africa   Demonstration on 21 March at Sharpeville fired on by South African police; 67 Africans killed.
Congo   Belgian Congo becomes independent; *Force publique* mutinies; United Nations troops sent into Congo.
Tanganyika   TANU wins election in Tanganyika and Julius Nyerere becomes Chief Minister.
Nigeria   Nigeria becomes an independent state within the Commonwealth.
Namibia   SWAPO (South West African People's Organization) founded.

1961 *Algeria*   Armed forces announce that they have taken over control of Algeria; OAS terrorism begins. Algerian peace talks begin in Evian, France.
Congo   Lumumba, the premier, murdered in Katanga.
Angola   Rebellion begins in Angola against the Portuguese.
Sierra Leone   Sierra Leone becomes an independent state within the Commonwealth.
South Africa   South Africa becomes a republic and leaves the Commonwealth.
Tanganyika   Tanganyika becomes an independent state within the Commonwealth.
Rhodesia   Rhodesia Front party formed.

1962 *Rwanda/Burundi*   Rwanda and Burundi become independent.
Ghana   Plots against President Nkrumah's life in Ghana.

Uganda	Uganda becomes an independent state within the Commonwealth.
Algeria	Algerian independence agreed to at end of Evian peace talks.
N. Rhodesia	First African government formed in Northern Rhodesia.
Mozambique	Frelimo headquarters set up in Dar es Salaam, Tanganyika.

1963
Congo	End of Katanga secession in Congo.
Togo	President Olympio killed in Togo coup.
Africa	Organization of African Unity (OAU) formed in Addis Ababa by thirty heads of state.
Rhodesia/Nyasaland	End of the Federation of Rhodesia and Nyasaland.
Kenya	Jomo Kenyatta becomes Prime Minister of Kenya.
Zanzibar	Zanzibar becomes an independent state within the Commonwealth.
Tunisia	French evacuate the naval base at Bizerta, Tunisia.
Kenya	Kenya becomes an independent state within the Commonwealth.

1964
Rwanda	Massacre of Tutsi in Rwanda.
Zanzibar	Revolution in Zanzibar; Sultan overthrown and Karume becomes President.
East Africa	Army mutinies in Kenya, Tanganyika and Uganda; British troops called in to help restore order.
Tanganyika	Union of Tanganyika and Zanzibar as Tanzania.
South Africa	Rivonia trial in South Africa; Nelson Mandela, nationalist leader, sentenced to life imprisonment.
Congo	Tshombe becomes President of Congo; revolts in Congo provinces; Belgian parachutists land at Stanleyville and elsewhere to rescue Europeans.
Malawi/Zambia	Malawi and Zambia become independent states within the Commonwealth.
Mozambique	Frelimo begins armed struggle against Portuguese in Mozambique.

1965
Fr. Colonies	*Organisation Commune Africaine et Malagache* (OCAM) formed at conference of French-speaking heads of state at Nouakchott.
Tanzania	Zhou Enlai (Chou En-lai), the Chinese premier, visits Tanzania; one-party state adopted in Tanzania.
S. Rhodesia	Rhodesia Front party wins general election in Southern Rhodesia; Ian Smith declares Rhodesia's 'unilateral declaration of independence' (UDI); UN Security Council embargo placed on Rhodesia.
Congo	General Mobutu takes over complete power in Congo.

1966
Africa	Commonwealth Conference in Lagos.
Nigeria	First military coup in Nigeria led by Ibo officers; a counter-coup follows six months later.

	Ghana	President Nkrumah deposed by military and police coup in Ghana.
	Uganda	Milton Obote seizes the Kabaka's palace in Kampala and makes Uganda into a centralized state.
	Botswana	Botswana becomes an independent state within the Commonwealth.
	Congo	*Union Minière du Haut-Katanga* taken over by Congo government.
1967	*Tanzania*	Arusha Declaration issued in Tanzania.
	Sierra Leone	Two army coups in Sierra Leone.
	Egypt	Arab-Israeli 'Six-Day War'; Israelis occupy Sinai and defeat Egypt.
	Congo	Uprising in eastern and northern Congo ended by foreign mercenaries employed by Gen. Mobutu's central government.
	E. Africa	East African Community established by Kenya, Tanzania and Uganda.
	Nigeria	Secession of Eastern Region as independent state of Biafra; beginning of civil war in Nigeria (see p. 295).
1968	*Malawi*	Malawi establishes diplomatic relations with South Africa.
	Rhodesia	Start of guerrilla war in Rhodesia.
	Nigeria	Tanzania, Ivory Coast and two other African states recognize Biafran independence.
	Eq. Guinea	Equatorial Guinea becomes independent of Spain.
	Mali	Military coup in Mali.
	Swaziland	Swaziland becomes an independent state within the Commonwealth.
1969	*Libya*	King Idris deposed by a military coup in Libya; Colonel Qadhafi comes to power.
	Ghana	General election in Ghana returns Dr Busia as Prime Minister. Ghana expels thousands of aliens.
	Kenya	Serious political disturbances in western Kenya.
1970	*Nigeria*	End of Nigerian civil war.
	Libya	British withdrawal from military bases in Libya.
	Uganda	President Obote's 'Common Man's Charter' introduced in Uganda.
	Tanzania	Chinese offer aid to Tanzania to build railway from Dar es Salaam, Zambian copper-belt.
	Egypt	Aswan High Dam in Egypt comes into operation.
1971	*Uganda*	General Amin leads military coup which overthrows President Obote of Uganda.
	South Africa	Central African Republic recognizes South Africa and receives economic aid from it.
	Congo/Zaire	Congo renamed Zaire.
	South Africa	Declaration of Mogadishu issued by eastern and central African states stating their intention to continue the armed struggle to liberate South Africa.

(see p. 295)

| | S. Rhodesia | African National Council (ANC) formed in Rhodesia by Bishop Muzorewa. |

1972 Zaire   'African authenticity' campaign launched by President Mobutu in Zaire.

Ghana   Army coup in Ghana; General Acheampong overthrows Busia government.

S. Rhodesia Pearce Commission in Rhodesia reports an over-whelming 'no' by African population to settlement proposals.

Uganda   President Amin begins to expel Asians from Uganda.

Sudan   Agreement in Sudan on 'southern problem'; regional autonomy granted to the south.

Burundi   Huto rising in Burundi suppressed with great loss of life.

Madagascar Military coup in Madagascar.

1973 S. Rhodesia/Zambia Zambia-Rhodesia border closed by President Kaunda.

South Africa Serious strikes by black workers in South Africa.

S. Rhodesia Prime Minister Smith of Rhodesia begins talks with African nationalists in an attempt to find some form of internal settlement.

Egypt   Israel-Egypt war; Egyptian troops retake part of Sinai.

Africa   Oil crisis brings great increase in prices for African states.

Ethiopia   Widespread drought in Ethiopia.

1974 Ethiopia   Emperor Haile Selassie overthrown by a military coup; Dergue established to rule the country.

Portuguese Colonies Coup in Lisbon by army officers disillusioned with the African wars brings down the Caetano regime and begins the process of decolonization in the Portuguese empire in Africa.

Guinea-Bissau Guinea-Bissau becomes independent.

1975 Africa   Lomé Agreement signed between EEC and 37 African states.

West Africa Economic Community of West African States (Ecowas) Treaty signed by 15 states.

Portuguese Colonies Portugal's withdrawal from Africa; independence for Cape Verde Islands, São Tomé and Principé. Mozambique (June) and Angola (Nov.). Civil war in Angola.

Zambia/Tanzania Tanzam railway officially opened between Zambia and Tanzania.

S. Rhodesia Four 'front-line' presidents at Quilemane pledge support for the Zimbabwe National Liberation Army.

Nigeria   General Murtala Mohamed, President of Nigeria, assassinated in Lagos.

Angola   South African troops invade Angola in support of UNITA forces.

1976 *South Africa*   Soweto riots and boycotts. Over 700 dead by 1977.
    Spanish Morocco   Spain withdraws from Western Sahara;
         territory partitioned between Morocco and
         Mauritania.
         Proclamation of Sahara Arab Democratic Republic,
         which through its armed Polisario Front wages a
         guerrilla war against both occupying states.
    South Africa   South Africa declares Transkei independent.
    Ethiopia   'Palace coup' in Addis Ababa.

1977 *Djibouti*   Djibouti became an independent state; final
         withdrawal of France from African territory.
    Zaire   Invasion of Shaba province, Zaire, by Katangese
         rebels.
    Ethiopia   Somali-supported forces invade Ogaden; serious
         fighting in the region. Cuban aid to Ethiopia in the
         war.
    Central African Rep.   Central African Empire proclaimed by
         Bokassa.
    Ethiopia   Widespread purge in Ethiopia by the Dergue.
    Nigeria   Constituent Assembly meets in Nigeria in
         preparation for a return to civilian government.

1978 *Tunisia*   Serious strikes in Tunisia.
    S. Rhodesia   Internal agreement in Rhodesia; transitional
         government formed.
    Ethiopia/Somalia   Somali forces defeated by Ethiopia in Ogaden
         war; Ethiopia steps up its attacks on Eritrean
         nationalist forces.
    Guinea   Reconciliation of Guinea with France.
    Uganda   Uganda invasion of Kagera salient in north-west
         Tanzania.
    South Africa   'Muldergate' scandal in South Africa.
    Ghana   Gen. Acheampong deposed in Ghana.

1979 *Tanzania/Uganda*   Tanzania supports Ugandan Liberation Front
         in invasion of Uganda; President Amin overthrown.
    Central African Rep.   Emperor Bokassa overthrown and Central
         African Republic re-established.
    Eq. Guinea   President Macias Nguema of Equatorial Guinea
         overthrown.
    Ghana   Junior officers coup in Ghana led by Flight-Lt.
         Rawlings; three former heads of state executed.
    Ghana/Nigeria   Elections in Ghana and Nigeria return both
         countries to civilian rule.
    S. Rhodesia/Zimbabwe   Lancaster House talks in London on a
         settlement for Zimbabwe; the country reverts to
         British rule for a transitional period.

1980 *Zimbabwe*   Elections in Zimbabwe result in an overwhelming
         victory for Robert Mugabe's ZANU-PF party.
         Mugabe becomes Prime Minister of an independent
         Zimbabwe.

Liberia   Military coup in Liberia by junior army officers.
Uganda   Military-backed coup in Uganda deposes President Binaisa; Dr Obote winner in first Ugandan elections for 18 years.
Tunisia/Libya   Tension between Tunisia and Libya after clashes at Gafsa.
Chad   Unrest in Chad leaves 700 dead.

1981 *Zimbabwe*   Serious clashes between ZANLA and ZIPRA guerrilla forces.
Egypt   President Sadat of Egypt assassinated in Cairo; vice-president Hosni Mubarrak becomes president.
Gambia   Coup in Gambia fails when British SAS free hostages held by rebels.

1982 *Uganda*   Further coup fails in Uganda.
South Africa   Dr Treurnicht launches ultra-right-wing Conservative Party in South Africa.
Kenya   Army coup in Kenya foiled.
Lesotho   South African raid on Lesotho.
Upper Volta   Army coup in Upper Volta.

1983 *Chad*   French troops sent to Chad to resist Libyan invasion.
Ethiopia   Serious drought and famine in Ethiopia, affecting between two and four million people; worldwide mobilization of aid.

1984 *Nigeria*   Major General Buhari takes power in Nigeria.
Mozambique/South Africa   Mozambique government signs peace accord with South Africa.
Nigeria   Serious religious riots in Yola, northern Nigeria.
Chad   French and Libyan forces agree to evacuate Chad.
South Africa   P. W. Botha returned to power as President of South Africa; new tri-racial Parliament opened.

1985 *Uganda*   President Obote overthrown by army coup in Uganda. Major-General Okello sworn in as country's new leader.
Nigeria   Further coup in Nigeria.
South Africa   Emergency legislation in South Africa; hundreds detained and many killed following serious violence and school boycotts. Press reporting restricted. Botha promises reform but at own pace.
Sudan   Sudanese army seizes power deposing President Nimeiri.
South Africa/Namibia   South African troops withdraw from Southern Angola; an independent government to be set up in Namibia.

1986 *Uganda*   Yoweri Musereri backed by the National Resistance Army overthrows President Okello in Uganda.
South Africa   South African backed coup in Lesotho; South African raids into Zambia, Zimbabwe and Botswana.

Widespread boycotts and violence leads to state of emergency; hundreds killed by Government forces and in communal violence; over eight thousand detained. US applies trade sanctions and disinvestment by US companies begins.

Mozambique   President Machel of Mozambique killed in plane crash; succeeded by Joachim Chissano.

Libya   US air attack on Libya for complicity with terrorism.

1987 *Tunisia*   President Habib Bourguiba overthrown in Tunisia.

1988 *South Africa*   Nelson Mandela moved into hospital accommodation.
'Free Nelson Mandela' campaign intensifies.

1989 *Sudan*   Coup in Sudan.

Namibia   Agreement on future independence of Namibia; UN peacekeeping force supervises departure of SWAPO guerrillas and South African forces.

South Africa   Botha suffers stroke. De Klerk President following narrow victory in General Election. Several killed during boycott and demonstrations during elections.

1990 *South Africa*   30-year ban on ANC lifted; final release from Victor Verster prison, Cape Town, of Nelson Mandela (11 Feb). Preliminary talks on future of South Africa between de Klerk and ANC delegation (May).

Namibia   Namibia achieves independence (20 March), becoming 50th member of Commonwealth and 160th member of United Nations.

Nigeria   Coup attempt by junior officers failed (April).

The development of South Africa 1912–1989

1912   South African Native National Congress formed (SANNC).

1914   National Party formed under Hertzog.
Delegation visits London to protest against Natives Land Act.
Afrikaner Rebellion following outbreak of war.

1915   Capture of German South-West Africa.

1916   Report of Beaumont Commission on Native Lands.

1917   Industrial Workers of Africa founded.

1919   South African Native National Congress delegation (SANNC) attends Versailles Peace Conference.
Death of Botha; Smuts becomes Prime Minister; Union Parliament accepts League of Nations' mandate for South West Africa.

1920   African mineworkers strike.
Smuts forms new government.
African demonstrators killed in Port Elizabeth.

1921   Smuts increases his majority in parliamentary election.
Communist Party of South Africa formed.

1922   Strike of white miners. Black strikes organized in the Rand and passive resistance against pass laws.

1923   Native Urban Areas Act.
National Party and Labour Party form electoral pact.
SANNC renamed African National Congress (ANC).

1924   National and Labour Party win election; Hertzog Prime Minister.

1925   Afrikaans becomes official language.

1926   Mines and Works Amendment Act introduces colour bar into workplace.

1927   Nationality and Flag Acts passed; Immorality Act limiting racial mixing; Native Administration Act.

1929   National Party wins General Election.

1930   Native (Urban Areas) Amendment Act. White women obtain the vote.

1931   Franchise amendments extend votes to almost all whites. Pass burning campaign in Durban area.

1932   Carnegie Commission reports on 'Poor Whites'.

1933   Hertzog and Smuts form coalition and win victory in general election.

1934   Malan forms purified National Party.
Formation of United Party.

1935   National Liberation League founded.
       First meeting of All African Convention in Bloemfontein.

1936   Representation of Natives Bill removes Africans from franchise.
       Native Trust and Land Act.

1937   Native (Urban Areas) Amendment Act restricts black settlement
       in urban areas; Native Laws Amendment Act enforces influx
       control.
       Native Representation Council begins work.

1938   United Party wins 111 seats to National Party's 27.

1939   House of Assembly votes 80–67 against neutrality in World War
       II; Hertzog resigns and Smuts becomes Prime Minister. War
       declared.

1940   Hertzog's and Malan's supporters merge to form reunited
       National Party.
       Xuma elected ANC President.

1941   Afrikaner Party formed.

1942   Draft Constitution for South African Republic published; coup
       attempt discovered and suspects interned.

1943   United Party wins General Election.
       ANC Youth League founded; formation of Non-European Unity
       Movement.

1945   Native (Urban Areas) Consolidation Act.

1946   Asiatic Land Tenure and Indian Representation Act; passive
       resistance by Indians begins.
       African mineworkers strike.
       Adjournment of the Native Representative Council.

1948   National Party under Malan and Afrikaner Party defeat Smuts.
       National Party begins implementation of apartheid policy.
       Apartheid introduced on surburban railways in the Cape
       Peninsula.

1949   Prohibition of Mixed Marriages Act.
       Rioting between Zulus and Indians in Durban.
       ANC adopts Programme of Action.

1950   Apartheid Laws passed including Immorality Act, Population
       Registration Act, Group Areas Act, Suppression of Communism
       Act. Communist Party dissolves itself.
       Stay-away campaign in Transvaal, 18 people killed by police.

1951   Bantu Authorities Act; Separate Representation of Voters Act
       removes 'Coloureds' from common voters' roll.

1952   Separate Representation of Voters Act ruled invalid. Passive
       resistance campaign against apartheid; arrest of campaign
       leaders and riots in various cities.

1953   Emergency powers introduced by South African government
       against passive resistance movement, including Criminal Law

Amendment Act and Public Safety Act.
Reservation of Separate Amenities Act, Bantu Education, and
Native Labour Act introduced. Strikes by African workers illegal.
National Party retains majority in General Election.
Liberal Party formed.

1954   Malan retires, Strijdom becomes Prime Minister.
Federation of South African Women established.

1955   Formation of South African Congress of Trade Unions.
Congress of the People Act. Cape Town adopts the 'Freedom
Charter'.

1956   Parliament validates removal of 'coloured' voters from common
roll.
ANC accepts Freedom Charter.
Mass women's anti-Pass Law demonstration in Pretoria.

1957   Amendments to Native Laws permits government to forbid
African-White contacts. Stay-away protests and bus boycotts.

1958   National Party wins 103 of 163 Parliamentary seats.
Death of Strijdom; Verwoerd succeeds as Prime Minister.

1959   Apartheid introduced into higher education.
Formation of Pan-Africanist Congress (PAC).
Progressive Party formed when eleven United Party members
resign.
ANC decides on anti-Pass Law campaign.

1960   African representation in Parliament abolished; riots in Durban.
Harold Macmillan makes 'Wind of Change' speech in Cape Town.
Demonstration at Sharpeville fired on by police, 67 killed.
Police announce suspension of Pass Laws (21 March).
ANC announces general strike; state of emergency proclaimed;
ANC and PAC banned; strike broken by detention of thousands
of people; Pass Laws reimposed.
Attempted assassination of Verwoerd.
Majority of voters vote in favour of a Republic.

1961   South Africa becomes a Republic and leaves Commonwealth
(31 May); renewed state of emergency leads to thousands of
detentions.
Verwoerd appoints Vorster Minister of Justice and Police.
Sabotage campaign begun by National Liberation Committee.
National Party wins General Election.

1962   Sabotage Act makes sabotage a capital offence; house arrests
introduced and banning powers extended.
United Nations votes for economic and diplomatic sanctions
against South Africa.

1963   90-day detention without trial introduced.
Arrest of leaders of sabotage movement at Rivonia,
Johannesburg.
Transkei given self-government after first elections for Transkei
Legislative Assembly.

1964   Rivonia trial in South Africa; Nelson Mandela sentenced to life imprisonment. Several sabotage trials; members of African Resistance Movement gaoled.

1965   Members of underground Communist Party gaoled; period of detention without trial extended to 180 days.

1966   National Party wins General Election.
Verwoerd assassinated; Vorster becomes Prime Minister.

1967   Terrorism Act provides for indefinite detention without trial; Planning Act controls influx of black population into urban areas.

1968   Progressive Party drops black members and becomes all-white party. Liberal Party dissolves itself.
'Coloured' Representatives in parliament abolished.

1969   Bureau of State Security (BOSS) established.

1970   Bantu Homelands Citizenship Act offers Africans citizenship only of homelands.

1971   Declaration of Mogadishu issued by eastern and central African states stating their intention to continue the armed struggle to liberate South Africa.
President Banda of Malawi makes state visit to South Africa; Ivory Coast delegation also visits South Africa.

1972   Black People's Convention formed; Africans in 'white areas' brought under Bantu Affairs Administration Boards.

1973   Strikes in Durban.

1974   National Party wins General Election.

1975   South African troops cross into Angola in support of UNITA forces; clashes with Cuban troops sent to support Angolan independence.

1976   South African troops withdraw to Namibian border following clashes with Cuban forces. Troops withdrawn into Namibia.
Uprising in Soweto black township; spreads to Cape Town. Widespread boycotts, rioting, detentions and shootings.
Over 700 deaths.
Transkei declared 'independent' state by South Africa.

1977   Steve Biko dies while under arrest.
Mandatory arms embargo imposed on South Africa by UN Security Council.
National Party wins 145 seats to Progressive Party's 16 at General Election.
Bophuthatswana declared 'independent' by South Africa.

1978   Eventual independence for Namibia accepted.
'Muldergate' scandal erupts discrediting government;
Vorster retires as Prime Minister and is succeeded by P.W. Botha.

1979   Vorster resigns from position as State President following

further 'Muldergate' revelations.
African trade unions recognized.
Talks between ANC and Chief Buthelezi, the Zulu leader, in London.

1980   Zimbabwe gains independence and elections result in overwhelming victory for Robert Mugabe's ZANU-PF party.
School boycotts in the Cape; 45 people shot in disturbances.
Sabotage destroys South Africa's major oil from coal plant.

1981   School boycott ends.
Major cross-border raids by South African forces into Angola and Mozambique.
Negotiations with western powers over future of Namibia.

1982   Dr Treurnicht and 16 rebel members of National Party form ultra-right-wing Conservative Party.
Constitutional proposals set up 'Coloured' and Indian participation in central and local government.

1983   Referendum supports political rights for 'Coloureds' and Indians but not Africans.
Banning orders tightened on Mrs Winnie Mandela.

1984   P. W. Botha returned to power as President of South Africa; new tri-racial Parliament opened.
Peace accord with Mozambique to end cross-border raids.

1985   Government announces end to ban on mixed marriages.
Hundreds detained under emergency laws in South Africa; Many deaths in rioting and school boycotts.
Botha pledges reform programme but at own pace.
Severe restrictions put on press.
South African troops withdraw from southern Angola in preparation for independence of Namibia.

1986   South African coup in Lesotho; South African raids into Zambia, Zimbabwe and Botswana.
Serious rioting in Alexandra township.
Bishop Desmond Tutu of Johannesburg calls for international sanctions against South Africa.
Strike by over million black workers in Johannesburg.
Crossroads squatters' camp broken up.
Indefinite State of Emergency declared; over 8,000 black activists, trade unionists and church leaders arrested.
Commonwealth 'Eminent Persons' Group predicts 'bloodbath' if reform delayed. US votes for sanctions against South Africa and disinvestment by US companies begins.

1987   National Party wins election, gaining 123 of 166 seats, but Conservative Party with 22 displaces Liberals as official Opposition.

1988   Nelson Mandela moved into hospital accommodation; campaign to free him from custody gathers pace.

1989   P. K. Botha suffers stroke; F. W. de Klerk becomes President
       following elections in which both Conservatives and Liberals
       make gains. Serious disturbances and mass boycotts of
       elections lead to several deaths.

1990   30-year ban on ANC lifted. Nelson Mandela released from
       Victor Verster prison, Cape Town (Feb). Triumphant return to
       Soweto. First talks of de Klerk with ANC delegation on future
       of South Africa.

The Far East

Modern Japan, 1914–1989

1914 Japan declares war on Germany; Japanese forces seize German Pacific islands and naval base in Shantung.

1918 Beginning of 'party government'. Hara Kei of the Seiyukai becomes Prime Minister, the first commoner to do so (Sept.); Japanese land with British forces at Vladivostok in Russia (April).

1920 Peace concluded with Germany (Jan.); Japan given control of former German Pacific islands.

1921 Assassination of Premier Hara (Nov.). Washington Naval Conference opens (Nov.), followed by Treaty in 1922 (see p. 256).

1922 Establishment of Japanese Communist Party. Japan restores Shantung and Kiaochow (Tsingtao) to China (Nov.). Withdraws from Vladivostok (Oct.).

1923 Great earthquake in Japan (Sept.).

1925 Russo-Japanese Treaty (Jan.). The Universal Manhood Suffrage Bill (increasing electorate from 3 million to 14 million) and the Peace Preservation Law are passed by the Diet.

1926 Taisho Emperor dies and is succeeded by Hirohito who assumes the title of Showa Emperor (25 Dec.).

1928 First election under universal manhood suffrage held (20 Feb.). Japan occupies Shantung peninsula in China. (April–May 1929); bomb attack on Chang Tso-lin in Manchuria (4 June).

1930 Japan agrees to London Naval Treaty. Prime Minister Hamaguchi is shot dead on Tokyo station.

1931 Japanese Kwantung army occupies Manchuria (Sept.).

1932 Manchukuo Republic is proclaimed (Jan.). 'May 15th Incident' – attempted coup by junior military officers. Saito forms a non-party cabinet. Shanghai campaign (28 March–3 May).

1933 Japan withdraws from the League of Nations (March), following Lytton Report on Japanese action in Manchuria.

1936 'February 26th Incident' – Japanese officers murder several ministers and generals. Hirohito forms a militarist cabinet. Anti-Comintern Pact signed in Berlin (Nov.).

1937 Outbreak of Sino-Japanese war after 'Marco Polo Bridge

Incident' (Sept.). By the end of the year Peking, Shanghai and Nanking are in Japanese hands.

1938   National Mobilization Bill passed (March).

1939   Fighting breaks out on Manchukuo-Mongolian border with Russia (April–July). Japan renounces 1911 Trade Treaty with USA (27 July).

1940   Dissolution of political parties (July–Aug.). Entrance of Japanese troops into French Indo-China (23 Sept.). Japan signs Tripartite Pact with Germany and Italy (27 Sept.).

1941   The Imperial Rule Assistance Association is established (Oct.). Soviet-Japanese neutrality pact (April). Tojo becomes Premier (Oct.). Japanese attack Pearl Harbour; USA and Britain declare war on Japan on 7 Dec. (For events in the Pacific War see pp. 106–7).

1945   Atomic bombing of Hiroshima and Nagasaki. Japan accepts the terms of surrender (Aug.) Authority passes to General MacArthur as Supreme Commander of the Allied Powers (SCAP).

1946   Emperor Hirohito makes the 'Human Being Declaration' (Jan.). New Japanese constitution is promulgated (Nov.); women obtain the vote. War Crimes trials begin.

1947   Japanese women obtain rights to property and divorce.

1948   Tojo, Hirota and five others are executed for war crimes (Dec.).

1950   The 'Red Purge' – dismissal of suspected communist sympathizers from office – begins (Feb.). The Japanese create the National Police Reserve (Oct.).

1951   Japanese peace treaty with Allies is signed in San Francisco. Japan signs the Mutual Security Agreement with USA (Sept.).

1952   The occupation of Japan ends.

1955   Liberals and Democrats in Japan merge to form the Liberal Democratic party.

1956   Japan is admitted to the United Nations.

1960   Demonstrations occur when the Mutual Security Agreement with USA is ratified (May). Prime Minister Ikeda announces the 'Income Doubling Plan' (Sept).

1964   Olympic Games held in Tokyo (Oct.).

1967   Demonstrations against Japan's support for USA's involvement in the Vietnam War (Oct.).

1968   Students occupy Tokyo University Campus (June–Jan. 1969).

1970   Mutual Security Agreement with USA renewed (Jun.). Mishima Yukio attempts a coup and then commits suicide (Nov.).

1971   USA agrees to return Okinawa to Japan (June).

1975   Investigation into 'Lockheed affair' begins (April).

1978   Treaty of Peace and Friendship between China and Japan signed (Aug.).

1980   Prime Minister Masayoshi Ohira dies (23 June). Zenko Suzuki forms government (July).

1982   Nakasone forms government (Nov.).

1983   Ex-Prime Minister Tanaka found guilty on charges arising from the Lockheed affair.

1986   Nakasone wins outright victory in general election after period of dependence on minority parties (July).

1987   Takeshita chosen to succeed Nakasone (Oct.).

1989   Death of Emperor Hirohito (7 Jan.); succeeded by Crown Prince Akihito. Takeshita forced to resign over 'Recruit' scandal (April). Foreign Secretary, Uno, succeeds, but forced to resign over sexual allegations (July). Toshiki Kaifu became Prime Minister on 9 Aug.

The making of the Chinese Revolution: 1914–49

1917 China declares war on Germany.

1918 China makes secret military agreements with Japan.

1919 At the Versailles Conference, former German concessions in China are passed to Japan instead of back to China on the basis of 1918 agreements. This leads to the 4th May protest movement.

1921 Chinese Communist Party (CCP) is founded (July).

1923 Period of Guomindang (Kuomintang)[1] and Russian collaboration signalled by the Sun-Joffe agreement. Sun Yat-sen publishes *San Min Chu I* ('Three Principles of the People').

1925 Death of Sun Yat-sen (12 March).

1926 Chiang Kai-shek comes to power. The Northern Expedition is launched (July).

1927 CCP is shattered by Chiang Kai-shek's coup in Shanghai (April). The Red Army is founded. Mao Zedong's Autumn Harvest Insurrection fails (Aug.).

1928 The Northern Expedition succeeds in uniting China under the National Government of Chiang Kai-shek (Oct.).

1930 The first 'Bandit Extermination Campaign' against the CCP is launched by Chiang Kai-shek (Dec.).

1931 Japanese invade Manchuria (Sept.). The Chinese Soviet Republic is founded by Mao Zedong in Jiangxi province.

1932 Manchukuo Republic proclaimed (Jan.). Japanese invade Jehol province (Dec.).

1934 The fifth anti-CCP extermination campaign fails to break into Jiangxi. The Long March begins (Oct.). and its survivors arrive in Shanxi in October 1935.

1936 Sian incident. Chiang Kai-shek captured and released (Dec.).

1937 The Marco Polo Bridge incident leads to the Sino-Japanese War. Guomindang and CCP form a 'united front'.

1938 Chiang Kai-shek withdraws to Chongqing (Chungking).

1945 Japan surrenders.

1946 The Marshall mission fails. Civil war resumes between the Guomindang and CCP.

[1] The Romanization of Chinese characters used to be based on the Wade system, but now follows the Pinyan system, as used here, e.g. Mao Zedong not Tse-tung, Beijing not Peking.

1948   Lin Biao begins the offensive against the remaining Nationalist strongholds in Manchuria (Jan.). CCP announces the creation of the North China People's Government (Sept.).

1949   Chiang Kai-shek resigns as President (Jan.). The Peoples' Republic of China is proclaimed in Beijing by Mao Zedong (1 Oct.). Chiang Kai-shek and Guomindang forces withdraw to Formosa (Taiwan).

China since 1949

1949   Chinese People's Republic proclaimed (1 Oct.). A People's Political Consultative Conference passes Organic Laws and a Common Programme setting up a multi-national, communist state with chairman of the Republic as head of state. Mao Zedong first Chairman (Oct.). Chinese Nationalist forces take refuge on Formosa (Taiwan) and garrison islands of Quemoy, Matsu and Tachen.

1950   Outbreak of Korean War (June.). Chinese troops intervene to repulse United Nations counter-offensive into North Korea (Oct.); 250,000 Chinese troops cross the Yalu River and force retreat of UN forces. Chinese invasion of Tibet (Oct.). Agrarian Law dispossesses landlords and gives land to peasants who are grouped together into collectives.

1951   UN condemns Chinese aggression in Korea (Feb.); further Chinese offensives held by UN troops (Feb.–May). Tibet signs agreement giving China control of Tibet's affairs (May); Chinese troops enter Lhasa (Sept.).

1953   Ceasefire in Korea (Jul.) First Five Year Plan nationalizes most of industry.

1954   Permanent constitution established; guarantees dominant place of the Communist Party.

1955   US Navy evacuates 42,000 Nationalist troops and civilians from Tachen Islands following artillery bombardment.

1956   Mao encourages criticism of regime – 'a hundred flowers' to bloom.

1958   Shelling of Quemoy leads to US military build-up. Mao Zedung inaugurates Second Five Year Plan and 'Great Leap Forward' to increase industrial production by 100% and agricultural output by 35%. Collective farms to be grouped in communes and industrial production based on them.

1959   Great Leap Forward yields disappointing results following huge dislocation of production; major famine in parts of China. Uprising in Tibet put down and Dalai Lama forced to flee to India (March).

1960   Quarrel with Russia over 'revisionism' leads to withdrawal of Russian advisers and technical support.

1962   Chinese war with India in Himalayas (see p. 291).

1964   China explodes first atomic bomb.

1966   Beginning of Cultural Revolution, attempt to introduce Maoist principles in all aspects of life. Red Guards inaugurate attacks on all hierarchic and traditional features of society. Intellectuals and others forced to undergo 'self-criticism'.

1967–8. Schools and educational institutions closed by Red Guards.

1969   Chairman of Republic, Liu Shaoqi disgraced. Border clash with Soviet Union (see p. 296).

1971   Lin Biao, deputy Prime Minister, disgraced and reportedly killed in air crash. Later reports suggest that he was executed.

1973   Deng Xiaoping, disgraced in Cultural Revolution, becomes Deputy Prime Minister.

1975   New constitution replaces single head of state with a collective, the Standing Committee of the National Peoples' Congress.

1976   Death of Mao Zedung (Sept.); Hua Guofeng becomes Chairman and Prime Minister. Begins action against 'Gang of Four' and Mao's widow, Jiang Qing.

1977   Deng Xiaoping reinstated. Jiang Qing expelled from Party and sentenced to death, but sentence commuted to life imprisonment. More pragmatic economic policy adopted.

1978   New constitution moderates constitution of 1975. China opens diplomatic relations with the United States.

1979   Chinese invasion of Vietnam (see p. 302). Demonstrations for greater freedom in Beijing. Cultural Revolution denounced as a disaster.

1980   Zhao Ziyang becomes Prime Minister, succeeding Hua Guofeng.

1981   Hu Yaobang succeeds Hua Guofeng as Chairman of Party until post abolished in 1982.

1982   New constitution approved for Communist Party abolishing posts of Chairman and Vice-Chairman. New constitution for China as a whole approved, increasing powers of Prime Minister.

1983   National People's Congress elect Li Xiannian to revived post of President; Deng Xiaoping chosen chairman of new State Military Commission. 'Rectification' campaign against corrupt officials.

1984   Modernization drive reverses emphasis on collective agriculture; relaxation of central quotas and price controls; factories given greater autonomy. Agreement reached with Britain on future of Hong Kong (Sept.).

1985   Five Year Plan announces slow down in pace of economic reform; fewer cities open to foreign investment and party control reasserted.

1986   Campaign for greater democracy suggested by leadership; student demonstrations in Shanghai and Beijing (Dec.).

1987   Backlash against reform; Hu Yaobang forced to resign and succeeded by Zhao Ziyang. Agreement with Portugal on return in 1999 of Macao to China. 13th Party Congress (Oct.) leads to retirement of eight senior politicians and promotion of younger technocrats. Li Peng becomes Prime Minister in place of Zhao Ziyang who is confirmed as General Secretary.

1988   Demand for greater speed in reform by Zhao Ziyang (March), but inflation and industrial unrest lead to freeze on price reforms for two years (Sept.).

1989   Death of Hu Yaobang (April) leads to student demands for his rehabilitation; sit-ins and demonstrations in several cities. 100,000 students march through Beijing (27 April). Students occupy Tiananmen Square (4 May). Hunger strike amongst students (13 May); million-strong pro-democracy march through Beijing (17 May); Li Peng announces martial law (20 May). Chinese troops disperse students in Tiananmen Square causing over a 1,000 deaths, and similar protests quelled in other Chinese cities (4 June). Chinese government arrests thousands of pro-democracy supporters in spite of world outrage at events of 4 June.

India and Pakistan 1914–47

1917   British government announces the development of self-governing institutions in India with a view to eventual introduction of responsible government.

1919   Rowlatt Act gives power to government to imprison without trial for up to two years and causes unrest. Gandhi orders a general strike; widespread riots. (March)
Amritsar massacre when General Dyer orders troops to fire on unarmed crowd, resulting in 379 deaths (13 April).
Government of India Act passed introducing the Montagu-Chelmsford reforms giving Indians a separate legislature, a share in provincial government, and control over lesser ministries.

1920   Gandhi wins control of Indian National Congress and launches non-operation campaign (Sept.). Mohammad Ali Jinnah, president of the Indian Muslim League, leaves Congress.

1921   Disobedience campaign reaches height. Peasant attacks on landlords. Killing of Hindu landlords leads to sectarian rioting and to growing split between the largely Hindu Congress and the Muslim League.

1922   Gandhi imprisoned.

1924   Gandhi released from prison owing to his ill-health.

1927   Commission appointed under Lord Simon to study workings of Montagu-Chelmsford reforms.

1928   Gandhi becomes leader of Congress; Congress demands complete independence for India within twelve months (Dec.).

1930   Nehru as President of Congress proclaims the independence of India (26 Jan.).
Gandhi starts civil disobedience campaign against the Salt Tax; marches to the sea in protest and is arrested (May). Congress outlawed and leaders arrested.
Britain summons Round Table Conference in London, but boycotted by Congress leaders.

1931   Gandhi holds talks with Viceroy of India, Lord Irwin. Second Round Table Conference in London attended by Gandhi.

1932   Congress leaders once again arrested.

1935   Government of India Act passed (Aug.), providing for complete parliamentary self-government in the provinces and a federal government for the whole of India including the princely states. Ministers responsible to the federal legislature were to be left in charge of all subjects except defence and external affairs, which remained the responsibility of the governor-general.

1937   Elections for the provincial assemblies under the Government of India Act. Congress Party forms ministries in seven of the eleven provinces. Projected federation delayed by failure of princely states to accede to it.

1939   Muslim League declares opposition to proposed federation because of fear of Hindu domination.

1940   Muslim League at session in Lahore demands that India be partitioned and that the Muslim areas of the north-west and north-east form separate 'independent states' *i.e.* 'Pakistan'. Introduction of federation adjourned indefinitely as a result of outbreak of Second World War.

1942   Sir Stafford Cripps sent from Britain with proposals to rally Indian opinion at time of Japanese advances in south-east Asia. British promise independence at the end of the war and a new constitution. British offer Muslims and princely states the prospect of staying out of the projected India union and forming separate unions. Both Congress and Muslim League reject offer. Congress begins 'Quit India' movement and most of its leaders arrested, meanwhile Jinnah consolidates his position as head of the Muslim League.

1945   New Labour government in Britain announces that it seeks 'an early realization of self-government in India'.
In Indian elections, Muslim League strengthens its hold on Muslim areas.

1946   British offer full independence to India. Negotiations between British Cabinet Mission and Indian leaders fail to agree a plan acceptable to both Congress and Muslim League.
Muslim League declares 'direct action' to achieve Pakistan. 'Direct Action Day' (16 Aug.) provokes massive communal rioting in Calcutta leaving over 4,000 dead; spreads to Bengal, Dacca and Bihar.
Lord Wavell succeeds in drawing Congress and League representatives into an interim government but fails to bring Congress and the League into a Constituent Assembly to create a constitution for a united India.

1947   British government declares (Feb.) it will transfer power not later than June 1948 to responsible Indian hands; announces that Lord Mountbatten to replace Lord Wavell as Viceroy.
Serious communal rioting in the Punjab and elsewhere in anticipation of partition (March).
Mountbatten becomes Viceroy (March) and advances the date for the transfer of power from June 1948 to 15 August 1947. British government announces plan for the partition of India and the creation of two separate dominions of India and Pakistan; the plan is accepted by Congress, the Muslim League and the Sikhs (June).
India and Pakistan become independent states (15 Aug.)
Savage communal rioting breaks out in the days before independence in eastern and western Punjab.
Mass exodus of Hindu and Sikh refugees from Pakistan and Muslims from India accompanied by massacres and rioting (Aug.–Oct.).

The Second World War in Asia and the Pacific 1937–1945

1937   Sino-Japanese War begins (July); Japanese take Shanghai (Nov.); Nanking (Dec.).

1938   Japanese take Canton and Wuhan (Oct.).

1939   Japanese occupy Hainan.

1940   US fleet moved to Pearl Harbour (May). Japanese forces begin to occupy French Indo-China (Sept.).

1941   Negotiations between US government and Japan propose neutral area in Indo-China; US freezes Japanese assets (July). Japanese propose withdrawal from Indo-China; America presents counter-demands (Nov.); Japanese task force puts to sea in readiness for attack on Pearl Harbour (26 Nov.). Tokyo tells its American ambassador that American demands are unacceptable (28 Nov.).

Tokyo orders departure of diplomatic staff from Washington (5 Dec.). Japanese attack Pearl Harbour (7 Dec.), destroying much of US Pacific fleet. US declares war on Japan.

Japanese invade Thailand and Malaya; attack Hong Kong; bombard Guam, Midway and Wake Island; attack air bases in Philippines (8 Dec.).

Japanese invade Gilbert Islands (9 Dec.); sink *Prince of Wales* and *Repulse* off Malaya and seize Guam (10 Dec.).

Japanese begin invasion of Burma (11 Dec.); make large-scale landing in Philippines (22 Dec.); capture Hong Kong (25 Dec.).

1942   Japanese capture Manila (2 Jan.); invade Dutch East Indies (11 Jan.); launch main invasion of Burma across Thai border (20 Jan.); seize Rabaul and Solomon Islands (23 Jan.).

Fall of Malaya to Japanese and surrender of Singapore with capture of 130,000 Allied troops (15 Feb.).

Japanese landings in New Guinea (March).

Japanese occupy Batavia (Jakarta) and rest of Java (6–9 March); take Rangoon (8 March).

Japanese cut supply route to China, the Burma Road (April). Fall of Mandalay to Japanese (1 May).

Battle of the Coral Sea (4–8 May) forestalls Japanese invasion of Australia through Port Moresby in New Guinea.

Surrender of last American and Filipino forces at Corregidor (6 May); last British forces leave Burma (20 May). Battle of Midway (2 June); major defeat for Japanese navy. Australian troops defeat Japanese assault on Port Moresby (Aug.–Oct.). Battle for Guadalcanal opens after US landing (Aug.). Allied offensive in Arakan (Burma) begins (Oct.).

1943   Japanese withdraw from Guadalcanal (1–7 Feb.). Arakan offensive defeated (March).

Admiral Yamamoto killed when his aircraft shot down (April).

Mountbatten becomes Supreme Allied Commander in Burma (Aug.). Americans land on Makin and Tarawa in Gilbert Islands (Nov.); beginning of island-hopping campaign. American landing in New Britain (Dec.).

1944   General Stillwell's advance into Northern Burma (Jan.).
Americans land in Marshall Islands (Feb.).
Japanese offensive into India – 'The March on Delhi' – battles of Imphal and Kohima defeat Japanese (Feb.–June).
Japanese launch major offensive in South China (April–Sept.).
Americans invade Saipan, Mariana Islands (15 June).
Battle of the Philippine Sea, Japanese carrier forces receive crippling defeat and retire to Okinawa (19–20 June).
Americans retake Saipan (9 July) and Guam (26 July).
Japanese withdraw from vital centre of Myitkyina in northern Burma (30 July).
US marines take Peleliu Island in Palau Group (Sept.–Oct.)
American forces land in Philippines (20 Oct.).
Battle of Leyte Gulf destroys much of remaining Japanese navy (23–26 Oct.).

1945   Americans capture Manila (3 Feb.); marines land on Iwo Jima (19 Feb.).
British forces cross Irrawaddy River in Burma (Feb.); American forces take Lashio in northern Burma, opening the 'Burma Road' to China (7 March); Japanese evacuate Mandalay (19 March).
Large-scale incendiary raids on Tokyo begin massive air assault on Japanese cities (25 Feb.–Aug.).
Americans land in Okinawa (1 April).
British take Rangoon (3 May).
Okinawa campaign completed (2 June).
Last Japanese forces in Burma killed or captured (4 Aug.).
Atomic bombs dropped on Hiroshima and Nagasaki (6 and 9 Aug.).
Russians invade Manchuria and Korea (9–12 Aug.).
Japan surrenders (14 Aug.).

Casualties in the Pacific Island Campaign[1]

Dates	Island	Strength of Japanese Garrison	Japanese killed	Americans killed
Aug. 1942–Feb. 1943	Guadalcanal	36,000	25,000	1,592
May 1943	Attu (N. Pacific)	2,650	2,622	549
Nov. 1943	Tarawa	4,600	4,580	1,090
June–Aug. 1944	Saipan	32,000	30,000	3,426
Sept.–Dec. 1944	Peleliu	10,500	10,000	1,500
Oct.–Dec. 1944	Leyte	70,000	65,000	3,593
Feb.–Mar. 1945	Iwo Jima	23,000	21,900	4,554
Apr.–June 1945	Okinawa	80,000	73,000	7,613

1 Ground fighting only

Source: C. J. Argyle, *Japan at War, 1937–45* (Arthur Barker, London, 1976), p. 139.

Warships launched in Japan and the United States, 1937–1945

		Battleships	Aircraft Carriers	Cruisers
1937–1940	Japan	2	5	4
	USA	2	2	7
1941	Japan	0	3	2
	USA	3	9	6
1942	Japan	0	6	3
	USA	3	35	10
1943	Japan	0	7	0
	USA	1	51	11
1944	Japan	0	5	1
	USA	1	44	20
1945	Japan	0	0	0
	USA	0	20	11

Source: C. J. Argyle, *Japan at War, 1937–45* (Arthur Barker, London, 1976), p. 186.

Aircraft production in Japan and the United States, 1939–1945

	Japan	United States
1939	4,467	2,141
1940	4,768	6,086
1941	5,088	19,433
1942	8,861	47,836
1943	16,693	85,898
1944	28,180	96,318
1945	8,263	46,001

Source: R. Goralski, World War II Almanac, 1931–1945 (Bonanza Books, New York, 1981), p. 438.

The Indian Sub-Continent since 1947

1947   India and Pakistan become independent states (15 Aug.); Nehru and Ali Khan lead their respective Cabinets. Rioting and massacres accompany the partition process in which up to 250,000 people die.

Mass exodus of refugees across new borders between India and Pakistan in the west, smaller flow and less violence in the east between India and East Pakistan.

Hindu ruler of Kashmir 'accedes' his largely Muslim state to India.

Sikh Punjab is scene of some of most serious violence; two million Sikhs flee across border into India where they begin demand for greater autonomy or independence for Sikh Punjab.

1948   Assassination of Mahatma Gandhi in Delhi (30 Jan.)

Ceylon becomes independent dominion (Feb.).

Mohammed Ali Jinnah dies.

UN truce line established in Kashmir leaving a third of the state in Pakistan hands and two-thirds in Indian.

Pakistan demands implementation of UN sponsored plebiscite on future of Kashmir.

India sets up Atomic Energy Commission.

1950   Constitution of Indian Union promulgated. India becomes a Republic within British Commonwealth.

1951   Liaquat Ali Khan assassinated.

1951–2   First National General Election in India confirms Congress Party dominance.

1954   Indo-Chinese treaty.

1955   Bulganin and Khrushchev visit India.

1956   States Reorganization Act in India.

New constitution declares Pakistan an Islamic state.

India begins Second Five Year Plan and builds several steel plants.

1958   Ayub Khan becomes President of Pakistan.

1959   Tibetan uprising; Dalai Lama flees to India.

Treaty of India and Pakistan over Indus waters.

1960   Union of Kashmir with India.

1962   Indian and Chinese forces fight in the Himalayas; ceasefire agreed (see p. 291).

1964   Death of Nehru; Lal Bahadur Shastri Prime Minister.

1965   Indo-Pakistan War (see p. 293).

Tamil riots against Hindi language; English confirmed as official language of India.

1966   Death of Shastri; Mrs Indira Gandhi becomes Prime Minister.

Indian government redraws boundary of the Punjab state to give it a majority of Sikhs, and attempts to appease Sikh separatist agitation.

1969   Yahya Khan President of Pakistan.

1971   Revolt in East Pakistan, which secedes from Pakistan to form state of Bangladesh (March). Revolt crushed (May), but guerrilla war continues.
Growing clashes with India and state of emergency in Pakistan (Nov.). War with India (Dec.) and Indian invasion of East Pakistan; Pakistan accepts ceasefire and recognizes new state of Bangladesh (see pp. 297–8).
Adjustment of border between India and Pakistan in Kashmir agreed at Simla Conference.
Zulfikar Ali Bhutto becomes President of Pakistan.
State of emergency declared in Ceylon following disclosure of plot to overthrow government by ultra-left JVP. Over 1,000 killed and 4,000 arrested.

1972   Pakistan leaves the Commonwealth.
Ceylon adopts new constitution and becomes Republic of Sri Lanka.

1973   Bhutto becomes Prime Minister of Pakistan under new constitution.

1975   State of emergency declared in India because of growing strikes and unrest; opposition leaders arrested.
Sheikh Mujibur Rahman, ruler of Bangladesh, is deposed and killed in military coup; Khandakar Mushtaque Ahmed is sworn in as President.

1977   Morarji Desai leads Janata Party to victory over Mrs Gandhi in general election – first defeat of Congress Party since independence.
Bhutto overthrown after allegations of ballot-rigging; constitution suspended.
Serious rioting in Tamil areas of Sri Lanka. Constitution amended to strengthen President.

1978   General Zia ul-Haq becomes President of Pakistan.

1979   Ex-prime minister Bhutto executed.

1980   Indira Gandhi wins election victory for Congress Party and returns to power.

1981   State of emergency declared in Sri Lanka because of attacks by Tamil Liberation Tigers.

1983   General Ershad assumes Presidency of Bangladesh.
Serious violence between Sinhalese and Tamils in Sri Lanka.
Emergency rule invoked in Punjab to suppress Sikh terrorism.

1984   Indian troops storm Golden Temple in Amritsar, centre of Sikh separatists (June). Indira Gandhi assassinated by Sikh members of her bodyguard and her son, Rajiv Gandhi becomes Prime

Minister; Hindu attacks on Sikhs kill an estimated 2,000 people. Talks between Tamils and President Jayawardene of Sri Lanka break down; conflict escalates in Tamil areas.
Fighting between Indian and Pakistan troops on the Sianchin Glacier in Kashmir (see p. 304).
General Zia confirmed as President by referendum.

1985   Further heavy fighting in Kashmir.
President Zia confirmed in office for five-year period.

1986   Tamils kill Sinhalese in further terror raids in Sri Lanka.
Ms Benazir Bhutto returns to Pakistan and demands end to martial law and free elections.

1987   Emergency rule imposed in Punjab.
Rajiv Gandhi and President Jayawardene sign an accord (July) offering more autonomy to Tamil areas; Indian peace-keeping force invited into Sri Lanka to supervise. Attacks on Indian army lead to assault on Tamil strongholds in Jaffna peninsula.

1988   President Zia of Pakistan killed in air crash (Aug.); Benazir Bhutto wins largest number of seats in general election (Nov.) and becomes Prime Minister.

1989   Amid continuing violence in Sri Lanka the Indian forces agree to withdraw.
Pakistan rejoins the Commonwealth.

Indo-China and Vietnam 1945–1975

1945   Japanese disarm French forces and an 'independent' Vietnam
       with Bao Dai as Emperor is proclaimed (March).
       Japan surrenders (15 Aug.); demonstrations in Hanoi spread
       throughout the country.
       Communist-dominated Viet Minh seize power; Ho Chi Minh
       declares Vietnam independent and founds Democratic Republic
       of Vietnam (2 Sept.).
       French troops return to Vietnam and clash with Communist
       forces; Chinese occupy Vietnam north of 16th Parallel (Sept.).

1946   Franco-Chinese accord allows French to re-occupy northern half
       of Vietnam (Feb.).
       France recognizes the Democratic Republic of Vietnam as a free
       state within the French Union (6 March).
       Breakdown of March accord, French bombard Haiphong and
       Ho Chi Minh calls for resistance to the French; beginning of
       Indo-Chinese war with surprise attack on French bases (Dec.).

1948   French create 'State of Vietnam' with Bao Dai as head of state
       (June).

1949   Laos recognized as an independent state linked to France (July).
       Cambodia recognized as an independent state linked to France
       (Nov.).

1950   Communist China and the Soviet Union recognize the
       Democratic Republic of Vietnam led by Ho Chi Minh (Jan.).
       United States announces military and economic aid for the
       French in Vietnam, Laos and Indo-China (May).

1951   Communist offensive takes most of northern Vietnam.

1954   Battle of Dien Bien Phu (March–May) ends in French defeat.
       Ngo Dinh Diem appointed Premier in South Vietnam by Bao Dai
       (July).
       Geneva Agreements on Vietnam, partitioning Vietnam along
       17th Parallel (July).
       Peace agreement signed in Geneva providing for a referendum
       in 1956 to decide government of a united Vietnam is not
       signed by the United States or South Vietnam (Aug.).
       South-East Asia Treaty Organization (SEATO) set up in Manila
       to combat communist expansion (8 Sept.).
       Viet Minh assume formal control of North Vietnam (Oct.).

1955   United States begins direct aid to government of South
       Vietnam (Jan.); US instructors requested (May).
       Cambodia becomes an independent state (Sept.).
       Diem deposes Bao Dai and proclaims the 'Republic of Vietnam'
       (Oct.).

1956   Prince Sihanouk renounces SEATO protection for Cambodia
       (Feb.).
       Communists share power in Laos (Aug.).

1957   Communist Pathet Lao attempt to seize power in Laos (May).

1958   Communist guerrillas involved in attacks in South Vietnam.

1959   Communist Party Central Committee sanctions greater reliance on military activity; communist underground activity increases; Diem government steps up repressive measures.
Communist Pathet Lao seek to gain control over northern Laos.

1960   Communist National Liberation Front of South Vietnam formed (Dec.). US advisers number 900.

1961   Pro-western government formed in Laos; North Vietnam and Soviet Union send aid to communist insurgents.
President Kennedy decides to increase military aid and advisers in South Vietnam (Nov.); US personnel reach over 3,000 by end of year.

1962   'Strategic hamlet' programme begun in South Vietnam (Feb.)
Australia 'Military Aid Forces' arrive in Vietnam (Aug.);
American forces reach 11,000 (Dec.).

1963   Buddhist riots in Hué against government repression; seven monks commit suicide by fire as part of protests; martial law introduced (May–Aug.)
American-backed coup overthrows Diem (1–2 Nov.); General Duong Van Minh takes over (6 Nov.).
President Kennedy assassinated; Lyndon Johnson takes over (22 Nov.).

1964   Military coup led by Major-General Nguyen Khanh replaces Minh government (Jan.).
US destroyers attacked in Gulf of Tonkin (2–4 Aug.); US aircraft retaliate against targets in North Vietnam (4 Aug.); US Congress passes Gulf of Tonkin resolution authorizing use of US forces in South-East Asia 'to prevent further aggression' (7 Aug.).
Number of US forces in South Vietnam reaches 23,000 by end of year.

1965   Sustained aerial bombardment of North Vietnam begins, 'Operation Rolling Thunder' (March).
US marines arrive at Da Nang (March); US announces its troops will now be used routinely in combat (June).
Period of political turmoil ends with Air Vice Marshal Nguyen Cao Ky as head of South Vietnamese government (June).
US military strength reaches 181,000 by end of year; widespread anti-war demonstrations in the US.

1966   Air attacks on North Vietnam resume after 37-day pause (31 Jan.).
B-52 bombers first used (April).
Buddhist and student protests against the war in Hué, Da Nang and Saigon, put down by South Vietnamese troops (March–June).
American strength reaches 385,000 by end of year.

1967   'Operation Cedar Falls' against Communist-held 'Iron Triangle'

north of Saigon (Jan.).
'Operation Junction City', biggest land offensive of the war along Cambodian border (Feb.)
General Nguyen Van Thieu elected President; Ky Vice-President (Sept.).

1968   Communist 'Tet' offensives against major cities of South Vietnam (30–31 Jan.); intense fighting in Hué and Saigon.
'My Lai Massacre' (March).
President Johnson announces withdrawal from presidential race and will seek negotiations (31 March).
Paris Peace Conference opens (31 May).
Bombing of North Vietnam halted (31 Oct.).
President Nixon elected and promises gradual troop withdrawal (Nov.).

1969   American troops in Vietnam reach peak of 541,500 (31 Jan.).
US raids against North Vietnam resume (5 June); Nixon announces first withdrawal of 25,000 combat troops (8 June).
Death of Ho Chi Minh (3 Sept.).
Laotian government requests US aid to resist Communist pressure (Oct.).
Widespread anti-war demonstrations in the US (Nov.–Dec.); 250,000 march in Washington (15 Nov.).

1970   US backed Lon Nol ousts President Sihanouk in Cambodia (March); Khmer Republic set up.
American and South Vietnamese forces invade Cambodia (March–April).
Anti-war demonstrations in American universities; six students shot at Kent State (4 May).
US ground troops withdraw from Cambodia (June).
US forces in Vietnam 335,800 (Dec.).

1971   South Vietnamese forces invade Laos to attack Ho Chi Minh trail (Feb.–March).
Nixon announces withdrawal of 100,000 US troops by end of year (7 April); 500,000 anti-war demonstrators march in Washington (24 April).
Australia and New Zealand announce withdrawal of troops from South Vietnam (Aug.).
Nguyen Van Thieu confirmed as President in one-man 'election' (3 Oct.).

1972   Nixon announces reduction of US forces to 69,000 by 1 May (13 Jan.).
North Vietnamese forces invade South Vietnam (30 March); renewed bombing of North authorized (April); mining of ports ordered (May).
Last American ground combat troops leave Vietnam (Aug.)
Peace negotiator Henry Kissinger reports substantial agreement on 9-point plan with North Vietnam (26 Oct.); US suspends talks (13 Dec.); bombing of North Vietnam resumed (18 Dec.); bombing halted after North Vietnamese agree a truce (30 Dec.).

1973   Kissinger and Le Duc Tho sign peace agreement ending the
        war (27 Jan.).
        Cease-fire in Laos concluded (21 Feb.).
        Last US military personnel leave Vietnam (29 March).

1974   War in South Vietnam resumes (Jan.).
        Communist insurgents advance on capital of Cambodia (July).
        President Nixon resigns (Aug.); US Congress puts ceiling on
        military aid to South Vietnam.

1975   North Vietnamese forces launch offensive; the north and
        central highlands fall to communists and South Vietnamese
        forces forced into headlong retreat (March).
        Cambodian capital, Phnom Penh, falls to communist insurgents
        (17 April).
        President Thieu resigns and flees to Taiwan (21 April); North
        Vietnamese troops enter Saigon (29 April) and unconditional
        surrender announced by President Van Minh (30 April).
        Pathet Lao consolidate communist takeover of Laos; Laos
        becomes a communist state (3 Dec.).

South-East Asia since 1945

1945 *Indonesia*   Unilateral declaration of independence by Republic of Indonesia (17 Aug.); Sukarno becomes President (18 Nov.).

     Vietnam   Ho Chi Minh seizes power and declares Vietnam independent.

1946 *Thailand*   King Ananda Mahidol shot dead; succeeded by Bhumibol Adulyadej (June)

     Philippines   Philippines gain independence from United States.

     Indonesia   Linggadjati agreement between Dutch and Indonesian Republic, agreeing Republic's control of Java, Madura and Sumatra as part of a federal United States of Indonesia in a Netherlands-Indonesian Union (17 Nov.).

     Vietnam   Outbreak of Indo-chinese war between French and Vietminh (see p. 282).

     Malaya   Malayan Union established (April); Sarawak and North Borneo ceded to Britain (May–July).

1947 *Indonesia*   Formal signature of Linggadjati agreement (March), but breakdown leads to 'police action' by Dutch (July).

     Philippines   United States signs 99-year lease for air and naval bases (March).

1948 *Vietnam*   French create 'state of Vietnam' (June).

     Burma   Burma becomes independent (Jan.).

     Malaysia   Malayan Union becomes Federation of Malaya (Feb.); beginning of Communist insurgency (May).

     Indonesia   Dutch and Indonesian truce agreement (Jan.), but communist rebellion leads to renewed fighting (Nov.–Dec.)

1949 *Laos*   Laos recognized as independent state (July).

     Cambodia   Cambodia recognized as independent state (Nov.).

     Indonesia   Peace Conference at the Hague opens (Aug.); transfer of sovereignty to United States of Indonesia agreed (Nov.) and formal independence granted (Dec.).

1954 *Vietnam*   Defeat of French forces at Dien Bien Phu (May); Vietnam partitioned (July).

1955 *Cambodia*   Cambodia becomes fully independent state (Sept.).

1957 *Malaysia*   Malay states become independent as Federation of Malaya (Aug.).

     Indonesia   Sukarno introduces authoritarian rule as 'guided democracy'.

1958 *Indonesia*   Revolt in Sumatra and Sulawesi.

1960 *Malaya*   Official end to 'emergency' (July).

1962 *Vietnam*   Major build-up of US forces in Vietnam begins.
     Burma   Military coup led by General Ne Win (March);
                    Revolutionary Council set up and publishes
                    programme, 'Burmese Way to Socialism'. Burma
                    Socialist Programme Party set up and all others
                    abolished (July).

1963 *Malaysia & Indonesia*   Federation of Malaysia established
                    (Sept.); beginning of 'confrontation' with Indonesia
                    (see p. 291).
     Vietnam   Diem regime overthrown (Nov.).

1964 *Vietnam*   Gulf of Tonkin incident and Tonkin Resolution (Aug.).

1965 *Philippines* Ferdinand E. Marcos elected President (Nov.).
     Indonesia   Following abortive coup, Communist Party banned
                    and thousands of members killed.
     Cambodia   Sihanouk breaks relations with United States (May).
     Singapore   Singapore becomes independent from Malaysia
                    (Aug.).

1966 *Indonesia*   General Suharto assumes emergency powers
                    (March).
     Malaysia   Agreement signed ending 'confrontation' with
                    Indonesia (June).

1967 *Indonesia*   President Sukarno hands over power to Suharto
                    (Feb.).

1968 *Vietnam*   'Tet' offensive by communists (Jan.).
     Indonesia   General Suharto elected President (Mar.) and
                    introduces 'New Order'.

1969 *Philippines* Marcos becomes first President to be re-elected.
     Vietnam   American troops in Vietnam peak at 542,000 (Jan.);
                    gradual withdrawal begins after pledges by
                    President Nixon.

1970 *Cambodia*   American-backed General Lon Nol ousts President
                    Sihanouk (March); American and South Vietnamese
                    forces cross into Cambodia (April).

1972 *Philippines* Marcos declares martial law and arrests Benigno
                    Aquino along with several hundred of oppositon
                    (Sept.).
     Burma   Ne Win and twenty army commanders retire and
                    become civilian members of government.
     Vietnam   Beginning of peace talks on Vietnam (Oct.).

1973 *Burma*   New Constitution agreed by referendum (Dec.).
     Vietnam   Americans sign peace agreement with North
                    Vietnam (Jan.); last US military personnel leave
                    (March).
     Laos   Cease-fire in Laos (Feb.).
     Thailand   Civilian rule returns to Thailand after resignation
                    of military rulers following death of 400 student
                    protesters (Oct.).

1974 *Burma*   Military rule formally ended and Revolutionary Council dissolved; Ne Win becomes first President of Burma as a one-party Socialist Republic (March).

1975 *Cambodia*   Phnom Penh falls to communist Khmer Rouge (April).
     Vietnam   Fall of Saigon to North Vietnamese forces and end of Vietnamese War (April).

1976 *Cambodia*   Democratic Kampuchea established under Pol Pot, who inaugurates programme of revolutionary upheaval and terror (Jan.).
     Burma   Attempted coup by young officers fails (July).
     Thailand   Army seize power after violent clashes between police and students (Oct.).

1979 *Cambodia*   Vietnamese invasion of Cambodia deposes Pol Pot and installs Heng Samrin as head of People's Republic of Kampuchea. Khmer Rouge and Pol Pot take up guerrilla war.
     Vietnam   Chinese troops launch invasion of Vietnam; withdraw after bitter fighting (Feb.–March).

1980 *Philippines* Opposition leader Benigno Aquino allowed to leave for United States (May).
     Thailand   General Prem Tinsulanonda sets up civilian-military government.

1981 *Philippines* Martial law lifted (Jan.).
     Burma   General San Yu becomes new President.
     Thailand   Unsuccessful coup attempt in Bangkok (April).

1982 *Cambodia*   Forces opposed to Heng Samrin regime form a coalition at Kuala Lumpur, including Khmer Rouge, Prince Sihanouk and Son Sann (June).

1983 *Philippines* Benigno Aquino assassinated at Manila airport on his return from the United States (21 Aug.).

1984 *Indonesia* Muslim riots in Jakarta suppressed by troops (Sept.).
     Cambodia   Vietnamese launch major offensive on guerrilla bases on Thai border; UN calls on Vietnam to withdraw from Cambodia/Kampuchea (Oct.).

1984 *Thailand*   Attempted coup in Thailand against Prem Tinsuland fails (Sept.).

1986 *Philippines* Corazon Aquino, widow of B. Aquino, elected President of Philippines; President Marcos goes into exile (Feb.); coup attempts in July and November suppressed.

1987 *Philippines* New Constitution approved (Feb.); coup suppressed (Aug.).
     Cambodia   Talks between Prince Sihanouk and Vietnamese Prime Minister Hun Sen in Paris on Cambodian settlement.

Indonesia   Official Golkar Party wins landslide victory in general elections (April).

1988 *Burma*   Student demonstrations against Ne Win's government suppressed by the army (March–July); Ne Win resigns as Party Chairman and San Yu as President (July). Brigadier-General Sein Lwin becomes President and Party Chairman and imposes martial law but resigns after riots (Aug.). General Saw Maung takes power but declares commitment to elections; BSPP becomes National Unity Party.

Cambodia   Vietnam announces it will remove all troops by December 1990 (May); Jakarta talks on peace settlement (June); resumed in Beijing (Aug.) and Jakarta (Feb. 1989) fail to reach earlier date for withdrawal.

1989 *Burma*   Military government announces elections will take place in May 1990 (Feb.).

Cambodia   Vietnamese forces begin withdrawal (Sept.).

Australasia

Australia and New Zealand since 1914

1914   War declared in Europe (Aug.); Australian and New Zealand forces seize German possessions in South-West Pacific.
German commerce raider *Emden* sunk by H.M.A.S. *Sydney* off Sumatra (9 Dec.).
Australian and New Zealand Army Corp (ANZAC) formed.
Labour Government formed in Australia (Sept.).

1915   Australian and New Zealand troops land at Gallipoli (25 April); evacuated (18–20 Dec.).
Labour's William Hughes Prime Minister of Australia (Oct.).

1916   Referendum in Australia votes against compulsory military service overseas; Hughes leaves Labour Party.
New Zealand introduces compulsory enrolment for war service.
New Zealand Labour Party formed.

1917   Coalition National Ministry formed in Australia under Hughes; Labour Party split; second referendum defeat for compulsory military service overseas.

1919   Women become eligible for seats in New Zealand Parliament.

1920   New Zealand given League of Nations mandate over former German Samoa; ANZAC Day instituted.

1921   Australia given League of Nations mandate over German New Guinea.

1926   Imperial Conference in London (Nov.) defines Dominion status.
Australia and New Zealand self-governing Dominions.

1927   Seat of Australian Government transferred to Canberra.

1929   Labour under James Scullin wins general election in Australia (Oct.).

1930   Statute of Westminster defines Dominion status.
Sir Isaac Isaacs first Australian Governor-General.
New Zealand introduces unemployment relief.

1931   Labour Government defeated in Australia by newly formed United Australia Party led by Lyons (Dec.).

1932   Sydney Harbour Bridge opened.
Imperial Economic Conference at Ottawa (July–Aug.) introduces limited imperial preferences.
Riots against pay cuts in New Zealand (April).

1933   Australia claims one third of Antarctica.

1934   United Australia Party wins Australian elections (17 Sept.);
       Lyons forms Australian Coalition Cabinet (7 Nov.).

1935   New Zealand National Government defeated and first Labour
       Government under Michael Savage takes office; guaranteed
       butter and cheese prices introduced; compulsory arbitration
       and basic wage; railways nationalized; and state mortgage
       system.

1938   Labour election victory in New Zealand.
       Australia embarks on three-year New Defence Programme;
       Trade Treaty with Japan.

1939   Menzies becomes Prime Minister of Australia (April) following
       death of Lyons.
       Australia and New Zealand declare war on Germany (3 Sept.);
       first Australian forces sent to the Middle East (Dec.).

1940   Death of New Zealand Premier Savage; succeeded by Peter
       Fraser.
       Australia opens direct diplomatic links with the United States
       with exchange of ministers.
       New Zealand Expeditionary Force sent to Middle East and
       ballot for military service introduced.

1941   Menzies deposed by his Cabinet (Aug.); Labour Government
       under Curtin formed (Oct.).
       State Health Service introduced in New Zealand.
       Australian forces sent to Malaya; Japanese attack on Pearl
       Harbour (7 Dec.); Australia and New Zealand declare war on
       Japan (9).

1942   Australia requests emergency military assistance from the
       United States and Britain (Jan.); Japanese land in New Guinea
       (Jan.); fall of Singapore (15 Feb.) over 18,000 Australians
       killed, wounded or captured in total during whole Malayan
       campaign.
       Darwin bombed by Japanese aircraft (19 Feb.).
       General Douglas MacArthur given command of Allied forces in
       the South-west Pacific with headquarters at Melbourne (March);
       Battle of the Coral Sea frustrates Japanese invasion of Australia
       (4–8 May).
       New Zealand introduces conscription and control of industrial
       manpower.
       Lend-lease extended to Australia and New Zealand.
       Japanese offensive in New Guinea held by Australians.

1943   Menzies begins reorganization of United Australia Party into
       Liberal Party. Japanese air raids on Darwin and Western
       Australia; beginnings of offensive in New Guinea.

1944   Australia-New Zealand Agreement (Pacific Pact) to collaborate
       on matters of mutual interest (Jan.). New Guinea mainland
       recovered from Japanese.

1945   Death of Australian Premier Curtin (July); Finance Minister
       Joseph Chifley succeeds. Cessation of hostilities with Japan

(15 Aug.); comprehensive social security system introduced.

1946   Commonwealth Government of Australia given powers in respect of social services.

1948   Australia introduces forty-hour week; rocket range at Woomera begun.

1949   Seven-week coal strike in Australia heightens fears of communist influence; Labour Government of Chifley defeated and Liberals under Menzies assume office.
Snowy Mountain hydro-electric scheme commenced.
New Zealand referendum approves compulsory military training; Labour Government of Peter Fraser defeated and National Government takes office in New Zealand.

1950   Menzies introduces bill to ban Communist Party, later modified.
Australian and New Zealand forces sent to Korea.

1951   USA, Australia and New Zealand sign ANZUS treaty for mutual military security in the Pacific.
State of emergency in New Zealand following dock strike.

1952   United Kingdom atomic bomb test at Monte Bello Islands, Western Australia; uranium discovered.

1953   Australian Atomic Energy Commission set up.

1954   Australia and New Zealand sign Manila Pact for collective defence against aggression in South East Asia and South West Pacific.

1956   Australia and United Kingdom agree on trade pact to replace Ottawa Agreement of 1932.

1957   Preferential treatment given to New Zealand dairy produce entering United Kingdom; New Zealand National Government defeated by Labour.

1959   Australian New Immigration Act opens way to non-English speaking immigrants.
Australia signs Antarctic Treaty at Worthington.

1960   Social service benefits extended to Aborigines in Australia.
Labour defeated in New Zealand elections and replaced by National Government under Keith Holyoake.

1961   Menzies Government returned in Australia; huge iron ore deposits discovered.

1962   Australian Aborigines given vote.
New Zealand trade pact with Japan.

1963   Huge bauxite deposits discovered in Australia; Australia adopts decimal currency. Liberal-Country Party returned, eighth Menzies Government.

1966   Menzies retires from office in Australia (Jan.).
Australian troops sent to Vietnam.

1967   Australian Prime Minister Harold Holt drowned; John McEwen sworn in as acting premier (Dec.).

1968   John Gorton becomes Prime Minister of Australia (Jan.).

1972   New Zealand Labour Party under Norman Kirk wins landslide victory (25 Nov.).
       Australian Labour Party wins election under Gough Whitlam.

1974   Death of Norman Kirk, New Zealand Prime Minister; succeeded by Wallace Rowling.
       Whitlam returned in Australia with reduced majority.

1975   Papua New Guinea becomes independent of Australian control. Constitutional crisis in Australia following blocking of Labour budget in Senate; Governor-General dismisses Labour Prime Minister Whitlam and caretaker Liberal Government formed (11 Nov.). Malcolm Fraser leads Liberal-Country Party to election victory (Dec.).
       Robert Muldoon of National Party defeats Labour in New Zealand election.

1978   Death of Robert Menzies (June).

1983   Australian Labour Party under Bob Hawke returns to power (March).

1984   Labour Party under David Lange defeats Muldoon in New Zealand (July). Hawke retains office in Australian election (Dec.).

1985   Crisis in ANZUS Pact because Lange Government declares the country a nuclear-free zone, refusing port facilities to American destroyer. Hawke refuses facilities for American ships monitoring missile tests (Feb.). New Zealand protests against French atomic tests at Muroroa Atoll. French secret service agents sink Greenpeace ship *Rainbow Warrior* in Auckland Harbour. Two French saboteurs arrested. South Pacific Forum declares South Pacific a nuclear-free zone.

1986   Australia Act makes Australia fully independent of United Kingdom (March); Queen remains sovereign.
       United States announces suspension of security obligations to New Zealand (Aug.).

1987   United States withdraws concessions to New Zealand on military equipment (Feb.); Labour wins general election (Aug.). Labour under Hawke confirmed in office in Australian general election (July).

1988   Australia celebrates Bicentenary of first settlement.

1989   David Lange resigns as New Zealand premier (July).

1990   New Zealand celebrated 150th anniversary of Treaty of Waitangi (original treaty between the Europeans and Maoris).
       Labour under Hawke wins narrow fourth election victory (March).

Latin America and the Caribbean

The Mexican Revolution, 1910–1917

1905	Francisco Madero stands in gubernational elections in Coahuila as a platform for protest at the *continuismo* of Porfirio Diaz, President since 1876. Madero emerges as a prominent critic of the Diaz regime.
1910 Oct.	Madero unveils his Plan de San Luis Potosi, a coherent platform of reform outlined during his imprisonment by Porfirio Diaz, and joins revolutionaries fighting Diaz in Chihuahua (Oct.).
1911 March	Emiliano Zapata initiates guerrilla struggle in Morelos.
May	The Treaty of Ciudad Juarez formally ratifies Diaz resignation of the Presidency.
Nov.	Madero is inaugurated as President after an emphatic victory in an October election. President Madero fails to replace the 'confessional' Congress of Diaz and does not purge the military leadership. Zapata's forces in the South are impatient for agrarian reform.
Nov.	The Plan de Ayala, the radical agrarian programme associated with Emiliano Zapata, is proclaimed.
1913 Feb.	A revolution erupts in Mexico City. Conservative General Victoriano Huerta takes the opportunity to oust Madero. Huerta assumes the Presidency and Madero is assassinated whilst in military custody. Huerta's regime obtains British loans but is confronted by the forces of Carranza, Villa and Zapata.
1914 April	Following the Tampico incident US forces occupy Veracruz, applying pressure to the Huerta regime.
July	Huerta is forced to resign but a civil war ensues between the forces that precipitated his downfall.
1915 Jan.	Venustiano Carranza issues a decree reconstituting *ejidos* (communal village landholdings) and calling for the expropriation of land to endow villages with sufficient land, also effectively undercutting Villa and Zapata's agrarian demands. General Obrégon's forces take Mexico City and march on Celaya where they later defeat Villa's army. Carranza is recognized

	as President by the US and eight Latin American states.
1916 Jan.	Francisco 'Pancho' Villa undertakes raids on US soil hoping to embarrass Carranza. In March he attacks Columbus, New Mexico.
June	The US expeditionary force of 12,000 men sent to pursue Villa clashes with Carranza's troops. Subsequently, the Pershing mission maintains a passive occupation until it is withdrawn from Mexico in February 1917.
Dec.	Hoping to formalize an existing ascendency over his rivals, Carranza summons a Constitutional Congress in Queretaro.
1917 Feb.	The new Constitution is ratified. Article 27 relates to agrarian reform and is influenced by Carranza's decree of 1915 and Zapata's Plan de Ayala of 1911.
May	Carranza assumes the Presidency. A bloody conflict continues which decimates the 'revolutionary family' by 1920 (see pp. 129–30). From December 1920 General Obrégon's Presidency brings some stability but intense factionalism remains within the revolutionary movement.

The United States as regional 'gendarme', 1912–1933

1912–25   US marines occupy Nicaragua.

1914–34   US marines occupy Haiti.

1916–24   US marines occupy Dominican Republic.

1917–23   US marines occupy Cuba.

1919   US marines occupy Honduran ports.

1924   US marines land in Honduras.

1926–33   US marines occupy Nicaragua and organize the National
          Guard. Control of the National Guard becomes the
          cornerstone of political power in Nicaragua and the
          guarantor of the Somoza 'dynasty' for 45 years.

1932   US navy on standby during the *matanza* in El Salvador.

1933   President Franklin Roosevelt initiates the 'good neighbour'
          policy.

Latin America 1916–1930

1916 *Argentina* In first election held by secret ballot, the candidate of the Radical Party, in opposition for thirty years, is triumphantly elected. Hipolito Irigoyen, a longstanding Radical *caudillo*, assumes Presidency and initiates long overdue reforms in labour working conditions.

1917 *Argentina* President Irigoyen maintains Argentina's strict neutrality in World War 1 despite pressure exerted by US President Woodrow Wilson.

Brazil The continued sinking of Brazilian shipping leads to a declaration of war on Germany. Brazil sends part of her navy to European waters and provides airmen for the Western front.

1919 *Peru* Augusto B. Leguia, President since 1908, resorts to increasingly authoritarian methods to maintain his rule.

Mexico Emiliano Zapata is shot dead by troops commanded by Jesus Guajardo in Cuatutla, Morelos (April). Zapata had been tricked by Guajardo's fabricated claim of mutiny against Carranza. Zapata's survival and international publicity of his activities had made him an increasing embarrassment to President Carranza.

Brazil Epitacio da Silva Pessoa is elected President (April) and his government's high expenditure including lavish schemes for the Brazilian Centenary Exposition in 1922 leads to budget deficits and large increases in the foreign debt.

1920 *Argentina* Leaves the League of Nations in protest at the Allies' repressive policy to defeated Germany, only re-joining in 1927.

Mexico General Alvaro Obrégon rebels due to Carranza's sponsorship of Ignacio Bonilla as Presidential candidate (May). Obrégon advances on Mexico City and Carranza attempts to flee to Veracruz. Carranza's forces are defeated at Aljibes, Puebla, and he is later murdered by one of his own supporters at Tlaxcalalongo in Puebla. De la Huerta is installed interim President in Mexico City but real power lies with Obrégon.

Chile Arturo Alessandri of the Liberal Alliance is narrowly elected President by an electoral court following a tied election (June). Alessandri attempts to rule despite a hostile conservative opposition, particularly in the Senate.

Mexico General Alvaro Obrégon becomes President (Dec.) and brings stable government during his term until 1924. The charismatic Obrégon able to nominate his successor, although choice of Plutarco Elias Calles alienates the faction of De la Huerta. Obrégon ruthlessly crushes a rebellion by De la Huerta and smashes the Co-operativist party, executing many revolutionary officers. Obrégon's agrarian and oil policies alienate US interests.

1922 *Brazil*   Artur Bernardes is elected President but faces considerable regional and radical opposition to his rule. A brief rebellion of the Fort Copacabana garrison in Rio de Janiero (July) led by Siquiera Campos is unsupported but constitutes a focal point to the growing *tenente* opposition to the politics of the old Republic.

Argentina   The Radical Party is returned at the General Election (Oct.). Marcelo T. de Alvear is elected President but Hipolito Irigoyen remains prominent within the Radical Party.

1923 *Peru*   Victor Raul Haya de la Torre forms the American Popular Revolutionary Alliance (APRA) whilst in exile in Mexico. As the proto-type populist reformist party in Latin America, it remains an important force in Peruvian politics to the 1980s.

Mexico   Francisco 'Pancho' Villa is assassinated (July). In 1920 the Federal government had bought Villa a large estate to induce him to disarm and 'retire'.

1924 *Brazil*   A rebellion erupts in São Paulo against President Bernardes (July). Three thousand federal troops influenced by the *tenentes* hold the city for a month and then withdraw. Rebel forces led by Luis Carlos Prestes, influenced by the *tenentes* and including many of the São Paulo rebels, march through Brazil from Rio Grande to the North East states as a 'revolutionary column' harrying the military forces of President Bernardes and eventually march into exile in Bolivia in Feb. 1927.

Chile   A military junta intervenes (Sept.) as a corrupt and irresponsible Congress renders Alessandri's Presidency ineffective.

Mexico   Plutarco Elias Calles, Industry Minister for President Carranza and Minister of the Interior under Obrégon, assumes the Presidency (Dec.). In 1926 Calles comes into conflict with the US government over agrarian and oil rights legislation and with Pope Pius X1 over the anti-clerical provisions of the 1917 Constitution. Calles remains the pre-eminent *caudillo* in Mexican politics to 1934.

1925 *Chile*   A 'young officers' coup removes the junta of General Altamirano and Major Carlos Ibanez comes to prominence as Minister of War (Feb.). Civilian politicians back the candidacy of Emiliano Figueroa for Presidency in December but Carlos Ibanez remains the power behind President Figueroa's chaotic government.

1926 *Brazil* Washington Luis, Minister of Justice in the previous two governments, is elected President in difficult times of conflicting regional factionalism exerting pressure upon the old Republic.

 Mexico The *Cristero* Rebellion by militant Catholics is precipitated by President Plutarco Elias Calles' rigorous enforcement of the anti-clerical provisions of the 1917 Constitution. Conservative peasant guerrillas particularly active in the Western and Northern States, attacking Federal Government and military personnel. Federal military authorities crush the rebellion in 1929.

1927 *Chile* An election confirms Carlos Ibanez domination of Chilean politics and he assumes the Presidency (July), wielding dictatorial powers as the economic crisis deepens in 1929. His harsh regime survives until July 1931.

1928 *Argentina* Hipolito Irigoyen is returned as President (April) and the Radical Party appears to be in a strong position to initiate a planned policy of social reform and industrialisation. However, in 1930 Irigoyen is removed in a conservative coup led by General Jose F. Uriburi, who installs a repressive regime.

 Mexico General Alvaro Obrégon is re-elected President but is assassinated by a religious fanatic two weeks later (July). Emilio Portes Gil becomes provisional President, but Plutarco Elias Calles remains the real power in Mexican politics.

1929 *Mexico* Plutarco Elias Calles forms the National Revolutionary Party (March). Under several names this party institutionalizes the Mexican revolution into a bureaucratic apparatus. By his control of the party Calles dominates Congress and Mexican politics beyond his Presidential term (1928) until 1934.

 Chile/Peru The longstanding territorial dispute between Chile and Peru is settled by treaty following US arbitration. Tacna is declared Peruvian and Arica Chilean.

1930 *Peru* The Arequipa rebellion led by General Luis Sanchez Cerro prevents the dictator Leguia attempting to stand for a third term of office.

 Colombia Bitter factionalism within the Conservative Party, in part over corrupt use of foreign loans, paves the way for the Liberal Party to gain the Presidency for the first time in forty years (Aug.). Moderate Liberal

Olaya Herrera assumes the leadership of a
government of National Concentration, which
includes some Conservative ministers.

Brazil   Getulio Vargas assumes the Presidency (Oct.) in a
successful revolt backed by the *tenente* movement
and other elements in Brazil disillusioned by the
power-broking regional cliques of the old Republic.
The support of powerful coffee-growing interests for
the government of Washington Luis evaporates
with the fall in foreign exchange earnings that
accompanied the 1929 depression.

Latin America, 1930–1939: the age of the dictators

In Central and Latin America the Depression years saw the rise of strong men who ensured *continuismo* principally by their control of the armed forces and the ruthless suppression of opposition:

1930 *Dominican Republic* A political crisis prompted by the possible re-selection of President Vasquez gives the army commander General Rafael Leonidas Trujillo Molina opportunity to take power. Rafael Trujillo's dictatorship is ended by his assassination in 1961.

1931 *El Salvador* Arturo Arango is elected President in first free election in twenty years (Jan.). Government ousted by General Maximilio Hernandez Martinez (Dec.). General Hernandez crushes the Salvadorean peasant movement in 1932; dictator until May 1944, when popular disgust at his brutality forces him to resign.

Guatemala General Manuel Orellana overthrows the government in a coup but unable to secure US recognition (Dec. 1930). General Jorge Ubico emerges strongman (Feb. 1931).
Ubico rules by a combination of 'constitutional amendment' and intimidation until ousted in coup 1944

Honduras General Tiburcio Carias Andino establishes a stranglehold on Honduran politics by his control of the army. In 1932, 1937 and 1944 he crushes peasant revolts; domination of Honduras lasts until 1948.

1931 *Peru* General Sanchez Cerro elected President, but internal opposition forces him to resort to emergency powers.

Argentina General Augustin Justo is elected President in a contest from which the Radical Party barred (Nov.).

1932 *Peru* Victor Raul Haya de la Torre is gaoled and his APRA reformist movement outlawed.

Chile Radical military coup removes ineffectual Liberal President and installs Carlos Davila (June). Davila flirts with a Socialist Republic. Colonel Marmaduke Grove is influential as socialist leader in this brief experiment which is ended by a second military coup (Sept.); Alessandri is compromise President.

Brazil Armed revolt in São Paulo (July), termed the 'Constitutionalist revolution', plays into hands of President Vargas who gains increasing powers in efforts to strengthen a centralized state. New constitution of 1934 codifies this change in power in favour of the Federal as against the State governments.

1932–34 *Colombia/Peru* The territorial dispute over Leticia (and possible oil rights) results in armed conflict (1933). League of Nations agreement in 1934 calls for Leticia to be returned to Colombia.

1932–35 *Bolivia/Paraguay* The Chaco War fought between Bolivia and Paraguay for possession of the Chaco Boreal lowland region of the Grand Chaco (north of Argentina and west of Brazil). Bolivia desired outlet to Atlantic and believed there were oil reserves to be developed. Bitter nineteenth century conflicts fuelled national rivalries that added to the intensity of the dispute. Bloody and exhausting conflict cost a total of 250,000 casualties (Bolivia suffering proportionately more). Paraguay in possession of the bulk of the disputed territory when truce agreed in 1935. A 1938 Peace Treaty ceded 70% of the Chaco Boreal to Paraguay and granted Bolivia a passage right through Paraguay to the sea. The political systems of both countries (particularly Bolivia) were destabilized by the strenuous war effort.

1933 *Peru* President Sanchez Cerro is assassinated and General Oscar Benavides is appointed by Congress to finish the Presidential term.

Nicaragua Liberal party rebel Augusto Cesar Sandino leads a guerrilla resistance against conservative forces and US marines until Feb. 1933, when he agrees a truce; US marines leave Nicaragua. National Guard under the control of Anastasio 'Tacho' Somoza Garcia is the centre of political power. In 1934 Sandino is shot when leaving talks in the Presidential Palace. Somoza Garcia does not assume the Presidency until 1937, but position always guaranteed by National Guard. In September 1957 Somoza Garcia is assassinated, but the Somoza 'dynasty's' rule continues until June 1979.

1934 *Colombia* Reformist Liberal leader Alfonso Lopez Pumarejo assumes the Presidency after victory in an election boycotted by the Conservatives (Aug.). 'Revolution on the March' promised by Lopez delivers only moderate agrarian and labour legislation, alienates many in the conservative Liberal elite.

Mexico Lazaro Cárdenas, Minister of the Interior since 1931, inaugurated as President (Dec.). Election a victory for the left wing of the party.
Cárdenas inevitably drawn into conflict with Plutarco Calles. Bolstered organized labour by encouraging the formation of the Mexican Labour Confederation (CTM) in 1936, stimulated the expropriation of land

for re-distribution and the nationalization of oil assets.

1935	*Brazil*	The uncoordinated communist rebellion in Rio, Recife and Natal is a failure (Nov.). Most Communist Party (PCB) leaders arrested immediately, Luis Carlos Prestes captured (March 1936). Rebellion used by Getulio Vargas to gain further centralized powers from Congress.
1936	*Chile*	A socialist general strike gives President Alessandri the excuse to suspend Congress and introduce martial law (Feb.).
	Paraguay	Colonel Rafael Franco, leader of the *Febrerista* movement, seizes power in a coup (Feb.) and initiates a semi-corporate state until August 1937, when removed by armed forces. Interim government established.
	Mexico	President Lazaro Cárdenas forces Plutarco Elias Calles into exile (April), resolving a power struggle within the revolutionary elite.
	Peru	APRA Presidential election victory is thwarted by right-wing forces in Congress which nullify the results and grant absolute powers to General Benavides.
1937	*Argentina*	Roberto Ortiz (Radical who had worked within the Justo government) is elected President ahead of former President Alvear in a contest full of electoral irregularities (Nov.).
	Brazil	President Getulio Vargas establishes the *Estado Novo*, centralised with some corporatist overtones (Nov.). Suspends payments on Brazil's foreign debt, abolishes all existing political parties (Dec.).
1938	*Colombia*	Eduardo Santos assumes the Presidency (Aug.). Election a victory for the conservative faction of the Liberal Party over the reformist wing of Alfonso Lopez. Brake on the reformism initiated by Lopez, causing the divisions within the Liberal Party to deepen.
	Chile	Pedro Aguirre Cerda is inaugurated as President after a narrow victory (Dec.). The socialists initially favoured Marmaduke Grove as candidate but supported the moderate radical Cerda as 'Popular Front' candidate when Nazi activity increased and Carlos Ibanez, darling of the right, returned from exile.
1939	*Peru*	General Benavides retires and is succeeded by Manuel Prado, the first civilian President for ten years.
	Paraguay	General Estigarribia, hero of the Chaco War, is elected President as unifying political figure (April); negotiates reconstruction loan from the US,

develops transport links with Brazil.

Argentina   Nazi Party is dissolved by Presidential decree (May). German ambassador directs the activities of the still intact party in 1940, 1941.

Latin America and the Caribbean 1940–1959

1940 *Mexico*   Avilo Camacho assumes Presidency (Dec.), rules until 1946. Camacho was victor in a power struggle within the Mexican Revolutionary Party (PRM); advocated an expansion of State Enterprises in the economy as outlined in the 1917 Constitution. He appeased the private sector by appointing its representatives onto some state agency boards.

1942 *Colombia*   Alfonso Lopez Pumajero (the Liberal Party leader) is elected President defeating the Conservative candidate, Carlos Aranjo Velez (May). Lopez does not rule with his old confidence; scandals and factionalism combine to weaken his authority by 1945.

Argentina   Ramon S. Castillo succeeds Roberto Ortiz as President (July).

1943 *Argentina*   President Castillo is removed in a military coup led by Brigadier General Arturo Rawson (June). The military rule Argentina until June 1946.

1944 *El Salvador*   General Maximilian Hernandez Martinez (dictator since March 1931) bows to popular pressure and resigns (May) after a determined protest, 'the folded arms strike', had paralysed San Salvador. Salvadorean politics quickly degenerates into a pattern of coup and counter-coup within a closed military caste.

Colombia   Whilst inspecting military manoeuvres, President Lopez and his advisers are temporarily held by the military commander of the Pasto garrison (July). Although the army remain loyal and Lopez is released, his authority is severely weakened.

Guatemala   General Jorge Ubico (President since February 1931) is ousted by a military coup encouraged by popular discontent at Ubico's increasingly rigid dictatorship (July). Juan Jose Arevalo, a cautious liberal reformer, is elected President and introduces legislation which allows trade union organisation in the foreign plantation and railway enclaves (Dec.).

1945 *Peru*   Jose Luis Bustamente, leader of the National Democratic Front, is elected President (June) but APRA emerges as the dominant force in Congress and Bustamente is forced to accept APRA cabinet members (to the chagrin of military and right-wing forces).

Colombia   Lopez resigns the Presidency (July) and Alberto Lleras Camargo finishes his term of office as the party political structure cracks under intense social pressure.

Venezuela   Revolt led by elements within the military co-operating with a revamped centrist political force formed in 1941 (Accion Democratica) removes dictatorship of Medina Angarita (Oct.). New junta appoints Romulo Betancourt, the leader of AD, as Provisional President until Feb. 1948.

Brazil   Getulio Vargas, President since 1930, is removed in a bloodless coup which dismantles the 'Estado Novo' corporate state and installs the head of the Supreme Court as provisional President (Oct.). Vargas remains prominent in Brazilian politics. General Enrico Gaspar Dutra of the Social Democratic Party (PSD) defeats the candidate of the National Democratic Union (UDN) in a Presidential contest restricted to the two traditional elite parties (Dec.).

1946 *Argentina*   Juan D. Peron is elected President (Feb.). In General Election his movement gains a majority in the Legislature, defeating an alliance of political groupings termed the Democratic Union. Peron is President June 1946–Sept. 1955.

Colombia   Split Liberal Party vote between the 'official' candidate Gabriel Turbay and the 'populist' Jorge Elicier Gaitan allows the Conservative Party candidate, Mariano Ospina Perez to 'steal' the Presidency (May), ruling until Aug. 1950 as acrimony and bitterness penetrate the political system.

Bolivia   The government of the National Revolutionary Movement (MNR) is deposed in a rebellion (July); Victor Paz Estenssoro escapes into exile.

Chile   Gabriel Gonzalez Videla is elected President by Congress (Sept.). Chilean politics hampered by the close balance of conflicting forces throughout the post-war period. Videla owes his election to a coalition of the Radical, Liberal and Communist parties in Congress.

Mexico   Miguel Aleman assumes the Presidency (Dec.) until 1952, a compromise candidate agreed upon by President Camacho, Lombardo Toledano and Lazaro Cárdenas. Aleman's former position of governor of the populous state of Veracruz aided his nomination, which was a defeat for the Callista faction within the Revolutionary Party.

1947 *Venezuela*   Accion Democratica gains a majority in Congressional elections (Dec.) and the party's Presidential candidate Romulo Gallego is victorious; assumes office in Feb. 1948.

1948 *Argentina*   The Peronist Party (PP) wins a majority in

Congressional Elections, consolidating Juan Peron's government (Feb.).

Colombia   Popular Liberal politician, Jorge Elecier Gaitan is assassinated in Bogota (April) unleashing mass violence which devastates the capital – the *Bogotazo* – and ushers in period of bitter civil conflict known as *La Violencia*. (between Conservative and Liberal party supporters) severely complicated by rural social pressures and agrarian disputes. Estimates of number of people killed (1948–57) are as high as 200,000.

Peru   President Bustamente is deposed in a coup led by General Manuel A. Odria (Oct.), who rules as head of military junta until June 1950, when he seeks Presidency.

Venezuela   Army coup ousts the Accion Democratica government (Nov.). President Gallego and party leader Romulo Betancourt exiled; Communist Party outlawed.

1949 *Bolivia*   Mamerto Urriolagoitia assumes the Presidency (May); despite MNR rebellion in August 1949, rules until May 1951.

Colombia   Political acrimony causes the Liberal Party candidate to withdraw and the right-wing Conservative Laureano Gomez is elected unopposed (Nov.) as the nation's political situation worsens.

1950 *Peru*   General Odria assumes the Presidency in an uncontested election (July) enabling him to continue autocratic rule until July 1956.

Brazil   Getulio Vargas returns to the centre of the political stage when, as the candidate of the re-vamped populist Brazilian Labour Party (PTB), he is elected President (Oct.) defeating Eduardo Gomez, the candidate of the traditionalist National Democratic Union (UDN). Vargas assumed the Presidency in Jan. 1951, ruling Brazil until his suicide in 1954.

Guatemala   Jacabo Arbenz of Partido Accion Revolucionario (PAR) is elected President in a contest in which suffrage is extended to all adult males and all adult literate females (Nov.). PAR also obtains majority in Congress, raising hopes for continued reform.

1951 *Bolivia*   Victor Paz Estenssoro, the MNR candidate, wins a large plurality whilst in exile (May). President Urriolagoitia hands over power to military rather than acknowledge an MNR victory. General Hugo Ballivian Rojas assumes Presidency and annuls election result.

Argentina   Juan Peron is re-elected President (Nov.) and PP maintains its majority in Congress.

1952 *Bolivia*   Social revolution led by the tin miners' union and labour confederation (COB) ousts the government

(April), installs Hernan Siles Zuazo as MNR interim President. Victor Paz Estenssoro assumes office until 1956, when the MNR retains the Presidency. Paz Estenssoro and Siles Zuazo remain prominent politicians in Bolivia but move substantially to the right. Bolivian political system remains unstable, oscillating between ineffective civilian government and harsh military rule.

Chile   Gen. Carlos Ibanez is elected President by vote in Congress as no candidate obtained majority (Sept.). Salvador Allende polled well for the Frente del Pueblo. Ibanez formed an unstable coalition cabinet, forced to endlessly re-shuffle it as Chile confronted economic difficulties.

Mexico   Adolfo Ruiz Cortines emerges as the most innocuous of the three precandidates as bureaucratic control of the Revolutionary Party (PRI) assumes greater importance than any 'Callista', 'Cardenista, or left/right polemic (Dec.). Ruiz Cortines introduces female suffrage on election and rules until 1958.

Venezuela   Colonel Marcos Perez Jimenez terminates a period of military chaos in government since the coup of 1950 by declaring himself President (Dec.). Imposes hardline dictatorship until 1958.

1953 *Colombia*   General Rojas Pinilla leads a bloodless coup which removes the Conservative Party government (June). Liberal Party boycotted elections and both national political parties involved in bitter conflict. Rojas Pinilla attempts to legitimize regime (1953–57) electorally in 1954.

1954 *Argentina*   Peronism continues to dominate Argentinian politics in general election (April).

Paraguay   General Alfredo Stroessner assumes Presidency (May)., confirmed by July contest, in which he runs unopposed as Colorado Party candidate. Stroessner installs one of harshest and most durable dictatorships in Latin America, intact until 1989 when factionalism within the Colorado Party prompted a coup. Stroessner forced into exile in Brazil.

Guatemala   CIA-sponsored invasion of exile forces from Honduras led by Colonel Carlos Castillo Arnes ousts the mildly reformist government of Jacobo Arbenz amidst allegations of communist influence in his government (June). In 1953 the Arbenz government had introduced a land reform programme which the United Fruit Company saw as a threat to its influence in Guatemala.

Brazil	Twenty-seven generals support a 'Manifesto to the Nation' demanding that the ageing President Getulio Vargas resign (Aug.). Investigation of attempted assassination of a government critic (Carlos Lacerda) had revealed a web of corruption in the Presidential entourage; Getulio Vargas committed suicide rather than resign.
1955 *Argentina*	Leading sectors of army and navy combined with some air force units to oust President Peron (Sept.). Five-man junta assumes dictatorial political power, led by General Pedro Eugenio Aramburu, President until May 1958. Bitter rivalry between the military elite and the Peronist movement continues to dominate Argentinian political life.
Brazil	Juscelino Kubitschek, candidate of the Social Democratic Party (PSD) is elected President (Oct.), defeating the former *tenente* Juarez Tavora who stood for the National Democratic Union (UDN). Joao 'Jango' Goulart, a populist figure within the Brazilian Labour Party (PTB), is elected Vice-President. Marshall Henrique Teixera Lott leads a constitutionalist coup to prevent a UDN Senate manoevre to block Kubitschek's inauguration as President (Nov.). Kubitschek and Goulart assume power in Jan. 1956. Kubitschek initiates 'development project' approach in his economic policy. Brasilia, the new capital, built during his Presidential term, which ended in 1961.
1956 *Chile*	Left-wing parties form an electoral alliance, the Frente de Accion Popular (FRAP) in an attempt to remove the impasse in Presidential contests (May).
Peru	Voters turn to a former President, Manuel Prado to ease out the regime of General Odria (June). In Congress APRA offers Prado its support in return for political concessions.
Nicaragua	Assassination of President Anastasio 'Tacho' Somoza Garcia (Sept.) fails to remove the Somoza dictatorship; his eldest son Luis Somoza Debayle, assumes Presidency.
1957 *Colombia*	General Rojas Pinilla attempts to amend the Constitutional provision of no re-selection for President and is ousted by a junta led by War Minister, General Gabriel Paris (May). Plebiscite held to legitimize the 'National Front' system of bi-partisan government. Scheme did bring an end to the main phase of social conflict (*La Violencia*) but tended to reinforce the oligarchic nature of the Colombian party system. Agreement guaranteed both parties equal representation in the Legislature, whilst the Presidential terms were to be held alternately by the two parties until 1970.

Haiti	Francois 'Papa Doc' Duvalier is elected to the Presidency amid accusations of fraud in a hectic contest (Sept.). Bans political parties and installs his repressive dictatorship (Nov.).

1958 *Venezuela*   General strike called by a civilian political alliance against the Jimenez regime (Jan.). Spontaneous riots prompt military rebels to oust Jimenez and install a provisional government.

Argentina   Return to civilian politics; Arturo Frondizi of the Radical Civic Union (UCRI) elected President with the aid of Peronist votes (Feb.). The UCRI has majority in Congress when Frondizi assumes the Presidency (May).

Chile   Jorge Alessandri Rodriguez (independent supported by Radical Party and the right) narrowly defeats both the Christian Democrat, Eduardo Frei (PDC) and Salvador Allende, the candidate of the left coalition (FRAP). Alessandri is elected by Congressional vote (Sept.).

Mexico   Performance of Adolfo Lopez Mateos as Labour Secretary to President Cortines gains him Presidential nomination and he rules until 1964. Quickly realizes the increase in importance of the middle classes in Mexican society that had accompanied economic growth and also makes skilful use of the 'Cuba card' in Mexican-US relations.

Venezuela   Romulo Betancourt (AD) defeats Junta's candidate in Presidential Election (Dec.), ushering in era of domination of Venezuelan politics by Accion Democratica (until 1968). Factionalism and division within AD ranks as much as corruption scandals weakened the party's hold over national politics although AD remains an important force.

Cuba   Batista flees Cuba as Santiago and Santa Clara fall to Castro's guerrillas on 31 Dec.

1959 *Cuba*   Official anniversary of Cuban Revolution, when Fidel Castro names Manuel Urrutia Lleo as President and Jose Miro Cardona as Prime Minister; new government formed in Havana (Jan.).

The Cuban Revolution 1917–1989

1917–23	US troops occupy Cuba to guarantee US economic interests.
1925 May	General Gerardo Machado, 'the butcher', assumes Presidency.
1933 Aug.	Economic depression and Machado's dictatorial style prompt increasing protest, culminating in general strike which forces Machado into exile. The popular movement dissipates, leaving a vacuum in Cuban politics.
1935–Dec. 1940	Succession of ineffectual Presidents hold office; the Commander-in-Chief of the army, Fulgencia Batista y Zaldivar, is real ruler of Cuba.
1940–Oct. 1944	Fulgencia Batista assumes the Presidency. Cuba joins the Allies in 1944. Batista does not circumvent the election of Grau San Martin, but goes abroad until Cuba's chaotic political life offers him further opportunity to assume power.
1948 June	Carlos Prio Socarras, candidate of the 'Autentico' Cuban Revolutionary Party (PRCA), is elected President.
1952 March	President Prio Socarras ousted by General Fulgencia Batista. The scheduled June 1952 election is cancelled. Congress is dissolved, political parties banned as Batista consolidates dictatorial power.
1953 July	Fidel Castro Ruiz is prominent in rebel force which unsuccessfully attacks Moncada barracks in Santiago (26). Most rebels are killed or imprisoned. Fidel Castro makes famous 'History Will Absolve Me' speech at his trial. In subsequent imprisonment on 'Isle of Pines', a revolutionary group coalesces.
1954 Nov.	Batista is re-elected in a contest boycotted by most political groupings amid allegations of fraud and government repression.
1955 May	An amnesty bill frees some political prisoners including Fidel Castro and members of the 'July 26th Movement'.
1956 Dec.	Fidel Castro and 82 men sail from Mexico to Cuba aboard the yacht *Granma*. Only 12 men survive the initial skirmishes with Batista's forces and retreat to the Sierra Maestra, whence a growing rural guerrilla resistance to Batista unfolds.
1958 Dec.	Santiago and Santa Clara fall to Castro's guerrillas on 31st. Batista flees (1 Jan.). Castro marches on Havana.

1959 Jan.	Castro names Manuel Urrutia Lleo as President and Jose Miro Cardona as Prime Minister.
Feb.	Miro Cardona and Cabinet resign and Castro becomes premier.
	First Soviet-Cuban trade agreement signed in Havana, pledging the Soviet Union to import one million tons of Cuban sugar annually for 5 years. Soviet importance as a sugar market and as source of economic aid becomes crucial to the Cuban economy.
May	Agrarian Reform Law passed, authorizing confiscation of estates of over 1,000 acres (30 *cabellerias*). Estates were either divided amongst landless peasants and sharecroppers, or formed the basis of State Farms in the Cash Crop Sector.
July	Castro provokes Urrutia into resigning and Osvaldo Dorticos Torrado becomes President, with Castro centrally placed as Premier. This marks the end of the initial phase of the revolution when there had been a dichotomy between the nominal political leaders and the Castroite forces.
Nov.	Ernesto 'Che' Guevara is made head of the National Bank.
1960 March	State Central Planning Board (JUCEPLAN) is established.
April	Interests of the United Fruit Company are expropriated.
	200 Cuban troops fight with the National Revolutionary Committee in the Congo against the forces of Moise Tshombe in a gesture of solidarity.
May	Cuba re-establishes diplomatic relations with the USSR.
June–July	Oil refineries in Cuba are nationalized.
July	Law passed instigating the State takeover of US-owned economic activity in retaliation for the US abolition of Cuba's share in the sugar quota.
Aug.	CIA approach John Roselli to persuade him to organize an attempt to poison Fidel Castro.
Sept.	Local political organization and participation developed by formation of nation-wide structure of 'Committees for the Defence of the Revolution'.
Oct.	Nationalization of all sugar mills and sugar-cane land. Major foreign banks nationalized.
	US embargo on all imports to Cuba.
Nov.	President Kennedy informed of CIA training of exile 'Brigade 2506' in Guatemala.
1961 Jan.	US severs diplomatic relations with Cuba.
	Fidel declares 1961 'the Year of Education' as mass literacy drive is undertaken. By December 1961 the illiteracy rate had plummeted from 24% of the population to 4%. Campaign later augmented by

	intensive study on Worker-Farmer Improvement Courses.
April	CIA-backed attempt to build an invasion beach-head in east Cuba. Cuban airfields bombed (15) but Castro's small air force isolates the 1,500 men of 'Brigade 2506' that reached the shore, in the 'Bay of Pigs' fiasco (16–17) (see p. 417).
	Castro for the first time asks the people to defend 'a socialist revolution'. In December 1962 the 1,200 prisoners are allowed to travel to the US.
July	Integrated Revolutionary Organization (ORI) is formed combining the '26th July Movement', the PSP (the old Communist Party) and student revolutionary directorate.
Nov.	The Partido Socialista Popular (PSP), the old Communist Party, is formally dissolved.
Dec.	Fidel Castro in a speech on Popular University TV declares himself a Marxist-Leninist, further disturbing the Kennedy administration in Washington.
1962 Feb.	Cuba suspended from the Inter-American System due to US pressure.
	A national campaign of polio vaccination is initiated.
March	Anibal Escalante and other 'old guard' communists purged from the government and the ORI.
	President Kennedy makes his 'We will build a wall around Cuba' speech in Costa Rica.
April	CIA agent William Hunter provides poison pills and money to Cuban contacts to undertake to poison Fidel Castro. Mission not attempted.
July	US embassy property in Havana is expropriated.
July–Aug.	Raul Castro, Cuban minister of the Armed Forces, and later Ernesto 'Che' Guevara, Minister for Industry, visit Moscow.
Sept.	Moscow statement confirms Cuba's request for arms and USSR's agreement to dispatch weapons and technical experts. Kennedy asks Congress for authority to call up 150,000 reservists.
Oct.	The Cuban Missile Crisis:
Oct. 16–17	US reconnaisance planes photograph Soviet intermediate-range missiles being installed in Cuba.
Oct. 22	Kennedy denounces the 'deliberately provocative and unjustified change in the status quo'.
	Nato Supreme Allied Commander in Europe alerted.
Oct 23	A Soviet broadcast denounces US blockade of Cuba. UN Security Council meets and US calls for dismantling and withdrawal of missiles.
Oct. 24	US blockade effective. U Thant (UN Secretary General) petitions both sides.
Oct. 26	Letter from Khrushchev to Kennedy offering to withdraw the missiles under UN supervision if US blockade of Cuba lifted and guarantee given that

	Cuba will not be invaded.
Oct. 27	Second letter from Khrushchev linking initial offer to conditional withdrawal of US missiles from Turkey. Kennedy replies on basis of first proposal.
Oct. 28	Firm undertakings given on removal of missiles under UN supervision. In Nov. Castro's 'Five Points' to guarantee Cuban territory are debated.
1963 Jan.	A diving-suit treated with poison fungi is prepared by the CIA as a 'present' for Castro, but attempted delivery of the suit is cancelled.
Feb.	ORI replaced by more formalized structure, the United Party of the Socialist Revolution (PURS).
Sept.	Symbolic attack by US planes on Las Villas province.
Oct.	Second Agrarian Reform confiscates all holdings in excess of 67 hectares. Agricultural smallholdings in private hands remain and constitute 40% of agricultural land.
Nov.	Conscription is introduced. Desmond Fitzgerald, head of CIA special affairs, offers a Cuban agent poisoning gadgetry to attempt to assassinate Castro. The agent rejects the equipment as too amateurish.
1964 Jan.	Fidel Castro visits Moscow.
Feb.	The US sacks Cuban workers at the controversial Guantanamo military base on the island.
1965 March	Cuba donates sugar supplies to Vietnam.
Sept.	Students are mobilized to help in the coffee harvest.
Oct.	Castro announces that the Cuban Communist Party (PCC), a politburo and secretariat is to replace the PURS.
1966 Jan.	First Tri-Continental Conference held in Havana. Revolutionaries from Africa, the Americas and Asia meet to discuss strategy and forms of solidarity.
Feb.	Fidel Castro attacks China's economic policy towards Cuba and accuses Chinese authorities of attempting to subvert the Cuban armed forces by distributing propaganda.
	Soviet-Cuban trade agreement increases trade volume by 22% and guarantees larger Soviet aid credits.
	Camilo Torres Restrepo (Colombian priest and revolutionary) is killed by the military in Santander, Colombia. Camilo Torres was a national hero who had joined and fought with the Cuban inspired National Liberation Army (ELN). Announcement of his death causes student riots in Bogota.
1967 Oct.	'Che' Guevara shot by Bolivian rangers at Hiquera, Bolivia, after being captured and wounded: a

demoralizing blow to insurgency in Latin America based upon the Cuban-style rural *foco* theory. Political groups on the left increasingly looked to the 'specific local conditions' in which they operated, and the Cuban revolutionary road became a secondary inspiration rather than a definitive model for the whole continent.

1968 May   Cuba refuses to sign the UN nuclear non-proliferation treaty.
Change in economic policy precipitates the nationalization of over 50,000 small private businesses.
The PCC is purged of a 'USSR micro-faction'.

1969 July   Soviet naval task force visits Havana to join tenth anniversary celebrations on symbolic 26th.

1970 Sept.   Soviet government assures the US that it has no intention of building a strategic submarine base in Cuba accusing Nixon administration of developing 'war psychosis'.
Economic problems continue; record sugar *zafra* but numerous economic dislocations caused by the concentration on drive for a 10 million ton harvest.

   Nov.   Salvador Allende's Popular Unity government renews diplomatic relations between Chile and Cuba.

1971 Oct.   The Cuban air force is strengthened by delivery of Mig-21 jets.

   Nov.   Castro visits Allende in Chile in a display of solidarity; later journeys to Peru and Ecuador.

1972 May   Cuba is re-elected as administrative member on UN Development Council.
Castro undertakes a two-month diplomatic tour to Africa, Eastern Europe and the Soviet Union.

   July   Cuba joins COMECON.
Peru's nationalist military government renews diplomatic relations with Cuba.

1973 Feb.   Cuba and US sign a five-year anti-hijacking pact to apply to aircraft and vessels. Similar agreement reached with Mexico in June.

   March   Completion of child health programme gives Cuba lowest child mortality in Latin America.

   May   Cuba and Argentina renew diplomatic relations.

   July   The US joins 15 Latin American countries in voting to lift OAS commercial sanctions against Cuba.

   Aug.   US eases some economic sanctions. Foreign subsidiary companies of US corporations allowed to sell goods to Cuba under licence.
Judicial reform restructures Cuba's legal system, establishes new People's Supreme Court.

Sept.	All Chilean assets in Cuba frozen, following military coup that ousts Allende.
Oct.	In an incident in the Panama Canal zone the US detains a Cuban merchant vessel.

1974 Jan. Soviet leader Brezhnev visits Cuba.

Oct. Committee established to supervise drafting of new Constitution.

1975 Jan. Cuba and West Germany renew diplomatic relations.

Mar.–May First commitment of military advisers to help MPLA forces in Angola.

July Castro offers evidence of attempts on his life to US Senate Committee on Intelligence investigating CIA 'dirty tricks' – eight such schemes between 1960 and 1965 alone.

Nov. A crack Cuban battalion is sent to Angola following increased South African intervention since August in the Angolan conflict.

Dec. First Congress of the Cuban Communist Party approves the new Constitution, instituted in 1976. Major provisions include directly elected municipal assemblies and indirectly elected provincial authorities and a National Assembly. Within the National Assembly the Council of State is the executive branch with the Chairman head of the government and C-in-C of the Armed Forces. Fidel Castro holds these positions.
Several troopships arrive in Angola as the Cuban commitment to the MPLA cause is deepened.

1976 Feb. Annual Soviet-Cuban trade treaty includes five-year commitment to double volume of trade. Soviet Union accounts for 50% of Cuba's total international trade.

April Terrorist campaign against Cuban interests.
Fishing vessels attacked and bomb explosions at the embassy in Lisbon and at the UN.

Oct. Cuban electorate vote for 170 municipal assemblies, 14 provincial assemblies and a new National Assembly.
Fidel Castro declares the hi-jacking agreement with the US void from April 1977 following the bombing of a civilian Cuban jet by anti-Castro terrorists. The Venezuelan government indicts four people for the bombing.

Dec. The National Assembly of People's Power is inaugurated.

1977 March Fidel Castro's African tour is a diplomatic offensive in part to explain Cuban involvement in Angola.
US government lifts ban on travel to Cuba.

April US-Cuban fishing treaty signed defining national fishing zones.

May The US and Cuba exchange diplomats and set up

'interest' offices in Havana and Washington.
The Republican Party opposes the move.

1978 April   New USSR-Cuba protocol strengthens trading
                   agreements.
     Sept.   Scientific and technical agreement is signed with
                   Spain.

1979 April   High turnout for Municipal Assembly elections.
                   Cuba establishes diplomatic relations with the
                   government of Maurice Bishop in Grenada and
                   offers aid.
     July   Cuba establishes diplomatic relations with the new
                   Sandinista government in Nicaragua and offers aid.
     Sept.   Havana is host to the the Sixth Conference of
                   Non-Aligned Countries.

1980 April   Over 100,000 emigrés leave Cuba for the US from
                   the port of Mariel.
     May   Liberalization of agricultural trading markets in an
                   effort to stimulate output of staple foodstuffs.
     Dec.   Second Congress of the Cuban Communist Party.

1981 Jan.   Cuba condemns the worsening human rights
                   situation in El Salvador.
     Feb.   Cuba denounces South African incursions into
                   Mozambique.
     Aug.   Cuba reaffirms commitment to aid MPLA
                   government in Angola in resisting South African
                   military pressure. Besides military aid, Cuba has
                   undertaken numerous social and health projects in
                   Angola.

1982 May   Cuba condemns British policy in the
                   Falklands/Malvinas dispute with Argentina.

1983 March   A Paris agreement reschedules Cuba's foreign debt.
     Oct.   In the US invasion of Grenada, 24 Cubans are killed
                   in fighting with US troops.

1984 April   High turnout in the election for a National Assembly
                   of People's Power.
                   US-Cuban discussions on migration levels.
                   Agreement that 3,000 criminals included in the
                   Mariel evacuation will be returned to Cuba.

1985 Nov.   The Cuban government acts as an intermediary
                   between the Colombian government and the M-19
                   guerrillas during the siege of the Colombian
                   Supreme Court.
     Dec.   Third Congress of the Cuban Communist Party
                   discusses mistakes in economic policy.

1986 May   Cuba forced to propose a postponement of debts
                   due in 1986.
     Dec.   Castro unveils the 'rectification' campaign to
                   reaffirm revolutionary ideals, reduce corruption and
                   bureaucratic inefficiency and improve economic

performance. In a desire to return to 'moral incentives', the campaign echoed concept of the 'new man' outlined by 'Che' Guevara in 1960s. 'Rectification' campaign uses methods which conflict with the *perestroika* championed by Gorbachev; Castro's commitment leads to cooling of Soviet-Cuban relations in 1988–89.

1987 Jan. Political prisoners go on hunger-strike at Combinado del Este prison.

July Paris Club debts fall due eventually forcing Cuba to reschedule a total of $850 million in 1988.

1988 Jan. Cuba dispatches elite troops and officers to Angola in response to the South African offensive of October 1987 committing an estimated 45,000 troops in the conflict.

Feb. Cuban and Angolan forces successfully defend Cuito Cuanavale in a crucial battle.

May Cuban and Angolan troops advance to Luena on the Namibian border in a successful counter-attack.

June Cuban Mig-23's provide crucial air support in heavy fighting which sees South African casualties rise prompting cease-fire negotiations.

Aug. Ceasefire agreement in Angola includes provision for the withdrawal of Cuban troops.

Sept. UN Human Rights Commission is invited to inspect Cuban prisons.

1989 Jan. Thirtieth Anniversary of the Revolution.
First Cuban troops to be withdrawn from Angola as part of cease-fire agreement arrive home.

April Gorbachev pays four-day visit to Cuba. Outlines Soviet desire to reduce the economic subsidies to Cuba and implies need for *perestroika*-type reforms. Castro emphasizes dangers of excessive reform.

June Following an investigation in April, and earlier US tip-offs, General Arnaldo Ochoa Sanchez (a hero of the Angolan campaign) is arrested with fellow officers and Ministry of Interior officials for their cooperation with the Medellin drug cartel.

July Following their court-martial General Arnaldo Ochoa and three other officers are executed by firing squad. Ten leading officials of the Ministry of the Interior are given long gaol sentences and Ministry purged.

Aug. Construction minister is sacked in a shake-up in the housing sector.
Two Soviet publications are banned including *Moscow News*, a leading advocate of *perestroika*. Soviet economic pressure upon Cuba increases. Oil shortages reveal a suspension of the thirty-year Soviet practice of exporting crude oil at a low price to Havana.

Latin America and the Caribbean, 1960–1989

1960 *Argentina*   President Frondizi's UCRI loses majority (March).
Peronist Party barred from participation.

Brazil   Janio Quadros is elected President with UDN
support (Oct.) defeating the candidate of the PSD,
Marshall Teixera Lott. Populist leader Joao 'Jango'
Goulart is re-elected Vice-President. Increasing
inflation and foreign debt produced by President
Kubitschek's ambitious development projects
hamper campaign of PSD candidate. Quadros
assumed the Presidency in January 1961 faced by a
hostile opposition majority in Congress.

1961 *Haiti*   'Papa Doc' Duvalier is re-elected (April). Consolidates
his regime by dissolving legislature and installing
rubber-stamp assembly.

Dominican Rep.   Dictator Rafael Trujillo assassinated (May).
Trujillo had dominated political life since 1931.
Although he at times assumed the Presidency, he
allowed his brother and Joaquin Balaguer to hold
the highest office for 'cosmetic' reasons. The Trujillo
'dynasty' rallied briefly under his son General Rafael
'Ramfo' Trujillo, but by December 1961 the family
was expelled from the island.

Brazil   President Quadros resigns in protest at
Congressional opposition to his agrarian and tax
reforms. Congress passes a constitutional
amendment to establish a parliamentary system and
much reduced powers for the Presidency (Sept).
This compromise allows Joao Goulart to assume the
Presidency, but military opposition to his rule
increases.

1962 *Argentina*   President Frondizi alienates the military hierarchy by
permitting Peronist participation in Congressional
elections (March). Peronists win a majority but
Frondizi is pressurised by the military to nullify
election results in provinces where Peronism
successful. The military removes President Frondizi
and installs the Leader of the Senate as an interim
president.

Jamaica   The Jamaican Labour Party, headed by its founder
Sir Alexander Bustamente, wins 26 of the 45 seats
available in the election (April), which followed
Jamaica's withdrawal from the Federation of the
West Indies (Sept. 1961).

Peru   Military Junta led by General Ricardo Perez Godoy
seizes power to block APRA's political ambitions,
and annuls June election (in which APRA leader

	successful). General Godoy ousted by officers in favour of an electoral contest in March 1963.
Argentina	Arturo Illia (UCRP) is elected President.
Jamaica	Becomes independent within the British Commonwealth (Aug.). Constitution guarantees opposition some representation in Upper House.
Trinidad	Trinidad and Tobago become independent within the British Commonwealth (Aug.). Eric Williams, who formed the People's National Party (PNP) in 1956, dominates both the PNP and politics in Trinidad until his death (March 1981).
Chile	Three right-wing organisations form an electoral alliance, the Frente Democratico (FD), to counter growing left-wing organisation before the 1964 Presidential Election.
Mexico	Gustavo Diaz Ordaz assumes Presidency. The organization of the Olympic Games in 1968 by the Diaz Ordaz administration provided an opportunity for protest by dissident groups, notably the student movement.
Dominican Rep.	Juan Bosch of the Democratic Revolutionary Party (PRD) is elected President and assumes office in February 1963.
1963 *Brazil*	The electorate votes to restore a full Presidential System and grant President Goulart extensive executive powers (Jan.), sowing the seeds of military alienation that lead to the coup of 1964.
Peru	In a return to civilian politics Fernando Belaunde Terry, candidate of new moderate force in Peruvian politics (Accion Popular), is elected (June).
Dominican Rep.	Democratically elected government of Juan Bosch is removed by Colonel Elias Wessen y Wessen; Bosch exiled (Sept.). Military factions develop around 'constitutionalist' and 'loyalist' positions.
1964 *Brazil*	President Joao Goulart removed in a coup (April) ushering in a long period of dictatorship. Marshall Humberto Castello Branco is approved by Congress; the first of a series of military nominees as President. Congress approves a constitutional amendment extending his term to March 1967.
Haiti	'Papa Doc' Duvalier installs himself as President for Life (April).
Chile	Eduardo Frei, the Christian Democrat candidate is elected President (Sept.), defeating the candidate of the left-wing coalition (FRAP) Salvador Allende.
1965 *Dominican Rep.*	US supports coup leader Colonel Wessen y Wessen in the conflict between military factions following the removal of Juan Bosch's civilian government. Lyndon Johnson sends the marines to the Dominican Republic to guarantee US interests.

Joaquin Balaguer, the trusted lieutenant of the dictator Trujillo, assumes the Presidency in 1966 and dominates the political system.

1966 *Guyana* British Guiana gains independence within the Commonwealth as the state of Guyana (May).

Argentina President Illia is deposed as the military re-enter politics (June). A hard-line junta led by Juan Carlos Ongania seizes power.

Brazil Congress approves Marshall Costa e Silva as sucessor to Castello Branco as military President in 1967.

1967 *Nicaragua* Major General Anastasio 'Tachito' Somoza Debayle assumes the Presidency on the death of his brother (Feb.). 'Tachito's' corrupt dictatorship provokes increasing popular opposition to the Somoza 'dynasty'.

Peru General Juan Velasco Alvardo leads a military coup which ousts the ineffectual Belaunde administration (Oct.). General Velasco introduces nationalist measures in the export sector and attempts to tackle Peru's structural socio-economic problems, particularly the land reform issue (1968–86).

Brazil Military President Costa e Silva suspends Congress indefinitely, initiating government by decree.

Guyana Forbes Burnham, leader of the People's National Congress Party (PNC) wins the election that establishes his stranglehold on Guyanese politics (Dec.).

1969 *Argentina* Military suppression of the *Cordobazo* – a mass insurrection in the city of Cordoba – prompts resignation of five ministers (May) and greatly weakens the Ongania regime.

Brazil Military high command choses General Emilio Garrastezu Medici as President following Costa e Silva's incapacity by a stroke. Medici assumes power in October.

1970 *Guyana* Becomes a 'co-operative' republic within the British Commonwealth. In March the National Assembly elects Raymond Chang of the ruling PNC as President, replacing Queen Elizabeth II as head of state.

Argentina Military President Juan Carlos Ongania is removed by a junta dissatisfied by his loss of political control. The terrorist murder of a former military President, Pedro Aramburu, in May 1970 sealed Ongania's fate.

Mexico Luis Echevarria Alvarez, candidate of the ruling Institutional Revolutionary Party (PRI), is elected President (July). PRI wins all sixty seats in the Senate and gains a majority in Congress. Luis Echevarria Alvarez had been the hard-line Minister of the Interior during the social protests of 1968.

	Chile	Salvador Allende, the candidate of the Left Coalition (Popular Unity) wins a plurality in a polarised contest (Sept.). Allende assumes Presidency in Nov.
1971	*Haiti*	'Papa Doc' Duvalier dies and his son Jean-Claude 'Baby Doc' Duvalier succeeds him as President for Life (April). The Duvaliers' repressive apparatus remains intact.
1972	*El Salvador*	Liberal Coalition led by José Napoleon Duarte and Guillermo Ungo win a rare free election, but are opposed by right-wing military elements which force both Duarte and Ungo into exile.
1973	*Chile*	The Popular Unity Government is ousted by a military coup (Sept.). Salvador Allende dies defending the Presidential palace; thousands of Popular Unity supporters are killed or imprisoned as the military junta led by General Augusto Pinochet installs a repressive dictatorship.
1976	*Argentina*	Chaotic Peronist government is removed by a military coup. A series of military dictatorships rule Argentina until October 1983. The original junta led by General Videla dissolved Congress and used State of Siege legislation to justify mass arrests, torture and political murder. Over 15,000 people 'disappear' during military rule. General Videla succeeded briefly by Genera Viola in 1981 before General Galtieri assumes power.
	Chile	Orlando Leterlier, former cabinet minister and diplomat in the Allende government is assassinated in Washington DC by members of the Chilean Secret Services (Sept.).
1979	*Grenada*	The New Jewel Movement led by Maurice Bishop ousts the repressive regime of Sir Eric Gairy (March).
	Brazil	General Joao Baptista Figuerado assumes the Presidency, last in a line of military Presidents. His 'abertura' (opening) policy unleashes popular pressures for democratic elections.
	Nicaragua	Popular resistance led by the Sandinista National Liberation Army (FSLN) forces Anastasio 'Tachito' Somoza out of power (June), ending the family's 'dynastic' control of Nicaragua politics since the 1920s. In the conflict against the Somoza regime 40,000 people died and a further 750,000 were made homeless.
	El Salvador	A young officers' coup ousts the repressive regime of General Romero and forms a reformist military-civilian junta, joined by Guillermo Ungo who returns from exile.
1980	*El Salvador*	Civilian members of the junta resign, ushering in 'Romerismo sin Romero' as the regime's emphasis moves from reform to repression. State of Siege is

declared, leading to civil war. The murder of
Archbishop Romero, a prominent human rights
activist, symbolizes the extent of official violence.
Subsequently over 70,000 people are killed, mainly
at the hands of the security forces and the
right-wing death squads.

Peru   The Maoist-influenced guerrilla group *Sendero
Luminoso* ('Shining Path') begins its insurgency in
the Andean province of Ayacucho. By 1989 *Sendero
Luminoso* threatens Lima by isolating the capital
from its hinterland.

Chile   A referendum held under State of Emergency
provisions (Sept.), with all political parties banned
and no use of electoral registers, adopts a new
constitution which appoints Pinochet as President
for a renewable eight-year term.

Jamaica   Edward Seaga's right-wing Jamaican Labour Party
(JLP) wins a violent electoral campaign (Oct.)
against Michael Manley's People's National Party
(PNP).

1982 Honduras   Roberto Suoza Cordova, a conservative civilian
politician, is elected to the Presidency (Jan.) but real
power is still firmly held by the armed forces, who
have dominated Honduran politics for over
twenty-five years.

Honduras/Nicaragua   First in a series of joint US/Honduran
military exercises began with simulated air and
amphibious landings in the Cabo Gracias a Dios
area, near Nicaragua (Feb.). These manoeuvres
expand annually, exerting considerable pressure
upon the Sandinista government.

Guatemala   General Lucas Garcia, who seized power in July
1978, becomes the most brutal of a series of military
dictators since 1954. 20,000 people died at the
hands of the security forces and the death squads
during his rule. Garcia ousted by a young officers'
coup (March). General Efrain Rios Montt, a
born-again Christian, assumed the Presidency but
the continued massacre of civilians by government
para-military groups removed grounds for any
guarded optimism. The suspension of US arms
shipments to Guatemala is lifted.

El Salvador   Roberto D'Aubuisson's far-right ARENA party gains
a majority in the Constituency Assembly, but
moderate Alvaro Magana is appointed President due
to US pressure (April).

Argentina   Argentina forces invade the Falkland Islands. Britain
declares a naval exclusion zone around the islands.
British navy sinks the Argentinian cruiser *Belgrano*
(May) on orders from the War Cabinet. General
Galtieri rejects Peruvian peace plan. British force
despatched from the Ascension Islands undertakes

landings at San Carlos and wins the Battle of Goose Green. British win the Battle of Port Stanley, prompting the surrender of Argentinian forces on the islands (see p. 303).

Colombia Belisario Betancur assumes the Presidency (Aug.) and attempts to draw dissident guerrilla forces into a political truce.

1983 Guatemala Defence Minister, General Mejia, ousts General Rios Montt from the Presidency in a near bloodless coup (Aug.), continuing Guatemalan political process of coup and counter-coup within a narrow political caste.

Argentina Leader of the Radical Party, Raul Alfonsin, is elected in return to civilian rule. President Alfonsin enjoys a 'honeymoon' period but his government's popularity worn away by failure to solve the aftermath of the 'Malvinas' (Falklands) fiasco, the undertaking of adequate judicial procedures against military personnel responsible for the 'disappearances' during military rule and Argentina's deep-rooted economic problems.

Grenada Maurice Bishop is ousted in Oct. (and later murdered) by a hard-line faction led by Deputy Prime Minister Bernard Coard and General Hudson Austin which provides an opportunity for US intervention. US naval task force (backed by a small contingent from the conservative Organisation of Eastern Caribbean States) successfully invades Grenada (Oct.) after three days' bitter fighting.

1984 Nicaragua CIA initiates the mining of Nicaraguan ports (Feb.). The Sandinista government takes its case to the World Court.

Colombia Assassination of Minister of Justice Lara Bonilla (April) prompts President Betancur to attempt a clampdown on the drugs mafia.

El Salvador In a bitter run-off election, the Christian Democrat, Jose Napoleon Duarte is elected President. The US administration guarantees his government unprecedented levels of economic aid. President Duarte holds first exploratory talks (Oct.) with guerrilla political leaders (the FDR-FMLN).

Nicaragua The Sandinistas win 65% of the votes in national elections. Daniel Ortega is elected President (Nov.)

Chile President Pinochet re-introduces State of Siege provisions (Nov.)

1985 Brazil Tancredo Neves, the candidate of the opposition alliance dominated by Brazilian Democratic Movement (PMBD), defeats the government candidate Paulo Maluf in a contest for the Presidency (Jan.).

Nicaragua	US administration initiates a three-year trade embargo against the Sandinista government (April). In 1988 President Reagan attempts to tighten the economic noose around Nicaragua.
Peru	Alan Garcia (APRA candidate) wins presidential election (April). He fails to improve Peru's dire economic situation or ease the civil conflict.
Brazil	Smooth transition to civilian rule is prevented by death of Tancredo Neves. Vice President Sarney is sworn in as President amid much confusion (April). José Sarney is the leader of the Liberal Front (PFL) a small conservative faction of the victorious opposition alliance.
Chile	The Democratic Alliance is formed (Aug.), unifying parties across the political spectrum opposed to General Pinochet's intransigent rule. Unsuccessful assassination attempt on General Pinochet by the increasingly active Manuel Rodriguez Patriotic Front (FPMR) associated with the illegal communist party (Sept.). Pinochet regime tightens existing press censorship, arrests trade union and socialist leaders, increases mass army raids on working class *poblaciones* in Santiago.
Guatemala	The Christian Democratic Party's candidate, Venecio Cerezo, is an easy victor in the Presidential election. Military leadership remains the power source in the Guatemalan political system.
1986 *Honduras*	José Azcona, dissident Liberal Party candidate, assumes the Presidency after his narrow November victory. The military leadership remain the real fulcrum of power.
Haiti	Mounting popular unrest forces 'Baby Doc' Duvalier into exile (Feb.). Popular celebrations cut short as the transitional military government, fronted by General Henri Namphy, is not over-rigorous in its dismantling of the dictatorship.
Peru	President Garcia's administration is tainted by indirect complicity with the military's massacre of over three hundred *Sendero Luminoso* prisoners whilst subduing prison protests (April).
El Salvador	President Duarte's government fails to halt growing economic dislocation despite massive aid from the Reagan administration. Economic austerity measures prompt greater unity of peasant and trade union groups, which organize May protests against the government.
Colombia	Virgilio Barco, the successful Liberal Party candidate, assumes the Presidency (Aug.). Efforts to open up the political system hampered by informal political power of drug interests, especially the 'Medellin Cartel'. The six major guerrilla groups

form the Simon Bolivar Guerrilla Coordinating Board as a reaction to increasing right-wing death-squad activity.

Brazil The initial success of the anti-inflationary package – the Cruzado plan – benefits the government alliance electorally: the Brazilian Democratic Movement (PMBD) sweeps to power in Congressional State elections (Nov.).

Chile Meeting between Christian Democratic and moderate conservative leaders with two junta members is first formal contact between government and opposition for thirteen years.

Argentina President Alfonsin rushes a 'final point' Bill through Congress designed to prevent further prosecution of military personnel after February 1987.

1987 *Brazil* As foreign exchange reserves fall below $4 billion, Brazil forced to suspend interest payments on its foreign debt (Feb.).

Haiti New constitution approved by the populace (April) but military rule casts shadow over forthcoming elections.

El Salvador An FDR-FMLN peace plan is rejected by Duarte (May) and talks are suspended.

Nicaragua Investigations into the Iran-Contra scandal prompt Congress to suspend aid to the Contras.

Panama Colonel Roberto Diaz, a retired deputy military commander, accuses General Manuel Antonio Noriega of murder and corruption. Noriega had dominated Panamanian politics since 1983 but since July 1987 has come under increased US pressure to resign.

Central America 'Guatemalan Pact' or Arias initiative is signed by Presidents of Central American countries. Hope of progress in solving the conflicts which envelop El Salvador and Nicaragua and enmesh Honduras and Guatemala.

Argentina The Congressional Elections (Sept.) are a triumph for the Peronist movement, taking 42% of the vote as against 37% for the government.

Colombia Jaime Pardo, the leader of Union Patriotica (UP) and its former Presidential candidate, is shot dead by unidentified gunmen (Oct.). Over 500 UP members are killed by right-wing death squads in 1986–87.

1988 *Argentina* Colonel Aldo Rico, freed by a military court to house arrest, leads a second unsuccessful insurrection against President Alfonsin.

Haiti In an electoral contest without a secret ballot or voting lists and boycotted by the four main opposition candidates, Leslie Mainigat is briefly elected President (Jan.). Following his first dispute with the military Mainigat is removed by General Henri Namphy, who reimposes rule by military junta.

Panama	General Noriega is indicted (in absentia) in Miami on drugs offences. President Delvalle attempts to remove Noriega as defence chief but the National Assembly ousts Delvalle and installs the anti-US nationalist Manuel Solis Palma as President (Feb.)
Mexico	The lacklustre candidate of the ruling Institutional Revolutionary Party (PRI), Carlos Salinas, is belatedly declared the winner in the controversial Presidential Election demonstrating the party's bureaucratic control of Mexican politics (July).
Chile	Opposition alliance of sixteen political parties forms the basis of successful 'No' vote against the Pinochet regime (Oct.).
Brazil	The murder of 'Chico' Mendes (Dec.), prominent ecologist and peasant leader, demonstrates the intransigence of the rural elite in the North to environmental pressures for conservation of the forest resources of Amazonia.

1989	*Paraguay*	General Andres Rodriguez ousts General Stroessner's thirty-four year dictatorship in Paraguay. General Alfredo Stroessner is sent into exile in Brazil. General Rodriguez receives over 70% of the votes in an unreliable Presidential election termed fraudulent by the opposition (May).
	Jamaica	Michael Manley's People's National Party (PNP) defeats the JLP incumbent Edward Seaga in a General Election (Feb.). The PNP wins 44 of the 60 parliamentary seats.
	El Salvador	The right-wing ARENA party wins both the Presidential and legislative elections. Cristiani is elected President (but hard-liner Roberto D'Aubuisson controls the party by his domination of its executive committee); as he assumes power in June the activity of death-squad organisations is again on the increase.
	Nicaragua	US administration claims that the Sandinista army's pursuit of Contra forces into Honduras constituted an invasion and dispatches 3,000 US troops for joint manoeuvres with Honduran forces. Later in the month Contra/Sandinista talks produce the fragile Sapoa truce.
	Argentina	Carlos Menem, the Peronist Candidate, defeats Eduardo Angeloz of the Radical party in the Presidential Election, and initiates severe programme of economic austerity in an attempt to combat inflation and the worsening foreign debt.
	Chile	The supporters of the military government have agreed upon Hernan Buchi as presidential candidate to face an opposition candidate the Christian Democrat, Patricio Aylwin. Patricio Aylwin is backed by the sixteen party opposition alliance and goes on to win the December election.

Colombia Murder of the leading Presidential candidate, Liberal Senator Luis Carlos Galan, by the drugs mafia steels the government of Virgilio Barco to declare war on the 'Drugs Mafia'. (Aug.). The narcotics interests answer the challenge by bombing the offices of the Liberal and Conservative parties.

Nicaragua The five Central American Presidents agree to the closure of 'Contra' bases in Honduras within three months (Aug.). US administration decreasing funds to Contras.

Panama US forces invade Panama (Dec). Major US operation to overthrow the Noriega regime and seize Noriega himself. US airborne troops seize Panama City and key towns. Noriega evades capture, seeking refuge in Vatican mission. Guillermo Endara installed as President of Panama. Noriega subsequently surrenders and is flown to the United States to face trial.

1990 *Nicaragua* Sandinistas defeated in General Election; Mrs Violetta Chamorro becomes President.

North America

United States 1914–1941

1914 Aug. 4		US makes formal proclamation of neutrality in war between European powers.
1915 Sept.16		Haiti becomes a US protectorate.
1916 Mar. 15		US troops invade Mexico in pursuit of revolutionary leader Gen. Pancho Villa and remain until 5 Feb. 1917.
	Nov. 7	Woodrow Wilson re-elected Democratic President.
	Nov. 29	US marines land in Dominican Republic and remain until 1924.
	Dec. 18	Wilson sends 'peace note' to all belligerents calling on them to end war and take steps to preserve future peace.
1917 Jan. 17		US pays Denmark $25 million for Virgin Islands.
	Feb. 3	US breaks off diplomatic relations with Germany in protest against sinking of American shipping.
	Feb. 5	Immigration Act excluding Asian labourers from US passed, despite presidential veto attempt.
	Mar. 2	Zimmermann Telegram (see p. 462) suggesting German-Mexican alliance against US made public in Washington.
	Mar. 2	Jones Act declares Puerto Rico a US territory and its inhabitants American citizens.
	Apr. 6	US declares war on Germany.
	June 26	First of 2 million US troops land in France.
	Nov. 3	US troops go into action in France for first time.
1918 Jan. 8		President Wilson announces Fourteen Points to Congress as basis of peace terms and post-war settlement.
1919 Jan. 29		18th Amendment to Constitution prohibits sale, manufacture and transportation of alcoholic drink from 16 Jan. 1920 (i.e. prohibition).
	Oct. 2	President Wilson crippled by stroke.
	Nov. 19	Senate refuses to ratify Versailles Treaty and US membership of League of Nations by 55 votes to 39.
	1919–1920	Mass arrests and deportations of left-wing and trade union activists.
1920 Aug. 26		19th Amendment to Constitution gives women the vote.
	Nov. 2	Republican Warren Harding defeats Democrat James Cox in Presidential election.

see p. 462

1921	Jan. 13	Census Bureau announces US an urban society with over half of population living in towns.
	Mar. 4	Harding inaugurated as 29th President.
	May 19	Immigration into US limited to 357,000 a year with quotas for nationalities.
	Aug.	Wave of Ku Klux Klan (see p. 437) terrorist activity sweeps through the Southern and Mid-West states.
1922	Feb. 6	US signs Washington Treaty with Britain, France, Italy and Japan limiting size of navies.
1923	Jan. 20	US withdraws occupation forces from Germany.
	Aug. 2	Harding dies. Calvin Coolidge sworn in as 30th President on Aug. 3.
	Sept. 15	Oklahoma placed under martial law because of extent of Ku Klux Klan activities.
	Oct. 25	Teapot Dome Scandal investigation begins into corruption in Harding's administration.
1924	Aug. 9	London Conference accepts US General Charles Dawes' plan for German war reparations payments. Germany to have $200 million international loan, two-year moratorium on payments, and submit to financial controls.
	Nov. 4	Coolidge wins Presidential election.
1926	May 10	US marines land in Nicaragua to quell insurrection and leave on June 5.
1927	Aug. 23	Execution of anarchists Sacco and Vanzetti for murder allegedly committed in 1920 arouses world-wide protests.
1928	Aug. 27	US and France sign Kellogg-Briand Pact outlawing war; 62 other states eventually sign.
	Nov. 6	Republican Herbert Hoover defeats Democrat Alfred Smith in Presidential election.
1929	Mar. 4	Hoover sworn in as 31st President.
	Aug. 6–31	Hague Conference accepts US businessman Owen Young's plan for future German war reparations payments. Germany to have $300 million international loan, reparations to be reduced, financial controls imposed by 1924 Dawes Plan to be removed, and payments to be completed in 1988.
	Oct. 24	'Black Thursday'. Wall Street Crash starts as 13 million shares change hands, beginning panic selling which lasts till the end of October. Shares lose $30,000 million in paper value over three weeks. Leads to Depression which spreads from US to Europe.
1930	Feb. 10	158 arrests in Chicago for violation of Prohibition by producing estimated 7 million gallons of whisky worth $50 million.
	Dec. 10	Congress passes legislation to provide $116 million public works scheme to alleviate unemployment.

1931	June 20	Hoover announces 'moratorium' on war debts payments to US, effectively abandoning German war reparations.
	Sept–Oct	Bank panic forces closure of 827 banks following run on funds by customers.
1932	Feb. 2	Reconstruction Finance Corporation set up to alleviate Depression. Lends $2 billion to banks, business and agriculture.
	May 29	Thousand-strong unemployed veterans 'Bonus Army' march arrives in Washington seeking relief. It is joined by supporters through the summer and rises to 17,000.
	July 28	Federal troops and tanks led by Gen. Douglas MacArthur break up and disperse unemployed demonstrators in Washington.
	Nov. 8	Democrat Franklin Roosevelt defeats Hoover in Presidential election.
1933	Mar. 4	Roosevelt sworn in as 32nd President.
	Mar. 6	Roosevelt declares Bank Holiday until Mar. 9 to prevent run on banks. Only financially solvent banks allowed to re-open.
	Mar. 9	100 days of 'New Deal' legislation to provide relief to banks, industry, agriculture and the unemployed begins. Results in over $15 billion expenditure by 1940.
	Mar. 12	Roosevelt broadcasts first of Sunday radio 'fireside chats'.
	Mar. 31	Reforestation Unemployment Act creates Civilian Conservation Corps to reduce unemployment through a reforestation programme.
	May 12	Agricultural Adjustment Act restricts production of some crops and finances farmers for not producing.
	May 12	Federal Emergency Relief Act passed.
	May 18	Tennessee Valley Act passed establishing Tennessee Valley Authority to create work by extending rural electrification.
	June 16	National Industrial Recovery Act creates the National Recovery Administration and the Public Works Administration.
	Aug. 5	National Labor Board established under Senator Robert Wagner to arbitrate in collective bargaining disputes.
	Nov. 8	Civil Works Administration established with initial $400 million funding to create 4 million jobs.
	Dec. 5	Prohibition on manufacture and sale of alcohol repealed by 21st Amendment to Constitution.
1934		Agriculture devastated in Mid-Western states by drought and inadequate conservation of land.
	Jan. 31	Farm Mortgage Refinancing Act passed to assist farmers with easier credit.
	June 28	Federal Farm Bankruptcy Act calls a moratorium on farm mortgage foreclosures.

1935	May 27	Sections of National Recovery Act declared unconstitutional by Supreme Court.
	July 5	Wagner-Connery Act establishes National Labor Relations Board with authority to encourage collective bargaining.
	Aug. 14	Unemployment and old-age insurance instituted by Social Security Act.
	Sept. 8	Louisiana Governor Huey Long assassinated in State Capitol building.
	Nov. 9	Committee for Industrial Organization formed as eventual breakaway from American Federation of Labor. Organizes occupations of car and steel works to encourage unionization in new industrial sectors.
1936	Jan. 6	Sections of Agricultural Adjustment Act declared unconstitutional by Supreme Court.
	July 30	US signs London Naval Treaty with Britain and France to limit naval armaments.
	Nov. 3	Roosevelt defeats Hoover to win Presidential re-election.
1937	July 22	Senate overturns Roosevelt's attempt to alter Supreme Court balance in his favour by appointment of liberal judges.
	Oct. 5	Roosevelt calls for international sanctions against aggressive powers.
	Dec. 12	Japanese aircraft bomb and sink US gunboat *Panjay* carrying Chinese refugees on Yangtse River. Japan apologizes.
1938	Jan. 28	Roosevelt calls on Congress to vote funds for expansion of Army and Navy.
	May 26	House of Representatives Committee to Investigate Un-American Activities formed.
	June 25	Minimum wage of 40c an hour and maximum working week of 40 hours guaranteed by 1940 under Wages & Hours Law. Child labour under 16 banned.
1939	July 1	Federal Works Agency established to co-ordinate New Deal activities.
	Aug. 2	Hatch Act outlaws political activity of federal employees below policy level.
	Sept. 1	Roosevelt declares in radio talk that US will remain neutral in war.
	Oct. 3	US and 20 members of Pan-American Conference sign Declaration of Panama establishing a 300-mile neutrality zone round American continent.
	Nov. 4	Neutrality Act amended at Roosevelt's insistence to allow 'cash and carry' arms sales to belligerents, effectively favouring Britain.
1940	July 30	Declaration of Havana by US and 20 American republics bans transfer of European colonies on American continent to other European powers.
	Sept. 3	US gives Britain 50 destroyers in exchange for bases in Newfoundland and the West Indies.

Sept. 16	US introduces first peace-time conscription measure to draft 900,000 recruits a year.
Nov. 5	Roosevelt wins third Presidential term by defeating Republican Alfred London.
1941 Mar. 11	Roosevelt authorized to supply war materials to Britain by Lease-Lend Act.
June 14	All German and Italian assets in US frozen.
Aug. 9–12	Meeting between Roosevelt and Churchill off Newfoundland produces Atlantic Charter setting out post-war aims.
Aug. 18	Roosevelt abolishes limitations on size of armed forces.
Dec. 7	Japanese mount surprise attack on US naval base at Pearl Harbor, Hawaii.
Dec. 8	Congress approves Roosevelt's declaration of war against Japan.
Dec. 11	Germany and Italy declare war on US.

For the events of the Pacific War, see pp. 106–7.

United States since 1945

1945 Apr. 12   Roosevelt dies. Harry Truman sworn in as successor.

      July 16   Atom bomb exploded near Alamogordo, New Mexico.

1946 Apr. 11   McMahon Act declares government monopoly over all US atomic energy activities.

      July 4   US grants Philippines independence.

1947 Jun. 23   Taft-Hartley Act outlawing trade union closed shop and allowing Government to impose 'cooling-off' period before strike passed by Congress despite Presidential veto.

      July 26   Defense Department formed to co-ordinate military organization.

1948 Nov. 2   Truman defeats Republican candidate Thomas Dewey in Presidential election.

1949 Oct. 14   11 Communist Party leaders jailed for advocating overthrow of Government.

      Oct. 26   Minimum Wage Bill raises minimum wage from 40c to 75c an hour.

1950 Jan. 21   Alger Hiss, a former State Department official, jailed for perjury after denying membership of a Communist spy organization.

      Jan. 31   Truman orders work to proceed on development of hydrogen bomb.

      Aug. 1   Guam becomes a United States territory.

      Aug. 28   Truman takes control of railways to avert a strike. Returned to private owners 23 May, 1952.

      Dec. 11   Supreme Court rules that 5th Amendment to the Constitution protects an individual from being forced to incriminate him or herself.

1951 Jan. 3   22nd Amendment to the Constitution limits Presidents to two terms in office.

1952 Apr. 8   Truman takes control of steel-works to avert strike; action ruled unconstitutional by Supreme Court.

      July 25   Puerto Rico becomes a self-governing US commonwealth territory.

      Nov. 1   First hydrogen bomb exploded at Eniwetok atoll, Marshall Islands.

      Nov. 4   Republican Dwight Eisenhower defeats Democrat Adlai Stevenson in Presidential election.

1953 Jan. 20   Eisenhower inaugurated as 34th President.

      Apr. 20   US Communist Party ordered to register with Justice Department as an organization controlled by the USSR.

      June 19   Julius and Ethel Rosenberg executed as spies for passing atomic secrets to USSR.

1954 Apr. 22   Senate hearings into Sen. Joseph McCarthy's claims of communist subversion in army begin. They continue until June 17.

    May 17   Supreme Court outlaws racial segregation in schools.

    May 24   Supreme Court declares Communist Party membership valid grounds for deportation of aliens.

    Dec. 2   Senate vote of censure against McCarthy effectively ends his witch-hunt campaign.

1955 Dec. 1   Black bus boycott led by Revd. Martin Luther King begins in Montgomery, Alabama, in protest against racial discrimination.

    Dec. 5   American Federation of Labour and Committee for Industrial Organization merge under leadership of George Meany.

1956 Nov. 6   Eisenhower defeats Stevenson in Presidential election.

    Nov. 13   Supreme Court outlaws racial segregation on buses.

1957 Sept. 24   Eisenhower despatches 1,000 paratroops to protect black high school students asserting their rights to non-segregated education in Little Rock, Arkansas.

1959 Jan. 3   Alaska becomes 49th state.
    Aug. 21   Hawaii becomes 50th state.

1960 Nov. 9   Democrat John Kennedy narrowly defeats Republican Richard Nixon in Presidential election.

1961 Jan. 20   Kennedy inaugurated as 35th President.
    Oct. 6   Kennedy declares that a 'prudent family' should possess a fall-out shelter to protect itself in event of nuclear war.

    Dec. 5   Kennedy announces 5 out of 7 Army recruits are rejected on physical grounds and calls for public to take up exercise and become 'athletes' rather than 'spectators'.

1962 Jan. 12   State Department announces that Communist Party members will be denied passports.

    Nov. 20   Kennedy signs order prohibiting racial discrimination in housing built with federal funds.

1963 June 17   Supreme Court rules religious ceremonies not essential in schools.

    Aug. 28   Martin Luther King leads 200,000 strong civil rights 'freedom march' in Washington.

    Nov. 22   Kennedy assassinated in Dallas, Texas, by Lee Harvey Oswald. Lyndon Johnson sworn in as 36th President.

1964 July 2   Civil Rights Act bans racial discrimination in services provision and by trade unions and businesses carrying on inter-state commerce.

    Aug. 30   Johnson signs anti-poverty Economic Opportunity Policy providing almost $1 billion for community action programmes.

Sept. 27	Warren Commission appointed to investigate Kennedy assassination declares there was no conspiracy and that Oswald acted alone.
Nov. 3	Johnson defeats Republican Barry Goldwater in Presidential election.
1965 July 30	Congress passes Medicare programme providing Federal medical insurance for over-65s.
Aug. 6	Government takes powers under Voting Rights Act to compel local authorities to register black voters and to remove obstacles to their voting.
Aug. 11	Black riots begin in Watts, Los Angeles, and continue until 16 Aug. 35 die.
Oct. 17	Demonstrations throughout US against involvement in Vietnam
Oct. 19	House Committee on Un-American Activities begins investigation into Ku Klux Klan.
Nov. 27	25,000 demonstrate in Washington against Vietnam War.
1966 July 1	Medicare comes into operation.
Nov. 8	Republican Edward Brooke becomes first black ever elected to Senate.
1967 July 23	Black riots in Detroit. Troops deployed as disturbances continue until 30 July; 40 die and over 2,000 injured.
Oct. 20	Major anti-Vietnam War demonstration in Washington.
1968 Feb. 29	National Advisory Committee on Civil Disorders (Kerner Commission) report condemns white racism in US and calls for aid to black communities.
Mar. 31	Johnson announces he will not run for second term as President.
Apr. 4	Martin Luther King assassinated in Memphis, Tennessee. Riots in over 100 cities follow.
May 2	Black 'Poor People's March' on Washington begins. Culminates in 3,000 strong camp at 'Resurrection city'.
June 5	Sen. Robert Kennedy shot in Los Angeles while campaigning for Democratic Presidential nomination. Dies on 6 June.
Aug. 26	Anti-Vietnam War demonstrations at Democratic convention in Chicago quelled by police and troops. Disturbances continue until 30 Aug.
Nov. 8	Republican Richard Nixon defeats Democrat Hubert Humphrey in Presidential election.
1969 Jan. 20	Nixon inaugurated as 37th President.
Oct. 15	Mass demonstrations against Vietnam War throughout US.
1970 May 4	National Guard kills four Anti-War students demonstrating at Kent State University, Ohio.

1971	Apr. 20	Supreme Court upholds bussing as a means of achieving racial balance in schools.
	May 2	Beginning of three day Anti-Vietnam War protest in Washington. Over 13,000 arrests.
	June 3	Publication of leaked 'Pentagon Papers' disclosing hidden background to Vietnam War. Supreme Court refuses to prevent publication, 30 June.
	July 5	26th Amendment to Constitution reduces voting age to 18.
	Aug. 11	Law enforcing educational desegregation in 11 Southern states comes into effect.
	Aug. 15	Nixon introduces anti-inflation wages and prices freeze; suspends convertability of dollar into gold.
1972	May 15	Alabama Governor George Wallace, in the past an uncompromising segregationalist, wounded and crippled in assassination attempt.
	June 17	Five men arrested burgling the Democratic National Committee offices at Watergate building, Washington. On June 22 Nixon denies White House involvement.
	Nov. 7	Nixon wins landslide victory over Democrat George McGovern in Presidential election.
1973	Jan. 8–30	Watergate burglary trial. Two of the seven convicted had been 'Committee to Re-elect the President' officials, and one a White House consultant.
	Feb. 7	Senate forms a committee to investigate the Watergate affair.
	Feb. 27	Indians protesting against Government treatment mount Siege of Wounded Knee. Two Indians die before it ends on 8 May.
	Apr. 30	White House advisers H. R. Haldeman and John Ehrlichman and staff member John Dean resign over participation in Watergate cover-up.
	May 11	'Pentagon Papers' case against Daniel Elsberg dismissed because government used burglary to obtain evidence.
	July 16	Revelation that Nixon has taped his White House conversations since 1970, eventually showing his active involvement in Watergate cover-up.
	Oct. 10	Vice-President Spiro Agnew forced to resign after disclosure of income tax evasion.
	Oct. 23	Nixon ordered to surrender White House tapes to Senate. Watergate investigation under threat of impeachment.
	Nov. 7	Congress votes to limit Presidential powers to wage war.
	Dec. 6	Gerald Ford sworn in as Vice-President.
1974	Jan. 1	Three former cabinet members and Nixon's two leading White House aides are convicted for their part in covering up Watergate events.
	July 24	Supreme Court orders Nixon to release his tape recorded conversations.

Aug. 9	Nixon resigns under threat of impeachment proceedings for involvement in Watergate. Ford sworn in as 38th President.
Sept. 8	Ford grants Nixon full pardon.
Sept. 16	Ford announces amnesty for Vietnam War draft evaders and deserters.

1976 Apr. 26   Senate Committee on Central Intelligence Agency demands stronger control over and greater accountability of intelligence services following concern over activities.

Nov. 1   Democrat Jimmy Carter defeats Ford in Presidential election.

1977 Jan. 20   Carter inaugurated as 39th President.

1978 June 6   Proposition 13 in California state referendum limits local taxes, triggering a campaign nationally to reduce federal and state taxation.

1979 Feb. 12   Carter appeals for voluntary conservation to limit effects of growing energy crisis.

Mar. 28   Serious atomic reactor accident at Three Mile Island, Pennsylvania, provokes loss of public confidence in nuclear power.

June 13 $100 million awarded to Sioux Indians as compensation for land taken from them in 1877.

Oct. 23   Congress grants Carter powers to introduce petrol rationing because of world oil crisis.

1980 Nov. 4   Republican Ronald Reagan gains landslide Presidential election victory over Carter.

1981 Jan. 20   Reagan inaugurated as 40th President.

Mar. 30   Reagan wounded in assassination attempt in Washington.

Aug. 13   Reagan's New Economic Programme projects 25% income tax reductions in 1981–84.

1986 Nov. 13   Reagan admits US arms sales to Iran, opening what becomes known as the Iran-Contra scandal.

Nov. 25   Further revelations about arms sales to Iran force resignation of National Security Adviser Adm. John Poindexter and Marine Col. Oliver North.

Dec. 2   Reagan appoints special prosecutor to investigate Iran-Contra scandal. As investigation develops details emerge of plan for proceeds of arms sales to Iran to be diverted to aiding Contra forces in Nicaragua.

1987 Mar. 3   Reagan says arms for Iran had been intended to help in release of hostages held in Middle East.

July 15   Adm. Poindexter says Reagan unaware of plan to divert Iran arms sales proceeds to aid Contras.

Aug. 12   Reagan accepts responsibility for Iran-Contra affair but denies knowledge of diversion of funds.

	Oct. 19	'Black Monday': massive slump in share prices on Wall Street.
1988	Mar. 16	Poindexter and North indicted on Iran-Contra charges.
	Nov. 8	George Bush defeats Democrat Michael Dukakis in Presidential election.
1989	Jan. 20	Bush sworn in as 41st President.

United States and the World from 1945

1945	May 8	V-E Day. End of war in Europe.
	June 26	50 nations sign United Nations Charter in San Francisco.
	July 17–2	Potsdam Conference between Truman, Stalin and Churchill (later Attlee) reaches decision on division of Germany and demand for Japan's unconditional surrender.
	Aug. 6	Atom bomb dropped on Hiroshima.
	Aug. 9	Atom bomb dropped on Nagasaki.
	Aug. 14	V-J Day. Japan acknowledges defeat.
	Sept. 2	Japan formally surrenders on USS *Missouri* in Tokyo.
1946	Aug. 1	Atomic Energy Act restricts exchange of nuclear information with other nations.
	Oct. 16	UN General Assembly opens in New York.
1947	Mar. 12	Truman signs Greek-Turkish Aid Bill promising the two states $400 million aid to resist Soviet aggression and internal Communist subversion. Becomes known as the 'Truman Doctrine'.
	June 7	Secretary of State George Marshall proposes Marshall Plan to assist European economic recovery.
1948	Apr. 3	Marshall's European Recovery Programme enacted. By 1952 Europe receives $17,000 million in aid.
	June 24	Berlin airlift begins, US and Britain fly in 2 million tons of supplies to counter Soviet rail and road blockade. Ends following negotiations 12 May 1949.
1949	Apr. 4	US signs North Atlantic Treaty in Washington with 11 other states to create NATO alliance.
1950	May 25	US, UK and France conclude Tripartite Agreement to reduce Middle East tension by guaranteeing existing borders and limiting arms sales.
	July 1	US troops arrive as part of United Nations force to assist South Korea, invaded by North Korea on 25 June.
	Sept. 26	US troops recapture South Korean capital Seoul.
	Oct. 7	US troops cross 38th Parallel into North Korea and advance by Nov. 20 to Manchurian border on Yalu River.
	Nov. 29	US troops forced to retreat in Korea by heavy Chinese attack.
	Dec. 19	US Gen. Dwight Eisenhower appointed Supreme Commander of NATO forces in Europe.
1951	Jan. 4	Seoul abandoned by US forces.
	Mar. 14	Seoul recaptured by US troops.
	Apr. 11	Gen. Douglas MacArthur dismissed by Truman from command in Korea and all military offices for

		defying policy by advocating attack on Communist China.
	Oct. 10	Truman signs Mutual Security Act authorizing over $7 billion expenditure overseas on economic, military and technical aid.
1952	Nov. 1	US explodes first hydrogen device at Eniwetok atoll, Marshall Islands.
1953	July 27	Armistice signed at Panmunjon ends fighting in Korea. 54,000 US servicemen died in war.
1954	Jan. 12	Secretary of State John Foster Dulles announces doctrine of 'massive retaliation' warning USSR that aggression will be met with nuclear attack.
	Mar. 8	US mutual defence agreement with Japan allows gradual re-arming of Japan.
	Sept. 8	Manila Treaty creates South East Asia Treaty Organization (SEATO) of US and seven other states for military and economic co-operation (see p. 260).
	Dec. 2	US signs Mutual Security Pact with Taiwan guaranteeing protection from Chinese attack. In effect until 1978.
1955	Feb. 12	Eisenhower despatches troops to South Vietnam as military advisers.
	Mar. 16	Eisenhower announces that atomic weapons would be used in event of war. US reported to have 4,000 bombs stockpiled.
	July 18–23	US attends summit meeting with Britain, France, USSR. Independence of East and West Germany recognized; Eisenhower proposes 'open skies' aerial photography plan as move towards disarmament.
	Aug. 15	US signs Austrian State Treaty with Britain, France and USSR restoring Austrian independence within 1937 borders.
1957	Jan. 5	Eisenhower Doctrine proposes military and economic aid to Middle East states threatened internally or externally by communism. Congress votes $200 million.
1958	July 15	US troops intervene in Lebanon Civil War under Eisenhower Doctrine following appeal from Lebanon President. Withdraw 25 Oct.
	Aug. 23	US military preparations provoked by fears that Chinese shelling of offshore Nationalist island of Quemoy is a prelude to invasion.
1959	Sept. 15–27	Eisenhower meets Soviet Prime Minister Nikita Khrushchev at Camp David and both agree on need for 'peaceful coexistence'.
	Dec. 1	US signs Antarctica Treaty with 11 other states guaranteeing the area's neutrality.
1960	Jan. 19	US and Japan sign mutual defence pact. Comes into effect June 23

	May 1	American U2 spy plane shot down over USSR and pilot captured.
	May 9	US announces suspension of U2 flights.
	May 16	Summit conference with USSR in Paris terminated when Eisenhower refuses to apologize to Khrushchev over U2 incident.
	July 11	American RB-47 reconnaissance bomber shot down over Soviet Union.
1961	Jan. 3	US breaks off diplomatic relations with Cuba over nationalization of American property without compensation.
	Mar. 1	Kennedy sets up Peace Corps as part of overseas aid programme.
	Apr. 17	1600-strong invasion of Cuba at Bay of Pigs by CIA-trained Cuban exiles with Kennedy's backing. Crushed by April 20.
	June 3–4	Kennedy and Khrushchev discuss German unification at unsuccessful summit conference in Vienna.
	Dec. 11	US despatches helicopters and crews to assist South Vietnam. 3,500 US troops in area.
1962	May 12	US troops deployed in Thailand to counter communist threat. They withdraw July 27.
	June 16	Defense Secretary Robert McNamara announces 'flexible response' to replace 'massive retaliation' strategy.
	June 27	Kennedy promises Taiwan military assistance in event of Chinese attack.
	Oct. 22–28	Cuban missile crisis. Kennedy announces aerial photography reveals Soviet missile sites in Cuba. Places Cuba under naval and air blockade to prevent delivery of missiles. Khrushchev removes missiles in return for US promise not to invade Cuba.
	Dec. 18	Nassau Agreement between Kennedy and UK Prime Minister Macmillan to provide Britain with Polaris nuclear missiles for submarines.
1963	Apr. 5	Hot line connected between White House and Kremlin.
	June 25	Kennedy announces on European tour that US 'will risk its cities to defend yours'.
	Aug. 5	Nuclear weapons tests in atmosphere, space and under water banned by treaty between US, UK and USSR.
	Oct. 7	White House announces aid to Vietnam will continue and that war could be won by end of 1965.
1964	Aug. 5	First US bombing of North Vietnam.
	Aug. 7	Congress grants Johnson sweeping military powers under Gulf of Tonkin Resolution, following alleged North Vietnamese attacks on US destroyers 2–4 Aug.
1965	Feb. 7	US begins heavy sustained bombing of North Vietnam.

Feb. 18	Defense Secretary McNamara announces deterrent strategy of 'mutually assured destruction'.
Mar. 8	US combat troops land in Vietnam bringing numbers involved to 74,000.
Apr. 28	400 US Marines land in Dominican Republic to prevent left-wing takeover. The force eventually rises to 24,000.
June 15	US troops in first action against Viet Cong.
July 28	Johnson announces numbers of US troops in Vietnam will be increased from 75,000 to 125,000.

1966 Feb. 8 — Declaration of Honolulu by Johnson and South Vietnam Premier Ky promises economic and social reforms in Vietnam.

Mar. 2 — Defense Secretary Robert McNamara announces US forces in Vietnam will be increased to 235,000.

June 11 — US forces in Vietnam to rise to 285,000.

1967 Jan. 27 — Space Treaty with UK and USSR outlaws use of nuclear weapons in space.

June 23–25 — Summit meeting between Johnson and Soviet Prime Minister Kosygin in Glassboro, New Jersey.

July 22 — Announcement of intention to deploy 525,000 US troops in Vietnam by end of 1968.

July 27 — Puerto Rico votes against independence and to remain a US commonwealth territory.

1968 Jan. 23 — North Korea seizes crew of USS *Pueblo* and accuses them of spying. They are released on 22 Dec.

Jan. 30 — Viet Cong open Tet Offensive. Although a military failure for the communists, the attack has a dramatic effect on US commitment to war in Vietnam.

Mar. 16 — US troops massacre 450 inhabitants in Vietnamese village of My Lai. News does not break until November. Lt. William Calley given life imprisonment 29 March 1971 but sentence reduced.

Mar. 31 — Johnson announces end to bombing of North Vietnam.

May 13 — Preliminary Vietnam peace talks open in Paris.

July 1 — US signs Nuclear Non-Proliferation Treaty with Britain and USSR.

1969 Jan. 25 — Full Vietnam peace talks begin in Paris.

Mar. — US troops in Vietnam reach their highest level at 541,000.

Nov. 3 — Nixon announces intention to withdraw US forces and to 'Vietnamize' the war.

Nov. 25 — US renounces use of biological weapons.

1970 Apr. 16 — Strategic Arms Limitation Talks (SALT) open between US and USSR in Vienna.

Apr. 21 — Nixon announces 150,000 US troop reduction in Vietnam over next year.

Apr. 30 — US troops deployed in Cambodia.

1971	June 10	US lifts 21-year trade embargo on China.
	Oct. 25	US signs Seabed Treaty with USSR, UK and other states banning nuclear weapons on ocean floor.
1972	Feb. 21–25	Nixon reverses US policy by visiting Communist China.
	Apr. 6	US resumes bombing of North Vietnam following communist offensive.
	May 22–30	Nixon and Brezhnev agree to limit atomic weapon production at Moscow summit. Senate ratifies agreement on 3 Aug.
1973	Jan. 28	Ceasefire ends US involvement in Vietnam War. Final combat troops leave 29 Mar.
	June 16–24	Nixon and Brezhnev summit meeting in US reaches agreement on co-operation to prevent nuclear war and on future arms negotiations.
	July 1	Congress orders end to US bombing of Cambodia and military action in area by 15 Aug.
	Oct. 17	Arab states ban oil supplies to US in protest against support for Israel. Ends 1974.
1974	Jan. 10	Defense Secretary James Schlesinger announces 'limited strategic strike options' as new nuclear doctrine.
	May 7	Ford declares Vietnam War era is over a week after Saigon falls to communists.
	July 3	US signs Threshold Test Ban Treaty with USSR, placing limits on underground nuclear testing.
1975	Aug. 1	US signs Helsinki Treaty with USSR guaranteeing European post-war boundaries and recognizing human rights.
1977	Sept. 7	Carter signs Panama Canal Zone Treaty agreeing to evacuate Canal Zone by the year 2000.
1978	Sept. 5–17	Carter mediates at Camp David negotiations between Egyptian President Sadat and Israeli Prime Minister Begin, culminating in outline Middle East peace treaty. Treaty signed at White House 26 March 1979; effective 25 April 1979.
1979	Jan. 1	US establishes full diplomatic relations with China and severs links with Nationalist government on Taiwan.
	Feb. 8	US withdraws support from President Somoza of Nicaragua ensuring his downfall to Sandinista revolution.
	Nov. 4	Iranian students occupy US Embassy in Tehran and seize 52 American hostages.
	Nov. 4	US establishes formal relations with German Democratic Republic.
1980	Apr. 24–25	8 US dead in unsuccessful helicopter attempt to rescue Tehran Embassy hostages.

Dec. 21	Iran demands $10,000 million payment for release of Embassy hostages.
1981 Jan. 20	US Embassy hostages released from Tehran as Reagan is sworn in as President.
1983 Oct. 23	241 US Marine members of peace-keeping force killed by suicide bombers in Beirut.
Oct. 25	US troops invade Grenada with forces of six Caribbean states to put down alleged left-wing threat. Suffer 42 dead in fighting with Grenada Army and Cuban construction workers.
1985 May 1	US bans all trade with Nicaragua.
Nov. 19–21	Reagan and Gorbachev summit in Geneva agrees on future annual meetings but fails to resolve differences over 'Star Wars' as obstacle to arms control.
1986 Jan. 7	Reagan orders US citizens to leave Libya and bans trade in retaliation for alleged Libyan involvement in international terrorism.
Feb. 18	Reagan announces $15 million military aid to anti-government guerrillas in Angola.
Mar. 20	House of Representatives rejects Reagan's $100 million aid package to anti-government Contra guerrillas in Nicaragua. Finally approves on 25 June and Reagan signs Bill on 18 Oct.
Mar. 24	US task force asserting sailing rights in Gulf of Sidra attacked by Libyan missile ships. US sinks two ships and bombs coastal radar installation.
Apr. 14	American F-111 bombers strike Tripoli and Benghazi following alleged Libyan links with international terrorism.
June 18	House of Representatives votes for trade embargo on South Africa and withdrawal by US companies.
June 27	International Court rules US support of Contras in Nicaragua illegal.
July 15	US troops deployed in Bolivia to assist in operations against cocaine producers.
Sept. 26	Reagan vetoes South African sanctions proposal by House of Representatives.
Oct. 2	US Senate defies Presidential veto and imposes trade sanctions on South Africa.
Oct. 10–11	Reagan and Gorbachev meet in Reykjavik, Iceland. Blame each other for failure to achieve arms control agreement.
1987 Nov. 24	US reaches agreement with USSR on scrapping of intermediate range nuclear missiles.
Dec. 8–11	Reagan and Gorbachev summit meeting in Washington. Intermediate range missiles treaty signed; agreement on further arms reductions proposals and for a meeting in 1988.

1988 May 29	Reagan and Gorbachev meet in Moscow and agree on further intermediate range missile reductions.
July 3	USS *Vincennes* shoots down Iranian airbus over Gulf of Iran, killing 290 passengers.
Dec. 14	US declares willingness to talk with Palestinian Liberation Organization following Yasser Arafat's 7 Dec. acceptance of Israel's right to exist. Discussions in Tunis take place 16 Dec.
1989 Jan. 4	US Navy jets shoot down two Libyan aircraft over Mediterranean.
Dec.	US forces invade Panama in operation to overthrow Noriega regime.

Canada since 1914

1914   Canada enters the First World War (Aug.); expeditionary force raised.

1917   Coalition government formed to pursue war. Canadian troops suffer heavy losses in capture of Vimy Ridge, France (April). Newfoundland obtains Dominion status. Conscription introduced (Aug.).

1918   Anti-conscription riots in Quebec; martial law imposed (April).

1919   Mackenzie King takes over from Sir Wilfrid Laurier as leader of Liberal Party.

1921   Liberal Party wins General Election; Mackenzie King becomes Prime Minister.

1926   King and Liberal Cabinet resign (June) as a result of a customs scandal; Liberals under Mackenzie King returned to power in elections in September. Canada becomes a self-governing Dominion within the Commonwealth.

1927   Richard Bennett becomes leader of Conservative Party.

1930   Conservative Government under Bennett wins election victory over Liberals (July); failure to reach agreement at London Conference on tariff preferences between Canada, the other Dominions, and Britain (Nov.).

1932   Bennett convenes Imperial economic conference at Ottawa (July–Aug.) and gains introduction of partial Imperial preference, gaining Canada access to United Kingdom markets on favourable terms.

1933   Royal Commission reports on bankruptcy of Newfoundland, recommending suspension of constitution and control by a nominated commission (Feb.).

1934   Commission appointed in Newfoundland and given British loans to assist economic recovery.

1935   Bennett announces 'New Deal'-style reforms (Jan.); Mackenzie King defeats Bennett by record majority in elections (Oct.).

1939   Canada enters war against Germany (Sept.); first Canadian troops sent to Britain (Dec.).

1942   Canadian Parliament votes for conscription (July); ends relations with Vichy France (Nov.). Canadian troops suffer heavily in Dieppe Raid (19 Aug.).

1943   Mackenzie King hosts Quebec Conference between Churchill and Roosevelt.

1945   King's Liberal Party returned in General Election (June).

1946   Arrests of Soviet spies allegedly involved in transfer of atomic secrets to Russia (Feb.). British Labour Government authorises the election of a Newfoundland Convention to discuss its future (June).

1948　Referendum on future of Newfoundland indecisive (June); second referendum (July) gives majority for federation with Canada. Louis St. Laurent becomes Liberal leader and Prime Minister in succession to MacKenzie King (Nov.).

1949　Newfoundland becomes 10th province of Canada (March); Canada signs North Atlantic Treaty (April). Official Languages Act establishes English and French as dual official languages. British North America Act gave federal parliament limited rights to amend constitution.

1950　Death of Mackenzie King (July).

1951　Old Age Security Act introduced.

1952　Collaboration on production of hydro-electric power with USA begins.

1953　Work begun on St. Lawrence Seaway system of canals and locks linking the Atlantic and the Great Lakes. General Election won by St. Laurent for the Liberals.

1956　John Diefenbaker becomes leader of Progressive Conservative Party (Dec.).

1957　St. Laurent loses General Election to Diefenbaker and the Conservatives form minority government (June), ending twenty-two years of Liberal Government.

1958　St. Laurent hands over as leader of opposition to Lester Pearson; Conservatives obtain clear majority of 158 seats in new election (March). Conference at Montreal institutes Commonwealth Assistance Loans.

1959　St Lawrence Seaway formally opened (June).

1963　Diefenbaker resigns (17 April); Pearson forms Liberal Government (22 April).

1964　Canada adopts Maple Leaf emblem for National flag. Growing discontent between French and English speaking Canadians and growing movement for separatism in Quebec.

1967　Diefenbaker retires from politics. De Gaulle angers Canadian government by references to autonomy for French Canada on visit to Quebec (July).

1968　Pearson resigns in favour of Pierre Trudeau (April): Trudeau increases Liberal majority at General Election (June).

1970　*Parti Quebeçois* gains six seats in Quebec National Assembly (of 110).

1972　Trudeau left as head of minority Liberal Government following General Election (Oct.).

1974　Trudeau regains majority in General Election.

1976　*Parti Quebecois* gains 70 seats in Quebec National Assembly.

1977   Visit of head of *Parti Quebeçois*, René Levesque, to France with full honours (Nov.).

1979   Trudeau defeated in General Election (May); Conservative Government under Joe Clark.

1980   Trudeau leads Liberals to General Election victory (Feb.). Trudeau proposes 'patriation' of the Constitution, severing last constitutional links with Britain, causing violent scenes in parliament. Referendum (20 May) in Quebec votes against proposal of *Parti Quebeçois* for negotiation for a looser political association with the rest of Canada.

1981   Canada formally asks Britain for 'patriation' of the constitution (Dec.).

1982   Canada Bill, approving patriation, passes British House of Commons. Queen Elizabeth visits Canada to formalize complete national sovereignty for Canada (April). New constitution replaces Acts of 1867 and 1949, provides a bill of rights and redefines ethnic, provincial and territorial rights.

1983   Brian Mulroney takes over as leader of Conservative Party from Joe Clark (June).

1984   John Turner succeeds Trudeau as Liberal leader and Prime Minister (June). Conservatives sweep to victory in General Election (Sept.), winning 211 of 282 seats.

1988   General Election on issue of free-trade agreement with the United States leads to further victory for Mulroney and the Progressive Conservative Party (Nov.). Free Trade agreement with United States enacted.

Heads of State and Selected Ministers/Rulers

Afghanistan

Kingdom of Afghanistan

Kings

Habibollah Khan	1901–19
Amanollah Khan	1919–29
Habibollah (usurper)	1929 (Jan.–Oct.)
Muhammad Nader Shah	1929–33
Muhammad Zahir Shah	1933–73

Prime Ministers

S. Khan	1929–46
S. Gazi	1946–53
S. Daoud	1953–63
M. Yussuf	1963–65
M. Maiwandwal	1965–67
A. Yakta (acting)	1967 (Oct.–Nov.)
N. Etemadi	1967–7l
A. Zahir	1971–72
M. Shafiq	1972–73

The monarchy was overthrown in a peaceful coup in July 1973 and a republic instituted.

Republic of Afghanistan

Presidents

Lt.-Gen. M. Daoud	1973–78
D. Kadir (acting)	1978 (Apr.–May)
N. Taraki	1978–79
H. Amin	1979 (Oct.–Dec.)
B. Karmal	1979–86
M. Najibullah	1986–

Prime Ministers

Lt.-Gen. M. Daoud	1973–78
Gen. D. Kadir (acting)	1978 (Apr.–May)
N. Taraki	1978–79
H. Amin	1979 (Mar.–Dec.)
B. Karmal	1979–81
A. Keshtmand	1981–88
M. Sharq	1988–

Albania

Principality of Albania

Regent and De Facto Ruler

Essad Pasha   1913–20

Prince Wilhelm held the throne from February until September 1914
but was unable to exercise authority.
Essad Pasha proclaimed himself King in 1919, controlling part of
Albania until his assassination in 1920. From 1920 to 1922 Albania
was without central control, under the nominal control of a Council of
Regents from 1920 to 1925.

Republic of Albania

President

Ahmed Bey Zogu   1925–28

He proclaimed himself King in September 1928.

Kingdom of Albania

King

Zog I   1928–39

Prime Minister

P. Evangheli   1933–39

Victor Emmanuel III of Italy was described as King of Albania from
1939 to 1943.

Prime Ministers

S. Verlazi	1939–41
M. Kruja	1941–43
E. Libohova	1943 (Jan.–Feb.)
M. Bushati	1943 (Feb.–May)
E. Libohova	1943–45
Col.-Gen. E. Hoxha (provisional)	1945–46

Socialist Republic

Presidents

O. Nishani	1946–53
Maj.-Gen. H. Leshi	1953–82
R. Alia	1982–

Prime Ministers

Col.-Gen. E. Hoxha	1946–54
Col.-Gen. M. Shehu	1954–82
A. Çarçani	1982–

First Secretaries, Albanian Workers' Party

Col.-Gen. E. Hoxha	1946–48
Col.-Gen. M. Shehu	1948–53
Gen. E. Hoxha	1953–85
R. Alia	1985–

Angola

Angola became independent from Portugal as a Republic in 1975.

Presidents

A. Neto	1975–79
J. dos Santos	1979–

Prime Minister

L. Ferreira do Nascimento	1975–78 (post abolished)

Argentina

Presidents

R. Sáenz Pena	1910–14
V. de la Plaza	1914–16
H. Irigoyen	1916–22
M. Torcuato de Alvear	1922–28
H. Irigoyen	1928–30
Gen. J. Uriburi	1930–32
Gen. A. Justo	1932–38
R. Ortiz	1938–42
R. Castillo	1942–43
Gen. A. Rawson	1943 (June)
Gen. P. Ramírez	1943–44
Gen. E. Farrell	1944–46
Gen. J. Perón	1946–55
Gen. E. Leonardi	1955 (Sept.–Nov.)
Gen. P. Aramburu	1955–58
A. Frondizi	1958–62
J. Guido (acting)	1962–63
A. Illia	1963–66
Gen. J. Ongania	1966–70
Military junta	1970 (June)
Brig.-Gen. R. Levingston	1970–71
Military junta	1971 (March)
Gen. A. Lanusse	1971–73
H. Campora	1973 (May–July)
R. Lastiri (acting)	1973 (July–Oct.)
Gen. J. Perón	1973–74
M. (Isabel) Perón	1974–75
I. Luder (acting)	1975 (Sept.–Oct.)
M. (Isabel) Perón	1975–76

Military junta	1976 (March)
Gen. J. Videla	1976–81
Gen. R. Viola	1981 (Mar.–Dec.)
Gen. L. Galtieri	1981–82
Gen. R. Bignone	1982–83
R. Alfonsin Foulkes	1983–89
C. Menem	1989–

Australia

Governors-General

Lord Denman	1911–14
Sir R. Munro-Ferguson	1914–20
Lord Forster	1920–25
Lord Stonehaven	1925–31
Sir I. Isaacs	1931–36
Henry, Duke of Gloucester	1936–47
Sir W. Dugan (acting)	1947 (Jan.–Mar.)
Sir W. McKell	1947–52
W. Slim, Viscount Slim	1952–60
W. Morrison, Viscount Dunrossil	1960—61
Sir R. Brooks (acting)	1961 (Feb.–Aug.)
Sir W. Sidney, Viscount de l'Isle	1961–65
Sir H. Smith (acting)	1965 (May–Sept.)
Sir R. Casey, Baron Casey	1965–69
Sir P. Hasluck	1969–74
Sir J. Kerr	1974–77
Z. Cohen	1977–82
Sir N. Stephen	1982–89
W. Hayden	1989–

Prime Minister

A. Fisher	1914–15
W. Hughes	1915–23
S. Bruce	1923–29
J. Scullin	1929–31
J. Lyons	1931–39
R. Menzies	1939–41
A. Fadden	1941 (Aug.)
J. Curtin	1941–45
F. Forde (acting)	1945 (July)
J. Chifley	1945–49
Sir R. Menzies	1949–66
H. Holt	1966–67
Sir J. McEwen	1967–68
J. Gorton	1968–71
W. McMahon	1971–72
E. Whitlam	1972–75
J. Fraser	1975–83
R. Hawke	1983–

Austria

Emperors of Austria-Hungary

Franz Joseph	1848–1916
Karl	1916–18

Principal minister

C. von Sturgkh	1912–16

A Republic was proclaimed in November 1918.

Presidents

X. Seits	1918–20
M. Hainisch	1920–27
W. Miklas	1927–38

Austria was incorporated in the German Reich, 1938–1945.

Chancellors

K. Renner	1919 (Mar.–Oct.)
M. Mayr	1919–21
J. Schober	1921–22
I. Seipel	1922–24
R. Ramek	1924–25
I. Seipel	1925–29
E. Streeruwitz	1929 (May–Sept.)
J. Schober	1929–30
I. Seipel	1931 (June)
K. Buresch	1931–32
E. Dollfuss	1932–34
K. Schuschnigg	1934–38
A. Seyss-Inquart	1938–45

Post-1945

Presidents

K. Renner	1945–50
L. Figl (acting)	1950–51
T. Körner	1951–57
J. Raab	1957 (Jan.–May)
A. Schärf	1957–65
J. Klaus (acting)	1965 (Feb.–June)
F. Jonas	1965–74
B. Kreitsky (acting)	1974 (Apr.–July)
R. Kirchschläger	1974–86
K. Waldheim	1986–

Belgium

Kings

Albert I	1909–34
Leopold III	1934–51

There was a Regency from September 1944 to July 1950. Leopold III returned to the throne in July 1950 and abdicated in July the following year.

Prince Charles (Regent)	1944–50
Leopold III	1950–51
Baudouin I	1951–

Prime Ministers

C. de Broqueville	1911–18
G. Cooreman	1918 (June–Nov.)
L. Delacroix	1918–20
H. de Wiart	1920–21
G. Theunis	1921–25
A. Vyvere	1925 (May)
P. Poulett	1925–26
H. Jaspar	1926–31
J. Renkin	1931–32
C. de Broqueville	1932–34
G. Theunis	1934–35
P. van Zeeland	1935–37
P. Janson	1937–38
P. Spaak	1938–39
H. Pierlot	1939–45
A. Van Acker	1945–46
P.-H. Spaak	1946 (Mar.)
A. Van Acker	1946 (Mar.–July)
C. Huysmans	1946–47
P.-H. Spaak	1947–49
G. Eyskens	1949–50
J. Duvieusart	1950 (June–Aug.)
J. Pholien	1950–52
J. Van Houtte	1952–54
A. Van Acker	1954–58
G. Eyskens	1958–61
T. Lefevre	1961–65
P. Harmel	1965–66
P. Vanden Boeynants	1966–68
G. Eyskens	1968–72
E. Leburton	1973–74
L. Tindemans	1974–78
P. Vanden Boeynants	1978 (Nov.–Dec.)
W. Martens	1979–81
M. Eyskens	1981 (Apr.–Sept.)
W. Martens	1981–

Brazil

Presidents

W. Pereira Gomes	1914–18
D. da Costa Ribeiro (acting)	1918–19
E. da Silva Pessoa	1919–22
A. da Silva Bernardes	1922–26
W. Pereira de Souza	1926–30
Military junta	1930 (Oct.)
G. Dornelles Vargas	1930–45
J. Linhares	1945–46
Gen. E. Gaspar Dutra	1946–51
G. Dornelles Vargas	1951–54
J. Café Filho	1954–55
C. Coimbra da Luz (acting)	1955 (Nov.)
N. de Oliveira Ramos (acting)	1955–56
J. Kubitschek de Oliveira	1956–61
J. da Silva Quadros	1961 (Jan.–Aug.)
P. Ranieri Mazzilli	1961 (Aug.–Sept.)
J. Marques Goulart	1961–64
P. Ranieri Mazzilli (acting)	1964 (April)
Marshal H. Castelo Branco	1964–67
Marshal A. da Costa e Silva	1967–69
Gen. E. Garrastazu	1969–74
Gen. E. Geisel	1974–79
Gen. J. Baptista de Fugueiredo	1979–85
J. Sarney	1985–89
F. Collor de Mello	1989–

Cambodia

Cambodia was a French protectorate from 1863, gained autonomy in 1945 and independence in 1953.

Kingdom of Cambodia

Governors-General of the Indochinese Union

A. Sarraut	1911–14
J. Van Vollenhoven	1914–15
E. Roume	1915–16
J. Charles	1916–17
A. Sarraut	1917–19
M. Monguillot	1919–20
M. Long	1920–22
F. Baudouin	1922
M. Merlin	1922–25
M. Monguillot	1925
A. Varennes	1925–28
M. Monguillot	1928

P. Pasquier	1928–34
E. Robin	1934–36
J. Brévié	1936–39
G. Catroux	1939–40
J. Decoux	1940–45

High Commissioners of the Indochinese Federation

G. d'Argenlieu	1945–47
E. Bollaert	1947–48
L. Pignon	1948–50
J. de Lattre de Tassigny	1950–52
J. Letourneau	1952–53

Kings

(under French protection)

Sisowath	1904–27
Monivong	1927–41
Norodom Sihanouk	1941–53

The Kingdom became independent in 1953.

Norodom Sihanouk	1953–55
Norodom Suramarit	1955–60
Council of Regency	1960 (Apr.–June)

Head of State

Prince Norodom Sihanouk	1960–68

Prime Ministers

Samdech Penn Nouth	1953 (Nov.)
Chann Ak	1953–54
Samdech Penn Nouth	1954–55
Leng Ngeth	1955 (Jan.–Sept.)
Prince Norodom Sihanouk	1955–56
Oun Cheang Sun	1956 (Jan.–Mar.)
Prince Norodom Sihanouk	1956 (Mar.)
Khmi Tit	1956 (Apr.–Sept.)
Prince Norodom Sihanouk	1956 (Sept.–Oct.)
San Yun	1956–57
Prince Norodom Sihanouk	1957 (Apr.–July)
Sim Var	1957–58
Samdech Penn Nouth	1958 (Jan.–Apr.)
Sim Var	1958 (Apr.–July)
Prince Norodom Sihanouk	1958–60
Pho Proeung	1960–61
Prince Norodom Sihanouk	1961–62
Chau Sen Cocsal	1962
Prince Norodom Kantol	1962–66
Gen. Lon Nol	1966–67
Son Sann	1967–68
Samdech Penn Nouth	1968 (Jan.–Mar)

State of Cambodia

Head of State

Cheng Heng   1968–70

Prime Ministers

Samdech Penn Nouth   1968–69
Gen. Lon Nol   1969–70

The Khmer Republic

Presidents

Cheng Heng   1970–72
Gen. Lon Nol   1972–75

Democratic Cambodia

Presidents

Prince Norodom Sihanouk   1975–76
Khieu Samphan   1976–81
Heng Samrin   1979–

Prime Ministers

Samdech Penn Nouth   1975–76
Pol Pot   1976 (Apr.–Sept.)
Nuon Chea (acting)   1976–77
Pol Pot   1977–79
Khieu Samphan   1979–81
Pen Sovann   1981–82
Chan Si   1982–84
Hun Sen   1985–

Canada

Governors-General

A. Albert, Duke of Connaught   1911–16
V. Cavendish, Duke of Devonshire   1916–21
J. Byng, Baron Byng   1921–26
F. Freeman-Thomas, Marquess of   1926–31
    Willingdon
V. Ponsonby, Earl of Bessborough   1931–35
J. Buchan, Baron Tweedsmuir   1935–40
A. Cambridge, Earl of Athlone   1940–46
H. Alexander, Viscount Alexander   1946–52
    of Tunis

V. Massey	1952–59
Maj.-Gen. G. Vanier	1959–67
D. Michener	1967–74
J. Léger	1974–79
E. Schreyer	1979–84
J. Sauvé	1984–

Prime Ministers

Sir R. Borden	1911–20
A. Meighen	1920–21
W. King	1921–26
A. Meighen	1926 (June–July)
W. King	1926–30
R. Bennett	1930–35
W. King	1935–48
L. St. Laurent	1948–57
J. Diefenbaker	1957–63
L. Pearson	1963–68
P. Trudeau	1968–79
J. Clark	1979–80
P. Trudeau	1980–84
J. Turner	1984 (June–Sept.)
B. Mulroney	1984–

Chile

Presidents

J. Luis Sanfuentes	1915–20
L. Barros Borgona (acting)	1920 (June–Dec.)
A. Alessandri Palma	1920–24
Military junta	1924–25
A. Alessandri Palma	1925 (Jan.–Oct.)
L. Altamirano	1925 (Oct.–Dec.)
E. Figueros Larrain	1925–27
Gen. C. Ibáñez del Campo	1927–31
P. Opazo (acting)	1931 (July)
J. Esteban Montero (acting)	1931 (July–Aug.)
M. Trucco (acting)	1931 (Aug.–Nov.)
J. Esteban Montero	1931–32
Military junta	1932 (June–July)
C. Dávila Espinoza (acting)	1932 (July–Sept.)
Gen. B. Blanche	1932 (Sept.–Oct.)
A. Oyanedel (acting)	1932 (Oct.–Dec.)
A. Alessandri Palma	1932–38
P. Aguirre Cerda	1938–41
G. Méndez (acting)	1941–42
J. Antonio Rios	1942–46
A. Duhale (acting)	1946 (June–Aug.)
Vice-Adm. V. Merino Bielech (acting)	1946 (Aug.–Nov.)
G. González Videla	1946–52

Gen. C. Ibáñez del Campo	1952–58
J. Alessandri Rodriguez	1958–64
E. Frei Montalva	1964–70
S. Allende Gossens	1970–73
Gen. A. Pinochet Ugarte (acting)	1973–74
President	1974–89
Patricio Aylwin	1989–

China

Presidents

Yuan Shih-k'ai	1912–16
Gen. Li Yüan-hung	1916–17
Gen. Feng Kuo-chang	1917–18

There was a temporary restoration of the Emperor and a division between north and south in 1917.

Emperor

| Hsüan-tung | 1917 (July) |

Northern Regime

Presidents

Hsü Shih Ch'ang	1918–22
Li Yüan-hung	1922–23
Ts'ao K'un	1923–24
Marshal Tuan Chi-jui	1924–26

De Facto Ruler

| Chang Tso-lin | 1926–28 |

Southern Regime

Presidents

| Sun Yat-sen | 1917–25 |
| Hu Man-min | 1925–27 |

Nanking Guomindang Regime (controlling the whole of China)

Head of Government

| Chiang Kai-shek | 1927–28 |

Republic of China (united)

Presidents

| Chiang Kai-shek | 1928–31 |
| Lin Sen | 1931–43 |

Chiang Kai-shek	1943–49
Gen. Li Tsung-jen	1949 (Jan.–Dec.)

Presidents of the Executive Yuan (Prime Minister)

T'an Yen-k'ai	1928–30
Soong Tzu-wen	1930 (Sept.–Nov.)
Chiang Kai-shek	1930–31
Sun Fo	1931–32
Chong Ming-shu (acting)	1932 (Jan.)
Wang Ching-wei	1932–35
Chiang Kai-shek	1935–38
Kung Hsiang-hsi	1938–39
Chiang Kai-shek	1939–45
Soong Tzu-wen	1945–47
Chiang Kai-shek	1947 (Mar.–Apr.)
Gen. Chang Chun	1947–48
Wong Wen-hao	1948 (May–Nov.)
Sun Fo	1948–49
Gen. Ho Ying-chin	1949 (Mar.–June)
Marshal Yen Hsi-shan	1949 (June–Dec.)

A Communist regime took power at the end of a civil war in 1949.

Chairmen of the Republic

Mao Zedong	1949–58
Marshal Zhu De	1958–59
Liu Shaoqi	1959–68
Dong Biwu	1968–75

(The office was abolished in 1975.)

Chairmen of the Communist Party

Mao Zedong	1949–76
Hua Guofeng	1976–81
Hu Yaobang	1981–82

(This office was abolished in 1982 and replaced by the post of General Secretary, which Hu Yaobang took.)

Prime Ministers

Zhou Enlai	1949–76
Hua Guofeng	1976–80
Zhao Ziyang	1980–88
Li Peng	1988–

Cuba

Presidents

Gen. M García Menocal	1913–21
A. Zayas y Alfonso	1921–25
Gen. G. Machado y Morales	1925–33
Gen. A. Herrera	1933 (12 Aug.)

C. de Céspedes y Quesada   1933 (Aug.–Sept.)
    Military junta   1933 (Sept.)
Gen. R. Grau San Martin   1933–34
C. Hevia (acting)   1934 (Jan.)
C. Mendieta   1934–35
J. Barnet y Vinageras   1935–36
M. Gómez y Arias   1936 (May–Dec.)
F. Laredo Bru   1936–40
Gen. F. Batista y Zalvidar   1940–44
R. Grau San Martin   1944–48
C. Prío Socarrás   1948–52
Gen. F. Batista y Zalvidar   1952–59
C. Piedra (acting)   1959 (Jan.)
M. Urrutia Lleo (acting)   1959 (Jan.–July)
O. Dórticos Torrado   1959–76
F. Castro Ruz   1976–

Prime Ministers

J. Miro Cardona   1959 (Jan.–Feb.)
F. Castro Ruz   1959–

(Castro also held the post of First Secretary of the Communist Party
Central Committee from 1965.)

Czechoslovakia

Czechoslovakia became an independent state in November 1918.

Presidents

T. Masaryk   1918–35
E. Beneš   1935–38
E. Hácha   1938–45

Czechoslovakia became a German Protectorate in March 1939. Benesě
presided over a Czech Government-in-Exile and returned to
Czechoslovakia in 1945.

E. Beneš   1945–48
K. Gottwald   1948–53
A. Zápotocky   1953–57
A. Novotny   1957–68
Gen. L. Svoboda   1968–75
G. Husák   1975–89
V. Havel   1989–

Denmark

Monarchs

Christian X   1912–47
Frederick IX   1947–72
Margarethe II   1972–

Prime Ministers

C. Zahle	1913–20
O. Liebe	1920 (Mar.–Apr.)
M. Friis	1920 (Apr.–May)
N. Neergard	1920–24
T. Stauning	1924–42
E. Scavenius	1942–45
K. Kristensen	1945–47
H. Hedtoft	1947–50
E . Eriksen	1950–53
H. Hedtoft	1953–55
H. Hansen	1955–60
V. Kampmann	1960–62
J. Krag	1962–68
H. Baunsgard	1968–71
J. Krag	1971–72
A. Jorgensen	1972–73
P. Hartling	1973–75
A. Jorgensen	1978–82
P. Schlüter	1982–

Egypt

Egypt was under British occupation from 1882 and was a British Protectorate from 1914 to 1936.

Sultans

Hussein Kemal	1914–17
Faud	1917–22

Faud was proclaimed King in 1922.

Kings

Faud I	1922–36
Farouk	1936–52
Regency for Ahmad Faud II	1952–53

Presidents

Gen. M. Neguib	1953–54
Col. G. Nasser	1954–70
A. Sadat	1970–81
S. Talib (acting)	1981 (Oct.)
Lt.-Gen. H. Mubarrak	1981–

El Salvador

Presidents

C. Meléndez (acting)	1913–14
A. Quiñónez	1914–15

C. Meléndez	1915–19
J. Meléndez	1919–23
A. Quiñónez	1923–27
P. Romero Bosque	1927–31
A. Araújo	1931 (Feb.–Dec.)
Gen. M. Hernández Martinez	1931–34
Gen. A. Ignacio Menéndez (acting)	1934–35
Gen. M. Hernández Martinez	1935–44
Gen. A. Ignacio Menéndez	1944 (May–Oct.)
O. Aguirre Salinas	1944–45
S. Castañeda Castro	1945–48
M. Cordoba	1948–49
O. Osorio	1949–56
J. Lemus	1956–60
C. Yanes Urias	1960–61
A. Portillo	1961 (Jan.–Feb.)
M. Castillo	1961–62
E. Cordón Cea	1962 (Jan.–July)
J. Rivera Carballo	1962–67
F. Sánchez Hernández	1967–72
A. Molina Barraza	1972–77
Gen. C. Romero Mena	1977–79
Civilian/military junta under A. Majano and J. Gutiérrez	1979–80
J. Napoleon Duarte	1980–82
A. Magaña	1982–84
J. Napoleon Duarte	1984–89
A Cristiani	1989–

Ethiopia

Emperors

Lidj Iyasu	1913–16
Empress Zauditu	1916–30
Haile Selassie	1930–74
Asfa Wossen (King-designate in exile)	1974–75

Prime Ministers

Aklilou Habte Wold	1960–74
Lij Endalkatchew Makonnen	1974 (Feb.–July)
Lij Mithail Imru Haile Selassie	1974 (July–Sept.)

There was a military coup in September 1974.

Heads of Military Council

Lt.-Gen. Aman Mikhail Andom	1974 (Sept.–Nov.)
Brig.-Gen. Teferi Benti	1974–75

A republic was established in March 1975.

Heads of State

Brig.-Gen. Teferi Benti	1975–77
Lt.-Col. Mengistu Haile Mariam	1977–
(from 1979 known as President)	

Heads of Government

Brig.-Gen. Teferi Benti	1975–76
Lt.-Col. Mengistu Haile Mariam	1976–

Finland

Finland became independent from Russia in December 1917 following the Russian Revolution.

Presidents

K. Stahlberg	1919–25
L. Relander	1925–31
P. Svinufvud	1931–37
K. Kallio	1937–40
R. Ryti	1940–44
Field-Marshal K. Mannerheim	1944–46
J. Paasikivi	1946–56
U. Kekkonen	1956–81
M. Koivisto	1981–

Prime Ministers

L. Ingman	1918–19
K. Castren	1919 (Apr.–Aug.)
J. Vennola	1919–20
M. Erich	1920–21
J. Vennola	1921–22
K. Kallio	1922–24
A. Kajander	1924 (Jan.–Nov.)
L. Ingman	1924–26
K. Kalio	1926 (Jan.–Dec.)
V. Tanner	1926–28
O. Hantere	1928–29
K. Kallio	1929–31
J. Sunila	1931–32
T. Kivimaki	1932–37
A. Kajander	1937–39
R. Ryti	1939–41
J. Rangell	1941–43
E. Linkomies	1943–44
A. Hackzell	1944 (Aug.–Sept.)
U. Castren	1944 (Sept.–Nov.)
J. Paasikivi	1944–46
M. Pekkala	1946–48
K. Fagerholm	1948–50

U. Kekkonen	1950–53
S. Tuomioja	1953–54
R. Törngren	1954 (May–Oct.)
U. Kekkonen	1954–56
K. Fagerholm	1956–57
V. Sukselainen	1957 (May–Nov.)
R. von Fieandt	1957–58
R. Kuuskoski	1958 (Apr.–Aug.)
K. Fagerholm	1958–59
V. Sukslainen	1959–61
M. Miettunen	1961–62
A. Karjalainen	1962–63
R. Lehto	1963–64
J. Virolainen	1964–66
R. Paasio	1966–68
M. Koivisto	1968–70
T. Aura	1970 (May–July)
A. Karjalainen	1970–71
T. Aura	1971–72
R. Paasio	1972 (Feb.–Sept.)
K. Sorsa	1972–75
K. Liinamaa	1975 (June–Nov.)
M. Miettunen	1975–77
K. Sorsa	1977–79
M. Koivisto	1979–82
K. Sorsa	1982–

France

Third Republic

Presidents

R. Poincaré	1913–20
P. Deschanel	1920 (Jan.–Sept.)
A. Millerand	1920–24
G. Doumergue	1924–31
P. Doumer	1931–32
A. Lebrun	1932–40

Marshal P. Pétain combined presidential powers with his own office of Prime Minister, July 1940, and created the post of Chief of State.

Chiefs of State

| Admiral Darlan | 1941–42 |
| P. Laval | 1942–45 |

Prime Ministers

P. Painlevé	1914–17
G. Clemenceau	1917–20
A. Millerand	1920 (Jan.–Oct)
M. Leygues	1920–21

M. Briand	1921–22
R. Poincaré	1922–24
F. Marsal	1924 (June)
E. Herriot	1924–25
P. Painlevé	1925 (May–Nov.)
M. Briand	1925–26
R. Poincaré	1926–29
A. Briand	1929 (July–Nov.)
A. Tardieu	1929–30
M. Steeg	1930–31
P. Laval	1931–32
A. Tardieu	1932 (Feb.–June)
E. Herriot	1932 (June–Dec.)
J. Paul-Boncour	1932–33
E. Daladier	1933 (Jan.–Oct)
A. Sarraut	1933 (Oct.–Nov.)
C. Chautemps	1933–34
E. Daladier	1934 (Jan.–Feb.)
G. Doumergue	1934 (Feb.–Nov.)
P.-E. Flandin	1934–35
F. Bouisson	1935 (June)
P. Laval	1935–36
A. Sarraut	1936 (Jan.–June)
L. Blum	1936–37
C. Chautemps	1937–38
L. Blum	1938 (Mar.–Apr.)
E. Daladier	1938–40
P. Reynaud	1940 (Mar.–June)
Marshal P. Pétain	1940–42

General C. de Gaulle led a National Unity government as head of state, 1945–1946. The Fourth Republic was constituted in December 1946.

Fourth Republic

Presidents

V. Auriol	1947–54
R. Coty	1954–59

Prime Ministers

F. Gouin	1946 (Jan.–June)
G. Bidault	1946 (June–Dec.)
L. Blum	1946–47
P. Ramadier	1947 (Jan.–Nov.)
R. Schuman	1947–48
A. Marie	1948 (July–Sept.)
H. Queuille	1948–49
G. Bidault	1949–50
H. Queuille	1950 (July)
R. Pleven	1950–51
H. Queuille	1951 (Mar.–Aug.)

R. Pleven	1951–52
E. Fauré	1952 (Jan.–Mar.)
A. Pinay	1952–53
R. Mayer	1953 (Jan.–June)
J. Laniel	1953–54
P. Mendès-France	1954–55
E. Fauré	1955–56
G. Mollet	1956–57
F. Gaillard	1957–59

The Fifth Republic was constituted in October 1958.

Fifth Republic

Presidents

Gen. C. de Gaulle	1959–69
A. Poher (interim)	1969 (Apr.–June)
G. Pompidou	1969–74
A. Poher (interim)	1974 (Apr.–May)
V. Giscard d'Estaing	1974–81
F. Mitterrand	1981–

Prime Ministers

M. Debré	1959–62
G. Pompidou	1962–68
M. Couve de Murville	1968–69
J. Chaban-Delmas	1969–72
P. Messmer	1972–74
J. Chirac	1974–76
R. Barre	1976–81
P. Mauroy	1981–84
L. Fabius	1984–86
J. Chirac	1986–88
M. Rocard	1988–

Germany

German Empire

Emperor

| Wilhelm II | 1888–1918 |

Chancellor

T. Bethmann-Hollweg	1909–17
G. Michaelis	1917
G. von Herling	1917–18
Prince Max of Baden	1918
F. Ebert	1918

Wilhelm II abdicated on 9 November 1918 and a Republic was proclaimed.

German Republic

Presidents

F. Ebert	1919–25
P. von Hindenburg	1925–34

Reich Chancellor

P. Scheidemann	1919 (Feb.–June)
G. Bauer	1919–20
H. Müller	1920 (Mar.–June)
C. Fehrenbach	1920–21
J . Wirth	1921–22
W. Cuno	1922–23
G. Stresemann	1923 (Aug.–Nov.)
W. Marx	1923–24
H. Luther	1925–26
W. Marx	1926–28
H. Müller	1928–30
H. Brüning	1930–32
F. von Papen	1932 (May–Nov.)
K. von Schleicher	1932–33

A. Hitler was appointed Chancellor in January 1933. Following the death of President Hindenburg in 1934 he took the title Chancellor and Führer.

Chancellor and Führer

A. Hitler	1934–45
Admiral C. Dönitz	1945 (Apr.–June)

Germany was occupied and divided by the Allies in 1945. The Western Zone became the Federal Republic of Germany in September 1949. The Eastern Zone became the German Democratic Republic the following month.

Federal Republic of Germany

Presidents

T. Heuss	1949–59
H. Lübke	1959–69
G. Heinemann	1969–74
W. Scheel	1974–79
K. Carstens	1979–84
R. von Weizsäcker	1984–

Federal Chancellor

K. Adendauer	1949–63
L. Erhard	1963–66
K. Kiesinger	1966–69
W. Brandt	1969–74
W. Scheel (acting)	1974 (May)
H. Schmidt	1974–82
H. Kohl	1982–

German Democratic Republic

President

W. Pieck	1949–60

The office of President was abolished in 1960. Its powers were transferred to that of the Chairman of the Council of State.

Chairman of the Council of State

W. Ulbricht	1960–73
W. Stoph	1973–76
E. Honecker	1976–89*
M. Gerlach (acting)	1989–

*Replaced briefly as Communist party leader by Egon Krenz. The reformist Hans Modrow became Prime Minister on 8 November. On 12 April 1990 he was succeeded by Lothar de Maizère.

Ghana

Until independence in 1957 Ghana was the British colony of the Gold Coast.

Governors

H. Clifford	1912–19
F. Guggisberg	1919–27
A. Slater	1927–32
T. Thomas	1932–34
A. Hodson	1934–41
A. Burns	1941–48
G. Creasy	1948–49
C. Arden-Clarke	1949–57

Governors-General

C. Arden-Clarke	1957 (May–Nov.)
Lord Listowel (W. Hare)	1957–60

Ghana became a Republic in 1960.

President

K. Nkrumah	1960–66
Eight man National Liberation Council under J. Ankrah	1966–69
Gen. A. Afrifa	1969 (Apr.–Aug.)
Three man Presidential Commission: A. Afrifa, J. Harley, A. Kwesi-Ocran	1969–70
E. Akufo-Addo	1970–1972
Col. I. Acheampong (Chairman, National Redemption Council, 1972–1975; Chairman, Supreme Military Council, 1975-1978)	1972–78

Lt.-Gen. F. Akuffo (Chairman, SMC)	1978–79
Flt.-Lt. J. Rawlings (Head, Armed Forces Revolutionary Council)	1979 (June–Sept.)
H. Limann	1979–81
Flt.-Lt. J. Rawlings	1981–

Prime Minister

| K. Nkrumah | 1957–66 |

The post was abolished from 1966 to 1969.

| K. Busia | 1969–72 |

The post was abolished in 1972.

Greece

Kings

Constantine I	1913–17
Alexander	1917–20
Constantine I	1920–22
George II	1922–23

Prime Ministers

T. Rangalos	1925–26
A. Zaimis	1926–28
E. Venizélos	1928–32
M. Papanastasiou	1932 (May–June)
E. Venizélos	1932 (June–Nov.)
P. Tasaldaris	1932–33
E. Venizélos	1933 (Jan.–Mar.)
Gen. N. Plastiras	1933 (Mar.)
Gen. A. Othonaios (interim)	1933–34
P. Tsaldarus	1934–35
Gen. G. Kondilis	1935 (Oct.–Nov.)
C. Demerdjis	1935–37

The monarchy was restored in 1935.

Kings

George II	1935–44
Regency	1944–46
George II	1946–47
Paul I	1947–64
Constantine II	1964–74

The monarchy was abolished in the 1974 referendum.

Prime Minister

| Gen. J. Metaxas (exercised power as dictator) | 1937–41 |

Greece was occupied by the Axis 1941–44.

Prime Minister of Government-in-Exile

E. Tsouderos	1941–44

Prime Ministers

S. Venizelis	1944 (Apr.)
G. Papandreou	1944–45
Gen. N. Plastiras	1945 (Jan.–Apr.)
Adm. P. Voulgaris	1945 (Apr.–Oct.)
Archbishop Damaskinos	1945 (Oct.–Nov.)
P. Kanellopoulos	1945 (Nov.)
T. Sofoulis	1945–46
P. Poulitsas	1946 (Apr.)
C. Tsaldaris	1946–47
D. Maximos	1947 (Jan.–Aug.)
C. Tsaldaris	1947 (Aug.–Sept.)
T. Sofoulis	1947–49
A. Diomedes	1949–50
J. Theotokis	1950 (Jan.–Mar.)
S. Venizelis	1950 (Mar.–Apr.)
Gen. N. Plastiras	1950 (Apr.–Sept.)
S. Venizelis	1950–51
Gen. N. Plastiras	1951–52
A. Papagos	1952–55
C. Karamanlis	1955–58
M. Georgakoloulos	1958 (Mar.–May)
C. Karamanlis	1958–63
G. Papandreou	1963 (Nov.–Dec.)
J. Paraskevopoulos	1963–64
G. Papandreou	1964–65
G. Athanasiadis-Novas	1965 (July–Aug.)
S. Stephanopoulos	1965–66
I. Paraskevopoulos	1966–67
P. Kanellopoulos	1967 (Apr.)

There was a military coup in April 1967.

Prime Ministers

C. Kollias	1967 (Apr.–Dec.)
Col. G. Papadopoulos	1967–73
S. Markeznis	1973 (Oct.–Nov.)
A. Androutsopoulos	1973–1974

Gen. G. Zoitakis was Regent from 1967–1972. Col. G. Papadopoulos became Regent in 1972. Restoration of the monarchy was rejected by plebiscite in 1974.

Presidents

G. Papadopoulos (provisional)	1973 (June–Nov.)
Gen. P. Ghizikis	1973–74
M. Stassinopoulos (interim)	1974–75
K. Tsatsos	1975–80
C. Sartzetakis	1985–90
K. Karamanlis	1990–

Prime Ministers

K. Karamanlis	1974–80
G. Rallis	1980–81
A. Papandreou	1981–89
T. Tzannetakis	1989 (July–Nov.)
X. Zolotas	1989–90
C. Mitsotakis	1990–1

Hungary

An independent Republic, November 1918.

Presidents

Count M. Karólyi (provisional)	1918–19

From March to August 1919 Hungary was a Soviet Republic under B. Kun.

K. Huskár	1919–20

Hungary was proclaimed a monarchy in 1920 but was without a monarch. Power was in the hands of a regent.

Regent

Adm. M. von Horthy	1920–45

Prime Ministers

A. Simonyi-Semadam	1920–21
Count I. Bethlen	1921–29
Count J. Károlyi	1929–31
G. Károlyi	1931–32
Capt. G. Gömbös	1932–36
K. Darányi	1936–38
B. Imrédy	1938–39
Count P. Teleki	1939–41
L. Bárdossy	1941–42
I. Kállay	1942–44
Gen. D. Sztöjay	1944 (Mar.–Aug.)
Gen. G. Lakatos	1944 (Aug.–Oct.)
F. Szálasi	1944 (Oct.–Dec.)
Gen. B. Miklos	1944–45

Hungary became a Republic in 1945.

Presidents[1]

Z. Tildy	1946–48
A. Szakasits	1948–50
S. Ronái	1950–52

[1] After the end of Communist rule in May 1990 Dr Arpad Gonez became interim President, then President in his own right.

Chairman of the Praesidium

I. Dobi   1952–67

Chairmen of the Presiding Council

P. Losonczi   1967–88
B. Straub   1988–

Prime Ministers

Z. Tildy   1945–46
F. Nagy   1946–47
L. Dinnyés   1947–48
I. Dobi   1948–52
M. Rákosi   1952–53
I. Nagy   1953–55
A. Hegedüs   1955–56
I. Nagy   1956 (Oct.–Nov.)
J. Kádár   1956–58
F. Münnich   1958–61
J. Kádár   1961–65
G. Kállai   1965–67
J. Fock   1967–75
G. Lázár   1975–87
K. Grósz   1987–89
M. Németh   1989–

India

Viceroys

C. Hardinge, Baron Hardinge   1910–16
F. Thesiger, Baron Chelmsford   1916–21
R. Isaacs, Marquess of Reading   1921–26
E. Wood-Halifax, Baron Irwin   1926–31
F. Freeman-Thomas, Marquess of   1931–36
  Willingdon
V. Hope, Marquess of Linlithgow   1936–43
A. Wavell, Viscount Wavell   1943–47
L. Mountbatten, Earl Mountbatten   1947

Governors-General

L. Mountbatten, Earl Mountbatten   1947–48
C. Rajagopalachari   1948–49

Presidents

R. Prasad   1949–62
S. Radhakrishnan   1962–67
Z. Hussain   1967–69
V. Giri (acting)   1969 (May–Aug.)
V. Giri   1969–74

F. Ahmed	1974–77
B. Jatti	1977 (Feb.–July)
N. Reddy	1977–82
G. Singh	1982–87
R. Venkataraman	1987–

Prime Ministers

J. Nehru	1949–64
G. Nanda (acting)	1964 (May–June)
L. Shastri	1964–66
G. Nanda (acting)	1966 (Jan.)
Mrs I. Gandhi	1966–77
M. Desai	1977–79
C. Singh	1979–80
Mrs I. Gandhi	1980–84
R. Gandhi	1984–89
V.P. Singh	1989–

Indonesia

Indonesia became officially independent from the Netherlands in December 1949.

Governors-General

A. Idenburg	1909–16
J. von Limburg Stirum	1916–21
D. Fock	1921–26
A. de Graaef	1926–31
B. de Jonge	1931–36
A. van Starkenborgh Stachouwer	1936–45

Lieutenant Governor-General

H. van Mook	1942–48

Commissioners-General

W. Schermerhorn	1946–48
M. van Poll	1946–48
F. de Boer	1946–48

Presidents

M. Sukarno	1945–67
Gen. R. Suharto	1967–

Prime Ministers

M. Sukarno	1945
S. Sjahrir	1945–47
A. Sjarifuddin	1947–48

M. Hatta	1948 (Jan.–Dec.)
S. Prawiranegara	1948–49
M. Hatta	1949–50
M. Natsir	1950–51
Dr. Sartono	1951 (Mar.–Apr.)
S. Wirjosandjojo	1951–52
Dr. Wilopo	1952–53
A. Sastroamidjojo	1953–54
M. Hatta (acting)	1954 (July–Aug.)
B. Harahap	1954–56
A. Sastroamidjojo	1956–57
Dr. Suwirjo (acting)	1957 (Mar.–Apr.)
D. Kartawidjaja	1957–63
M. Sukarno	1963–66
Gen. R. Suharto	1966–67

The office was abolished in 1967.

Iran

Shahs

Ahmed Mirza Shah	1909–25
Reza Shah Pahlevi	1925–41
Mohammad Reza Shah Pahlevi	1941–79

Prime Ministers

A. Furanghi	1941–42
A. Solheily	1942 (Mar.–Aug.)
Q. es-Sultaneh	1942–43
A. Solheily	1943–44
M. Saed	1944 (Mar.–Nov.)
N. Bayatt	1944–45
I. Hakimi	1945 (May–June)
M. Sadr	1945 (June–Oct.)
I. Hakimi	1945–46
Q. es-Sultaneh	1946–47
S. Hekmat	1947 (Dec.)
I. Hakimi	1947–48
A. Hajir	1948 (June–Nov.)
M. Saed	1948–50
A. Mansur	1950 (Mar.–June)
Gen. A. Razmara	1950–51
H. Ala	1951 (Mar.–Apr.)
M. Mussadeq	1951–52
Q. es-Sultaneh	1952 (July)
M. Mussadeq	1952–53
Gen. F. Zaheda	1953–55
H. Ala	1955–57
M. Eghbal	1957–60
J. Emami	1960–61

A. Amini	1961–62
A. Alam	1962–64
H. Mansur	1964–65
A. Hoveida	1965–67
J. Amouzegar	1977–79

The Shah fled from Iran in January 1979. Ayatollah Ruhollah Khomeini became head of a provisional government in February. As supreme religious leader he was acknowledged as the Islamic Republic of Iran's highest authority until his death in 1989.

Presidents

A. Bani-Sadr	1980–81
M. Raja'i	1981 (July–Aug.)
H. Khamenei	1981–89
H. Rafsanjani	1989–

Iraq

Iraq was part of the Ottoman Empire until occupied by Britain in 1916. It was held by Britain as a League of Nations' mandate until the granting of independence in 1932.

Kings

Faisal I	1921–33
Ghazi	1933–39
Faisal II	1939–58

Prime Ministers

Gen. N. Pasha es-Said	1932–33
S. Ali el Gailani	1933 (Mar.–Nov.)
J. Midfai	1933–34
A. Jaudat Bey	1934–35
J. Midfai	1935 (Mar.)
Gen. Y. Pasah el Hashimi	1935–36
S. Hikmat Sulaiman	1936–37
J. Midfai	1937–38
Gen. N. Pasha es-Said	1938–40
S. Ali el Gailani	1940–41
J. Midfai	1941 (May–Oct.)
Gen. N. Pasha es-Said	1941–44
H. el-Pachichi	1944–46
T. Suwaidi	1946 (Feb.–June)
A. el-Umari	1946 (June–Nov.)
Gen. N. Pasha es-Said	1946–47
S. Jabr	1947–48
M. el-Sadr	1948 (Jan.–June)
M. el-Pachichi	1948–49
Gen. N. Pasha es-Said	1949 (Jan.–Dec.)

S. Jawdat Ayubi	1949–50
T. el-Suweidi	1950 (Feb.–Sept.)
Gen. N. Pasha es-Said	1950–52
S. Mustafa el-Umari	1952 (July–Nov.)
Gen. N. Mohammed	1952–53
J. Midfai	1953 (Jan.–Sept.)
M. Fadil Jamali	1953–54
Gen. N. Pasha es-Said	1954–57
S. Jawdat Ayubi	1957 (June–Dec)
A. Wahab Mirjan	1957–58
Gen. N. Pasha es-Said	1958 (Mar.–May)
A. Mukhtar Baban	1958 (May–July)

The monarchy was overthrown and a republic formed in July 1958.

Presidents

Gen. M. Najib Rubai	1958–63
Col. A. Mohammed Aref	1963–66
Maj.–Gen. A. Rahman Aref	1966–68
Maj.–Gen. A. Hassan Bakr	1968–79
S. Hussain al-Takriti	1979–

Ireland

From 1922 Ireland was a self-governing British Dominion. It became an independent sovereign state in 1937.

Presidents

D. Hyde	1938–45
S. O'Kelly	1945–59
E. de Valéra	1959–73
E. Childers	1973–74
C. Dalaigh	1974–76
P. Hillery	1976–

Prime Ministers

M. Collins	1922
W. Cosgrave	1922–32
E. de Valéra	1932–48
J. Costello	1948–51
E. de Valéra	1951–54
J. Costello	1954–57
E. de Valéra	1957–59
S. Lemass	1959–66
J. Lynch	1966–73
L. Cosgrave	1973–77
J. Lynch	1977–79
C. Haughey	1979–81

G. FitzGerald	1981–82
C. Haughey	1982 (Mar.–Dec.)
G. FitzGerald	1982–87
C. Haughey	1987–

Israel

Presidents

C. Weizmann (acting)	1948–49
C. Weizmann	1949–52
J. Springzak (acting)	1952 (Nov.–Dec.)
I. Ben-Zvi	1952–63
K. Luz	1963 (Apr.–May)
Z. Shazar	1963–68
E. Katzir	1968–78
Y. Navom	1978–83
C. Herzog	1983–

Prime Ministers

D. Ben-Gurion	1948–53
M. Sharett	1953–55
D. Ben-Gurion	1955–63
L. Eshkol	1963–69
Mrs G. Meir	1969–74
Gen. Y. Rabin	1974–77
M. Begin	1977–83
Y. Shamir	1984–84
S. Peres	1984–86
Y. Shamir	1986–

Italy

Kings

Victor Emmanuel III	1900–46
(Emperor of Ethiopia 1936;	
King of Albania 1939)	
Umberto	1946 (May–June)

Prime Ministers

A. Salandra	1914–16
P. Boselli	1916–17
V. Orlando	1917–19
F. Nitti	1919–20
G. Giolitti	1920–21
I. Bonomi	1921–22

L. Facta	1922 (Feb.–Oct.)
B. Mussolini	1922–43
Marshal P. Badoglio	1943–44

Italy became a Republic by referendum in June 1946.

Presidents

A. de Gasperi (acting)	1946 (June)
E. de Nicola	1946–48
L. Einaudi	1948–55
G. Gronchi	1955–62
A. Segni	1962–64
G. Saragat	1964–71
G. Leone	1971–78
A. Fanfani (acting)	1978 (June–July)
A. Pertini	1978–85
F. Cossiga	1985–

Prime Ministers

F. Parri	1945 (June–Nov.)
A. de Gasperi	1945–53
G. Pella	1953–54
A. Fanfani	1954 (Jan.–Feb.)
M. Scelba	1954–55
A. Segni	1955–57
A. Zoli	1957–58
A. Fanfani	1958–59
A. Segni	1959–60
F. Tambroni	1960 (Mar.–July)
A. Fanfani	1960–63
G. Leone	1963 (June–Dec.)
A. Moro	1963–68
G. Leone	1968 (June–Dec.)
M. Rumor	1968–70
E. Colombo	1970–72
G. Andreotti	1972–73
M. Rumor	1973–74
A. Moro	1974–76
G. Andreotti	1976–79
F. Cossiga	1979–80
A. Forlani	1980–81
G. Spadolini	1981–82
A. Fanfani	1982–83
B. Craxi	1983–87
G. Andreotti	1987 (Feb.–June)
G. Goria	1987–88
C. De Mita	1988–89
G. Andreotti	1989–

Japan

Emperors

Yoshihito	1912–26
Hirohito	1926–89
Akihito	1989–

Prime Ministers

T. Hara	1918–21
Y. Uchida	1921 (Nov.)
K. Takahashi	1921–22
T. S. Kato	1922–23
Adm. G. Yamamoto	1923–24
K. Kyoura	1924 (Jan.–June)
T. Kato	1924–25
R. Wakatsuki	1925–27
G. Tanaka	1927–29
O. Hamaguchi	1929–31
R. Wakatsuki	1931 (Apr.–Dec.)
T. Inukai	1931–32
Adm. M. Saito	1932–34
Adm. K. Okado	1934–36
F. Goto	1936 (Feb.)
Adm. K. Okado	1936 (Feb.–Mar.)
K. Hirota	1936–37
Gen. S. Hayashi	1937 (Feb.–June)
Prince F. Konoye	1937–39
K. Hiranuma	1939 (Jan.–Aug.)
Gen. N. Abe	1939–40
Adm. M. Yonai	1940 (Jan.–July)
Prince F. Konoye	1940–41
Lt.–Gen. H. Tojo	1941–44
Gen. K. Koiso	1944–45
Adm. K. Suzuki	1945 (Apr.–Aug.)
N. Higashikuni	1945 (Aug.–Oct.)
K. Shidehara	1945–46
S. Yoshida	1946–47
T. Katayama	1947–48
H. Ashida	1948 (Feb.–Oct.)
S. Yoshida	1948–54
I. Hatoyama	1954–56
T. Ishibashi	1956–57
N. Kishi	1957–60
H. Ikeda	1960–64
E. Sato	1964–72
K. Tanaka	1972–74
T. Miki	1974–76

T. Fukuda	1976–78
M. Ohira	1978–80
M. Ito (acting)	1980 (June–July)
Z. Suzki	1980–82
Y. Nakasone	1982–87
N. Takeshita	1987–89
S. Uno	1989 (June–Aug.)
T. Kaifu	1989–

Jordan

Part of the Ottoman Empire until taken by Britain in World War I.
Britain occupied Transjordan from 1918 until it became a protectorate
under Emir Adbullah ibn Hussein in 1923. The area gained
independence in 1946 and became known as Jordan in 1949.

Residents (Transjordan)

H. Philby	1921–24
C. Cox	1924–39
A. Kirkbride	1939–46

Kings

Abdullah ibn Hussein	1946–51
Talal ibn Abdullah	1951–52
Hussein ibn Talal	1952–

Prime Ministers

Sayed Pasha el-Mufti	1950 (Apr.–Dec.)
Samir Pasha Rifai	1950–51
Tewfik Pasha Abulhuda	1951–53
Fawzi el-Mulki	1953–54
Tewfik Abulhuda	1954–55
Sayed el-Mufti	1955 (May–Dec.)
Hazza el-Majali	1955 (Dec.)
Ibrahim Hashim	1955–56
Samir Rifai	1956 (Jan.–May)
Sayed el-Mufti	1956 (May–July)
Ibrahim Hashim	1956 (July–Oct.)
Suliman Nabulsi	1956–57
Hussein Khalidi	1957 (Apr.)
Ibrahim Hashim	1957 (Apr.–May)
Samir Rifai	1957–59
Hazza el-Majali	1959–60
Bahjat Talhouni	1960–62
Wasif al-Tell	1962–63
Samir Rifai	1963 (Mar.–Apr.)
Hussein bin Nasser	1963–64
Bahjat Talhouni	1964–65
Wasif al-Tell	1965–67

Hussein bin Nasser	1967 (Mar.–Apr.)
Saad Jumaa	1967 (Apr.–Oct.)
Bahjat Talhouni	1967–69
Abdul Moneim Rifai	1969 (Mar.–Aug.)
Bahjat Talhouni	1969–70
Abdul Moneim Rifai	1970 (June–Sept.)
Brig. Mohammed Daoud	1970 (Sept.)
Ahmed Toukan	1970 (Sept.–Oct.)
Wasif al-Tell	1970–71
Ahmed Louzi	1971–73
Zaid Rifai	1973–76
Mudar Badran	1976–79
Ahmed Obaidat	1979–80
Mudar Badran	1980–84
Zaid Rifai	1985–89
Mudar Badran	1989–

Korea

The Empire of Ta'ehan, as Korea was known, was under Japanese occupation from 1910 to 1945. In May 1945 the country was divided into Soviet and American zones.

Republic of Korea (South Korea)

Presidents

Syngman Rhee	1948–60
Huh Chung (acting)	1960 (Apr.–Aug.)
Yoon Bo Sun	1960–62
Gen. Park Chung Hi	1962–79
Choi Kyu-hah	1979–80
Gen. Chun Doo Hwan	1980–88
Roh Tae–Woo	1988–

Prime Ministers

Gen. Lee Bum Suk	1948–50
John Myun Chang	1950–52
Chang Paik Song	1952 (Apr.–Oct.)
Paik Too Chin	1952–54
Pyun Yung Tai	1954 (June–Oct.)

The office was abolished between 1954 and 1960.

Huh Chung	1960 (Apr.–Aug.)
John Myun Chang	1960–61
Supreme Council for National Reconstruction following coup	1961 (May)
Lt.–Gen. Chang Do Yung	1961 (May–July)
Maj.–Gen. Song Yo Chan	1961–62
Gen. Park Chung Hi	1962 (June–July)

Kim Hyun Chul	1962–63
Choi Doo Sun	1963–64
Gen. Chung Il Kwon	1964–70
Paik Too Chin	1970–71
Kim Chong Pil	1971–75
Choi Kyu Hah	1975–88
Kang Young-hoon	1988–

Korean People's Democratic Republic (North Korea)

Presidents

Kim Du Bon	1948–57
Choi Yong Kun	1957–72
Marshal Kim Il-sung	1972–

General Secretary, Korean Workers' Party

| Marshal Kim Il-sung | 1948– |

Lebanon

Originally part of the Ottoman Empire, Lebanon was a French
mandate from 1920 and became independent in January 1944.

Presidents

Bishara al-Khuri	1944–52
Camille Chamoun	1952–58
Gen. Fouad Chehab	1958–64
Charles Hélou	1964–70
Suleiman Franjieh	1970–76
Elias Sarkis	1976–82
Bachir Gemayel	1982 (Aug–Sept)
Amin Gemayel	1982–88
(Resigned in 1988 with no successor appointed until 1989)	
R. Moawad	1989 (5–22Nov)
E. Hrawi	1989–

Prime Ministers

Riad Sohl	1944 (Jan.–Dec.)
Abdul Hamed Karami	1945 (Jan.–Aug.)
Sami Sohl	1945–46
Saadi Mounla	1946 (May–Dec.)
Riad Sohl	1946–51
Hussein Oueni	1951 (Feb.–June)
Abdullah Aref al-Yafi	1951–52
Sami Sohl	1952 (Feb.–Sept.)
Nazim Akkari	1952 (Sept.)

Gen. Fouad Chehab	1952 (Sept.–Oct.)
Khelab Chebab	1952–53
Saeb Salam	1953 (Apr.–Aug.)
Abdullah Aref al-Yafi	1953–54
Sami Sohl	1954–55
Rashid Abdul Hamid Karami	1955–56
Abdullah Aref al-Yafi	1956 (Mar.–Nov.)
Sami Sohl	1956–58
Rashid Abdul Hamid Karami	1958–60
Ahmed Daouk	1960 (May–Oct.)
Saeb Salam	1960–61
Rashid Abdul Hamid Karami	1961–64
Hussein Oueni	1964–65
Rashid Abdul Hamid Karami	1965–66
Abdullah Aref al-Yafi	1966 (Apr.–Dec.)
Rashid Abdul Hamid Karami	1966–68
Abdullah Aref al-Yafi	1968-69
Rashid Abdul Hamid Karami	1969–70
Saeb Salam	1970–73
Amin Hafez	1973 (Apr.–June)
Takieddine Sohl	1973–74
Rashid Sohl	1974–75
Brig. Noureddin Rifai	1975 (May)
Rashid Abdul Hamid Karami	1975–76
Selim al-Hoss	1976–80
R. Karami	1980–87
N. Berri	1987–88

From 1988 there were two rival Prime Ministers: the Syrian-backed S. al-Hoss and the Maronite Christian militia commander Gen. M. Aoun. In November 1989, Selim al-Hoss was again named Prime Minister.

Libya

Libya was controlled by Italy from 1912, became a United Nations mandate in 1945 and an independent Kingdom in 1951. Libya became a Republic in 1969 and has been known as the Libyan Arab Republic (1969–1976), the Libyan Arab People's Republic (1976–1977), and the Socialist People's Libyan Arab Jamahiriya (State of the Masses) from 1977.

Kingdom of Libya

King

Idris I	1951–69

Prime Ministers

Mahmud Muntasser	1951–54
Mohammed Saqizly	1954 (Feb.–Apr.)

Mustafa Halim	1954–57
Abdul Majid Coobar	1957–60
Mohammed bin-Othman al Said	1960–63
Mohieddine Fekini	1963–64
Mahmud Muntasser	1964–65
Husain Maziq	1965–67
Abdel Kader al Badri	1967 (July–Oct.)
Abdel Hamid Bakkouche	1967–68
Wanis al Geddafi	1968–69

The monarchy was overthrown in September 1969.

President

| Col. Mu'ammar Muhammad Qadhafi | 1969– |

Prime Ministers (until 1977, when post abolished)

Mahmoud Sulaiman al Maghrabi	1969–70
Col. Mu'ammar Muhammad al-Qadhafi	1970–72
Maj. Abdul Salam Ahmed Jallud	1972–77
Abdullah Obeidi	1977

Secretary of the General People's Committee

Jadallah at-Talhi	1979–84
Muhammad az-Zarrouk Ragab	1984–86
Jadallah Azouz at-Talhi	1986–89
Omar al-Muntasir	1989–

Malawi

The country was known as Nyasaland from 1907 and was under British control. It was federated with Rhodesia between 1953 and 1963 and became independent in 1964.

Governors

G. Smith	1913–23
C. Bowring	1923–29
T. Thomas	1929–32
H. Young	1932–34
H. Kittermaster	1934–39
H. Mackenzie-Kennedy	1939–42
E. Richards	1942–47
G. Colby	1948–56
R. Armitage	1956–61
G. Jones	1961–64

Federation of Rhodesia and Nyasaland (1953–1963)

Prime Minister

| Sir G. Higgins | 1953–56 |
| Sir R. Welensky | 1956–63 |

Governor-General

Sir G. Jones   1964–66

Prime Minister

H. Banda   1964–66

Malawi became a Republic in 1966.

President

H. Banda   1966–

Malaysia

Malaya became independent from Britain in 1957. It federated with
Sabah, Sarawak and Singapore to form Malaysia in 1963. Singapore
seceded in 1965.

Malaya

Heads of State

Abdul Rahman   1957–60
Hisamuddin Alam Shah   1960 (Apr.–Sept.)
Syed Putra   1960–63

Prime Ministers

Abdul Rahman   1957–59
Abdul Razak   1959 (Apr.–Aug.)
Abdul Rahman   1959–63

Malaysia

Heads of State

Syed Putra   1963–65
Ismail Nasiruddin Shah   1965–70
Abdul Halim Mu'azzam Shah   1970–75
Yahya Putra   1975–80
Mahmood Iskandar ibni Sultan Ismail   1980–85
Mahmood Iskandar ibni Al-Marhum   1985–

Prime Ministers

Abdul Rahman   1963–70
Abdul Razak   1970–76
Hussein bin Onn   1976–84
Mahathir Mohamad   1984–

Mexico

Presidents

V. Huerta	1913–17
V. Carranza	1917–20
Gen. A. Obrégon	1920–24
P. Calles	1924–28

Gen. Obrégon was elected in 1928 but was assassinated before taking office. Calles acted as head of a government formed under a National Revolutionary Party from 1928–1934.

Gen. L. Cárdenas	1934–40
Gen. M. Ávila Camacho	1940–46
M. Aleman Valdés	1946–52
A. Ruiz Cortines	1952–58
A. Lopez Mateos	1958–64
G. Díaz Ordaz	1964–70
L. Echeverría Alvarez	1970–76
J. Portillo y Pacheco	1976–82
M. de la Madrid Hurtado	1982–88
C. de Gortari	1988–

Mozambique

Mozambique achieved independence from Portugal in 1975.

Presidents

S. Machel	1975–1986
J. Chissano	1986–

Netherlands

Queens

Wilhelmina	1890–1948
Juliana	1948–80
Beatrix	1980–

Prime Ministers

P. van der Linden	1913–18
R. de Beerenbrouck	1918–25
H. Colijn	1925–26
D. de Geer	1926–29
R. de Beerenbrouck	1929–33
H. Colijn	1933–39
D. de Geer	1939–40
P. Gerbrandy	1941–45
W. Schermerhorn	1945–46
L. Beel	1946–48
W. Drees	1948–58

L. Beel	1958–59
J. de Quay	1959–63
V. Marijnen	1963–65
J. Cals	1965–66
J. Zijlstra	1966–67
P. de Jong	1967–71
B. Biesheuvel	1971–73
J. den Uyl	1973–77
A. van Agt	1977–82
R. Lubbers	1982–

New Zealand

Governor

A. Foljambe, Earl of Liverpool	1912–17

Governors-General

A. Foljambe, Earl of Liverpool	1917–20
Sir R. Stout (acting)	1920 (Aug.–Sept.)
J. Jellicoe, Earl Jellicoe	1920–24
Sir. R. Stout (acting)	1924 (Dec.)
Sir. C. Fergusson	1924–29
Sir M. Myers	1929–30
Sir C. Bathurst, Viscount Bledisloe	1930–35
G. Monckton-Arundell, Viscount Galway	1935–41
Sir C. Newall, Baron Newall	1941–46
Sir B. Freyberg, Baron Freyberg	1946–52
Sir C. Norrie, Baron Norrie	1952–57
Sir C. Lyttelton, Viscount Cobham	1957–62
Sir B. Fergusson	1962–67
Sir A. Porritt	1967–72
Sir E. Blundell	1972–77
Sir K. Holyoake	1977–80
Sir D. Beattie	1980–85
Sir P. Reeves	1985–

Prime Minister

T. Mackenzie	1912–15
W. Massey	1915–25
Sir F. Bell	1925 (May)
J. Coates	1925–28
Sir J. Ward	1928–30
G. Forbes	1930–35
M. Savage	1935–40
P. Fraser	1940–49
Sir S. Holland	1949–57
K. Holyoake	1957 (Sept.–Dec.)
Sir W. Nash	1957–60
K. Holyoake	1960–72
Sir J. Marshall	1972 (Feb.–Dec.)

N. Kirk	1972–74
H. Watt (acting)	1974 (Aug.–Sept.)
W. Rowling	1974–75
R. Muldoon	1975–84
D. Lange	1984–89
G. Palmer	1989–90

Nicaragua

Presidents

A. Diaz	1911–16
E. Chamorro Vargas	1917–20
D. Manuel Chamorro	1920–23
B. Martinez (acting)	1923–24
C. Solorzano	1924–26
E. Chamorro Vargas	1926 (Jan.–Nov.)
A. Diaz	1926–29
Gen. J. Moncada	1929–32
J. Bautista Sacasa	1932–36
C. Brenes Jarquin (acting)	1936–37
Gen. A. Somoza García	1937–47
L. Argüello	1947 (May)
B. Lescayo-Sacasa	1947 (May–Aug.)
V. Roman y Reyes	1947–50
A. Somoza García	1950–56
L. Somoza Debayle	1956–63
R. Shick Gutiérrez	1963–66
L. Guerrero Gutiérrez	1966–67
Gen. A. Somoza Debayle	1967–72
Three-member military junta (Gen. R. Martinez Laclayo, Gen. A. Lobo Cordero, E. Papua Irias)	1972–74
Gen. A. Somoza Debayle	1974–79
Five-member junta	1979–81
Three-member junta with D. Ortega Saavedra as co-ordinator	1981–85
D. Ortega Saavedra	1985–90
Mrs Violeta Barrios de Chamorra	1990–

Nigeria

Nigeria became independent from Britain in 1960 and a republic in 1963.

Governors

F. Lugard	1914–19
H. Clifford	1919–25
G. Thomson	1925–31
D. Cameron	1931–35
B. Bourdillon	1935–42

A. Burns	1942–43
A. Richards	1943–47
J. Macpherson	1948–54

Governors-General

J. Macpherson	1954–55
J. Robertson	1955–60
N. Azikiwe	1960–63

Presidents

(Title not used January 1966 – October 1977, and after December 1983.)

N. Azikiwe	1963–66
N. Orizu (acting)	1966 (Jan.)
Maj.-Gen. J. Aguiyi-Ironsi	1966 (Jan.–July)
Lt.- Col. Y. Gowon	1966–75
Gen. M. Ramat Mohammed	1975–76
Lt.-Gen. O. Obasanjo	1976–79
A. Shehu Shagari	1979–83
Maj.-Gen. M. Buhari	1983–85

Prime Minister

| A. Tafawa Balewa | 1957–66 |

Under military rule from 1966.

Head of State and Commander-in-Chief of Armed Forces

Maj.-Gen. J. Aguiyi-Ironsi	1966–68
Lt.-Col. Y. Gowon	1968–75
Gen. M. Ramat Mohammed	1975–76
Lt.-Gen. O. Obasanjo	1976–79
A. Shehu Shagari	1979–83
Maj.-Gen. M. Buhari	1983–85
Maj.-Gen. I. Babaginda	1985–87
Col. Ali Seybou	1987–

Norway

Kings

| Haakon VII | 1905–57 |
| Olaf V | 1957– |

Prime Ministers

G. Knudsen	1919–20
O. Halvorsen	1920–21
O. Blehr	1921–23
O. Halvorsen	1923 (Mar.–May)
A. Berge	1923–24
J. Mowinckel	1924–26

I. Lykke	1926–28
J. Mowinckel	1928–31
N. Kolstad	1931–32
J. Hundseid	1932–33
J. Mowinckel	1933–35
J. Nygaardsvold	1935–45
E. Gerhardsen	1945–51
O. Torp	1951–55
E. Gerhardsen	1955–63
J. Lyng	1963 (Aug.–Sept.)
E. Gerhardsen	1963–65
P. Borten	1965–71
T. Bratteli	1971–72
L. Korvald	1972–73
T. Bratteli	1973–76
O. Nordli	1976–81
G. Brundtland	1981 (Feb.–Oct.)
K. Willoch	1981–86
G. Brundtland	1986–89
J. Syse	1989–

Pakistan

Presidents

Q. Ali Jinnah	1947–48
K. Nazimuddin	1948–51
G. Muhammed	1951–55
Maj.-Gen. I. Mirza	1956–58
Field Marshal M. Ayub Khan	1958–69
Maj.-Gen. A. Yahya Khan	1969–71
Z. Ali Bhutto	1971–73
F. Elahi Chaudri	1973–78
Gen. M. Zia ul-Haq	1978–88
I. Khan	1988–

Philippines

Under US control from 1898. The Philippines became a
commonwealth in 1935 and an independent republic in 1946.

Presidents

M. Quezon	1935–44
(in exile 1941–44)	
S. Osmena	1944–46
M. Roxas y Acuna	1946–48
E. Quirino	1948–53
R. Magsaysay	1953–57
C. Garcia	1957–61
D. Mascapagal	1961–65
F. Marcos	1965–86
Mrs C. Aquino	1986–

Poland

Poland became an independent state in November 1918.

Presidents

Marshal J. Pilsudski	1918–22
G. Narutowicz	1922
S. Wojciechowski	1922–26
I. Mosciki	1926–39

Marshal Pilsudski seized power in a coup in 1926 and Poland was under military dictatorship until 1939. In September 1939 Poland was occupied and divided by Germany and the USSR.

Polish Government-in-Exile

President

W. Raczkiewicz	1939–45

Prime Ministers

Gen. W. Sikorski	1939–43
S. Mikolajczyk	1943–45

Poland was controlled by a Provisional Government of National Unity from July 1945. Elections in 1947 gave communist-socialist candidates a majority.

President

B. Bierut	1945–52

In 1952 the office of President was replaced by a Council of State.

Chairmen of the Council of State

A. Zawadski	1952–64
E. Ochab	1964–68
Marshal M. Spychalski	1968–70
J. Cyrankiewicz	1970–72
H. Jablonski	1972–85
Gen. W. Jaruzelski	1985–

First Secretaries, Communist Party Politburo

W. Gomulka	1945–48
B. Bierut	1948–56
E. Ochab	1956 (Mar.–Oct.)
W. Gomulka	1956–70
E. Gierek	1970–80
S. Kania	1980–81
Gen. W. Jaruzelski	1981–

Gomulka was Poland's dominant political figure 1956–70; Gierek 1970–1980. Jaruzelski took this position from 1981.

Prime Ministers

J. Cyrankiewicz	1954–70
P. Jaroszewicz	1970–80
E. Babiuch	1980 (Feb.–Aug.)
J. Pinkowski	1980–81
Gen. W. Jaruselski	1981–85
Z. Messner	1985–88
M. Rakowski	1988–89
Gen. Kiszcak	1989 (Aug)
T. Mazowiecki	1989–

Portugal

Presidents

M. de Arriaga	1911–15
B. Machado	1915–I7
S. Paes	1917–18
J. Antunes	1918–19
A. de Almeida	1919–23
M. Gomes	1923–25
B. Machado	1925–26
Marshal A. Carmona	1926–51
A. Salazar (provisional)	1951 (Apr.–July)
Marshal F. Lopez	1951–58
Rear-Adm. A. Tomás	1958–74
Gen. A. de Spinola	1974 (May–Sept.)
Gen. F. Gomes	1974–76
Gen. A. Eanes	1976–86
M. Soares	1986–

Prime Ministers

A. Baptista	1920–21
B. Machada	1921–22
A. da Silva	1922–23
A. de Castro	1923–25
V. Guimarães	1925 (Feb.–Dec.)
A. da Silva	1925–26
A. Carmona	1926–28
J. de Freitas	1928–30
D. de Oliveira	1930–32
A. Salazar	1932–68
M. Caetano	1968–74
A. Carlos	1974 (May–July)
V. Goncalves	1974–75
P. de Azevedo	1975–76
M. Soares	1976–78
N. da Costa	1978 (Aug.–Oct.)
C. Pinto	1978–79
M. Pintassilgo	1979 (July–Dec.)
F. Carneiro	1979–80

| D. do Amaral | 1980 (Dec.) |
| P. Balsemão | 1980–82 |

Balsemão resigned on 19 Dec. 1982. P. Crespo was appointed Prime Minister but was unable to form a government. Balsemão formed a caretaker government Jan.–June 1983.

| M. Soares | 1983–85 |
| A. Silva | 1985– |

Romania

Kings

Carol I	1880–1914
Ferdinand II	1914–27
Michael (under Regency)	1927–30
Carol II	1930–40
Michael	1940–47

Prime Ministers

I. Brătianu	1914–18
Gen. A. Averescu	1918 (Feb.–Mar.)
A. Marghiloman	1918 (Mar.–Nov.)
Gen. Coandă	1918 (Nov.–Dec.)
I. Brătianu	1918–19
A. Vaida-Voevod	1919–20
Gen. A. Averescu	1920–22
I. Brătianu	1922–26
Gen. A. Averescu	1926–27
I. Bratianu	1927 (Mar.–Nov.)
I. Maniu	1928–30
G. Mironescu	1930–31
N. Iorga	1931–32
A. Vaida-Voevod	1932–33
I. Duca	1933 (Feb.–Dec.)
G. Tătărescu	1933–37
O. Goga	1937
M. Cristea	1937–39
A. Călinescu	1939 (Mar.–Sept.)
Gen. I. Antonescu (as dictator)	1940–44
Gen. C. Sănătescu	1944 (Aug.–Dec.)
N. Rădescu	1944–45
P. Groza	1945 (Mar.)

Romania became a republic in 1947.

Presidents

C. Parhon	1948–52
P. Groza	1952–58
I. Maurer	1958–61
G. Gheorghiu-Dej	1961–65
C. Stoica	1965–67

N. Ceausescu   1967–89*
I. Iliescu   1989–

* Ceausescu was executed on 25 December 1989 during the
Romanian revolution. Iliescu became interim President.

Saudi Arabia

United as a kingdom in 1932.

Kings

Abdul Aziz ibn Abdur-Rahman   1932–53
   al-Faisal Al Sa'ud
Saud ibn Abdul Aziz   1953–64
Faisal ibn Abdul Aziz   1964–75
Khalid ibn Abdul Aziz   1975–82
Fahd ibn Abdul Aziz   1982–

Singapore

Singapore became independent from Britain in 1963 and almost
immediately joined the Malaysian federation. It seceded in 1965.

Governors

F. Gimson   1946–52
J. Nicoll   1952–55
R. Black   1955–57
W. Goode   1957–59

Head of State

Inche Yusuf bin Ishak   1963 (Aug.–Sept.)

Prime Ministers

D. Marshall   1955–56
Lim Yew Hock   1956–59
Lee Kuan Yew   1959–63

Republic of Singapore

President

Inche Yusuf bin Ishak   1965–70
B. Sheares   1971–81
D. Nair   1981–85
W. K. Wee   1985–

Prime Minister

Lee Kuan Yew   1965–

South Africa

Governors-General

Viscount Gladstone	1910–14
Viscount Buxton	1914–24
Earl of Athlone	1924–31
Earl of Clarendon	1931–37
Sir P. Duncan	1937–43
N. de Wet	1943–46
G. van Zyl	1946–50
E. Jansen	1951–59
L. Steyn (acting)	1959–60
C. Swart	1960–61

In 1961 South Africa became a republic and left the British
Commonwealth.

Presidents

C. Swart	1961–67
J. Naudé (acting)	1967–68
J. Fouché	1968–75
N. Diederich	1975–78
M. Viljoen (acting)	1978 (Aug.–Oct.)
B. Vorster	1978–79
M. Viljoen (acting)	1979–84
P. Botha	1984–89
F. de Klerk (acting until Sept. 1989)	1989–

Prime Ministers

Gen. L. Botha	1910–19
Gen. J. Smuts	1919–24
Gen. J. Hertzog	1924–39
Gen. J. Smuts	1939–48
D. Malan	1948–54
J. Strijdom	1954–58
C. Swart (acting)	1958 (Aug.–Sept.)
H. Verwoerd	1958–66
B. Vorster	1966–78
P. Botha	1978–84

The post of Prime Minister was abolished in 1984 and combined with
that of President.

Spain

King

Alfonso XIII	1886–1931

Prime Ministers

A. Maura	1917–23

Gen. M. Primo de Rivera mounted a coup in 1923 and held power until 1930.

Gen. Dánaso Berenguer	1930–31
Adm J. Bautista Aznar (interim)	1931 (Feb.–Apr.)

Spain became a republic in April 1931.

Presidents

N. Alcalá-Zamora	1931–36
M. Azaňa	1936–39

Prime Ministers

N. Alcalá-Zamora (provisional)	1931 (Apr.–Oct.)
M. Azaňa	1931–33
A. Lerroux	1933–34
R. Samper	1934 (Apr.–Oct.)
A. Lerroux	1934–35
M. Portela Valladares	1935–36
M. Azaňa	1936 (Feb.–-May)
S. Casares Quiroga	1936 (May–July)
J. Giral	1936 (July–Sept.)
F. Largo Caballero	1936–37
J. Negrín	1937–39

Chief of State

Gen. F. Franco Bahamonde	1939–75

Franco designated Prince Juan Carlos as his eventual successor in 1969.

King

Juan Carlos I	1975–

President of Council of Ministers (Prime Minister)

Gen. F. Franco Bahamonde	1939–73
Adm. L. Carrero Blanco	1973–74
C. Arias Navarro	1974–75
A. Súarez Gonzalez	1975–81
L. Calvo Sotelo	1981–82
F. González Márquez	1982–

Sri Lanka

Sri Lanka was known as Ceylon while under British contol, and achieved its independence in 1948.

Governors

R. Chalmers	1913–16
J. Anderson	1916–18

W. Manning	1918–25
H. Clifford	1925–27
H. Stanley	1927–31
G. Thomson	1931–33
R. Stubbs	1933–37
A. Caldecott	1937–44
H. Moore	1944–48

Governors-General

H. Moore	1948–49
H. Ramsbotham, Viscount Soulbury	1949–55
O. Goonetilleke	1955–62
W. Gopallawa	1962–72

Prime Ministers

S. Senanayake	1948–52
D. Senanayake	1952–53
Sir J. Kotelawala	1953–56
S. Bandaranaike	1956–59
W. Dahanayake	1959–60
D. Senanayake	1960 (Mar.–July)
Mrs S. Bandaranaike	1960–65
D. Senanayake	1965–70
Mrs S. Bandaranaike	1970–72

Sri Lanka became a Republic in 1972.

Presidents

W. Gopallawa	1972–78
J. Jayawardene	1978–88
R. Premadasa	1988–

Prime Ministers

Mrs S. Bandaranaike	1972–77
J. Jayawardene	1977–78
R. Premadasa	1978–88
D. B. Wijeratne	1988–

Sweden

Kings

Gustav V	1907–50
Gustav VI Adolf	1950–73
Charles XVI Gustaf	1973–

Prime Ministers

H. Hammarskjöld	1911–17
C. Swartz	1917 (Mar.–Oct.)
N. Eden	1917–20

H. Branting	1920–21
O. von Sydow	1921 (Feb.–Oct.)
H. Branting	1921–23
E. Trygger	1923–25
R. Sandler	1925–26
C. Ekman	1926–28
A. Lindman	1928–30
C. Ekman	1930–32
F. Hamrin	1932 (Aug.–Sept.)
P. Hansson	1932–36
M. Pehrsson	1936 (June–Sept.)
P. Hansson	1936–46
T. Erlander	1946–69
O. Palme	1969–76
T. Fälldin	1976–78
O. Ullsten	1978–79
T. Fälldin	1979–82
O. Palme	1982–86
I. Carlsson	1986–

Syria

President

H. al-Atassi	1936–39

France, which held Syria as a League of Nations' mandate, suspended the constitution in 1939. Syria was under Anglo-French occupation 1941–46.

S. Shukri al Quwwatli	1943–49
Col. H. Zaim	1949 (June–Aug.)
Col. S. Hinawi (acting)	1949 (Aug.)
H. al-Atassi	1949–51
Col. A. es-Shishaqli (Dictator)	1951–53
Col. A. es-Shishaqli (President)	1953–54
H. al-Atassi	1954–55
S. Shukri al Quwwatli	1955–58

(Union with Egypt under the Egyptian head of state, 1958–1961.)

N. el-Kudsi	1961–63
Maj.-Gen. L. Atassi	1963 (Mar.–July)
Gen. A. el-Hafez	1963–66
N, Atassi	1966–70
A. Khatib	1970–71
Lt. -Gen. H. al-Assad	1971–

Taiwan

Following the communist victory in the Chinese civil war in 1949, the Nationalist Government held only the island of Taiwan.

Presidents

Gen. Li Tsung-jen	1949–50
Chiang Kai-shek	1950–75
Yen Chia-kan	1975–78
Chiang Ching-kuo	1978–88
Lee Teng-hui	1988–

Prime Ministers

Marshal Yen Hsi-shan	1949–50
Gen. Chen Cheng	1950–54
O.K. Yui	1954–58
Gen. Chen Cheng	1958–63
Yen Chia-kan	1963–72
Chiang Ching-kuo	1972–78
Sun Yun-hsuan	1978–84
Yu Kuo-hwa	1984–89
Lee Huan	1989–90
Gen. Hau Pei-tsun	1990–

Tanzania

Tanzania was made up of Tanganyika (German until World War I;
British Trust Territory until independence in 1961) and Zanzibar
(British Protectorate from 1890 until independence in 1963). They
combined in 1964.

Tanganyika

Governors

H. Byatt	1916–24
D. Cameron	1924–31
G. Symes	1931–33
H. MacMichael	1933–38
M. Young	1938–42
W. Jackson	1942–45
W. Battershill	1945–49
E. Twining	1949–58
R. Turnbull	1958–61

Dominion of Tanganyika

Governor-General

Sir R. Turnbull	1961–62

Prime Ministers

J. Nyerere	1961–62
R. Kawawa	1962 (Jan.–Dec.)

Republic of Tanganyika

President

J. Nyerere	1962–64

Prime Minister

R. Kawawa   1962–64

Zanzibar

Residents

F. Pearce   1914–22
J. Sinclair   1922–24
A. Hollis   1924–30
R. Rankine   1930–37
J. Hall   1937–40
H. Pilling   1941–46
V. Glenday   1946–51
J. Rankine   1952–54
H. Potter   1954–60
G. Mooring   1960–63

Sultanate of Zanzibar

Sultan

Seyyid Jamshid bin-Abdullah   1963–64
  bin-Khalifah

Prime Minister

Muhammed Shamte Hamadi   1963–64

Republic of Zanzibar

President

Abeid Amani Karume   1964 (Jan.–Apr.)

Prime Minister

Abdullah Kassim Hanga   1964 (Jan.–Apr.)

Tanzania

President

J. Nyerere   1964–85
N. A. H. Mwinyi   1985–

Prime Minister

(The office was abolished until 1972)

R. Kawawa   1972–77
E. Sokoine   1977–80
C. D. Msuya   1980–83
E. Sokoine   1983–84
S. A. Salim   1984–85
J. Warioba   1985–

Thailand

Generally known before 1939 as Siam.

Kings

Vajiravudh	1910–25
Prajadhipok	1925–35
Ananda Mahidol	1935–46
Bhumipol Adulyadej	1946–

Prime Ministers

Marshal Luang Pibul Songgram	1938–44
Kuang Aphaiwongse	1944–45
Nai Thawi Bunyakat	1945–46
Kuang Aphaiwongse	1946 (Jan.–Mar.)
Nai Pridi Phanomjong	1946 (Mar.–Aug.)
Luang Dhamrong Nawassat	1946–47
Marshal Luang Pibul Songgram	1947 (Nov.)
Kuang Aphaiwongse	1947–48
Marshal Luang Pibul Songgram	1948–57
Marshal Sarit Thanarat	1957 (Sept.)
Pote Sarasin	1957–58
Gen. Thanom Kittikachorn	1963–73
Sanya Thammasak	1973–74
Sanya Dharmasakti	1974–75
Seni Pramoj	1975 (Feb.–Mar.)
Kukrit Pramoj	1975–76
Seni Pramoj	1976 (Apr.–Oct.)
Thanin Kraivichien	1976–77
Gen. Kriang Chananand	1977–81
Gen. Kriangsak Chomanan	1981–83
Gen. Prem Tinsulanonda	1983–88
Maj-Gen. Chatichai Choonhavan	1988–

Turkey

Sultans

Mohammed V	1909–18
Mohammed VI	1918–22

The office of Sultan was abolished in November 1922 and Turkey declared a Republic in October 1923.

Presidents

M. Kemal Atatürk	1923–38
Gen. I. Inönü	1938–50
M. Bayar	1950–60
Gen. C. Gürsel	1961–66
Gen. C. Sunay	1966–73
Adm. F. Korutürk	1973–80

I. Caplayangil	1980 (Apr.–Sept.)
Gen. K. Evren	1980–89
T. Özal	1989–

Prime Ministers (as Grand Vizier until 1921)

Damad Ferid Pasha	1920 (Apr.–Oct.)
Tewfik Pasha	1920–23
Reouf Bey	1923 (Feb.–Oct.)
Ismet Pasha	1923–35
I. Inönü	1935–37
J. Bayar	1937–39
R. Saydam	1939–43
S. Saracoglu	1943–46
R. Peker	1946–47
H. Saka	1947–49
S. Gunaltay	1949–50
A. Menderes	1950–60
C. Gursel	1960–61
I. Inönü	1961–65
S. Urguplu	1965 (Feb.–Oct.)
S. Demirel	1965–71
N. Erim	1971–72
F. Melen	1972–73
N. Talû	1973–74
B. Ecevit	1974 (Jan.–Nov.)
S. Irmak	1974–75
S. Demirel	1975–77
B. Ecevit	1977 (June–July)
S. Demirel	1977–78
B. Ecevit	1978–79
S. Demirel	1979–80
B. Ülüsü	1980–83
T. Özal	1983–89
Y. Akbulut	1989–

Union of Soviet Socialist Republics

Until the 1917 Revolution, Russia was a monarchy.

Tsar

Nicholas II	1894–1917

Prime Ministers

W. Kokovtsov	1911–14
I. Goremykin	1914–16
B. Stürmer	1916 (Feb.–Nov.)
A. Trepov	1916–17
N. Golitsin	1917 (Jan.–Mar.)

Prime Ministers of the Provisional Government

G. Lvov	1917 (Mar.–July)
A. Kerensky	1917 (July–Nov.)

A Bolshevik Government took power in November 1917 and adopted the constitution of a Federal Republic in July 1918.

President of the Council of People's Commissars

V. Lenin	1917–22

Presidents

M. Kalinin	1922–46
N. Shvernik	1946–53
Marshal K. Voroshilov	1953–60
L. Brezhnev	1960–64
A. Mikoyan	1964–65
N. Podgorny	1965–77
L. Brezhnev	1977–82
Y. Andropov	1983–84
K. Chernenko	1984–85
A. Gromyko	1985–88
M. Gorbachev	1988–

The dominant figure from 1917 to 1990 was the General Secretary of the Communist Party. Since 1990 Gorbachev has been the first Executive President.

General Secretaries

V. Lenin	1917–22
J. Stalin	1922–53
N. Khrushchev	1953–64
L. Brezhnev	1964–82
Y. Andropov	1982–84
K. Chernenko	1984–85
M. Gorbachev	1985–

United Kingdom

Sovereigns

George V	1910–36
Edward VIII	1936 (abdicated, uncrowned)
George VI	1936–52
Elizabeth II	1952–

Prime Ministers

H. Asquith	1908–16
D. Lloyd George	1916–22
A. Bonar Law	1922–23
J. R. MacDonald	1924 (Jan.–Nov.)
S. Baldwin	1924–29
J. R. MacDonald	1929–35
S. Baldwin	1935–37
N. Chamberlain	1937–40
W. Churchill	1940–45
C. Attlee	1945–51

Sir W. Churchill	1951–55
Sir A. Eden	1955–57
H. Macmillan	1957–63
Sir A. Douglas-Home	1963–64
H. Wilson	1964–70
E. Heath	1970–74
H. Wilson	1974–76
J. Callaghan	1976–79
Mrs M. Thatcher	1979–

United States

Presidents

W. Wilson	1913–21
W. Harding	1921–23
C. Coolidge	1923–29
H. Hoover	1929–33
F. Roosevelt	1933–45
H. Truman	1945–53
D. Eisenhower	1953–61
J. Kennedy	1961–63
L. Johnson	1963–69
R. Nixon	1969–74
G. Ford	1974–77
J. Carter	1977–81
R. Reagan	1981–89
G. Bush	1989–

Vatican

Popes

Pius X	1903–14
Benedict XV	1914–22
Pius XI	1922–39
Pius XII	1939–58
John XXIII	1958–63
Paul VI	1963–78
John Paul I	1978
John Paul II	1978–

Venezuela

Presidents

Gen. J. Vicente Gómez	1908–35
Gen. E. López Conteras	1935–41
Gen. I. Medina Angarita	1941–45

R. Betancourt	1945–48
R. Gallegos Freire	1948 (Feb.–Nov.)
Lt.-Col. C. Delgado Chalbaud	1948–50
G. Suarez Flamerich	1950–52
Col. M. Pérez Jiménez	1952–58
Rear-Adm. W. Larrazábal Ugueto	1958 (Jan.–Nov.)
E. Sanabria	1958–59
R. Betancourt	1959–64
R. Leoni	1964–69
R. Caldera Rodriguez	1969–74
C. Pérez Rodriguez	1974–79
L. Herrera Campins	1979–84
J. Lusinchi	1984–89
C. Pérez Rodriguez	1989–

Vietnam

The central Vietnam region of Annam was a French protectorate from 1883 and part of the Indochinese Union from 1887. Between 1940 and 1945 it was controlled by Japan. French rule was restored in 1945, local autonomy within an Indochinese Federation was granted in 1946, and Vietnam became independent in 1954.

Governors-General of Indochinese Union

A. Sarraut	1911–14
J. Van Vollenhoven	1914–15
E. Roume	1915–16
J. Charles	1916–17
A. Sarraut	1917–19
M. Monguillot	1919–20
M. Long	1920–22
F. Baudouin	1922
M. Merlin	1922–25
M. Monguillot	1925
A. Varennes	1925–28
M. Monguillot	1928
P. Pasquier	1928–34
E. Robin	1934–36
J. Brévié	1936–39
G. Catroux	1939–40
J. Decoux	1940–45

High Commissioners of Indochinese Federation

G. d'Argenlieu	1945–47
E. Ballaert	1947–48
L. Pignon	1948–50
J. de Lattre de Tassigny	1950–52
J. Letourneau	1952–53

Empire of Annam

Emperors (under French protection)

Duy Tan	1906–16
Khai Dinh	1916–25
Bao Din	1925–45

Democratic Republic of Vietnam (North Vietnam)

Presidents

Ho Chi Minh	1945–69
Ton Duc Thang	1969–76

Prime Ministers

Ho Chi Minh	1945–55
Pham Van Dong	1955–76

Empire of Vietnam

Emperor

Bao Dao	1954–55

Prime Ministers

Buu Loc	1954–55
Ngo Dinh Diem	1955 (June–Oct.)

Republic of Vietnam (South Vietnam)

Presidents

Ngo Dinh Diem	1955–63
Maj.-Gen. Duong Van Minh	1963–64
Mej.-Gen. Nguyen Khanh	1964 (Jan.–Feb.)
Maj.-Gen. Duong Van Minh	1964 (Feb.–Aug.)
Maj.-Gen. Nguyen Khanh	1964 (Aug.–Sept.)
Maj.-Gen. Duong Van Minh	1964 (Sept.–Oct.)
Phan Khac Suu	1964–65
Gen. Nguyen Van Thieu	1965–75
Tran Van Huong	1975 (April)
Maj.-Gen. Duong Van Minh	1975 (April)

Prime Ministers

Ngo Dinh Diem	1955–63
Nguyen Ngoc Tho	1963–64
Maj.-Gen Nguyen Khanh	1964 (Feb.–Aug.)
Nguyen Xuan Oanh	1964 (Aug.–Sept.)
Gen. Nguyen Khanh	1964 (Sept.–Oct.)
Tran Van Huong	1964–65
Nguyen Xuan Oanh (acting)	1965 (Jan.–Feb.)
Phan Huy Quat	1965 (Feb.–June)
Air Vice-Marshal Nguyen Cao Ky	1965–67

Nguyen Van Loc	1967–69
Tran Van Huong	1969 (May–Aug.)
Gen. Tran Thien Khiem	1969–75
Bguyen Ba Can	1975 (April)
Vu Van Mau	1975 (April)

South Vietnam fell to the North in April 1975 and the two states were united in 1976.

Socialist Republic of Vietnam

Presidents

Ton Duc Thang	1976–80
Nguyen Huu Tho	1980–81
Truong Chinh	1981–86
Nguyen Van Linh	1986–87
Vo Chi Cong	1987–

Prime Ministers

Pham Van Dong	1976–87
Pham Hung	1987–89
Do Muoi	1989–

Secretaries-General Vietnamese Party of Labour (Communist Party)

Le Duan	1976–86
Truong Chinh	1986 (July–Dec.)
Nguyen Van Linh	1986–90

Yugoslavia

The Serb, Croat and Slovene State formed in December 1918 became known as Yugoslavia in October 1929.

Kings

Peter I (originally King of Serbia)	1903–21
Alexander I	1921–34
Peter II	1934–45

Prime Ministers

S. Protić	1921 (Feb.–Dec.)
N. Pašić	1921–26
N. Uzunović	1926–28
V. Vukitćević	1928–29
Gen. P. Zivković	1929–32
V. Marinković	1932 (Apr.–July)
M. Serškie	1932–34
N. Uzonivić	1934 (Jan.–Dec.)
B. Jević	1934–35
M. Stojadinović	1935–39
D. Cvetković	1939–41

Yugoslavia was occupied by the Axis in 1941. A government-in-exile was based in London and then in Cairo.

S. Jovanović	1942–43
M. Trifimović	1943 (June–Aug.)
B. Purić	1943–45

A republic was proclaimed in 1945.

Presidents of the Praesidium

I. Ribar	1945–53
Marshal J. Broz Tito	1953–80

Since 1980 Yugoslavia has had a 'Collective Presidency'. A President is selected annually from this eight-member committee.

Heads of the Collective Presidency

L. Kolisevski	1980 (May)
C. Mijatović	1980–81
S. Krajger	1981–82
P. Stambolić	1982–83
M. Spiljac	1983–84
V. Djuranović	1984–85
R. Vlajković	1985–86
S. Hasani	1986–87
L. Mojson	1987–88
R. Dizdarević	1988–89
M. Rožicé	1989–90
B. Jovic	1990–

Prime Ministers

Marshal J. Broz Tito	1945–63
P. Stambolić	1963–67
M. Spiljak	1967–69
R. Ribičić	1969–71
D. Bijedić	1971–77
V. Djuranović	1977–82
M. Planinc	1982–86
B. Mikulić	1986–88
A. Marković	1988–

Zaire

The Belgian Congo until independence in 1960.

Governors-General

P. Ryckmans	1934–46
E. Jungers	1946–51
L. Pétillon	1951–58
H. Cornelis	1958–60

Presidents

J. Kasavubu	1960–65
J.-D. Mobutu (became Mobutu Sésé Séko Kuku Ngbendu Wa Zabanga)	1965–

Prime Ministers

P. Lumumba	1960 (July–Sept.)
J. Ileo	1960 (Sept.)
Powers held by a College of Commissioners	1960–61
J. Ileo	1961 (Feb.–Aug.)
C. Adoula	1961–64
M. Tshombe	1964–65
E. Kimba	1965 (Oct.–Nov.)
Gen. L. Mulamba	1965–66

The office of Prime Minister was temporarily abolished and its powers taken over by the President. Prime Ministers since 1979 have been relatively insignificant politically.

Zimbabwe

Southern Rhodesia was annexed to the British Crown in 1923. A white regime declared illegal unilateral independence in 1965 and a republic in 1970. The area became independent as Zimbabwe in 1980.

Administrator

F. Chaplin	1914–23

Governors

J. Chancellor	1923–28
C. Rodwell	1928–34
H. Stanley	1934–42
E. Baring	1942–44
W. Tait	1944–46
J. Kennedy	1947–53
P. William-Powlett	1954–59
H. Gibbs	1959–65

Prime Ministers

Sir C. Coghlan	1923–27
H. Moffat	1927–33
G. Mitchell	1933 (July–Sept.)
Sir G. Huggins (later Lord Malvern)	1933–53
G. Todd	1953–58
Sir E. Whitehead	1958–62
W. Field	1962–64
I. Smith	1964–80

Between 1953 and 1963 Rhodesia was part of the Federation of Rhodesia and Nyasaland.

Prime Ministers

Sir G. Huggins	1953–56
Sir R. Welensky	1956–63

President (during period of illegal independence)

C. Dupont	1970–76
J. Wrathall	1976–80

Zimbabwe

President

C. Banana	1980–87

Prime Minister

R. Mugabe	1980–

(from 1987 executive President)

Wars and international affairs

Section II
Wars and international affairs

Principal international organizations and groupings

Arab League

Established in 1945 to promote co-operation between member states. All the Arab countries including Mauritania, Sudan and Somalia are normally members, but Egypt was suspended in 1979 after its overtures to Israel. Palestine (i.e. the PLO) also holds membership. The League sent a peace-keeping force to Lebanon in June 1976, and has tried to mediate in the civil war in the 1980s.

Secretaries-General

Abdul Azzem (Egypt)	1945–1952
Abdul Hassouna (Egypt)	1952–1972
Mahmoud Riad (Egypt)	1972–1979
Chedli Klibi (Tunisia)	1979–1990

Members

Algeria (1962)	Oman (1971)
Bahrain (1971)	Palestine (PLO)
Djibouti (1977)	Qatar (1971)
Egypt (suspended 1979)	Saudi Arabia
Iraq	Somalia (1974)
Jordan	Sudan (1956)
Kuwait (1961)	Syria
Lebanon	Tunisia (1958)
Libya (1951)	United Arab Emirates (1971)
Mauritania (1973)	Yemen
Morocco (1958)	

Association of South East Asian Nations (ASEAN)

This association was formed on 8 August 1967, with headquarters in Jakarta, to promote active collaboration and mutual assistance in economic, social, cultural, technical, scientific and administrative fields. The founding members were Indonesia, Thailand, the Philippines, Malaysia and Singapore. Brunei joined in 1984. It was hoped through the association to increase the political stability of South-East Asia and to improve the rate of economic development. There is an annual meeting of Foreign Ministers, and progress has been made not only in economic co-operation but also in joint research, education, transport and tourism.

Secretaries-General

Hartono Dharsono (Indonesia)	1967–1978
Umarjadi Njotowijona (Indonesia)	(Feb–July) 1978
Datuk Ali bin Abdullah (Malaysia)	1978–1980
Narciso Reyes (Philippines)	1980–1982

Chan Kai Yau (Singapore)   1982–1984
Phan Wannamethee (Thailand)   1984–

Members

Brunei (1984)   Singapore (1967)
Indonesia (1967)   Thailand (1967)
Malaysia (1967)
Philippines (1967)

Commonwealth, the

A grouping of states, numbering 50 in 1990, which evolved from the
former territories of the British Empire. The statute of Westminster (31
December 1931) defined the structure of the British Commonwealth and
recognized the dominions as 'autonomous communities'. The
organisation works to improve economic collaboration and other
forms of co-operation between member states. Not all former
territories of the British Empire are members. Burma never joined; the
Republic of Ireland is not a member. South Africa left in 1961,
Pakistan left in 1972 and rejoined in 1989, Fiji left after the military
coup in 1987. Namibia (joined 1990) is the most recent member.

Secretaries General of the Commonwealth

Arnold Smith (Canada)   1965–1975
Sir Shridath S Ramphal (Guyana)   1975–1989
Chief Emeka Anyaoku (Nigeria)   1989–

Council for Mutual Economic Assistance (COMECON)

Organization established in Moscow in January 1959 to improve trade
between the Soviet Union and other Eastern European states.
Regarded by Stalin as an instrument to enforce an economic boycott
on Yugoslavia, and also used as a Soviet response to growing
Western European economic interdependence. Apart from the East
European countries, Mongolia joined in 1962, Cuba in 1972 and
Vietnam in 1978. Changes in Europe since 1989 have left its future
role uncertain, whilst in January 1990 Czechoslovakia called for its
dissolution.

Secretaries

Nikolai Faddeyev (USSR)   1949–83
Vyacheslav Sychev (USSR)   1983–

Council of Europe

Organization established in 1949 to achieve greater European unity
based on the common heritage of its member states. Matters of
national defence are excluded. The original states were Belgium,
Britain, Denmark, France, Ireland, Italy, the Netherlands, Norway and
Sweden. They were also joined by Greece, Iceland and Turkey later in
1949, West Germany in 1951, Austria in 1956, Cyprus in 1961,

Switzerland in 1963 and Malta in 1965. It is quite separate from the European Community (q.v.).

Secretaries-General

Jacques Camille-Paris (France)	1949–1953
Leon Marchal (France)	1953–1957
Ludovico Benvenuti (Italy)	1957–1964
Peter Smithers (UK)	1964–1969
Lujo Toncic-Sorinj (Austria)	1969–1974
Georg Kahn-Ackermann (Federal Republic of Germany)	1974–1979
Franz Karasek (Austria)	1979–1984
Marcelino Oreja Aguirre (Spain)	1984–

European Community (EC)

Also frequently referred to as the Common Market. Came into being on 1 January 1958, following the signing by the original six states (Belgium, France, Italy, Luxembourg, the Netherlands and West Germany) of the Treaty of Rome on 25 March 1957. The original six states, who bound themselves to work together for economic and political union, have been enlarged with the entry of Denmark, Ireland and the UK on I January 1973, Greece on 1 January 1981 and Spain and Portugal on 1 January 1986. Under the Lomé Convention of 31 October 1979, the Community has trade agreements with 58 countries in Africa, the Caribbean and the Pacific.

Presidents of the European Commission

Walter Hallstein (Federal Republic of Germany)	1958–1966
Jean Rey (Belgium)	1966–1970
Franco Malfatti (Italy)	1970–1972
Sicco Mansholt (Netherlands)	1972–1973
Francois-Xavier Ortoli (France)	1973–1977
Roy Jenkins (UK)	1977–1981
Gaston Thorn (Luxembourg)	1981–1985
Jacques Delors (France)	1985–

Presidents of the European Parliament

Robert Schuman (France)	1958–1960
Hans Furler (Federal Republic of Germany)	1960–1962
Gaetano Martino (Italy)	1962–1964
Jean Duvieusart (Belgium)	1964–1965
Victor Leemans (Belgium)	1965–1966
Alain Poher (France)	1966–1969
Mario Scelba (Italy)	1969–1971
Walter Behrendt (Federal Republic of Germany)	1971–1973
Cornelius Berkhouwer (Netherlands)	1973–1975
Georges Spénale (France)	1975–1977

Emilio Colombo (Italy)	1977–1979
Simone Veil (France)	1979–1982
Pieter Dankert (Netherlands)	1982–1984
Pierre Pflimlin (France)	1984–1987
Lord Plumb (UK)	1987–1989
Enrico Barón Crespo (Spain)	1989–

European Free Trade Association (EFTA)

Grouping of European countries whose aims are to achieve a free trade in industrial goods between members, to help achieve the creation of a general Western European market and to expand world trade in general. Three members (Denmark, Portugal and the United Kingdom) subsequently left to join the European Economic Community. Indeed, EFTA had arisen partly as a response to the original veto by France on Britain joining the European Community.

Secretaries-General

Frank Figgures (UK)	1960–1965
John Coulson (UK)	1965–1972
Bengt Rabaeus (Sweden)	1972–1975
Charles Muller (Switzerland)	1976–1981
Magnus Vahlquist (Sweden) (Acting)	1981 (Oct.–Nov.)
Per Kleppe (Norway)	1981–1988
Georg Reisch (Austria)	1988–

League of Nations

International organization set up as an integral part of the Versailles Settlement in 1920 (see p. 8) to preserve the peace and settle disputes by negotiation. Although the United States refused to participate, it comprised 53 members by 1923. Based in Geneva, the League relied upon non-military means to coerce states, such as 'sanctions' (q.v.), but found itself virtually powerless in the face of the Japanese invasion of Manchuria and the Italian invasion of Abyssinia. The League was discredited by 1939 and was dissolved in April 1946 with the formation of the United Nations. (See also pp. 264–66 for a chronology of the League.)

Secretaries-General

Sir Eric Drummond (Earl of Perth) (UK)	1919–1932
Joseph Avenol (France)	1933–1940
Sean Lester (Ireland) (Acting)	1940–1946

North Atlantic Treaty Organization (NATO)

Created by the North Atlantic Treaty of 4 April 1949. The organization represented the first US commitment to European defence in peacetime. NATO came in response to Western fears about the power of the Soviet Union and the failure of the UN Security Council to operate in the face of the Soviet veto. The treaty states are obliged to take such action as they deem necessary to assist a fellow signatory subjected to aggression, although there is no obligation to fight. The treaty states are Belgium, Luxembourg, the Netherlands, Britain, the United States, Canada, Italy, Norway, Denmark, Iceland and Portugal who were original signatories plus Greece and Turkey (1952) and West Germany (1955). France was an original signatory, but withdrew from the organization in 1966.

Secretaries-General

Lord Ismay (UK)	1952–1957
Paul-Henri Spaak (Belgium)	1957–1961
Alberico Casardi (Acting)	1961–(Mar.–Apr.)
Dirk Stikker (Holland)	1961–1964
Manlio Brosio (Italy)	1964–1971
Joseph Luns (Holland)	1971–1984
Lord Carrington (UK)	1984–1988
Manfred Wörner (Federal Republic of Germany)	1988–

Supreme Allied Commanders, Europe

Dwight D. Eisenhower (US)	1950–1952
Matthew Ridgway (US)	1952–1953
Alfred M. Gruenther (US)	1953–1956
Lauris Norstad (US)	1956–1963
Lyman L. Lemnitzer (US)	1963–1969
Andrew J. Goodpaster (US)	1969–1974
Alexander Haig (US)	1974–1979
Bernard Rogers (US)	1979–

Organization for Economic Co-operation and Development (OECD)

The organization consists of over 20 countries, mostly the richer nations. Its aims are to encourage and co-ordinate the economic policies of members, to contribute to the expansion of developing countries and to promote the development of world trade on a multi-lateral basis. It publishes economic statistics and compiles reports on specific aspects of world economics. It is the successor to the Organization for European Economic Co-operation (OEEC).

Secretaries-General

Thorkil Kristensen (Denmark)	1961–1969
Emile van Lennep (Netherlands)	1969–1984
Jean-Claude Paye (France)	1984–

Organization of African Unity

Grouping of African states set up in 1963 after a meeting in Addis Ababa. Its formation united the rival Monrovia and Casablanca groups as well as including nearly all the independent black African states. At its first meeting the members agreed to accept inherited colonial boundaries, thus preventing many border incidents. The members also voted to boycott South Africa. It has mediated successfully in disputes amongst its members (as in 1972, in the dispute between Guinea and Senegal) and has campaigned against the vestiges of colonialism in southern Africa (as in Namibia in the 1980s).

Secretaries-General

Diallo Telli (Guinea)	1964–1972
Nzo Ekangaki (Cameroon)	1972–1974
William Eteki Mbomua (Cameroon)	1974–1978
Edem Kodjo (Togo)	1978–1983
Peter Onu (Nigeria) (Acting)	1983–1985
Ide Oumarou (Niger)	1985–

Organization of American States (OAS)

Regional political organization consisting of the United States and over 30 Latin-American and Caribbean republics, created at the Bogota Conference in 1948. The organization has an Inter-American Conference which meets every five years to discuss general policies, and each member state is represented by an ambassador on its council, which oversees the implementation of OAS policy. There are provisions for *ad hoc* consultative meetings of foreign ministers and special conferences which promote co-operation in dealing with technical problems. The whole organization is served by a secretariat known as the Pan-American Union, which operates through its general headquarters in Washington.

Secretaries-General

Alberto Lleras Camargo (Colombia)	1948–1954
Carlos Davila (Chile)	1954–1956
José Mora Otero (Uruguay)	1956–1968
Galo Plaza Lasso (Ecuador)	1968–1975
Alejandro Orfila (Argentina)	1975–1984
Valerie McComie (Barbados) (Acting)	1984 (Mar.–June)
João Clemente Baena Soares (Brazil)	1984–

Organization of Petroleum Exporting Countries (OPEC)

This organization, whose membership is open to any country with substantial exports of crude petroleum, works to unify and coordinate the oil policies of its members, helps to stabilize prices in international oil–markets and generally to safeguard the interests of its members. It originated in September 1960 when, after a Baghdad meeting, such leading oil-producers as Saudi Arabia, Iran and Venezuela banded together to form OPEC. In 1973, OPEC precipitated a world economic crisis by agreeing price increases which eventually quadrupled the price of oil. Britain is not a member.

Secretaries-General

Faud Rouhani (Iran)	1961–1964
Abdul Rahman Al-Bazzaz (Iraq)	1964–1965

Ashraf Lutfi (Kuwait)	1965–1966
Mohammed S. Joukhdar (Saudi Arabia)	1967
Francisco R. Parra (Venezuela)	1968
Elrich Sanger (Indonesia)	1969
Omar El-Badri (Libya)	1970
Nadim Pachachi (UAE)	1971–1972
Abderrahman Khene (Algeria)	1973–1974
M.O. Feyide (Nigeria)	1975–1976
Ali M. Jaidah (Qatar)	1977–1978
Rene G. Ortiz (Ecuador)	1979–1981
Marc S. Nan Nguema (Gabon)	1981–1983
Dr. Subroto (Indonesia)	1983–

United Nations, the

International peace-keeping organization set up in 1945 to replace the League of Nations (q.v.). From the 50 states who signed the Charter of the UN in 1945, numbers had more than doubled by 1970 with the rise of independent ex-colonial states. All states have one vote in the General Assembly and its executive, the Security Council, can call on member states to supply armed forces. UN troops have been involved in peace-keeping duties in many parts of the world since 1945, notably in the Middle East, Africa and Cyprus. (See also pp. 267–69 for a chronology of the United Nations.)

Secretaries-General

Trygve Lie (Norway)	1946–1953
Dag Hammarskjold (Sweden)	1953–1961
U Thant (Burma)	1961–1971
Kurt Waldheim (Austria)	1972–1981
Javier Perez de Cuellar (Peru)	1982–

Warsaw Pact

Military grouping of Russia and East European states, with a political consultative committee intended to meet twice a year with rotating venue and chairmanship. In fact meets every alternate year, with delegations led by first secretaries of the party. Committee of defence ministers meets annually. Committee of foreign ministers has met since 1976 annually. Military Council of national chiefs of staff meets twice a year.

Commanders-in-Chief

Marshal I. S. Konev (USSR)	1955–1960
Marshal A. A. Grechko (USSR)	1960–1967
Marshal I. I. Yakubovsky (USSR)	1967–1976
Marshal Viktor G. Kulikov (USSR)	1977–

Members

Albania (ceased to participate in
1961 because of Stalinist and
pro-Chinese attitudes. Withdrew in 1968)
Bulgaria
Czechoslovakia

German Democratic Republic
Hungary
Poland
Romania
USSR

Major treaties and international agreements

1914   London Agreement, 15 June, between Britain and Germany concerning the Baghdad railway.
London Declaration, 5 September, by Britain, France, and Russia not to make separate peace with the Central Powers.

1915   Treaty of London, 25 April, between Britain, France and Italy offers Italy territorial gains at expense of Austria-Hungary in return for entering War.

1916   Sykes-Picot Agreement between British and French divides between them the Middle East provinces of the Turkish Empire after Turkey's defeat, 16 May.

1917   Secret agreement of St. Jean de Maurienne offers Italy part of Turkish territory after her defeat.
Secret treaty between Britain and Japan apportions German Pacific colonies between them.
Balfour Declaration supports the idea of a Jewish homeland in the Middle East, 2 November.

1918   Treaty of Brest-Litovsk, 3 March, between Russia and the Central Powers. Russia ceded territory, and made Finland and the Ukraine independent. Later invalidated.

1919   Treaty of Versailles, 28 June, between Germany and the Allies. Germany ceded territory and all her colonies to the Allies, returned Alsace-Lorraine to France, promised to pay large reparations and had her armed forces restricted. The Rhineland was demilitarized and occupied, and the League of Nations was created. Germany admitted 'war guilt'.
Treaty of Saint-Germain, 10 September, between Austria and the Allies, reduced Austria to a rump state following concessions to Czechoslovakia, Poland, Yugoslavia, Hungary, Italy and Romania, from the old Austria-Hungary.
Treaty of Neuilly, 27 November, between Bulgaria and the Allies reduced Bulgaria and provided for reparations payments.
Anglo-Afghan Treaty of Rawalpindi, 8 August.
Anglo-French agreement on Syria, 15 September.

1920   Treaty of the Trianon, 4 June, between Hungary and the Allies, reduced Hungary to a rump state and provided for reparations payments.
Treaty of Sèvres, 10 August, between Turkey and the Allies, reduced Turkey in size but was not accepted by the Turks. US Senate refuses to ratify Versailles Treaty; US Congress votes to terminate war with Germany, 9 April.
Treaties of Tartu, 2 February, between Russia and Estonia, of Moscow, 12 July, between Russia and Lithuania, and of Riga 11 August, between Russia and Latvia, establish Baltic States.
Treaty of Tartu, 14 October, between Russia and Finland creates an independent Finland.

Peace of Alexandropol, 2 December, Armenia cedes half her territory to Turkey.

1921   Alliance between France and Poland, 19 February; Treaty of Riga, 18 March, between Russia and Poland, ended war between them and defined their mutual border.
Paris Conference of Allies, 24–29 January, sets figure on reparations by Germany; London Ultimatum to Germany on payment accepted, 5–10 May.
Peace treaties of USA with Austria, Germany and Hungary, 25–29 May.
Four Power Pacific Treaty signed in Washington, 14 December.

1922   Washington Naval Agreement, 6 February, between Britain, France, the United States, Japan, Italy and others restricted the size of navies.
Treaty of Rapallo, 16 April, formed an alliance between Russia and Germany.
The 'Little Entente', 31 August, formed between Czechoslovakia, Yugoslavia and Romania under French auspices.
Turko-Greek armistice, 10 October.
US Protectionist Tariff introduced, 20 September.
Nine-Power Treaty secures independence of China, 6 February, Japan restores Shantung to China.

1923   Treaty of Lausanne, 24 July, between Turkey and the Allies replaced the Treaty of Sèvres. Confined Turkey to Asia Minor and the area around Constantinople.
Anglo-American War Debt Convention, 19 June.

1924   London Reparations Conference, 18 August, accepts Dawes Plan on reduced German reparations. Geneva Protocol on Wars of Aggression, 2 October.

1925   Locarno Pact between Britain, France, Germany, Italy and Belgium, 1 December, guaranteed the current West European borders.
Geneva Protocol, 17 June, prohibited use of 'inhumane' methods of warfare.
Russo-Japanese Treaty, 20 January.
Russo-Turkish Treaty of Security.

1926   Reassurance Treaty between Russia and Germany, 24 April.
Anglo-Turkish agreement on Mosul, 5 June.
Alliance between USA and Panama, 28 July.
Treaty of Friendship between Italy and Albania, 27 November.

1927   Anglo-Iraqi Treaty, 14 December.
Alliance between Albania and Italy, 22 November.
Russo-Persian non-aggression Pact, 1 October.

1928   Briand-Kellogg Pact, 27 August, between Britain, France, the United States, Germany, Italy and Japan, renounced war as a means to settle disputes. Later adhered to by other states.
Italo-Abyssinian Treaty of Friendship, 2 August; Italo-Greek Treaty of Friendship, 23 September.

1929   Eastern Pact between Russia, Estonia, Latvia, Poland, Romania,
        9 February; joined by Turkey, 27 February.
        Lateran Treaties of Italy and Vatican, 11 February; Young
        Report on Reparations by Germany, 7 June.
        Kellogg Pact came into force, 24 July.
        Inter-American treaty of arbitration, 5 January.

1930   London Naval Agreement, 22 April, between Britain, France,
        the United States, Japan and Italy, expanded the 1922
        Washington agreements.
        Young Plan came into force, 17 May.
        Britain recognized independence of Iraq, 30 June.

1931   Russo-Turkish agreement on naval reductions in Black Sea, 8
        March.
        Protocol on Hoover Plan, 11 August, to suspend German
        reparations for one year.
        Statute of Westminster, 31 December, defined structure of
        British Commonwealth and recognized dominions as
        'autonomous communities'.

1932   Geneva Protocol on Germany's equality of rights, 11 December.
        Anglo-French Pact of Friendship, 13 July.
        Imperial Economic Conference at Ottawa signed Ottawa
        Agreements, 20 August, introducing limited preferential tariffs
        within British Empire.
        Franco-Russian non-aggression pact, 29 November.
        Russo-Polish non-aggression pact, 25 January and 27
        November.

1933   London Convention on definition of aggression signed by ten
        states, 3–5 July.
        Russo-German treaties of 1926 and 1929 extended, 5 May.
        Four-Power Pact signed in Rome, 15 July. (Britain, France, Italy
        and Germany).
        Anglo-German trade pact, 27 April.
        Non-aggression pact between Latin American countries signed
        in Rio, 11 October.

1934   Non-aggression pact between Germany and Poland, 26
        January. Balkan Pact, 9 February, with Romania, Greece,
        Yugoslavia and Turkey.
        USA agrees independence of Philippines from 1945, 24 March.
        Russo-Finnish non-aggression pact for ten years, 7 April.
        Peruvian-Colombian settlement over Leticia Bay, 24 May.
        Sudanese-Libyan border agreed, 20 July.
        Baltic States Collaboration Treaty, 12 September.

1935   Franco-Italian agreement, 6 January, concerning colonies and
        Austria.
        Alliance between France and Russia, 2 May, providing for
        mutual aid against aggression.
        Anglo-German naval agreement, 18 June.
        Russo-Czech Pact of mutual assistance, 16 May.
        Russo-Turkish Treaty extended for ten years, 7 November.

1936   Peace Treaty between Bolivia and Paraguay ending Chaco War,
        21 January.
        Treaty between USA and Panama, 2 March.
        Convention on the Straits signed at Montreux, 20 July; Turkey
        recovers control over Bosphorus and Dardanelles.
        Anglo-Egyptian Treaty, 26 August, terminates military
        occupation.
        Non-intervention agreement between Britain, France, Germany
        and Italy, 7 August, against involvement in Spanish affairs.
        Germany and Japan sign Anti-Comintern Pact, 24 November.

1937   Anglo-Italian agreement signed, 2 January.
        Polish-Danzig agreement, 7 January.
        Italo-Yugoslav Pact, 26 March.
        Non-aggression Pact between Afghanistan, Iran and Turkey, 8
        July.
        Anglo-Russian and Anglo-German naval agreements signed, 17
        July.
        Italy joins Anti-Comintern Pact, 6 November.

1938   Britain and Republic of Ireland signed agreement, 25 April.
        Munich Agreement, 29 September, between Britain, France,
        Germany and Italy forces Czechoslovakia to cede territory to
        Germany, Hungary and Poland.
        Libya declared part of Italy, 25 October.
        Eighth Pan-American Conference in Lima issues 'Declaration of
        Lima' against 'all foreign intervention', 26 December.
        Russo-Polish declaration of friendship, 28 December.

1939   France and Britain guarantee Polish integrity, 31 March.
        'Pact of Steel', 22 May, between Germany and Italy formalized
        Rome-Berlin 'Axis'.
        German-Soviet non-aggression pact, 23 August, for mutual aid,
        neutrality and spheres of influence in eastern Europe.
        Russo-Japanese armistice, 16 September.
        Russia secures naval and air bases in Estonia, Latvia and
        Lithuania, 28 September-10 October.
        Anglo-French-Turkish pact of mutual assistance, 19 October.

1940   Treaty of Moscow, 12 March, established peace between
        Russia and Finland after 'Winter War', Finns cede territory.
        Tripartite Pact between Japan, Germany and Italy, 27
        September.

1941   America signed Lend-Lease Bill for aid to Britain, 11 March.
        Soviet-Japanese Neutrality Pact, 13 April.
        German non-aggression pact with Turkey, 18 June.
        Atlantic Charter by Roosevelt and Churchill, 11 August.

1942   Washington Pact of 26 United Nations, 1 January.
        Anglo-Soviet 20-year treaty, 20 May.

1943   Casablanca conference of Allies agreed on demand for
        'unconditional surrender' of Germany, 26 January.
        Marshal Badoglio of Italy signed secret armistice with Allies, 25
        July.

Quebec meeting on Allied strategy, 11-24 August.
Cairo meeting of Roosevelt, Churchill and Chiang Kai-shek,
22-26 November.
Teheran meeting of Roosevelt, Churchill and Stalin, 26
November-2 December.

1944   Bretton Woods Agreement, July, to set up a World Bank and
International Monetary Fund.
Russia signed armistice with Finland, 4 September, ending
Finnish involvement in war.
Russia signed armistice with Romania, 12 September.
Moscow conference between Churchill and Stalin, 9-19 October.

1945   Armistice signed with Hungary, 20 January.
Yalta Agreement, 11 February, between Britain, Russia and the
United States on the future of Germany, Europe and world
security.
Pact of Union of Arab States in Cairo, 22 March, set up Arab
League.
United Nations Charter, 26 June, established new world forum
with Britain, Russia, France, the United States and China as
leading powers.
Potsdam Agreement between Britain, Russia and the United
States, 2 August, expanded on the Yalta Agreement.

1946   Treaty of London recognizes Transjordan as independent state,
25 May.
Linggadjati Agreement, 15 November, between Dutch and
Indonesians on creation of Indonesian Republic.
World Bank set up, 27 December.

1947   Peace Treaties, 10 February, with Italy, Finland, Hungary,
Bulgaria and Romania.
Treaty of Dunkirk, 4 March, between Britain and France
promised mutual aid against German aggression.
Benelux customs union created, 14 March, between Belgium,
Holland and Luxembourg.
Marshall Plan, 5 June; aid for reconstruction accepted by 16
European countries through European Recovery Programme.
British announced Indian Independence, setting up states of
India and Pakistan, 5 July.
UN voted for partition of Palestine into Jewish and Arab states,
29 November.

1948   Brussels Treaty, 17 March, between Britain, France, Belgium,
Holland and Luxembourg, providing for mutual aid against
aggression, and for economic and social co-operation.
Organization for European Economic Co-operation (OEEC) formed
by sixteen West European nations, 16 April.
Treaty forming Organization of American States (OAS) for joint
resistance to attack, signed 30 April, by United States and 20
other Central and Latin American states to come into force in 1951.

1949   Comecon (Council for Mutual Economic Assistance) set up, 25

January by USSR and communist eastern European states for economic co-ordination and development.

North Atlantic Treaty, 4 April, between the United States, Canada, Britain, France, Belgium, Holland, Luxembourg, Norway, Denmark, Portugal and Iceland for mutual aid against aggression.

Statute of the Council of Europe, 5 May, by ten West European states.

Israel signed armistice with Egypt, 24 February; Jordan, 3 April; Syria, 20 July, establishing effective borders of new Israeli state.

The Hague conference reached agreement on independence of Indonesia, 2 November.

1950   US-South Korea defence agreement, 26 January.
Colombo Plan formed, 28 November, for economic development of Commonwealth countries in Asia.

1951   Pacific Security Treaty between United States, Australia, and New Zealand (ANZUS Pact), 1 September.
Japanese Peace Treaty, 8 September, with 48 other powers; Japan signed Mutual Security Pact with the United States permitting them to remain indefinitely in Japan.

1952   US-Japanese Agreement, 28 February, on bases in Japan.
Treaty between France, West Germany, Italy, Belgium, Holland and Luxembourg, 27 May, created European Defence Community.
US-Israeli defence agreement, 23 July.

1953   Armistice signed in Korean War, 27 July, at Panmunjon.
Mutual defence agreement between United States and Spain, 26 September, allowing US bases.
Mutual Defence Treaty of United States with South Korea, 1 October.

1954   Truce signed in Indochinese War, 21 July, partitioning North and South Vietnam.
Peace agreement in Geneva, 11 August, about future of Vietnam, not signed by US or South Vietnam.
South East Asia Collective Defence Treaty, 8 September, signed by US and 7 other nations pledging joint action to protect South Vietnam and other nations in the area.
London Agreement, 3 October, extends Brussels Pact to West Germany and Italy, forming the West European Union.
Mutual Defence Treaty with Nationalist China by United States, 2 December.

1955   US-Canadian agreement on operation of Early Warning System, 5 May (extended in 1958 to set up NORAD, North American Air Defence Command).
London and Paris Agreements, 5 May, gave West Germany full sovereignty and brought her into North Atlantic Treaty Organization.
Warsaw Pact formed, 13 May, between Russia and eastern bloc powers for mutual assistance in the event of war.

Austrian State Treaty, 15 May, between Britain, the United States, Russia and France established Austria as neutral, sovereign state.

1957   Treaty of Rome, 22 March, between France, West Germany, Italy, Belgium, Holland and Luxembourg established European Economic Community.
UN International Atomic Energy Agency for peaceful use of atomic energy set up, 29 July.

1959   Ten-Power Committee on Disarmament set up, 7 September, representing Britain, Canada, France, Italy, the United States, Bulgaria, Czechoslovakia, Poland, Romania and the Soviet Union.
Treaty for peaceful use of Antarctica opened for signature, 1 December.

1960   Japanese-US Treaty of mutual security, 19 January.
Stockholm Convention, 3 May, between Britain, Denmark, Norway, Portugal, Austria, Sweden and Switzerland set up European Free Trade Association.
Indus Waters Treaty, 19 September, between Pakistan and India.

1961   Organization for Economic Co-operation and Development (OECD), 30 September, replaced the OEEC and includes United States and Canada.

1963   Treaty of Co-operation between France and West Germany, 22 January.
Partial Test-Ban Treaty, 5 August, between Britain, the United States and Russia limiting nuclear testing.
'Hot-line' agreement reached between the United States and Soviet Union, 5 April.

1966   Malaysian-Indonesian Agreement, 1 June, ending 'confrontation'.

1967   Treaty banning nuclear weapons in space opened for signature in London, Moscow and Washington, 27 January.
Treaty of Tlatelolco, prohibiting nuclear weapons in Latin America, agreed for signature in Mexico City, 14 February.
Egypt and Jordan signed anti-Israel Pact, 30 May.
Iraq joined anti-Israel Pact, 4 June.

1968   UN Security Council called for permanent peace settlement in Middle East, 22 November.
Nuclear Non-Proliferation Treaty agreed and opened for signature, 1 July.

1969   Disarmament Committee renamed Conference of the Committee on Disarmament with 24 members, 26 August.

1970   Standstill cease-fire between Egypt and Israel in Suez Canal Zone, 7 August.
Treaty between West Germany and Russia, 12 August, renounced use of war.
Treaty between West Germany and Poland, 18 November, renounced use of war and confirmed existing borders.

1971   Sea-bed Treaty prohibiting use of sea-bed for nuclear weapons opened for signatures, 11 February.
        Five-power agreement of Britain, Australia, New Zealand, Singapore and Malaysia on defence of Singapore and Malaysia, 9 January.

1972   Salt I anti-ballistic missile (ABM) agreement and five-year interim agreement on limitation of strategic arms signed by US and Soviet Union, 26 May.
        Simla Peace Agreement between India and Pakistan, 3 July; 'Line of control' in Kashmir agreed, 11 December.

1973   Israeli-Egyptian agreement on cease-fire line following Yom Kippur War, 11 November.

1974   Protocol to the US-Soviet Salt ABM agreement limited deployment to a single area, 3 July; US-Soviet Threshold Test Ban Treaty signed, limiting underground nuclear tests, 3 July.
        Vladivostok Accord between United States and Soviet Union, 24 November, established framework for future negotiations controlling strategic arms race.
        Israeli-Egyptian Agreement on disengagement of forces on Suez Canal, 18 January.
        Israeli-Syrian agreement on disengagement on Golan Heights, 5 June.

1975   Act of the Helsinki Conference, 'Helsinki Agreement', 1 August, between 35 nations regarding European security, including a reaffirmation of human rights and proposals for economic collaboration between eastern and western 'blocs'.
        Israeli-US agreement on establishment of early warning system in Sinai, 1 September.
        Israeli-Egyptian agreement for Israeli withdrawal from Sinai and establishment of a buffer zone, 4 September.

1976   US-Soviet Treaty restricting nuclear explosions for peaceful purposes, 28 May.

1978   Camp David agreements between Israel and Egypt for conclusion of peace treaty and overall Middle East settlement, 17 September.

1979   Israeli-Egyptian Peace Treaty, 26 March.
        Salt II Agreement signed by United States and Soviet Union restricting numbers of strategic offensive weapons, 18 June, ratification withheld by the United States.
        Lancaster House Agreement, London, 15 December, ended war in Zimbabwe and created independent state from April 1980.

1981   US, Israel and Egypt signed agreement for peace-keeping force in Sinai, 10 July.
        Inhumane Weapons Convention signed in Geneva, 18 May.

1982   Israeli-Egyptian agreement on Sinai, 19 January, completed Israeli withdrawal.

1984   Lusaka Accord between Angola and South Africa, 16 February;

South Africa agreed to withdraw from Angola and SWAPO to withdraw from Namibia.

Nkomati Accord between Mozambique and South Africa, 1 March; mutual non-aggression agreement and to seek end to civil war in Mozambique.

US-Soviet agreement to expand and improve 'Hot Line', 17 July.

Sino-British declaration on return of Hong Kong to China, 26 September.

1985   All Pacific nations sign Treaty of Raratonga, aimed at creating a nuclear-free zone in the Pacific.

1987   Cease-fire agreement reached in Iran-Iraq War, 20 August, policed by UN.

Arias Peace Plan signed by Presidents of Central American states to end war in Nicaragua, 1 August.

Intermediate Nuclear Force (INF) Treaty signed between United States and Soviet Union, 8 December.

1988   Geneva accord, 14 May, for withdrawal of Soviet forces from Afghanistan, beginning 15 May 1988 and to be concluded by February 1989; Pakistan and Afghanistan agreed non-interference in each others' affairs.

Cease-fire agreement in Geneva, 1 August, reached over Namibia; timetable for withdrawal of Cuban forces from Angola reached in November; UN Transition Assistance Group to supervise progress to full Namibian independence on 1 April 1990.

All Cuban forces to leave Angola by July 1991.

The League of Nations

1916   President Wilson first suggests the need for a 'Peace League'.

1918   Wilson's 'Fourteen Points' includes the idea of an association of nations (Jan.); Jan Smuts publishes *The League of Nations: A Practical Suggestion* (Nov.), proposing a wide-ranging organization to deal with problems of international co-operation, disarmament, colonies, and social and labour problems.

1919   At Paris Peace Conference, 27 nations agree to Wilson's proposal for a League of Nations (Feb.). The Agreement or Covenant setting up the League is written into the Treaties of Versailles (28 June) and Saint-Germain (10 Sept.). Headquarters of League set up in Geneva. Albert Thomas, French Socialist, first director of the International Labour Organization, one of the League's committees; other committees established to deal with world health, communications, and education, not restricted to signatories of the Covenant. League begins allocation of mandates of former colonies to victorious powers and their allies. First defiance of League's authority when Italian poet and adventurer D'Annunzio seizes part of Fiume from the League on behalf of Italy (Sept.).
Germany condemns the League of Nations as biased in favour of the Allies (June); first signs of hostility to the Covenant in the United States – Wilson goes on pro-League tour of the United States (Sept.).
United States Senate votes against amended League of Nations in two votes (Nov.).

1920   United States boycotts first meeting of the League (Jan.); membership of League finally rejected by Senate (March).
Turks repudiate Treaty of Sèvres and defy League of Nations (see p. 9).
League fixes German war reparations of 3,000,000,000 million marks for 30 years (April).
Poland launches war against Russia in defiance of League and seizes Vilna from Lithuania.
Permanent Court of Justice set up in The Hague to advise on legal matters.
China and Austria admitted to the League (Dec.).

1921   New US President Harding rejects the League of Nations (April); Baltic States join the League (Sept.). League arbitrates dispute between Sweden and Finland over Aaland islands.

1922   League arbitrates between Colombia and Venezuela.

1923   Lithuania seizes Memel from League; League eventually approves its possession (May 1924).
Italy bombards and occupies Greek island of Corfu after Italian general killed on Greek-Albanian border, in defiance of League of Nations. Paris-based Conference of Ambassadors agrees to ask for Greek apology and compensation and Italians withdraw.

1924   League accepts draft of protocol outlawing war (Sept.); presented to League Assembly (Oct.) with provision for economic sanctions to enforce judgements. 47 League members agree to compulsory arbitration of conflicts.

1925   League successfully arbitrates between Chile and Peru; induces Greeks to withdraw from Bulgaria and pay compensation (Oct.).

1926   Turkey accepts League of Nations' arbitration over Mosul. League's Disarmament Commission arranges Disarmament Conference. Disarmament Commission urges world disarmament and begins preparation of draft convention on disarmament.
Germany admitted to the League.
Brazil and Spain leave the League.

1927   League given supervisory role over German rearmament with end of Allied military control of Germany.

1928   28 League members accept Kellogg-Briand Pact.

1930   League's Disarmament Commission puts forward draft convention on disarmament but USSR and Germany vote against it.

1931   China appeals to League of Nations over Japanese aggression in Manchuria. League sends Commission under Lord Lytton.

1932   Japanese refuse to leave Manchuria and declare it to be the state of Manchukuo. Lytton Commission reports, condemning Japanese aggression and demanding their withdrawal (Oct.). League pressure leads to Japanese withdrawal from Shanghai but not from Manchuria.

1932–34   World Disarmament Conference meets but fails to make any substantial progress; Hitler leaves the Conference (Oct. 1933).

1933   Japan leaves the League of Nations after her condemnation over Manchuria (March) and extends her conquests into Jehol in Northern China.

1934   USSR joins the League of Nations (Sept.)
Italy rejects League arbitration in dispute with Abyssinia (Ethiopia) (Dec.)

1935   Abyssinia's plea for League assistance (Jan.) is debated (Feb.) but no action taken.
Saar plebiscite under League supervision permits Saar to be reunited with Germany (Jan.).
League condemns German rearmament (April) but with no effect.
League appoints five-power Commission on Abyssinia (May); Italy offered concessions in Abyssinia but refused by Abyssinia (Sept.) Mussolini's invasion of Abyssinia (Oct.) condemned as aggression by League which imposes economic sanctions.
Germany leaves the League (Oct.).

1936   Italy threatened with oil embargo if it continues war against Abyssinia (March).

Haile Selassie addresses League calling for assistance against Italian aggression (June).
Sanctions against Italy abandoned (July).

1937   League condemns Japanese invasion of China (Sept.)
Italy leaves the League (Dec.).

1939   Spain leaves the League (May); USSR expelled for invasion of Finland (Dec.).

1944   Meeting in San Francisco of delegates of 46 states to replace the League of Nations with the United Nations Organization (April).

1946   League of Nations formally dissolved (April); some of its committees, such as the ILO and World Health Organization, become agencies of the United Nations.

The United Nations

1941 June 12   Inter-Allied Declaration signed in London by all nations then at war with Germany to work for a 'world in which, relieved of the menace of aggression, all may enjoy economic and social security'.

Aug. 14   Atlantic Charter issued by US President Franklin D. Roosevelt and British Prime Minister Winston Churchill detailing eight points to 'base their hopes for a better future for the world'.

1942 Jan. 1   Declaration by United Nations signed by 26 nations in Washington approving basic points of Atlantic Charter; first official use of name 'United Nations'.

1943 Oct. 30   Moscow Declaration on General Security signed by Britain, China, Soviet Union and United States, recognizing 'the necessity of establishing at the earliest practicable date a general international organization, based on the principle of sovereign equality'.

1944 Aug. 21   Dumbarton Oaks Conference in Washington, D.C. at which representatives of 39 nations discuss over three months proposals for establishing United Nations organization, agreeing on Security Council as executive branch of UN.

1945 June 26   UN Charter approved by delegates of 50 nations at international conference in San Francisco.

Oct. 16   Food and Agriculture Organization of United Nations established to improve consumption, production and distribution of food throughout world.

Oct. 24   UN Charter goes into effect upon ratification by majority of nations, including Britain, China, France, Soviet Union, and United States. Date celebrated annually as United Nations Day.

1946 Jan. 10   UN General Assembly begins first meeting in London with delegates of 51 nations as members. Trygve Lie of Norway is elected first Secretary-General of UN.

June 25   International Bank for Reconstruction and Development begins operations to assist nations by government loans.

Nov. 4   UNESCO, United Nations Educational, Scientific and Cultural Organization, formed to promote international co-operation in solving problems such as illiteracy.

Dec. 14   Gift of $8,500,000 from US millionaire John D. Rockefeller Jr. accepted by UN to buy 18 acres in New York City as site of permanent headquarters.

1947 Apr. 4	International Civil Aviation Organization established to develop international standards and regulations for civil aviation.
1948 Apr. 7	World Health Organization established to promote world health.
Sept. 17	UN peace negotiator Count Folke Bernadotte of Sweden assassinated in Jerusalem while trying to arrange truce in fighting between Arabs and Israelis.
Dec. 10	Universal Declaration of Human Rights adopted by UN General Assembly.
1949 Jan. 1	Cease-fire between India and Pakistan obtained by UN to end two years of fighting over control of Kashmir.
Feb.–July	Cease-fire agreements arranged between Israel and Arab states by UN negotiator Ralph J. Bunche.
Dec. 27	Netherlands grants independence to Indonesia after conference arranged by UN to settle fighting.
1950 Mar. 23	World Meteorological Organization established to promote international reporting and observations of weather.
June 27	UN Security Council calls for member nations to send troops to aid South Korea, which had been attacked by communist North Korea. Soviet Union was boycotting meetings of Security Council at this time and so could not veto measure. Troops of US and 15 other nations dispatched to aid South Korea.
1953 July 27	UN signs truce with North Korea, ending over three years of fighting.
1956 Nov. 7	UN obtains cease-fire in Suez Canal fighting between Egypt and Israeli-British-French forces; sends UN Emergency Force to supervise truce.
1957 July 29	International Atomic Energy Agency created to promote peaceful uses of atomic energy.
1961 Sept. 13	UN troops begin fighting in Congo (now Zaire) to restore order in civil war.
Sept. 18	UN Secretary-General Dag Hammarskjold killed in air crash in Africa while on Congo peace mission.
Nov. 3	U Thant of Burma elected as UN's third Secretary-General to succeed Dag Hammarskjold.
1964 Mar. 4	UN peace-keeping force sent to Cyprus to prevent fighting between Turkish and Greek forces.
1966 Dec. 16	UN Security Council asks member nations to stop trading with Rhodesia because of its policies against Blacks.
1967 June 10	UN negotiates truce in Six-Day Israeli-Arab War.

1971 Oct. 25	Communist China admitted to UN and Nationalist China expelled by 76–35 vote of General Assembly.
Dec. 13	UN General Assembly votes 79 to 7 with 36 abstentions for Israel to restore to Arab countries territories acquired by force.
1972	Kurt Waldheim appointed UN Secretary-General on resignation of U Thant.
1973 Oct. 22	Cease-fire in 17-day-old Middle East War ordered by UN Security Council.
Oct. 25	UN peace-keeping force sent to Middle East to prevent further fighting between Arab nations and Israel.
1974	Special session of UN General Assembly establishes emergency relief fund for poor nations of world.
1975	International Women's Year declared by UN to promote women's equality.
1977 Nov. 4	Mandatory embargo on military supply shipments to South Africa ordered by UN; first such action against UN member.
1978	UN 6,100-man peace-keeping force stationed in southern Lebanon: Brings withdrawal of Israeli troops that invaded in March.
1982	Perez de Cuellar becomes Secretary-General.
1987 Aug. 20	UN Secretary-General, Perez de Cuellar, negotiates cease-fire in Iran-Iraq War. UN observer group police the truce.
1988	UN Transition Assistance Group supervise cease-fire in Namibia and elections prior to independence.
1990	UN membership reaches 160 with admission of Namibia.

The new nations since 1914[1]

Algeria	French Algeria until 1962.
Angola	Portuguese Angola until 1975.
Austria	rump state, created in 1918 from German-speaking part of former Austro-Hungarian Empire.
Bangladesh	prior to 1947 part of British Indian Empire; 1947–71 known as East Pakistan.
Belize	British Honduras until 1973, independent in 1981.
Benin	until 1960 part of French West Africa; then Dahomey until 1975.
Bhutan	formerly semi-autonomous kingdom linked to British Indian Empire.
Botswana	British Bechuanaland until 1966.
Brunei	former British protectorate in British Borneo.
Burkina Faso	formerly French Upper Volta; then Upper Volta until 1984.
Burundi	formerly part of German East Africa (to 1919), thereafter part of Belgian controlled Ruanda-Urundi. Urundi became Burundi in 1962.
Cameroon	formerly French and British Cameroon. French Cameroon became independent in 1960, and in 1961 part of British Cameroon acceded to the independent, former French Cameroon to form a two-state Federal Republic, the United Republic of Cameroon in 1972 and the Republic of Cameroon in 1984.
Cape Verde	Portuguese Cape Verde until 1975.
Central African Republic	formerly part of French Equatorial Africa.
Chad	formerly part of French Equatorial Africa.
Congo	formerly part of French Equatorial Africa.
Czechoslovakia	formerly part of Austro-Hungarian Empire (pre-1918).
Djibouti	French Somaliland until 1967, then French territory of Afars and Issas.
Egypt	British Protectorate until 1922.
Equatorial Guinea	formerly Spanish Territory of the Gulf of Guinea.

1 *Some smaller states have been excluded.*

Finland	part of Russian Empire until 1917 as autonomous Grand Duchy.
Gabon	formerly part of French Equatorial Africa.
Gambia	formerly British Gambia, now part of Confederation of Senegambia (with Senegal).
German Democratic Republic	(East Germany) formerly part of the united German state, divided as a result of World War II, but excluding part of former German state lost to present state of Poland.
German Federal Republic	(West Germany) formerly part of the united German state divided as a result of World War II.
Ghana	formerly British Gold Coast, including British Togoland, formerly German Togoland (to 1922).
Greenland	formerly a province of Denmark (to 1979).
Grenada	formerly part of British Windward Islands.
Guinea	formerly French Guinea.
Guinea-Bissau	formerly Portuguese Guinea.
Guyana	formerly British Guiana.
Hungary	up to 1918 part of the dual monarchy of Austria-Hungary and the Austro-Hungarian Empire.
India	formerly part of the British Indian Empire, then comprising present-day Pakistan and Bangladesh.
Indonesia	formerly Dutch East Indies.
Ireland, Republic of	formerly the Irish Free State, a dominion of Great Britain (1921–48), previous to 1921 part of the United Kingdom. Also known as Eire, 1921–48.
Israel	created in 1948 out of Palestine, a British mandated territory from 1920, previously part of Turkish Empire.
Ivory Coast	formerly French Ivory Coast.
Jamaica	British colony of Jamaica until 1962.
Jordan	formerly Transjordan (from 1922), part of the united Palestine mandate of Britain (1920–22), previously part of Turkish Empire.
Kampuchea	formerly Cambodia (from 1953), previously part of French-Indochina.
Kenya	formerly British colony of Kenya (to 1963), known as British East Africa to 1920.
Korea, North	formerly part of Japanese-controlled Korea (1910–45); created separate state in 1948.

Korea, South	formerly part of Japanese-controlled Korea (1910–45); created separate state in 1948.
Kuwait	protected status under Britain until independent state in 1961.
Laos	formerly part of French Indochina.
Lebanon	French mandated territory 1920–43, previously part of Turkish empire.
Lesotho	British protectorate of Basutoland until 1966.
Libya	formerly Tripoli (as Italian colony, 1911–45).
Malawi	formerly part of Federation of Rhodesia and Nyasaland (1953–64), previously British protectorate of Nyasaland.
Malaysia	formerly the Federation of Malaya (to 1963), previously known as the Straits Settlements and the Federated Malay States.
Mali	formerly (with Senegal) the Federation of Mali (1959–60); previously part of French West Africa.
Mauritania	French colony of Mauritania until 1960.
Mongolia	prior to 1924 Outer Mongolia.
Morocco	formerly French Morocco (to 1956) and Spanish Morocco which became part of independent Morocco in 1969.
Mozambique	Portuguese Mozambique until 1975.
Myanmar	formerly Burma until 1989. Burma was part of British India before Independence.
Namibia	formerly South West Africa (to 1990), prior to 1920 German South-West Africa.
Niger	formerly French West Africa.
Pakistan	prior to 1947 part of British Indian Empire.
Papua New Guinea	formerly (from 1920–45) Australian mandated territory, thereafter Australian-governed to 1975. Prior to 1920 the area comprised German New Guinea and Australian-run Papua.
Philippines	American colony from 1898 until independence in 1946.
Poland	an ancient kingdom, but prior to 1918 Poland's territory formed part of the German, Austro-Hungarian and Russian Empires. In 1945 its boundaries were substantially altered.
Rwanda	part of German East Africa to 1919, then mandated to Belgium as part of Ruanda-Urundi and following World War II part of United Nations trust territory of Ruanda-Urundi under Belgian administration. In 1962 Ruanda became the separate state of Rwanda.

Saudi Arabia	proclaimed the kingdom of Saudi Arabia in 1932, previously comprising kingdom of Hejaz and Arabia.
Senegal	formerly part of French West Africa, in 1959 joined with French Sudan, present day Mali, in Federation of Mali, but from 1960 independent. In 1982 formed Confederation of Senegambia with Gambia.
Sierra Leone	British Sierra Leone until 1961.
Singapore	British Crown Colony, then part of Malaysia 1963–65.
Somalia	formerly British and Italian Somaliland, united as an independent state in 1960.
Sri Lanka	British colony of Ceylon to independence in 1948; in 1972 changed name to Sri Lanka.
Sudan	Anglo-Egyptian Sudan until independence in 1956.
Surinam	Dutch Guiana to 1954 when became an autonomous part of the Netherlands, independent from 1975.
Syria	prior to 1918 part of Turkish Empire, then placed under French League of Nations mandate until independence in 1946.
Taiwan	ceded to Japan in 1895, the island of Formosa returned to China in 1945, but from 1949 became base for Nationalist Chinese State under Chiang Kai-Shek.
Tanzania	formerly German East Africa (to 1918), then League of Nations mandated territory of Tanganyika under British control. Following independence in 1961, it joined with Zanzibar (independent in 1963) in 1964 to form Tanzania.
Thailand	known as Siam until 1939.
Togo	German Togoland until 1918 when mandated under British and French control, then United Nations Trust territory. In 1957 British Togoland joined with the Gold Coast and became part of independent Ghana. French Togoland became independent in 1960.
Trinidad and Tobago	British colony of Trinidad and Tobago until 1962.
Tunisia	French protectorate until independence in 1956.
Turkey	formerly the central part of the Turkish Empire which included much of the Middle East and Arabia. The Turkish Republic was founded in 1923, comprising most of the modern area of Turkey.
Uganda	British protectorate until independence in 1962.
Union of Soviet Socialist Republics	formerly the Russian Empire (to 1917).

United Arab Emirates	known as the Trucial States prior to 1971.
Vietnam	part of French Indochina to 1954 when separated into North and South Vietnam, reunited as a single state in 1975.
Western Sahara	formerly known as Spanish Morocco to 1956 when divided between Mauritania and Morocco; in 1979 Mauritania relinquished its claim but it remains disputed between Morocco and an independence movement, the Polisario Front.
Yemen Arab Republic	part of the Turkish Empire until 1918, when passed to local tribal control, becoming the Yemen Arab Republic in 1962.
Yemen, Peoples' Democratic Republic	formerly under British control, including part of Aden as the protectorate of Aden; independent from 1967.
Yugoslavia	before 1918 the independent kingdom of Serbia and parts of the Austro-Hungarian Empire and Bulgaria. In 1918 Yugoslavia created as kingdom of Serbs, Croats and Slovenes.
Zaire	formerly Belgian Congo until independence in 1959; name changed to Zaire in 1971.
Zambia	formerly known as Northern Rhodesia and a British protectorate; in 1953 combined with Southern Rhodesia and Nyasaland in a Federation, dissolved in 1963, becoming independent Republic of Zambia in 1964.
Zimbabwe	formerly known as British Southern Rhodesia; in 1953 combined with Northern Rhodesia and Nyasaland in a Federation, dissolved in 1963, becoming British colony of Rhodesia. It declared independence in 1965 as Rhodesia, but following the war and agreement of 1979 became Zimbabwe.

Wars and major armed conflicts

Mexican Revolution and American interventions 1910–17

The Mexican Revolution began as peasant uprisings in the north, led by Madero in the state of Chihuahua, and in the south led by Zapata, in Moretos state. In 1911 President Diaz was forced to resign and Madero became President after an interim period. Initially disbanding his rebel armies, he used the Federal army to defeat a rising in the north and to contain the more leftward leaning forces of Zapata, who broke out into open revolution at the end of 1911 demanding radical land reform. A counter-revolution in Mexico City in 1914 led to three years of confused civil war with numerous factions led by irregular leaders, such as Francisco Villa in the north, who formed an unstable alliance with Zapata in the south. In 1914 American troops occupied Veracruz in retaliation for the arrest of American sailors, contributing to the overthrow of the counter-revolutionary regime in Mexico. In July, the moderate Carranza assumed the Presidency and was recognized by the US in 1915, but was forced to continue fighting the forces of Villa and Zapata. Villa's forces won an important battle at Torreon in 1914, but were defeated at Celaya in April 1915. Crossing the American border, Villa sacked Columbus, New Mexico in March 1916 and was pursued by General Pershing into Mexico until requested to withdraw by Carranza. A Congress summoned to Mexico in 1917 established a new constitution, bringing most large-scale fighting to an end.

The First World War 1914–18

On 28 July 1914 Austria-Hungary declared war on Serbia, whom she blamed for the assassination of the Austrian heir to the throne a month earlier. Austria was supported by her ally Germany, but they were faced by the 'Entente' powers, Russia, France and Britain. In late 1914 the Germans failed to capture Paris despite the boldness of their invasion plan (the Schlieffen Plan), and the war settled into the deadlock of trench warfare on the Western Front. In the East the Germans defeated the Russian invasion of East Prussia at Tannenberg and the Masurian Lakes. In 1915 the Entente tried to break the deadlock on the Western Front by expeditions to the Dardanelles and Salonika in south-east Europe, and by inducing Italy to attack Austria, but to no avail. In 1916 both sides launched grand offensives on the Western Front, the Germans against Verdun and the Allies on the Somme, but despite enormous casualties the deadlock continued. At sea the British and Germans fought the drawn battle of Jutland. In 1917 both sides were given hope, the Germans by the Russian Revolution (which eventually removed Russia from the war) and the Allies by the United States' entry into the war. The next year proved decisive. The Germans launched a last great offensive in spring 1918 but this was halted and American support tipped the scales the Allied way. Germany agreed to an armistice in November. Her allies, Austria and Turkey, had already given up the fight, the Austrians defeated at Vittorio Veneto in Italy and the Turks defeated by the British in Palestine and Mesopotamia. Although the major engagements were fought in Europe, British and Arab forces fought major campaigns against the Turks in Arabia and Palestine and Mesopotamia. In Africa, the German colonies of South-West Africa and Tanganyika were also the scene of fighting. In the Far East Japanese forces seized the German base of Kiaochow.

Anglo-Irish conflict 1916–21: Irish Civil War 1922–23

Rebellion broke out in Dublin on Easter Monday, 24 April 1916 (the 'Easter Rising'). The rebellion was suppressed by 1 May, and Sir Roger Casement and leaders of the rising were tried and executed. Open warfare began again in 1919, and atrocities by the Irish Republican Army were matched by those committed by a special force brought in by the British, the Black and Tans. Peace was formally established by a treaty recognizing the dominion status of the Irish Free State, signed on 8 December 1921. A Republican faction led by De Valera refused to acknowledge the Treaty and demanded inclusion of Ulster in the Irish state. Anti-treaty forces made raids on Ulster and arms raids in the south, but after seizing the Four Courts building in Dublin were forced to surrender and hunted down elsewhere by Free State forces. A cease-fire was accepted by Republican leaders in 1923.

Chinese Civil War and 'Northern Expedition' 1916–34

An unstable Government was formed in China following the Revolution of 1911. The death of the first President in 1916 brought into the open conflicts already just short of outright civil war. Although a semblance of government was maintained in Beijing, much of China fell prey to rival warlords who fought one another. From 1922 the communists and nationalists in the Guomindang began to co-operate, creating an army with which to reunite China. From the nationalist base in Canton, Chiang Kai-shek emerged after the death of Sun Yat-sen (1925) to lead the nationalist troops on the 'Northern Expedition', defeating the warlords of central and eastern China; in 1927 he occupied Nanjing, which became the capital. Following the seizure of Shanghai in the same year, Chiang Kai-shek turned against the communists, killing thousands of their activists and forcing many of them to flee south. Chiang carried his campaign across the Yellow River against the northern warlords. Although meeting a reverse when he attacked the Japanese forces in Shantung, Chiang entered Beijing on 8 June 1928 when it was evacuated by the northern warlord, Marshal Chang Tso-lin. Chiang Kai-shek now turned against the communist-controlled areas of the south in Jiangxi, Hunan, Fujian, and Hebei. In a series of campaigns, initially unsuccessful, Chiang forced the communists to evacuate their last bases in Jiangxi and undertake the 'Long March' in 1934. Meanwhile nationalist control of northern China remained weak, and growing Japanese involvement in Manchuria lead to its full-scale invasion of Manchuria in 1931–2.

The Russian Civil War and Russo-Polish War 1917–20

In November 1917 the communists seized power in Russia but were opposed by counter-revolutionary tsarist or 'White Russian' forces. In 1918 the victorious Allied powers intervened to assist the anti-Bolshevik forces. Allied and 'White Russian' forces attacked the Bolshevik strongholds around Moscow and Petrograd from the north, based on Archangel, from the Ukraine and Caucasus in the south and from Siberia along the route of the Trans-Siberian Railway. Poland also invaded Russia in April 1919. Gradually, the Red Army organized by Trotsky was able to defeat the individual 'White' armies, leading to the withdrawal of the Allied intervention forces and a Russian counter-attack on Poland. By 1920 the Bolshevik forces had defeated their rivals for power and secured control over the Soviet Union.

Third Afghan War 1919

In May 1919 Amir Amanullah declared a holy war (Jihad) against Britain, crossed the border and occupied Bagh. While Jalalabad and Kabul were bombarded by the RAF, a British expedition drove the Afghans out of Bagh and forced the Khyber Pass into Afghanistan. An armistice was agreed on 31 May and the treaty of Rawalpindi was signed on 8 August.

The Hungarian-Romanian War 1919

In 1919 a communist government under Bela Kun took power in Hungary. Resentful of the armistice terms proposed by the Allies after the war, the Hungarians invaded Slovakia and the Romanians, fearing that they too would be invaded themselves attacked Hungary to forestall any further communist advances. In August the Romanians captured Budapest and Bela Kun fled. The Romanians left in November. In 1920 Hungary's territorial losses were confirmed by the Treaty of the Trianon.

The Greek-Turkish War 1920–23

By the Treaty of Sèvres, 1920, the Allies handed territory in Asia Minor to Greek control, but the Turks refused to accept this change, and General Mustapha Kemal resisted the Greek occupation. In 1922 he drove the Greeks from their last stronghold at Smyrna, secured control of the area around Constantinople and overthrew the Ottoman Sultan. In 1923 the Allies renegotiated the peace treaty with Turkey at Lausanne.

The Moroccan Revolt – 'the Revolt of the Rif' – 1921–26

Abd el Krim led a revolt against Spanish colonial forces, defeating Spanish armies at Das Abara and Anual, in the latter killing 10,000 Spanish troops. In 1922 Abd el Krim set up a 'Rif Republic' and in 1924 defeated another Spanish army at Sidi Messaoud. An invasion of French Morocco was halted and a Franco-Spanish army under the command of Marshal Pétain defeated the Rifs, forcing Abd el Krim to surrender in 1926, ending the Rif Republic.

Sandino Revolt in Nicaragua and American intervention 1926–34

United States Marines had occupied Nicaragua since 1912 to support a conservative regime and protect American interests. In 1926 the Marines withdrew and a peasant army organized by Augusto Cesar Sandino took up arms in revolt. In 1927, 2,000 American troops returned but were unable to defeat the Sandino forces. Following a treaty giving some concessions to the peasants, troops were withdrawn in 1933. In 1934 Sandino was assassinated by the National Guard and two years later its commander, Somoza, became President with American support. The subsequent guerrilla movement founded in 1961, the Sandinista National Liberation Front (FSLN) was named in honour of Sandino while Somoza's son continued to rule until 1979 (see pp. 137–142).

Wahabi tribal unrest, 1928

Several thousand Wahabi tribesmen threatened Iraq and Kuwait, launching raids from the Arabian desert. Britain deployed armoured trains and squadrons of RAF planes to bomb and strafe the tribesmen.

Japanese invasion of Manchuria 1931–32

From their base in Kwantung, the Japanese seized the city of Mukden, alleging Chinese sabotage of the Japanese–financed South Manchurian Railway, and went on to over-run all of Chinese Manchuria by early 1932. Chinese appeals to the League of Nations led to no decisive action against the Japanese who created a puppet state, Manchukuo, in the conquered territory, under the deposed Manchu emperor Pu Yi. A Japanese attempt to seize the city of Shanghai, however, was frustrated by opposition from the League.

El Salvador peasant revolt 1931–32

Asturo Araujo became President in 1931 with popular peasant support but was immediately overthrown by General Hernandez. The coup sparked off a peasant revolt in 1932, led by Farabundo Marti, which was crushed by Hernandez's troops killing 20–30,000 peasants.

The Chaco War 1932–35

Minor wars in 1928–9 and 1931–2 between Bolivia and Paraguay over control of the disputed Chaco area of Paraguay flared into major war in May 1932, following the election of the hard-liner Daniel Salamanca as President of Bolivia. Although it had a larger population and resources, Bolivia's invading forces were repulsed and eventually pursued by Paraguayan forces into Bolivia. The defeats led to the overthrow of President Salamanca in December 1934, and in June

1935 Bolivia was forced to conclude a truce leaving Paraguay in possession of all the disputed area.

The Italo-Abyssinian War 1935–36

In October 1935 Mussolini invaded Abyssinia (Ethiopia) and caused an international outcry. An Anglo-French plan to partition Abyssinia between Italy and its ruler, Haile Selassie, failed, as did economic sanctions against Italy to force her to end her aggression. In May 1936 the Italian conquest was complete.

The Spanish Civil War 1936–39

In July 1936 Spanish generals, led by Franco, rose against the Republican government and plunged Spain into civil war. Despite international declarations against foreign involvement, Italy, Germany and Portugal aided the generals, and Russia and France helped the Republicans. In addition, International Brigades were formed by volunteers from many countries to fight for the Republicans, and helped to defeat the Nationalists in the battle of Guadalajara, 1937. But by early 1939 the Nationalists held most of Spain. They finally captured Madrid on 28 March. (See pp. 31–4).

The Sino-Japanese War 1937–45

In July 1937 the Japanese seized upon the pretext of fighting between Chinese and Japanese troops at the Marco Polo Bridge in Beijing to launch an all-out invasion of China, which the Japanese dubbed the 'China Incident'. The Japanese seized Shanghai after fierce fighting and took Nanjing and Guangzhou (Canton). The Chinese government was forced to abandon most of the Chinese coast and set up its capital in Chongqing (Chungking). Japanese forces were unable to conquer the whole of China, being resisted both by nationalist Chinese troops under Chiang Kai-shek and increasingly by the communist forces under Mao Zedong. Over half of all Japanese forces were still involved in China when war with the United States and Britain broke out in 1941. America gave assistance to the Chinese forces by airlifts from India. Communist forces waged a mainly guerrilla war in North China, while the nationalists stood on the defensive in the south-west. Clashes between the nationalist and communist forces in the run-up to Japanese surrender in August 1945 prefigured the struggle for control of China which brought Civil War (see p. 279) and eventual communist triumph.

The Russo-Japanese conflict, 1937–39

Russia and China signed a non-aggression pact in 1937 but when Japanese forces moved to the border of Manchuria, there was fighting with Russian forces. In 1939 there was further heavy fighting in Manchuria in which the Russians inflicted a sharp defeat on Japan. An armistice was followed by a non-aggression pact between Russia and Japan in April 1941.

The Russo-Finnish War (the 'Winter War') 1939–40 and 'Continuation War' 1941–44

War broke out on 30 November 1939 over Russian claims to Karelia, but Finnish resistance under Mannerheim led to several defeats before Finland was forced to make peace and to cede territory in Karelia and the northern border area with Russia. In June 1941 the Finns joined the Germans in war against Russia, fighting mainly on the Karelian front north of Leningrad. Finland made peace with Russia in 1944, when the defeat of Germany seemed inevitable.

Second World War 1939–45

German forces invaded Poland on 1 September 1939, which led to declarations of war by Britain and France on 3 September. The Germans invaded the Low Countries on 10 May 1940, and France was compelled to sign an armistice on 22 June. The British army was evacuated from Dunkirk, while in the 'Battle of Britain' the German Luftwaffe failed to defeat the RAF and establish air superiority which would have made an attempted invasion of Britain possible. Italy declared war on 10 June 1940, and Britain attacked Italian forces in North Africa. For over a year Britain and her Empire stood alone against the Axis powers. In 1941, however, the war was vastly extended, Japan joining the Axis and Russia, China and America joining Britain. The Japanese rapidly overran many of the European colonies in South-East Asia, but Hitler's invasion of Russia (June 1941) eventually proved a decisive mistake. In 1942 the Germans were defeated in North Africa and Russia, in 1943 the Allies invaded Italy, and in 1944 Britain and America opened the 'Second Front' in France. The Allies linked up with the Russians on the Elbe on 28 April 1945 and the Germans accepted unconditional surrender terms on 7 May. In the Far East, major Japanese forces remained committed to the indecisive war in China, but American forces in the 'island-hopping' campaign in the Pacific, and British forces via Burma, inflicted defeats on the Japanese forces. A huge bombing and submarine offensive had brought Japan near to defeat when atomic bombs were dropped on Hiroshima and Nagasaki in early August 1945. Japan surrendered on 14 August 1945.

The Greek Civil War, 1944–49

The Greek Civil War developed out of the rivalry between communist and monarchist partisans for control of Greece as the Axis forces retreated at the end of the Second World War. British troops were sent to aid the pro-monarchist forces in 1944, while the Soviet Union took the side of the communist insurgents. After 1945, American aid enabled British troops to remain in Greece and assist the return of the monarchy. Communist resistance was seriously weakened by the break between Yugoslavia and Russia in 1948, resulting in the closure of much of Greece's northern border to infiltration and aid. The Greek communists announced an end to open conflict in October 1949.

Palestine 1945–48

Guerrilla warfare was waged by Jewish Zionists against British mandate forces and the Arab population, to achieve an independent Jewish nation. On 22 July 1945 the King David Hotel in Jerusalem, housing the British headquarters, was blown up, leaving 92 dead or missing. With the proclamation of the independence of Israel on 14 May 1948, Britain surrendered her League of Nations mandate over Palestine and withdrew her armed forces.

Indonesian War of Independence 1945–49

The independence of the Republic of Indonesia (formerly Netherlands East Indies) was proclaimed by the nationalist leaders, Sukarno and Hatta, on 17 August 1945. British, Indian and Dutch troops began to arrive on 29 September 1945. British troops captured the rebel capital of Surabaya on 29 November 1945. The Dutch recognized the Indonesian Republic (comprising Java, Sumatra and Madura) on 13 November 1946. The withdrawal of British troops was completed on 30 November 1946. A nationalist uprising on West Java on 4 May, 1947 led to Dutch military action on Java on 20 July 1947. A truce arranged under UN auspices on 17 January 1948, broke down, and the Dutch occupied the rebel capital, Jogjakarta, on 19 December 1948. International opposition and guerrilla warfare led to the Dutch decision to withdraw, and to the independence of Indonesia on 27 December 1949.

Chinese Civil War 1946–49

Civil war between the national government under Chiang Kai-shek and the communist forces resumed after the defeat of Japan in August 1945. Through the mediation of General George C. Marshall, a truce was arranged on 14 January 1946. It broke down and American supplies to the nationalists were halted on 29 July 1946. A nationalist offensive in Shaahxi took the communist capital, Yenan, on 19 March 1947, but it was retaken in April 1948. As communist forces advanced, Beijing fell on 22 January 1949, Nanjing on 22 April 1949 and Shanghai on 27 May 1949. Mao Zedong proclaimed the People's Republic of China on 1 October 1949. The nationalists withdrew to Taiwan on 7 December 1949.

Philippines, Hukbalahap Insurgency 1946–54

When the Philippines became independent on 4 July 1946, the war-time communist Anti-Japanese People's Liberation Army, or Hukbalahaps, waged a guerrilla campaign against the government of the republic. By 1950 the Hukbalahaps, with an army of 15,000 men and support of the peasantry, had established control over central Luzon. With American backing, however, a new defence secretary, Ramon Magsaysay, revitalized the Philippine armed forces. Counter-insurgency operations, together with a programme of land reform and the resettlement of dissidents, meant that by 1954 the revolt had petered out. The Hukbalahap leader, Luis Taruc, surrendered on 17 May 1954.

First Indochina War 1946–54

Following the surrender of Japan, Ho Chi Minh proclaimed the Democratic Republic of Vietnam at Hanoi on 2 September 1945. French and British forces regained control in Saigon, and after negotiations, French troops entered Hanoi on 16 March 1946. After French naval forces shelled the Vietnamese quarter of Haiphong on 23 November 1946, an abortive Viet Minh uprising took place in Hanoi on 19 December 1946. Guerrilla warfare grew into full-scale conflict between the French and the Viet Minh forces under General Giap. On 20 November 1953 the French established a forward base at Dien Bien Phu to lure the Viet Minh into a set-piece battle, but the garrison of 15,000 men was overwhelmed on 7 May 1954. An agreement for a cease-fire and the division of the country at latitude 17°N was signed at the Geneva Conference on 27 July 1954.

Indo-Pakistan War 1947–49

A rebellion by the Muslim majority in Kashmir led the Hindu maharajah to accede to the Indian Union, and Indian troops were flown into Kashmir on 27 October 1947. Pakistan sent aid to the Muslim Azad ('free') Kashmir irregulars, and Pakistani army units crossed into Kashmir in March 1948. An undeclared state of war between India and Pakistan continued until UN mediation brought about a cease-fire on 1 January 1949. India formally annexed Kashmir on 26 January 1957.

Israeli War of Independence 1948–49

Israel was invaded by the armies of its Arab neighbours on the day the British mandate ended, 15 May 1948. After initial Arab gains, Israel counter-attacked successfully, enlarging its national territory. Only the British-trained Arab Legion of Jordan offered effective opposition. Separate armistices were agreed with Egypt (23 February 1949), Jordan (3 April 1949) and Syria (20 July 1949).

Burmese Civil War 1948–55

In the year after gaining independence on 4 January 1948, the Burmese government faced armed opposition from a wide range of dissident groups: the communists, themselves divided into the White Flag Stalinists and the Red Flag Trotskyites; a private army of war-time 'old comrades' known as the People's Volunteer Organization, who made common cause with army mutineers; ethnic minorities seeking autonomy, such as the Mons and Karens; and bands of Muslim terrorists, Mujahids, in the north of Arakan. By 12 March 1949, when Mandalay fell to the Karen National Defence Organization and the communists, most of Burma was in rebel hands. But the rebels were disunited, and Mandalay was retaken by government forces on 24 April 1949. The rebel capital, Toungoo, was captured on 19 March 1950. The government held the initiative and was able to deal with a new threat posed by Chinese Guomindang refugees in the eastern Shan states. An offensive in November 1954 reduced the Mujahid menace, and Operation 'Final Victory' was launched against the Karens on 21 January 1955. Outbreaks of fighting have occurred since 1955, but never on the scale of the early years of independence.

Colombian Guerrilla War 1948 – continuing

Civil war – 'La Violencia' – in 1948 allowed the military wing of the Communist Party, the Colombian Revolutionary Armed Forces (FARC), to establish itself. It was joined by other guerrilla groups from the 1960s, including the pro-Cuban ELN, the Maoist APL, the leftist M-19, and the Trotskyite ADO. Guerrilla warfare in the hinterland tied down over 57,000 troops and 50,000 paramilitary police. Attempts at a peace accord collapsed after a cease-fire in 1984–5 with all groups except the ELN. Financed by cocaine profits, the guerrilla groups have carried out kidnappings, murders and robberies, but also have fought pitched battles with Colombian troops. The largest and oldest, the FARC, has an estimated 36,000 men under arms. The war has been estimated to have cost over 200,000 lives since 1948.

Karen Insurgency in Burma 1948 – continuing

Since independence in 1948 the Burmese state has been faced with guerrilla insurgency from the four-million-strong Karen population, based near the Thai border, as well as by other ethnic minorities. The Karen National Liberation Army is one of six groups fighting for autonomy or complete independence. Drug traffic via Thailand supplies funds for the Karen forces, who are opposed by 170,000 men of the Burmese forces. Guerrilla attacks, mainly in the Irrawaddy Delta, have been countered by 'search and destroy' missions by the Burmese army, so far with little success.

Malayan Emergency 1948–60

The Federation of Malaya was proclaimed on 1 February 1948. Communist guerrilla activity began, and on 16 June a state of emergency was declared. In April 1950 General Sir Harold Briggs was appointed to co-ordinate anti-communist operations by Commonwealth forces. He inaugurated the Briggs Plan for resettling Chinese squatters in new villages to cut them off from the guerrillas. After the murder of the British high commissioner, Sir Henry Gurney, on 6 October 1951, General Sir Gerald Templer was appointed high commissioner and director of military operations on 15 January 1952, and on 7 February a new offensive was launched. On 8 February 1954 British authorities announced that the Communist Party's high command in Malaya had withdrawn to Sumatra. The emergency was officially ended on 31 July 1960.

Costa Rican Civil War and rebel invasion 1948

Civil war broke out in March 1948 when President Teodoro Picado attempted to annul the elections. He allowed the Communists to organize a 2,000-strong militia to support the regular army. But the forces of the National Liberation Party, led by Colonel Jose Figueres, gradually took control of the country and entered the capital, San Jose, on 24 April 1948. President Picado resigned and the regular army was disbanded. On 10 December 1948 Costa Rica was invaded from Nicaragua by 1,000 armed supporters of the ex-president, Calderon Guardia. The town of La Cruz fell, but the rebels had been driven out by 17 December 1948.

Korean War 1950–53

North Korean troops invaded the South on 25 June 1950. The United Nations decided to intervene following an emergency session of the Security Council, which was being boycotted by the Soviet Union. The first American troops landed at Pusan airport on 1 July 1950. General MacArthur mounted an amphibious landing at Inchon on 15 September 1950, and Seoul was recaptured on 26 September. The advance of the UN forces into North Korea on 1 October 1950 led to the entry of China into the war on 25 November 1950. Seoul fell to the Chinese on 4 January 1951, but was retaken by UN forces on 14 March 1951. General MacArthur was relieved of his command on 11 April 1951 after expressing his desire to expand the war into China. Truce talks began on 10 July 1951, and an armistice was finally signed at Panmunjon on 27 July 1953.

Chinese invasion of Tibet 1950–59

The Chinese invaded across the eastern frontier of Tibet on 7 October 1950. An agreement was signed on 23 May 1951, giving China control of Tibet's affairs, and Chinese troops entered Lhasa in September 1951. The Dalai Lama remained as a figurehead ruler, but there was widespread guerrilla activity against the Chinese forces of occupation. The last serious resistance came in 1959. On 10 March 1959 an uprising took place in Lhasa, but it was suppressed by Chinese tanks, and on 30 March the Dalai Lama fled to asylum in India.

Indonesian Civil War 1950–62

In 1950 prolonged guerrilla campaigns began by a fanatical Muslim sect, Darul Islam, and by the South Moluccans, who proclaimed their independence on 26 April 1950. In 1957 objections to Javanese domination of Indonesian affairs and suspicion of Dr Sukarno's left-wing policies led the military commanders in Borneo, Sumatra and Celebes to refuse to acknowledge the authority of the cabinet. A Revolutionary Government of the Indonesian Republic was proclaimed on 15 February 1958. The authorities took military action against the right-wing rebels, capturing their headquarters at Bukittingi on 5 May 1958, and their capital, Menado, on 26 June 1958. The rebel movement finally collapsed when an amnesty was offered on 31 July 1961, and the civilian leaders surrendered. Opposition from Darul Islam was also suppressed by 1962.

Tunisian War of Independence 1952–56

In February 1952 Habib Bourguiba and other leaders of the New Constitution Party were arrested, and the ensuing disorders led to the introduction of martial law. In the countryside the Tunisian nationalists waged a guerrilla campaign, while in the towns there were terrorist outrages by nationalists and by the 'Red Hand', a secret settler organization. Preoccupied with the Algerian revolt, France granted Tunisia independence on 20 March 1956.

Mau Mau Revolt 1952–60

Violence by the Mau Mau, an African secret society in Kenya, led to a British declaration of a state of emergency on 20 October 1952. Leading Kikuyu nationalists were arrested and Jomo Kenyatta was given a seven-year prison sentence in October 1953. A separate East African command consisting of Kenya, Uganda and Tanganyika was set up under General Sir George Erskine. In campaigns in the first half of 1955 some 4,000 terrorists in the Mount Kenya and Aberdare regions were dispersed. Britain began to reduce her forces in September 1955; the state of emergency in Kenya ended on 12 January 1960.

East German Workers' Uprising 1953

Demonstrations by building workers in East Berlin on 16 June 1953 spread to a number of factories the following day. More than 300 places in East Germany were affected, including major towns such as Magdeburg, Jena, Gorlitz and Brandenburg. The disorders were suppressed by security police, and curfew and martial law restrictions remained in force until 12 July 1953.

Moroccan War of Independence 1953–56

Nationalist agitation grew when Sultan Muhammad V was forced into exile on 20 August 1953 after refusing to co-operate with the French authorities. The Army of National Liberation, composed of Berber tribesmen who had seen service with the French army during the Second World War and the First Indochina War, began a large-scale guerrilla campaign in 1955. The Sultan returned on 5 November 1955, and a Franco-Moroccan declaration on 2 March 1956 ended the French protectorate and established the independence of Morocco.

Cuban Revolution 1953–59

An attempted uprising led by Fidel Castro in Santiago and Bayamo on 26 July 1953 was suppressed. Castro was imprisoned but granted an amnesty in May 1955. He led an unsuccessful landing in Oriente

Province on 30 November 1955, but commenced a successful guerrilla campaign based in the Sierra Maestro. Castro launched a final offensive in October 1958, and General Batista fled the country on 1 January 1959.

Guatemalan Invasion 1954

An army of Liberation, composed of Guatemala exiles and supported by the US Central Intelligence Agency, invaded Guatemala from Honduras and Nicaragua on 18 June 1954. The left-wing government of President Arbenz was overthrown by 27 June and the leader of the exiles, Colonel Carlos Castillo Armas, was declared president on 8 July 1954.

Costa Rican Invasion 1954

On 25 July 1954 Costa Rican exiles based in Nicaragua crossed the border, but were repelled. A Nicaraguan plane was hit and both sides mobilized on the border, but the United States sent planes to Costa Rica to deter further Nicaraguan action.

Algerian War of Independence 1954–62

Algerian nationalists staged attacks on French military and civilian targets on 1 November 1954. In August 1956 the guerrilla groups formed the Armée de Liberation Nationale. The French army conducted a brutal counter-insurgency campaign, which, while effective, alienated its supporters. On 13 May 1956 criticism of army methods led the commander-in-chief in Algeria, General Massu, to refuse to recognize the government of France. General de Gaulle, returned to power on 1 June 1958, set a course for Algerian self-determination. A mutiny by the French army in Algeria, led by generals Challe and Salan, began on 22 April 1961, but was suppressed. Despite terrorism by French settlers of the OAS, peace talks began at Evian-les-Bains in May 1961, and a cease-fire was agreed on 18 March 1962. Algeria was declared independent on 3 July 1962.

Cyprus Emergency 1955–59

Agitation for union with Greece (Enosis) led in April 1955 to the start of a campaign of terrorism and guerrilla warfare by EOKA, the militant wing of the Enosis movement. A state of emergency was declared on 27 November 1955. Archbishop Makarios of Cyprus was deported to the Seychelles on 9 March 1956. A cease-fire came into effect on 13 March 1959, and the state of emergency was lifted on 4 December 1959. Cyprus became an independent republic on 16 August 1960.

Sudanese Civil War 1955 – continuing

The conflict began in 1955 with riots in Yambio in July and mutinies by southern troops in August. The Anya Nya rebels, demanding secession for southern Sudan, began a guerrilla campaign in 1963.

Peace talks between the insurgents and the government began in Addis Ababa in February 1972. A cease-fire came into effect on 12 March 1972 and the south was granted a measure of autonomy. However a mutiny of southern troops in May 1983 and opposition to President Nimeiri's imposition of Islamic law on the country in September 1983 led to renewed civil war. The Sudan People's Liberation Army was formed under Colonel John Garang and President Nimeiri declared a state of emergency on 29 April 1984; fighting continues.

Costa Rican rebel invasion 1955

On 11 January 1955 a 500-strong force of rebels invaded from Nicaragua. After an 11-day campaign, and pressure brought to bear on the Nicaraguan government through the council of the Organization of American States, the invaders were driven out.

Polish Workers' Uprising 1956

A revolt of workers seeking better conditions broke out in Poznan on 28 June 1956. It was suppressed by the security forces.

Hungarian Uprising 1956

Student demonstrations in Budapest on 23 October 1956 led to a general uprising against the government of Erno Gero. On 27 October Soviet troops were withdrawn from Budapest. On 1 November 1956 Imre Nagy, the new Prime Minister, announced Hungary's withdrawal from the Warsaw Pact and asked the United Nations to recognize its neutrality. Soviet reinforcements surrounded Budapest and entered the city early on 4 November. Resistance ended on 14 November 1956.

Suez Invasion 1956

Egypt nationalized the Suez Canal on 26 July 1956. After secret talks with Britain and France, Israel invaded Sinai on 29 October 1956. When Egypt rejected a cease-fire ultimatum by France and Britain, their air forces began to attack Egyptian air bases on 31 October. On 5 November British and French forces invaded the Canal Zone. Pressure from the United Nations and world opinion forced a cease-fire at midnight on 6/7 November 1956.

Honduras border conflict with Nicaragua 1957

On 18 April 1957 Nicaraguan troops crossed the Coco river and invaded Honduras to seize disputed border territory. Honduras recaptured the town of Morocon on 1 May. The Organization of American States arranged a cease-fire and withdrawal of forces on 6 May 1957.

Ifni Incident (Morocco) 1957

On 23 November 1957, some 1,200 Moroccan irregulars attacked the

Spanish territory of Ifni. The Spanish garrison was strengthened and Madrid announced that order had been restored on 8 December 1957.

Lebanese Civil War 1958

Civil war broke out in Lebanon in April 1958 between the pro-Western government of President Chamoun, dominated by Maronite Christians, and pro-Nasserite Muslims. Following the overthrow of the monarchy in an army coup in Iraq on 14 July 1958, President Chamoun appealed for aid, and on 15 July American troops landed in Beirut. On 23 September 1958, the neutralist General Chehab took over from President Chamoun. The last American troops were withdrawn from Lebanon on 25 October 1958.

Tunisian conflict with France 1958–61

On 8 February 1958 the French air force bombed the Tunisian town of Sakiet, killing 79 people, in retaliation for Tunisian assistance to the Algerian rebels. Clashes took place as Tunisia demanded the evacuation of French bases. On 17 June 1958 the French agreed to withdraw from all bases except Bizerte. On 5 July 1961 Tunisia made a formal claim to the French Bizerte base and imposed a blockade on 17 July. France sent reinforcements, who occupied the town of Bizerte in heavy fighting on 19–22 July. An agreement for the withdrawal of French troops from the town was signed on 29 September 1961, and the French base was evacuated by 15 October 1963.

Laotian Civil War 1959–75

The arrest of Prince Souphanouvong and other leaders of the communist Pathet Lao on 28 July 1959 marked the end of attempts at coalition government and the beginning of a three-way conflict between neutralists under Premier Prince Souvanna Phouma, rightists under General Nosavan, and the Pathet Lao. International efforts to find a settlement led to a cease-fire on 3 May 1961 and recognition of the neutrality of Laos at a conference in Geneva on 23 July 1962. But fighting resumed in Laos, with growing involvement by North Vietnam, Thailand and the United States. The South Vietnamese army attacked Laos on 8 February 1971 to disrupt the Ho Chi Minh trail. A new cease-fire agreement was reached on 21 February 1973, and a coalition government formed in 1974. But communist victories in Vietnam and Cambodia in April 1975 opened the door to a takeover by the Pathet Lao in Laos. The Pathet Lao declared Vientiane liberated on 23 August 1975, and Laos was proclaimed the Lao People's Democratic Republic on 2 December 1975, with Prince Souphanouvong as president.

Vietnam War 1959–75

Following the division of Vietnam at the Geneva Conference in 1954, Ngo Dinh Diem became president of South Vietnam and secured American support. His government became increasingly authoritarian and repressive, and unrest grew. The communists in South Vietnam (the Viet Cong) built up their strength and launched their first attack on the South Vietnamese armed forces on 8 July 1959 near Bien Hoa, killing two American advisers. A state of emergency was proclaimed in the south on 19 October 1961. After attacks on the USS *Maddox* and *Turner Joy*, the US Congress passed the Gulf of Tonkin resolution on 7 August 1964, giving President Johnson wide military powers in South Vietnam. The sustained bombing of North Vietnam by US aircraft (Operation 'Rolling Thunder') began on 7 February 1965. The first American combat troops landed at Da Nang on 8 March 1965 and engaged the Viet Cong on 15 June. On 30 January 1968, Communist forces launched their Tet offensive with heavy attacks on Saigon, Hue and 30 provincial capitals. On 31 March 1968 President Johnson announced the end of the bombing of the north, and on 13 May 1968 peace discussions began in Paris. On 25 January 1969 these discussions were transformed into a formal conference. American and South Vietnamese troops invaded Cambodia in 1970, and the South Vietnamese made an incursion into Laos in 1971. A new communist offensive against the south began on 30 March 1972, and this led to a resumption of American bombing of the north on 6 April. The last American ground combat units were withdrawn on 11 August 1972. American bombing was halted on 15 January 1973, and a peace agreement was signed in Paris on 27 January. Two years later, a North Vietnamese offensive, which began on 6 January, overran the South, and Saigon was occupied on 30 April 1975.

Congolese Civil War 1960–67

Belgium granted independence to the Congo (now Zaire) on 30 June 1960. Widespread disorder followed. The army mutinied, and on 11 July 1960 Moise Tshombe declared the rich mining province of Katanga an independent state. The prime minister of the Congo, Patrice Lumumba, appealed to the United Nations and the establishment of a peace-keeping force was approved by the Security Council on 14 July 1960. On 14 September 1960 the army chief of staff, Colonel Mobutu, seized power. Lumumba was seized by Mobutu's troops, handed over to the Katangese and murdered on 9 February 1961. For the next two years, periods of armed conflict and negotiation (during which Dag Hammarskjold, UN Secretary-General, was killed in a plane crash on 18 September 1961) failed to solve the Congo's problems. Katanga's secession eventually ended when a UN offensive in December 1962 forced Tshombe into exile (15 January 1963). The last UN forces left the Congo on 30 June 1964. Violence continued until November 1967, when a revolt by mercenaries in the eastern provinces, which had begun on 5 July, was finally suppressed.

Revolt of the Kurds in Iraq 1961 – continuing

The Kurdish minority in north-east Iraq, led by General Mustafa Barzani, rose in revolt in March 1961 after the failure of negotiations on autonomy with General Kassem's regime. The Kurdish militia, the Pesh Merga ('Forward to Death'), fought a prolonged campaign, growing in strength up to 1974, thanks to support from Iran. Then on 13 June 1975 Iran and Iraq signed the Algiers Pact, by which Iran agreed to stop its supplies and close its borders to the Kurds. The revolt collapsed and although guerrilla warfare continued, it was on a much-reduced scale. Fighting was renewed during the Iran-Iraq war (see p. 303) when Iraq was widely condemned for using chemical weapons against Kurdish insurgents, many of whom fled across the Turkish border.

Angolan War of Independence 1961–75

The liberation struggle commenced in Portuguese Angola on 3 February 1961, when insurgents attempted to free political prisoners in Luanda. The risings were suppressed with great bloodshed, but a guerrilla campaign developed, and by 1974 Portugal was maintaining an army in Angola of 25,000 white and 38,000 locally-enlisted troops. After the coup in Portugal on 25 April 1974, negotiations began, and on 15 January 1975 the Portuguese agreed to Angolan independence. As rival liberation groups fought for control of the country, the independence of Angola was proclaimed on 11 November 1975.

Bay of Pigs Invasion 1961 (Cuba)

Some 1,500 anti-Castro exiles landed in the Bay of Pigs, Cuba, on 17 April 1961, in an operation sponsored by the US Central Intelligence Agency. The invasion was defeated after three days' fighting, when the expected general anti-Castro uprising failed to take place.

Guerrilla Insurgency in Guatemala 1961 – continuing

Guerrilla warfare began soon after the revolt against the government of President Ydigoras Fuentes on 13 November 1960 by junior army officers, who objected to the presence of American-sponsored training camps for Cuban exiles. The rebels were defeated, but soon launched a guerrilla campaign. In the late 1960s they allied themselves with the Guatemalan Communist Party to form the Fuerzas Armadas Rebeldes (Insurgent Armed Forces), a name later changed to the Guerrilla Army of the Poor. American special forces assisted in government operations against the insurgents, who were forced to switch their attacks from the countryside to the cities for a time. Retaliation by right-wing death squads resulted in thousands of deaths on both sides. In 1977 the United States halted military aid to Guatemala over human-rights violations, but the embargo was lifted on 17 January 1982. A state of siege was introduced on 1 July 1982.

Conflict on Irian Jaya 1962 – continuing

Following a clash between Indonesian and Dutch naval forces on 15 January 1962, President Sukarno ordered military mobilization and sent armed units into West New Guinea. In a settlement negotiated through the United Nations, the Dutch agreed on 15 August 1962 to hand over West New Guinea, which was incorporated into Indonesia as Irian Barat on 1 May 1963. The Free Papua Movement, opposed to Indonesian control and desiring unification with Papua New Guinea, undertook small-scale guerrilla operations. Fighting in

1984 led to the movement of over 11,000 refugees to Papua New Guinea.

Indo-Chinese War ('Himalayan War') 1962

After a series of incidents in the disputed border areas, Chinese forces attacked on 20 October 1962 and drove the Indian forces back on the north-east frontier and in the Ladakh region. India declared a state of emergency on 26 October 1962, and launched an unsuccessful counter-offensive on 14 November 1962. On 21 November, the Chinese announced that they would cease fire all along the border and withdraw $12\frac{1}{2}$ miles behind the line of actual control that existed on 7 November 1959.

North Yemen Civil War 1962–70

The royal government of North Yemen was overthrown in an army coup led by Colonel Sallal on 26 September 1962. A civil war began, in which the republican regime was supported by up to 70,000 Egyptian troops and the royalist tribesmen were assisted by arms supplies and technicians from Saudi Arabia. Egypt's defeat in the Six-Day War in 1967 led to an agreement with Saudi Arabia for a disengagement of forces from North Yemen, signed at a meeting of Arab heads of state in Khartoum on 31 August 1967. Sporadic fighting continued until Saudi Arabian mediation secured the formation of a coalition government on 23 May 1970.

Algerian Conflict with Morocco 1963

A series of border clashes between Moroccan and Algerian forces in the Atlas mountains took place in September and October 1963. Ethiopia and Mali mediated a cease-fire on 30 October 1963, and an agreement for the establishment of a demilitarized zone was signed on 20 February 1964.

'Confrontation' between Indonesia and Malaysia 1963–66

When the Federation of Malaysia was established on 16 September 1963, President Sukarno of Indonesia announced a policy of 'confrontation' on the grounds that the federation was 'neo-colonialist'. There followed a campaign of propaganda, sabotage and guerrilla raids into Sarawak and Sabah. An agreement ending 'confrontation' was signed in Bangkok on 1 June 1966 (ratified 11 August).

Cypriot Civil War 1963–68

President Makarios's proposals for constitutional reform led to fighting between Greek and Turkish Cypriots on 21 December 1963. There was a cease-fire on 25 December. A United Nations peace-keeping force was established in Cyprus on 27 March 1964. On 7–9 August 1964,

Turkish planes attacked Greek Cypriot positions on the north-west coast in retaliation for attacks on Turkish Cypriots. There was renewed fighting between Turkish and Greek communities in 1967. A settlement was reached after mediation by the UN and the United States on 3 December 1967, and the withdrawal of Greek regulars from Cyprus and the demobilization of Turkish forces held in readiness to invade was completed by 16 January 1968.

Kenyan Conflict with Somalia 1963–67

The 1960 independence constitution of the Somali Democratic Republic contained a commitment to recover its 'lost territories', which included the northern frontier district of Kenya. Serious border clashes between the Kenyans and Somalis began in March 1963 and diplomatic relations were broken off in December. Sporadic fighting continued until the two countries agreed to end the dispute by the Declaration of Arusha on 28 October 1967.

Guinea-Bissau War of Independence 1963–74

Armed resistance to Portuguese rule was launched by PAIGC in 1963. PAIGC proclaimed the independence of the republic on 24 September 1973. Following the *coup d'etat* in Lisbon on 25 April 1974, led by General Antonio de Spinola (who had been governor and commander-in-chief in Guinea), the Portuguese recognized the independence of Guinea on 10 September 1974.

Eritrean Revolt 1963 – continuing

Eritrea was integrated into the Ethiopian Empire on 14 November 1962, and a separatist movement, the Eritrean Liberation Front, took up arms the following year. Taking advantage of the instability caused by the overthrow of Haile Selassie on 12 September 1974, separatist guerrillas succeeded in taking control of most of Eritrea except the capital, Asmara, by the end of 1977. The conclusion of the Ogaden War in March 1978 (see p. 301) enabled the Ethiopian army, with Cuban and Soviet assistance, to launch a major counter-offensive in Eritrea on 15 May 1978. The last major town in rebel hands, Keren, fell to government troops in November 1978. Guerrilla warfare has continued, although the division of the Eritrean separatist movement into warring factions reduced its effectiveness.

Ethiopia, Invasion by Somalia 1964

After a series of border clashes, Somali armed forces crossed into Ethiopia on 7 February 1964 to assert the Somali Republic's claim to the Ogaden desert region. The Organization of African Unity called for an end to hostilities, and President Abboud of Sudan secured a cease-fire based on the original boundary on 30 March 1964.

Mozambique War of Independence 1964–74

FRELIMO launched its first attacks in September 1964, and gradually took control of large areas of the countryside. By 1974 Portugal was forced to maintain an army in Mozambique of 24,000 white and 20,000 locally enlisted troops. After the coup in Portugal of 25 April 1974, negotiations were opened with FRELIMO. Despite a violent revolt by white settlers in Lourenco Marques (now Maputo) on 3 September 1974, a cease-fire agreement was signed on 7 September 1974 and Mozambique officially became independent on 25 June 1975.

Aden 1964–67

On 18 January 1963 Aden acceded to the South Arabian Federation. British troops were involved in frontier fighting with the Yemen, and in suppressing internal disorders in Aden. A large-scale security operation was launched in January 1964 in the Radfan region, north of Aden. On 26 November 1967 the People's Republic of South Yemen was proclaimed, and the British military withdrawal from Aden was completed on 29 November. In the period 1964–67, British security forces lost 57 killed and 651 wounded in Aden.

Indo-Pakistan War 1965

Border clashes took place in the Rann of Kutch in April 1965, but a cease-fire agreement came into effect on 1 July. More serious fighting in Kashmir and the Punjab began on 5 August 1965, when Muslim irregulars invaded east Kashmir. The Indian army contained these incursions, but on 1 September 1965 Pakistani regular forces crossed the frontier. India launched a three-pronged attack towards Lahore on 6 September. As a military stalemate developed, the UN Security Council called for a cease-fire which came into effect on 23 September 1965.

Dominican Civil War 1965

Civil war broke out on 24 April 1965 between the Constitutionalists, supporting former President Bosch, and the Loyalist forces of President Reid Cabral. On 28 April 1965, 400 US Marines were sent in to prevent a left-wing takeover and during the next month a further 24,000 American troops were landed. A cease-fire was signed on 6 May and at the end of May an Inter-American peace-keeping force, comprising units from the United States, Honduras, Nicaragua, Costa Rica, Brazil and El Salvador, under the auspices of the Organization of American States, was formed to keep the warring factions apart.

Oman, War in the Dhofar 1965–75

Civil war broke out in 1965 between the Sultan's armed forces and dissident tribesmen in the Dhofar, who had won control of most of the region by 1970. On 23 July 1970 Sultan Said bin Taimur was deposed by his son, Qaboos, who greatly strengthened the armed forces. With foreign assistance, including an Iranian expeditionary force of 2,000 men, the revolt was suppressed and the Sultan officially declared the war ended on 11 December 1975.

Rhodesian War of Independence 1965–79

Black nationalist guerrilla activity in Southern Rhodesia grew after the unilateral declaration of independence by Ian Smith's white minority regime on 11 November 1965. Two guerrilla forces were operating: ZIPRA, the military wing of Joshua Nkomo's Zimbabwe African People's Union, based in Zambia and recruiting from the Ndebele peoples; and ZANLA, the military wing of Robert Mugabe's Zimbabwe African National Union, based in Mozambique and recruiting from the Shona peoples. These two groupings united to form the Patriotic Front on 9 October 1976. A settlement for an end to the conflict based on a new constitution was reached at the conclusion of a conference at Lancaster House, London on 15 December 1979. Zimbabwe became an independent republic on 18 April 1980.

Chad, Civil War 1965 – continuing

The civil war in Chad originated in the mid-1960s as a conflict between the French-backed government of President Tombalbaye and a number of separatist factions in the Muslim north of the country, grouped into the Front de Libération Nationale and supported by Libya. By the mid-1970s FROLINAT controlled three-quarters of the country. On 6 February 1978 the head of state, General Malloum, who had overthrown President Tombalbaye in 1975, announced a cease-fire with FROLINAT. Conflict then developed between two factions in FROLINAT: FAN, under Hissene Habré, and the more militant FAP, under Goukouni Oueddei, backed by Libya. Habré's army defeated FAP and captured the capital, N'Djamena, on 7 June 1982. Fighting resumed in 1983 when FAP and Libyan troops advanced and took the strategically important town of Faya-Largeau on 24 June. Habré appealed for foreign assistance and troops were sent by Zaire on 3 July and France on 14 August. The Libyan advance was halted, and France and Libya signed a withdrawal agreement on 17 September 1984. Libyan troops remained in the north of Chad, however, and created a *de facto* partition of the country until Goukouni Oueddei was shot and wounded in an argument with Libyan troops, and his men changed sides in 1986. A united Chadian force mounted a surprise attack and captured the Libyan air base at Ouadi Doum in March 1987, forcing the Libyans to evacuate most of the territory they had occupied.

Namibian War of Independence 1966–89

Namibia was mandated to South Africa by the League of Nations on 17 December 1920. South Africa refused to recognize the South West Africa People's Organization, which was designated the 'sole authentic representative of the Namibian people' by the United Nations in 1973. SWAPO launched a guerrilla campaign in October 1966 and this was stepped up in 1978 from bases in Angola and Zambia. South Africa carried out a series of attacks on SWAPO camps in Angola. SWAPO guerrilla activity in Namibia continued, despite the non-aggression pact signed by Angola and South Africa on 16 February 1984. A cease-fire supervised by the UN took effect from 1989, providing for the withdrawal of Cuban and South African forces from the region to be followed by elections in Namibia and independence in 1990.

Israeli-Arab 'Six-Day' War 1967

Israel decided on a pre-emptive strike following Egypt's request for the withdrawal of the UN peace-keeping force from Sinai on 16 May, the closure of the Gulf of Aqaba to Israeli shipping on 22 May, and the signature of an Egyptian-Jordanian defence pact on 30 May. On 5 June 1967 Israel launched devastating air attacks on Egyptian air bases. Israeli forces then invaded Sinai and reached the Suez Canal on 7 June. By nightfall on 7 June Jordan had been defeated and Jerusalem and the West Bank were in Israeli hands. On 9 June Israeli troops attacked Syria and occupied the Golan Heights. A cease-fire was agreed on 10 June 1967.

Nigerian Civil War 1967-70

On 30 May 1967 the military governor of the Eastern Region of Nigeria, Colonel Ojukwu, declared the Ibo homeland an independent sovereign state under the name of the Republic of Biafra. Troops of the Nigerian federal army attacked across the northern border of Biafra on 7 July 1967. The Biafrans invaded the neighbouring Mid-West Region on 9 August 1967. The federal army recaptured Biafra on 22 September 1967, and Port Harcourt fell on 20 May 1968. Supply shortages and starvation finally led to the collapse of Biafran resistance after a four-pronged federal attack in December 1969. The Biafran army surrendered on 15 January 1970.

Philippine Communist and Muslim Insurgency 1968 – continuing

The Hakbalahap insurgency (see pp. 281–2) had faded by the mid-1950s, but in December 1968 a congress of re-establishment was held on Luzon, which reconstituted the Communist Party. Its New People's Army (NPA) began a guerrilla campaign. The government also faced armed opposition from Muslim separatists of the Moro National Liberation Front (MNLF) on Mindanao. President Marcos declared martial law on 23 September 1972. A cease-fire with the MNLF was announced on 22 December 1976 after talks held in Libya, but fighting continued. President Aquino signed a 60-day truce with the NPA on 27 November 1986, but fighting resumed when it expired in 1987.

Soviet invasion of Czechoslovakia 1968

During the night of 20/21 August 1968 some 250,000 Soviet troops, accompanied by token contingents from Warsaw Pact Allies Poland, Hungary and Bulgaria, crossed the Czech frontier and occupied Prague and other leading cities to reverse the liberalizing reforms of Alexander Dubcek's government, the so-called 'Prague Spring'. The

Czech army was ordered to offer no resistance, but there were extensive civilian demonstrations against the occupying forces. The Soviet invasion led to the installation of a new Soviet-backed government and the end of the 'Prague Spring'.

Honduran 'Soccer' War with El Salvador 1969

Hostilities were sparked off by the harassment of a visiting Honduran soccer team in San Salvador (in retaliation for the treatment of the Salvadorean team in Honduras) and the victory of El Salvador over Honduras in a World Cup soccer match on 15 June 1969. The underlying cause was the presence of some 300,000 Salvadorean workers living, many illegally, in Honduras. Riots led to the deaths of two Salvadoreans and the expulsion of 11,000 others. In response, the Salvadorean army crossed the border at several points on 14 July 1969. Honduras accepted an Organization of American States cease-fire call on 16 July, but El Salvador continued fighting. The OAS formally branded El Salvador as the aggressor and voted to impose sanctions on 29 July. El Salvador began to withdraw on 30 July and withdrawal was completed by 5 August.

Chinese border conflict with Soviet Union 1969

Long-standing Sino-Soviet border disputes erupted into serious fighting on Damansky Island in the Ussuri river on 2 March 1969. Each side blamed the other for the clash, in which 31 Soviet frontier-guards were killed. The fighting spread further west to the border between Xinjiang (Sinkiang) and Kazakhstan. On 11 September 1969 the Soviet Prime Minister, Alexei Kosygin, who was returning from the funeral of Ho Chi Minh in Hanoi, stopped briefly at Beijing airport for a meeting with Zhou Enlai. Talks were arranged and tension on the border subsided.

Northern Ireland, civil insurgency 1969 – continuing

In 1968 long-standing sectarian animosity between the Catholic and Protestant communities in Northern Ireland degenerated into violent conflict, sparked by the campaign for Catholic civil rights. British troops were deployed in Londonderry on 14 August 1969 and Belfast on 15 August at the request of the government of Northern Ireland. The first British soldier to be killed was shot by an IRA sniper in Belfast on 6 February 1971. Internment without trial was introduced on 6 August 1971, and direct rule from London was imposed on 30 March 1972. On 'Bloody Sunday', 30 January 1972, British troops opened fire on a Catholic civil rights march, and 13 people were killed. At the peak, in August 1972, there were 21,500 British soldiers in Northern Ireland, but this was reduced to 10,000 by the mid-1980s. Over 3,000 people had died in the conflict by 1990.

South Yemen conflicts with Saudi Arabia and rebel exiles 1969–72

An unsuccessful attempt by the new left-wing government in South

Yemen to assert a claim to disputed border territory led to clashes with Saudi Arabia in November 1969. Saudi Arabia provided training and a base at ash-Sharawrah for South Yemeni exiles, organized into an 'Army of Deliverance', which raided into South Yemen. In 1972 fighting spread to the border between North and South Yemen. In August 1972 South Yemeni exiles in the north formed a United National Front of South Yemen. Their forces, supplied by Saudi Arabia, mounted attacks on 26 September 1972, which led to full-scale fighting. Arab mediation brought agreement between North and South Yemen in Cairo on 28 October 1972 to meet for discussions on a merger of the two countries.

Kampuchean Civil War 1970–75

On 18 March 1970, Lieutenant General Lon Nol ousted the head of state, Prince Norodom Sihanouk, who was out of the country. Sihanouk allied himself with his former enemies, the Marxist Khmer Rouge, to form the National United Front of Cambodia. Lon Nol appealed for aid on 14 April 1970, and on 29 April, American and South Vietnamese troops mounted an incursion into Kampuchea to attack North Vietnamese Viet Cong and Khmer Rouge forces. The last American troops withdrew on 29 June 1970. The communists took control of the countryside, and in 1975 cut supply routes to the capital, Phnom Penh. Lon Nol left the country on 1 April 1975 and the Khmer Rouge occupied Phnom Penh on 17 April.

Jordanian Civil War 1970–71

After serious clashes between Palestinian guerrillas and the Jordanian army, King Hussein declared martial law on 16 September 1970. Civil war broke out in Amman on 19 September as the army attacked the Palestinian refugee camps. Some 250 Syrian tanks entered Jordan in support of the Palestinians, but suffered losses in Jordanian air strikes and withdrew on 23 September 1970. A cease-fire was agreed on 25 September 1970. Further heavy fighting took place early in 1971 and the PLO guerrillas withdrew from Amman on 13 April. Their expulsion from Jordan was completed by 18 July 1971.

Indo-Pakistan War and Bangladeshi War of Independence 1971

Elections in December 1970 resulted in a landslide victory in East Pakistan for the Awami League. On 26 March 1971 Sheikh Mujibur Rahman, the head of the League, proclaimed East Pakistan an independent republic under the name of Bangladesh. He was arrested, and West Pakistani troops and locally-raised irregulars, *razakars*, put down large-scale resistance by 10 May 1971. Awami League fighters, the Mukti Bahini, began a guerrilla campaign, and clashes between India and Pakistan increased as millions of refugees fled into India. President Yahya Khan declared a state of emergency in Pakistan on 23 November 1971. On 3 December 1971 the Pakistani air force launched surprise attacks on Indian airfields. On 4 December some 160,000 Indian troops invaded East Pakistan. Pakistani forces in East Pakistan surrendered on 16 December 1971, and a general cease-fire came into effect the following day.

Burundi Civil War 1972-73

On 29 April 1972 guerrillas from the majority Hutu tribe in Burundi attacked the ruling Tutsi minority, killing between 5,000 and 15,000 in an abortive coup. The Burundi armed forces, under Tutsi command, retaliated with assistance from Zaire, and by the end of May 1972 the death toll amongst the Hutu had risen to an estimated 100,000. Refugees poured into neighbouring states. On 10 May 1973 Hutu rebels from Rwanda and Tanzania invaded Burundi. The Burundi army in response crossed into Tanzania on 29 June and killed 10 people. President Mobutu of Zaire mediated an accord between the presidents of Tanzania and Burundi on 21 July, 1973.

Uganda rebel invasion 1972

On 17 September 1972 some 1,000 armed supporters of ex-president Milton Obote, who had been overthrown by General Amin in January 1971, invaded Uganda from Tanzania. The guerrillas were easily repulsed, and the Ugandan air force bombed the Tanzanian towns of Bukoba and Mwanza in reprisal. The Organization of African Unity and the Somali foreign minister mediated a peace agreement between Uganda and Tanzania, which was signed on 5 October 1972.

Yom Kippur War 1973

On 6 October 1973, the day of a Jewish religious holiday, Egyptian forces crossed the Suez Canal, overwhelming Israel's Bar-Lev defence line in a well-planned surprise attack. Syrian forces attacked the Golan Heights, but initial gains were surrendered by 12 October. In a daring counter-stroke on 15 October 1973, Israeli forces crossed to the west bank of the Suez Canal and encircled the Egyptian Third Army. A cease-fire became effective on 24 October 1973.

Turkish invasion of Cyprus 1974

In July 1974 a coup in Cyprus brought to power a government favouring 'enosis' (union) with Greece, but Turkey quickly responded by invading the island to safeguard the Turkish half of the population. An armistice was agreed on 16 August, which left Turkish rule over one-third of the island.

Western Sahara, Polisario Insurgency 1975 – continuing

The Spanish colony of Western Sahara was claimed by both Morocco and Mauritania, while there was also an independence movement, the Polisario, formed in 1973 and supported by Algeria. On 6 November 1975 King Hassan of Morocco sent 350,000 unarmed Moroccans in a 'Green March' into the Western Sahara. They were recalled after three days, but agreement was reached in Madrid on 14 November 1975 for a Spanish withdrawal and joint administration of the territory after 28 February 1976 by Morocco and Mauritania. Their armed forces came into conflict with the Polisario, which proclaimed the Saharan Arab Democratic Republic. The Polisario concentrated on Mauritanian targets, mounting a daring raid on the capital, Nouakchott, on 7 June 1976. Morocco and Mauritania formed a joint military command on 13 May 1977, and Mauritania received support from the French air force. On 5 August 1979 Mauritania came to terms with Polisario, but Morocco moved to occupy the whole of the western Sahara. Libya recognized the Polisario in April 1980. In 1984 Morocco built a 1,600-mile defensive wall from the Moroccan town of Zag to Dakhla on the Atlantic coast, protecting the economically important north of the territory and creating an effective stalemate.

Lebanese Civil War and invasions 1975 – continuing

Tensions between the Christian and Muslim communities in Lebanon were exacerbated by the influx of Palestinian guerrillas expelled from Jordan in 1971. A state of civil war existed after a massacre of Palestinians by Phalangist gunmen on 13 April 1975. Syrian forces were drawn into the conflict on 1 June 1976. A cease-fire was agreed on 17 October 1976, backed by an Arab Deterrent Force consisting mainly of Syrian troops, but fighting soon resumed. Palestinian raids into Israel led to an Israeli incursion into the Lebanon 15 March–13 June 1978. Israel launched a full-scale invasion of Lebanon on 6 June 1982 and forced a Palestinian evacuation from Beirut, beginning on 22 August 1982. An agreement between Israel and the Lebanese government on 17 May 1983 proved a dead letter, but Israel withdrew its forces from the Lebanon during 1985. Fighting between the various factions continued unabated. Eventually, Syrian forces occupied West Beirut in strength on 22 February 1987 to separate the warring militias, but a Christian attempt to resist Syrian domination led to renewed bitter fighting in 1989.

East Timor, Indonesian annexation and guerrilla war 1975 – continuing

In June 1975 Portugal announced its intention of holding independence elections in its colony of East Timor. On 11 August 1975 the moderate UDT, which favoured continuing links with Portugal, attempted to stage a coup, but by 20 August civil war had broken out with the communist group FRETILIN. As increasing numbers of refugees fled into Indonesian West Timor, Indonesian troops entered East Timor on 7 December 1975 to forestall a left-wing takeover. By 28 December, the Indonesians were in control, and East Timor was officially integrated into Indonesia on 17 July 1976. Guerrilla war by FRETILIN continued against Indonesian forces, with harsh reprisals leading to a death toll in excess of 100,000 by 1985.

Angolan Civil War 1975–89

The three rival liberation movements signed an agreement with Portugal on 15 January 1976 regarding Angolan independence, but were soon engaged in a civil war for control of the country. Major fighting between the MPLA and FNLA broke out in the capital, Luanda, on 27 March 1975. During July 1975 the MPLA gained control of Luanda. In the ensuing conflict the Marxist MPLA received aid from the Soviet Union and was supported by some 15,000 Cuban troops, whilst the FNLA/UNITA alignment received supplies from the US via Zaire, and South African military support from October 1975. When independence was declared on 11 November 1975, FNLA/UNITA established a rival government in Huambo. The MPLA drove FNLA forces into Zaire and captured Huambo on 8 February 1976. The US had halted its aid to FNLA/UNITA on 27 January 1976. The Organization of African Unity recognized the MPLA government on 11 February 1976, and South Africa announced the withdrawal of its forces on 25 March 1976. UNITA continued to wage a guerrilla campaign in Angola with aid from South Africa, which sought a counter to Angola's support for the South West Africa People's Organization guerrillas fighting for the independence of Namibia. In April 1989 a cease-fire was arranged, leading to the withdrawal of Cuban and South African forces and a cessation of UNITA attacks.

Mozambique Civil War 1976 – continuing

From 1976 Rhodesia fostered a guerrilla campaign by anti-FRELIMO dissidents in Mozambique, which was harbouring Robert Mugabe's ZANLA (see p. 294). After 1980, South Africa took over the support of the MNRM as part of its policy of 'destabilizing' its neighbours. The MNRM concentrated on sabotage and guerrilla raids on communications, power lines and foreign-aided development projects. Mozambique and South Africa signed a non-aggression pact, the Nkomati accord, on 16 March 1984, but MNRM activity had scarcely slackened by the end of the 1980s.

Soweto Uprising 1976

Large scale rioting in the black townships of South Africa, triggered by measures to enforce learning of Afrikaans in schools, led to over 500 African deaths in the ensuing repression.

Libyan conflict with Egypt 1977

Strained relations and border incidents led Egypt to mount a limited punitive action against Libya on 21 July 1977 in the shape of an armed incursion and air attacks on the major Libyan air-base at Al Adem. A cease-fire was agreed, through the mediation of Yasser Arafat, chairman of the PLO, and others, on 24 July, 1977.

Zaire, rebel invasions from Angola 1977–78

On 8 March 1977 Zaire's Shaba province (formerly Katanga) was invaded from Angola by some 2,000 insurgents claiming to be members of the Congolese National Liberation Front. President Mobutu accused Cuban troops of leading the invasion and appealed for African support on 2 April 1977. On 10 April French transport aircraft carried 1,500 Moroccan troops to Zaire and they helped the Zaire army to repel the invasion. On 11 May 1978 a second invasion from Angola by some 3,000 rebels took place. French and Belgian paratroopers were sent to Kolwezi to rescue white hostages on 19 May 1978 and the invaders were dispersed. Zaire and Angola signed a non-aggression pact on 12 October 1979.

Ethiopian conflict in the Ogaden 1977–78

The turmoil in Ethiopia after the overthrow of Emperor Haile Selassie on 12 September 1974 led the Somali Republic to pursue its claim to the Ogaden by fostering a guerrilla movement in the area, the Western Somali Liberation Front. A Somali-backed offensive in 1977 gave the guerrillas control of the southern desert area, and an attack launched against Harar on 23 November 1977 narrowly failed. With Cuban and Soviet support, Ethiopia launched a counter-offensive on 7 February 1978 and recovered control of the Ogaden. On 9 March 1978 Somalia announced the withdrawal of its forces from the Ogaden.

Sri Lanka, communal strife 1977–continuing

Tension between the Tamil minority and the Sinhalese majority in Sri Lanka led to rioting in the northern town of Jaffna, beginning on 14 August 1977, in which 125 people died. The situation grew more serious in the 1980s. Acts of terrorism by the Tamil Liberation Tigers provoked violence by the army against the Tamil community. A state of emergency was declared on 4 June 1981. Two soldiers, the first military victims, were killed in an ambush in Jaffna in October 1981. Talks between President Jayawardene and the Tamil United Liberation Front failed to find a political solution. In 1987 Indian troops were requested to assist the Sri Lankan government and a force of 100,000 Indian troops attacked Tamil positions in the Jaffna peninsula. Guerrilla war continued and in 1989 Indian troops began to withdraw. In the south the ultra-left JVP movement active from 1971 has conducted an increasingly bitter terror campaign since 1987. Over 3,000 people died in civil disorder in the first three months of 1989.

Vietnamese invasion of Kampuchea 1978–89

After a series of clashes on the border, Vietnamese forces and Kampuchean rebels launched an invasion of Kampuchea on 25 December 1978. The capital, Phnom Penh, was occupied on 7 January 1979, and a People's Republic of Kampuchea was proclaimed, with Heng Samrin as president. Guerrilla operations against the Vietnamese occupying forces were carried out by three groups: the Khmer Rouge; guerrillas loyal to the former head of state, Prince Sihanouk; and the non-communist Khmer People's National Liberation Front. These groups formed a loose coalition in Kuala Lumpur, Malaysia on 22 June 1982. Warfare continued, especially on the Thai border, although talks aiming at a settlement began in 1987, leading to agreement on a withdrawal of Vietnamese forces in 1989.

Ugandan conflict with Tanzania 1978–79

On 27 October 1978 Uganda invaded Tanzania and occupied some 700 square miles of Tanzanian territory known as the Kagera salient. A Tanzanian counter-offensive on 12 November 1978 ejected the Ugandans from the salient. In January 1979, Tanzanian forces, with armed Ugandan exiles, advanced into Uganda. Kampala fell on 11 April 1979 and President Amin fled the country.

Nicaraguan Civil War 1978–90

Civil war was precipitated by the murder of President Anastasio Somoza's leading opponent, newspaper editor Pedro Joaquin Chamorro, on 10 January 1978. The FSLN made steady advances, and Somoza finally fled the country on 17 July 1979. Civil war continued as the Sandinista government faced two military threats: the first, the Democratic Revolutionary Front, a group of rebels led by dissident Sandinist Eden Pastora, mounted raids from its base in Costa Rica; the second, the Nicaraguan Democratic Front or 'Contras', was a force of ex-National Guardsmen who operated from their exile in Honduras and who received extensive American aid until the US Congress halted funding on 25 June 1984. The Sandinista regime declared a state of emergency in May 1982, but disunity among its enemies enabled it to function despite the guerrilla threat. On 8 August 1987 leaders of the five Central American countries, including Nicaragua, met in Guatemala City to sign a peace accord calling for the democratization of Nicaragua and for Contra-Sandinista negotiations. A 60-day cease-fire was announced in Sapoa on 23 March 1988. With the election defeat of the Sandinistas in 1990, the civil war effectively ended.

El Salvador guerrilla insurgency 1979 – continuing

Guerrilla activity by the left-wing Farabundo Marti National Liberation Front intensified after 1979. Conflict between the 40,000-strong Salvadorean army, backed by the United States, and 9,000 Liberation Front guerrillas reached a stalemate by the end of 1986.

Chinese invasion of Vietnam 1979

Chinese forces launched an invasion of Vietnam on 17 February 1979 in retaliation for Vietnam's intervention in Kampuchea (see p. 301). Following the fall of the provincial capital, Lang Son, on 3 March 1979, the Chinese government announced that it had accomplished its aims, and the withdrawal of its forces was completed by 16 March 1979.

Soviet invasion of Afghanistan and Civil War 1979 – continuing

The instability of the Soviet-backed regime and growing resistance to reforms led to a full-scale Soviet invasion of Afghanistan on 27 December 1979. A new government was installed under Babrak

Karmal, but a considerable Soviet military presence had to be maintained in the country to combat the Mujaheddin guerrillas. Following Babrak Karmal's resignation on 4 May 1986, his successor, Major-General Najibollah announced a six-months' cease-fire on 15 January 1987, but this was rejected by the Mujaheddin. Russian troops began to withdraw in 1988 and completed withdrawal in early 1989, having lost 15,000 dead. Contrary to expectation the Kabul regime did not collapse, and attempts by the Mujaheddin forces to take Kabul and other principal cities were repulsed.

Iran-Iraq War 1980–88

Hoping to exploit the instability of Iran after the fall of the Shah, Iraq abrogated the Algiers pact of 1975, by which it had been forced to accept joint control of the Shatt al-Arab waterway, and invaded Iran on 12 September 1980. Khorramshahr fell on 13 October, 1980, but the Iranian government did not collapse and its armed forces began to counter-attack successfully. Each side bombed the other's oil installations and attacked international shipping in the Gulf. Iran rejected Iraq's cease-fire overtures as the military stalemate deepened. On 9 January 1987 Iran launched a major offensive – codenamed Karbala-5 – with the aim of capturing Basra. The Iranians advanced some distance towards their objective, while suffering heavy casualties. In 1987 and 1988 Iraq made major advances and a cease-fire was organized in August 1988. The war is estimated to have cost almost a million casualties, with some of the heaviest land-fighting since the Second World War.

Falkland Islands (Malvinas) 1982

Argentina maintained a long-standing claim to the sovereignty of the Falkland Islands and on 2 April 1982 the Argentine dictatorship, under General Galtieri, launched a successful invasion of the islands, forcing its garrison of 18 Royal Marines to surrender. Argentine forces also seized the island of South Georgia. On 5 April a British Task Force set sail to recapture the islands and on 7 April an exclusion zone of 200 miles was declared around the island. On 25 April South Georgia was recaptured and on 1 May air attacks began on the Argentine garrison on the Falklands. The next day the Argentine cruiser *Belgrano* was sunk by a British submarine and on 4 May HMS *Sheffield* was hit by an Exocet missile. On 21 May British troops went ashore at San Carlos. Two British frigates, the *Ardent* and *Antelope,* were sunk and others damaged by air attack, but British troops took Darwin and Goose Green by the end of May and on 11–14 June an attack on Port Stanley led to the surrender of the Argentine forces. During the conflict 255 British and 720 Argentine troops were killed. A large permanent garrison and modern airstrip have been placed on the island for its future security.

Invasion of Grenada 1983

On 19 October 1983 the army took control in Grenada after a power struggle led to the murder of Prime Minister Maurice Bishop. On 21

October the Organisation of Eastern Caribbean States appealed to the United States to intervene, and on 25 October US Marines and airborne troops invaded Grenada, together with token contingents from six other Caribbean countries. Resistance from the Grenadian army and 700 Cuban construction workers with paramilitary training was overcome, and order restored by 27 October 1983.

Sikh separatist unrest 1984 – continuing

Separatist unrest amongst Sikhs had led to several hundred deaths in the Punjab by early 1984 and the introduction of emergency rule. Following the stock-piling of arms at the Golden Temple, Amritsar, the Sikhs' holiest shrine, the Indian army stormed the complex and in fierce fighting killed the leading Sikh militant Jarnail Sing Bhindranwale and over 700 of his followers. On 31 October the Indian Prime Minister, Indira Gandhi, was assassinated by two Sikh bodyguards and in ensuing 'revenge' attacks over 2,000 Sikhs were killed. Terrorism by Sikh extremists and communal riots have led to several thousand deaths by 1990 and the reintroduction of emergency rule in the Punjab.

Indo-Pakistan conflict in Kashmir 1984 – continuing

The UN has policed the cease-fire line established in the wake of the 1971 Indo-Pakistan war, but in the high Himalayan ranges, sporadic fighting has taken place, principally around the Sianchin glacier. In May 1984 the Pakistanis launched a major infantry-artillery attack to dislodge Indian troops who had moved onto the glacier. In 1985 Pakistani planes bombed Indian positions and air combat took place. Renewed tension brought India and Pakistan to the verge of war in 1990.

New Caledonia separatist movement 1984 – continuing

In 1984 the indigenous Melanesian population, the Kanaks, began violent resistance to elections which it was expected would confirm in power French settlers opposed to independence. Kanak separatists resisted any compromise short of a referendum on independence amongst the indigenous population. As violence spread, 7,000 French soldiers and riot police were sent to New Caledonia in 1987 to allow a referendum election to take place. In September 1987 residents of New Caledonia, including the 40% who are French, voted to remain a French territory.

Burkina Faso (Upper Volta) conflict with Mali 1985

In December 1985 Burkina Faso forces invaded northern Mali over a border dispute, with each side backed respectively by Libya and Algeria. Three days of fighting left 400 dead, but arbitration by the international court at the Hague was accepted.

Uprising or 'Intifada' in Arab West Bank and Gaza 1987 – continuing

In December 1987, widespread unrest amongst Palestinian refugees erupted in the Israeli-occupied West Bank and Gaza strip against Israeli security forces. Rioting and terrorist incidents had led to over 600 dead by end 1989. In April 1988, an Israeli special unit assassinated the PLO military commander, Abu Jihad, believing he was masterminding the violence.

Romanian Revolution and Civil War, 1989

On 17 December 1989 security forces fired on protesters in the Romanian city of Timisoara. On 18 December, Romania closed its frontiers. On 20 December, troops surrendered in Timisoara. Fighting spread to Bucharest and other major cities. The army switched sides, joining the popular uprising against the Ceausescu (q.v.) dictatorship and the hated security police (the *Securitate*). By 24 December all strategic points were controlled by the revolutionary National Salvation Front. Ceausescu and his wife were executed by firing squad on 25 December 1989, having been found guilty of genocide by a military court. Provisional casualty figures gave 689 dead and 1200 injured in the revolution.

Panama: US invasion of, 1989

Tension between America and the corrupt Noriega (q.v) dictatorship mounted during 1989, especially after the annulment of the May elections. On 20 December, US forces launched a ground and air invasion to overthrow the Panamanian regime and seize Noriega. Despite some resistance from the Panamanian Defence Forces and the pro-Noriega civilian militia (the 'Dignity Battalions'), US forces rapidly occupied Panama City and other key areas. Noriega fled, finding refuge in the Vatican embassy, before surrendering and being extradited to the United States. By 31 December 1989, 23 Americans had died and 320 had been wounded in the invasion.

Nuclear development and arms control

1902   Rutherford and Soddy investigate the radioactive transmutation of the elements.

1905   Planck and Einstein develop the idea of energy being transmitted in finite steps or 'quanta'.
        Einstein proposes the special theory of relativity, predicting the mutual conversion of mass and energy.

1908   Geiger develops a counter for detecting radioactive rays.

1911   Rutherford proposes the existence of the atom; Bohr and Rutherford suggest structure of the atom.

1916   Einstein puts forward general theory of relativity.

1919   Rutherford splits the atom and demonstrates the existence of sub-atomic particles.

1925   Heisenberg and Schrodinger establish the theory of 'quantum mechanics' and the basis for atomic physics.

1932   Existence of the neutron discovered by Chadwick, particles which could split the atom.

1934   Fermi discovers that nuclei could be made to disintegrate if bombarded with neutrons themselves produced by nuclear disintegrations.

1938   Hahn and Strassmann split the uranium atom and demonstrate the release of further neutrons to produce a chain reaction.

1940   Professors Peierls and Frisch at Birmingham University in Britain produce memorandum on the design of an atomic bomb (Feb.); increased support given to research.
        Soviet Union sets up committee to investigate the 'uranium problem'.
        Germans set up research institute in Berlin, code-named 'The Virus House' to explore atomic developments.

1941   British Maud Committee reports favourably on possibility of atomic weapon (June).
        Russian programme disrupted by German invasion and removed beyond the Urals (July).

1942   Anglo-Norwegian sabotage team wreck German 'heavy water' plant at Rjukan in Norway, crucial to German atomic research (April).
        Americans set up 'Manhattan Project' under US Army Corps of Engineers to administer work on the production of an atomic bomb (June). Several processes tried to achieve separation of fissile Uranium 235 from Uranium 238.
        First nuclear chain reaction using plutonium takes place at the University of Chicago under direction of Fermi (Dec.).

1943   Quebec agreement between Churchill and Roosevelt agrees cooperation on atomic bomb programme (Aug.).

1944   Both uranium enrichment and plutonium reaction developed in the United States to produce atomic weapons.
Discovery of captured German documents reveals lack of progress in their atomic research.

1945   The first successful explosion of an experimental atomic device takes place at Alamogordo, New Mexico (16 July).
USAAF B29 bomber, *Enola Gay*, dropped the first atomic bomb, nicknamed 'Little Boy', on the Japanese city of Hiroshima (6 Aug.). Second atomic bomb, nicknamed 'Fat Man', dropped on Nagasaki (9 Aug.).

1946   United Nations General Assembly passes a resolution to establish an Atomic Energy Commission (Jan.).
At the first meeting of the Atomic Energy Commission, the American delegate, Bernard M. Baruch, puts forward a plan by which the United States would surrender its atomic weapons and reveal the secrets of controlling atomic energy to an International Control Agency. The Baruch Plan rejected by the Soviet Union (June).
United States carries out the first nuclear test in peace-time at Bikini Atoll in the Marshall Islands (1 July).
President Truman signs the Atomic Energy Act, restricting exchange of information with other nations on atomic energy, thus ending co-operation between the United States and Britain in the development of nuclear weapons (6 Aug.).

1949   Soviet Union explodes an atomic bomb, ending the American monopoly of nuclear weapons (29 Aug.).

1950   Soviet Union withdraws from the Atomic Energy Commission (Jan.).

1952   Britain tests its first atomic bomb (3 Oct.).
United States explodes the first hydrogen device at Eniwetok atoll in the Marshall Islands (1 Nov.).

1953   Soviet Union tests its first hydrogen bomb in Siberia (12 Aug.).
'Atoms for Peace': President Eisenhower announces a plan at the UN General Assembly for a pool of fissile material to be available for peaceful purposes (Dec.).

1954   'Massive Retaliation': in the aftermath of the Korean War, John Foster Dulles, US Secretary of State, announces that 'Local defence must be reinforced by the further deterrent of massive retaliatory power', that is, by the threat of nuclear weapons (12 Jan.).
First atomic power station opened at Obninsk, USSR (27 June).
USS Nautilus, first American atomic powered submarine, commissioned (Sept.).

1955   At the Geneva Summit, President Eisenhower puts forward his 'open skies' proposal for mutual aerial photography of each other's territory by the Soviet Union and United States as a step towards disarmament (July).

1956   Britain opens first large-scale commercial nuclear power station at Calder Hall, Cumbria (23 Oct.), but mainly used for defence purposes.

1957   First British hydrogen bomb exploded near Christmas Island (15 Aug.).
        UN International Atomic Energy Agency established to promote the safe use of atomic energy for peaceful purposes (July).
        Soviet Union announces the successful launch of an inter-continental ballistic missile (26 Aug.).
        Adam Rapacki, Foreign Minister of Poland, proposes in a speech to the UN General Assembly the creation of a nuclear-free zone in central Europe. Plan rejected by NATO on the grounds that nuclear weapons are essential to offset Soviet superiority in conventional forces (2 Oct.).

1958   First meeting of Britain's Campaign for Nuclear Disarmament (CND) held in London (17 Feb.).
        Successful firing of America's first inter-continental ballistic missile, the liquid-fuelled Atlas (Nov.).

1959   Establishment of the Ten-Power Committee on Disarmament, comprising representatives from Britain, Canada, France, Italy, United States, Bulgaria, Czechoslovakia, Poland, Romania and Soviet Union (7 Sept.). Treaty for the peaceful use of Antarctica opened for signature in Washington.

1960   France explodes its first atomic device in the Sahara (13 Feb.).
        First successful underwater firing of a Polaris missile from the USS *George Washington* (20 July).
        First Polaris nuclear submarine, USS *George Washington*, becomes operational (15 Nov.).
        United States offers 5 submarines with 80 Polaris missiles to create a NATO Multilateral Nuclear Force at the NATO ministerial meeting in Paris (Dec.).

1962   First meeting in Geneva of the Eighteen Nation Disarmament Committee, the former Ten-Power Committee with the addition of Brazil, Burma, Egypt, Ethiopia, India, Mexico, Nigeria and Sweden (14 March).
        US Secretary of Defence, Robert McNamara, announces in a speech at the University of Michigan, Ann Arbor, a new strategy of 'flexible response' to replace that of 'massive retaliation' (June).
        Cuban missile crisis: President Kennedy announces on 22 October that aerial reconnaissance has established that offensive missile sites are being constructed by the Soviet Union in Cuba and that a naval and air 'quarantine' is being imposed until the sites are dismantled.
        On 28 October Mr Khrushchev agrees to remove the missiles from Cuba in return for an American guarantee not to invade (Oct.).
        President Kennedy meets British Prime Minister, Harold Macmillan, at Nassau in the Bahamas and agrees to make US Polaris missiles available to Britain for use with British warheads (Dec.).

1963   'Hot Line' agreement between the United States and the Soviet Union (5 Apr.).

Partial Test-Ban Treaty, outlawing nuclear tests in the atmosphere and outer space and underwater (5 Aug.).

1964   First Chinese atomic explosion takes place at Lop Nor in Sinkiang province (16 Oct.).

1965   US Secretary of Defence, Robert McNamara, announces that the United States would rely on threat of 'assured destruction' to deter a Soviet attack (18 Feb.).

1966   NATO establishes the Nuclear Defence Affairs Committee (all members except France, Iceland and Luxembourg) and the Nuclear Planning Group (all members except France and Iceland). (14 Dec.).

1967   Treaty banning all nuclear weapons in outer space opened for signature in London, Moscow and Washington (28 Jan.).
Treaty of Tlatelolco, prohibiting nuclear weapons in Latin America, opened for signature in Mexico (14 Feb.).
First Chinese hydrogen bomb test carried out (17 June).

1968   Non-Proliferation Treaty opened for signature in London, Moscow and Washington (1 July).
France explodes its first hydrogen bomb (25 Aug.).

1969   President Nixon announces the decision to deploy a ballistic missile defence system, 'Safeguard', primarily to defend ICBM sites (14 March). Eight new members join the Eighteen Nation Disarmament Committee, renamed the Conference of the Committee on Disarmament (Aug.).
Five additional members join on 1 Jan. 1975.
Preparatory negotiations on Strategic Arms Limitation Talks (SALT) between the United States and the Soviet Union begin in Helsinki (17 Nov.).

1970   Strategic Arms Limitation Talks open in Vienna (16 April).
First Minuteman III missiles to be equipped with multiple independently targeted re-entry vehicles (MIRVs) become operational in the United States (June).
First successful underwater launch of a Poseidon missile from USS *James Madison* (Aug.).

1971   Sea-bed Treaty prohibiting the emplacement of nuclear weapons on the sea-bed opened for signature in London, Moscow and Washington (11 Feb.).

1972   SALT I anti-ballistic missile agreement and five-year interim agreement on the limitation of strategic arms signed by the United States and the Soviet Union (26 May).

1973   Mutual and Balanced Force Reduction talks between NATO and the Warsaw Pact begin in Vienna (30 Oct.).

1974   US Secretary of Defence, James Schlesinger, announces new doctrine of 'limited strategic strike options' in the event of a nuclear war, in which a broad spectrum of deterrence would be available before the resort to large-scale strategic strikes (10 Jan.).

1974   India explodes its first atomic device at Pokharan in the
        Rajasthan desert (18 May).
        Protocol to the US-Soviet SALT ABM agreement, limiting ABM
        deployment to a single area (3 July).
        US-Soviet Threshhold Test Ban Treaty signed, limiting
        underground nuclear tests (3 July).
        Vladivostok Accord between the United States and the Soviet
        Union, setting out the framework for future negotiations on
        controlling the strategic arms race (24 Nov.).

1976   US-Soviet treaty restricting nuclear explosions for peaceful
        purposes (28 May).

1977   United States announces that it had tested an Enhanced
        Radiation Weapon or 'neutron bomb' (7 July).

1978   President Carter announces the postponement of a decision on
        the production and deployment of the neutron bomb (7 April).

1979   Major nuclear accident in the United States at Three Mile
        Island, Harrisburg, Pennsylvania: thousands of gallons of
        radioactive water and a plume of radioactive gas released (28
        March).
        SALT II agreement signed by United States and Soviet Union,
        restricting numbers of strategic offensive weapons. United
        States withholds ratification of the treaty following the Soviet
        invasion of Afghanistan in December 1979 (18 June).
        NATO announces its intention to modernize its long-range
        theatre nuclear systems by the deployment of 464
        ground-launched Cruise missiles and 108 Pershing II
        medium-range ballistic missiles in Europe (12 Dec.).

1980   Agreement to site 'Cruise missiles' in Europe (June).
        President Carter signs Presidential Directive 59, emphasizing
        the possibility of flexible, controlled retaliation against a range
        of military and political targets in a prolonged nuclear war (25
        July).
        US Department of Defense announces its intention to build an
        Advanced Technology, or 'stealth', bomber with a greatly
        reduced radar detectability (22 Aug.).

1981   In Operation BABYLON Israeli F-16 aircraft drop sixteen tons of
        explosives on Iraq's Osirak nuclear plant on the grounds that
        Iraq is manufacturing nuclear weapons (7 June).
        President Reagan orders the production and stockpiling of the
        neutron bomb, but says that it would not be deployed in
        Europe without NATO's consent (6 Aug.).
        President Reagan authorizes the updating of US strategic
        forces, including the production of one hundred MX missiles
        and the new BI bomber (2 Oct.).
        US-Soviet negotiations on intermediate-range nuclear forces
        open at Geneva (30 Nov.).

1982   Strategic Arms Reduction Talks (START) between United States
        and Soviet Union begin at Geneva (29 June).

1983   President Reagan announces the Strategic Defense Initiative, or

'Star Wars' project, which aims to employ lasers and satellite technology to neutralize a missile attack on the United States (23 Jun.).
Intermediate-range 'Cruise missiles' deployed in Britain, Holland and Germany (Nov.).

1986   Major nuclear accident in the Soviet Union at the Chernobyl site, north of Kiev, involving explosions, fire and release of radioactivity from No. 4 Reactor (26 April).
Summit meeting on arms control between President Reagan and Mr Gorbachev at Reykjavik, Iceland, founders on the issue of the US Strategic Defense Initiative (11–12 Oct.).

1987   President Reagan announces imminent arms control deal and superpower summit with Mr Gorbachev (18 Sept.).
Deployment of Cruise missiles halted in NATO countries (Nov.).
US and USSR reach historic agreement to scrap intermediate range nuclear weapons (24 Nov.), when INF Treaty signed in Washington (8 Dec).

1988   Moscow summit talks between Reagan and Gorbachev (29 May).

1989   Mr Gorbachev offers unilateral cuts in short-range missiles (10 May).
Cruise missiles removed from NATO countries (June), including the Greenham Common site in England, the scene of continuous women's demonstrations in the 1980s. President Bush announces cuts in Strategic Defense Initiative programme; 'stealth bomber' unveiled (July).

Strategic nuclear weapons of the superpowers 1963–1985

	1963	1968	1976	1980	1985
United States					
ICBM	424	1054	1054	1054	1026
SLBM	224	656	656	656	640
LRB	630	600	373	338	241
Soviet Union					
ICBM	90	858	1477	1398	1398
SLBM	107	121	845	1028	979
LRB	190	155	135	156	170

Key: ICBM   Intercontinental ballistic missiles
        SLBM   Submarine-launched ballistic missiles
        LRB   Long-range bombers (range over 6,000 miles)

Source: The International Institute for Strategic Studies, *The Military Balance*, *1976–1977* (London, 1976), p. 75.

The strategic nuclear arsenals of other states 1960–1986

	1960	1976	1986
United Kingdom			
Aircraft	50	50	–[1]
Land-based missiles	–	–	–
SLBM	–	64	64
France			
Aircraft	–	36	34[1]
Land-based missiles	–	18	18
SLBM	–	48	80
China			
Aircraft	–	65	110
Land-based missiles	–	50–80 (est.)	140–180 (est.)
SLBM	–	–	26

Note: SLBM: Submarine launched ballistic missiles.
[1] Aircraft designated for strategic nuclear role only. In 1986 the United Kingdom possessed 201 land-based, short range aircraft capable of carrying a nuclear payload plus 30 carrier-borne aircraft; France had 75 land-based, short range aircraft, plus 36 carrier-borne.

Source: The International Institute for Strategic Studies, The Military Balance, 1976–1977 (London, 1976), pp. 18, 21, 50; Royal United Services Institute and Brassey's Defence Yearbook, 1987 (London, 1987), pp. 462, 465.

Major acts of Terrorism and Assassinations

1914 June 28   Assassination of Archduke Franz Ferdinand at Sarajevo by Gavrilo Princip.

July 30   Assassination of Jean Jaurès, French socialist leader, in Paris.

1918 July 16   Execution of Tsar Nicholas and Russian royal family at Ekaterinburg.

1922 June 22   Assassination of Field-Marshal Sir Henry Wilson, Northern Irish MP, in London, by Irish Republicans.

June 24   Assassination of Walter Rathenau, German foreign minister, by anti-Semitic group.

Aug. 22   Assassination of Michael Collins, leader of pro-treaty Irish, by anti-treaty faction in County Cork.

1923 July 20   'Pancho' Villa assassinated at Parral, Mexico.

1924 June 10   Giacomo Matteotti, prominent Italian socialist, murdered by Fascists.

1927   Kevin O'Higgins, Vice-President of Irish Free State, killed by Irish Republican Army.

1928 July 17   President of Mexico, Alvaro Obrégon, assassinated.

1932 May 1   President of France, Paul Doumer, assassinated by Russian emigré.

1933 Apr. 30   President of Peru, Luis Sanchez Cevro, assassinated.

Nov. 8   King of Afghanistan, Nadir Shah, assassinated.

1934 June 30   Nazis organize murder of leaders of S.A. and other potential rivals the ('Night of the Long Knives').

July 25   Chancellor of Austria, Engelbert Dollfuss, murdered by Austrian Nazis.

Oct. 9   King Alexander of Yugoslavia and Louis Barthou, French foreign minister, assassinated by a Bosnian terrorist in Marseilles.

Dec. 1   Sergei Kirov, a Bolshevik leader, assassinated, almost certainly at Stalin's behest to justify purge of opponents.

1935 Sept. 8   Senator Huey Long assassinated at Baton Rouge.

1939 Sept. 8   Leader of Romanian Iron Guard, Professor Cristescu, and Prime Minister, Armand Calinescu, assassinated.

1940 Aug. 21   Leon Trotsky assassinated in Mexico.

1941   French socialist leader, Marx Dormoy assassinated in bombing at Montelimar, France.

1942 June 5   Yves Paringaux, French chief of staff in Vichy Government, assassinated at Melum, France.

May 31   Reinhard Heydrich, German Governor of Bohemia and Moravia, assassinated by Czech partisans.

Dec. 24	Admiral Darlan, commander of French North Africa, assassinated by French right-winger in Algiers.
1944 July 20	Bomb attempt on Hitler's life at his East Prussian HQ fails.
1945 Feb. 24	Prime Minister of Egypt, Ahmed Maher Pasha, assassinated in Cairo Parliament.
Apr. 28	Benito Mussolini shot by Italian partisans.
1946 July 22	Jewish terrorist bombing of King David Hotel, British Military HQ in Jerusalem, kills forty-two with 52 missing.
1948 Jan. 20	Mahatma Gandhi assassinated in Delhi by a Hindu extremist.
Sept. 17	Count Folke Bernadotte, UN mediator, killed by Jewish terrorists in Jerusalem.
Dec. 28	Prime Minister of Egypt, Nokrashi Pasha, assassinated.
1951 July 20	King Abdullah of Jordan assassinated in Jerusalem.
Oct. 6	High Commissioner of Malaya, Henry Gurney, assassinated in Malaya.
Oct 16	Prime Minister Ali Khan of Pakistan assassinated.
1958 July 14	King Faisal II and the Prime Minister of Iraq, Nuri-es-Said, assassinated in Baghdad.
1959	Prime Minister of Ceylon (Sir Lanka), Solomon Bandaranaike, assassinated by a Buddhist monk (25 Sept, died 27 Sept.)
1960 Aug. 29	Prime Minister of Jordan, Hazza el-Majali, assassinated.
1963 Feb. 8	Prime Minister of Iraq, Abdul Karim Kassem, assassinated in Baghdad.
Nov. 1	Prime Minister of South Vietnam, Ngo Dinh Diem, killed during coup.
Nov. 22	President John F. Kennedy assassinated in Dallas, Texas.
1965 Feb. 21	Malcolm X, American Black Muslim leader, killed in New York.
1966 Sept. 6	Dr Verwoerd, Prime Minister of South Africa, assassinated in Cape Town.
1968 Apr. 4	Dr Martin Luther King, civil rights leader, assassinated in Memphis, Tennessee.
June 5	Robert Kennedy, brother of John and presidential candidate, assassinated by Sirhan Bishara.
July 23	Israeli Boeing 707 hijacked and flown to Algiers by Popular Front for the Liberation of Palestine; first major episode of air piracy.
Aug. 25	US Ambassador to Guatemala killed.
Nov. 22	Car bombing in Jerusalem kills twelve Israelis.

	Dec. 26	Palestinians attack Israeli 707 at Athens airport, killing one passenger.
	Dec. 28	Israeli commandos take over Beirut airport and destroy thirteen Arab aircraft.
1969	Feb. 18	Arab gunmen attack Israeli plane at Zurich airport.
	Aug. 22	US airplane en route to Tel Aviv hijacked and forced to fly to Damascus where it is destroyed; hostages exchanged for Syrian prisoners.
	Dec. 12	Bomb in Milan kills sixteen people.
1970	Feb. 10	Arab attack at Munich airport kills one Israeli and injures eleven others.
	Mar. 31	German Ambassador to Guatemala kidnapped; found dead (5 April).
	July 31	American diplomat kidnapped and killed by Tupamaros guerrillas in Montevideo, Uruguay.
	Sept. 6–12	Palestinian terrorists hijack three planes en route for New York, a fourth hijack is foiled. Two are flown to Jordan and one to Cairo. A fourth plane is hijacked and taken to Jordan; all four aircraft destroyed by bombs and passengers exchanged in deal for Arab terrorists in prison in Europe.
	Oct. 10–18	Pierre Laporte, Quebec Labour Minister, seized by separatists in Montreal and killed.
1971	Mar. 14	Sabotage of fuel tanks in Rotterdam by pro-Palestinians.
	Apr. 15	Yugoslav Ambassador to Sweden shot by Croatian extremists in Stockholm.
	Aug. 21	Ten killed, seventy-four wounded in grenade attack on opposition rally in Manila, Philippines.
	Nov. 28	Jordanian Prime Minister, Wasif al-Tell, assassinated by Black September terrorists in Cairo.
1972	Feb. 6	Sabotage of gas-processing plants in Rotterdam by Black September.
	Feb. 6	Black September kill five Jordanians in Cologne.
	Feb. 21–23	Hijack of Lufthansa jet from New Delhi to Athens; crew and passengers released after Palestinians paid $5 million.
	Feb. 22	Provisional IRA bomb at barracks in Aldershot, Britain, kills seven soldiers.
	Mar. 18	Toronto supermarket bombing kills two.
	Mar. 21	Fiat executive Oberdan Sallustro kidnapped by Argentinian urban guerrillas; killed (10 April).
	May 8	Belgian airplane hijacked en route from Vienna to Tel Aviv; Israeli soldiers kill two hijackers.
	May 11	Bombs explode at US Army HQ at Frankfurt, killing one.
	May 30	Japanese Red Army terrorists attack aircraft passengers at Lod airport near Tel Aviv, killing twenty-six.
	July 8	Car bomb kills leader of Popular Front for the Liberation of Palestine.

July 21	Bombings in Northern Ireland kill nine people in Belfast.
Sept. 5	Black September attack Israeli athletes at Munich Olympics; two athletes, nine hostages, five terrorists, and one policeman die.
Dec. 8	PLO representatives in Paris assassinated.
1973 Mar. 1	US Ambassador to Sudan and a Belgian diplomat killed when Black September seize embassy in Khartoum.
Mar. 10	Governor of Bermuda and aide assassinated.
May 17	Bombing in Milan kills four.
Aug. 5	Attack on Athens airport by Palestinians kills five and wounds fifty.
Sept. 20	Spanish Prime Minister, Luis Carrero Blanco, assassinated by Basque terrorist bomb in Madrid.
1974 Feb. 3	IRA suitcase bomb kills eleven British soldiers on a coach in Yorkshire.
Feb. 5	Patty Hearst kidnapped by Symbionese Liberation Army.
Apr. 11	Arab terrorists kill eighteen people in apartment block in Kiryat Shmona and are killed themselves.
May 15	Palestinians kill twenty-five people in Israeli village.
May 17	Car bombs in Dublin and Monaghan, Ireland, kill thirty.
May 28	Bomb at anti-fascist rally in Brescia, Italy, kills seven.
June 17	Bomb on Rome-Munich train by neo-Fascist Black Order kills twelve.
June 17	IRA bomb at Tower of London kills one person.
Aug. 30	Bomb in Tokyo kills eight.
Oct. 5	IRA plant bomb in Guildford, England, killing five and wounding seventy.
Nov. 21	Birmingham, England, pubs bombed by IRA, killing twenty-one.
1975 Mar. 5	Attack on hotel in Tel Aviv by Palestinians kills eleven.
Mar. 25	King Feisal of Saudi Arabia assassinated
July 4	Palestinian bomb in Jerusalem kills fourteen.
Oct. 24	Turkish Ambassador to France assassinated in Paris.
Nov. 13	Six killed by bomb in Jerusalem.
Dec. 2–14	South Moluccan terrorists seize train in Netherlands, killing two people before surrender.
Dec. 21	OPEC HQ in Vienna seized by Palestinians and Baader-Meinhof terrorists.
Dec. 29	Eleven killed by bomb at La Guardia airport.
1976 Jan. 4	Five Catholics assassinated in Belfast.
Jan. 5	Ten Protestant workmen assassinated in Belfast.
Feb. 13	Nigerian head of state, General Mohammed, killed in attempted coup.
June 16	American Ambassador to Lebanon and aide kidnapped and killed.

June 27–July 3   Palestinian and Baader-Meinhof terrorists hijack Air France airbus en route from Tel Aviv to Paris and fly to Entebbe, Uganda. Israeli forces make surprise assault, killing seven hijackers and twenty Ugandan troops; most hostages safely released.

July 21   British Ambassador to Ireland, Mr. Christopher Ewart-Biggs, and his secretary killed by an IRA landmine near Dublin.

Aug. 11   Palestinians kill four people at Istanbul airport awaiting El Al flight.

Aug. 20   Right-wing death-squads kill forty-seven people in Buenos Aires.

Oct. 28   Vice-President of Provisional Sinn Fein assassinated by Protestant paramilitaries.

Nov. 17   Palestinian terrorists attack Intercontinental Hotel in Amman; three killed by Jordanian troops.

1977 Apr. 7   Baader-Meinhof terrorists kill West German chief federal prosecutor and two others.

Apr. 10   Former Yemeni Prime Minister assassinated with Yemeni ambassador in London.

May 23   South Moluccan terrorists seize a train at Assen and a school at Bovinsmilde; two hostages and six terrorists killed in ending incidents.

July 30   Bank chairman assassinated near Frankfurt.

Sept. 5–Oct. 19   German industrialist, Hans-Martin Schleyer, kidnapped and murdered by terrorists.

Oct. 11   President of Yemen and brother assassinated.

Oct. 13   Lufthansa aircraft hijacked to Aden, then to Mogadishu where stormed by German commandos, killing three terrorists.

1978 Feb. 14   Bomb attack in Jerusalem kills two people.

Feb. 17   IRA bomb at restaurant in Belfast kills twelve.

Feb. 18–19   Palestinian gunmen seize hostages in Cyprus after killing Egyptian newspaper editor, Yusuf el Sebai; Egyptian troops attempt to seize plane but fifteen of them killed in gun battle.

Mar. 10   Italian judge Rosario Berardi killed by Red Brigades.

Mar. 11   Palestinian terrorists kill thirty-five people on a bus travelling between Haifa and Tel Aviv.

Mar. 16   Aldo Moro, former Italian premier kidnapped and five bodyguards killed; found dead (10 May).

May 20   Arab attack on El Al flight passengers at Orly airport, Paris; three terrorists and one policeman killed.

July 9   Former premier of Iraq, General al-Naif, assassinated in London.

Aug. 6   PLO office in Islamabad attacked killing four people.

Aug. 6   Bomb in Harare, Rhodesia (Zimbabwe) kills seven.

Aug. 13   Bombing of PLO office in Beirut kills 150.
Theatre bomb in Abadan, Iran, kills over four hundred.

Sept. 11   Bulgarian exile, Georgei Markov, assassinated in London.

1979 Jan. 29   Red Brigades assassinate public prosecutor Emilio
                 Alessandria in Milan.
     Feb. 14   US Ambassador to Afghanistan kidnapped in Kabul
                 and dies in release attempt.
     Mar. 22   British ambassador to Netherlands, Sir Richard
                 Sykes, assassinated by the IRA in The Hague.
     Mar. 30   Airey Neave, British Conservative politician,
                 assassinated by IRA at House of Commons.
     June 16   Muslim Brotherhood kill sixty-three Syrian cadets at
                 Aleppo.
     July 13   Palestinian attack on Egyptian embassy in Istanbul
                 kills three.
     Aug. 27   IRA bomb kills eighteen British soldiers at
                 Warrenpoint, Northern Ireland.
     Aug. 27   Lord Mountbatten and three others assassinated by
                 IRA in Sligo, Ireland, by IRA bomb.
     Sept. 21   Red Brigades murder Fiat executive Carlo Ghigliano
                 in Turin.
     Nov. 20–Dec. 4   Grand Mosque, Mecca, seized by Muslim
                 extremists, over 160 killed.
     Dec. 14   American Boeing workers gunned down near
                 Istanbul.
     Dec. 15   Two top PLO men assassinated in Nicosia.

1980 Jan. 31   Thirty-five killed when police storm Spanish
                 embassy in Guatemala seized by guerrillas.
     Mar. 24   Archbishop of San Salvador assassinated by
                 right-wing death-squad; thirty-nine killed at his
                 funeral (30 March).
     Apr. 7   Gun battle with Palestinian terrorists at kibbutz
                 in north Israel leaves seven dead.
     Apr. 30   British SAS storm Iranian embassy in London
                 following seizure of embassy and hostages by
                 Iranian gunmen; two hostages and five terrorists
                 killed.
     July 19   Former Turkish Premier assassinated in Istanbul.
     July 21   Former Premier of Syria assassinated in Paris.
     Aug. 2   Bombing of Bologna railway station by neo-fascist
                 terror group kills eighty-four.
     Sept. 17   Assassination of Anastasio Somoza, former
                 President of Nicaragua, in Paraguay.
     Sept. 26   Bomb at Munich beer festival kills twelve.
     Oct. 3   Bombing of French synagogue kills four.
     Dec. 31   Bombing of Norfolk Hotel in Nairobi, Jewish-owned,
                 kills sixteen.

1981 Jan. 21   Sir Norman Strange and son assassinated by IRA in
                 South Armagh.
     Mar. 2–14   Pakistan Boeing 720 hijacked by Muslim terrorists to
                 Kabul and Damascus; Pakistan diplomat killed.
     Mar. 28   Indonesian aircraft hijacked to Bangkok; shoot-out
                 kills four hostages (28 Mar.).
     May 13   Assassination attempt on Pope John Paul II by
                 Turkish terrorist, Mahmet Ali Agca.

	May 30	President Ziaur Rahman of Bangladesh killed by rebel army officers at Chittagong.
	Aug. 30	President and Prime Minister of Iran killed by bomb.
	Sept. 5	Prosecutor-General of Iran assassinated in Tehran.
	Oct. 6	President Sadat of Egypt assassinated at military review in Cairo.
	Sept. 14	President-elect of Lebanon, Bashir Gamayel, killed by bomb.
	Nov. 28	Muslim Brotherhood bombing in Damascus kills sixty-four.
1982	Mar. 30	Bomb on Paris-Toulouse train kills six.
	June 3	Israeli ambassador to London shot.
	July 20	IRA bombs in Hyde Park and Regent's Park kill 10 bandsmen and soldiers.
	Aug. 7	Armenian terrorists kill eleven in attack on Ankara airport, Turkey (7 Aug.).
	Aug. 9	Gun attack on Jewish restaurant in Paris kills six.
	Aug. 21	Benigno Aquino, Philippine opposition leader, killed at Manila airport.
	Dec. 6	IRA pub-bombing at Ballykelly, Northern Ireland, kills seventeen.
1983	Apr. 18	Bomb attack on American embassy, Beirut, kills sixty.
	May 20	Car bomb in Pretoria, South Africa, kills eighteen.
	July 15	Armenian terrorist bomb at Orly airport, Paris, kills seven.
	July 27	Armenian terrorists seize Turkish embassy in Lisbon; shoot-out leaves five terrorists and one hostage dead.
	Oct. 9	Four South Korean cabinet ministers and seventeen others killed by bomb attack in Rangoon.
	Oct. 19	Prime Minister of Grenada and three others killed by rebels.
	Nov. 4	Suicide truck-bombings of US Marine headquarters and French barracks in Beirut kills 241 Americans and 58 French; Suicide bombing of Israeli HQ in Tyre kills sixty.
	Dec. 17	Bombing of Harrods store in London by IRA kills six.
1984	Feb. 15	Red Brigades kill Leamon Hunt, director-general of Sinai peace-keeping force in Rome.
	Aug. 2	Bomb at Madras airport kills twenty-nine people.
	Aug. 23	Bombing of Tehran railway station kills seventeen.
	Oct. 12	Bombing of Grand Hotel, Brighton, by IRA kills five, and narrowly misses killing British Prime Minister and senior ministers.
	Oct. 31	Mrs Indira Gandhi, Indian Prime Minister, assassinated by members of bodyguard.
	Dec. 23	Bomb on train in Florence kills fifteen.
1985	Apr. 12	Bombing by Muslim extremists in Madrid kills eighteen.

June 14–30	American jet hijacked by Lebanese Shi'ite terrorists, one American passenger killed, before hostages exchanged for Shi'ite prisoners held by Israel.
June 19	Bomb at Frankfurt airport kills three.
July 24	Mine attack on train in Burma kills seventy.
Sept. 25	Muslim extremists kill three Israeli civilians on a boat in Cyprus.
Oct. 7	Palestinians seize Italian cruise liner *Achille Lauro*, killing one passenger.
Nov. 6	M-19 guerrillas in Colombia seize Palace of Justice in Bogota; storming of building leaves all terrorists and seventy-two others dead.
Nov. 23–24	Egyptian airliner hijacked by PLO splinter group; one hostage and sixty others die when plane stormed by Egyptian commandos.
Dec. 27	Arab terrorist attack on Rome airport kills fourteen.
Dec. 27	Arab terrorists kill three in attack on Vienna airport.
1986 Feb. 28	Swedish Prime Minister Olaf Palme assassinated in Stockholm.
Apr. 5	West Berlin discotheque bombed, one US serviceman and a woman killed.
Apr. 25	Five Civil Guards killed by Basque bomb in Madrid.
May 31	Tamil extremist bomb on train in Sri Lanka kills eight.
July 14	Basque separatists kill eleven Civil Guards in Madrid.
Sept. 6	Terrorist attack on synagogue in Istanbul kills twenty-one worshippers.
Sept. 7	President Pinochet of Chile escapes assassination attempt, but five bodyguards die.
Sept. 14	Bomb attack on Seoul airport kills five.
Oct. 25	Basque separatists kill Provincial Military Governor, his wife and son, in bomb attack at San Sebastian.
Nov. 17	Action Directe terrorists kill Georges Besse, Chairman of Renault, in Paris.
Nov. 30	Sikh terrorists kill twenty-four Hindus in bus ambush in northern India.
1987 Feb. 9	Car bomb in Beirut's Muslim quarter kills fifteen.
Mar. 20	Director of Italian Space and Air Armaments Division killed in Rome.
Apr. 17	Over a hundred killed in Tamil bus ambush in Sri Lanka.
Apr. 21	Bomb in Colombo (Sri Lanka) bus station kills 150.
Apr. 25	Northern Irish judge and his wife killed by IRA bomb.
May 20	Car bomb in Johannesburg kills three police.
May 24	Twelve Tamils killed by bomb in Sri Lanka.
June 1	Lebanese Premier, Mr Rashid Karami, assassinated.
June 2	Thirty Buddhist monks killed by Tamil guerrillas.
June 19	Car bomb in Barcelona by Basque separatists kills seventeen.
July 6	Thirty-six bus passengers killed by Sikh extremists in Punjab; another thirty-four killed next day.

	July 14	Bombing in Karachi kills seventy-two.
	Nov. 8	Bomb at Remembrance Day ceremony in Enniskillen, Northern Ireland, kills seventeen.
	Nov. 9	Bomb in Colombo by Tamil separatists kills thirty-two.
	Nov. 29	Bomb on Korean airliner kills all 116 passengers.
	Dec. 11	Basque separatist bomb kills twelve in Saragossa.
1988	Jan. 22	Bomb attacks on funeral in Jalalabad (Afghanistan) kill five.
	Feb. 14	Three PLO officials killed by bomb in Limassol, Cyprus.
	Feb. 19	Bomb attack in Namibia kills fourteen.
	Mar. 6	Three IRA bombers shot by British SAS in Gibraltar.
	Mar. 16	Loyalist gunman kills three at IRA funeral.
	Apr. 14	Car bomb in Naples kills five US servicemen.
	Apr. 22–May 5	Seventeen killed in shoot-out with Kanak separatists in New Caledonia following seizure of hostages.
	Apr. 30	Tamil attacks on buses kill thirty-seven in Sri Lanka.
	June 1	Car bomb in East Beirut kills sixteen.
	June 15	Six soldiers killed by IRA bomb at Lisburn, Northern Ireland.
	Aug. 17	President Zia of Pakistan killed by bomb on aircraft.
	Aug. 20	Eight soldiers killed by bus bomb in Northern Ireland.
	Sept. 30	Sixty killed by gunmen in Hyderabad, Pakistan.
	Oct. 30	Petrol bomb attack by Palestinians at Jericho kills four.
	Dec. 21	Terrorist bomb kills 270 on Pan Am jet which crashes in Lockerbie, Scotland, killing eleven residents.
1989	Jan. 23	Guerrilla attack on army barracks in Argentina leaves thirty-eight dead.
	Mar. 17	Car bombing in Beirut kills twelve.
	Apr. 13	Forty-five killed in Tamil bombing at Trincomalee (13 Apr.).
	Sept. 22	IRA bomb attack on barracks at Deal, England, kills twelve bandsmen.

Section III
Economic and social

Estimated world population 1900–2025

	millions
1900	1,625
1925	1,950
1950	2,516
1975	4,076
2000	6,122 (projected)[1]
2025	8,206 (projected)[1]

[1] Projected figures are the medium variant offered on current assessments of growth. High and Low variants are as follows:

	High	Low
2000	6,340	5,927
2025	9,088	7,358

Source: United Nations, *World Population Prospects: Estimates and Projections as assessed in 1984* (New York, 1986)

Estimated world population 1950-2000

	millions
1950	2,516
1955	2,751
1960	3,019
1965	3,335
1970	3,693
1975	4,076
1980	4,450
1985	4,837
1990	5,246[1]
1995	5,678[1]
2000	6,122[1]

[1] Medium variant of projected population. High and Low variants are:

	High	Low
1990	5,334	5,189
1995	5,827	5,562
2000	6,340	5,927

Source: United Nations, *World Population Prospects: Estimates and Projections as assessed in 1984* (New York, 1986)

Average annual growth of world population 1950–1990

	percentage
1950–55	1.79
1955–60	1.86
1960–65	1.99
1965–70	2.04
1970–75	1.97
1975–80	1.75
1980–85	1.67 (est.)
1985–90	1.63 (est.)

Source: United Nations, *World Population Prospects: Estimates and Projections as assessed in 1984* (New York, 1986)

World population and projections by major areas 1950–2000
(millions)

	Africa	Latin America	North America	Far East[1]	South Asia[2]	Europe	Oceania	USSR
1950	224	165	166	671	704	392	13	180
1960	280	217	199	791	877	425	16	214
1970	361	283	227	986	1,116	459	19	242
1980	479	361	252	1,176	1,408	485	23	265
1985	555	405	264	1,250	1,568	492	25	279
1990[3]	645	451	275	1,324	1,734	499	26	292
2000[3]	872	546	297	1,475	2,074	512	30	315

[1] China, Japan, Korea
[2] India, Pakistan, Bangladesh, South-East Asia
[3] Projected

Source: United Nations, *World Population Prospects: Estimates and Projections as assessed in 1984* (New York, 1986)

Population of individual countries
(millions, rounded to nearest thousand)

Afghanistan	1928	6,500 (est.)
	1950	8,420
	1960	10,016
	1970	12,457
	1980	14,607
	1988	19,340
Algeria	1936	6,000 (est.)
	1950	9,000 (est.)
	1966	11,822
	1972	15,270
	1977	17,422
	1988	23,820
Argentina	1930	10,500
	1947	15,894
	1960	20,011
	1970	23,362
	1980	27,947
	1985	31,730
Australia	1921	5,436
	1947	7,561
	1961	10,508
	1971	12,756
	1984	15,540
Bangladesh	1961	50,854 (East Pakistan)
	1974	71,479
	1981	87,120
	1988	103,630
Brazil	1930	41,100
	1950	51,976
	1960	79,967
	1970	92,342
	1980	118,675

Canada	1921	8,788[1]
	1931	10,376[1]
	1951	14,009
	1971	21,568
	1981	24,343
	1985	25,660

[1] excludes Newfoundland

China	1900	450,000 (est.)
	1930	485,000 (est.)
	1953	590,195
	1965	700,000 (est.)
	1975	933,000 (est.)
	1982	1,081,883
	1985	1,080,920

Cuba	1950	5,858
	1960	7,029
	1970	8,572
	1985	10,038

Egypt	1947	18,967
	1957	22,997
	1966	30,076
	1976	36,626
	1988	51,320

France	1921	39,210
	1931	41,835
	1946	40,507
	1962	46,510
	1975	52,656
	1985	55,730

| Germany | 1925 | 62,400 |
| | 1939 | 69,500 |

		West Germany	East Germany
	1950	47,696	17,199

	1961	53,977	15,940
	1984	61,675	16,660
Ghana	1921	2,078	
	1950	4,242	
	1960	6,772	
	1970	8,614	
	1980	11,457	
	1988	14,045	
India	1921	319,361 (inc. Pakistan)	
	1951	356,879	
	1961	435,512	
	1971	548,160	
	1981	685,120	
	1988	789,120	
Indonesia	1950	79,538	
	1960	96,194	
	1970	120,280	
	1980	150,958	
	1988	172,450	
Iran	1928	12,000 (est.)	
	1956	18,955	
	1966	25,785	
	1976	33,708	
	1988	47,680	
Iraq	1921	2,849	
	1947	4,816	
	1957	6,317	
	1965	8,047	
	1977	12,030	
	1988	16,745	
Israel	1921	757[1]	
	1950	1,748	
	1961	2,183	

	1972	3,148
	1985	4,315

[1] Territory of British Palestine Mandate

Italy	1921	37,404
	1931	40,300
	1951	47,159
	1961	49,904
	1971	53,745
	1985	57,115

Japan	1900	43,763
	1930	60,000
	1950	83,200
	1960	93,419
	1970	103,720
	1980	117,060
	1988	122,400 (est.)

Korea, South	1950	20,357
	1960	25,003
	1970	31,923
	1980	38,124
	1985	42,130

Korea, North	1965	11,100
	1975	16,000 (est.)
	1985	21,185

Malaysia	1921	3,306[1]
	1960	10,992[2]
	1970	8,809[3]
	1980	14,157
	1989	16,640

[1] Former Malay states, including Sarawak and Singapore
[2] Includes Singapore, Sarawak and Sabah
[3] Excludes Singapore which became a separate state, 1965

Mexico	1921	14,800
	1950	25,791

	1960	34,923
	1970	48,225
	1980	67,396
	1988	83,040
Netherlands	1920	6,865
	1930	7,936
	1947	9,625
	1960	11,462
	1971	13,061
	1985	14,454
Nigeria	1921	18,500 (est.)
	1953	30,418
	1963	55,670
	1975	74,870
	1989	110,240
Pakistan	1951	75,842[1]
	1961	93,832[1]
	1972	64,980
	1981	83,782
	1989	105,720

[1] Includes the population of East Pakistan which in 1971 became Bangladesh

Philippines	1950	20,551
	1960	27,904
	1970	37,540
	1980	48,317
	1988	57,410
Poland	1921	27,200
	1931	32,107
	1946	23,900[1]
	1960	29,776
	1985	38,060

[1] The boundaries of the Polish state were substantially altered in 1945; figures for 1946 also reflect very large losses of population in the Second World War

South Africa	1921	6,928
	1946	11,416
	1960	16,003
	1970	21,488
	1980	24,886
	1989	34,335
Spain	1920	21,303
	1930	23,600
	1950	27,977
	1960	30,431
	1970	34,041
	1981	37,746
	1989	39,690
Sri Lanka	1921	4,505
	1960	10,965
	1971	12,711
	1981	14,850
	1987	16,550
Sudan	1921	5,850
	1955	10,260
	1973	12,428
	1983	20,564
	1988	24,235
Taiwan	1953	7,591
	1960	12,345
	1982	18,271
Tanzania	1921	4,122
	1948	8,000 (est.)
	1967	12,231
	1978	17,552
	1985	23,600 (est.)
Thailand	1930	11,000 (est.)
	1950	19,000 (est.)

	1967	29,700	
	1979	45,221	
	1985	50,610	
Turkey	1927	13,648	
	1940	17,821	
	1955	24,065	
	1965	31,391	
	1975	40,348	
	1988	53,230	
United Kingdom	1922	44,372	
	1939	47,762	
	1951	50,225	
	1961	52,709	
	1971	55,907	
	1985	56,618	
USSR[1]	1926	147,000	
	1939	170,500	
	1959	208,800[1]	
	1970	241,700[1]	
	1987	284,580[1]	

[1] Population includes those areas added to the Soviet Union as a result of boundary changes since 1939

United States of America	1920	105,710	
	1930	122,775	
	1940	131,669	
	1950	151,868	
	1960	179,979	
	1970	203,984	
	1980	227,236	
	1987	245,650	
Vietnam	1930	16,500 (est.)[1]	
	1950	26,000[1]	
		North	*South*
	1964	17,900	15,715

	1970	23,787	21,154 (est.)
	1979	52,742[2]	
	1988	64,120[2]	

[1] As part of French Indochina
[2] North and South Vietnam were united in 1975

Yugoslavia	1921	11,985
	1931	13,934
	1948	15,700[1]
	1961	18,549
	1971	20,523
	1981	22,428

[1] Includes territory annexed in 1945

Zaire	1947	10,805[1]
	1958	12,769[1]
	1970	21,637
	1983	31,944

[1] As Belgian Congo

Zambia	1921	807
	1950	2,000
	1974	4,751
	1982	6,242

Zimbabwe	1921	807
	1931	1,130
	1951	2,320
	1974	6,100
	1982	7,532

Sources: United Nations, Demographic Yearbook (New York, 1985)

Population density and urbanization: selected countries

	Population density (per sq. km.)		Urban population (percentage)		
	1975	1985	1950[1]	1970[1]	1985[1]
Afghanistan	30	30	5.8	11.0	18.5
Algeria	7	10	–	–	43.0
Angola	5	8	–	–	25.0
Argentina	9	11	62.5	80.7	85.0
Australia	2	2	68.9	85.6	86.0
Bangladesh	533	720	–	–	12.0
Bolivia	4	6	–	–	48.0
Brazil	13	17	36.2	55.9	73.0
Burma (Myanmar)	45	57	–	–	24.0
Canada	2	2	62.9	76.1	76.0
Chad	3	4	–	–	27.0
Chile	14	17	60.2	76.0	84.0
China	86	112	13.5	16.7	21.0
Colombia	18	26	37.1	57.2	67.4
Cuba	81	94	49.4	60.2	71.8
Czechoslovakia	116	126	51.2	55.5	65.0
Ecuador	24	35	–	–	52.0
Egypt	37	51	30.1	39.8	46.0
Ethiopia	23	37	–	–	12.0
France	96	102	55.9	70.0	73.0
Germany E.	156	153	68.8	73.8	77.0
Germany W.	249	245	71.1	–	86.0
Ghana	41	59	14.5	29.1	39.6
Greece	69	76	36.8	64.7	69.7
Guatemala	57	79	30.5	35.7	41.4
Haiti	165	197	–	–	27.0
Hong Kong	4,179	5,337	–	–	92.0
Hungary	113	114	36.5	45.2	54.3
India	182	246	17.3	19.9	26.0

	1975	1985	1950[1]	1970[1]	1985[1]
Indonesia	69	90	12.4	17.1	25.3
Iran	20	29	30.1	44.0	52.0
Iraq	26	38	33.8	51.1	71.0
Israel	162	212	71.7	85.3	90.0
Italy	185	190	–	47.7	67.0
Japan	297	324	37.5	72.1	77.0
Kampuchea	45	37	–	–	11.0
Kenya	23	39	–	–	20.0
Korea N.	132	176	–	–	64.0
Korea S.	352	428	21.4	40.7	65.0
Laos	14	16	–	–	16.0
Libya	2	2	–	–	65.0
Madagascar	11	18	–	–	22.0
Malawi	43	64	–	–	12.0
Malaysia	36	50	–	–	38.0
Mexico	30	42	42.6	58.7	70.0
Morocco	39	55	–	–	45.0
Mozambique	12	18	–	–	19.0
Nepal	89	122	–	–	8.0
Netherlands	334	351	54.6	78.0	88.4
New Zealand	11	12	–	–	84.0
Nicaragua	17	27	34.9	47.0	59.4
Niger	4	6	–	–	16.0
Nigeria	68	119	10.2	16.1	23.0
Pakistan	87	120	10.4	25.5	29.1
Peru	12	16	–	–	67.0
Philippines	142	191	27.1	33.0	39.6
Poland	109	122	39.8	52.3	61.0
Portugal	103	113	19.3	26.2	31.2
Romania	89	97	31.3	38.2	49.0
Saudi Arabia	3	6	–	20.8	72.0
Senegal	26	34	–	–	36.0
Sierra Leone	43	54	–	–	28.0
Singapore	3,872	4,274	–	–	100.0

	1975	1985	1950[1]	1970[1]	1985[1]
Somalia	5	13	–	–	34.0
South Africa	20	31	42.6	47.9	56.0
Soviet Union	11	13	47.9	56.3	66.0
Spain	70	79	37.0	54.7	76.0
Sri Lanka	213	256	–	–	21.0
Sudan	6	8	–	–	21.0
Sweden	18	19	47.5	81.4	83.0
Switzerland	155	158	–	–	58.0
Syria	40	60	–	43.5	50.0
Taiwan	–	550	–	–	66.0
Tanzania	16	25	–	–	22.0
Thailand	81	99	–	–	20.0
Tunisia	35	47	–	–	57.0
Turkey	51	68	28.8	34.4	46.0
Uganda	49	67	–	–	10.0
United Kingdom	229	236	80.8	78.0	92.0
United States	23	26	64.0	73.5	74.0
Uruguay	16	18	–	–	85.0
Venezuela	13	20	53.8	75.7	87.0
Vietnam	136	195	–	–	20.0
Yemen	27	50	–	–	20.0
Yugoslavia	83	92	18.5	38.6	46.0
Zaire	11	14	15.8	21.6	37.0
Zambia	6.5	10	–	–	50.0
Zimbabwe	16	22	–	–	25.0

[1] Or nearest equivalent date

Population of major world cities*
(thousands)

	1921	1951	1956	1960	1966	1971	1981	1985
Accra	–	136	–	338	–	564	–	860
Addis Adaba	–	–	–	–	–	1,083	–	1,408
Alexandria	–	919	1,278	–	1,081	–	2,576	–
Ankara	–	–	451	1,853	971	1,553	–	1,877
Athens	301	1,379	–	–	–	2,101	3,027	–
Auckland	164	–	–	–	–	797	–	–
Baghdad	–	–	656	–	1,657	2,184	–	2,200
Beijing (Peking)	–	–	4,010	–	–	7,570	–	9,452
Belgrade	112	368	–	585	–	746	–	936
Berlin	3,801	3,337[1]	–	3,261[1]	3,268	–	–	3,049
Bogota	–	648	–	–	1,681	2,978	–	3,968
Bombay	1,176	2,839	–	4,152	–	5,971	8,227	–
Brussels	685	956	–	1,020	1,075	–	997	982
Bucharest	309	–	1,237	–	1,519	–	1,979	1,995
Budapest	1,185	–	1,850	–	1,960	–	–	2,071
Buenos Aires	–	4,603	–	7,000	–	8,925	9,927	–
Cairo	–	–	2,877	–	4,220	–	5,650	–
Calcutta	1,327	4,578	–	4,405	–	7,031	9,166	–

City								
Cape Town	207	578	—	807	—	1,108	—	—
Caracas	—	694	—	—	1,764	—	2,944	2,992
Chicago	—	3,621	—	3,550	—	3,369	3,005	—
Colombo	244	—	409	—	618	—	1,251	—
Damascus	304	—	—	—	—	923	2,359	—
Delhi	—	1,384	—	—	—	3,647	5,714	—
Freetown	—	—	—	—	—	—	—	—
Guatemala City	—	284	—	439	—	707	793	1,600
Hamburg	986	—	1,760	—	1,851	1,400	—	—
Hanoi	—	—	—	644	—	1,825	—	—
Ho Chi Minh City[2]	—	—	—	—	—	—	—	5,364
Hong Kong	600	—	2,240	—	938	—	5,109	—
Houston	—	596	—	—	—	1,234	2,948	1,595
Istanbul	—	—	1,269	—	2,053	3,135	—	—
Jakarta	—	1,865	—	2,907	—	4,576	6,503	—
Johannesburg	288	884	1,153	—	—	1,441	1,534	—
Kabul	—	154	—	—	400	318	377	913
Karachi	—	1,126	—	—	2,721	3,499	5,103	—

[1] East and West Berlin.

[2] Previously known as Saigon.

* The definition of urban areas for individual countries is often at variance with that of other countries; also, the definition of urban areas concerned has sometimes changed in the course of the past century. Figures here are for urban agglomeration unless otherwise stated.

	1921	1951	1956	1960	1966	1971	1981	1985
Khartoum	–	–	–	–	–	228	–	476
Kiev	366	–	–	1,104	1,413	–	2,355	–
Kinshasa	–	–	290	–	508	2,008	–	2,654
Kuala Lumpur	80	–	–	–	–	452	–	938
Lagos	–	272	–	665	–	1,080	–	1,404
Lahore	282	849	–	–	1,674	2,165	2,922	–
Leningrad	722[2]	–	–	3,300	3,706	–	4,779	–
Lima	–	–	–	–	–	3,318	5,259	–
Lisbon	486	790	–	817	–	762	–	807
London	7,488	8,348	–	8,172	7,914	7,281	6,754	6,851
Los Angeles	–	1,970	–	2,479	–	2,812	2,967	3,097
Madras	523	1,416	–	1,729	–	3,170	4,277	–
Madrid	751	–	1,775	2,260	2,559	–	3,188	3,217
Managua	–	109	–	235	–	399	608	644
Manila	–	984	–	1,139	–	1,436	1,630	–
Melbourne	795	–	1,524	–	2,108	2,584	2,604	–
Mexico	–	2,335	–	2,698	–	7,315	–	8,831
Montreal	619	–	1,621	–	2,437	–	2,862	–
Moscow	1,050	–	–	5,032	5,507	–	8,396	8,408
New York	–	7,892	–	7,782	–	7,896	7,072	7,165
Osaka	–	–	2,547	–	3,133	–	–	2,632

City								
Paris	2,907	2,850	4,823	2,790	–	–	8,510	–
Pusan	–	474	–	1,271	–	1,842	3,160	–
Rio de Janeiro	–	2,303	–	3,124	–	4,252	5,093	–
Riyadh	–	–	150	–	225	668	–	1,250
Rome	692	1,652	2,188	–	2,485	–	2,840	2,832
Rotterdam	511	–	712	–	1,048	–	–	1,021
São Paulo	–	2,017	–	3,674	–	5,870	7,034	–
Santiago	–	–	1,539	–	2,314	–	4,132	–
Seoul	–	1,446	–	2,983	–	5,433	8,364	9,646
Shanghai	–	–	6,900	–	–	10,820	–	12,048
Singapore	303	–	–	–	–	2,278	–	2,529
Stockholm	419	744	–	809	1,262	1,493	–	1,562
Sydney	906	–	1,863	–	2,445	2,874	3,022	–
Tehran	–	–	1,512	–	2,695	3,150	–	5,734
Tel Aviv	–	–	364	–	392	1,091	1,305	–
Tokyo	–	–	7,867	–	11,005	–	–	8,389
Toronto	521	–	1,358	–	2,158	–	3,067	–
Vancouver	117	–	665	–	892	–	1,311	–
Vienna	1,866	1,766	–	1,628	–	1,615	1,516	1,531
Warsaw	931	804	–	–	1,261	–	1,621	1,649

[2] The population of Leningrad was artificially depressed in 1921 as a result of the Russian Revolution; its population in 1911 was 1,962,000

Sources: B. R. Mitchell, European Historical Statistics, 1750–1975 2nd edn. (Macmillan, 1980), pp. 76–8; J. Paxton (ed.), The Statesman's Year Book, 1985–86 (Macmillan, 1985)

Life expectancy at birth for world and world areas 1950–1985

	World	Africa	Latin America	North America	East Asia	South Asia	Europe	Oceania	USSR
1950–55	46.0	37.8	51.1	69.1	42.7	39.9	65.3	60.8	64.1
1975–80	58.0	47.6	62.6	73.3	66.6	52.7	72.3	66.5	69.6
1980–85	59.5	49.3	64.2	74.4	68.4	54.9	73.1	67.9	70.9

Source: United Nations, *World Population Prospects: Estimates and Projections as Assessed in 1984* (New York, 1986)

Infant mortality rate for world and world areas 1950–1985

(deaths by age 1 year per 1,000 live births)

	World	Africa	Latin America	North America	East Asia	South Asia	Europe	Oceania	USSR
1950–55	156	191	125	29	182	180	62	67	73
1975–80	85	124	70	14	39	115	19	36	28
1980–85	78	112	62	11	36	103	15	31	25

Source: United Nations, World Population Prospects: Estimates and Projections as Assessed in 1984 (New York, 1986)

Median age of the world population by major areas 1950–1985

	World	Africa	Latin America	North America	East Asia	South Asia	Europe	Oceania	USSR
1950	23.4	18.8	19.7	30.0	23.5	20.4	30.5	27.9	24.7
1975	21.9	17.5	19.1	28.6	21.5	19.0	32.3	25.7	29.1
1985	23.5	17.3	20.8	31.3	24.7	20.3	33.9	27.6	30.3

Source: United Nations, World Population Prospects: Estimates and Projections as Assessed in 1984 (New York, 1986)

Major population and refugee movements

1914   Outbreak of First World War halts massive outflow of emigrants from Europe. Thousands of Belgian refugees flee to Britain and France with German occupation of most of Belgium.

1915–20   Massacres of Armenians by Turks drive hundreds of thousands of Armenians to seek refuge in Soviet Armenia and the Near East.

1917–21   Over a million 'White Russians' flee Russia during the Revolution and Civil War, mainly to France, Britain, Turkey and the United States.

1919–22   Almost 2 million Greeks expelled from Turkey and Bulgaria to Greece and Crete; over 400,000 Turks returned from Crete and Greece to Turkey; 250,000 Bulgarians leave Greece for Bulgaria.

1933–40   Between 250,000 and 300,000 Jewish refugees flee to parts of Europe, Palestine, the United States and Latin America to escape Nazi persecution. Another 70,000 flee the Baltic States to Russia.

1939–40   130,000 *Volksdeutsche* transferred from Soviet Poland to German area of Poland.

1940   Approximately 400,000 Finns evacuate area of Karelia ceded to the USSR. 100,000 Germans from Russia and Bessarabia transferred to Poland or Germany. Several million French and Belgians flee into unoccupied southern France.

1941   Stalin deports 400,000 Volga Germans and other minorities suspected of disaffection to Siberia and Central Asia.

1944   Approximately 7 million foreign workers employed in Germany at peak of war effort.

1944–5   1.2 million Germans flee westward in face of Russian advance.

1945–50   An estimated 1 million German POWs remain in the USSR after peace. 1.4 million 'displaced persons' in Germany, mainly consisting of persons unwilling or unable to return to their home country. Continued flight from east into Allied-occupied Germany, approximately a third of West German population by 1950 consists of people not born in its territory. Repatriation of approximately 3 million Japanese from Co-Prosperity Sphere, Manchuria, Korea and China to Japanese mainland.

1947   At partition of India over 17 million Hindu and Muslim refugees flee to join co-religionists in the new independent states of India and Pakistan.

1948   Jewish population of Palestine rises to 800,000 from 84,000 in 1922 as a result of increased flow of immigrants.

1948–9   Creation of state of Israel and Arab-Israeli War lead to displacement of about a million Palestinian Arab refugees to Syria, Lebanon, Jordan and Egypt.

1948–60   Almost a million Jews, many from eastern Europe and north Africa, emigrate to Israel.

1949   Approximately 2 million Nationalist Chinese under Chiang Kai-shek flee to Formosa (Taiwan) after communist victory in Chinese Civil War.

1950–3   Korean War displaces approximately 3 million Koreans from North to South Korea.

1956   Approximately 200,000 Hungarians flee to West following uprising.

1958   First arrivals of Commonwealth immigrants from West Indies in United Kingdom; beginnings of mass immigration to United Kingdom from West Indies and Indian sub-continent of approximately 1.5 million. By 1985 a total of 2.4 million non-whites in Britain, 40 per cent born there.

1959   Australia alters immigration rules to facilitate non-English speaking immigrants; by 1963 there are 250,000 Italian immigrants. Dalai Lama heads flight of Tibetan refugees to India after Chinese crush revolt.

1960   Beginning of 'guest-worker' system in Germany; by 1970s approximately 2.5 million workers come from Yugoslavia and Turkey.

1971   Thousands of Bangladeshis flee into India to escape fighting in aftermath of declaration of independence.

1972   Ugandan ruler Idi Imin expels 50,000 Ugandan Asians.

1975   Communist victory in Vietnam leads to exodus of 'boat people' to other countries of South-East Asia.

1979   Soviet invasion of Afghanistan leads to an estimated 2 million Afghan refugees in camps in Pakistan.
            Thousands of refugees flee Cambodia for Thailand following Vietnamese invasion to end Pol Pot regime; Red Cross estimates 2 million people in danger inside and outside Cambodia as a result of disruption.

1980   Relief agencies report two million refugees in East Africa, mainly in Somalia, Ethiopia and Sudan, as a result of war and drought. Somalia estimated to have biggest refugee problem in the world and a million refugees have fled to Sudan from Ethiopia, Zaire, Chad and Uganda.

1985   Massive drought in East Africa uproots millions of people.

1987   400,000 refugees flee from Somalia to Ethiopia to escape fighting.

1989   Opening of Hungarian part of 'iron curtain' with Austria permits start of exodus of East Europeans to West. This gathers momentum with the lifting of similar restrictions in Czechoslovakia, East Germany etc. and the symbolic opening of the Brandenburg Gate in December 1989.

Output of wheat 1913–1983: selected countries
(millions of metric tons)

	1913	1924	1938	1950	1962	1972	1983
Argentina	–	–	–	–	7.5	7.9	11.7
Australia	–	–	–	–	8.2	8.4	21.7
Canada	–	–	–	–	15.4	14.5	26.9
France	8.7	7.7	9.8	7.7	14.1	17.9	24.8
Germany[1]	5.1	3.1	6.3	2.6	4.6	7.1	9.0
India	–	–	–	–	11.2	26.4	42.5
Italy	5.7	4.5	8.2	7.8	9.5	9.4	8.5
Pakistan	–	–	–	–	4.2	6.9	12.4
Turkey	–	–	–	–	8.6	12.3	16.4
USSR	28.0	13.0	40.8	31.0	70.8	86.0	82.0
USA	–	–	–	–	33.0	42.0	66.0

[1] West Germany only after 1945.

Sources: B. R. Mitchell, *European Historical Statistics, 1750–1970* (Macmillan, 1975), pp. 249–75; J. Paxton (ed.), *The Statesman's Year Book, 1985–86* (Macmillan, 1985), p. xiii

Output of rice, 1962–1985: major producers
(in thousand metric tons)

	1962	1972	1980	1985
Bangladesh	15,034	15,134	20,821	21,700
Brazil	6,123	6,761	9,776	7,760
Burma (Myanmar)	7,786	7,361	13,100	14,500
China	86,038	105,197	142,993	172,184
India	52,733	58,868	80,312	90,000
Indonesia	12,393	18,031	29,652	34,300
Japan	16,444	15,319	12,189	12,958
Korea, South	4,809	5,500	5,311	7,608
Korea, North	–	3,783	4,960	5,200
Pakistan	1,824	3,495	4,679	5,210
Philippines	3,957	4,898	7,836	8,150
Thailand	11,267	12,413	17,368	18,535
USA	3,084	3,875	6,629	4,523
Vietnam, North	4,600	4,400	11,679	14,500
Vietnam, South	6,029	6,348		

Source: J. Paxton, The Statesman's Year-Book, 1977–78, (Macmillan, 1977), p. xviii; The Statesman's Year-Book, 1985–86 (Macmillan, 1985), p. xviii

Output of coal and lignite 1910–1985: selected countries
(in million metric tons)

	1910	1920	1940	1950	1960	1975	1985
United States[1]	470	521	466	468	377	643	828
United Kingdom	264	230	224	220	197	124	91
USSR	27	11	133	261	509	701	716
Japan	16	29	57	49	51	20	17
Germany	247	250	267	188	240	214	207
(E. Germany after 1945)				140	228	245	278
India	n.a.	20	n.a.	n.a.	n.a.	92	125
Australia	–	–	–	–	–	70	107
China	–	–	–	–	–	425	715
South Africa	–	–	–	–	–	70	146
Poland	–	32	47	83	114	211	117

[1] Short tons

Sources: B. R. Mitchell, *European Historical Statistics, 1750–1970* (Macmillan, 1975), pp. 365–8; J. Paxton (ed.), *The Statesman's Year Book, 1985–86* (Macmillan, 1985)

Output of steel 1910–1985: selected countries
(annual production in million metric tons)

	1910	1918	1930	1940	1950	1960	1975	1985
United States[1]	26.5	45.2	41.4	60.8	96.4	99.3	116.6	84.6
United Kingdom	6.5	9.7	7.4	13.4	16.6	24.7	20.2	15.1
Germany[2]	13.7	15.0	11.5	19.0	12.1	34.1	40.4	35.7
USSR	3.5	0.4[3]	5.8	18.0	27.3	65.2	141.3	154.0
France	3.4	1.8	9.4	4.4	8.7	17.3	27.0	23.3
Japan	0.1	0.8	2.3	5.3	4.8	22.1	114.0	99.5[4]
Italy	0.7	0.3	0.5	1.0	2.4	8.2	21.8	21.7
India	–	–	–	–	–	–	4.9	10.9[4]
China	–	–	–	–	–	–	25.0	29.0
Brazil	–	–	–	–	–	–	7.5	14.7

[1] Figures in net tons of 2,000 lb.
[2] West Germany only after 1945.
[3] Figure reflects the disruption of the Revolution in 1917.
[4] 1982 figures.

Sources: B. R. Mitchell, European Historical Statistics, 1750–1970 (Macmillan, 1975), pp. 399–402; J. Paxton (ed.), The Statesman's Year Book, 1985–86 (Macmillan, 1985)

Motor vehicles produced 1921–1985:
selected countries
(in thousands, commercial and private)

	1921	1929	1938	1965	1975	1985
France	55	142	227	1,616	1,694	3,148
Germany	–	96	338	3,063	3,172	3,334
Italy	–	47	71	1,186	1,459	1,575
Japan	–	–	30	1,876	6,942	11,122
Spain	–	–	–	234	967	1,226
United Kingdom	95	136	445	2,180	1,647	1,313
USA	1,900	4,900	3,947[1]	9,306[3]	6,713[3]	6,739[3]
USSR	–	4	231	814	–	1,300

[1] 1935
[2] 1983
[3] Passenger cars only

Sources: B. R. Mitchell, *European Historical Statistics, 1750–1970* (Macmillan, 1975), pp. 467–9; J. Paxton (ed.), *The Statesman's Year Book, 1985–6* (Macmillan, 1985)

Output of electricity 1920–1985: selected countries

(in million kWh)

	1920	1935	1955	1975	1985
France	5.8	17.5	49.6	180.0	262.8[1]
Germany[2]	15.0	35.7	78.9	301.8	366.9
Italy	4.0	12.6	25.6	140.8	182.9[3]
Russia	0.5	26.2	170.2	1039.0	1418.0[3]
Spain	1.0	3.3	11.9	76.3	117.3[3]
Sweden	2.6	6.9	24.7	80.6	100.1[1]
United Kingdom	8.5	26.0	89.0	272.1	297.3
China	–	–	55.0	121.0	–
India	–	–	25.5[4]	54.6	122.0[1]
United States	43.0	–	–	–	–
Canada	–	–	–	263.3	395.4[3]
Brazil	–	–	–	56.3[5]	152.0[1]
Japan	3.8	24.7	65.2	459.0	581.1[1]

[1] 1982
[2] West Germany only after 1945
[3] 1983
[4] 1964
[5] 1972

Sources: B. R. Mitchell, *European Historical Statistics, 1750–1970* (Macmillan, 1975), pp. 479–82; J. Paxton (ed.), *The Statesman's Year Book, 1985–6* (Macmillan, 1985)

Output of crude oil 1950–1984: selected countries

(million metric tons)

	1950	1960	1975	1984
Americas				
USA	285.2	384.1	411.4	487.0
Canada	3.8	27.5	70.0	82.0
Mexico	10.3	14.1	41.4	150.0
Trinidad	3.0	6.1	11.1	8.0
Venezuela	78.2	148.7	122.1	95.0
Argentina	3.5	9.2	20.2	24.0
Brazil	.1	4.0	9.4	24.0
Middle East				
Iraq	6.7	47.5	111.0	58.5
Iran	32.3	52.1	266.7	105.0
Saudi Arabia	26.6	61.1	352.1	235.0
Kuwait	17.3	81.7	104.8	58.0
Abu Dhabi	–	–	67.3	36.0
Qatar	1.6	8.2	20.8	18.8
Egypt	2.4	3.6	11.7	36.0[1]
Africa				
Nigeria	–	1.0	88.0	68.0
Libya	–	–	72.4	52.5
Algeria	–	8.6	88.0	29.5
Angola	–	–	8.4	9.5
Gabon	–	1.0	13.1	8.0
Far East & Oceania				
China	–	5.0	77.0	110.0
Indonesia	6.5	20.6	65.5	70.5
India	–	–	8.1	28.0
Brunei	4.3	4.7	9.5	8.0
Malaysia	–	–	–	21.0
Australia	–	–	19.3	23.0

	1950	1960	1975	1984
Europe				
United Kingdom	–	–	1.6	125.0
Norway	–	–	1.6	34.5
Romania	4.1	11.5	14.6	12.0
USSR	37.5	148.0	489.8	615.0

Source: J. Paxton, *The Statesman's Year-Book, 1977–78*, (Macmillan, 1977), pp xxvv–xxiii; *The Statesman's Year-Book, 1985–86* (Macmillan, 1985), pp xxii–xxiii

World oil reserves (as assessed in 1985)

	Billions of barrels	% of World Total
Gulf States and Middle East		
Neutral Zone	5.4	0.8
Iran	48.5	6.9
Iraq	44.5[1]	6.4
Kuwait	92.7[1]	13.3
Oman	3.5	0.5
Qatar	3.35	0.5
United Arab Emirates	32.49	4.6
Saudi Arabia	171.7[1]	24.6
Syria	1.45	0.2
Total Middle East	398.38	57.0
Africa		
Algeria	9.0	1.3
Angola	1.8	0.3
Egypt	3.2	0.5
Libya	21.1	3.0
Nigeria	16.7	2.4
Total Africa	55.5	7.9
Western Hemisphere		
USA	27.3	3.9
Mexico	48.6	7.0
Canada	7.1	1.0
Venezuela	25.9	3.7
Total Western Hemisphere	117.7	16.8
Western Europe		
United Kingdom	13.6	1.9
Norway	8.3	1.2
Total Western Europe	24.4	3.5
Asia-Pacific		
Australia	1.5	0.2
Brunei	1.4	0.2

	Billions of barrels	% of World Total
India	3.0	0.4
Indonesia	8.7	1.2
Malaysia	3.5	0.5
China	19.1	2.7
Total Asia-Pacific	37.6	5.4
USSR	63.0	9.0
Other	2.0	0.2
Total World	698.7	100.0

[1] These figures are believed to represent a considerable underestimation.

Source: Adapted from Oil and Gas Journal, December 1984 and December 1985

Gross National Product 1952–1985: major states
($ Billion)

	1952	1960	1970	1975	1985
United States	350	511	977	1,509	3,635
Japan	16	39	195	495	1,158
West Germany	32	71	185	409	613
France	29	60	148	305	489
United Kingdom	44	72	121	215	426
USSR	113	201	390	666	2,063
India	–	–	–	92	194
China	–	–	–	–	262
Brazil	–	–	–	108	209
Canada	–	–	–	152	337

Sources: Various

Inflation rates 1950–1980: selected countries
(percentages)

	UK	USA	W. Germany	France	Italy	Japan
1950–60	4.1	2.1	1.8	5.7	3.0	4.0
1960–70	3.9	2.6	2.6	4.0	4.0	5.7
1970–80	13.7	7.8	5.1	9.6	14.1	9.0

Source: OECD, Main Economic Indicators

Index of consumer prices, 1950–1980: major countries
(1970 = 100)

	1950	1960	1970	1975	1980
UK	44.8	67.2	100	184.4	362.2
USA	61.7	76.2	100	138.6	212.3
W. Germany	64.5	76.9	100	134.7	164.7
France	38.6	67.3	100	152.8	250.4
Italy	50.6	67.9	100	171.1	375.1
Japan	38.7	57.2	100	172.4	237.6

Source: OECD, Main Economic Indicators

Share of world manufacturing exports 1913–1980: major countries
(percentages)

	1913	1929	1937	1950	1960	1970	1980
USA	12.6	20.7	19.6	29.1	17.9	15.3	11.5
UK	29.9	23.6	22.4	25.0	12.7	8.6	6.8
Japan	2.4	3.9	7.2	3.3	5.3	9.3	10.4
Germany[1]	26.4	21.0	22.4	7.1	14.8	15.8	13.9
Italy	3.6	3.7	3.6	3.8	3.9	5.7	5.5
France	12.9	11.2	6.4	10.2	7.4	6.9	6.9

[1] West Germany only after 1945

Sources: H. Tyszynski, 'World Trade in Manufactured Commodities, 1899–1950' The Manchester School, 19 (1951), pp. 278–86; Cambridge Economic Policy Review (1979); National Institute Economic Review

Famines and major natural disasters since 1914

1914 Estimated 9 million starving on northern island of Hokkaido, Japan (Jan.); 2,500 die in Turkish earthquake (Oct.).

1915 29,000 die in earthquake in Central Italy.

1918–19 Central Europe and Germany face mass starvation as a result of wartime Allied blockade and breakdown of government.

1920 Severe famine reported in China.

1921–22 Estimated 18 million suffering from starvation in Russia as a result of Civil War; estimates rise to 33 million in early 1922.

1922 1,000 die in Chilean earthquake.

1923 20,000 die in Persian earthquake (June); between 140,000 and 300,000 dead in Tokyo earthquake (Sept.) with over 2.5 million homeless.

1924 50,000 dead in floods in China.

1928–30 Widespread famine in China; estimated 2 million deaths.

1929 3,000 dead in Persian earthquake.

1930 6,000 dead in earthquake at Pegu, Burma (May); 3,000 die at Naples in earthquake (July).

1931 Over 1,000 killed at Managua, Nicaragua, in earthquake.

1931–3 Widespread famine in Russia and the Ukraine accompanying forced collectivization, several million dead.

1934 Earthquake in Northern India and Nepal kills 10,000 people; typhoon in Japan kills 1,500 (Sept.).

1935 Earthquake at Quetta in Pakistan kills 20,000 people (May); 1,000 die when Oveda dam bursts in Italy (Aug.).

1937 Flooding of Ohio River, USA, makes 750,000 people homeless.

1938 Flooding of Yellow River, China, causes large casualties.

1939 Chilean earthquake kills 30,000 people (Jan.); earthquake in Turkey kills 45,000 people (Dec.).

1941–3 Siege of Leningrad causes an estimated 600,000 civilian deaths, mainly through starvation and disease.

1942–3 Famine in Bengal causes an estimated 1.5–3.5 million deaths.

1944–5 The 'Hunger Winter' in the Netherlands; approximately 15,000 die of shortages.

1945 Tidal wave in East Pakistan (Bangladesh) kills 4,000.

1948 4,000 killed in earthquake in Japan.

1949   7,000 killed in earthquake in Ecuador.

1950   Three earthquakes in Iran kill 1,500.

1953   Over 1,200 people die in coastal floods in Low Countries and Britain (Feb.); 1,000 killed by tidal wave in Greek isles (Aug.).

1954   1,600 killed at Orleansville, Algeria, in earthquake.

1956   Typhoon in China kills over 2,000.

1957   Earthquake in northern Iran kills 2,000 people.

1958   Typhoon in Japan kills 1,300 people.

1959   Over 3,000 killed in typhoon in Madagascar.

1960   Earthquake at Agadir, Morocco, kills 12,500 (Feb.); 1,500 die in earthquake at Lars, Iran (April): 3,000 die in East Pakistan floods (Oct.).

1962   Avalanche in the Peruvian Andes kills 3,000 people (Jan.); over 12,000 killed in Iranian earthquake (Sept.).

1963   10,000 die in East Pakistan hurricane (May); Skopje earthquake kills 1,000 people in southern Yugoslavia (July); dam burst in Italy kills 3,000 (Oct.); 4,000 die in Haiti hurricane (Oct.).

1964   Burst reservoir kills 1,000 people in India; typhoon kills 7,000 in Ceylon and Madras.

1965   Typhoon kills 10,000 in East Pakistan.

1966   2,000 die in Turkish earthquake.

1968   Iranian earthquake kills between 11,000 and 20,000 people.

1970   Massive floods in East Pakistan kill between 250,000 and 500,000 people (Nov.); Peruvian earthquake kills an estimated 70,000 people.

1971   5,000 killed by typhoon floods in India.

1972   Earthquake in Managua, Nicaragua kills 10,000 people.

1973   Drought and famine in Sahel area of Mauritania, Senegal, the Gambia, Upper Volta, Mali, Niger and Chad kill an estimated 250,000 people; 100,000 die in Ethiopia.

1974   20,000 feared dead in Chinese earthquake (May); monsoon floods in Bangladesh kill 2,000 (Aug.); typhoon floods in Honduras kill 8,000 (Sept.); earthquake in Pakistan kills 4,000 (Dec.).

1975   Earthquake centred on Lice, Turkey, kills 3,000 people.

1976   Earthquake in Guatemala kills 22,000 people (Feb.); almost a 1,000 killed in Italy by earthquake (May); earthquake in Philippines kills 3,000 (Aug.); 3,700 killed at Van, Turkey, by earthquake (Nov.).

1977   Romanian earthquake kills 1,570 people.

1978   Flood of Jumna river in India kills 10,000 (Sept.); between 5,000 and 20,000 killed in Iranian earthquake (Sept.).

1978–80 Drought and famine in east Africa threaten estimated 10 million with starvation in Sudan, Ethiopia, Somalia and Djibouti.

1979 1,000 killed by hurricanes on Dominica.

1980 Algerian earthquake at El Asnam kills between 2,000 and 20,000 people (Oct.); earthquake in southern Italy kills 3,000–4,000 people (Nov.). UN relief agencies estimate 2 million facing starvation in Cambodia.

1981 Floods in Shansi province, China, kill 5,000 people.

1982 Monsoon floods in India kill several hundred and leave millions homeless (Sept.): earthquake in Yemen kills nearly 3,000 people (Dec.).

1983 2,000 killed in Turkish earthquake.

1984 10,000 killed by typhoon floods in Philippines.

1984–5 Famine in Ethiopia and neighbouring area affects millions, prompting huge relief effort.

1985 10,000 killed in typhoon floods in Bangladesh (May); Mexican earthquake kills 2,000 people (Sept.).

1987 Failure of Ethiopian harvest prompts fresh famine scare.

1988 Armenian earthquake kills thousands.

World health, disease and medicine

1914–16   Widespread government campaigns against venereal diseases amongst troops in Europe, including use of drugs.

1916   First birth-control clinic opened in the USA, in New York by Margaret Sanger and Ethyl Byrne.

1918–19   Influenza pandemic claims an estimated 27 million lives world-wide; first outbreaks in USA and France in spring 1918; spread rapidly to Africa, Asia and China; slackened in winter of 1918–19, but renewed outbreak in March 1919.

1921   First birth-control clinic opened in Britain in Walworth, London. First BCG tuberculosis vaccination carried out in France. Insulin isolated by Banting and Best in Canada, offering prospect of control of diabetes.

1922   Prohibition in the United States produces drop in alcohol-related deaths.
Discovery of link between Vitamin B deficiency and rickets.
Freud publishes *The Ego and the Id*.

1923   Glenny and Hopkins introduce diphtheria and tetanus immunization. League of Nations Health Organization set up in Geneva with branches in Paris, Washington, Alexandria, Sydney and Singapore to act as intelligence centre on epidemics. Scope of activities later widened to include standardization of drugs and sera. Committees set up to investigate malaria, leprosy, cancer, rural hygiene, housing and nutrition. Also action against drug traffic.

1924   Rabies baccillus isolated at Pasteur Institute, Paris. Calmette and Guerin introduce tuberculosis vaccine for general use amongst infants.

1925   Dr. Henry Soutter carries out first heart-valve surgery.

1926   Pasteur Institute produces anti-tetanus serum. Doctors link smoking with mouth cancer.

1927   Vitamin C identified as ascorbic acid.

1928   Fleming makes accidental discovery of penicillin and observes its ability to kill bacteria; first patented 'sticking plasters'. First use of an 'iron lung' in Boston, USA.

1929   Butenandt and Doisy isolate the first sex hormone, oestrone. Discovery of anti blood-clotting agent, heparin.

1930   Fluoride discovered to prevent dental caries. First intra-uterine contraceptive device.

1932   Vaccine developed against yellow fever. Vitamin C isolated.

1933   Virus responsible for influenza pandemic in 1918–19 isolated.

1935   Vitamin E isolated in United States.

1941   Successful use of first antibiotic, penicillin; becomes widely available within next three years for dealing with infections.

1944   Quinine artificially produced.

1946   US research links smoking to cancer.

1948   Antibiotic streptomycin introduced for treatment of tuberculosis. World Health Organization established, based in Geneva with offices in New York and regional offices elsewhere. WHO launches campaign against TB.

1949   Cause of sickle cell anaemia found.

1950   First kidney transplant carried out in Chicago.

1952   Artificial heart pump first used to keep patient alive in United States.

1953   Dr Salk produces successful vaccine against polio. First full chemical analysis of a protein, insulin, carried out by Dr Sanger at Cambridge. Watson and Crick discover structure of DNA. Drs Bunge and Sherman demonstrate that deep-frozen sperm remains fertile, paving way for sperm banks.

1957   Asian flu epidemic.

1958   First heart 'pacemaker' implanted in patient. The drug Thalidomide is associated with birth defects in children. Oral contraceptive – 'The Pill' – becomes available.

1963   First successful kidney transplant to overcome rejection problems.

1966   WHO campaign against TB has completed 400 million tests and 180 million vaccinations.

1967   First heart transplant by Dr Christian Barnard in South Africa.

1969   Human egg fertilized in test tube for first time.

1971   First heart-lung transplant.

1975   WHO announces smallpox eradicated from Bangladesh, leaving Ethiopia only infected area.

1978   First 'test-tube baby' born with use of egg and sperm fertilized outside the womb.

1979   'Body-scanner' for diagnosis developed in Britain.

1980   WHO announces eradication of smallpox.

1981   Identification of an immune deficiency disease, AIDS, affecting homosexual groups in the United States.

1984   AIDS-causing virus discovered. World Health Organization estimates potential deaths at several million, with deaths affecting the heterosexual community also.

1985   Gorbachev launches anti-alcohol campaign in USSR.

1987   Widespread anti-AIDS campaign begun in several countries.

1989   World-wide research on anti-AIDS drugs produces first
       treatments likely to slow progress of disease. Some 200,000
       full-blown cases reported spread over 150 countries; 6–10
       million estimated to be affected by the HIV virus.

The environment and pollution: major events since 1945

1945   First atomic explosions in New Mexico and at Hiroshima and Nagasaki.

1946   First nuclear test at Bikini Atoll in the Marshall Islands.

1952–3 First Hydrogen bomb tests in the Pacific Marshall Islands by the United States, and in Siberia by the USSR.

1952   London 'smog' kills an estimated 4,000 people; beginning of serious action to tackle air pollution in United Kingdom; London declared a smokeless zone (1955); Clean Air Act passed (1956). Britain explodes atomic bomb off western Australia.

1957   Major radioactive leak at Windscale nuclear plant in Cumbria, Britain.

1959   Treaty for peaceful use of Antarctica opened for signature.

1960   France begins atomic bomb testing in the Sahara.

1961   World Wildlife Fund opened.

1962   Recognition of the effects of Strontium 90.

1967   *Torrey Canyon* oil spillage off south-western Britain reveals first major concern with effects of pollution on marine environment. Treaty banning nuclear weapons from space.

1971   Sea-bed Treaty prohibits the emplacement of nuclear weapons on the sea-bed. Friends of the Earth founded.

1972   UN Conference on the Human Environment held at Stockholm.

1975   Greenpeace organization founded.

1976   Explosion at chemical plant at Seveso, Italy, releases dioxins into a large area; town evacuated and massive clean-up operation involving removal of thousands of tons of top-soil.

1977   UNESCO sets up fund to save the Acropolis, Athens, from effects of air pollution.

1979   International agreement on trans-national air pollution signed. A major nuclear accident in the United States at Three Mile Island, near Harrisburg, Pennsylvania; thousands of gallons of radioactive water and a plume of radioactive gas released. Temporary evacuation of population puts effective end to nuclear power station construction in United States.

1983   First Green deputies elected to West German parliament; first representation of specific environmental party in Western Europe.

1984   240 killed by gas explosion in Mexico (Nov.); explosion at
        Bhopal, India, and gas leak kills 3,000 people and injures
        200,000 more (Dec.).

1986   Explosion at Chernobyl nuclear reactor in USSR spreads
        radio-active pollution over wide area of the Soviet Union and
        western Europe. Population of Chernobyl evacuated and
        emergency action taken to seal the nuclear core.

1987   Widespread concern about effects of 'acid rain' on western
        European forest areas and waters; agreements to reduce some
        emissions of sulphur dioxide by power stations.
        Nimbus 7 satellite confirms hole in ozone layer over Antarctica
        (Oct.).

1988   Widespread deaths of seals in North Sea from viral infection
        claimed a result of growing pollution.
        Explosion from leak in trans-Siberian pipeline in the Urals,
        USSR, kills several thousand people in railway trains.
        International recognition of global climatic change in depletion
        of 'ozone layer' and 'greenhouse effect'. First measures to
        reduce use of harmful CFC gases and to encourage further
        research.

1989   Massive spillage from oil-tanker *Exxon Valdez* off Alaska
        contaminates large area of coastline.
        Euro-elections show continued growth of Green Movement as a
        political force.
        Crippled Iranian oil-tanker *Kharg V* creates 260 square km oil
        slick off coast of Morocco (Dec.).

Section IV
Biographies

Abbas, Ferhat (1900–): Algerian nationalist. One of the leaders of the Algerian independence movement. Prime Minister of the 'provisional government' in exile in Tunisia, 1958–61. President of the National Assembly, 1962–63, after independence, but after mounting differences with Ben Bella he resigned.

Acheampong, Ignatius Kutu (1931–): Ghanaian military leader who led the coup whih overthrew Kofi Busia (q.v.) in 1972. He became Chairman of the National Redemption Council government with responsibility also for defence and finance. On 9 October 1975 he became Chairman of the Supreme Military Council. He was deposed in the coup of July 1978.

Acheson, Dean (1893–1971): American statesman. As US Secretary of State from 1949 to 1955 played a key role in establishing NATO (q.v.) and in formulating American policy during the Korean War (q.v.).

Adenauer, Konrad (1876–1967): German statesman. Mayor of Cologne, 1917–33. Removed by Nazis. Prominent member of Catholic Centre Party in Weimar Republic. President of Prussian State Council, 1920–33. Twice imprisoned by Nazis. Founded Christian Democratic Union, 1945. Elected first Chancellor of Federal Republic, 1949; re-elected 1953, 1957. Also Foreign Minister, 1951–55. Negotiated German entry into NATO, EEC. Established diplomatic relations with USSR, 1955. Resigned 1963.

Agnew, Spiro (1918–): Vice-President of the United States, 1969–73. Republican politician, distinguished only as Nixon's (q.v.) surprise running-mate (chosen to secure the Southern vote) and also for his forced resignation in 1973 over his financial affairs.

Allende, Salvador (1908–1973): A founder member of the Chilean Socialist Party, he became its General Secretary in 1942. In 1945 he was elected to the Senate and served as its Vice-President and President. In 1970, as the candidate for the Popular Unity Front, he was narrowly elected as President. His policies 'to open the road to socialism' included land reforms, nationalization of industry and the mines, and opposition to American economic dominance. Following a worsening economic situation and considerable opposition to these policies, a right-wing military junta, backed by the US, overthrew his government in September 1973. Allende died whilst being overthrown in the coup.

Amin, Idi (1925–): Ugandan dictator. As Uganda's army commander he overthrew the government of Milton Obote (q.v.) on 25 January 1971. His period as dictator (1971–79) was marked by massacre and brutality. In 1972 he ordered the mass expulsion of Asians from Uganda. Fled to Libya in 1979 after his overthrow following a Tanzanian invasion.

Aquino, Corazon (1932–): Philippine politician. Entered politics in 1985 following the 1983 assassination of her husband, opposition leader Benigno Aquino. Won 1986 Presidential election despite rigging attempt by Marcos (q.v.). Pro-Aquino demonstrations and the withdrawal of US support forced Marcos's flight. Faced five early attempted coups, but success in a 1987 plebiscite confirmed her as President until 1992. A further coup attempt occurred in 1989.

Arafat, Yasser (1929–   ): Chairman of the PLO (q.v.) since 1969 and head of the Executive Committee of al-Fatah (q.v.) since 1968. He is also known as Abu Ammar. He was a founding member of al-Fatah in 1956 and worked as an engineer in Kuwait between 1957 and 1965. He has steered the PLO in a moderate direction since the October 1973 war.

Assad, Hafez Ali (1928–): President of Syria since 1971, he has shown extraordinary political longevity for a Syrian ruler. He is a member of the Ba'ath Party (q.v.) and became Defence Minister and Commander of the Air Force in 1966. In October 1970 he mounted the *coup d'état* which placed him in office. His support for terrorist activity led Britain to break off relations with Syria in 1986.

Attlee, Clement Richard, 1st Earl Attlee (1883–1967): Elected leader of the Labour Party in 1935. In the war-time coalition government he took office as Lord Privy Seal, 1940–2, Secretary for the Dominions 1942–43 and Lord President of the Council 1943–45. He was Deputy Prime Minister 1943–45 and Prime Minister from 1945 to 1951. As Labour Prime Minister he presided over an active and able cabinet which introduced the National Health Service, comprehensive social welfare and nationalized many basic industries. He presided over the granting of independence to India, Pakistan, Ceylon (Sri Lanka) and Burma, the British withdrawal from Palestine and the onset of the Cold War.

Ayub Khan, Mohammed (1907–1974): Commander-in-Chief of the Pakistani army and Minister of Defence from 1954–55. He became President in 1958. He was re-elected in January 1965, but after widespread strikes and riots, especially in East Pakistan, he resigned in March 1969.

Azana, Manuel (1881–1940): Spanish President. Founded Republican Party, 1924. Subsequently imprisoned. War Minister, 1931. First Prime Minister of Second Republic, 1931–3, and again in 1936. Imprisoned for advocacy of Catalan self-rule, 1934. President 1936–9. Fled to France, February 1939.

Azikiwe, Mhamdi (1904–   ): Premier of Eastern Nigeria from 1954–59, he became Nigeria's Governor-General in 1960 after independence. When Nigeria became a Republic on 1 October 1963 he was its first President. He was deposed in a military coup which occurred while he was in Britain in January 1966.

Balewa, Sir Abubakar Tafawa (1912–66): Nigerian statesman. The first federal Prime Minister of independent Nigeria, 1960–66. On 15 January 1966 he was murdered in a military *coup d'état*.

Banda, Hastings Kamazu (1906–   ): African nationalist. Practised as a doctor in Britain and Ghana before returning to Nyasaland, where he became President-General of the African National Congress in 1958. Riots led to the declaration of a state of emergency, and the arrest of Banda. He was released in April 1960 and became leader of the Malawi Congress Party and first Prime Minister on independence. He has been President of the Republic of Malawi since its declaration on 6 July 1966.

Bandaranaike, Mrs Sirimavo (1916–   ): Sri Lankan politician. Prime Minister 1960–65, the first woman Prime Minister. Prime Minister again from 1970 to 1977, responsible for the 1972 constitution by which Ceylon became the Republic of Sri Lanka.

Batista, Fulgencio (1901–1973): Cuban politician. Army sergeant. Joined a coup against President Machado in 1933, took rank of colonel and attempted to develop a fascist state. Allowed formation of opposition parties, 1937; elected President, 1939. Voluntary exile in Dominican Republic, 1944. Returned as dictator after coup, 1952. Increasingly unpopular with the army and harried by guerrilla forces under Fidel Castro (q.v.) he fled from Cuba, 1958.

Begin, Menachem (1913–   ): Israeli politician. Prime Minister, 1977–83. Became Prime Minister of Israel when his right-wing alignment Likud won a greater number of seats than any other political party in the May 1977 elections. However, since Likud did not gain a majority, it was necessary to form a coalition with other groups represented in Parliament. Begin had commanded the Irgun, a terrorist group operating first against the British in the 1940s. After independence he led the Herut party which became part of the Likud group. He was Minister without portfolio in the National Unity Government formed just before the Six Day War. He opposed any withdrawal from the West Bank but presided over relaxation of tension with Egypt. Joint recipient of Nobel Peace Prize with Sadat (q.v.) in 1978.

Ben Bella, Mohammed Ahmed (1916–   ): Algerian revolutionary leader. Imprisoned by French for political activities, 1950, escaped in 1952. Founded and led *Front de la Libération Nationale* (FLN) in armed struggle against France, 1954. Arrested in 1956, he was freed under terms of Evian Agreements in 1962 to become Algerian President. Overthrown in 1965 and under house arrest till 1979.

Beneš, Eduard (1884–1948): Czech statesman. Worked with Masaryk in Paris during First World War, seeking Czech independence. Principal Czech representative at Paris Peace Conference. Prime Minister, 1921–2, Foreign Minister, 1918–35. Active diplomat, chief proponent of Little Entente (Czechoslovakia, Romania and Yugoslavia, with French support). President of League of Nations Assembly, 1935. Succeeded Masaryk as President, 1935. Resigned, 1938, following Munich Agreement. President of Czech government-in-exile in London, 1941–5. Re-elected president, 1946. Resigned shortly after Communist coup, 1948.

Ben-Gurion, David (1886–1973): Zionist leader. Chairman of the Jewish Agency, 1935–48. Proclaimed the independence of the state of Israel and subsequently became its first Prime Minister (1948–53). He was a key figure in the creation of the modern democratic state of Israel.

Beria, Lavrenti Pavlovich (1899–1953): Soviet secret police chief. Bolshevik organizer in Russian Revolution. Led secret police in Georgia, 1921–31. First Secretary of Georgian Communist Party, 1931. Appointed by Stalin (q.v.) to head Commissariat for Internal Security (NKVD), 1938–53. Deputy Prime Minister, 1941. Politburo member, 1946. Arrested and executed by rivals in Party power struggle following Stalin's death.

Bernadotte, Count Folke (1895–1948): Swedish Red Cross president and United Nations mediator. Arranged exchanges of wounded Allied and German prisoners, 1943–44. Involved by Himmler in rejected peace approaches to Western Allies, January 1945. Appointed UN mediator between Arabs and Jews in Palestine, May 1948. Assassinated by Jewish terrorists, September 1948.

Bhutto, Benazir *see below*

Bhutto, Zulfikar Ali (1928–79): Pakistani politician. Appointed Prime Minister in December 1971 after India's victory over Pakistan. As Foreign Minister, 1963–66, he had favoured close links with China and urged a tough line with India over the disputed state of Kashmir. After a period marked by political and social reforms he was ousted from power in 1977. Executed 1979. His daughter, Benazir Bhutto, became Prime Minister ten years later.

Biko, Steve Bantu (1946–73): South African black nationalist leader. Medical student, helped found South African Students' Organization in 1968, becoming its president, and the Black People's Convention. Organized Black Community Programme to encourage black pride and opposition to apartheid. Banned by South African government, 1973. Death in police custody aroused international condemnation.

Blum, Léon (1872–1950): French Socialist statesman. Elected to Chamber of Deputies, 1919. By 1925, established as a leader of Socialist Party. First Socialist Prime Minister, 1936, leading 'Popular Front'. Introduced important social reforms, including 40-hour working week. Formed second Popular Front, 1938. Imprisoned by Vichy regime, 1940. Accused of being responsible for French military weakness and tried, 1942. Interned in Germany during Second World War. Briefly Prime Minister of caretaker government, 1946.

Botha, Pieter (1916–): South African politician. Entered National Party government in 1958, held a number of posts, becoming party leader and Prime Minister in 1978. He became state President in 1984. His policy of modifying apartheid failed to satisfy black aspirations and international opinion but increasingly alienated his own right wing. Relinquished party leadership following a stroke in January 1989,

retaining presidency until his angry resignation, August 1989.
Resigned from National Party, May 1990, in protest at talks with ANC.

Boumedienne, Colonel Houari (1925–1978): Algerian Prime Minister
and head of government, 1965–78. Ousted Ben Bella (q.v.) from
power in 1965. From 1960–62 he was chief-of-staff of the Algerian
forces fighting for independence from France. In 1962, after
independence, he became Defence Minister. From 1963–65 he was
Vice Premier.

Bourguiba, Habib (1902–): President of Tunisia, 1957–88. A leading
Tunisian nationalist, in 1934 he formed the Neo-Destour Party which
was outlawed by France. He spent several years in prison during the
struggle for independence. Bourguiba has favoured close relations
with the West. In 1975 he was elected President for Life. Deposed in
1988 after he became increasingly senile.

Brandt, Willy (1913–): West German Social Democratic statesman.
Active in opposition to Hitler. Member of Bundestag, 1949–57.
President of Bundesrat, 1955–57. Mayor of West Berlin, 1957–66.
Chairman of Social Democratic Party, 1964. Joined coalition with
Christian Democrats under Chancellor Kiesinger, 1966. Chancellor in
SPD-Free Democrat coalition, 1969. Awarded Nobel Peace Prize, 1971.
Resigned following spy scandal, 1974, remaining Chairman of SPD.
Consistent advocate of improved relations with Eastern Europe
('*Ostpolitik*').

Brezhnev, Leonid Ilyich (1906–1982): Soviet politician. Communist
Party official in Ukraine and Moldavia. Held military posts, 1933–4.
Member of Praesidium of Supreme Soviet, 1952–7. President of
Praesidium, 1960–4, succeeding Marshal Voroshilov. Succeeded
Khrushchev as First Secretary of Central Committee, 1964. General
Secretary of Central Committee, 1966. Chairman of Praesidium, 1977.

Bunche, Ralph (1904–71): United Nations official. Academic turned
State Department official. Involved in establishing the United Nations;
Director of Trusteeship Division, 1947; UN Under-Secretary, 1955–71.
Nobel Peace Prize for work in Palestine, 1950. Led UN peace-keeping
operations in Suez (1956), the Congo (1960) and Cyprus (1964).

Bush, George Herbert Walker (1924–): 41st President of the United
States. Republican politician. Gained lengthy experience as
Vice-President, 1981–89, serving under Reagan (q.v.). The first
Vice-President to be elected President since Martin van Buren in 1836.
Inherited Reagan's legacy of massive budget deficit, a drugs crisis
and external problems in Panama. Bush ordered the December 1989
invasion of Panama to overthrow the Noriega (q.v.) regime and seize
the dictator.

Busia, Kofi Abrefa (1913–78): Nigerian politician. After the deposition of
Nkrumah (q.v.) in 1966 he was made adviser to the National
Liberation Council. On 1 October 1969 he became Prime Minister

when power was handed over to civilian government again. His government encouraged the Africanization of foreign firms. On 13 January 1972 he was overthrown by the military and went into voluntary exile.

Caetano, Marcelo (1906–1980): Portuguese politician. Minister under Salazar (q.v.) in the 1940s and 1950s; retired to academic life in 1959. Following Salazar's retirement was Prime Minister, 1966–74. Attempted liberalization, but its limited nature and his failure to resolve colonial wars in Angola and Mozambique led to 1974 revolution and his exile.

Carter, James Earl (Jimmy) (1924–): 39th US President. Democrat Senator for Georgia, 1962–66. Elected Governor of Georgia 1971. Defeated Ford (q.v.) in Presidential election, 1976. Negotiated Panama Canal Treaty, treaty between Egypt and Israel at Camp David (see p. 420) and the unratified SALT II. Weakened by bad relations with Congress, failure to surmount world oil crisis and economic recession. Bungled rescue attempt of American Embassy hostages in Iran contributed to defeat by Reagan (q.v.) in Presidential election, 1980.

Castro, Fidel (1927–): Cuban revolutionary leader. Prime Minister since 1959. Formerly a lawyer, he was imprisoned in 1953 for an attack on an army barracks in Cuba. Following his release during an amnesty, he went to Mexico and organized the Cuban revolutionary movement. After attempts in 1956 and 1958, the rebels finally occupied Havana in 1959 and overthrew President Batista. He became Prime Minister and head of the armed forces on 16 February 1959. A Marxist, he instituted reforms in agriculture, industry and education and broke away from American economic dominance. In 1961 he routed an invasion of US-supported exiles at the Bay of Pigs (q.v.). The following year his acceptance of Russian help and the installation of Soviet rockets led to the so-called 'Cuban missile crisis'. In 1976 he became head of State and President of the Council of State.

Ceausescu, Nicolae (1918–89): Romanian dictator. Member of underground Communist Party, 1936. Party Secretariat member, 1954. Deputy leader, 1957–65. General Secretary, 1965. Head of State, 1967. Combined independent foreign policy, notably criticism of the 1968 Warsaw Pact invasion of Czechoslovakia, with authoritarian regime, massive repression and personality cult. Repressed demonstrations prompted by economic crisis, 1967. Showed little sympathy for the Soviet line instituted by Gorbachev (q.v.). His corrupt regime and bankrupt economy provoked riots in 1989. Their savage repression led to the December 1989 'winter revolution' (see p. 305). Executed by firing squad after secret trial, 25 December 1989.

Chamberlain, Neville (1869–1940): British Conservative politician. Son of Joseph Chamberlain. Lord Mayor of Birmingham, 1915–16. Director General of National Service, 1916–17. Member of parliament, 1918–40. Postmaster General, 1922–3. Paymaster General, 1923. Minister of Health, 1923, 1924–9. Chancellor of the Exchequer, 1923–4, 1931–7.

Prime Minister, 1937–40. Resigned, 1940, becoming Lord President of the Council in war-time coalition, following rebellion by Conservative MPs in favour of Churchill. Much criticized for attempts to appease Germany and Italy, especially Munich Agreement, 1938. Retired from politics, 1940.

Chiang Ching-kuo: Son of Chiang Kai-shek (q.v.).

Chiang Kai-shek (1887–1975): Chinese general and statesman. He took part in the 1911 Chinese revolution and became chief of staff to the revolutionary leader Sun Yat-sen. In 1928 he became commander of the Guomindang army and head of the government established at Nanking. His forces fought local war-lords, Japanese invaders and communists. He led the government during the Second World War but in 1949 was defeated by the communists and retired to Formosa (Taiwan), from where he continued to lead the Nationalist China government until his death in 1975.

Chou En-lai, (1898–1976): Chinese communist leader. He organized the revolt in Shanghai in 1927, established a partnership with Mao in 1931 and took part in the Long March of 1934–5. After talks with Chiang (q.v.) to establish a coalition failed, he became Prime Minister and Foreign Minister of the new China in 1949. During the Cultural Revolution he used his influence to restrain extremists. He died in office in January 1976.

Churchill, Sir Winston (1874–1965): British statesman. Conservative MP, 1900–4. Became a Liberal in protest at Tariff Reform policies. Liberal MP, 1906–8, 1908–22. Constitutionalist, later Conservative MP, 1924–45. Conservative MP for Woodford, 1945–64. Under-secretary at Colonial Office, 1906–8. President of the Board of Trade, 1908–10. Home Secretary, 1910–11. First Lord of the Admiralty, 1911–15. Chancellor of the Duchy of Lancaster, 1915. Minister of Munitions, 1917–19. Secretary for War and Air, 1919–21. Secretary for Air and Colonies, 1921. Colonial Secretary, 1921–2. Chancellor of the Exchequer, 1924–9. First Lord of the Admiralty, 1939–40. Prime Minister and Minister of Defence, 1940–5. Leader of the Opposition, 1945–51. Prime Minister, 1951–5. Minister of Defence, 1951–2. Knighted, 1953. Resigned 1955. Chequered career. During First World war involved in disputes over Admiralty policy and Gallipoli campaign. Opposed Conservative policies over India and rearmament during 1930s. Advocated prevention of German expansion. War-time leadership earned him legendary status, though not returned to power in 1945. Negotiated war-time alliance with USA and USSR. After Second World War, favoured alliance with USA against USSR.

Coolidge, (John) Calvin (1872–1933): 30th US President. Massachusetts Republican State legislative member 1912–15, Lieutenant Governor 1916–18, Governor 1918. Elected as Harding's Vice-President in 1920. Succeeded to the Presidency on Harding's death, August 1923, going on to win the 1924 Presidential election. Conducted *laissez-faire* policy domestically and non-intervention abroad. Declined nomination for further term, 1928. Apparent

prosperity of Coolidge era exposed as illusory by the Wall Street
Crash seven months after he left office.

Cuellar, Perez de *see under* Perez de Cuellar

Dayan, Moshe (1915–1981): Israeli politician and defence chief.
Foreign Secretary under Begin, 1978–79. Defence Minister between
1967 and 1974, he was blamed for being caught unprepared when the
1973 October war came. From 1953 to 1957 he was chief-of-staff of
the Israeli Defence Forces. He left the army to be active in the Labour
Party and he served as the Agriculture Minister from 1959 to 1964. A
member of Ben Gurion's faction, he left the Labour Party with Ben
Gurion in 1965 but rejoined the government after the 1967 Arab-Israeli
war. He opposed the return of the Arab territory occupied in 1967.

De Gaulle, Charles (1890–1970): French soldier and statesman.
Member of French military mission to Poland, 1919–20. Lectured at
Staff College. Sought to modernize Army. Published 'The Army of the
Future', 1932–4. Ideas subsequently employed by German Army.
Briefly a member of Reynaud's government, 1940. Fled to Britain after
fall of France. Became head of Committee of National Liberation ('Free
French'), 1943. Claimed status of head of government. Led
unsuccessful attempt to recapture Dakar. Entered Paris, August 1944.
President of provisional government, 1945. Suspected of authoritarian
ambitions. Resigned, 1946. Founded political group *Rassemblement du
Peuple Français* (RPF), retiring from its leadership in 1953. During
Algerian Crisis, 1958, invited by President Coty to form temporary
government with wide executive powers. Won overwhelming victory
in referendum on new Constitution. Elected first President of Fifth
Republic, 1959. Granted independence to former French colonies in
Africa, 1959–60. Granted Algeria independence, 1962. Developed
independent nuclear deterrent. Encouraged closer ties with Federal
Germany. Twice vetoed British entry to EEC, 1962–63, 1967.
Re-elected on second ballot, 1965. Re-elected after May 1968 'Events',
but resigned in 1969, following opposition to his plans to reform
Constitution.

Deng Xiaoping, (1904–): Veteran Chinese politician. Secretary-General
of the Chinese Communist Party. Purged during the Cultural
Revolution, but reinstated in 1973. Fell from power again, 1976.
Reinstated and led attack on 'Gang of Four'. Ordered army to attack
democracy gathering in Tiananmen Square, June 1989. Retired from
sole remaining formal Communist Party post, November 1989.

Desai, Morarji (1896–): Indian politician. Long-serving Congress
politician. Deputy Prime Minister, 1967. Out of favour with Indira
Gandhi (q.v.). Formed Janata Party, leading it to victory in March
1977 general election. Became Prime Minister of India at the age of 81.

D'Estaing Valéry Giscard (1926–): French politician. National
Assembly member, 1956–74. Led Independent Republicans. Finance
Minister, 1962–74. Defeated Gaullist and Left opponents in Presidential
election, 1974. Gaullist backing gave him a National Assembly

majority but this weakened in the face of scandals, including one over gifts received from Central African President, Bokassa. Defeated in Presidential election by Mitterrand, 1981.

De Valera, Eamon (1882–1975): Irish statesman. Led group of Irish volunteers in Easter Rising, 1916. Imprisoned, released 1917. Elected MP, 1917. Leader of Sinn Fein, 1917–26. Elected president of Dail Eireann. Opposed 1921 treaty with Britain. Led extreme nationalists during Civil War, 1922–3. Leader of Fianna Fail, winning 1932 elections. Between 1932–8, reduced links with Britain. After 1937, Prime Minister under revised Constitution. Maintained Irish neutrality during Second World War. Lost power, 1948. Re-elected, 1951–4, 1957–9. President, 1959–73

Diem, Ngo Dinh *see under* Ngo Dinh Diem

Dollfuss, Engelbert (1892–1934): Austrian politician. Leader of Christian Social party. Chancellor, 1932–4. Opposed by Nazis and Socialists. Used political violence as pretext for dictatorial government. Suspended parliamentary rule, 1933. Provoked and suppressed Socialist revolt. Granted authority by parliament to implement new fascist-style constitution. Murdered during attempted Nazi coup.

Drummond, Sir James Eric (1876–1951): British diplomat. Joined Foreign Office, 1900. Member of British delegation to Peace Conferences, 1918–19. First Secretary of the League of Nations, 1919–33. British Ambassador to Rome, 1933–39. 16th Earl of Perth, 1937.

Dubcek, Alexander (1921–): Czech politician. First Secretary of the Czechoslovak Communist Party and key figure in the 'Prague Spring' (q.v.) reform movement, which culminated in the Soviet invasion of Czechoslovakia in August 1968; dismissed from his post, he was first President of the New Federal Assembly (August 1968–September 1969) then ambassador to Turkey (December 1969–June 1970) before being expelled from the Communist Party. This attempt to build a national socialism with a 'human face' posed a threat to Soviet control of Eastern Europe. By 1989, however, circumstances had changed. In December 1989 Dubcek was elected Chairman (Speaker) of the Czech parliament.

Dulles, John Foster (1888–1959): American Secretary of State, 1953–59. An advocate of a hard line against Communism, his foreign policy was obdurately opposed to negotiation with Russia and to American recognition of Communist China. Strongly opposed the Anglo-French invasion of Egypt in 1956 – the 'Suez Crisis' (q.v.). *See also* Massive Retaliation.

Eden, Sir Robert Anthony, 1st Earl of Avon (1897–1977): Conservative politician. Eden sat as Conservative MP for Warwick and Leamington from 1925 until he retired in 1957. He acted as parliamentary private secretary to Sir Austen Chamberlain (Foreign Secretary), 1926–9, was under-secretary at the Foreign Office, 1931–3, Lord Privy Seal, 1934–5,

minister without portfolio for League of Nations Affairs, 1935 and
Foreign Secretary 1935–8. In 1938 he resigned in protest at the
government's policy of appeasement. War-time Foreign Secretary,
1940–5. From 1942 to 1945 he was also Leader of the Commons. He
returned to the Foreign Office in 1951 and remained there until 1955.
He was Prime Minister from 1955 to 1957, resigning in 1957 because
of ill-health. Eden was an extremely experienced diplomat but he
miscalculated domestic and world opinion when authorizing the
ill-fated invasion of Suez in 1956.

Einstein, Albert (1879–1955): Great scientist. Mathematical scientist
famous for his theory of relativity. Awarded Nobel Prize, 1921 for his
work in quantum theory. Driven from Germany by the Nazis. Warned
Roosevelt in August 1939 of Nazi research into uranium and alerted
Roosevelt to the urgency of possible use of atomic energy in bombs.

Eisenhower, Dwight David (1890–1969): American statesman and
military commander. After the Japanese attack on Pearl Harbor on 7
December, 1941 he became assistant chief-of-staff in charge of the
Operations division in Washington. He was in command of the
European theatre of operations in 1942, and successively Commander
of the Allied forces in north Africa from 1942–44, Supreme
Commander of the Allied Expeditionary Force in the Western zone of
Europe from 1944–45, Commander of the US Occupation Zone in
Germany in 1945, Chief of Staff of the United States Army from
1945–48, and Supreme Commander of the North Atlantic Treaty
Forces in Europe from 1950–52. In 1952, Eisenhower won the
Republican nomination for the presidency, and then the presidency
itself. In September 1955 he suffered a severe heart attack, and in
June 1956 underwent a serious operation for intestinal disorder. He
nevertheless secured re-election in November 1956. He was succeeded
in office by President John F. Kennedy (q.v.) in February 1961.

Faisal, Abdul Aziz Saud Al- (1905–75): King of Saudi Arabia. After
filling various government posts he became Crown Prince and Prime
Minister in 1953. He competed with King Saud for power and between
1958 and 1964, when Saud was deposed, he had full control of the
Saudi government. In 1964 he was proclaimed king. A conservative
monarch, he had no sympathy with radical Arab regimes and
maintained close relations with the United States. It was under his
rule that Saudi Arabia first claimed huge profits from oil and began to
use that resource for political purposes.

Farouk, King (1920–1965): King of Egypt, 1936–52. His attempts at
land reform and economic development failed in the face of
institutional corruption. Appointed increasingly anti-British
governments, 1944–52. Egypt's military failure against Israel in 1948
and Farouk's personal extravagance led to his overthrow and exile,
1952.

Foch, Ferdinand (1851–1929): French soldier, Marshal of France.
Served as military instructor, 1894–99. Director of *Ecole de Guerre*,
1907–11. Wrote *Principles and Conduct of War*, 1899. Appointed Chief

of Staff, 1917. Created Generalissimo of Allied forces from March 1918; architect of Allied victory on Western Front. Field Marshal, 1919. Supervised implementation of military provisions of Treaty of Versailles.

Ford, Gerald Rudolph (1913–): 38th US President. Michigan Republican Congressman, 1948–73. Nixon's Vice President on resignation of Agnew (q.v.), 1973. Appointed President following Nixon's resignation over the Watergate scandal, 1974. Unique in holding both offices without election. Pardoned Nixon and amnestied Vietnam War draft evaders, 1974. Defeated by Carter (q.v.) in Presidential election, 1976.

Franco, Francisco (1892–1975): Spanish soldier and military dictator. Held command of Foreign Legion in Morocco. Chief of Staff, 1935. Governor of Canaries, 1936. On outbreak of Civil War, integrated Foreign Legion and Moorish troops into rebel army. Became leader of nationalist forces, 1936. Defeated Republican Government, 1939. Established corporatist, authoritarian state, acting as 'Caudillo' (Leader), and ruling Spain as absolutist leader until his death.

Galtieri, Lieut.-Gen. Leopoldo Furtunato (1926–): Argentinian dictator, December 1981 to June 1982. President of Argentina during the invasion of the Falklands (Malvinas) in May 1982. The military failure of the policy led to his removal in June 1982.

Gandhi, Indira (1917–1984): The daughter of Nehru, she joined the Congress Party in 1938. In 1964 she became Minister of Information and in 1966 succeeded Shastri, becoming India's first woman Prime Minister. She survived temporary expulsion from the party leadership in 1969 and in 1971 was re-elected. In 1975 a crisis developed when the High Court declared her election as invalid. This led to the declaration of a state of emergency. Her unpopular measures resulted in an overwhelming defeat for the Congress Party in the March 1977 elections and the loss of her seat. This loss of power was only temporary. Returned as Prime Minister in 1980. Assassinated by Sikh extremists, 1984. Succeeded by her son, Rajiv (q.v.).

Gandhi, Mohandas (Mahatma) (1869–1948): Indian patriot, social reformer and moral teacher. He lived in South Africa from 1893–1914, before returning to India to lead the independence movement. He was a dominating influence in Congress with his policies of non-violence and civil disobedience and was frequently arrested. After independence he continued his fight to rid India of the caste system and to unite Hindu and Moslem, but was assassinated in 1948 on his way to a prayer meeting.

Gandhi, Rajiv (1944–): Indian politician. An airline pilot, he entered politics on the death in 1981 of his elder brother, Sanjay. Held a number of offices under his mother, Indira Gandhi, before succeeding her as Prime Minister at her assassination, 1984. Despatched troops to Sri Lanka to quell militant Tamil separatists, 1987. Defeated by a relatively united opposition in December 1989 elections.

Giap, Vo Nguyen (1912–86): Vietnamese general who defeated the French at Dien Bien Phu (q.v.). Withstood American intervention in the Vietnam war which followed. Deputy prime minister and commander-in-chief, North Vietnam.

Goebbels, Joseph (1897–1945): German Nazi propagandist. Early recruit to Nazi Party. Party chief in Berlin, 1926–30. Became Party's propaganda chief, 1929. Elected to Reichstag, 1930. Minister of Propaganda, 1933–45. Held powerful position in Nazi leadership. Made skilful use of oratory, parades, demonstrations and radio. Attracted to 'radical' aspect of Nazi ideology. Death by suicide.

Goering, Hermann (1893–1946): German Nazi military and political leader. First World War ace pilot. Joined Nazi Party, 1922. Given command of Storm Troopers, 1923. Elected to Reichstag, 1928. President of Reichstag, 1932–3. Entered government, 1933, as Reich Commissioner for Air, Minister President of Prussia and Prussian Minister of the Interior (hence controlled Prussian police). Created Gestapo, 1933. Head of Luftwaffe. Responsible for preparing Germany's war economy. Created General, 1933, Field Marshal, 1938 and Reich Marshal, 1940. Became Hitler's deputy during Second World War. Influence declined after Battle of Britain, 1940. Disgraced after plotting to oust Hitler, 1945. Condemned to death at Nuremberg Trials. Death by suicide.

Gorbachev, Mikhail (1931–): Soviet statesman who succeeded Chernenko as general secretary of the Communist Party in 1985. His advent to power after a succession of ailing, old-guard leaders marked a major departure in the Soviet leadership. Succeeded Gromyko as President, 1988. His reforming policies, especially *perestroika* and *glasnost* have been threatened by nationalism in such areas as Azerbaijan and the Baltic. His policy of non-interference was vital in the 1989 revolutions in Eastern Europe which overthrew the old Communist regimes. Became Executive President, 1990.

Gowon, Yakubu (1934–): Nigerian officer and politician. Head of Federal Military Government, 1966–75. On 29 July 1966 he became Head of State of Nigeria and Commander-in-Chief of the army, following a coup which overthrew the regime of General Ironsi. He led the federal troops in the civil war (1967–70) but was overthrown in a coup on 29 July 1975.

Grivas, George (1898–1974): Greek army officer. Served in World War Two; supported royalists in Greek Civil War. Led EOKA guerrilla movement in Cyprus from 1953 in fight for independence from Britain and union with Greece (Enosis). Commander of post-independence Greek Cypriot National Guard. Recalled to Greece, 1967. Returned to Cyprus to wage underground struggle for Enosis which alienated Turkish Cypriot community, leading to 1975 Turkish invasion and partition of Cyprus.

Gromyko, Andrei Andreevich (1909–1989): Soviet statesman. Attached to Soviet embassy in Washington, 1939. Ambassador in Washington,

1943. Attended Tehran, Yalta and Potsdam Conferences. Elected deputy of Supreme Soviet, 1946. Became Deputy Foreign Minister, and permanent delegate to United Nations Security Council, using veto frequently. Ambassador to Britain, 1952–3. Foreign Minister, 1957–85. Signed partial nuclear test ban agreement, 1963. President of the USSR, 1985–88.

Guevara, Ernesto (Che) (1928–1967): Latin American revolutionary and guerrilla fighter who became a cult figure in the 1960s. Che Guevara was born in Argentina in 1928 and trained as a doctor. He joined Castro's revolutionary army and landed in Cuba in 1956. After the overthrow of Batista in 1959, he acted as a diplomat and administrator in Cuba, and wrote a book analysing the principles and practice of guerrilla warfare. In 1966 he launched a guerrilla campaign in Bolivia, but was captured and executed by Bolivian government forces on 9 October 1967. He became a symbol and martyr for radical students world-wide.

Haig, Alexander Meigs (1924–): American soldier and politician. Brigade commander in Vietnam, 1966–67. President Nixon's military adviser, 1969–73, and White House chief-of-staff, 1973–74. Supreme Allied Commander NATO Forces Europe, 1974–78, where he survived an assassination attempt. Appointed Reagan's Secretary of State, 1981, he resigned in 1982 after increasing conflict with the administration.

Haile Selassie (1892–1975): Emperor of Ethiopia from 1930–74. He was exiled to Britain, 1936–41, during the Italian occupation. He was an active supporter of Pan-African unity and was a President of the Organization of African Unity (q.v.) whose headquarters are in Addis Ababa. He acted as mediator in the Sudanese and Nigerian civil wars but was himself deposed and stripped of his powers by the army in 1974.

Hammarskjold, Dag (1905–61): Swedish statesman. Became Secretary-General of the United Nations in 1953. Killed in an air crash whilst attempting to mediate in the Congo. Posthumously awarded the 1961 Nobel Peace Prize. He previously conducted the UN through the 1956 Suez Crisis with skill and impartiality.

Harding, Warren Gamaliel (1865–1923): 29th US President. Ohio Republican State Senator, 1890–1902. Lieutenant Governor, 1904–06. Elected to Senate, 1914. Won landslide presidential election victory on 'back to normalcy' platform, 1920. Facing depression, Harding reduced taxes, increased tariffs and introduced immigration controls. Called 1921–22 Washington Disarmament Conference to limit size of navies. Death in office, 1923, followed by revelations of administrative corruption (notably the Teapot Dome scandal), though the extent of Harding's awareness was unclear.

Hassan II (1929–): King of Morocco since 1961. Exiled with his father by the French, he returned to Morocco in 1955 and assumed command of the armed forces. He became Prime Minister in 1960. He has survived *coup d'état* and assassination attempts and gradually has assumed wider powers.

Havel, Vaclav (1936–   ) President of Czechoslovakia since unanimous election, 29 December 1989. Former dissident and political prisoner. Born Prague; playright; co-founder of Charter 77. Jailed for 4 months. Victim of smear campaign. Jailed again, 1979, for 4½ years for subversion. Co-founder of Civic Forum, November 1989. Reluctantly accepted popular draft as presidential candidate, December 1989.

Heath, Edward (1916–   ): British Conservative politician. Entered Parliament, 1950. Party Whip, 1951–5. Chief Whip, 1955–9. Minister of Labour, 1959–60. Lord Privy Seal, 1960–3. Secretary for Trade and Industry, 1963–4. First leader of Conservative Party to be elected by ballot, 1965. Prime Minister, 1970–4. Proponent of European integration. Achieved British entry into EEC, January 1973. Failed to tackle problems of inflation and industrial relations. Improved British relations with China. Following electoral defeats of 1974, replaced as leader of Party by Margaret Thatcher, 1975. Has frequently attacked policies of Thatcher from back benches.

Himmler, Heinrich (1900–1945): German Nazi leader and chief of Police. Early member of Nazi Party. Involved in Munich Putsch, 1923. Head of Schutzstaffel (SS), 1929. Head of Gestapo, 1934, subsequently of all police forces, 1936. Head of Reich administration, 1939. Minister of the Interior, 1943. Commander-in-Chief of Home Forces, 1944. Used elaborate system of terror, espionage, detention and murder to reinforce totalitarian state. Bore major responsibility for racial extermination policies. Made attempts to negotiate unconditional surrender before end of war. Tried at Nuremberg. Death by suicide.

Hirohito (1901–1989): Emperor of Japan. Regent, 1921; survived assassination attempt, 1924; succeeded to throne, 1926. Backed Tojo's urging of war against Britain and US, 1941. Threw weight behind those arguing for peace in 1945, accepting Allied unconditional surrender demand in August. Avoided trial as war criminal because General Douglas MacArthur saw him as crucial factor in post-1945 Japanese political stability. Discarded traditional divine status, 1946. Official visits abroad in the 1970s marked recognition of Japan's growing economic status. His culpability in Japan's road to war still disputed by historians.

Hitler, Adolf (1889–1945): Dictator of Germany. Born in Austria. Served in Bavarian Army during First World War, becoming lance corporal, twice decorated with Iron Cross. Joined German Workers' Party in Munich, 1919, transforming it into National Socialist German Workers' Party (NSDAP/Nazi Party), based on extreme nationalism and anti-Semitism. Attempted putsch in Munich, 1923, which proved abortive, though making him a national figure. While in prison wrote his political testament, *Mein Kampf*. Began to reorganize Nazi Party, 1925. Established unrivalled position as leader of Party. Created efficient propaganda machine and organised elite guard, Schutzstaffel

(SS). Helped to power by Great Depression. Nazi Party won 107 seats in 1930 Reichstag elections, becoming second largest party. In elections, July 1932, won 230 seats (highest they ever achieved). Appointed Chancellor by Hindenburg, January 1933, though Nazis still a minority in Reichstag. Following Reichstag fire and Enabling Act, assumed dictatorial powers. Other political parties dissolved. Nazi Party purged of rivals by 1934. On death of Hindenburg, 1934, became President, uniting position with that of Chancellor as Führer ('Leader'). Internal opposition ruthlessly suppressed. Rearmament programme expanded in 1935, aiding economic recovery. Occupied Rhineland, 1936. Rome-Berlin 'Axis' negotiated, 1936. Annexed Austria, 1938 (Anschluss). Gained Sudetenland after Munich Agreement, 1938. Seized remainder of Czechoslovakia, 1939. After non-aggression Pact with USSR (Molotov-Ribbentrop Pact, August 1939), invaded Poland, 1 September 1939, precipitating Second World War. Achieved swift military successes through 'Blitzkrieg' campaigns, but fatal error was in attacking Russia, June 1941. Ordered "final solution" (i.e. mass genocide) of the Jewish people in such camps as Auschwitz and Treblinka where millions died. Faced combined opposition of USSR, USA and Britain. Survived assassination attempt, July 1944. Committed suicide during closing stage of war.

Ho Chi-minh (1890–1969): Vietnamese nationalist and revolutionary. Leader of the Vietnam revolutionary nationalist party of Indo-China, which struggled for independence from France during and after the second world war. In 1945 the independent republic of Vietnam was formed with Ho Chi-minh as president. In 1954 the decisive victory over the French at Dien Bien Phu (q.v.) led to the Indo-China armistice and the Geneva Agreements. Holding power until his death in 1969, he succeeded in welding together the elements of nationalism and communism in North Vietnam. Troops were sent against South Vietnam and, largely through his efforts, a unified socialist Vietnam was brought about in 1975.

Hoover, Herbert Clark (1874–1964): 31st US President. Businessman and organizer of relief operations following World War One, appointed Secretary of Commerce by President Harding, 1921. Elected Republican President in 1928, his attempts to combat the Depression through a Reconstruction Finance Corporation and the relief of state debts failed. Defeated by Roosevelt in 1932 presidential election. Appointed co-ordinator of food supplies to war-ravaged countries, 1946. Headed Hoover Commission to reorganize federal government structure, 1947–49, 1953–55.

Hoover, (John) Edgar (1895–1972): Head of US Federal Bureau of Investigation. Lawyer in Department of Justice, 1917. Special assistant to Attorney General, 1919. FBI Assistant Director, 1921; Director, 1924–72, serving under eight Presidents. Reorganized the Bureau, concentrating on gangsters in the 1930s, enemy spies in the 1940s and communist subversion after 1945. His role became increasingly controversial in the 1960s, when the FBI was accused of harassing anti-Vietnam War and black civil rights activists.

Hoxha, Enver (1908–85): Albanian politician. Joint founder and General Secretary of the Albanian Communist Party (now the Albanian Labour Party) from 1941 to 1985. His significance in the international communist movement has been his support of China in the Sino-Soviet dispute. He broke diplomatic relations with the USSR in 1961, officially withdrew Albania from the Warsaw Pact in 1968. He kept Albania in isolation under a rigid Stalinist regime.

Hua Kuo-feng (1922–   ): Chinese Communist leader. Rapid rise to power from the obscurity of party secretary in a part of Hunan in 1955 to membership of the Central Committee in 1969 and the Ministry of Public Security. In 1973 he moved up to the politburo. Following Chou's death in January 1976 he was a surprise appointment as acting Prime Minister. This post was confirmed in April. After the death of Chairman Mao in October 1976 he became Chairman of the Central Committee of the Chinese Communist Party.

Hussein, King Ibn Talal (1935–): King of Jordan since 1952. Succeeded to the throne upon the abdication of his father. His crown is supported primarily by the tribes and the army as well as subsidies from the United States. His pro-Western sympathies have often been at odds with his more radical neighbours. His relations with Syria and with the PLO (q.v.) have improved after the 1970 civil war against the guerrillas.

Jagan, Dr Cheddi (1918–   ): Independent nationalist. The first Prime Minister of independent Guyana.

Jaruzelski, General Wojcieck (1923–   ): Polish soldier and politician. Long and distinguished army career. Became Chief of General Staff, 1965, Minister of Defence, 1968, and member of Politburo, 1971. Became Prime Minister after resignation of Pinkowski, 1981. Declared martial law in effort to tackle economic crisis and to counter growth of Solidarity movement. Solidarity banned and its leaders detained and tried. Lifted martial law, July 1983. Elected President, 1989.

Jinnah, Mohammed Ali (1876–1948): Pakistani statesman. One of the makers of modern Pakistan. President of the Muslim League. First Governor-General of independent Pakistan.

John Paul II, Pope (1920–): Born Karol Wojtyla. Student and actor, 1938. Quarry-worker in German-occupied Poland. Ordained as priest, 1946. Appointed bishop, 1958, Archbishop of Cracow, 1964, Cardinal, 1967. In October 1978 elected as first non-Italian Pope since 1552. Doctrinally conservative, an extensive world traveller, his popular appeal much in evidence at mass rallies. Survived assassination attempts in May 1981, when he suffered gunshot wounds, and in 1982.

Johnson, Lyndon Baines (1908–1973): 36th President of the United States, 1963–68. Elected to the House of Representatives in 1938 and to the Senate in 1948. Became Democratic leader in the Senate in 1953. Despite suffering a severe heart attack in 1955, he held the post until he became Vice President of the United States in January, 1961.

After completing the presidential term to which the assassinated President Kennedy had been elected, he was nominated to run as Democratic candidate for the presidency in 1964, and election which he won by a large majority. Because of disenchantment within the Democratic Party over his administration's policies towards Vietnam, he did not run for re-election in 1968. He was succeeded by Richard M. Nixon (q.v.).

Kasavubu, Joseph Ileo (1910–1969): Zairean politician who favoured a federal state. He became President in 1960 with Lumumba (q.v.) as Prime Minister after a post-independence election gave neither a majority. He was deposed by the army in November 1965 in a military coup led by Mobutu (q.v.).

Kaunda, Kenneth David (1924–): Zambian politician. President of Zambia since 1964. As leader of the Zambia National Congress, he was imprisoned for nine months, but was released in 1960 and became leader of the United National Independence Party. He has been President of Zambia since 1964, is the creator of the political philosophy of humanism and as one of the front-line presidents (q.v.) he has played an important part in the independence negotiations in Rhodesia and Mozambique. He assumed autocratic powers in 1972 to prevent tribal break-up but, after a new constitution in 1973, his presidency was confirmed. One of the most respected leaders of Africa and the Commonwealth.

Kemal Ataturk (Mustafa Kemal) (1881–1938): Creator of modern Turkish nation. Joined Young Turk reform movement. Entered army, winning quick promotion. Fought Italians in Tripoli, 1911, and in Balkan Wars. Involved in Gallipoli campaign during First World War. Led national resistance after Greek invasion following Turkey's defeat. Renounced loyalty to Sultan and formed provisional government in Ankara, 1920. Led Turks in War of Independence until 1922, expelling Greeks, deposing Sultan and establishing republic. Became first President of Republic, 1923–38. Architect of modern secularized state. Emancipated women. Sought to build strong nation from homelands of Anatolia and residue of European Turkey. Did not attempt to regain former Arab possessions. Territorial settlement with Greece achieved at Treaty of Lausanne, 1923.

Kennedy, John Fitzgerald (1917–1963): American statesman and 35th President. Born May 1917 in Boston, Massachusetts. The son of Joseph Kennedy, a successful businessman and ambassador to the United Kingdom, and a Roman Catholic. He graduated from Harvard University in 1940 and served in the US Navy. Elected to the House of Representatives in 1946. He defeated Henry Cabot Lodge for one of the Massachusetts Senate seats in 1952, and in November, 1960 defeated Richard Nixon (q.v.) in the presidential election by a narrow margin. On 22 November 1963 he was assassinated in Dallas, Texas. A commission under the Chief Justice of the United States Supreme Court, Earl Warren, concluded that he had been killed by one Lee Harvey Oswald, acting alone. He was succeeded by the Vice President, Lyndon Baines Johnson, on the afternoon of his death. His short period as President witnessed the Cuban Missile Crisis. His style and charisma made him one of the most admired and popular presidents of modern times.

Kennedy, Robert Francis (1925–1968): American politician. Presidential campaign manager for his brother, John F. Kennedy, 1960. US Attorney General, emphasizing civil rights and investigating institutionalized crime, 1961–64. Democratic Senator for New York, 1965–68. Assassinated in Los Angeles, June 1968, while campaigning for Democratic presidential nomination on black rights and anti-Vietnam War platform.

Kenyatta, Mzee Jomo (1893–1978): Kenyan national leader. President of Kenya, 1964–78. In 1952 he was arrested on suspicion of leading the Mau Mau rebellion (q.v.) and sentenced to seven years' imprisonment followed by detention. He was released in 1961 and as President of the Kenya African National Union became Prime Minister in 1963 and President in December 1964.

Keynes, John Maynard, 1st Baron Keynes (1883–1946): British economist. Worked at Treasury during First World War. Chief representative at negotiations prior to Treaty of Versailles. Criticized reparations plans in *The Economic Consequences of the Peace*, 1919. Made radical proposals for dealing with unemployment by provision of public works. Ideas influenced Liberal Party's election manifesto, 1929. Full proposals on economic controls in interests of maintaining full employment appeared in *The General Theory of Employment, Interest and Money*, 1936. Inspired 'Keynesian Revolution' during and after Second World War. Rejected classical belief in self-regulating economy. Argued need for government expenditure to be adjusted to control level of public demand. Advised Chancellor of the Exchequer during Second World War. Chief British delegate at Bretton Woods Conference, 1944. Involved in discussions leading to creation of International Monetary Fund and World Bank.

Khama, Sir Seretse (1921–): Botswana national leader. A lawyer exiled from Botswana from 1950–56, he founded the Botswana Democratic Party in 1962 and in 1966 became the first President of Botswana at independence. As a front-line president (q.v.) he played a leading role in Rhodesian independence negotiations and in discussions of the subsequent problems of Southern Africa.

Khomeini, Ayatollah (1900–89): Iranian religious leader of Shi-ite Muslims. His denunciation of the Shah's westernizing reforms and female emancipation led to arrest and exile in France. Urged Iranian army to overthrow Shah and institute Islamic republic. Returned to Tehran when the Shah fled, 1979, and remained the dominant figure until his death, severing relations with the West, enforcing religious fundamentalism, and waging 1980–88 Gulf War with Iraq. Issued death threat against Salman Rushdie, author of the *The Satanic Verses*.

Khrushchev, Nikita Sergeyevich (1894–1971): Soviet politician. Joined Communist Party, 1918. Fought in Civil War. Member of Central Committee of Party, 1934. Full member of Politburo and of Praesidium of Supreme Soviet, 1939. Organized guerrilla warfare against Germans during Second World War. Premier of Ukraine, 1944–47. Undertook major restructuring of agriculture, 1949. Became First Secretary of All Union Party on death of Stalin, 1953. Sensational denunciation of Stalinism, 1956. Relegated Molotov, Kaganovich and Malenkov (potential rivals), 1957. Succeeded Bulganin as prime minister, 1958–64. Official visits to USA, 1959, India and China, 1960. Deposed, 1964, after criticism of his reforms.

Kim Il-sung (1912–): Korean communist. Communist leader of the Democratic Republic of Korea since 1948. He took the title of President in 1972 and has been the centre of an ever-growing personality cult. With Soviet backing he instigated the Korean War (q.v.) in 1950.

King, Martin Luther (1929–68): American black civil rights leader. Ordained as Baptist minister, 1947. Began non-violent civil rights campaign in Montgomery, Alabama, leading boycott of racially segregated buses, 1955–56. Founded Southern Christian Leadership Conference, 1957. An effective orator, notably in his Washington 'I have a dream' speech, 1963. Awarded Nobel Peace Prize, 1964. His assassination in Memphis, Tennessee, April 1968, provoked widespread black riots throughout America.

Kissinger, Henry (1923–): American academic and politician. German-born; US citizen, 1943. Professor of Government, Harvard, 1958–71. Adviser in Nixon's (q.v.) Presidential campaign, 1968. White House National Security Adviser, 1969–73, playing a greater foreign policy role than the Secretary of State. Conducted diplomatic missions in Middle East, Southern Africa and Vietnam. Joint Nobel Peace Prize winner with Vietnamese negotiator Le Duc Tho for extricating US from Vietnam. Secretary of State under Nixon and Ford (q.v.), 1973–77.

Kosygin, Alexei (1904–1980): Soviet politician. Communist Party Central Committee member, 1939. Minister for Economic Planning, 1956–57. State economic planning commission chairman and first Deputy Prime Minister, 1960. Succeeded Khrushchev as Chairman of the Council of Ministers (Prime Minister), 1964. Increasingly overshadowed by Brezhnev (q.v.), his moves towards industrial and agricultural decentralization and consumer goods production largely failed. Resigned on health grounds, 1980.

Laval, Pierre (1883–1945): French politician. Member of Chamber of Deputies, 1914–19, and from 1924 onwards. Originally a socialist, became independent after 1927, on elevation to Senate. Minister of Public Works, 1925. Minister of Justice, 1926. Prime Minister, 1931–32, 1935–36. Foreign minister, 1934–36. Negotiated Hoare-Laval Pact with Britain, 1935. Proponent of closer ties with Germany and Italy. After fall of France, 1940, played major role in creation of

Pétain's Vichy regime. Prime Minister, 1942–44. Collaborated with Germany, e.g. in supply of forced labour. Fled to Germany, then Spain, after liberation of France. Repatriated, tried, and executed for treason.

Lawrence, Thomas Edward (1888–1935): 'Lawrence of Arabia'. British archaeologist sent to persuade Arabs to intensify anti-Turkish campaign, 1916. Skilled guerrilla tactician. Entered Damascus with British troops at head of Arab army, October 1918. Felt Arab interests were betrayed by post-war treaties. Because of this, and other more complex personal motives, sought anonymity by joining the Army and the Air Force under assumed names. Killed in a motor cycle accident.

Le Duc Tho (1911–): Veteran Vietnamese nationalist. A founder member of the Viet Minh (q.v.), he led the North Vietnamese delegation at the Paris peace talks.

Lee Kuan Yew (1923–): Singapore elder statesman. He was one of the founders of the Singapore Socialist People's Action Party in 1954 and has been Prime Minister since 1959. Under his leadership, Singapore has seen remarkable economic development, but political opposition has often been stifled.

Lenin, Vladimir Ilyich (V.I. Ulyanov) (1870–1924): Russian revolutionary leader and architect of Soviet State. After expulsion from Kazan University for political activity, absorbed writings of Marx. In St Petersburg organized League for the Liberation of the Working Class. Exiled to Siberia, 1897. In London, 1903, when Russian Social Democratic Labour Party divided into Mensheviks and Bolsheviks. Led Bolshevik wing and published newspaper, *Iskra* ('The Spark'). Involved in abortive Russian Revolution, 1905. Controlled revolutionary movement from exile in Switzerland. Smuggled into Russia by Germans, 1917. Overthrew Kerensky's provisional government and became head of Council of People's Commissars. Ended war with Germany and concluded treaty of Brest-Litovsk, March 1918. Civil war with 'White' armies continued until 1921. As Chairman of Communist Party, established virtual dictatorship and dissolved Constituent Assembly. Created Communist International.

Liaquat, Ali Khan (1896–1951): Pakistan politician. Prominent pre-World War Two member of Muslim League. First Prime Minister of independent Pakistan, 1947–51, and after death of Jinnah (q.v.) in 1948, the nation's dominant figure. His refusal to declare Pakistan an Islamic state and attempts at friendlier relations with India aroused extremist anger, and he was assassinated in 1951.

Lie, Trygve (1896–1968): Norwegian social democratic politician. First Secretary-General of the United Nations, 1946–53. Advocated admission of Communist China to UN. Helped secure UN aid for South Korea to fight aggression by North Korea.

Lin Biao (1908–1971): Chinese communist military leader. Party member, 1927. Led an army on the Long March and against the

Japanese. Waged successful campaign against Guomindang forces, 1948. Led Chinese armies in Korean War, 1950–52. Appointed Marshal, 1955, and Minister of Defence, 1959. Co-operated with Mao in Cultural Revolution and nominated at 1969 Party Congress as his eventual successor. Reportedly died in a plane crash in Mongolia, after attempting a coup in Beijing, September 1971.

Liu Shao-chi (1898–1974): Chinese Communist leader. Elected to Party Central Committee, 1927. Party principal vice-chairman on establishment of People's Republic, 1949. Chairman of People's Republic, 1959. His position weakened in the Cultural Revolution when he faced criticism for viewing workers as the main revolutionary force rather than, as Mao argued, the peasantry. Stripped of all political posts, October 1968.

Lloyd George, David, 1st Earl Lloyd George of Dwyfor (1863–1945): British Liberal statesman. Member of Parliament, 1890–1945. President of the Board of Trade, 1905–08. Chancellor of the Exchequer, 1908–15. Introduced controversial People's Budget, 1909, proposing increased taxation to fund social reform and naval rearmament. Budget rejected by House of Lords, causing constitutional crisis leading to Parliament Act, 1911. Minister of Munitions, 1915–16. Secretary for War, 1916. Prime Minister, 1916–22. Leader of the Liberal Party, 1926–31. Created Earl Lloyd George, 1945. Dynamic and efficient war-time leader. Attended Paris Peace Conference, 1919. Opposed calls for draconian penalties on Germany. Faced economic problems at home in post-war period. Continuing violence in Ireland led to creation of Irish Free State, 1921, weakening Lloyd George's position, as did revelations of his sale of honours. Forced to resign, 1922, when Conservatives left coalition. Never held office again.

Lon Nol, Marshal (1913–): Former Prime Minister and Minister of Defence in Cambodia. Leader of the coup which overthrew Prince Sihanouk (q.v.) in March 1970. He headed the Republican forces in the civil war, as well as holding the office of President, but was exiled following their defeat by the Khmer Rouge (q.v.) in 1975.

Lumumba, Patrice (1925–61): Zairean politician who favoured central government as opposed to a federation. He became Prime Minister and Minister of Defence in 1960, with Kasavubu (q.v.) as President, after a post-independence election gave neither side a majority. He was dismissed by Kasavubu in September 1960, and captured and reportedly shot by Katangan rebels.

Luthuli, Albert (1899–1967): African Nationalist. Former Zulu chief who became a leading figure in the ranks of the African non-violent resistance leadership. Awarded Nobel Prize for Peace in 1960.

Luxemburg, Rosa (1870–1919): Polish-born German revolutionary leader. Major theoretician of Marxism. Imprisoned for opposition to First World War, 1915–18. Founded German Communist Party in 1918 with Karl Liebknecht, based on earlier Spartacist group. Opposed the nationalism of existing socialist groups, as shown by their participation in War. Critical of German Social Democrats in government. Sought to restrain more violent colleagues, but unable to prevent Spartacist uprising, January 1919. Brutally murdered by counter-revolutionary troops.

MacArthur, Douglas (1880–1964): US General. Army Chief of Staff, 1930–35. Supreme Allied Commander, South West Pacific, World War Two. Received Japanese surrender, 1945. Led occupation forces in Japan, 1945–51, playing a decisive role in preserving Japanese stability. Commander-in-Chief UN forces in Korean War, 1950–51. Dismissed by Truman (q.v.) for urging spread of war into China, contrary to official policy. Failed to win nomination as candidate in 1952 Presidential election.

McCarthy, Joseph (1908–1957): American politician. Republican Senator for Wisconsin. McCarthy alleged in 1950 that over 200 Government employees were either Communist Party members or sympathisers, though he provided no evidence. Chairman of the Senate Sub-committee on Investigations, 1953, where he accused numerous Democrats and Liberals of communist sympathies. His attacks on the Army aroused President Eisenhower's antagonism, leading to a Senate motion of censure against McCarthy in 1954 which ended his career.

Machel, Samora (1933–1986): Mozambique nationalist leader. First President of Mozambique, 1975–86. President of Frelimo (q.v.) from 1970, Machel became President of the transitional government in Mozambique in 1974 and President on independence in 1975. As one of the front line Presidents (q.v.), he was involved in Rhodesian independence negotiations. Killed in plane crash, 1986.

Macmillan, (Maurice) Harold, Earl of Stockton (1894–1987): Conservative politician. Macmillan was Conservative MP for Stockton-on-Tees 1924–29, 1931–45, and for Bromley 1945–64. Served as minister resident at Allied HQ in NW Africa, 1942–45, Secretary for Air, 1945, Minister for Housing and Local Government, 1951–54, Minister of Defence, 1954–55, Foreign Secretary, 1955, Chancellor of the Exchequer, 1955–57 and Prime Minister, 1957–63. As early as the 1930s Macmillan revealed himself as an advocate of the Tory paternalist tradition in the Conservative Party, a stance which suited the mood of the 1950s and facilitated his rise to the premiership. His term in Downing Street was seen as something of a high point of post-war prosperity. But by the time of his resignation in 1963, it appeared to many people that Macmillan's style of leadership was dated and out of touch with the new decade. He retired due to ill-health. Famous also for his 'Wind of Change' speech, recognising the need for decolonisation in Africa.

Makarios, Archbishop (1913–1977): President of Cyprus from 1960 to his death, except for a short interval in 1974. Also, head of the Greek Orthodox Church in Cyprus. Originally a supporter of enosis, or union with Greece, he conducted negotiations with the British in the mid-1950s and was deported by them in 1956. He was released in 1957 but did not return to Cyprus until 1959. He was elected President in 1960 and during his time in office supported Cypriot independence. Forced into 5-month exile after attack on Presidential palace in 1974. He returned to a divided island, and was unable to reassert Greek supremacy over the Turkish Cypriot minority.

Malan, Daniel (1874–1959): South African politician. Dutch Reformed Church preacher, 1905–15. Elected as Nationalist MP, 1918. Intense Afrikaaner nationalist, opposed South African involvement in Second World War. Prime Minister, 1948–54. Instituted apartheid, dividing South Africa on racial lines between black, coloured and white.

Mandela, Nelson Rolihlahlia (1918–): South African nationalist leader. A lawyer. Member of African National Congress (ANC) executive, 1952; advocated multi-racial democracy. Went underground on banning of ANC, 1961; organized *Umkonto we Sizwe* ('Spear of the Nation') for non-terrorist violent action. Arrested and imprisoned for five years, 1962. Life imprisonment at trial for sabotage under Suppression of Communism Act, 1963. Remained a national symbol of resistance to apartheid. Rejected offer of release in return for renouncing political violence, 1986. His wife, Winnie has played an active (if occasionally controversial) political role in South Africa and internationally. Finally released, February 1990.

Mao Tse-tung   *see under* Mao Zedong

Mao Zedong (1893–1976): Chinese Communist leader. Full-time revolutionary, 1923. Saw the peasantry as the main revolutionary force rather than, as in classical Marxism, the urban working class. Chairman of Kiangsi Soviet Republic, 1931. Driven out by Guomindang forces, led the Long March to North West China. Allied with Guomindang against Japanese, 1937. Rejected Stalin's post-war urging to continue alliance with Guomindang, and won a civil war, becoming People's Republic chairman, 1949. Initially followed Soviet model of agricultural collectivisation and industrial development. 'Let a hundred flowers bloom' policy, 1956, sought intellectual support by encouraging ultimately unwelcome criticism of Party. The 1958 'Great Leap Forward' was a turn to small scale labour intensive programmes and was followed by a bitter ideological split with the Soviet Union. The 1966–69 'Great proletarian Cultural Revolution' attempted to accelerate radicalism by rallying the masses and students against the Party bureaucracy. The ensuing chaos and its consequent brake on Chinese development remained unresolved at Mao's death.

Marcos, Ferdinand Edralin (1917–89): Philippine politician. President of the Philippines, 1965–86; also Prime Minister, 1973–86. His regime was marked by massive corruption. Ousted from power in a peaceful coup by Corazon Aquino (q.v.) after rigged elections in February 1986. Given exile haven in Hawaii by the US, where he died in 1989. His wife Imelda was also reknowned for extravagance.

Mariam, Lt.-Col. Mengistu Haile (1937–): Ethiopian leader. Came to power in the 1971 revolution which overthrew Emperor Haile Selassie. Mengistu became first President of Ethiopia in 1987 after a plebiscite approved the country's new constitution.

Meir, Golda (1898–1978): Israeli Prime Minister from 1969 to 1974. After independence, she was very active in the Labour party and was appointed Minister to the Soviet Union in 1948. In 1949 she became the Minister of Labour, a post she held until she was appointed Minister for Foreign Affairs in 1956. She resigned as Minister in 1965 and served as Secretary of the Labour Party until 1968. Elected Prime Minister, 1969. Resigned unexpectedly, 1974.

Menzies, Robert Gordon (1894–1978): Australian politician. Member of Victoria Legislative Assembly, 1928–34. United Australia Party MP, 1934. Appointed Attorney General, 1935. Resigned, becoming party leader and Prime Minister, 1939. His concentration on the war lost him his party's leadership in 1941. Transformed the UAP into the conservative Liberal Party, 1943–45. Prime Minister, 1949–66, encouraging industrial development and an active foreign policy. Succeeded Churchill as Lord Warden of the Cinque Ports, 1965.

Mitterrand, François Maurice (1916–   ): French politician. Socialist deputy, 1946. Ministerial office in 11 governments under the 4th Republic. Unsuccessful Left candidate against de Gaulle (q.v.) in presidential election, 1965. Socialist Party secretary, 1971. Defeated in presidential election, 1974. Elected President, defeating Giscard D'Estaing (q.v.), 1981. Backed by a National Assembly Socialist majority, attempted radical economic policy, 1981–83. After 1986 Assembly elections, shared power with Gaullist majority led by Chirac (q.v.) and moderated policy. Re-elected President, 1988, defeating Chirac. Failed to win Socialist majority in ensuing Assembly elections.

Mobutu, Sese Seke (1930–   ): Zairean politician. President of Zaire since 1965. At the independence of Zaire he was colonel chief of staff of the army. Following the dismissal of Lumumba (q.v.) by Kasavubu (q.v.) he set up a caretaker government, and in 1961 he restored Kasavubu and led attacks on Katanga. In 1965 he deposed Kasavubu and became President and in 1966 Prime Minister and Minister of Defence.

Moi, Daniel Arap (1924–   ): Kenyan politician. Legislative Council member, 1957. Chairman, Kenya African Democratic Union, 1960–61. Minister for Education, 1961–62; Local Government, 1962–64; Home Affairs, 1964–68. Vice President, 1967–78. President following death of Kenyatta (q.v.), 1978. Instituted one-party state and survived coup attempt, 1982. As increased power shifted to the presidency, faced growing international accusations of human rights' abuses.

Molotov, Vyacheslav Mikhailovich (1890–1986): Soviet politician. Emerged as prominent Bolshevik during November Revolution, 1917. Loyal colleague of Stalin, 1921 onwards. Member of Politburo, 1926–57. Helped implement Five Year Plan, 1928. Premier, 1930–41.

Foreign Minister, 1939–49. Negotiated Pact with Ribbentrop, August 1939. Deputy premier, 1941–57. Negotiated treaties with Eastern Bloc countries, 1945–49. Became member of ruling triumvirate following death of Stalin, 1953. Negotiated Austrian State Treaty, 1955. Minister of State Control, 1956–57. Became Foreign Minister again, 1957. Influence declined with rise of Khrushchev. Ambassador to Mongolia, 1957–60. Retired, 1961–62.

Monnet, Jean (1888–1979): French politician, economist and diplomat. Member of Inter-Allied Maritime Commission, 1915–17. First deputy secretary-general of League of Nations, 1919–23. Chairman, Franco-British Economic Co-ordination Committee, 1939–40. Became Minister of Commerce, 1944. Fostered establishment of National Planning Council, becoming head of Council, 1945–47. Architect of European Community. Chairman, Action Committee for United States of Europe, 1955–75. Instrumental in foundation of European Coal and Steel Community. President of ECSC, 1952–55.

Mountbatten (of Burma), Louis Mountbatten, 1st Earl (1900–1979): Naval commander. At the outbreak of the Second World War Mountbatten was commanding the Fifth Destroyer Flotilla. In 1941 his ship, HMS *Kelly,* was sunk in the Mediterranean and he was nearly drowned. He was then appointed adviser on combined operations. His largest operation was the Dieppe Raid in August 1942, which though a failure, taught valuable lessons. Mountbatten was then appointed supreme commander in South-East Asia, arriving in India in October 1943 to find a diversity of problems. After the war he was Viceroy of India, and presided over the partition of the sub-continent and the independence of India and Pakistan. He later returned to a naval career. In 1955 he was First Sea Lord and in 1959 Chief of the Defence Staff. He was assassinated by Irish extremists in 1979.

Mubarrak, Hosni (1928–   ): Egyptian politician. Air Force Chief of Staff 1969–72 commander-in-chief, 1972–75. Vice President, 1975–81. Vice Chairman of National Democratic Party (NDP), 1976–81; NDP Secretary General, 1981–82. President following assassination of Sadat (q.v.) 1981. Renewed relations with Jordan and the Palestine Liberation Organisation. Faced rioting over economic problems, 1986. Further six-year term as President confirmed by referendum, 1987.

Mugabe, Robert Gabriel (1924–   ): Zimbabwean politician. Entered politics, 1960. Deputy Secretary General of Zimbabwe African People's Union (ZAPU), 1961. Arrested, 1962; fled to Tanzania, formed Zimbabwe African National Union (ZANU), 1963. Detained in Rhodesia, 1964–74. Joint leader with Nkomo (q.v.) of Mozambique-based Patriotic Front guerrilla campaign, 1976–79. Attended Lancaster House independence conference, 1979. First Prime Minister of Zimbabwe following election victory over Nkomo and Muzorewa (q.v.), 1980. Moved towards one-party state. Merged ZANU and ZAPU, 1987. Executive President since 1987.

Mujibur Rahman, Sheikh (1920–1975): Bangladesh politician who led the Awami League (q.v.) to victory in the 1970 general election. In

March 1971 he proclaimed the independence of Bangladesh and was arrested and convicted of treason. After the intervention of India in the civil war he was released and became Prime Minister and later President of the new nation. In August 1975 he and his family were assassinated.

Mussadeq, Mohammed (1880–1967): Iranian politician. Foreign Minister, 1922–24. Withdrew from politics but returned to Parliament, 1942. Violently nationalist speeches against Anglo-Iranian Oil Company carried him into office as Prime Minister, 1951. Falling output following nationalization of company and loss of Western expert advisers prevented promised social reforms. Overthrown in coup encouraged by Shah, with CIA support, and arrested, 1953.

Mussolini, Benito (1883–1945): Dictator of Italy. Originally a socialist. Imprisoned for political activities, 1908. Editor of socialist national newspaper, *Avanti*, 1912–13. Resigned from party having been criticised for supporting war with Austria. Founded newspaper, *Il Popolo d'Italia*, Milan, 1914. Organized groups (*fasci*) of workers to campaign for social improvements. Amalgamated into Fascist Party, 1919. Elected to Chamber of Deputies, 1921. During period of civil unrest, led 'March on Rome', 1922. Appointed Prime Minister by King Victor Emmanuel III, 1922. Headed fascist/nationalist coalition, as Duce. Acquired dictatorial powers, 1922. Dictatorship established, 1925. Single party, corporatist state instituted, 1928–29. Large-scale public works introduced. Lateran Treaty settled Church/State relations, 1929. Expansionist foreign policy: Corfu incident, 1924; invasion of Abyssinia, 1935. Created 'Axis' with Hitler, 1936. Left League of Nations, 1937. Annexed Albania, 1939. Declared war on France and Britain, 1940. Invaded Greece, 1940. Military setbacks in East Africa and Libya. Heavily dependent on Germany by 1941. Forced to resign following coup by Victor Emmanuel III and Marshal Badoglio, 1943. Detained, but freed by Germans. Established republican fascist government in German-controlled North Italy. Captured and executed by Italian partisans, April 1945.

Muzorewa, Bishop Abel (1925–): Zimbabwean bishop of the United Methodist Church and nationalist leader. Led the ANC (q.v.) opposition to the Smith-Home proposals in 1971. In 1975 he led the ANC delegation at the Victoria Falls talks and in 1976 represented them at Geneva. Formerly in exile in Lusaka, he returned to Rhodesia to lead the internal group of the ANC after the split in 1977, and in March 1978 was one of the nationalist leaders to sign the internal Rhodesian settlement. Member, transitional government, Zimbabwe-Rhodesia, 1978–80. Heavily defeated by Mugabe (q.v.) in 1980 elections.

Nagy, Imre (1896–1958): Hungarian politician. Lived in USSR, 1930–44. Reforming Agriculture Minister in Hungarian Provisional Government, 1945–46. Prime Minister, 1953–55. Attempted liberalization led to loss of office and expulsion from Communist Party. Re-appointed in October 1956 Hungarian Rising; overthrown by Soviet intervention,

November 1956. Arrested and secretly executed, 1958. Officially rehabilitated, 1988.

Nasser, Gamal Abdel (1918–1970): Leading Arab Nationalist. President of Egypt, 1954–70. Educated at the Royal Military Academy, he fought in the 1948 Arab-Israeli war and, like all officers, was disgusted with King Farouk's provision of faulty arms to his troops. Founded the Free Officers group which overthrew the monarchy in 1952. For the first two years, Nasser hid behind the figurehead of Neguib. But as Neguib was building a popular following and demanding more power, Nasser ousted him in 1954. Nasser then became Prime Minister and Chairman of the Revolutionary Command Council, Egypt's governing body. After decades of unstable governments, Nasser did bring political stability to Egypt although this was done at the cost of increasing government control. The economy, under constant strain from the Arab-Israeli conflict and a rapidly increasing population, was quite another matter. Nasser committed Egypt to a course of socialism and nationalized first foreign firms and then Egyptian. His policies contributed to the 1956 Suez crisis (q.v.). State planning controlled most of the economy. Nasser had an active Middle Eastern policy and sought to foster Arab unity and lead the Arabs. This often caused bad relations with the more conservative Arab states, and involved him in a misbegotten unity with Syria and in the Yemen misadventure. Despite this, he was a widely-respected figure in the Arab world for the pride he had brought to its people. He tried to resign after the June 1967 defeat, but his people refused to permit it.

Neguib, Mohammed (1901–84): Egyptian general and politician. As member of Free Officers Movement overthrew King Farouk (q.v.), 1952. President of Egypt, 1952–54. Forced to resign and placed under temporary house arrest by young officers led by Nasser (q.v.), 1954.

Nehru, Pandit Jawaharlal (1889–1964): Indian national leader and stateman. First Prime Minister and Minister of Foreign Affairs when India became independent in 1947. A leading member of the Congress Party, he had been frequently imprisoned for political activity. Under his leadership India progressed, and in world affairs his influence was for peace and non-alignment.

Neto, Agostino (1922–79): Angolan politician. Imprisoned four times between 1952–60 and from 1960–62 for nationalist activities. Led guerrilla war against Portugal as President of People's Movement for the Liberation of Angola (MPLA), 1962–74. President of Angola since 1975. Defeated South African backed rivals with Cuban assistance, 1976.

Ne Win, U (1911–   ): Burmese political leader. Member of anti-British 'We Burmans Association' in 1980s. Chief of staff of collaborationist army in Japanese-occupied Burma, 1942–44. Led guerrilla force supporting Allies against Japan, 1944. General and second in command of army on Burmese independence, 1948. Caretaker Prime

Minister, 1958–60. Seized power in coup, 1962, leading the Burmese Socialist Programme Party (BSSP) to create a one party state. President, 1974–81. Faced increasing resistance from communist and minority groups. Resigned as BSSP chairman following violently suppressed anti-government demonstrations, 1988.

Ngo Dinh Diem (1901–1963): First President of South Vietnam. Provincial governor 1929–32, but became increasingly anti-French. Founded anti-colonialist and anti-communist National Union Front, 1947. Banned and exiled by French. Following 1954 Geneva Agreements, he returned to become Prime Minister of an anti-communist government. President of South Vietnam following a rigged election in 1955, his authoritarian regime was increasingly unpopular. Victim of a CIA-engineered coup, he was assassinated, 1963.

Nguyen Van Thieu (1923–): President of South Vietnam, 1967–75. Previously he had pursued an army career, becoming Chief of Staff in 1963. His period in office saw the fall of Saigon and the final communist takeover of South Vietnam.

Nimeiry, Gaafar Mohamad al- (1930–): President of the Sudan, 1969–85. Educated in the Military Academy, he served in the army and became its Commander-in-Chief. In 1969 he mounted a *coup d'etat* and became Prime Minister and President of the Revolutionary Command Council. He survived several attempts to oust him from power until his overthrow in a military coup in April 1985.

Nixon, Richard Milhouse (1913–): 37th US President. Elected as Republican to House of Representatives, 1946; Senate, 1950. Vice President under Eisenhower (q.v.), 1953–61. Narrowly defeated by Kennedy (q.v.) in presidential election, 1960. Won presidential election, 1968. Ended American involvement in Vietnam, eased US-Soviet relations and opened diplomatic links with Communist China. Re-elected President, 1972. Controversial second term saw resignation of Vice President Agnew (q.v.), 1973, and Nixon's own resignation, 1974, under threat of impeachment for involvement in Watergate conspiracy.

Nkomo, Joshua (1917–): Zimbabwean politician. President, African National Congress, 1957–59. In exile, 1959–60. President, National Democratic Party, 1960. Helped found and became President of Zimbabwe African People's Union, 1962. Imprisoned, 1964–74. Joint leader with Mugabe (q.v.) of Patriotic Front guerrilla movement, 1976–79. ZAPU defeated by Mugabe's Zimbabwe African National Union (ZANU) in post-independence elections, 1980. Minister of Home Affairs in coalition government, 1980–81. Co-operation with Mugabe ended by violent tribal differences, 1982. Party vice-president on merger of ZANU and ZAPU, 1987.

Nkrumah, Kwame (1909–72): African Nationalist. President of Ghana, 1960–66. He became Prime Minister of Ghana in 1951 and was Prime Minister at independence in 1957. On 1 July 1960 he became first President of the Republic of Ghana and was a leading advocate of

Pan-Africanism. His government, hit by economic depression and an increasingly dictatorial nature, was overthrown by a military coup in February 1966. He took refuge in Guinea until his death.

Noriega, General Manuel Antonio (1938–): Panamanian dictator. Military background. Became chief of G-2, the Panama intelligence agency in 1969. After President Torrijos was killed in an air crash in 1981, took over control of armed forces, becoming in 1983 de facto ruler of Panama. Subverted 1984 presidential election. Indicted by US juries of drug trafficking and racketeering, 1988. Survived coup attempt, October 1989. Fled US invasion force seeking to capture him, December 1989, taking refuge in Vatican embassy. Surrendered to US forces, 3 January 1990. Flown to Florida to face drug trafficking charges.

Nyerere, Julius Kambarage (1922–): President of Tanzania, 1964–85. He was a founder member of the Tanganyika African National Union, Prime Minister at independence and in 1964 became President of Tanzania. Internationally known as a political philosopher, putting forward many of his views on the theory and practice of socialism in the Arusha declaration (q.v.). One of the most respected African nationalists and Commonwealth statesmen until his retirement in 1985.

Obasanjo, Olusegun (1937–   ): Nigerian politician. Became Nigerian Head of State in February 1976 after an unsuccessful coup in which President Mohammed was killed.

Obote, Opolo Milton (1924–): Ugandan politician. President of Uganda, 1966–71 and from 1980–85. Led the opposition party in Uganda before becoming Prime Minister in 1962. He was President from 1966 to 1971 when he was deposed by Idi Amin (q.v.) whilst attending the Commonwealth Conference in Singapore. He was exiled to Tanzania. Following the invasion by Ugandan dissidents in 1979, aided by the Tanzanian army, he was elected President in 1980. Deposed, 1985.

Ojukwu, Chukwenmeka Odumegwu (1933–): President of Biafra, 1967–70. As military governor of the Eastern states of Nigeria he announced their secession as Biafra. In January 1970, as the rebellion collapsed, he escaped to the Ivory Coast, leaving Colonel Effiong to surrender.

Ortega Saavedra, Daniel (1945–): Nicaraguan politician. Underground activist against Somoza (q.v.) regime, 1959. Member, National Directorate of Sandinista Liberation Front (FSLN), 1966–67. Imprisoned, 1967–74. Resumed anti-Somoza activity, fighting successful guerrilla campaign, 1977–79. Member of the Junta of national Reconstruction, 1979. President, 1981–90.

Pahlevi, Muhammed Reza Shah (1919–): Ruler of Iran after his father's abdication in 1941, until 1979. His coronation was not until 1967. His position during the early years of his reign was precarious, and in 1953 he was forced to flee Iran for a short time. He later became an absolute ruler. In 1962, to gain popular support, he decreed the White Revolution, an extensive reform programme which included such items as land reform, a literacy campaign and the emancipation of women. He maintained close relations with the US and built up a formidable defence capacity with her help. However, his dictatorial rule, and the excesses of the Savak (the secret police) helped fuel the fundamentalist Islamic movement led by Ayatollah Khomeini (q.v.), which overthrew him in a mass popular uprising in 1979.

Park, General Chung Hee, (1917–   ): South Korean general. Led the military coup in South Korea (q.v.) in 1961. He was at first acting President but was elected to office in 1963 and was re-elected in 1967 and 1971.

Peres, Shimon (1923–): Israeli Defence Minister from 1974 to 1977 and Labour Party candidate for Prime Minister in the May 1977 elections. During the 1948 war, Peres commanded the Israeli navy, and afterwards became an arms purchaser for the new state. He remained a member of Ben Gurion's faction, and when Ben Gurion left the ruling Labour Party in 1965, Peres followed. He helped the faction return to power after the 1967 Arab-Israeli war. In 1974 and 1977 he narrowly lost the nomination for Prime Minister to Rabin, but with Rabin's resignation as leader of the party in April 1977, Peres achieved the nomination. Considered moderate on the Arab-Israeli conflict, he does not believe that Israel can return to its 1967 borders.

Perez de Cuellar, Javier (1920–): Peruvian diplomat. Peru's United Nations representative, 1971–75, presiding over the UN Security Council in 1974. From 1979–81 he was UN Under–Secretary General for special political affairs and became Secretary General in 1982. Successfully negotiated cease-fire between Iran and Iraq in their eight-year Gulf War, August 1988.

Peron, Juan Domingo (1895–1974): Argentine general and President. Influenced by fascism, participated in a military coup, 1943, becoming Minister of Labour and Social Security. Elected President, 1946 and 1951. Attempted to rally urban working class against traditional landed interests with anti-American nationalism and welfare policies. Eva Duarte de Peron (1919–52), his politically astute wife, played a central role. Her death, and growing confrontation with the Church, weakened his popularity. Ousted by the military and exiled, 1955. A *peronista* revival encouraged his return to victory in the 1973 Presidential election.

Pétain, Henri Philippe (1856–1951): French soldier and politician. Entered army, 1876. Lectured at Ecole de Guerre, 1906 onwards. Became colonel, 1912. Commanded an army corps, 1914. National renown followed defence of Verdun, 1916. Commander-in-chief of French armies in the field, 1917. Created Marshal of France, 1918. Vice-president, Higher Council of War, 1920–30. Led joint French-Spanish campaign against insurgents in Morocco, 1925–26. Inspector-general of army, 1929. Became Minister of War, 1934. Ambassador to Spain, 1939. Became Prime Minister, June 1940.

Secured Armistice with Germany. Given powers by National Assembly to rule by authoritarian means, July 1940. Became head of state in unoccupied ('Vichy') France, 1942. Obliged to flee France with retreating Germans, 1944. Sentenced to death for treason, 1945, but sentence commuted to life imprisonment by de Gaulle.

Pilsudski, Josef (1867–1935): Polish soldier and statesman. Exiled to Siberia for political activities, 1887–92. Founded Polish Socialist Party, 1892. Became editor of Polish underground socialist newspaper, *Robotnik*. Increasingly nationalist in outlook. Sought Japanese support for Polish rising during Russo-Japanese War, 1904. Recruited by Austria to lead Polish legion against Russia, 1914. Interned by Germans, 1917. On release, became commander of all Polish armies. Elected Chief of State, 1918. Remained dictator until Constitution established, 1922. Led Polish campaign against Bolsheviks, 1919–20. Created field marshal, 1920. Commanded army unit until retirement, 1923. Carried off military coup in 1926. Served as Prime Minister, 1926–28, 1930. Retained dictatorial powers until his death in 1935. Unable to convince France of threat from Nazi Germany, he concluded Non-Aggression Pact with Germany, 1934.

Pinochet, Augusto (1915–): Chilean general. Led right-wing military coup against socialist President Allende, 1973. Outlawed political parties and repressed Left and liberals. Commander-in-chief of armed forces, 1973–80. President of Government Council, 1973–74. President of Chile, 1974–89. An October 1988 referendum calling for elections represented a personal rejection of Pinochet. Stood down as President but retained control over armed forces.

Pol Pot, Saloth Sar (1928–): Kampuchean political leader. Joined underground Communist Party, 1946. Student in Paris, 1950–53. Became Kampuchean Communist Party secretary in 1963 and organised Khmer Rouge guerrillas who captured capital Phnom Penh in April 1975. His programme to destroy western influence and return to agricultural society led to 3–4 million deaths. Prime Minister, 1976–79. Overthrown by invading Vietnamese army, sentenced to death in absence. Reformed guerrilla army with Chinese support, but believed to have given up leadership in 1985. His supporters active after Vietnam's withdrawal from Kampuchea in 1989.

Pompidou, Georges (1911–1974): French politician. Member of resistance, during Second World War. Aide to General de Gaulle, 1944–46. Member of Council of State, 1946–54. Deputy director-general of tourism, 1946–49. Director-general of Rothschild's (banking house), 1954–58. Chief of de Gaulle's personal staff, 1958–59. Involved in drafting of Constitution of Fifth Republic. Negotiated cease-fire agreement with Algerian nationalists, 1961. Prime Minister, 1962–68. President, 1969–74. Pursued policies similar to those of de Gaulle (q.v.).

Qadhafi, Colonel Muammar al- (1941–): Libyan leader. Entered the Libyan army in 1965 and overthrew the monarchy in a coup in 1969. He has headed the Libyan government since. Of fundamentalist religious beliefs, he has sought to remould Libyan society in accordance with socialist Islamic beliefs. He supports the Palestinian hard-line approach, and also funds other radical movements abroad, such as the IRA in Ulster. He has been the father of many unsuccessful schemes to unite with his neighbours.

Quisling, Vidkun (1887–1945): Norwegian soldier, politician and traitor. Military attaché in Petrograd, 1918–19, Helsinki, 1919–21. Minister of War, 1931–33. Expanded right-wing National Unity Party. Visited Germany, 1939. Advised Hitler on creation of sympathetic regime in Norway. Headed puppet regime following German occupation, 1940. Tried and executed, 1945. His name is synonymous with treachery.

Rabin, Yitzhak (1922–): Israeli politician. Prime Minister from 1974 to 1977. He resigned in April 1977 as head of the Labour Party and its candidate for Prime Minister over his wife's illegal bank account in the United States. Two weeks earlier he had defeated Shimon Peres (q.v.) for the Labour nomination. Rabin had a long career in the army and served as its chief of staff between 1960 and 1964. He was ambassador to the United States from 1968 to 1973. Returned as Minister of Defence, 1984.

Rahman, Tunku Abdul (1903–): First Prime Minister and Minister of External Affairs in the Federation of Malaya. He became first Prime Minister of Malaysia in 1963. Following rioting and the declaration of a state of emergency, he resigned in 1970. The 'founding father' of independent Malaysia.

Reagan, Ronald (1911–): 40th US President. Film actor. Republican Governor of California, 1967–74. Defeated Carter (q.v.) in 1980 Presidential election; re-elected, 1984. First term marked by 'Reaganomics': tax-cutting, reductions in public spending which hit the poor, and maintenance of high military expenditure. Expressed intense anti-Soviet rhetoric. Military intervention in Grenada, 1983. In second term developed warmer relations with Soviet Union under Gorbachev (q.v.), with summit meetings at Geneva and Reykjavik. Reagan's hitherto impregnable personal popularity was undermined from 1986 by controversy over covert arms sales to Iran and support for Contra forces in Nicaragua.

Ribbentrop, Joachim von (1893–1946): German Nazi diplomat. Involved in negotiations between Hitler and German government. Helped organize Nazi government, 1933. Ambassador at large, 1935. Concluded Anglo-German Naval Treaty, 1935, and Anti-Comintern Pact, 1936. Ambassador in London, 1936–38. Foreign Minister, 1938–45. Responsible for giving German foreign policy a distinctly 'Nazi' character. Negotiated Molotov-Ribbentrop Pact, 1939, and Pact with Italy and Japan, 1940. Tried as war criminal at Nuremberg. Hanged, 1946.

Rommel, Erwin (1891–1944): German soldier. Served on Romanian and Italian fronts during First World War. Lectured at War Academy. Joined Nazi Party, 1933. Commanded 7th Panzer Division, penetrated Ardennes, May 1940. Became commander of 'Afrika Corps', 1941,

earning nickname 'The Desert Fox'. Defeated by campaigns of
Alexander and Montgomery, 1942–43. Given task of strengthening
defences in France, 1944. Active in resistance to Allied landings in
Normandy, June 1944. Implicated in plot to assassinate Hitler.
Apparently forced to commit suicide, October 1944.

Roosevelt, Franklin Delano (1882–1945): 32nd US President. Democrat
State Senator, New York, 1911–12. Assistant Secretary to the Navy,
1913–20. Crippled by polio, 1921. Governor of New York, 1928.
Defeated Hoover in Presidential Election, 1932. Instituted 'New Deal'
to counter Depression, with 'Hundred Days' of legislation, 1933.
Devalued dollar and extended federal government role through public
works, agricultural support, labour legislation and business protection.
Re-elected 1936, 1940, 1944. Attacked for radicalism, some legislation
was declared unconstitutional by the Supreme Court, 1937.
Maintained wartime neutrality, 1930–41, but supported Britain
materially through Lend-Lease. Declared war on Axis powers,
December 1941. Attended war-time conferences with Stalin and
Churchill, notably Yalta, which delineated East-West post-war spheres
of European influence. Died in office at moment of victory over
Germany.

Sadat, Anwar al- (1919–1981): President of Egypt, 1970 to 1981.
Joined the Free Officers (q.v.) in 1950 and participated in the 1952
coup which overthrew the constitutional monarchy. Sadat held various
important positions in the government, and was Vice President at the
time of Nasser's death. He was one of the very few of the Free
Officers left in power at this point, probably because he had never
sought to build a following of his own and so constituted no threat to
Nasser. He became provisional President at Nasser's death and later
was elected to the post. His dramatic peace initiative, including a
historic visit to Jerusalem, altered the diplomatic status quo in the
Middle East, and led to the Camp David peace treaty of 1978. Sadat
was assassinated in 1981.

Sakharov, Andrei Dimitrievich (1921–1989): Russian nuclear physicist.
Achieved international fame as a human rights campaigner and
dissident. Awarded Nobel Prize, 1975. Rehabilitated by Gorbachev,
1988.

Salazar, Antonio de Oliveira (1889–1970): Portuguese dictator.
Professor of economics at Coimbra University, 1916. Minister of
Finance, 1926, 1928–32. Prime Minister, 1932–68. Also Minister of
War, 1936–44, Foreign Minister, 1936–37. Principal architect of
authoritarian constitution introduced in 1933. Implemented fascist-type
government on virtually dictatorial lines, stifling political opposition.
Restored public finances and modernised transport system. Organized
public works schemes. Maintained Portuguese neutrality during
Second World War and maintained Portuguese empire in Angola and
Mozambique.

Shamir, Yitzhak (1914–): Israeli politician. Served as Prime Minister
after Begin's resignation in 1983. In 1984, entered into a coalition with
the Labour Party, sharing the position of Prime Minister with Peres on

a rotating basis. Foreign Minister, 1984 to 1986, then Prime Minister again according to the agreement. Adopted hard-line repressive policies against the *intifada,* the uprising of the Arabs in the occupied territories.

Shastri, Shri Lal Bahadur (1904–66): Indian politician. Succeeded Nehru (q.v.) as Prime Minister in 1964. Died of a heart attack after the Soviet-backed Tashkent talks aimed at bringing about peace between India and Pakistan.

Sihanouk, Prince Norodom (1922–): Cambodian leader. Elected head of state in Cambodia following the death of his father in 1960. He was deposed in 1970 and set up the Royal Government of National Union for Cambodia (GRUNC) in exile in Beijing. He returned to power in April 1975, following the defeat of the Republican forces, but resigned on 5 April 1976.

Singh, Vishwanath Pratap (1931–): Prime Minister of India since 1989. Former Congress (I) politician. Various posts, including Defence Minister, under Indira Gandhi. Broke with Congress, 1987. President, Janata Dal coalition which ousted Rajiv Gandhi from power in 1989 election.

Sithole, Revd Ndabaningi (1920–): Zimbabwean churchman and nationalist. A Congregational minister, he was originally Chairman of ZAPU (q.v.). When it split in August 1963, he became leader of ZANU (q.v.). He spent ten years in gaol and after his release in the 1974 amnesty, went into exile in Zambia with a section of the ANC led by Muzorewa (q.v.). In 1976 he withdrew a section of ZANU from the ANC and attended the Geneva Conference, contesting with Mugabe the claim to be leader of ZANU. He returned to Rhodesia in July 1977 and allied himself with Muzorewa again. In March 1978 he became a party to the internal Rhodesian agreement.

Smith, Ian Douglas (1919–): Leader of White Rhodesia. After posts as Deputy Prime Minister, Minister of Treasury, Defence and External Affairs he became leader of the ruling Rhodesia Front and Prime Minister in 1964. After winning an overwhelming majority in the general election in May 1965 he made a Universal Declaration of Independence (UDI) on 11 November 1965. In June 1969 his decision to declare a Republic and introduce an apartheid-type constitution was endorsed by a referendum. Forced to negotiate an internal settlement with Bishop Muzorewa (q.v.) in 1978. Smith became Minister without Portfolio in the Zimbabwe-Rhodesia government of Muzorewa. Came to London in 1979 for the talks which settled the Rhodesia crisis.

Smuts, Jan Christian (1870–1950): South African statesman and soldier. Fought on behalf of the Boers in the Boer War (1899–1902). Prime Minister of the Union of South Africa, 1919–24 and again 1939–48. Worked to heal differences within South Africa and maintain membership of the Commonwealth. Seen as too pro-British by Afrikaaners. Defeated in 1948 by the National Party under Malan (q.v.).

Solzhenitsyn, Alexander Isayevich (1918–): Russian novelist and leading dissident. Author of *One Day in the Life of Ivan Denisovich*, a damning indictment of life in one of Stalin's prison camps (where Solzhenitsyn himself was imprisoned). Expelled from Soviet Writer's Union, 1969. Nobel Prize for Literature, 1970. Expelled from Russia in 1974, he lives in the USA.

Somoza, Anastasio (1925–1980): Nicaraguan general and politician. Member of family ruling Nicaragua from 1936–79. President 1967–73, 1974–79. Imposed martial law, 1972. Lost US support through human rights violations. Overthrown by Sandanista Liberation Front guerrilla forces, 1979. Assassinated in Paraguay, 1980.

Souphanouvong, Prince (1902–): Laotian leader. Fought with independence troops against the French in Laos and later led the Pathet Lao (q.v.) in their struggle against the government of Souvanna Phouma. In the 1974 coalition government he led the Joint National Political Council and became President of the Lao People's Democratic Republic in December 1975.

Stalin, Josef Visarionovitch (J. V. Djugashvili) (1879–1953): Soviet leader. Expelled from seminary for political activities, 1899. Exiled to Siberia twice. Attended conferences of Russian Social Democrats in Stockholm, 1906, and London, 1907. Expert on racial minorities in Bolshevik Central Committee, 1912. Became editor of *Pravda*, 1917. Worked with Lenin in Petrograd during Revolution, 1917. Member of Revolutionary Military Council, 1920–23. People's Commissar for Nationalities, 1921–23. General Secretary of Central Committee of Communist Party, 1922–53. During Civil War, supervised defence of Petrograd. Co-operated with Kamenev and Zinoviev to exclude Trotsky from office, 1923. (Secured Trotsky's exile, 1929). Gained control of Party at Fifteenth Congress, 1927. Embarked on policy of 'Socialism in One Country' through Five Year Plans, 1928. Achieved rapid economic development. Eliminated political opponents in series of 'show trials', 1936–38. Massive machinery of repression created. Chairman of Council of Ministers, 1941–53. During Second World War, as Commissar of Defence and Marshal of the Soviet Union, took over direction of war effort. Present at Tehran, Yalta and Potsdam conferences. Established firm control of Eastern European Communist 'satellites', with exception of Yugoslavia, during post-war period. 'Personality cult' of Stalin officially condemned by Khrushchev at Party Congress, 1956.

Stevens, Siaka Probyn (1905–): Sierra Leone politician. Elected Prime Minister of Sierra Leone on 21 March 1967, but was overthrown and exiled without taking office. He was restored to power on 26 April 1968, and became President when Sierra Leone became a Republic in 1971.

Stevenson, Adlai Ewing (1900–1965): American politician. Democrat Governor of Illinois, 1949–53. Unsuccessful Democrat candidate against Eisenhower in presidential elections, 1952 and 1956. US Ambassador to the United Nations, 1960–65.

Stresemann, Gustav (1878–1929): German statesman. Elected to Reichstag, 1907–12, 1914–29. Leader of National Liberals, 1917. Took nationalistic position during First World War, supported High Command. Became more moderate after war. Founded People's Party (DVP), 1919. Advocated meeting Germany's commitments under Treaty of Versailles, thereby gaining confidence of Allies. Became Chancellor during crisis year, 1923. Foreign Minister, 1923–29. Restored Germany's diplomatic position. Concluded Locarno Pact, 1925. Achieved German entry into League of Nations, 1926. Secured reduction of reparations demands. Negotiated terms for Allied evacuation of Rhineland. Supported Dawes Plan, 1924, and Young Plan, 1929. Awarded Nobel Peace Prize, 1926.

Strijdom, Johannes (1893–1958): South African politician. Elected Nationalist MP, 1929; acknowledged by 1934 as an ultra-Afrikaaner leader. Prime Minister following the death of Malan (q.v.), 1954–58. Extreme advocate of apartheid, responsible for legislation removing voting rights from Cape Coloureds, for undermining liberal multi-racial universities, and for the 1956–58 Treason Trial.

Suharto, General (1921–): Indonesian general and politician. Leader of the army who took over control in Indonesia in March 1966. Power was handed over to him by Sukarno (q.v.) in February 1967. He was acting President until March 1968, when he was elected to office by the People's Consultative Assembly. He was re-elected in March 1973 and also became Prime Minister and Minister of Defence.

Sukarno, Ahmed (1901–70): Indonesian nationalist leader. First President of Indonesia. After an abortive communist coup in 1965 in which he was implicated, the army took over in March 1966. He nominally held power until February 1967, when he handed over to General Suharto (q.v.).

Sun Yat-sen (1867–1925): Chinese revolutionary and nationalist. Lived abroad after failure of attempted rising in 1895. After further unsuccessful risings, he succeeded in 1911 in overthrowing the ruling Manchu dynasty. Became first President of Republican China. He shortly afterwards resigned in favour of Yuan Shih-kai.

Syngman Rhee (1875–1965): South Korean politician. Elected President of the Republic of Korea (South Korea) in 1948 and held office until April 1960 when he was forced to resign and leave the country. His regime was corrupt and authoritarian.

Thant, Sithu U (1909–74): Burmese diplomat. Secretary-General of the United Nations, 1962–72.

Thatcher, Margaret Hilda (*née* Roberts) (1925–): Mrs Thatcher has been Conservative MP for Finchley since 1959. She was parliamentary secretary to the Ministry of Pensions and National Insurance 1961–64, and secretary of state for education and science 1970–74. In 1975 she was elected leader of the Conservative Party. Between 1975 and 1979 she led the party away from the centrist policies of Heath (q.v.) and adopted a monetarist (q.v.) stance on economic problems and a tough line on law and order, defence and immigration. In May 1979 she became Britain's first woman prime minister, following her election victory. In spite of considerable unpopularity and very high unemployment, Mrs Thatcher's conduct of the Falklands War and Labour's disarray led to a landslide victory at the polls in 1983. Her second term was marked by growing emphasis on liberalizing the economy, especially the privatization (q.v.) of major public concerns. In 1987 she achieved a record third term of office with a majority of over 100 in parliament but rapidly encountered mounting political and economic difficulties.

Tito, Josip Broz (1892–1980): Yugoslav statesman. Member of Yugoslav Communist party since early 1920s, becoming its secretary-general, 1937. Led Yugoslav partisan forces during Second World War. Become marshal, 1943. After war, pursued independence from USSR, 1948. First President of Yugoslav Republic, 1953–80. Pursued independent foreign policy, encouraging co-operation among non-aligned nations.

Todd, Reginald Stephen Garfield (1908–): Prime Minister of Southern Rhodesia in 1953 at the formation of the Federation with Northern Rhodesia and Nyasaland. In 1958 his liberal policies led to his rejection by his party, the United Federal Party. Between 1965–66 and 1972–76 he was under government restriction orders. At the Geneva talks in 1976 he was adviser to Joshua Nkomo (q.v.).

Tojo, Hideki (1884–1948): Japanese general and politician. Chief of State in Manchuria, 1938–40. Minister of War, 1940–41. Prime Minister 1941–44. Identified with militant expansionist war party from 1931; created military dictatorship; authorized Pearl Harbour attack, bringing US into Second World War, 1941. Resigned as Japan suffered military reverses, 1944. Attempted suicide on Japan's defeat, 1945. Tried and executed as war criminal, 1948.

Touré, Sekou (1922–): Guinean politician and trade unionist. Became Head of State in Guinea in October 1958 on independence. He was awarded the Lenin Peace Prize in 1960.

Trotsky, Lev Davidovich (L. D. Bronstein) (1879–1940): Russian revolutionary of Ukrainian-Jewish descent. Exiled to Siberia, 1898. Joined Lenin in London, 1902. Became an independent socialist, 1902. Hoped to achieve reconciliation between Bolsheviks and Mensheviks. Returned to Russia, 1905, and organized first soviet in St Petersburg. Exiled to Siberia again. Returned to St Petersburg from New York, May 1917. Chairman of Petrograd Soviet, November 1917. First Commissar for Foreign Affairs. Delayed conclusion of Treaty of Brest-Litovsk, 1918. Commissar for War during Civil War, creating Red Army. After death of Lenin, and disagreements with Stalin, excluded from office. Theory of 'Permanent Revolution' condemned by Communist Party. Lost influence over Party policy, 1925. Expelled from Communist Party, 1927. Deported, 1929. Wrote *History of the*

Russian Revolution while in France (1931–33). Murdered by Stalinist agent in Mexico, 1940.

Trudeau, Pierre (1919–): Canadian politician. Elected as Liberal member of the Federal Parliament, 1965. Minister of Justice and Attorney General, 1967. Succeeded Lester Pearson as Prime Minister, 1968. Strong opponent of separatism for French-speaking Quebec. Defeated in 1979 election. Returned to office as Prime Minister, 1980–84.

Truman, Harry S. (1884–1972): 33rd US President. Served US Army in France, 1918. Democratic Senator, Missouri, 1935–44. Elected as Roosevelt's Vice President 1944, succeeded him on death in April 1945. Authorized dropping of atomic bombs on Japan, August 1945. Surprise victor in 1948 Presidential election on 'Fair Deal' civil rights and social reform platform, but unable to push legislation through conservative Congress. Vigorous anti-communist foreign policy: Truman Doctrine; Marshal Plan for European recovery; Berlin airlift; creation of NATO, and US participation in UN forces in Korea.

Tshombe, Moise Kapenda (1919–1969): Congolese Prime Minister and President, 1964–65. He announced the secession of Katanga from Zaire in July 1960 and led the Katanga forces until 1963, when UN forces took control and he went into exile. In 1964 he was recalled to lead the central government, but was dismissed in 1965 and again went into exile. Having been sentenced to death by the Kinshasa High Court, his plane was hijacked to Algiers where he was placed under house arrest until his death.

Verwoerd, Hendrik Frensch (1901–1966): South African Prime Minister, 1958–66. In 1950 he became Minister of Native Affairs in South Africa, where he was responsible for putting apartheid (q.v.) into practice He then became leader of the Nationalist Party and on 2 September 1958 became Prime Minister. He was assassinated on 6 September 1966. Strong advocate of a South African Republic outside the Commonwealth (which South Africa left in 1961).

Vorster, Balthazar Johannes (1915–1983): South African Prime Minister, 1966–78. Formerly Minister of Justice, he became South African Prime Minister in 1966 following the assassination of Verwoerd (q.v.). As Prime Minister he tried to make diplomatic contacts with black African states and attempted to help solve both the Rhodesian and Namibian problems. He maintained strict apartheid, winning a landslide victory from the white electorate in 1977. Forced to resign by the Muldergate scandal (q.v.).

Waldheim, Kurt (1918–): Austrian diplomat and politician. Diplomat, 1945–64, mainly at United Nations. Foreign Minister, 1968–70. Failed to win presidential election, 1971. UN Secretary-General, 1971–82. Largely unsuccessful term because of East-West mutual mistrust. President of Austria, 1986. During election campaign reputation was undermined by questions about his war-time activities and the extent of his awareness of Nazi atrocities.

Walesa, Lech (1943–): Polish trade unionist. Former Gdansk shipyard worker. Emerged as leader of independent 'Solidarity' trade union. Solidarity comprised some 40 per cent of Polish workers by late 1980. Mounted outspoken opposition to economic and social policies of government. Detained following imposition of martial law, December 1981. Released eleven months later. During his detention, Solidarity was banned. Continued to hold prominent position. Granted audience with Pope John Paul II, 1983. Awarded Nobel Peace Prize, 1983. Guided Solidarity throughout 1980s, but declined to hold office when, in September 1989, Solidarity became part of Poland's first non-Communist government for forty years.

Weizmann, Chaim (1874–1952): Zionist leader. Headed British Zionist movement before First World War. Advised Foreign Office during planning of Balfour Declaration, 1917. Head of World Zionist Movement after 1920. Became head of Jewish Agency for Palestine, 1929. Elected first President of Israel, 1948.

Welensky, Roland (Roy) (1907–): Deputy Prime Minister and Minister of Transport of the Central African Federation from 1953–56 when he became Prime Minister and Minister of External Affairs. He remained Prime Minister until the break-up of the Federation in 1963.

Wilson, Sir (James) Harold, Lord Wilson of Rievaulx, (1916–   ): Labour MP for Ormskirk, 1945–50, and for Huyton from 1950. He served as parliamentary secretary to the Ministry of Works, 1945–47, secretary of overseas trade, 1947, and President of the Board of Trade, 1947–51. In 1951 he resigned in protest at the government's decision to impose National Health prescription charges. In 1963 he was elected leader of the Labour Party. He was Prime Minister 1964–70 and 1974–76, when he resigned office. In 1976 he was appointed a Knight of the Garter. Perhaps Wilson's greatest achievement was in keeping an inexperienced government in power with a precarious majority from 1964 to 1966, and in steering a minority government through the months from February to October 1974. Wilson led the Labour Party to office in four out of five consecutive elections.

Wilson, Thomas Woodrow (1856–1924): 28th US President. Lawyer and academic. Democratic Governor, New Jersey, 1910. Inaugurated President, 1913. Liberal domestic policy. 'Big Stick' policy in Latin America. Determined on neutrality in First World War. Re-elected to Presidency, 1916; declared war on Germany, 1917. Announced Fourteen Points for reshaping of post-war world on basis of national self-determination and the creation of an international forum, January 1918. Congress refused to ratify Wilson's signing of Versailles Treaty, particularly objecting to participation in League of Nations. Awarded Nobel Peace Prize, 1919. Suffered incapacitating stroke, 1919.

Section V
Glossary of terms

African National Congress (ANC)   Black South African pressure group, formed in 1912 at Bloemfontein to promote the welfare of Blacks in South Africa. Its origins date from the formation in Cape Colony in 1882 of the Native Education Association. Banned from South Africa in 1961. Its leader, Nelson Mandela (q.v.) the symbol of black African hopes, was convicted of sabotage in 1964 and sentenced to life imprisonment. Mandela was released in 1990 and the ANC ban lifted.

African National Council (ANC)   Black Rhodesian pressure group, initially set up in 1971 to oppose the Smith-Home settlement proposals for Rhodesia (q.v.). In 1975, with the backing of the Organization of African Unity (q.v.), Muzorewa (q.v.) led an ANC delegation to the Victoria Falls conference representing all the nationalist groups. This unity did not last and, by 1977, after groupings and regroupings, the ANC was divided into two main wings, led respectively by Muzorewa and Nkomo.

al-Fatah   The Syrian branch of the Palestinian liberation movement. It became the most powerful force in the Palestine Liberation Organization (q.v.) after the Arab-Israeli war of 1967.

aliya   Jewish term meaning the 'going-up' or return of Jews from the diaspora to what they consider their homeland, first to Palestine and later to Israel, during the twentieth century.

Alliance for Progress   Conceived and implemented during the Kennedy administration (1961–63). An attempt to promote economic development in Latin America through extensive and varied United States' assistance. The Alliance for Progress began in August 1961 with the signature of a charter by representatives of twenty American states at Punta del Este in Uruguay. Action began in March 1962, with the declared aim of increasing living standards in these countries by $2\frac{1}{2}$% per annum.

ANC   *see under* African National Congress

Anschluss   The idea of union between Austria and Germany, current after the collapse of the Habsburg Monarchy in 1918 and given further impetus after Hitler became German Chancellor in 1933. The deliberate destabilization of the Austrian government by the Nazis in 1938 led to the resignation of Chancellor Schuschnigg and his replacement by Arthur Seyss-Inquart, a Nazi nominee who invited the Germans to occupy Austria. The union of Austria with Germany was proclaimed on 13 March 1938.

anti-clericalism   Term applied to the opposition to organized religion, largely directed against the power of the Roman Catholic Church. Anti-clericalism was prevalent during the revolutionary period in France and throughout the nineteenth century. Also apparent in Spain, especially during the Second Republic, 1931–39, in Germany as a result of the *Kulturkampf* and sporadically in Italy.

Anti-Comintern Pact   The agreement between Germany and Japan signed on 25 November 1936 which stated both countries' hostility to international communism, also signed by Italy in 1937. In addition to its commitment to oppose the Soviet Union, the pact also recognized the Japanese regime which had ruled Manchuria since 1931.

anti-Semitism   Term used to describe animosity towards the Jews, either on a religious or a racial basis. Originally coined by racial theorists of the later nineteenth century, anti-Semitism can take a number of different political, economic or racial forms. A number of political parties in Germany and Austria were based on anti-Semitism, and it also appeared in France via the Action Française. Economic and political anti-Semitism was also a feature of Tsarist Russia with frequent pogroms (q.v.) against Jewish communities, a form of activity which seems to have recurred in the Soviet Union in 1958–59 and 1962–63.

ANZAC   Acronym for Australian and New Zealand Army Corps. It became famous in the Gallipoli Campaign of 1915.

Anzus Pact   Name given to the Pacific Security Treaty signed by Australia, New Zealand and the United States on 1 September 1951. It is of indefinite duration, and marked a reorientation and new independence in defence policy by Australia and New Zealand towards the United States and away from the United Kingdom. New Zealand later withdrew from the Pact as part of its anti-nuclear policy.

apartheid   The South African doctrine of racial segregation, put forward by the National Party under Dr Malan in 1948, and subsequently practised under successive governments of Strydom, Verwoerd, Vorster and Botha. Although virtually universally condemned by the world outside, the South African defence of apartheid is that it allows for the separate development of the Bantu population along their own lines, ultimately leading to self-governing African states (Bantustans, q.v.) in South Africa. In practice, under apartheid the Black African population has been the subject of a continuing stream of discriminatory legislation, including the 1949 Prohibition of Mixed Marriages Act, the 1950 Suppression of Communism Act, the 1950 Group Areas Act, and the much-criticized 1963 'Ninety-Day Law' under which the police have powers of arbitrary confinement without recourse to the courts. The result was the suppression of all internal opposition to White supremacy. The Africans have been consigned to a role as a disenfranchised and politically powerless labour force. For recent developments in South Africa, see pp. 90–5.

arms race   The Cold War rivalry between the USSR and the Western powers, particularly the USA, to establish supremacy in arms production.

Arusha Declaration   Socialist theory of development put forward by President Nyerere (q.v.) of Tanzania in February 1967. He was sceptical about the motives of countries offering aid in Africa and felt that a developing country should control its own resources and encourage self-reliance. His theories have been put into practice in Tanzania through nationalization of banks and insurance companies, Africanization of foreign assets and nationalization of many European-owned firms, as well as the setting up of 'Ujamaa' villages which concentrate people into co-operative settlements.

Aryan The name given to a 'superior' European race, whose existence was promulgated by the Nazis. Their racial theory is, of course, nonsense.

ASEAN or Association of South-East Asian Nations see p. 247–8

Atlantic Charter A statement of principles agreed by Churchill and Roosevelt on behalf of Britain and the United States in August 1941, on the conduct of international policy in the postwar world. These included no territorial or other expansion; no wish for territorial changes other than those agreed by the peoples concerned; respect for the rights of all peoples to choose their form of government; desire for general economic development and collaboration; the need to disarm aggressor nations, and the wish to construct a general system of international security. Although mainly a propaganda exercise, the US refused to acknowledge any future international obligations in spite of British pressure. The Charter was endorsed by the Soviet Union and fourteen other states at war with the Axis powers in September 1941.

autarky The policy of economic self-sufficiency, as witnessed in Nazi Germany prior to World War II, aiming at total home production to the exclusion of all imported items.

Awami League A political party proposing independence for East Pakistan, which won 167 seats out of 300 in the Pakistan general election held in December 1970. The Pakistan authorities refused to open the new National Assembly and civil war broke out. The leader of the Awami League, Sheikh Mujibur Rahman (q.v.), became Prime Minister of the new nation of Bangladesh but in January 1975 abolished all political parties and replaced them by a single party.

Axis A term first used by Mussolini on 1 November 1936 to describe fascist Italy's relationship with Nazi Germany, established by the October protocols of 1936. He referred to the Rome-Berlin Axis, which was reinforced by a formal treaty in May 1939, the Pact of Steel. In September 1940, Germany, Italy and Japan signed a tripartite agreement which led to the term 'Axis Powers' being used to describe all three, as well as their Eastern European allies.

ayatollah Islamic title, given to the most learned teachers and scholars in Shi'ite Iran. The title came into prominence to refer to Ayatollah Khomeini (q.v.), the leader of the 1979 Islamic revolution in Iran.

Azania Term used by black nationalists to denote South Africa.

AZAPO Azanian People's Organization. Black consciousness movement formed in South Africa in 1977.

Baader-Meinhof Group An anarchist terrorist group active in West Germany in the 1970s. It was led by Andrea Baader (1943–77) and Ulrike Meinhof (1934–76) with funds channelled via East Germany. Both were captured, and died in high-security prisons.

Ba'ath Party Syrian political party founded in 1941, whose name means 'renaissance' in Arabic; its goals are Arab unity, socialism and freedom. It has branches in several Arab countries but has seen its greatest power in Iraq and Syria. Its support has come mainly from the military, intellectuals and the middle class.

Baghdad Pact *see under* Central Treaty Organisation p. 421.

balance of power A theory of international relations which aimed to secure peace by preventing any one state or group of states from attaining political or military strength sufficient to threaten the independence and liberty of others. It was based on the maintenance of a counterforce equal to that of the potential adversaries, and was the central theme of British policy in Europe against the French, and from 1904 to 1914, the Germans. This was epitomized by the creation of the Entente Cordiale (q.v.) with France to counter the threat from Germany, and later the Triple Entente (q.v.) of Britain, France and Russia to balance the Triple Alliance (q.v.) of Germany, Austria-Hungary and Italy. In the inter-war period, Britain again attempted to create a balance against French power by encouraging the rapid recovery of Germany. The policy was abandoned in the 1930s as Germany and Japan began to pursue more aggressive foreign policies, which could not be countered by the League of Nations' security system, nor by further alliances.

Balfour Declaration A crucial document fundamental to an understanding of Jewish claims to Palestine. In a letter of 2 November 1917 to the British Zionist leader Lord Rothschild, Arthur Balfour, the Foreign Secretary, stated Britain's support for the establishment of a Jewish national home in Palestine. It included the provision that nothing should be done to prejudice the civil and religious rights of the non-Jewish communities in the area. The letter's terms were incorporated into Britain's League of Nation's mandate for Palestine. The real commitment in the Balfour Declaration has been hotly contested ever since.

bamboo curtain Term used to describe the isolation of communist China from 1948 to 1971 when, with the admission of China to the United Nations and the visit of Nixon (q.v.) to Peking, the 'bamboo curtain' was lifted. The term is analogous to 'Iron Curtain' (q.v.) used to denote Russia and Eastern Europe.

Bandung Conference Conference in 1955 largely organized at the initiative of the Colombo Powers and China, to herald a new era of Afro-Asian solidarity. Its guiding principles were the 'Five Principles' of Peaceful Co-existence which had emerged from the settlement of the Sino-Indian conflict over Tibet (29 April 1954). These were: mutual respect for territorial integrity and sovereignty; non-aggression; non-interference in each other's internal affairs; equality and mutual benefit; peaceful co-existence and economic co-operation. Despite general agreement, not all countries accepted the neutralist position in world affairs advocated by China. Division and dissent marked the Second Bandung Conference in 1965.

banning order An order used in South Africa to prohibit a person engaging in, say, political activity, being interviewed or quoted by the media.

Bantustan The supposedly independent tribal homelands in South Africa (e.g. Transkei). None has received international recognition.

Barbarossa, Operation Code name for German invasion of Russia, June 1941.

Battle of Britain see p. 280.

Bay of Pigs (Cochinos Bay) A coastal area in southern Cuba. On 17 April 1961, Cuban exiles trained and assisted by the US Central Intelligence Agency (CIA) landed at the Bay of Pigs in an attempt to overthrow the communist regime of Fidel Castro. The operation was planned during the later stages of the Eisenhower Administration, but inherited and implemented by the Kennedy Administration. The failure of the insurgents was due to many factors: the unfavourable terrain surrounding the Bay of Pigs; lack of support from local inhabitants, and the absence of sufficient military support for those who landed on the island. The result of the attempt was disastrous for the Cuban exiles, of whom more than eighty were killed and over one thousand captured; it also represented the first, and most serious, diplomatic failure of the Kennedy Administration. The claims of the United States of non-involvement in the affair were scarcely credible, and the Castro regime was made to appear stronger and less vulnerable.

Biafra The name given to the eastern region of Nigeria on its attempted secession in 1967.

'Big Five' Permanent members of the UN Security Council: the USA, USSR, Britain, China and France.

'Big Four' Representatives of the major victorious powers of World War I at the Paris Peace Conference of 1919. They were Lloyd George, Woodrow Wilson, George Clemenceau and the Italian Prime Minister, Vittorio Orlando.

'Big Three' Leaders of the major Allied powers during World War II: Churchill, Stalin and Roosevelt.

Black Monday   Term applied to the collapse of the New York Stock Exchange on 19 October 1987, when the Dow Jones Industrial Average fell by 22.6%, bringing major falls in other markets around the world. It was the worst fall since 1929. See Black Thursday.

Black Muslims   American Negro movement whose twin pillars of belief are Negro superiority and racial separation. Its best known leader was perhaps Malcolm X, who was assassinated in February 1965.

Black Panther Party   Name derived from the symbol used by Black Power candidates in 1966 when fighting elections in Alabama. See below.

Black Power   Radical black movement which emerged in the United States, partly reflecting dissatisfaction with the lack of progress of the civil rights movement. It was at its most aggressive in the late 1960s, and there were fears in the USA that inter-racial strife of civil war dimensions might erupt in the cities. However, the 1970s saw some improvement in the position of American Blacks and that, together with the deaths of Black Power leaders such as George Jackson and Malcolm X, weakened the movement.

Black September   Extremist Palestinian terrorist group founded in 1971 and named after the Black September of 1970, during which King Hussein (q.v.) virtually eliminated the guerrilla presence in Jordan. The commando group has piled up a long series of outrages, among them the assassination of the Jordanian Prime Minister, Wasif al-Tell and the attempted assassinations of the Jordanian ambassadors to Switzerland and the United Kingdom 1971; the murder of a number of Israeli athletes at the Munich Olympics 1972; and the murder of the American ambassador and two other foreign diplomats in Khartoum in 1973.

Black Thursday   24 October 1929, the day the Wall Street crash began, when the first major fall in confidence in the US stock market occurred. The 'Crash of 29' led to the slump of the 1930s.

Blitzkrieg   (Ger: lightning war) A theory of warfare which involved a rapid attack on a very narrow front to create penetration in depth. The technique involved prior aerial bombing to reduce enemy resistance and then the deployment of highly mobile armoured columns. Used extensively by the German army in the Second World War, and especially by General Guderian in the campaign against France in 1940. Also abbreviated to 'Blitz' in English to describe the heavy bombing and night attacks on British cities by the German air force during the Second World War.

boat people   Term used to describe those persons, both Chinese and non-communist Vietnamese, seeking to escape from Vietnam after 1975 when South Vietnam fell to communist North Vietnam. Many escaped, in overladen small boats, to Malaysia, Hong Kong, etc. Many fell prey to pirates. The problem became acute again in the

1980s as economic hardship in Vietnam provoked further waves of refugees into Hong Kong. Against an international outcry, Britain began repatriation to Vietnam in December 1989.

Bolshevik (Russ: member of the majority) A term applied to the radical faction of the Russian Social Democratic Party, which split in 1903. Lenin led the Bolsheviks in opposition to the more moderate Mensheviks (q.v.). The Bolsheviks came to power in Russia after the October Revolution of 1917, and the name was retained by the Soviet Communist Party until 1952.

BOSS Bureau of State Security, the South African Secret police force accused of many illegal actions both inside and outside South Africa.

Brains Trust Originally the nickname of the group of advisers, mainly economists and businessmen, who helped Roosevelt (q.v.) formulate his New Deal policies. Now the term is more generally applied to any such small advisory group.

brainwashing Term originating from the mental and frequently physical torture used by the communists in the Korean War (see p. 284) to persuade their captured prisoners to alter their view of society.

Bretton Woods The scene of an international conference held in July 1944 to consider British, Canadian and American proposals for a post-war international monetary system. The final agreement was largely based on American plans and proposed the convertibility of currencies and stable exchange rates in order to encourage multilateral trade. One of the results of Bretton Woods was the setting up of the International Monetary Fund (q.v.) and World Bank.

Brezhnev Doctrine The doctrine was developed by Leonid Brezhnev, First Secretary of the Communist Party of the Soviet Union, as a justification for the invasion of Czechoslovakia by five Warsaw Pact countries in 1968; it maintained that the Socialist community of nations may intervene in the affairs of one of its members, if it sees it as necessary and for the public good. Under Gorbachev, the doctrine has been abandoned and there was no intervention in 1989 as Eastern Europe reshaped its political system.

brinkmanship Term used to describe the policy of going to the brink (i.e. of nuclear war) to force another power to climb down or seek a negotiated settlement. An example is the policy of Kennedy during the Cuba Missile Crisis (q.v.). The term originated with John Foster Dulles, American Secretary of State, 1953–59.

Broederbond White secret society formed after the Boer War to maintain Afrikaaner dominance in South African cultural, economic and political life, and which influenced National Party policy.

buffer state A small state established or maintained between two larger states to prevent clashes between them or to prevent either taking control of strategic territory.

Bundestag   The West German federal parliament established in May 1949, elected for a four-year term by universal suffrage.

Bushido   The Samurai code of honour dating from the twelfth century which is a continuing influence in Japanese life. Similar to medieval European chivalry, it promotes a concept of personal honour based on courage, honesty, justice and simplicity.

Bussing   American practice of moving children by bus to schools in different areas, to prevent educational facilities in the 1970s becoming entirely black or white. The intention was to encourage racial harmony, but many white parents complained the practice infringed the right to choose where their children were educated.

Camp David   The US Presidential retreat in Maryland. On 5–17 September 1978 President Carter chaired talks at Camp David between President Sadat of Egypt and Prime Minister Begin of Israel and agreement was reached on a treaty finally signed on 26 March 1979. Israel pledged to withdraw from Sinai; to stop settlement on the West Bank and the Gaza Strip; to end Israeli military government of the West Bank within five years, after which the Palestinian inhabitants of the area would elect a government. Syria and the PLO rejected the agreement.

Canal Zone   An area five miles each side of the forty-mile-long Panama Canal in Central America, granted to the United States in 1903. The zone is administered by a United States governor and controlled by the US army. Following increasing agitation for return of the zone, President Carter and Panamanian General Torrijos signed a treaty on 7 September 1977 promising its return by 1 January 2000.

CAP   *see under* Common Agricultural Policy.

Casablanca Powers   A loose association of more radical African states consisting of Ghana, Guinea, Mali, Morocco, U.A.R. and Algeria, set up in 1961. They combined with the Monrovia states (q.v.) to form the Organization of African Unity (q.v.).

caudillismo   Term used in Spanish and Latin American politics denoting the almost absolute power of the head of state and the personal loyalty of his supporters. Examples are Franco in Spain (see below), and Peron in Argentina.

Caudillo, El (Sp: the leader)   Title assumed by Francisco Franco in 1937 as head of the insurgent nationalist forces in the Spanish Civil War, and of the so-called Burgos Government. His authority was reinforced in July 1947 with the declaration that he should remain 'Caudillo' or head of state for life, pending the restoration of the monarchy.

Cento   see p. 421.

Central Intelligence Agency (CIA)   An American agency, headed by a director appointed by the President with Senate approval, that works under the National Security Council to co-ordinate intelligence activities in the interest of national security. The CIA evaluates intelligence information supplied by the Army, Navy, Air Force, State Department and other intelligence-gathering civilian and military agencies. This information is disseminated among various units of the national government to aid the formulation of foreign and defence policy. The CIA also engages in world-wide intelligence-gathering activities. The Congressional Charter establishing the CIA specifically prohibits the use of its resources for internal surveillance. As a result of alleged breaches of the charter, Congress has created a 'watchdog' select committee to oversee CIA operations.

Central Powers   Initially members of the Triple Alliance created by Bismarck in 1882, namely Germany, Austria-Hungary and Italy. As Italy remained neutral in the First World War, the term was applied to Germany, Austria-Hungary, their ally Turkey and later also Bulgaria.

Central Treaty Organization (Cento)   The Baghdad Pact was signed by Turkey and Iraq on 24 February 1955. The Pact was joined by the United Kingdom on 4 April 1955, by Pakistan on 23 September 1955 and by Iran on 3 November 1955. Iraq withdrew on 24 March 1959, and the name was changed to the Central Treaty Organization on 21 August 1959. The United States signed bilateral defence agreements with Iran, Turkey and Pakistan on 5 March 1959. The Treaty provides for mutual co-operation for security and defence. The Islamic Revolution in Iran dealt a major blow to the organization.

Charter 77   Group of civil rights activists formed in Czechoslovakia in 1977 in the wake of the Helsinki Agreement (see p. 262) to monitor abuses by the authorities. They were themselves subject to imprisonment and harassment.

Cheka   Extraordinary commission, or secret political police force, established by the Bolsheviks (q.v.) in post-revolutionary Russia to defend the regime against internal enemies.

Chetniks   Originally Serbian guerrillas seeking liberation from the Ottoman Empire. Active against German supply lines in occupied Balkan states during the First World War. They also opposed German occupation in the Second World War and were aided by the British until 1944. Some commanders collaborated with the Germans and Italians against Tito's partisans.

Christian Democracy   Anti-communist, moderate political movement formed in many European countries with the development of a mass electorate in the late nineteenth and twentieth centuries. Amongst the largest was the Italian Christian Democrat Party founded in 1919, and the major representative of Catholic, moderate opinion. The German

National People's Party, formed in 1918, and the German Centre Party, formed in 1870, also represent this tradition, latterly taken up by Adenauer's Christian-Democratic Union, formed in 1945. Many other European countries have political parties with this or similar labels.

CIA   *see under* Central Intelligence Agency

civil disobedience   The policy of non-violent, non-co-operation with the British in India during the struggle for independence. The policy was propagated by Gandhi with great success.

civil rights movement   Movement to secure access for American blacks to voting and citizenship rights guaranteed by the 14th and 15th amendments to the US Constitution in 1868 and 1870. A National Association for the Advancement of Colored People was formed in 1909, but little progress was made for fifty years. In 1957 Federal troops were used in Little Rock, Arkansas, to enforce a 1954 Supreme Court ruling banning segregated education. A black campaign of sit-ins, boycotts and demonstrations in which Dr Martin Luther King (1929–68) emerged as a leader prompted civil rights legislation by the 1960s Kennedy and Johnson administrations. Riots in Harlem (1964) and Watts (1965) revealed dissatisfaction with the pace of achievement and encouraged the growth of black militancy. In the 1970s and 1980s many Blacks felt their progress towards full equality, particularly in education and employment, was weakened by what they saw as unsympathetic Republican administrations.

Cod War   Popular term for the fishing dispute between Iceland and Great Britain between 1972 and 1976.

Cold War   Protracted state of tension between countries, falling short of actual war. The term was first used in a US Congress debate on 12 March 1947 on the doctrine expounded by Harry S. Truman (1894–1972) promising aid to 'free peoples who are resisting attempted subjugation by armed minorities or by outside pressures'. A direct product of the civil war in Greece (1946–49), the doctrine bore the wider implication that the US would actively respond anywhere in the world to what it saw as direct encroachment by the USSR. The practical division of Europe occurred as a result of the Eastern European states' rejection of US Marshall Aid (q.v.), often under pressure from the Soviet Union, and their subsequent membership of Comecon (q.v.). This division into two hostile camps was completed by the creation of NATO in 1949–50 (q.v.) and the Warsaw Pact in 1955 (q.v.). The Cold War between the Soviet Union and the USA continued into the 1970s before being superceded by a period of detente. The main crises within the Cold War period were the Russian invasion of Hungary in 1956; of Czechoslovakia in 1968; the Berlin Blockade of 1948, and the Cuban Missile Crisis of 1962. Western outrage at these supposed manifestations of Soviet expansion was tempered by the British and French involvement in Suez in 1956, and the US involvement in Vietnam during the 1960s and early 1970s. The advent of Gorbachev in Russia and the events of 1989 in Eastern Europe are regarded as marking the end of the Cold War.

collaboration   Support by the population (or part of it) for an enemy occupier of a country. The term was much used in World War II in such countries as France and Norway.

collective security   The policy of guaranteeing the security of one country jointly by several others. Originated in the 1924 Geneva Conference,

collectivism   Political concept which demands that the state plays a more interventionist role in the society to promote the development of the society along collectivist lines. Rights and obligations in collectivist theory are socially derived and are based upon the conception that a notion of common good pervades, or ought to pervade, the society.

collectivization   The process of transferring land from private to state or collective ownership. Extensively operated in the Soviet Union during the early 1930s, when peasants' individual holdings were combined to form agricultural collectives (*Kolkhoz*) or in some cases state-owned farms (*Sovkhoz*), run by state employees.

Colombo Plan   Coming into force on 1 July 1951, the plan was a co-operative attempt by both developed and developing countries to further the economies and raise living standards in South and South East Asia. It was originally intended to last until 1957, but has been successively extended.

Colonels, Greek   Term applied to the Greek right-wing military junta led by two colonels which seized power in April 1967. The authoritarian regime collapsed in 1974, after the failure of its intervention in Cyprus.

colour bar   The separation of people along racial divisions. Usually manifested, as in South Africa, by prohibiting black people from entering white-only areas. See apartheid.

Comintern   Abbreviated title of the Third International established in March 1919 to promote revolutionary Marxism. By 1928 it had become a vehicle for Stalin's ideas. Finally dissolved in May 1943 as a goodwill gesture to the Soviet Union's western allies. Though its stated purpose was the promotion of world revolution, the Comintern functioned chiefly as an organ of Soviet control over the Communist movement.

Common Agricultural Policy (CAP)   The controversial policy of the European Community which subsidises farmers from a Common Agricultural Fund contributed to by member states.

Common Market   see p. 249–50

Commonwealth   see p. 248.

Comrades   Radical Black militants in the townships of South Africa, e.g. Soweto. The more moderate Blacks are known as the 'Fathers'.

concentration camp   Camp for the detention of political and other opponents. Such camps as Belsen and Auschwitz claimed millions of victims – Jews, gypsies and ethnic minorities – in Nazi-controlled Europe. The first camps in Nazi Germany were established in 1933 in Dachau and Oranienburg. The name was originally coined to describe the camps used to intern the rural civilian population by the British during the Boer War (1899–1902) in South Africa.

Conducator (leader, führer)   Title used by the Romanian communist dictator Nicolae Ceausescu (q.v.).

Confrontation   Term applied to the armed conflict between Indonesia and Malaysia in the 1960s. See p. 291.

Congress   (1) the two chambers of the US legislature – i.e. the more powerful Senate, and the 435-member House of Representatives. (2) Common abbreviation for the Indian National Congress, formed in 1885 and the main vehicle of Indian nationalism. See p. 433–4.

containment   US policy aimed at preventing the extension of communist influence. George Kennan argued in 1947 that the USSR should be faced with a 'patient but firm and vigilant containment of Russian expansive tendencies.' Examples in practice have been economic aid to Europe under the Marshall Plan, and military engagement in Korea and Vietnam.

Contras   Exiles from Nicaragua after the 1979 victory of the Sandanista revolution, who continued to support former right-wing dictator Anastasio Somoza Debayle from neighbouring Honduras and mounted armed attacks in north-west Nicaragua. After Somoza's death in 1980 the Contras continued their anti-Sandinista campaign with American backing, but the electoral defeat of the Sandinistas in 1990 effectively ended their activities.

co-prosperity sphere   The term used by Japan between the wars to describe the area of Asia which it hoped to control and develop, stretching from the USSR's Pacific coast to Timor in the south, and east from Burma to New Guinea. Japan succeeded in occupying a large part of the area in World War Two.

Cuban Missile Crisis   On 22 October 1962 President Kennedy (q.v.) announced on television that United States surveillance had established the presence of Soviet missile sites in Cuba, and that he was imposing a quarantine on Cuba to prevent the shipment of further offensive weapons. With the threat of nuclear war imminent, tense negotiations took place. On 28 October Khrushchev agreed to remove the missiles, and in return Kennedy lifted the blockade and agreed not to invade Cuba.

Cultural Revolution   The term used to describe the convulsions in Chinese society caused in 1965 by Mao Zedong's movement to purge the country of his opponents and to bring about a revolution in popular ideology.

Dalai Lama   The spiritual and also temporal leader of the Tibetan people. After Chinese troops occupied Tibet in 1951, a major rebellion took place in 1959. The Dalai Lama subsequently fled to India. Awarded Nobel Peace Prize, 1989.

Dawes Plan   Proposals drawn up by American banker Charles G. Dawes (1865–1951) in 1924 for the settlement of German war reparations by an annual payment of 2,000 million marks.

D-Day   Code name for 6 June 1944, the first day of Operation Overlord, the allied landings in Normandy. Three British and Canadian divisions landed on 'Gold', 'Juno' and 'Sword' beaches and two American divisions landed on 'Omaha' and 'Utah' beaches. By the evening a beach-head 24 miles long and 4 miles deep was established, at the cost of 10,000 casualties.

decolonization   The European withdrawal from overseas possessions after World War II. Britain withdrew from India and Pakistan in 1947, and the majority of her African colonies gained independence by the 1960s. France freed Indo-China, Algeria and Tunisia after liberation wars in the 1950s. Belgium, the Netherlands and Portugal had relinquished the last of their colonies by the 1970s.

Demilitarized Zone   An area following approximately the 38th parallel which divides North and South Korea. Following cessation of hostilities in the 1950–53 Korean War, it was agreed that no military forces should enter the area. A similar zone divided Vietnam along the 17th parallel.

Dengism   Chinese economic modernization programme introduced by Deng Xiaoping in 1984. China turned to decentralized management in industry, the encouragement of market forces, individual enterprise and foreign investment. By the late 1980s there were fears of inflation and unemployment and complaints of corruption. Harshly suppressed demands for political liberalization in 1989 appeared to force a step back in the programme.

Destalinization   The overturning of the 'cult of personality' that had surrounded Soviet dictator Stalin (q.v.) who died in 1953. At the 20th Party Congress in Russia, the attack on Stalin and his purges was led by Khrushchev (q.v.). The process included renaming Stalingrad (which became Volgograd in 1961). Under Gorbachev's *glasnost,* there have been further revelations of the evils of the Stalin era.

detente   A French diplomatic term meaning a reduction in tension between two adversary states, widely used to describe Soviet-American and Sino-American relations since 1968. The policy of detente has been characterized by a large number of personal summit meetings between US and Soviet and US and Chinese leaders, which have resulted in agreements on trade, cultural exchanges and limited arms control. The Helsinki Agreement of 1975 represented the existence of a more general detente between the western and communist nations. With the advent of Gorbachev in Russia, detente and co-operation had effectively ended the Cold War (q.v.) by the end of the 1980s.

deterrence Strategy by which one country deters an adversary from launching a nuclear attack by the threat of instant nuclear retaliation. A so-called 'balance of terror' exists between two countries when both have a high level of assured destruction capability – that is, when neither can expect by a first strike against the enemy's nuclear force to do sufficient damage to prevent a retaliatory second strike causing unacceptable destruction to its own cities. The United States and the Soviet Union operate a range of retaliatory systems to ensure that they maintain this assured destruction capability.

Dien Bien Phu, Battle of The crucial battle which lost the French Empire in Indo-China. In November 1953, the French commander in Indo-China, General Navarre, fortified Dien Bien Phu, a valley 200 miles west of Hanoi, with 15,000 men to cut the supply routes of the Viet Minh guerrillas (q.v.) into Laos and to draw them into a pitched battle. But the French had underestimated the capability of General Giap (q.v.), the Viet Minh commander, to concentrate men and heavy artillery on the hills overlooking Dien Bien Phu. The vital airfield was rendered unusable, and the French garrison was overwhelmed on 7 May 1954. The defeat ended French power in Indo-China, and this was confirmed at the conference taking place in Geneva. See also p. 282.

Dirty War Term applied to the vicious Argentine military campaign used against such left-wing guerrilla groups as the Monteneros from 1976 to 1978.

dissidents Term used particularly in the context of Russia, Eastern Europe and China to refer to those who refuse to conform to the politics and beliefs of the society in which they live. They have frequently been imprisoned and persecuted. Among the most famous are Alexander Solzhenitsyn, the Nobel Prize-winning novelist, expelled from Russia in 1974. Under *glasnost* a new, more liberal climate has developed in, for example, Russia, Poland and Hungary.

dollar diplomacy Term used first by Latin Americans, later more generally, to refer disapprovingly to the use of economic influence by the United States in promoting its overseas interests.

domino theory Refers to the existence of relations of political dependence between several states. Should any one power fall under communist control, the theory argued that others would also fall, like a row of dominoes. The first explicit formulation of the theory appeared in 1954 in support of arguments for American military assistance to certain non-communist regimes in Indo-China. Both South Vietnam (q.v.) and Laos (q.v.) were seen as 'first dominoes', and their alleged strategic relationship to the rest of South East Asia was the explanation of the importance attached by successive US administrations to preventing the forcible overthrow of their regimes by communist-supported insurgents.

Drang nach Osten (Germ: push to the east)   The German desire for territorial gains in eastern Europe.

Duce   Title assumed by Benito Mussolini (q.v.). The title means, literally, leader.

Eastern bloc   Term which referred to the communist states of eastern Europe, including the Balkan states of Yugoslavia and Albania. With the dramatic changes in such eastern European countries as Hungary and Poland in 1989, the political and economic cohesion of this 'bloc' has been considerably weakened.

Eastern Front   Term used in both World Wars to describe the battle-front between Germany and Russia.

Enosis   From the Greek word meaning 'to unite' the term used to describe the aims of the Greek Cypriot movement for the political union of Cyprus and Greece. The Turkish minority (c.20% of the population) has consistently feared and opposed such a union. The coup by EOKA supporters (q.v.) in July 1974 prompted a Turkish invasion of Cyprus, and the island is now divided, with the 40% of the island in Turkish control proclaimed as a Turkish federated state.

Entebbe Raid   Daring Israeli commando operation to rescue hostages. On 27 June 1976 an Air France Airbus from Tel Aviv to Paris with 12 crew and 247 passengers was hijacked by members of the Popular Front for the Liberation of Palestine (q.v.) and forced to fly to Entebbe in Uganda. Negotiations began over the hijackers demands, and non-Israeli hostages were released. During the night of 3–4 July, three Israeli Hercules C-130 transport aircraft landed at Entebbe airport, rescued the hostages and flew them back to Israel, refuelling en route at Nairobi, Kenya.

EOKA   The anti-British, Greek-Cypriot terrorist movement, founded and led by Colonel Grivas to force a British withdrawal from Cyprus. It was most active from 1955 to 1959, with Cyprus becoming an independent country within the Commonwealth in 1960. See also Enosis (above) and Makarios (p. 392).

escalation   Term for increasing the intensity or area of a conflict. It was particularly associated with the increases in the scope of the American effort in the Vietnam War. Significant stages in the process of escalation were the first bombing of North Vietnam in August 1964, after incidents in the Gulf of Tonkin, followed by the decision to begin regular bombing of the North in February 1965 and to commit ever-increasing numbers of combat troops.

ETA   Initials of the militant Basque terrorist group in Spain seeking to re-create in northern Spain the short-lived republic of Euzkadi (October 1936–June 1937). It has been responsible for numerous acts of violence.

Eurocommunism   The policy of individual communist parties in western European countries to seek and pursue their own political paths, not dominated by or taking orders from Russia – as had happened under the domination of the Comintern (q.v.) in the inter-war period.

European Community   see p. 249–50.

Fair Deal   The political programme advocated by US President Truman (q.v.) in 1948, when running for his second term as President. It was a progressive set of policies which, although denying the need for a planned economy, advocated housing, health and education policies all aimed at extending social justice at home, as well as economic and military aid programmes abroad.

Falange   The only political party permitted in Franco's Spain. Founded by José Antonio Primo de Rivera in 1933 as a right-wing movement opposed to the Republic. Primo de Rivera was assassinated in November 1936, in the early months of the Spanish Civil War. The movement survived his death to be used by Franco when the Grand Council of the Falange replaced the Cortes as the legislative body in Spain between June 1939 and July 1942.

Fascism   An Italian nationalist, authoritarian, anti-communist movement developed by Mussolini after 1919, which became the only authorized political party in Italy after the March on Rome in 1922. The movement derived its name from the *fasces* (bundle of sticks), the symbol of state power in ancient Rome. More generally applied to authoritarian and National Socialist movements in Europe and elsewhere (q.v. Nazi).

February Revolution   The revolution in Russia on 8 March 1917 (February in the Julian Calendar). Demonstrators protesting in St Petersburg at food shortages and against the war were joined by troops, and the Duma appointed a provisional government under Prince Lvov. Tsar Nicholas II abdicated on 15 March and Russia attempted to move towards constitutional democracy under the liberal intelligentsia, until the October Revolution.

fedayeen   Palestinian guerrillas who raided Israel under the leadership of the Grand Mufti, following their expulsion from Palestine by the Israelis in 1948–49. The word derives from the Arabic for those who risk their lives for a cause. The fedayeen eventually came under the leadership of the PLO.

fellow traveller   Term, most often used in connection with the Communist Party, describing an individual who sympathizes with the position of a political group but is not a member.

Fifth Column   Expression used by Gen. Mola during the Spanish Civil War (1936–39). He claimed that his four columns advancing on Madrid would be aided by a 'fifth column' of sympathizers in the city itself. The term was used widely in World War Two to describe secret enemy sympathisers.

Final Solution   Translation of the German *entlösung,* used to describe the destruction of European Jewry carried out by Nazi Germany in occupied countries between 1941 and 1945.

Five Year Plan   System of economic planning first adopted in the Soviet Union between 1928 and 1933. The plan laid down short term aims and targets for the development of heavy industry and the collectivization of agriculture. The second plan, 1933–37 aimed at increased production of consumer goods but the third, 1938–42 returned to the primacy of heavy industry, largely directed towards rearmament. The five year plan has since been adopted as a planning method by other socialist countries.

Food for Peace   An important part of America's foreign aid programme. Congress established 'Food for Peace' in 1954 in order to reduce American farm surpluses, to increase foreign consumption of American produce and to strengthen America's position with the developing nations. Vast quantities of wheat have been sold to nations for their local currencies which are usually returned to preserve economic stability. By 1973, Congress had authorized a four-year programme involving an annual sum of $2.5 million. One of the major recipients of such American assistance has been India, a state which has not always associated itself diplomatically with the United States.

Four Freedoms   Freedoms enumerated as basic human rights by President Franklin D. Roosevelt (1882–1945) in his annual message to the US Congress in January 1941. They are the freedoms (1) of speech and expression, (2) of religion, (3) from want and (4) from fear.

Fourteen Points   A peace programme put forward by President Woodrow Wilson to the US Congress on 8 January 1918 and accepted as the basis for an armistice by Germany and Austria-Hungary. Later it was alleged that the Allied powers had violated the principles embodied in the Fourteen Points, especially in relation to the prohibition of *Anschluss* (q.v.), the union of Germany with Austria. The original points were: the renunciation of secret diplomacy; freedom of the seas; the removal of economic barriers between states; arms reductions; impartial settlement of colonial disputes; evacuation of Russia by Germany and her allies; restoration of Belgium; German withdrawal from France and the return of Alsace-Lorraine; readjustment of the Italian frontiers; autonomous development of nationalities in Austria-Hungary; evacuation of Romania, Serbia and Montenegro and guarantees of Serbian access to the sea; free passage through the Dardanelles and the self-determination of minorities in the Ottoman Empire; creation of an independent Poland with access to the sea; and the creation of a general association of states.

Free French   The *Forces Françaises Libres* made up of French troops and naval units who continued the fight against Nazi Germany after the fall of France in the summer of 1940. In opposition to the Vichy regime in France, General de Gaulle established a 'Council for the Defence of the Empire', and later the *Comité National Français*. The Free French were active against Vichy forces in Syria and Miquelon and St Pierre in 1941. On 19 July 1942 the Free French were renamed the *Forces Françaises Combatantes* (French Fighting Forces). The FFC represented de Gaulle's main claim as the true representative of French liberation. As the Allied forces liberated France in the summer of 1944, the FFC were able to provide the first Allied troops to enter Paris, after an uprising organised by the *Forces Françaises de l'Intérieur*.

Free Officers   Radical Egyptian nationalist and republican movement of young army officers, nominally led by Mohammed Neguib but Gamal Abdel Nasser (1918–1970) was its most influential figure. Egypt's military failure against Israel in 1948 encouraged growing support and the movement mounted a bloodless coup against King Farouk on 23 July 1952. Neguib became President but was deposed by Nasser in November 1954.

free world   Term used in the west to describe non-communist countries.

Frente de Libertação de Mocambique (FRELIMO)   The nationalist guerrilla movement in Mozambique which, in 1964, launched an armed struggle for independence. By the early 1970s they claimed control over much of the north. The leader of FRELIMO became President of the provisional government in 1974 and President on independence in 1975.

Frente Nacional de Libertação de Angola (FNLA)   This anti-Marxist Angolan group was in control of the north of Angola at independence. Joint FNLA/UNITA troops were virtually defeated by the MPLA (q.v.) by February 1976, but sporadic fighting has been reported since.

Front-line Presidents   The term used to designate the black African Presidents actively involved in attempts to bring about a peace settlement in South Africa: Presidents Neto of Angola, Khama of Botswana, Chissano of Mozambique, Nyerere of Tanzania, Kaunda of Zambia and Mugabe of Zimbabwe.

Führer (Ger: leader)   Title first coined in 1921 to describe Hitler as head of the Nazi party. After his appointment as Chancellor in 1933, the term was used more widely to describe him as 'führer' of Germany.

Gang of Four   Radical Chinese Communist leaders – Wang Hongwen,

Zhang Chungqiao, Yao Wenyuan and Jiang Qing – denounced by
party moderates who gained power in 1976 after the death of Mao
Zedong. The Gang, which argued for continuing revolutionary purity
rather than economic pragmatism, was arrested and accused at a
show trial of plotting to take control of the army. Jiang Qing – Mao's
widow – was given a suspended death sentence in 1981.

GATT   *See under* General Agreement on Tariffs and Trade

Gaullist   A follower of General de Gaulle (q.v.), usually associated
with authoritarianism and nationalist sentiment.

Gaza Strip   Disputed territory under Israeli occupation. Swollen with
refugees and taken by Egyptian troops in the 1948 war, Gaza was
under harsh Egyptian rule 1948–67. Israel occupied Gaza briefly in
1956–57, and had hoped to prevent its being used to mount guerrilla
attacks on Israel, but was forced to return it to Egypt. Israel
conquered the area in June 1967 and put it under military
administration. At first the Arab population was extremely restive and
difficult to control, but the situation quietened after a time. Gazans
were permitted to enter Israel to work, and were a useful source of
skilled and unskilled labour. The Israeli government has established
Jewish settlements in Gaza. Like the West Bank (q.v.), the Strip has
been the scene of many demonstrations and riots in recent years.
(See also *intifada*, p. 434.)

General Agreement on Tariffs and Trade (GATT)   An international
agreement which came into force in 1948. The countries belonging to
GATT account for over 80% of world trade, and are pledged to
encourage free trade. To date there have been six negotiating
conferences on the reduction of tariffs and the abolition of import
restrictions.

Gestapo   The Secret State Police (*Geheime Staatspolizei*) established
by Goering in Prussia in April 1933 to arrest and murder Nazi
opponents. In April 1934 the Gestapo was enlarged under Himmler,
and eventually became part of the SS.

glasnost   The liberalizing 'openness' of the Soviet intellectual
atmosphere encouraged by Mikhail Gorbachev, following his
appointment as Communist Party secretary in March 1985. *Glasnost*
appeared to set few limits on the discussion of contemporary Soviet
society and politics and of Soviet history, particularly the Stalin period.

Gold standard   A country on the gold standard is in the position
where its central bank will exchange gold for its currency on demand.
The UK came off the gold standard in 1914, returning briefly 1925–31.
The gold standard provided a convenient method of fixing exchange
rates, but has now been generally abandoned.

Golkar   The political party ruling Indonesia under President Suharto
in the 1970s and 1980s.

good neighbour policy   Foreign affairs position taken by US President Franklin D. Roosevelt (1882–1945) in an effort to move from isolationism towards closer relations with other states, particularly in South America.

Great Crash   The Wall Street stock market collapse, beginning on 24 October 1929 when 132 million shares were sold in panic trading following a two-year speculative boom. The crash forced an American business slump, which affected European financial stability and led to the 1930s Depression.

Great Leap Forward   The Chinese Communist attempt in 1958–61 to make a rapid move towards communism. Large scale agricultural collectivization was instituted and private consumption reduced. Bad harvests and the ending of technical assistance from the USSR following ideological disputes undermined the attempt.

'Great Society'   Expression used by US President Lyndon Johnson (1908–73) to describe what he hoped would emerge from his administration's 1963–68 progressive civil rights and welfare legislation.

Green revolution   The expansion of agricultural production in developing countries since 1945 by the increasing use of chemical fertilizers, pesticides and high-yield crop seeds. These techniques have been increasingly criticized for their environmental effects.

Greens   The West German ecology party which made a dramatic advance in state elections in 1979 and which, despite internal divisions, remains an influential force. In the late 1980s Green parties in other European countries have been gaining significant support in elections and, while winning few seats, have forced an acknowledgement of environmental issues on other political parties.

guided democracy   The ideology of President Sukarno's regime in Indonesia from 1959–65. Sukarno attempted to unite national, religious and communist forces under a strong executive government, but was overthrown by the army in October 1965.

Gulag Archipelago   The title of Alexander Solzhenitsyn's denunciation of the Russian communist system, based on his and other victims' experience of the Soviet labour camps. Gulag is an acronym for the Russian name of the State Administration of Correctional Labour Camps.

Guomindang *see* Kuomintang

Haganah   Secret force formed in 1936 by the Jews in Palestine to defend themselves against Arab attacks. Haganah fought in April and May 1948 to prevent Arabs severing links between Tel Aviv and Jerusalem, and the force became the basis of the army when Israel was created.

hawks Term used to describe Americans who argued that intensification and escalation of US involvement in the 1965–72 Vietnam War provided the best guarantee of its most effective conclusion.

Herrenvolk (Ger: master race) A doctrine expounded by the Nazis who used the supposed superiority of the 'Aryan' race as a justification for German territorial expansion and the enslavement of 'inferior races'.

Hezbollah Militant Iranian-backed terrorist group active in Lebanon in the 1980s. Its name means 'Party of God'.

Holocaust, the Name given to the death of around six million Jews at the hands of the Nazis during the Second World War. (See table, p. 51.)

Hot Line A direct telecommunications link between the White House and the Kremlin, which was set up by a memorandum of understanding signed by the United States and the Soviet Union in Geneva on 20 June 1963. The need for such a direct channel of communications for negotiations in times of crisis had been demonstrated by the Cuban Missile Crisis of October 1962. It was used, for example, during the Middle East War in June 1967.

Huk Originally the Philippine 'People's Army against Japan' formed among communist-led peasants in March 1942, which came increasingly under Chinese communist influence. Outlawed in 1948 and 1957 for its campaign against landlords and the government, the Huk was reorganized as the 'New People's Army' in the early 1970s. The movement continued its campaign despite the fall of President Marcos in 1986.

Hundred Flowers Chinese communist government attempt to win intellectual support in 1956–7, based on Mao Tse-tung's declaration, 'Let a hundred flowers bloom and a hundred schools of criticism compete'. The policy was abandoned when it became clear how extensive the resulting criticism would be.

ILO *see under* International Labour Organization

India, Partition of The division of British India on independence in to India, Pakistan, (and now Bangladesh), Burma (Myanmar) and Ceylon (Sri Lanka).

Indian National Congress Party formed as an educational association in 1885 to encourage Indian political development and which grew into an opponent of British rule. Mohandas Karamchand Gandhi (1869–1948) became its leader in 1915, and Congress conducted a non-violent civil disobedience campaign through the 1920s and 1930s. Its leaders were interned by Britain between 1942 and 1945. On independence in 1947 Congress president Jawaharlal Nehru (1889–1964) became India's first Prime Minister, with a policy of industrialization and non-alignment in foreign affairs. The Congress Party, apart from a period in opposition from 1977–80, formed every government since independence to the defeat of Rajiv Gandhi in 1989.

Indo-China   French south-east Asian colonies in Annam, Cambodia, Cochin-China, Laos and Tonkin. They were held by France from the 1860s until July 1954, when the Geneva Agreements recognized Cambodia, Laos and Vietnam as independent states.

International Brigades   Volunteer brigades formed to support the Republican cause in Spain during the Spanish Civil War. Composed mainly of left-wing and communist sympathisers from all parts of Europe and the United States, the volunteers saw the fight against Franco's nationalist insurgents as part of the wider struggle against European fascism.

International Labour Organization (ILO)   Originally established in 1919 as an independent body which would act in association with the League of Nations (q.v.) to improve working conditions, wage levels, industrial health care, etc. It is now a specialist agency of the United Nations.

International Monetary Fund (IMF)   Organization set up at the Bretton Woods conference in 1944 which came into operation in 1947. Members contribute a quota to the fund and can negotiate a loan if they are in debt. The intention was that the IMF would help to stabilize exchange rates, but since floating exchange rates have developed, countries tended to allow their currencies to lose value rather than borrow from the IMF.

Intifada   Name given to the Arab uprising which began in 1988 in the Israeli-occupied Gaza Strip (q.v.) and West Bank (q.v.).

Iran-Contra Affair   Term used for scandal under Reagan administration involving diversion of funds to Contras in Nicaragua. For details, see pp. 170–1.

Iron Curtain   A symbol of the frontier between the 'communist' and the 'free' world. The term was used by Winston Churchill with reference to Eastern Europe, when he said at Fulton, Missouri in March 1946: 'From Stettin in the Baltic to Trieste in the Adriatic an iron curtain has descended across the Continent.' The term was much in use during the Cold War. However, the advent of Gorbachev to power and the revolutionary changes in Eastern Europe in 1989, including the effective dismantling of the Berlin Wall and the symbolic opening of the Brandenburg Gate crossing, have made the term redundant.

Islamic Revolution   An outgrowth of the reassertion of Islamic values in the late 1970s, initially in Saudi Arabia, encouraged by the confidence flowing from wealth based on oil. In March 1979 Iran was declared an Islamic Republic following the overthrow of the Shah and his replacement by a Shi'ite dominated Revolutionary Council under Ayatollah Khomeini. The regime rejected Western influence and values and enforced Islamic law. Gen. Mohammed Zia ul-Haq's military government in Pakistan similarly based itself on Islamic law, and there has been pressure within other Muslim states to follow this pattern.

isolationism Policy of avoiding alliances and having minimal involvement in international affairs. The USA remained isolationist until the early twentieth century and returned to the policy in the 1920s and 1930s following its involvement in World War 1. After 1945, America's role as leader of the West forced an abandonment of isolationism but a return to the policy has been a recurring demand of some conservative Republicans, first in the early 1960s and again after the 1965–72 Vietnam War.

Jamahiraya Libyan expression meaning 'the state of the masses'. In March 1977 Col. Muammar Qadhafi proclaimed his country to be the Socialist People's Libyan Arab Jamahiraya.

Janata Alliance of opposition groups formed against the Indian Congress Party in 1977. Morarji Desai led Janata to victory against Mrs Gandhi in the July 1979 election but the alliance succumbed to internal divisions and went down to electoral defeat in 1980.

July Conspiracy Otherwise known as the Hitler Bomb Plot, this was an attempt by disaffected sections of the German officer corps to assassinate Hitler and end Nazi rule in order that negotiations could take place with the Western Allies. The plot involved a bomb placed in Hitler's East Prussian headquarters by Col. von Stauffenberg on 20 July 1944 and was assumed to have succeeded by accomplices in Berlin, who thus committed themselves to a new government. Hitler's almost miraculous survival signalled the failure of the plotters and the attempt was used as an excuse by Hitler to purge the army and execute other high-ranking officials known to oppose the regime.

Kadets The 'Constitutional Democrats', a Russian liberal party which emerged after the 1905 Revolution. Strongly represented in the pre-1917 Duma, the Kadets argued for a democratic republic between the February and October 1917 Revolutions, but were banned by the Bolsheviks in January 1918.

Kaiser Emperor of Germany after German unification in December 1870. The title derived from 'Caesar' and was held by successive kings of Prussia until William II's abdication in November 1918.

Kamikaze Bomb-laden Japanese aircraft which made suicidal attacks on Allied warships in World War II. The word, which also described the pilots, derived from the Japanese 'divine wind'.

KANU Kenya African National Union. Led by Jomo Kenyatta (1897–1978) from 1947 onwards, the party's base was in the Kikuyu tribe and it soon became the only legal party following Kenyan independence in 1963.

Kellogg-Briand Pact The General Pact for the Renunciation of War formulated by US Secretary of State Frank B. Kellogg and French Foreign Secretary Aristide Briand. Nine powers signed and formally renounced war in August 1928. They were eventually joined by fifty-six other states.

Kemalism   Ideology of Kemal Ataturk, who as President from 1923–38 attempted to modernize and secularize Turkey by encouraging industrial development, imposing Western dress and lifestyles, outlawing polygamy and replacing the Arabic with the Latin script.

Keynesianism   Theory and practice derived from the economist Maynard Keynes, particularly his General Theory (1936). It encouraged state intervention to secure economic growth through the management of overall demand by fiscal means, and laid the basis for post-1945 welfare capitalism.

Khalistan   The name of the independent homeland in the Indian sub-continent sought by militant Sikh activists.

Khalsa   The Sikh Commonwealth in the Punjab, India, known as the 'brotherhood of the pure.' Derived from the Arabic for pure, sincere, free.

Khedive   Title granted by the Ottoman Empire to the hereditary pasha of Egypt between 1867 and 1914. It was replaced by the title Sultan when Britain occupied Egypt.

Khmer Rouge   The communist guerrilla troops who defeated the republican forces in the Cambodian civil war (q.v.).

Knesset   The 120-member single-chamber Israeli legislature. Members are elected for four years by universal suffrage under proportional representation.

Korean War   The country of Korea was occupied by the Japanese from 1910–45 when the area was partitioned, the USSR occupying the land to the north of the 38th parallel and the US that to the south. No agreement was reached concerning the eventual reunification of the country, and in 1950 troops from North Korea invaded the south and civil war broke out. The invasion of South Korea by North Korea on 25 June 1950 led to intervention by UN forces following an emergency session of the Security Council, which was being boycotted by the USSR. The advance of UN forces into North Korea on 1 October 1950 brought the Chinese into the war on 27 July 1953. In 1972 talks took place about reunification, but little progress has been made and the country remains divided into the Democratic People's Republic of Korea and the Republic of Korea.

Kremlin (Russ: citadel)   Refers to the citadel in Moscow occupied by the former Imperial Palace. Now the administrative headquarters of, and synonymous with, the government of the USSR.

Ku Klux Klan   A white supremacist secret society formed in the US southern states following their defeat in the American Civil War in 1865. The Klan's terrorist violence forced the imposition of martial law in some areas and it was suppressed by the 1880s. It revived in 1915 and extended its terror campaign to Catholics, Jews and the Left. A further resurgence came in response to 1960s civil rights legislation.

Kulaks (Russ: tight-fisted person)   Term used to describe Russian peasants who were able to become landowners as a result of the agrarian reforms of 1906 and were encouraged by Lenin's NEP.

Kuomintang   Nationalist Chinese democratic republican party founded in 1891 by Sun Yat-sen, led from 1925 by Chiang Kai-shek. The party governed China from 1928 and led the resistance to Japanese occupation from 1937 to 1945. Under Chiang the Kuomintang degenerated into a military oligarchy, and he was overthrown by the Communists in 1949. Chiang and his followers retreated to Taiwan, with American support.

Lateran Treaties   Agreement signed between Mussolini and Pope Pius XI on 11 February 1929 establishing a Concordat between Fascist Italy and the Catholic Church, recognizing the Vatican City State's sovereignty and compensating the Papacy for possessions confiscated in 1870.

League of Nations   see p. 250.

Lebensraum (Ger: living space)   Slogan adopted by German nationalists and especially the Nazi party in the 1920s and 1930s to justify the need for Germany to expand territorially in the East. The theory was based on the alleged over-population of Germany and the need for more territory to ensure their food supplies. Interpreted by some Germans as the desire for a return to the frontiers of 1914, the attack on the Soviet Union suggests that Hitler's interpretation of the concept was much wider.

Lend-lease   Act passed by the US Congress on 11 March 1941, authorizing President Roosevelt to lend or lease arms and equipment to states 'whose defence the President deems vital to the defence of the United States', despite America's neutrality. Aid went to Britain, China and the USSR.

Liberation theology   The attempt by some Central and South American Roman Catholic priests to work with a 'bias to the poor' by reconciling in practice Christian theology with Marxist economic and social analysis.

Likud   An alliance of Israeli right-wing parties which won the May 1977 general election under Menachem Begin's leadership, replacing Mapai and the Labour Party for the first time. Likud went on to further success in the 1988 elections.

Little Boy   The name given to the first atomic bomb, dropped on Hiroshima by the US aircraft *Enola Gay* on 6 August 1945.

Little Entente   Complex of alliances between Yugoslavia and Czechoslovakia (1920), Czechoslovakia and Romania (1921), and Yugoslavia and Romania (1921), consolidated in the May 1929 Treaty of Belgrade, to deter Austria and Hungary from retrieving territory lost in 1918. The term was used disparagingly and the Entente collapsed under the pressure of events in the 1930s.

Lomé Conventions, the   Signed on 28 February 1975 between the European Community and forty-six African, Caribbean and Pacific countries, of which twenty-two are members of the Commonwealth, eighteen were formerly associated with the Six (q.v.) under the Yaoundé Convention, and six had no previous links with members of the European Community. The Convention includes provisions to allow duty-free entry into the Community of all imports from the ACP States except about four per cent of imports of agricultural products. It also set up the Stabex Scheme and the European Development Fund and concerned general industrial, technical and financial co-operation. The negotiations leading up to the Convention conducted on behalf of the Community by the Commission were notable for large numbers of countries involved and the degree of common purpose achieved between the ACP States, who were represented by a single spokesman. Six states which have achieved independence since 1975 have also joined.

Long March   The 8,000-mile retreat of Communist forces from October 1934 to October 1935 under Guomindang attack. The march, led by Mao Zedong, Zhu De and Lin Biao, was from the beleaguered Jiangxi Soviet to the more defensible Yenan region in north-west China. Of the 100,000 who set out only 30,000 survived, but the march was seen as an inspiring epic of the Chinese Revolution.

Luftwaffe   The German air force, illegal by the Treaty of Versailles, but openly developed by the Nazis from 1935 onwards under Marshal Hermann Goering. Initially impressive in the *Blitzkrieg* of 1939–40, it was eventually overwhelmed by superior Allied air power.

McCarthyism   Unsubstantiated accusations of disloyalty and abuse of legislative investigatory power that engender fear of real or imagined threats to national security. The term derives from the behaviour of Senator Joseph R. McCarthy (1909–57) of Wisconsin who, in the early 1950s, made repeated unsubstantiated accusations of treachery against public officials (particularly in the State Department) under the protection of his Senatorial immunity.

Maginot Line   French defensive fortifications stretching from Longwy to the Swiss border. Named after French minister of Defence, André Maginot, the line was constructed between 1929 and 1934 as a means of countering a German attack. Due to the Belgians' refusal to extend the line along their frontier with Germany, and French reluctance to appear to 'abandon' Belgium and build the line along the

Franco-Belgian border to the sea, the defensive strategy relied on the Germans' inability to penetrate the Ardennes forest. This hope was seen as misguided when the Germans were able to turn the French flank by an advance through Belgium, and the Maginot Line was still virtually intact when France surrendered on 22 July 1940.

Mahatma Title (from the Sanskrit 'great soul') bestowed on Indian national leader Mohandas Karamchand Gandhi (1869–1948) by his Hindu followers, in recognition of his asceticism, simplicity and what they saw as saintly qualities.

Malvinas The Argentinian name for the Falklands Islands in the South Atlantic, which both Britain and the Argentine claim. The islands were occupied by Argentina on 2 April 1982 and retaken by Britain on 14 June.

Manchukuo The name given to the Chinese province of Manchuria by the Japanese when they occupied it in 1931. They installed a puppet regime under the last Chinese Manchu emperor, Henry Pu Yi, which was overthrown by Chinese Communists and the USSR in 1945.

mandates Rights granted to certain states at the end of the First World War by the League of Nations to administer the colonies and dependencies of Germany and the Ottoman Empire. The mandates came in three forms. Some territories were only under a limited term mandate while they prepared for independence; the British control over Iraq, Palestine and Transjordan, and the French control of Lebanon and Syria came into this category. Others were to be administered indefinitely because of their lack of development. This included all the German colonies in Africa, except for South West Africa. The third category were also to be administered indefinitely but could be treated as part of the mandate powers' territory. South West Africa, New Guinea and Samoa were included in these.

Manhattan Project Code name for the development from August 1942 of the atomic bomb at Oak Ridge, Tennessee, by a team of British, German and US scientists. The first experimental explosion was made in the New Mexico desert on 17 June 1945.

Maoism Revision of Marxism to suit Chinese conditions undertaken by Mao Zedong (1893–1976). Mao argued that in non-industrialized countries the peasantry rather than the urban proletariat was the main force for revolutionary change. The peasantry would ally with the working class to overthrow the feudal classes, and advance to socialism without an intervening capitalist stage. Revolution had in Mao's view to be permanently renewed, as the 1966–69 Cultural Revolution demonstrated. His ideas brought China into conflict with the USSR, which claimed that it was the fount of Marxist ideology. Following Mao's death China appeared to have stepped back from a rigorous application of his thought.

Mapai The Israeli Workers' Party (Miphlegeth Poalei Israel), formed in Palestine in 1930. Dominated by David Ben-Gurion (1886–1973) from 1930 to 1965, the party served in every coalition government from 1948 to 1977. Mapai combined with two small socialist parties in 1968 to form the Israeli Labour Party.

Maquis   Guerrilla resistance fighters, who liberated Corsica in 1943. Maquis groups in mainland France increased greatly in 1943 and 1944, and those in Brittany were particularly effective in hampering German movements prior to D-Day on 6 June 1944.

Marshall Plan   United States plan for the economic reconstruction of Europe, named after Secretary of State General George C. Marshall. The Organization for European Economic Co-operation was established to administer the aid in April 1948, but the Soviet rejection of the Plan meant that most of the monetary aid went to Western Europe. Between 1948 and 1952 the US provided some $17,000 million which was a crucial element in European post-war recovery.

Marxism   The ideological basis of state socialism and of communism formulated by Karl Marx (1818–83) and Friedrich Engels (1820–95), since subject to much revision and development. Marx claimed to have discovered that history moved dialectically towards socialism through a developing thesis, antithesis and synthesis. This dialectic showed itself in class struggle. The basis of any society lay in its means of production and the ownership of those means. The culture, politics and morality of any society were a superstructure built upon the economic base and reflected the interests of the ruling class. Revolution came when developing productive methods came into irreconcilable conflict with the system of ownership. Industrialism had emerged out of agricultural feudalism and the bourgeoisie had overthrown the nobility to enable itself to carry capitalist development forward. Capitalism, which faced its own contradictions, would in turn be overthrown by the industrial working class which would create socialism. Whatever the weaknesses of Marx's claim to have discovered a scientific truth, his analysis did provide many socialists with a strong ideological self-confidence.

Marxism-Leninism   An interpretation of Marxism made by Lenin (1870–1924), whose leadership of the Bolshevik seizure of power in Russia in 1917 gave his ideas great influence. Lenin's analysis of imperialism sought to explain capitalism's continuing survival. Imperialism enabled capitalist states to find new markets and sources of raw materials, and to wean a domestic 'labour aristocracy' from revolution with a share in the fruits of colonial exploitation. He saw the working class as incapable of realizing the need for socialism unaided, and developed the concept of the Party, a professional elite which would lead the struggle against capitalism and exercise a post-revolutionary dictatorship of the proletariat.

massive retaliation   Name given to a defence doctrine announced by John Foster Dulles (q.v.) in January 1954, which laid down that the correct way for the United States to meet local communist aggression was by responding 'vigorously at places and with means of our own choosing'. The implied threat was that the United States would no longer observe the self-imposed restraints of the Korean War (q.v.) but might use her full nuclear capability against the Soviet Union in response to acts of communist aggression anywhere in the world. The advantage of the policy was that it meant a saving on conventional forces, but there was a problem of credibility, as it would be extremely difficult to convince the Russians that the United States would really initiate nuclear war to counter all minor acts of aggression.

Mau Mau The Mau Mau was a militant African secret society active in Kenya between 1952 and 1960. A state of emergency was declared and some 10,000 British troops sent to Kenya. About 13,500 people were killed during the troubles, and the Mau Mau emergency was a vital factor persuading Britain to decolonize.

May events Paris student demonstrations on 2 May 1968 over educational issues developed into broader political protests. After violent riots on 10–11 May, ten million workers mounted a general strike and work-place occupations, threatening the Republic's stability. Concessions to workers and students ended *les événements,* but the position of President Charles de Gaulle was undermined.

Muldergate South African political scandal in 1978 over alleged misuse of State funds by Information Minister Connie Mulder, which led ultimately to the resignation of President Vorster in June 1979. The name was a reference to the Nixon Wateryate scandal.

multilateralists Term most often used with reference to nuclear weapons, describing the position taken by those arguing that a state possessing nuclear arms should not relinquish them alone – the argument of unilateralists – but should negotiate mutual disarmament with other states.

Multilateral Nuclear Force (MNF) An abortive American proposal of the early 1960s for the creation of a mixed-manned NATO force of 25 surface vessels. They would be armed with Polaris nuclear missiles, but there would be an American veto on their use. Despite French and British rejection of the plan, the United States and West Germany decided to go ahead in June 1964, but this decision was later reversed. An alternative British scheme, the Atlantic Nuclear Force, was also dropped.

Muslim Brethren Founded in 1928 in Egypt by Hassan al-Banna as an Islamic revival movement. By 1939 the Brethren played a considerable role in the nationalist movement and were a powerful organization with mass support. The society often clashed with the government and was dissolved in 1948 because of its use of violence and assassination as political weapons. Following the 1948 assassination of the Prime Minister by one of the Brethren, al-Banna was himself assassinated. By 1951 the organization was permitted to reconstitute itself. Initially the society enjoyed good relations with the officers who led the 1952 revolution, but these soon deteriorated. The Brethren saw their political role evaporating and tried to undermine the government. In 1954 they made an unsuccessful attempt to assassinate Nasser. Hundreds of arrests followed. The society went underground, but was further decimated by more arrests in 1965–66. Branches were established in Syria in 1937. The Brethren there also sided with the nationalists but they never formed a paramilitary movement. In 1952 the government dissolved the society, but permitted it to reform again in 1954. Its activity was also curbed during Syria's union with Egypt.

My Lai   A Vietnamese village where US troops massacred 450 inhabitants on 16 March 1968 during an operation against the Viet Cong. The incident became public in November 1969, further undermining the already unpopular US position in Vietnam. On 29 March 1971 Lt. William Calley was sentenced to life imprisonment for his part in the crime, but his sentence was later reduced.

Nassau Agreement   An agreement concluded on 18 December 1962 between President Kennedy and Harold Macmillan, under which America provided Britain with Polaris nuclear missiles. This 'favoured nation' treatment proved a major factor in de Gaulle's decision to veto Britain's Common Market application shortly afterwards.

NATO   see p. 250.

Nazi   Popular contraction of 'National Socialist' and used to describe both the NSDAP as a party and its individual members. The party was ideologically attached to right-wing authoritarianism (c.f. Italian fascism q.v.) but also included strong anti-Semitism and a belief in the racial supremacy of the 'Aryan' race. The party was led by Adolf Hitler from 1921 until his death in 1945. It was initially based in Munich and suffered a setback in its involvement in the Beer Hall Putsch of November 1923. Nevertheless, the party under Hitler's guidance underwent a resurgence in the late 1920s and achieved a major electoral breakthrough when it captured 107 seats in the Reichstag. Their electoral success continued into 1932 and, in an attempt to provide some form of consensus government, Hitler was offered the Chancellorship in 1933. After the 'seizure of power', Nazi party organizations such as the SS and DAF came to dominate many facets of life in Germany. The party organization collapsed at the end of the Second World War and was made illegal after the German surrender.

New Economic Policy (NEP)   Introduced in Russia by Lenin at the tenth Party Congress in March 1921. Disturbances and food shortages had made it impossible to impose communism and some amelioration was introduced. Private commerce was permitted and some banks reintroduced. The incentives this provided helped to improve food production and created a more contented peasantry. The NEP was finally abandoned in January 1929 in favour of the Five Year Plan and the collectivization of agriculture.

New Deal   The economic and social programme of US President Franklin D. Roosevelt to combat the Depression in his first two terms

(1932–1940). The first phase involved devaluing the dollar, expanding business credit, aiding small farmers, and creating employment through public works. From this emerged the Civilian Conservation Corps, the Civil Works Administration and the Tennessee Valley Authority. The second phase introduced social insurance through a Social Security Act and strengthened union rights with a National Labor Relations Act. Always controversial and arousing accusations of 'socialism', sections of the programme were declared unconstitutional by the Supreme Court, but the New Deal helped reduce unemployment from 17 to 10 million.

New Order   The economic and political integration of Europe under German domination which, according to Nazi propaganda, would have benefited the whole continent rather than simply provide Germany with economic resources to exploit.

Night of the Long Knives   The night of 29–30 June 1934, when the SS murdered Capt. Ernst Röhm and 150 SA leaders on Hitler's orders, together with a large number of other potential opponents of the regime. The SA was alleged to be planning a coup, and on this basis the massacre was retrospectively legalized.

Nine, the   Belgium, Denmark, France, Italy, Ireland, Luxembourg, the Netherlands, the United Kingdom and West Germany, that is, the nine members of the European Community (q.v.) after its enlargement in January 1973. Norway, which had signed the Treaty of Accession, failed to ratify it and did not join. In 1982 the Nine became Ten when Greece joined the Community, and Twelve when Spain and Portugal joined.

Nixon Doctrine   Policy of distributing the burden of collective defence more equitably as between the United States and her allies. The doctrine was first enunciated on the island of Guam in 1969, when President Nixon expressed the willingness of the United States to provide military supplies and economic assistance to friendly nations, but seemed to rule out the likelihood of providing American ground troops for local conflicts in S.E. Asia. The doctrine required allies to assume 'primary responsibility' for their own defence, and was at first thought to apply exclusively to S.E. Asia. Later, the concept of 'limited assistance' was developed in a series of statements and actions by members of the Nixon administration into a general principle which would guide the relations between the United States and her allies.

non-interventionist   The policy of avoiding involvement in the wars or internal conflicts of other states. Britain and France played a rigidly non-interventionist role in the 1936–39 Spanish Civil War, virtually ensuring the collapse of the Republic. Germany and Italy supported the nationalist insurgents and the USSR, to a lesser extent, aided the Republic, while all declared a nominal non-intervention.

Non-Proliferation Treaty   Treaty intended to prevent the proliferation of nuclear weapons signed in Washington, London and Moscow on 1 July 1968. It came into force on 5 March 1970.

Nuremberg rallies Mass rallies orchestrated by Propaganda Minister Joseph Goebbels at Nazi Party Congresses in Nuremberg from 1933 to 1938, intended to rouse participants and impress observers with oratory and militaristic display.

OAS 1. Organization of American States see p. 252. 2. *Organisation de l'Armée Secrète,* a right-wing French terrorist organization led by Gen. Raoul Salan, which threatened the 5th Republic in 1961–62. Most members were ex-Algerian colonists who opposed President Charles de Gaulle's attempts to extricate France from Algeria, and they attempted to assassinate him several times.

OAU see p. 251–2.

Oder-Neisse Line This is the boundary line of the river Oder and its tributary, the Western Neisse which was established as a frontier between Poland and Germany after World War II. It was accepted by the UK, the USA and the USSR at the Potsdam Conference, on the understanding that a final delimitation would take place later. An agreement made between the German Democratic Republic and Poland in 1950 described the line as a permanent frontier, and in 1955 the East German and Polish governments made a declaration to this effect. It was not accepted by the German Federal Republic, the UK and the USA. In pursuit of improved relations with Eastern Europe the Chancellor of the German Federal Government, Willy Brandt, signed a treaty with Poland in December 1970 in which both countries accepted the existing frontiers.

OECD see p. 251.

OGPU Soviet security police agency, established in 1922 as the GPU and retitled OGPU after the formation of the USSR in 1923. Founded to suppress counter-revolution and enemies of the system, it was used by the leadership to uncover political dissidents and, after 1928, in enforcing the collectivization of agriculture. After 1930 it monopolized police activities in the Soviet Union before being absorbed by the NKVD in 1934.

oil embargo In response to the October 1973 Arab-Israeli war, seven Arab states imposed an embargo on oil shipments to the United States to persuade her to press Israel to withdraw from territory occupied in the 1967 war. The embargo on the United States was lifted in January 1974.

Organization for Economic Cooperation and Development (OECD) see p. 251.

Organization of African Unity (OAU) see p. 251–2.

Organization of American States (OAS) see p. 252.

Ostpolitik Eastern policy developed in the German Federal Republic by Kurt Kiesinger to normalize relations with communist countries other than the Soviet Union who recognized the German Democratic Republic. It led to the conclusion of peace treaties with the USSR and Poland (1972), and border agreements over traffic and communications between East and West Berlin.

Overlord Code name for the Allied landings in Normandy to liberate German-occupied France in June 1944. The name emerged from a conference in Quebec between Churchill and Roosevelt in August 1943.

Pact of Steel The military alliance concluded between Fascist Italy and Nazi Germany in May 1939, despite which Italy remained a 'non-belligerent' for the first nine months of World War II.

Palestine Liberation Organization *see under* PLO

Partisans Originally Russians who harried Napoleon's supply lines during his advance on Moscow in 1812, the term is now generally used to describe guerrilla bands fighting behind enemy lines. In World War Two partisan forces were often communist-led, notably in German-occupied Russia and in Yugoslavia under Tito.

Pass Laws The requirement that black South Africans should carry pass-books to be produced on demand, a humiliating procedure intended to restrict their movements. The laws were increasingly the source of black anger.

Pathet Lao A Laotian rebel movement led by Prince Souphanouvong (q.v.) and established in 1949. It collaborated with the Viet Minh (q.v.) in the invasion of Laos in 1953. During the civil war it fought against the Royal Lao government troops and took part in the coalition government set up in 1974. In early 1975 it effectively took over control of the country and in December its leader Prince Souphanouvong became President of the Lao People's Democratic Republic.

Patriotic Front The unexpected grouping of Zimbabwean nationalists Mugabe (q.v.) and Nkomo (q.v.) in Geneva in 1976 led to the formation of the Patriotic Front which had the support of the OAU (q.v.). Smith refused to negotiate with them. Their military forces were divided into two separate groups: ZANU led by Mugabe from Mozambique and ZAPU led by Nkomo from Zambia.

Peace Corps A US agency that administers the foreign aid programme adopted in 1961, under which American volunteers are sent to developing countries to teach skills and generally to assist in raising living standards. Most developing countries have taken advantage of the availability of this service, but others have been highly critical and have refused to allow the volunteers into their countries.

Pearce Commission   A Commission led by Lord Pearce and set up in Rhodesia following the Smith-Home agreement of November 1971. The report disclosing the result of the 'test of acceptability' was published on 23 May 1972 and showed that the people as a whole did not regard the proposals as an acceptable basis for independence.

Pearl Harbor   The US naval base in Hawaii attacked by Japanese carrier-borne aircraft on 7 December 1941, destroying five US battleships, 14 smaller vessels, 120 aircraft and killing over 2,000. America declared war on Japan the following day.

Pentagon   The five-sided US Department of Defense building in Virginia on the outskirts of Washington, DC. Often used as a synonym for American military interests.

perestroika   From the Russian 'restructuring', an attempt led by Mikhail Gorbachev (Communist Party Secretary, 1985, President, 1988) to regenerate the stagnant Soviet economy by encouraging market forces, decentralizing industrial management, and democratizing the Party and government machinery. By mid-1990 a definite political liberalisation did not appear to have been matched by practical economic results.

petrodollar   Following the massive increases in oil prices in 1975, OPEC members had huge balance of payment surpluses in dollars which they wished to invest. This money, known as petrodollars, was partly lent to developing countries for purchase of machinery, but much was invested in US government securities and in the money markets of London and New York.

Phoney War   The phase of military inactivity on the Western Front between the fall of Poland in September 1939 and the German attack on Norway and Denmark in April 1940. The period was also known by Britain as the 'Bore War', by the French as *la drôle de guerre*, and as the 'Sitzkrieg', a pun on the German *blitzkrieg*.

PLO   Palestine Liberation Organization formed in May 1964 in Jordan to unite Palestinian Arabs against Israel. It is dominated by the Syrian al-Fatah, led by Yasser Arafat. The PLO has mounted guerrilla attacks on Israel and Israeli-occupied territory and been involved in international terrorism. Israel refuses to recognize the PLO, but recently PLO representatives have spoken at the United Nations and had discussions with Western officials.

pluralism   A pluralistic society is one in which a plurality of interests are represented by the institutions which constitute the society. Pluralism demands that independent organizations should be able to operate in the same social/political system.

pogrom   Attacks on Jews encouraged by the Tsarist authorities in 1881. The word comes from the Russian for 'destruction' and pogroms extended into eastern Europe, forcing many Jews to emigrate. Hitler ordered such an attack on Jews in November 1938, during which synagogues, businesses, homes and hospitals were damaged or destroyed.

Polaris   The United States Navy's contribution to the United States strategic offensive forces consists of 41 nuclear-powered submarines, each initially equipped with 16 Polaris intermediate-range ballistic missiles, which first became operational in 1961 and can be fired while the submarine is submerged.

Polish Corridor   The Treaty of Versailles decided that the new Polish state should have direct access to the sea. In order to provide this, a large area of West Prussia and Posen, where many Germans lived, was assigned to Poland. The 'Corridor' also had the effect of cutting East Prussia off from the rest of Germany. Danzig (Gdansk), standing at the mouth of the Vistula and the natural artery of Polish trade, but a German city and formerly part of Germany, was placed under League of Nations' control, Poland remaining responsible for her foreign relations. The creation of the 'Corridor' was bitterly resented by German nationalists, and Hitler's demands for the return of Danzig and parts of the 'Corridor' formed part of the crisis which brought about war in September 1939.

Politburo   The Political Bureau of the Communist Party, the party's executive committee and the centre of power in communist-controlled states.

Popular Democratic Front for the Liberation of Palestine (PDFLP)   Marxist resistance movement which was formed under the leadership of Nayef Hawatmah in 1969 as a splinter group from the PFLP (q.v.). Originally it was Syrian-backed. The PDFLP, along with al-Fatah (q.v.) has taken a more moderate stance on the Palestinian problem since the 1973 October War. It supports participation in negotiations at Geneva and has indicated a willingness to form a national authority on whatever territory can be liberated from Israel. However it has not recognized Israel's right to exist. Its members fought on the side of the Leftists in the Lebanese civil war and in November 1976 clashed with the Syrian-backed Palestinian guerrilla organization.

Popular Front   Name used to describe the alliance of communists, socialists and liberal democrats which was designed to combat fascism in Europe between 1935 and 1939. Alliances under this name gained power in Spain, and in France under Léon Blum.

Popular Front for the Liberation of Palestine (PFLP)   Founded in 1967 when several smaller resistance groups merged. The organization was led by George Habash. Of Marxist-Leninist orientation, the PFLP has seen its role as that of midwife to revolutionary change in the Arab world. It has believed that only with that change could the unity necessary for a successful confrontation with Israel be achieved. It did not join the PLO (q.v.) until 1970, and since the 1973 October War has formed part of the rejectionist front – supported by Iraq and Libya – which asserts the need to continue the armed struggle with Israel and opposes a negotiated settlement. The PFLP withdrew from the PLO in September 1974 and also cut its ties with the Palestine Central Council, but remained a member of the Palestine National Council. The intervention of Syria in the Lebanese civil war brought about a limited rapprochement between the rejectionist front and the PLO, but it was short-lived. The rejectionist front has condemned the PLO's 1977 improvement in relations with Jordan.

Potsdam Conference   The last inter-allied conference of World War II, held at Potsdam outside Berlin (11 July–2 August 1945). The meeting between Winston Churchill (until 26 July when a general election brought Attlee and the Labour Party into power), President Truman and Marshal Stalin (with Bevin, Eden, Byrnes and Molotov attending) was to formulate future Allied policies, to lay the basis for definitive peace settlements and to reach agreed policies on the treatment of Germany. The idea of partitioning Germany into a number of states was dropped and principles governing the treatment of the whole of Germany leading to disarmament, de-Nazification and demilitarization were agreed upon. The differing views of the Russians and the Western Powers on reparations were amongst the most intractable problems of the conference. It was agreed that the city of Königsberg (now Kaliningrad) was to be transferred to the USSR and that the Polish-German frontier should be on the Oder-Neisse line (q.v.). The western interpretation of the Yalta Declaration on Liberated Europe could not be realized and the question of the Turkish Straits remained unsettled.

'Prague Spring'   Name given to the period of attempted liberalization in Czechoslovakia under Dubcek, who was Secretary of the Communist Party in spring 1968. The attempt was brought to an end by the intervention of Warsaw Pact troops in August 1968 and Dubcek's replacement by Husak.

Pravda   Soviet newspaper. Organ of the Central Committee of the Communist Party of the Soviet Union. First Marxist daily with a mass circulation; founded in 1912.

Puppet government   A government allowed to retain a façade of independence but which is controlled by an external power. An example was Manchukuo, Japanese-occupied Manchuria from 1932–45.

Quai d'Orsay   The Seine embankment in Paris on which the French Foreign Office is situated: by extension, a term for the Foreign Office itself.

Quisling   Eponym for leader of an enemy-sponsored regime, deriving from Vidkun Quisling (1887–1945) (q.v.).

Rabat Conference   The 1974 Arab summit meeting which confirmed the PLO in its role as the only legitimate representative of the Palestinians. For the first time King Hussein of Jordan agreed that the

Palestinians had a right to sovereignty in all of liberated Palestine, under PLO leadership.

Rapacki Plan   Proposal in February 1958 by Polish Foreign Minister Adam Rapacki (1909–70) to create a nuclear-free zone by banning the manufacture and stationing of nuclear weapons in Czechoslovakia, Poland, East and West Germany. Rejected by Britain and the US because the USSR would retain conventional military superiority in the area.

rapprochement   Diplomatic expression deriving from the French, signifying the re-establishment of friendly relations between hitherto hostile states.

Red Brigades   Italian left-wing urban guerrilla group which emerged in the early 1970s. As well as carrying out numerous terrorist actions, the Brigades kidnapped and murdered former prime minister Aldo Moro in 1978, intending to destabilize the Italian state.

Red China   The People's Republic of China, set up in Beijing on 1 October 1949 following Communist victory over Nationalist forces in the civil war.

Red Guards   Youths in the Chinese People's Liberation Army given authority to agitate through the country spreading radicalism. They became prominent for their enthusiasm as Mao Zedong's shock-troops in the 1966–69 Cultural Revolution, denouncing 'revisionism' and 'bourgeois decay'.

Reich   The term used to describe the German Empire. The First Reich was considered to have been the Holy Roman Empire and thus the unified Germany after 1870 was known as the Second or *Kaiserreich*. This enabled Hitler's ideas of an enlarged Germany to be known as the Third Reich, although this name was officially dropped in the 1930s.

Reichstag   The German parliament (building) in Berlin created by the Constitution of 1871. Representatives were elected by universal suffrage and represented a concession to democracy, although the Reichstag could not initiate legislation and could only block certain measures. Moreover, government ministers were not appointed by, nor responsible to, the Reichstag. Nevertheless, it became the focal point of politics (if not decision making) in the 1890s during the reign of Wilhelm II. The building was destroyed by fire on 28 February 1933; its destruction was used by the Nazis for propaganda purposes against the Left and to pass a number of restrictive decrees.

reparations   Payments imposed on powers defeated in war to recompense the costs to the victors. Most commonly associated with the payments inflicted on Germany at the end of the First World War, although the actual amount was not fixed until April 1921, when the sum was set at £6,600 million plus interest. The Dawes and Young Plans later reduced the repayments until the effects of the Depression caused reparations payments to be abandoned after the Lausanne agreement in 1932. Apart from their international ramifications, reparations payments played an important part in the domestic politics of the Weimar Republic.

resistance The popular term for the opposition to the Nazi regime, both inside Germany and in the occupied countries, 1940–45. From January 1942, the Free French began to organize resistance groups and in May 1943, the Maquis (q.v.) liberated Corsica. By 1945 resistance groups were active throughout Europe but were often divided amongst themselves on ideological grounds, providing the basis for post-war political conflicts.

revisionist Term applied by orthodox Marxists to one who attempts to reassess the basic tenets of revolutionary socialism. Originating in Germany in the 1890s and 1900s, its chief exponents were Edouard Bernstein and Karl Kautsky. Regarded as heresy in the Soviet Union, the Cuban, Chinese and Albanian Communists have since used the same term to describe the Moscow line.

Rhodesian Front White Rhodesian party led by Ian Smith (q.v.). In the 1977 elections the Rhodesian Front held all 50 white seats in the Rhodesian parliament.

SA Abbreviation of the German *Sturmabteilung* or Storm Battalion, sometimes known as 'Brownshirts' from their uniform. Groups of ex-soldiers organized in quasi-military formations from 1923 to support the Nazis. Under their leader, Rohm, the force grew rapidly to an estimated four and a half million men by June 1934, when both Hitler's and the army's fear of its power prompted Hitler's murder of Rohm and the leaders of the SA in the 'Night of the Long Knives' (q.v.). Although it remained in existence, the power of the SA as a political force was broken.

Sadat Initiative Proposal by Egyptian President Anwar Sadat (1919–1981), prompted by Egypt's inability to maintain high military expenditure, that he should visit Israel to explain the Arab position on the Middle East before the Knesset. The offer was accepted by Israeli Prime Minister Menachem Begin (b. 1913) and a visit took place on 19–21 November 1977. Sadat's tacit recognition of Israel was condemned by the PLO and a number of Arab states and led to his assassination in 1981.

SALT *see under* Strategic Arms Limitation Talks

sanctions Term usually applied to economic boycott of one country by another. Sanctions were the chief weapon of the League of Nations (q.v.) against countries who were thought not to be fulfilling their international obligations. An economic boycott was imposed on Italy in October 1935, following the invasion of Abyssinia, but its terms were limited and largely ineffective. These were finally lifted in July 1936. Similar sanctions were imposed on Rhodesia in 1965 by

Britain and the UN, but proved ineffective.

Sandinistas The Sandinista Liberation Front which waged a guerrilla war against Nicaraguan dictator Gen. Anastasio Somozo, driving him from power in July 1979. The Sandinistas won the sympathy of the Church, the unions and the middle classes and ruled post-revolutionary Nicaragua until their surprise election defeat in 1990.

SAVAK Name of the Iranian Secret Police.

Schlieffen Plan The plan devised in 1905 by Gen. Count Alfred von Schlieffen (1833–1913), Chief of the German General Staff, to attack France through Belgium. Though modified, it laid the basis for the German army's advance in August 1914, the violation of Belgian neutrality bringing Britain into the war.

SDI Strategic Defense Initiative, also known as 'Star Wars', a plan announced by President Reagan in March 1983 to protect the United States from nuclear attack by destroying missiles with satellites outside the atmosphere. Reagan offered to share the technology to demonstrate its peaceful intent.

Sea-bed Treaty Treaty banning the installation of weapons of mass destruction on the sea-bed and ocean floor or in the subsoil thereof beyond a 12-mile coastal zone. Signed in Washington, London and Moscow on 11 February 1971. It came into force on 18 May 1972.

Second Front The invasion of Normandy agreed upon at the Quebec Conference in August 1943 and mounted in June 1944. Stalin had appealed to the Western Allies to launch a Second Front in the West to ease German pressure on Russia since 1941.

Securitate The Romanian secret police under the Ceausescu (q.v.) dictatorship. Their brutal suppression of disturbances in Timisoara in December 1989 sparked the Romanian revolution. Their loyalty and fanaticism caused hundreds of deaths in the civil war. Disbanded by the provisional government. Many were summarily executed. See p. 305.

segregation The separation of white and black races in public and private facilities. Laws requiring the segregation of the races have been on the statute books of several American states. In 1896, the Supreme Court ruled that such laws were valid under the separate but equal doctrine under which Blacks could be segregated if they were provided with equal facilities. As a result of this doctrine, segregation spread to schools, public transport, recreation and housing. By the 1940s the Supreme Court began to weaken the doctrine of 'separate but equal' by insisting on facilities being, indeed, equal. Finally, in 1954, the Court reversed the separate but equal formula, ruling that segregation based on race or colour was, in fact, incompatible with equality. Since this judgement, court-order desegregation coupled with legislation on civil rights in 1957, 1960, 1964, 1965 and 1968, has removed the edifice of government-sanctioned segregation.

Sendero Luminoso   The Communist Party of Peru, a Marxist guerrilla movement founded in 1970. The title – which means 'Shining Path' – derived from the Peruvian Marxist José Carlos Mariátegui's declaration that 'Marxism-Leninism will open the shining path to revolution'.

Sharpeville   In March 1960 South African security forces fired on Africans demonstrating against pass laws outside a police station: 67 were killed and many injured. A state of emergency was declared, African leaders arrested and the two leading African political parties, the ANC and PAC were banned under the Suppression of Communism Act.

Shi'ites   Members of the Iranian Muslim sect Shiah, which believes Muhammad's son-in-law Ali was his true successor, unlike the orthodox Sunni, who acknowledge the succession of Omar. The divergence between the two branches of Islam is now doctrinal.

shuttle diplomacy   After the 1973 Arab-Israeli War, American Secretary of State, Henry Kissinger, began a series of visits to facilitate negotiations between the countries involved in the conflict. These made clear the American preference for a piecemeal approach to the conflict rather than a reconvening of the Geneva Conference. Although three disengagement agreements involving small Israeli withdrawals from Syrian and Egyptian territory were achieved, this method left unresolved the central question of the Palestinians. Nothing further was accomplished after 1975.

Sinn Fein   Gaelic for 'Ourselves alone'. Irish Nationalist party founded in 1902 by Arthur Griffiths (1872–1922) and formed into the Sinn Fein League in 1907–08 when it absorbed other nationalist groups. The group rose to prominence in the 1913–14 Home Rule crisis, when many Sinn Feiners joined the Irish Volunteers and many Dublin workers joined the organization. Sinn Fein members were involved in the Easter Rising in 1916. It is still the name of the political wing of the IRA (the Irish Republican Army).

Six, the   The original six countries, Belgium, France, Italy, Luxembourg, the Netherlands and West Germany, who together created the European Coal and Steel Community in 1952, and the European Economic Community and Euratom in 1958.

Six Day War   The 5–10 June 1967 war between Israel and the Arab states, provoked by an Egyptian blockade of the Gulf of Aqaba. Israel bombed Egypt, Iraq, Jordan and Syria on 5 June; destroyed Egyptian armoured forces, reached the Suez Canal, and captured the West Bank of the Jordan on 7 June; then captured the strategic Syrian

Golan Heights. These territories are still occupied by Israel.

Smithsonian Agreement In December 1971, agreement was reached by the finance ministers of the Group of Ten in an attempt to restore stability to the world monetary system. The US dropped its 10% surcharge on imports and devalued the dollar by 8·5% and some European currencies were revalued. This did not, in fact, lead to a return to fixed exchange rates, but does provide a landmark for currency value charges.

Social Democracy Non-doctrinaire, socialist or socialist-inclined political movement of the nineteenth and twentieth centuries, combining concern for greater equality with acceptance of a mixed economy and representing a non-communist left-wing tradition, often drawing support from organized labour. Notable examples include the Social Democratic Party of Germany, founded in 1875, and the Swedish Social Democratic Labour Party, formed in 1880.

Social Fascist Term of abuse used by communists against Social Democratic and Labour Parties from 1928–34, in line with the Comintern view that rivals for working class support were 'the left wing of Fascism'.

Socialism in One Country Doctrine expounded by Stalin in Russia after it became clear that the Revolution of 1917 was not going to affect the other states of Europe. The main task was to create a socialist society without help from outside, either political or economic.

Solidarity Polish trade union and reform movement formed in the 1970s in the shipyards of Gdansk to demand liberalization of the Polish communist regime and the formation of free trade unions. Under its leader, Lech Walesa, the movement won important concessions from the government before the threat of Soviet invasion and the assumption of power by the Polish army led to the banning of the organization and the imprisonment of its leaders. It survived as a clandestine organization. Solidarity continued throughout the 1980s, representing the voice of the mass of the workers in Poland. In 1989, it joined in forming the first non-communist government in Poland since 1948.

South-West Africa People's Organization (SWAPO) An independence movement founded in 1959, which in 1966 began guerrilla activity against South African forces. It was banned from Namibia and operated over the border. In 1989 its leader, Sam Numoja (q.v.), returned to Namibia in anticipation of independence in 1990.

Soviet Workers' councils which emerged spontaneously in the 1905 Russian Revolution and re-appeared in 1917. Intended to encourage and reflect direct working-class participation in political activity, they were effectively dominated by the Bolsheviks (later the Communists) after 1917, and became national administrative organs.

Soweto Riots occurred here in 1976 following widespread strikes and general unrest in the South African townships. The immediate cause of trouble was opposition to the compulsory use of Afrikaans for instruction in schools.

Spartacists German Socialist Party (SPD) radicals led by Rosa Luxemburg and Karl Liebknecht, who went on to form the German Communist Party (KPD) in 1918 and led a bloodily suppressed revolutionary rising in January 1919. The name came from Spartacus, the leader of a slave rebellion in Rome in 73 BC.

special relationship The relationship between Britain and the United States, one allegedly based on historical links of culture and kinship running deeper than diplomatic expediency.

SS Abbreviation of German *Schutzstaffel* or Guard Detachment. Hitler's personal bodyguard of dedicated Nazis founded in 1923 as a rival to Rohm's SA (q.v.). Placed under the command of Heinrich Himmler in 1929, the SS carried out the liquidation of the SA leadership in June 1934 and in July became an independent organization with its own armed units. *SS-Verfugunstruppe* (Special Task Troops), organized as regular soldiers, were formed from 1935 and as the *Waffen-SS* comprised a group of elite regiments, separate from army control. Other sections of the SS provided concentration-camp guards – the *SS-Totenkopfverbande* – and police squads in occupied territory.

Stalinism The arbitrary bureaucratic rule, personality cult and political purges underpinning Stalin's attempt to create 'Socialism in One Country' through enforced agricultural collectivization and a rapid build-up of heavy industry. More recently the term has been used as a synonym for the Soviet and East European communist regimes.

state capitalism Lenin's expression for the compromise with financial interests which, combined with increased central economic control, was an attempt to preserve Bolshevik power in 1918. Latterly, a pejorative left-wing description of Soviet society, in which a privileged bureaucratic elite allegedly exploits the working class through its own monopoly of economic and political power.

Strategic Arms Limitation Talks (SALT) The United States and the Soviet Union embarked on SALT with the object of limiting the level of competition between them and reducing the size of their strategic nuclear armaments. Preliminary negotiations took place in Helsinki in November and December 1969, and an agreement on anti-ballistic missile systems and an interim agreement on strategic offensive arms were concluded by President Nixon (q.v.) in Moscow on 26 May 1972. The second phase of the negotiations, SALT II, opened in Geneva on 21 November 1972. In talks between President Ford (q.v.) and Chairman Brezhnev (q.v.) at Vladivostok in November 1974, an agreement was reached setting down guidelines for a pact to control the strategic arms race for the period 1977–85. However, the technical and political problems involved in framing such a pact have meant that no definitive treaty has yet been signed.

succession states The states formed after the First World War from the territory of the former Austro-Hungarian Empire, or incorporating parts of it. These included Poland, Czechoslovakia, Yugoslavia, Romania, Hungary and Austria.

Sudetenland German-speaking area of northern Bohemia assigned to Czechoslovakia in 1919. Claimed by Hitler for the Reich, the Sudetenland became the centre of an international crisis in 1938 over Germany's attempt to revise the Versailles Treaty by force. The threat of general European war was temporarily averted by the Munich Agreement, in which Czechoslovakia was forced to cede the Sudetenland to Germany.

Suez Crisis Major diplomatic crisis in 1956. Following Egyptian nationalization of the Suez Canal on 26 July 1956, Israel invaded Sinai on 29 October. When Egypt rejected a cease-fire ultimatum by France and Britain, their air forces began to attack Egyptian air bases on 31 October. On 5 November Franco-British forces invaded the Canal Zone and captured Port Said. Hostilities ended at midnight on 6–7 November following a cease-fire by the UN, and the Franco-British forces were evacuated.

summit conference Meeting between the leaders of great powers to discuss issues of major long-term interest or to resolve specific areas of tension. The expression was used by Winston Churchill (1874–1965) when he called for a 'parley at the summit'

swastika Ancient religious symbol in the shape of a hooked cross. In European mythology it became linked with the revival of Germanic legends at the end of the nineteenth century. Adopted by a number of extreme right-wing groups in Germany after the First World War, including the Erhardt Brigade, a *Freikorps* unit active in the Kapp Putsch. It was also adopted by Hitler as the symbol of National Socialism and in September 1935 became Nazi Germany's national emblem.

syndicalism Theory which advocates the ownership and organization of industry by workers and their organizations, usually trade unions. This is in contrast to the socialist theory of ownership by the state. Syndicalism is also associated with the belief in the power of trade unionism and the use of the general strike as a weapon to bring about major social and political change. Although often associated with anarchists, many of the syndicalists in the 1920s joined the communist or fascist parties.

Tanker War Attacks made on oil tankers in the Persian Gulf in the 1980–88 Iran-Iraq War. Iraq attacked shipping trading with Iran in 1984: Iran replied with attacks on tankers using the ports of Iraq's Arab supporters.

Tashkent Agreement   A declaration of truce took place between India and Pakistan after a conference convened at Tashkent in the USSR (3–10 January 1966). Alexei Kosygin, Chairman of the Council of Ministers of the USSR, acted as mediator between Lal Bahadur Shastri (q.v.), Prime Minister of India and Ayub Khan (q.v.), President of Pakistan, in a settlement which ended the war on the Kashmir border and restored Indian-Pakistan relations.

Tehran Conference   Wartime meeting in Tehran, Persia (28 November–1 December 1943) between Winston Churchill, President Franklin D. Roosevelt and Marshal Stalin (with the combined chiefs of staff, Anthony Eden and Harry Hopkins attending) to plan military strategy in Europe and the Far East. It was agreed that 'Overlord', the Anglo-American invasion of northern France, would take place on 1 May 1944. Stalin promised that Russia would join in the war against Japan in the Far East after victory over Germany had been achieved. The future of Poland and Germany was also discussed.

terrorism   A tactic intended to achieve political ends or gain publicity for a cause by creating a climate of fear through assassination, bombing, kidnapping and the seizure of aircraft. Most non-communist countries have suffered terrorism since the 1960s.

Test-Ban Treaty   Treaty signed by the USA, USSR and Britain after five years' negotiation on 5 August 1963, agreeing not to test nuclear weapons in outer space, the atmosphere or under the ocean. In the following two years over 90 other states signed, though France and China refused and have carried out atmospheric nuclear tests.

Tet   Communist Viet Cong and North Vietnamese attack on Saigon (now Ho Chi Minh City) and 140 other towns and villages during the Tet lunar new year festival. The 'Tet Offensive' ran from 20 January to 25 February 1968. The communists gained nothing materially, casualties on both sides were heavy, but the South Vietnamese government was undermined and America's commitment to the Vietnam War significantly weakened.

Third International   Otherwise known as the Communist International or the Comintern. Founded by Lenin in March 1919 to unite revolutionary socialists. Finally disbanded by Stalin in May 1943 as a concession to his western allies.

Third Reich   Term used to describe the Nazi dictatorship in Germany, 1933–45. Originally coined by the Nazis to describe the expanded Germany of their theories, the term was dropped from official usage in the 1930s.

Third Republic   The term used to describe the government of France from the Franco-Prussian War in 1871 to the fall of France in 1940 and the establishment of the Vichy Regime (q.v.).

Third World   Under-developed and poor nations in Africa, Asia and

Latin America which are neither part of the capitalist industrialized west nor of the communist eastern bloc.

Thirty-eighth Parallel   The line of latitude 38° north dividing South Korea from communist North Korea, established at the 1945 Yalta Conference. The intention that the two states should ultimately unite was ended by the 1950–53 Korean War.

'Thousand Days'   The period in office of US President John F. Kennedy (1917–1963) from his inauguration in January 1961 to his assassination in November 1963. Kennedy initiated civil rights legislation, moves towards a nuclear test ban, authorized the Bay of Pigs invasion, outmanoeuvered the USSR in the Cuban Missile Crisis, and drew the US more deeply into the Vietnam War.

Tiananmen Square   Massacre of pro-democracy demonstrators (mainly students) in the main square of Beijing by hard-line Chinese government forces, 4 June 1989. See p. 103.

Tlatelolco, Treaty of   Treaty prohibiting nuclear weapons in Latin America signed in Mexico City on 14 February 1967 by 14 countries.

Tonkin resolution   Following alleged North Vietnamese attacks on American shipping in the Gulf of Tonkin, both Houses of the US Congress gave US President Lyndon Johnson (1963–69) sweeping powers to use force in the area on 7 August 1964. Immediate escalation of US involvement in the Vietnam War followed.

total war   The mobilization of a nation's entire economic, ideological and military resources in wartime to achieve victory, as with Britain, Germany and the Soviet Union in World War II.

Trotskyist   Follower of Leon Trotsky (1870–1940), the Soviet revolutionary leader who lost the power struggle with Stalin in 1924 and was assassinated in Mexico in 1940. Trotsky condemned Stalin's excessive Russian nationalism and the increasingly bureaucratic and dictatorial nature of his socialism. Trotskyism found support among disillusioned Western communists following the 1956 Soviet invasion of Hungary, and among student activists in the 1960s and 1970s.

Tupamaros   Marxist urban guerrilla movement in Uruguay named after Tupac Amarus who led an eighteenth century Peruvian Indian revolt against Spain. Initially effective, the 1,000-strong movement was weakened by a police and right-wing paramilitary offensive in 1972.

Twenty-One Demands   Demands made upon China by Japan on 18 January 1915 with a threat of military action if they were not met. They were an attempt to make China a Japanese protectorate by forcing the appointment of advisers. Japan was restrained by Britain, but gained control over Manchuria and Shantung, a 50% interest in

China's leading iron and steel company, and a limitation on foreign influence in China's coastal regions.

U-boats German submarines (*untersee*) which operated widely in both World Wars, particularly in the North Atlantic, sinking merchant shipping carrying supplies to Britain.

UDI The illegal and widely condemned Unilateral Declaration of Independence made by Ian Smith's white Rhodesian Front government on 11 November 1965 in an attempt to avoid moving towards black majority rule in Southern Rhodesia.

unequal treaties Term used by the Chinese to describe conditions imposed upon them by imperialist states, particularly the agreement on an Open Door policy in China reached by Belgium, Britain, France, Italy, Japan, the Netherlands, Portugal and the United States at the 1921 Washington Conference.

Uniho Nacional Para a Independencia Total de Angola
(UNITA) Angolan nationalist group which was in control of the south of Angola at independence. Joint UNITA and FNLA troops were defeated by the MPLA (q.v.) by February 1976, but UNITA continued a guerrilla struggle from its strongholds in the south of Angola.

United front The Communist Party tactic of forming alliances with socialist and working-class parties to face what is seen to be a common enemy, for example fascism, usually during a period of communist weakness.

United Nations see p. 253.

U-2 Incident On 1 May 1960 an American U-2 high-altitude reconnaissance aircraft was brought down over the Soviet Union near Sverdlovsk while on a photographic mission. As a result, the Russians cancelled the summit meeting with President Eisenhower in West Berlin on 16 May 1960. The pilot, Francis Gary Powers, was sentenced to ten years' imprisonment, but was exchanged for the Soviet spy, Colonel Abel, on 10 February 1962.

urban guerrillas Groups using military methods and terrorist tactics in cities to achieve political ends. The most notable are the Red Brigades in Italy and the Red Army Faction in Germany in the 1970s, and the Provisional IRA in Northern Ireland from the early 1970s onwards.

Versailles, Treaty of Treaty ending World War I signed by Germany and the victorious powers in 1919. Germany lost her colonies; ceded territory to Belgium, Lithuania and Poland; returned Alsace-Lorraine to France; had its army reduced to 100,000 with limitations on weapons and a ban on submarines and an air force; acknowledged war guilt and promised to pay reparations. The treaty also established the League of Nations. Germany complained of the

Treaty's harshness and it remained a source of bitterness, used by the Nazis in their rise to power.

Vichy   French provincial spa town where the interim autocratic French government was established between July 1940 and July 1944. The Vichy regime was anti-republican, and collaborated extensively with the Germans who occupied the areas it controlled in November 1942. After the liberation of France in 1944, Pétain and the Vichy ministers established a headquarters in Germany.

Viet Cong   Communist guerrilla troops who fought in South Vietnam on behalf of the National Liberation Front.

Viet Minh   A communist political group in North Vietnam founded by Ho Chi-minh (q.v.) in 1941 to work for independence. In 1945 its forces entered Hanoi and formed a provisional government under Ho Chi-minh. From 1951 it worked as part of the Deng Lao Dong Vietnam (Vietnam Workers' Party).

Wafd   The leading Egyptian nationalist party between the wars, forming a government under Nahas Pasha in 1936. He was dismissed by King Farouk in 1938 and his restoration to office by Britain in 1941 (on the grounds that he favoured the Allies) weakened Wafd's nationalist standing. Returned to power in the 1950 elections, the Wafd faced civil disorder, was sacked by Farouk in 1952 and dissolved in 1953.

Waffen SS   An elite military force, part of the Nazi SS (*Schutzstaffeln*), made up of Germans and anti-communist volunteers from most European states. Forty divisions were deployed in World War II.

War Communism   The Bolshevik attempt begun in 1918 to overcome economic collapse by nationalizing larger enterprises, partially militarizing labour, requisitioning agricultural produce by force, and introducing a state monopoly of exchange. Its unpopularity and ultimate ineffectiveness led to the New Economic Policy of 1921.

war criminal   A concept which emerged at the end of World War I in a 'Hang the Kaiser' campaign. At the Nuremburg Trials after World War Two, 177 Nazis were accused by the Allies of planning to wage an aggressive war and of genocide, and ten were sentenced to death.

warlords   Generals who dominated provinces in a politically fragmented China between 1916 and 1928, waging war on one another with private armies.

Warsaw Pact   see p. 253–4.

Watergate   General term given to a variety of illegal acts perpetrated by officials in the Nixon (q.v.) administration (1969–74), and subsequent efforts to 'cover-up' their responsibility for these acts, which led eventually to the resignation of President R. M. Nixon and the succession to the Presidency of Vice-President Gerald R. Ford (q.v.). Specifically, 'Watergate' refers to a burglary, by a group of seven men acting under the orders of the White House, of the Democratic national party headquarters located in the Watergate building in Washington D.C. Other illegal acts included within the general term 'Watergate' were: bribery, illegal use of the CIA, FBI and other government agencies for political and partisan purposes, income tax fraud, the establishment and use by the White House of an unofficial 'plumbers' group designed to discover the source of leaks to the press, the use of 'dirty tricks' during the 1972 election campaign, and illegal campaign contributions. As a result of these Watergate crimes many cabinet officers, presidential assistants and other administration officials were convicted of various crimes. It produced a spate of new laws concerning secrecy in government and regulation of campaign practices. It also produced a Supreme Court decision which, for the first time, limited the doctrine of 'executive privilege' by holding that the privilege cannot be used to prohibit disclosure of criminal misconduct.

Weimar   Town where the German National Constituent Assembly met in February 1919. It gave its name to the German Republic of 1918–33. The town was chosen to allay fears of the Allied powers and the other German states about Prussian domination in Berlin, and also to escape from the associations attached to the former capital city. The economic problems which beset the Weimar Republic and the concomitant unemployment facilitated the rise of Hitler, and in March 1933 he suspended the Weimar Constitution of July 1919 to make way for the Third Reich (q.v.).

West Bank   The West Bank of the Jordan River was annexed by King Abdullah of Jordan after the 1948 war. It was taken by Israel in 1967 and placed under military administration. East Jerusalem was not only annexed but its boundaries were extended, in defiance of international law. To establish a firm hold on the city, Israel had evicted Arab families and replaced them with Jews. In 1970 a government plan to double the Jewish population of the city by 1980 was published. The United Nations has condemned Israel several times for its actions in East Jerusalem. Archaeological excavations have also called forth UN protest. The Israeli government insists on maintaining secure borders in any settlement but there is conflict over how much territory this involves. Groups of religious extremists, like Gush Emunim, opposed the return of any territory and insist on the right to settle in all of Biblical Israel. They have gone so far as to set up illegal settlements which the government has been loath to dislodge. The government itself has set up Jewish settlements on the West Bank. These, in turn, undermine its claim to be willing to return Arab territory and are an obstacle to peace. In the past few years Arabs on the West Bank have grown increasingly restive. Riots and demonstrations have culminated in the uprising known as the '*intifada*' (q.v.). There is also considerable division within Israel over policy towards the West Bank.

Western Front   The zone of British, French and German military operations in World War I. It extended, largely in lines of trenches, for Nieuport on the Belgian coast, through northern France to the area around Verdun.

White Russians   Term for Russians living on western border of Soviet Union, but used generally to describe counter-revolutionary forces in the aftermath of the Bolshevik Revolution of 1917.

Winter War   The war from 30 November 1939 to 12 March 1940 which followed the Soviet invasion of Finland. Finland surrendered, ceding territory to the USSR and promising not to join an alliance against her.

Yalta Conference   The most crucial 'Big Three' meeting of the war held at Yalta in the Crimea (4–11 February 1945). Agreements reached between Winston Churchill, President Franklin D. Roosevelt and Marshal Stalin (with the chiefs of staff, Molotov, Stettinus, Anthony Eden and Harry Hopkins attending) virtually determined the reconstruction of the post-war world. France was admitted as an equal partner of the Allied Control Commission for Germany but the practical details of Allied control were not worked out in Protocols III, IV, V and VI. The future of Poland, one of the most contentious issues of the conference, was referred to in the ambiguously worded Declaration on Poland in Protocol VII, where no agreement was made as to the reconstruction of the Polish government. Being anxious to secure a firm Russian undertaking to join in the war against Japan, Roosevelt acceded to Stalin's condition that Russia should resume her old rights in China, lost as a result of the Russo-Japanese war of 1904–05, and a secret tripartite agreement was signed to this effect on 11 February 1945. Protocol I set out the agreement reached on the creation of a World Organization of the United Nations and the voting formula for the Security Council. It was agreed to call a conference in San Francisco in April 1945, to draw up a charter for the United Nations.

Yezhovschina   A word used to describe the Stalinist purges of the 1920s and 1930s. The name derives from the head of the Soviet secret police, N.I. Yezhov.

Yom Kippur   The Jewish day of atonement, a period of religious observance. During this period Egyptian and Syrian forces moved against Israel on 6 October 1973. Israel counter-attacked on 8 October, threatening Cairo and Damascus. The 'Yom Kippur war' ended with a United Nations arranged cease-fire on 24 October.

Young Plan   The proposal made on 7 June 1929 by US businessman Owen D. Young (1874–1962) for a settlement of German war reparations. Payments were to be reduced by 75% and made annually until 1988. Germany accepted the plan, but Hitler refused to make further payments after 1933.

Zionism   The belief that the Jews should create a homeland in Palestine, suggested by Theodor Herzl (1860–1904) who felt the Jews were threatened by east European pogroms. Until then Palestine had been generally seen by Jews as a spiritual rather than physical homeland. An initial reluctance among many Jews who felt assimilated in Europe was overcome by the experience of the Nazi Holocaust. The state of Israel was set up in 1948.

Zimmermann Telegram   Coded message of 19 January 1917 from the German foreign minister, Arthur Zimmermann, to the German minister in Mexico, urging the conclusion of a German-Mexican alliance in the event of a declaration of war on Germany by America when Germany resumed unrestricted submarine warfare against shipping on 1 February. Mexico would be offered the recapture of her 'lost territories' in New Mexico, Arizona and Texas. Intercepted by British Naval Intelligence, the telegram was released to the American press on 1 March, greatly inflaming feeling against Germany, and helping to precipitate the American Declaration of War against Germany on 6 April 1917.

Section VI
Bibliography

This bibliography is arranged in broadly geographical terms to allow concentration on particular aspects of world history in the twentieth century and the sub-themes within it. Some topics such as imperial expansion and decolonization are of world-wide scope, and contain works relating to more than one geographical area.

i. Introductory works

The later sections of J. M. Roberts, *A History of the World* (1976) and W. H. McNeill, *A World History* (1967) are excellent introductions to the modern world. See also J. M. Roberts, *The Triumph of the West* (1985) for a principal theme of world history this century. H. A. S. Grenville, *A World History of the Twentieth Century, 1900–84* (2 vols., 1980–5) and P. Calvocoressi, *World Politics since 1945* (5th edn., 1987) deal exclusively with the present century. J. Major, *The Contemporary World: a historical introduction* (1970) and G. Barraclough, *An Introduction to Contemporary History* (1967) are useful analyses of some of the major themes, while D. C. Watt, F. Spencer and N. Brown, *A History of the World in the Twentieth Century* (1967) examines international relations. The development of the world beyond Europe is examined in P. Worsley, *The Third World* (1967) and C. E. Black, *The Dynamics of Modernization: a study in comparative history* (1967). Important studies of the development of the modern world are I. Wallerstein, *The Modern World System* (1974) and J. A. Hall, *Powers and Liberties: the causes and consequences of the rise of the West* (1985)

The economic history of the twentieth century is considered in W. Ashworth, *A Short History of the International Economy since 1850* (4th edn. 1987) and A. G. Kenwood and A. L. Longheed, *The Growth of the International Economy: an introductory text* (1971). The excellent Penguin series of the history of the world economy should also be consulted: G. Hardach, *The First World War, 1914–1918* (1977); D. H. Aldcroft, *From Versailles to Wall Street, 1919–1929* (1977); C. P. Kindleberger, *The World in Depression, 1929–1939* (1977); and A. S. Milward, *War, Economy and Society, 1939–1945* (1977).

For the world monetary system as a whole, see D. Calleo, *The Imperious Economy* (1982); on America's role and more generally, M. Moffitt, *The World's Money* (1945); L. Tson Kalis (ed.) *The Political Economy of International Money* (1985); C. P. Kindleberger, *Power and Money: the economics of international politics and the politics of international economics* (1970); S. E. Rolfe and J. L. Burkle, *The Great Wheel: the world monetary system: a reinterpretation* (1974); and A. Shonfield, *Modern Capitalism: the changing balance of public and private power* (1966). The specific role of the multinational companies is discussed in L. Turner, *Invisible Empires: multinational companies and the modern world* (1970) and *Multinational Companies and the Third World* (1973), E. T. Penrose, *The Large International Firm in Developing Countries: the international petroleum industry* (1968), and M. Wilkins, *The Maturing of Multinational Enterprise: American business abroad from 1914 to 1970* (1974). P. Bairoch, *The Economic Development of the Third World since 1900* (1975); H. Myint, *The Economics of Developing Countries* (4th edn., 1973) and G. Myrdal, *The Challenge of World Poverty: a world anti-poverty programme in outline* (1970) specifically examine the world beyond the major industrial powers. The role of aid as part of the nexus linking the developed and less developed world is considered from various points of view in J. A. White, *The Politics of Foreign Aid* (1974), T. Hayter, *Aid as Imperialism* (1971), L. D. Black, *The Strategy of Foreign Aid* (1968) and M. I. Goldman, *Soviet Foreign Aid (1967)*.

The energy question is considered in G. Foley and C. Nassim, *The Energy Question* (1976), P. R. Odell, *Oil and World Power* (4th edn., 1974), and G. C. Tugendhat and A. Hamilton, *Oil the Biggest Business* (rev.edn., 1975). The rise of OPEC is examined in M. S. Al-Otaiba, *OPEC and the Petroleum Industry* (1975), and Z. Mikdashi, *The Community of Oil Exporting Countries: a study in governmental co-operation* (1972). More recent concerns, such as the rise of Third World debt, are considered in H. Lever and C. Huhne, *Debt and Danger: the world financial crisis* (1985).

For population developments there is an excellent survey of world population from earliest times in C. McEvedy and T. Jones (eds), *Atlas of World Population History* (1978) and for more contemporary pre occupations see K. and A. F. K. Organski, *Population and World Power* (1961), T. McKeown, *The Modern Rise of Population* (1976), W. D. Barrie, *The Growth and Control of World Population* (1970) and R. Symonds and M. Carter, *The United Nations and the Population Question, 1945–70* (1973). For particular areas see S. Chandrasekhar (ed.) *Asia's Population Problems: with a discussion of population and immigration in Australia* (1967), D. Chaplin (ed.), *Population Policies and Growth in Latin America* (1971), W. A. Hance, *Population, Migration, and Urbanization in Africa* (1970) and J. I. Clarke and W. B. Fisher, *Populations of the Middle East and North Africa* (1971).

Urban development is considered generally in J. H. Lowry, *World City Growth* (1975), K. Davis, *World Urbanization, 1950–1970* (2 vols., 1969–72), P. M. Houser and L. F. Schnore (eds.) *The Study of Urbanization* (1965), T. H. Elkins, *The Urban Explosion* (1973), W. D. C. Wright and P. H. Steward, *The Exploding City* (1972) and P. Hall, *The World Cities* (2nd edn., 1977). Urban change in Europe and North America is considered in the last section of L. Mumford, *The City in History: its origins, its transformation, and its prospects* (1961) and his *The Urban Prospect* (1968), P. Hall (ed.), *Europe 2000* (1977), J. Gottman (ed.), *Megalopolis: the urbanized northeastern seaboard of the United States* (1962), and A. Sutcliffe (ed.), *Metropolis, 1890–1940* (1984) which includes an essay on the Tokyo area. Third-world studies include D. J. Dwyer, *The City in the Third World* (1968) and *The City as a Centre of Change in Asia* (1972), T. G. McGee, *The Urbanization Process in the Third World: explorations in search of a theory* (1971), G. W. Breese, *Urbanisation in Newly-Developing Countries* (1966), W. A. Hance, *Population, Migration and Urbanization in Africa* (1970) and G. K. Payne, *Urban Housing in the Third World* (1977). P. Lloyd, *Slums of Hope? Shanty towns of the Third World* (1979) digests an enormous amount of literature on the processes and effects of urban migration and has an excellent bibliography. Also on the social effects of urbanization see W. Mangin (ed), *Peasants in Cities: readings in the anthropology of urbanization* (1970), R. E. Pahl, *Patterns of Urban Life* (1970), A Southall (ed.), *Urban Anthropology: cross-cultural studies of urbanization* (1973), and B. J. L. Berry, *The Human Consequences of Urbanization: divergent paths in the urban experience of the twentieth century* (1973).

Amongst the ideologies affecting twentieth century development, nationalism is of great importance. A. D. Smith, *Theories of Nationalism* (1971) looks at various approaches, see also his edited collection, *Nationalist Movements* (1976). E. Kedourie, *Nationalism* (1960) is an introduction to the ideology, see also H. Seton-Watson, *Nations and States: an enquiry into the origins of nations and the politics of nationalism* (1977) and E. Gellner, *Nations and Nationalism* (1983). Also valuable are B. Akzin, *States and Nations* (1964), K. W. Deutsch, *Nationalism and Social Communication: an inquiry into the foundations of nationality* (2nd edn., 1966) and the older F. O Hertz, *Nationality in History and Politics* (1944). Nationalism as a phenomenon of particular regions can be studied in A. Cobban. *The Nation State and National Self-Determination* (1969) and R. Pearson, *National Minorities in Eastern Europe, 1848–1944* (1983), E. Kedourie (ed.), *Nationalism in Asia and Africa* (1971), F. R. Von der Mehden, *Religion and Nationalism in Southeast Asia: Burma, Indonesia, the Philippines* (1963), G. Antonius, *The Arab Awakening: the story of the Arab national movement* (1938), S. Haim (ed.), *Arab Nationalism: an anthology* (1962), T. Hodgkin, *Nationalism in Colonial Africa* (1956), D. A. Rustow, *A World of Nations: the problems of political modernization* (1967), A. P. Whitaker and D. C. Jordan, *Nationalism in Contemporary Latin America* (1966) and R. Emerson, *From Empire to Nation: the rise to self-assertion of Asian and African peoples* (1970).

Of the other powerful ideologies, socialism and communism, there are introductory texts in D. McLellan, *Marx* (1975) and *Engels* (1975), G. Lichtheim, *Marxism, an Historical and Critical Study* (1961) and *A Short History of Socialism* (1969), R. N. C. Hunt, *The Theory and Practice of Communism* (1963), and F. Claudin, *The Communist Movement: from Comintern to Cominform* (1975). The anarchist tradition is discussed in G. Woodcock, *Anarchism* (1963) and J. Joll, *The Anarchists* (1969).

Liberalism is less well served, although it had an important legacy from the nineteenth century, but see H. J. Laski, *The Rise of European Liberalism* (2nd edn., 1947) and A. Arblaster, *The Rise and Decline of Western Liberalism* (1984). The important force of social democracy can be examined in R. J. Harrison, *Pluralism and Corporation: the political evolution of modern democracies* (1980), J. Haywood, *Trade Unions and Politics in Western Europe* (1980), M. Kolinsky and W. Paterson (eds.), *Social and Political Movements in Western Europe* (1976), R. Miliband, *Parliamentary Socialism* (1961), I. Campbell and W. Paterson, *Social Democracy in Post-War Europe* (1974) and W. Paterson and A. Thomas, *Social Democratic Parties in Western Europe* (1977).

Two general works which deal with the nature of regimes are Barrington Moore, *Social Origins of Dictatorship and Democracy* (1966) and R. Ason, *Democracy and Totalitarianism* (1968). See also P. Wiles, *Economic Institutions Compared* (1977) and A. Ellis and K. Kumar (eds.), *Dilemmas of Liberal Democracies* (1983), T. Skocpol, *States and Social Revolutions* (1979), M. Olson, *The Rise and Decline of Nations* (1982) and J. H. Goldthorpe (ed.), *Order and Conflict in Contemporary Capitalism* (1984).

The role of revolution in the modern world is discussed in J. Dunn, *Modern Revolutions: an introduction to the analysis of a political phenomenon* (2nd edn., 1989), Chalmers Johnson, *Revolution and the Social System* (1964) and *Revolutionary Change* (1968), P. Calvert, *Revolution* (1970) and *A study of Revolution* (1970). Third world revolutions are specifically examined in F. J. Carrier, *The Third World Revolutions* (1976), G. Chaliand, *Revolution in the Third World: myths and prospects* (1977), J. S. Migdal, *Peasants, Politics and Revolution: pressures towards political and social change in the third world* (1975) and E. R. Wolf, *Peasant Wars of the Twentieth Century* (1969).

Almost inseparable from the idea of revolution in the less developed world is guerrilla warfare and terrorism. For the former, Che Guevara, *Guerrilla Warfare* (1969) and G. Fairbairn, *Revolutionary Warfare: the Countryside Version* (1974) are particularly relevant. For terrorism see G. Wardlaw, *Political Terrorism* (2nd edn., 1989.), W. Laqueur, *Terrorism* (1977), P. Wilkinson, *Political Terrorism* (1974) and S. Segaller, *Invisible Armies: terrorism into the 1990s* (2nd edn., 1987). The specific phenomenon of urban guerrilla warfare is considered in R. Moss *Urban Guerrillas* (1972), A. Burton *Urban Terrorism* (1975), and R. Clutterbuck, *Protest and the Urban Guerrilla* (1973), while the implications for societies are discussed in P. Wilkinson, *Terrorism and the Liberal State* (1977) and R. Clutterbuck, *Living with Terrorism* (1975).

The political role of the military is discussed in S. E. Finer, *The Man on Horseback: the role of the military in politics* (2nd edn., 1976) and M. E. Howard (ed.), *Soldiers and Governments: nine studies in civil-military relations* (1957); specifically on the role of the military in the third world, see M. Janowitz, *Military Institutions and Coercion in the Developing Nations* (1977). S. Andreski, *Military Organisation and Society* (2nd edn., 1968) is a classic exposition of the role of warfare in society, but see also A. Marwick, *War and Social Change in the Twentieth Century* (1974), M. R. D. Foot (ed.), *War and Society* (1973), B. Brodie, *War and Politics* (1973) and A. Buchan, *War in Modern Society* (1968). Much of recent discussion has been focused on the issue of 'total war', for which see Marwick (above) and N. F. Dreisziger (ed.), *Mobilisation for Total War: the Canadian, American and British Experience, 1914–1918, 1939–1945* (1981).

The influence of nuclear weapons upon the world scene is considered in J. Newhouse, *The Nuclear Age: a history of the arms race from Hiroshima to Star Wars* (1989), B. Brodie (ed.), *The Absolute Weapon: atomic power and world order* (1972), G. H. Quester, *Nuclear Diplomacy: the first twenty-five years* (1970), and L. Freedman, *The Evolution of Nuclear Strategy* (1981).

For the evolution of warfare, see J. F. C. Fuller, *The Conduct of War, 1789–1961: a study of the impact of the French, Industrial and Russian Revolutions on War and its Conduct* (1961). C. McInnes and G. D. Sheffield (eds.), *Warfare in the twentieth century: theory and practice* (1988) is a more recent collection of studies, while C. Cook and J. Stevenson, *The Atlas of Modern Warfare* (1978) provides an account and analysis of military history since 1945. There are excellent maps in T. Hartman (with J. Mitchell), *A World Atlas of Military History* (1984) and see also L. W. Martin, *Arms and Strategy: an international survey of modern defence* (1973). The geopolitics of military power is discussed over a long period in P. Kennedy, *The Rise and Fall of the Great Powers: economic change and military conflict, 1500–2000* (1988).
There are now regular updates of world-wide armed conflicts in J. Laffin (ed.), *War Annual* (1986–) and in the Royal United Services and Brassey's *Defence Yearbook*. The definitive assessment of size of the world's armed forces and their composition, including nuclear armouries, can be found in the International Institute for Strategic Studies, *The Military Balance*, published annually. L. A. Sobel (ed.), *Political Terrorism* (1975) contains a narrative of terrorist activity from 1968 to 1974.

A good atlas is essential to the understanding of twentieth century world affairs. G. Barraclough (ed.), *The Times Atlas of World History* (1978) and R. I. Moore (ed.), *The Newnes Historical Atlas* (1981) are two excellent examples though neither is concerned solely with the twentieth century. M. Gilbert, *Recent History Atlas: 1870 to the Present Day* (1966) is a useful supplement concentrating on the modern era. For reference purposes there is a wealth of statistical material in B. R. Mitchell, *European Historical Statistics, 1750–1975* (2nd edn., 1980) and *International Historical Statistics: Africa and Asia* (1986). There is a wide range of data in J. Paxton (ed.), *The Statesman's Yearbook*, published annually since 1864, while the United Nations *Statistical Yearbooks* (1945–) provide valuable additional material, and for the earlier period see the League of Nations *Statistical Yearbooks* (1920–). For demographic data, see the United Nations, *Demographic Yearbooks* (1945–). For chronological outlines of events see S. H. Steinberg, *Historical Tables, 58BC – AD1978* (10th edn., 1979) and D. Mercer (ed.), *Chronicle of the 20th Century* (1988).

ii European history

There are excellent overviews in J. M. Roberts, *Europe, 1880–1945* (1967), J. Joll, *Europe since 1870* (1973), F. Gilbert, *The End of the European Era, 1890 to the Present* (3rd edn., 1984) and A. Grant and H. Temperley, *Europe in the Nineteenth and Twentieth Centuries* (7th edn., rev. A. Ramm, 2 vols., 1984). See also G. Lichtheim, *Europe in the Twentieth Century* (1972) and the two versions of the Cambridge Modern History, Vol XII, D. Thomson (ed.), *The Era of Violence* (1960) and G. L. Monat (ed.), *The Shifting Balance of World Forces, 1898–1945* (1968). W. Laqueur, *Europe since Hitler* (1970) and D. Urwin, *Western Europe since 1945* (1981 edn.) deal specifically with post-1945 developments, while F. Fejto, *A History of the People's Democracies* (1971) and Z. Brzezinski, *The Soviet Bloc* (1974) deal specifically with eastern Europe. For the economic history of the continent, see the later sections of D. Landes, *The Unbound Prometheus: technological change and industrial development in Western Europe from 1750 to the present* (1972) and C. Cipolla (ed.), *The Fontana Economic History of Europe* (1973). For social change, see D. Geary, *A Social History of Western Europe, 1848–1945* (1985), P. N. Stearns, *European Society in Upheaval* (1967) and G. Mosse, *The Culture of Western Europe: the nineteenth and twentieth centuries* (1961).

On individual countries, for France see A. Cobban, *A History of Modern France, 1715–1945, vol. III; 1870–1945* (1965), D. Johnson, *France 1914–1983: The Twentieth Century* (1986), P. Bernard and H. Dubief, *The Decline of the Third Republic, 1914–1938* (1985) and J. F. McMillan, *Dreyfus to De Gaulle: Politics and Society in France* (1985). Also helpful is G. Dupeaux, *French Society, 1848–1945* (1976). On Spain, the standard history is R. Carr, *Spain, 1808–1975* (rev. edn., 1980) and for Italy, see D. Mack Smith, *Italy* (1959) and M. Clark, *Modern Italy 1871–1982* (1984). German history is examined in W. Carr, *A History of Germany, 1815–1985* (rev. edn., 1987), W. R. Berghahn, *Modern Germany: Society, Economy and Politics in the Twentieth Century* (1982), and G. A. Craig, *Germany: 1866–1945* (1978). For Russia, see H. Rogger, *Russia in the Age of Modernisation and Revolution, 1881–1917* (1983), M. McCauley, *The Soviet Union since 1917* (1981) and G. Hosking, *A History of the Soviet Union* (1985). Eastern Europe is discussed in C. A. Macartney, *The Hapsburg Empire, 1790–1918* (1971), R. A. Kann, *The Multi-National Empire* (2 vols., 1950), A. Sked, *The Decline and Fall of the Habsburg Empire, 1815–1918* (1989), and R. Pearson, *National Minorities in Eastern Europe, 1848–1945* (1983). For the British Isles, see R. K. Webb, *Modern England: From the Eighteenth Century to the Present* (1969) as an overview, and specifically on the twentieth century M. Beloff, *Wars and Welfare, Britain 1914–1952* (1984); R. Blake, *The Decline of Power, 1915–1970* (1985), A. Sked and C. Cook, *Post-War Britain*: a *political history* (1984) and D. Childs, *Britain since 1945* (1979). For Ireland see F. S. L. Lyons, *Ireland since the Famine* (rev. edn., 1973) and R. Foster, *Modern Ireland, 1600–1972* (1988).

The First World War

The origins of the First World War have attracted a vast literature, of which J. Joll, *The Origins of the First World War* (1985) is a good overview. The diplomatic background to war and its repercussions have received recent analysis in D. Stevenson, *The First World War and International Politics* (1988), while the older A. J. P. Taylor, *The Struggle for Mastery in Europe, 1848–1918* (1954) remains valuable. R. J. W. Evans and H. Pogge von Strandman (eds.), *The Coming of the First World War* (1988) is a series of essays on the views of the belligerents in 1914. B. Schmitt, *The Outbreak of War in 1914* (Historical Association pamphlet, 1964) is a brief account of the traditional interpretation that the alliance system was to blame for the outbreak of the war. See also his longer study, *The Coming of the War* (2 vols., 1930). The great classic of this school of thinking is L. Albertini, *The Origins of the War of 1914* (3 vols., 1952–57). Shorter and more recent accounts are L. C. F. Turner, *The Origins of the First World War* (1970) and H. W. Koch, *The Origins of the First World War* (1984 edn.). Also useful is the short account of the break-up of the nineteenth century international system, R. Langhorne, *The Collapse of the Concert of Europe, 1890–1914* (1981), while M. S. Anderson, *The Eastern Questions, 1774–1923* (1966) provides a wider perspective on that particular problem. Amongst the most important recent interpretations has been F. Fischer, *Germany's War Aims in the First World War* (1967) which sees the war as a result of Germany's pre-war expansionism, see also his *War of Illusion* (1972). On Germany see also I. Geiss, *German Foreign Policy, 1871–1914* (1976) and G. Ritter, *The Schlieffen Plan* (1958). On France see J. Keiger, *France and the Origins of the First World War* (1983) and on Russia D. Lieves, *Russia and the Origins of the First World War* (1983). Z. S. Steiner, *Britain and the Origins of the First World War* (1977) is the most detailed account of British involvement. The classic study of Anglo-German naval rivalry is E. L. Woodward, *Great Britain and the German Navy* (1935), but now updated on the naval side by A. J. Marder, *From the Dreadnought to Scapa Flow, vol. i: The road to war, 1904–14* (1961) and on the political by P. Kennedy, *The Rise of the Anglo-German Antagonism, 1860–1914* (1980). Broader interpretations of the social and psychological factors have gained some currency in recent years, see for example M. Howard, 'Reflections on the First World War' in his *Studies in War and Peace* (1970). There are numerous general histories of the war but among the most approachable are A. J. P. Taylor, *The First World War: an illustrated history* (1966), invaluable because of its illustrations, C. Falls, *The First World War* (1960) and B. H. Liddell-Hart, *History of the First World War* (1970). M. Ferro, *The Great War* (1963) is another short, readable introduction. See also, J. Terraine, *The Western Front, 1914–18* (1964). For works which place the military aspects of the war in a broader context see K. Robbins, *The First World War* (1984), B. Bond, *War and Society in Europe, 1870–1970* (1984) and G. Hardach, *The First World War* (1977). The nature of warfare is discussed in J. Ellis, *Eye-Deep in Hell* (1976) and A. E. Ashworth, *The Trench Warfare* (1980), while A. Horne, *The Price of Glory: Verdun, 1916* (1964), L. Macdonald, *They Called it Paschendaele* (1983) and M. Middlebrook,

The First Day on the Somme (1971) and *The Kaiser's Battle* (1983) (on
Germany's 1918 offensive) give full treatment of individual battles, as
does J. Keegan, *The Face of Battle* (1979).

The effect of the war on individual societies can be traced in J. Kocka,
Facing Total War: German Society, 1914–1918 (1985), A. J-J. Becker,
The Great War and the French People (Eng. edn. 1985), A. Marwick,
The Deluge: British Society and the First World War (1965), A. J. May,
The Passing of the Habsburg Monarchy (2 vols., 1966), L. Kochan,
Russia in Revolution, 1890–1918 (1966), and N. Stone, *The Eastern
Front* (1978). General coverage of such issues is provided by A.
Marwick, *War and Social Change in the Twentieth Century* (1974).

The revolutionary effects of the war are discussed in C. L. Bertrand
(ed.) *Revolutionary Situations in Europe, 1917–1922* (1977) and F. L.
Carsten, *Revolution in Central Europe, 1918–1919* (1972). For
Germany, see A. J. Ryder, *The German Revolution* (1966) and D.
Geary, 'Radicalism and the Worker: Metalworkers and Revolution,
1914–1923' in R. J. Evans (ed.), *Society and Politics in Wilhelmine
Germany* (1978).

War aims and the failure of early peace attempts are discussed in F.
Fischer, *Germany's aims in the First World War* (1967), V. Rothwell,
British War Aims and Peace Diplomacy (1971), C. Andrew and A.
Kanya-Forstner, *France Overseas* (1981), as well as A. J. P. Taylor,
The Struggle for Mastery and D. Stevenson, *The First World War*. See
also, M. Kitchen, *The Silent Dictatorship* (1976), on the growing role
of the German General Staff.

Versailles and international relations, 1919–39

For the Versailles settlement, A. Adamthwaite, *The Lost Peace* (1980)
provides a valuable documentary source for the whole inter-war
period, while J. M. Keynes, *The Economic Consequences of the Peace*
(1919) remains a powerful criticism of the settlement. E. H. Carr, *The
Twenty Years Crisis* (new edn., 1981) remains a stimulating account of
the period. G. N. Gathorne Hardy, *A Short History of International
Affairs, 1920–39* (1950) has aged less well and, among general
accounts, H. Gatzke, *European Diplomacy between the Two World
Wars* (1972) is to be preferred, and R. Albrecht-Carrié, *A Diplomatic
History of Europe from the Congress of Vienna* (1961) provides the
wider background. R. A. C. Parker, *Europe, 1919–1945* (1969) is also a
good general introduction. On 1919 and its immediate aftermath A. J.
Mayer, *The Policy and Diplomacy of Peacemaking* (1968), G. Shulz,
Revolution and Peace Treaties (1972) and S. Marks, *The Illusion of
Peace* (1976) are useful, whilst F. P. Walters, *A History of the League
of Nations* (1960) remains the most thorough account of that body.

On the origins of war in 1939, A. J. P. Taylor, *The Origins of the
Second World War* (1963) is still exciting and very readable, though
its views have been challenged. P. Bell, *The Origins of the Second
World War in Europe* (1986) is a recent overview of the issues, but
see also D. C. Watt, *The Coming of War*, 1938–9 (1989),

A. Adamthwaite, *The Making of the Second World War* (1977), and
W. Carr, *Poland to Pearl Harbour: the Making of the Second World
War* (1985). On specific events and issues, N. Rostow, *Anglo-French
Relations, 1934–6* (1984) analyses western policies at a key period,
whilst K. Robbins, *Munich* (1968) and T. Taylor, *Munich* (1979) look at
the most criticized episode in 1930s diplomacy. S. Newman, *March,
1939* (1976) concentrates on the British guarantee to Poland, which
was so vital in the outbreak of war. On French policy see especially,
A. Adamthwaite, *France and the Coming of the Second World War*
(1977) and on Germany, G. L. Weinberg, *The Foreign Policy of Hitler's
Germany* (1970) and W. Carr, *Arms, Autarky and Aggression* (1972).
And on British appeasement in general see especially M. Gilbert, *The
Roots of Appeasement* (1966), K. Middlemas, *Diplomacy of Illusion*
(1972) and W. R. Rock, *British Appeasement in the 1930s* (1976). See
also the essays by N. Medlicott and M. Howard in D. Dilks (ed.)
*Retreat from Power: Studies of Britain's Foreign Policy of the
Twentieth-Century: Volume One, 1906–1939 (1981).*

The Russian Revolution

Good starting points for the breakdown of the regime are H.
Seton-Watson, *The Russian Empire, 1801–1917* (1967), J. N.
Westwood, *Endurance and Endeavour: Russian History, 1812–1971*
(1973) and L. Kochan and P. Abraham, *The Making of Modern Russia*
(1983). R. B. McKean, *The Russian Constitutional Monarchy,
1907–1917* (Historical Association, 1977) synthesizes much recent
research. There are also useful essays in R. Pipes (ed.), *Revolutionary
Russia* (1968) and a short interperative essay in J. Dunn, *Modern
Revolutions* (2nd edn., 1989), ch. 1. B. Williams, *The Russian
Revolution, 1917–1921* (1987) and R. Service *The Russian Revolution*
(1989) are introductory volumes, while E. H. Carr, *A History of Soviet
Russia: The Bolshevik Revolution* (3 vols., 1966) provides the standard
account of these years, although his *The Russian Revolution from
Lenin to Stalin* (1980) is shorter. Other accounts on aspects of this
period are provided by G. Katkov, *Russia, 1917: the February
Revolution* (1967), R. Pipes, *The Formation of the Soviet Union* (1954)
and M. Ferro, *October 1917: a social history of the Russian Revolution*
(1980), while M. Wood, *The Russian Revolution* (1979) provides a
short analysis and some documents.

Several works approach the period from a biographical viewpoint
including B. Wolfe, *Three who made a revolution* (1966), on Lenin,
Trotsky and Stalin, D. Shub, *Lenin* (1966), C. Hill, *Lenin and the
Russian Revolution* (1971), A. B. Ulam, *Lenin and the Bolsheviks*
(1965), I. Deutscher, *Stalin* (1966), and *The Prophet Armed: Trotsky,
1879–1921* (1963). On the Marxist background to Bolshevik thinking,
see E. Wilson, *To the Finland Station* (1947).

The civil war period and Allied intervention are discussed in J.
Bradley, *Allied Intervention in Russia* (1968), R. Ullman, *Intervention
and the War: Anglo-Soviet Relations, 1917–21* (1961), whilst R.
Service, *The Bolshevik Party in Revolution*, 1917–23 (1979) and T.

Rigby, *Lenin's Government* (1979) look at Soviet institutions in this period.

A work looking beyond 1924, and rather general, is S. Fitzpatrick, *The Russian Revolution, 1917–32* (1982). The long-term development of foreign policy is considered in A. B. Ulam, *Expansion and Coexistence, Soviet Foreign Policy, 1917–73* (1968).

Stalin

For the Stalin era, M. McCauley, *Stalin and Stalinism* (1983) has some useful documents and a brief appraisal. There is excellent testimony from the period in memoirs such as V. Serge, *Memoirs of a Revolutionary* (1963) and E. Ginsberg, *Into the Whirlwind* (1968). On Stalin himself, see I. Deutscher, *Stalin* (1966) A. B. Ulam, *Stalin* (1973) and R. H McNeal, *Stalin; Man and Ruler* (1988).

The aftermath of Lenin's death is discussed in E. H. Carr, *The Interregnum, 1923–4* (1978), *Socialism in one Country 1924–6* (1978) and his *The Russian Revolution from Lenin to Stalin, 1917–29* (1970). The demise and exile of Trotsky are dealt with in I. Deutscher, The *Prophet Outcast* (1963) and R. Segal, *The Tragedy of Leon Trotsky* (1983). For the debates after Lenin's death, see A. Erlich, *The Soviet Industrialization Debate, 1924–1928* (1960).

On 'Stalinism' in the 1930s see A. Nove, *An Economic History of the U.S.S.R.* (1972), as an introduction, and the work by R. W. Davies, *The Socialist Offensive* (1980) on the collectivization of agriculture and H. Kuromiya, *Stalin's Industrial Revolution: Politics and Workers 1928–1932* (1988). R. Conquest, *The Great Terror* (1968) concentrates on the purges, but see also J. Arch Getty, *Origins of the Great Purges: the Soviet Communist Party reconsidered, 1933–1938* (1988). L. Schapiro, *The Communist Party of the Soviet Union* (1970) is excellent and more wide-ranging than the title suggests.

For the war period see A. Werth, *Russia at War* (1965) and A. Dallin, *German Rule in Russia, 1941–5* (1957).

Stalin's foreign policy is discussed in G. F. Kennan, *Russia and the West under Lenin and Stalin* (1961), A. B. Ulam, *Expansion and Co-existence* (1967), J. Haslam, *Soviet Foreign Policy, 1930–3* (1983) and *The Soviet Union and the Struggle for Collective Security* (1984).

France and the fall of the Third Republic

J. F, McMillan, *Dreyfus to De Gaulle: Politics and Society in France, 1898–1969* (1985) is the most recent study, see also the older J. P. T. Bury, *France, 1870–1940* (1951), A. Cobban, *A History of Modern France, vol. 3* (1965); and D. W. Brogan, *The Development of Modern France* (1940). There is also a short account by P. Williams, 'From Dreyfus to Vichy' in J. M. Wallace-Hadrill (ed.) *France, Government and Society* (1957). For the Popular Front see J. Jackson, *The Popular Front in France* (1988), D. Levy, 'The French Popular Front, 1936–37' in H. D. Graham and P. Preston (eds.), *The Popular Front in Europe* (1987) and J. Coulton, *Leon Blum* (1974). For working-class responses see R. McGraw 'France' in S. Salter and J. Stevenson (eds.), *The Working Class and Politics in Europe and North America, 1929–45* (1990) and D. Brower, *The New Jacobins: the French Communist Party and the Popular Front* (1968). For other political groupings see P. Larmour, *The French Radical Party in the 1930s* (1964), W. D. Irvine, *French Conservatism in Crisis* (1979), C. A. Micaval, *The French Right and Nazi Germany, 1933–9* (1972) and the section on France in E. Weber, *Varieties of Fascism* (1964).

On the demise of the Republic see A. Adamthwaite, *France and the Coming of the Second World War* (1977) and, specifically on 1940, A. Horne, *To Lose a Battle: France, 1940* (1979). Also useful is R. Collier, *1940: the world in flames* (1980). Similar issues are tackled from the point of view of a leading politician in G. Warner, *Pierre Laval and the Eclipse of France* (1968).

Much has been written on Vichy, notably R. Aron, *The Vichy Regime, 1940–4* (1958), R. Paxton, *Vichy France* (1972) and R. Cobb, *French and Germans, Germans and French* (1983). For the Resistance see the section in M. R .D. Foot, *Resistance* (1976), H. R. Kedward, *Resistance in Vichy France* (1978) and *Occupied France: Collaboration and Resistance, 1940–1944* (1985) and M. Dank, *The French against the French* (1978). For De Gaulle see D. Cook, *Charles de Gaulle* (1984).

Eastern Europe between the wars

General introductions to the period are provided by H. Seton-Watson, *Eastern Europe between the Wars* (1962) and the more recent *East Central Europe between the Two World Wars* (1974) by J. Rothschild, whilst a wider perspective is given in A. Palmer, *The Lands Between: a history of east central Europe since the Congress of Vienna* (1970). C. A. Macartney and A. Palmer, *Independent Eastern Europe* (1962) and H. and C. Seton-Watson, *The Making of a New Europe* (1981) are also helpful.

A. Polansky, *The Little Dictators* (1975) covers each east European state since 1918 in turn, and there are various individual works on east European states, notably R. Clogg, *A Short History of Modern Greece* (1979), M. Macdermott, *A History of Bulgaria* (New York, 1962), S. Pollo and A. Puto, *The History of Albania* (1981), S. Fischer-Galati, *Twentieth Century Rumania* (1970) and J. K. Hoensch, *A History of Modern Hungary, 1867–1956* (1988). With regard to German expansion in the 1930s, Austria is discussed in J. Gehl, *Austria, Germany and the Anschluss, 1931–9* (1963) and G. Brook-Shepherd, *Anschluss* (1963). See also T. Kirk, 'Austria' in S. Salter and J. Stevenson (eds.), *The Working Class and Politics in Europe and North America, 1929–45* (1990).
On Czechoslovakia see J. W. Bruegel, *Czechoslovakia before Munich* (1973), E. M. Smelser, *The Sudeten Problem, 1933–8* (1975) and J. Korbel, *Twentieth Century Czechoslovakia* (1977). Standard works on

Poland are R. F. Leslie (ed.), *A History of Poland since 1863* (1983) and A. Polonsky, *Politics in Independent Poland, 1921–39* (1972).

Mussolini and fascist Italy

M. Clark, *Modern Italy, 1871–1982* (1984) is a substantial modern study and a helpful guide to the fascist era, as is M. Blinkhorn, *Mussolini and Fascist Italy* (1984). On the pre-fascist era C. Seton-Watson, *Italy from Liberalism to Fascism* (1967) is standard and on the rise of fascism see A. Lyttleton, *The Seizure of Power, 1919–29* (1973), P. Corner, *Fascism in Ferrara* (1975) and F. Snowden *The Fascist Revolution in Tuscany* (1989). The development of fascism is discussed in A. Lyttleton, *Italian Fascism from Pareto to Gentile* (1973) and F. Chabod, *A History of Italian Fascism* (1961) provides a general political survey, whilst E. R. Tannenbaum, *Fascism in Italy, 1922–45* (1972) looks at social and cultural aspects. Also useful is E. Wiskemann, *Fascism in Italy* (1969). Church-state relations are covered in A. Jemolo, *Church and State in Italy, 1850–1950* (1960) and R. A. Webster, *The Cross and the Fasces: Christian Democracy in Italy, 1860–1960* (1960). The experience of the workers under fascism is discussed in P. Corner, 'Italy' in S. Salter and J. Stevenson (eds.), *The Working Class and Politics in Europe and North America, 1929–45* (1990).

Of the biographies of Mussolini, C. Hibbert, *Benito Mussolini* (1962) is accessible, see also L. Fermi, *Mussolini* (1961). D. Mack Smith, *Mussolini's Roman Empire* (1977) and E. M. Robertson, *Mussolini as Empire Builder* (1977), which concentrates on 1932–6, for foreign policy, whilst E. Wiskemann, *The Rome-Berlin Axis* (1949) concentrates on the German alliance, as does F. W. Deakin, *The Brutal Friendship* (2 vols., 1966). The economic performance of fascist Italy is examined in W. G. Welk, *Fascist Economic Policy: An Analysis of Italy's Economic Experiment* (1938) and R. Sarti, *Fascism and Industrial Leadership in Italy, 1919–1940* (1971).

The Spanish Civil War

R. Carr, *Spain, 1808–1939* (Oxford, 1966; rev. edn., *Spain, 1808–1975*, Oxford, 1980) is an essential starting point, rooting the Civil War in Spanish development, as does his *The Spanish Tragedy* (1977). G. Brenan, *The Spanish Labyrinth* (1943) is widely recognized as a modern classic for its deep understanding of the Spanish context. P. Preston (ed.), *Revolution and War in Spain, 1931–1939* (1984) has an extremely useful historiographical essay by the editor and several important essays. For a synoptic view of the experience of the lower classes, see M. Blinkhorn 'Spain' in S. Salter and J. Stevenson (eds.), *The Working Class and Politics in Europe and North America, 1929–45* (1990) and the essays by Graham and Preston in H. Graham and P. Preston (eds.), *The Popular Front in Europe* (1987). H. Thomas, *The Spanish Civil War* (rev. edn., 1977) remains a well-balanced narrative, but see also G. Jackson, *The Spanish Republic and the Civil War* (1965). On the origins of the war, P. Preston, *The Coming of the Spanish Civil War* (1978) gives emphasis to the land question, as does

E. E. Malefakis, *Agrarian Reform and Peasant Revolution* (1970). R. Carr (ed.), *The Republic and the Civil War in Spain* (1971) is another useful collection of essays. On the right-wing forces, see R. Robinson, *The origins of Franco's Spain* (1970), S. Payne, *Falange* (1961) and the biographies of Franco by J. Trythall, *Franco* (1970) and B. Crozier, *Franco* (1967). On the left, see S. Payne, *The Spanish Revolution* (1970) and P. Broue and E. Temime, *The Revolution and the Civil War in Spain* (1972), the latter critical of the communists' role. Two books sympathetic to the anarchists are V. Richards, *Lessons of the Spanish Revolution* (1957) and M. Bookchin, *The Spanish Anarchists* (1977). The role of the communists is also considered in D.T. Cattell, *Communism and the Spanish Civil War* (1955) and B. Balloten, *The Grand Camouflage* (1961), reissued as *The Spanish Revolution: the Left and the Struggle for Power during the Civil War* (1979). A fascinating case study of a group which exemplifies the complexities of Spanish politics in M. Blinkhorn, *Carlism and Crisis in Spain, 1931–1939* (1975).

Interventionism is discussed in D. Puzzo, *Spain and the Great Powers, 1936–41* (1962), V. Bromo, *The International Brigades* (1965), J. F. Coverdale, *Italian Intervention in the Spanish Civil War* (1977), J. Edwards, *Britain and the Spanish Civil War* (1979), and E. H. Carr, *The Comintern and the Spanish Civil War* (1984). G. Weintraub, *The Last Great Cause* (1976) is an exposé of the war of propaganda carried out by both sides to enlist support and on the most famous episode – the bombing of Guernica – see G. Thomas and M. Witts, *Guernica* (1975) and H. R. Southworth, *Guernica! Guernica! A Study of Journalism, Diplomacy, Propaganda and History* (1977). R. Fraser, *Blood of Spain* (1979) has eyewitness accounts of the conflict, while George Orwell, *Homage to Catalonia* (1938) and J. Gurney, *Crusade in Spain* (1974) are two accounts from British volunteers who fought for the Republic. See too, P. Toynbee, *The Distant Drum: Reflections on the Spanish Civil War* (1976).

Germany from Weimar to Hitler

E. Eyck, *History of the Weimar Republic* (2 vols., 1962, 1963) is a full and useful introduction to the period. A. J Nicholls, *Weimar and the Rise of Hitler* (1968) is shorter and more analytical, whilst R. J. Bessel and E. J. Feuchtwanger (eds.), *Social Change and Political Development in the Weimar Republic* (1981) is an important group of essays. For the revolution of 1918–19 see A. J. Ryder, *The German Revolution* (1967) – see also the shorter account in his Historical Association pamphlet of the same title (1959). F. L. Carsten, *Revolution in Central Europe, 1918–1919* (1971) is excellent on the 'grass roots' establishment of workers' and soldiers' councils, and J. P. Nettl, *Rosa Luxemburg* (2 vols.) provides a biography of a leading revolutionary. R. Cooper, *Failure of a Revolution: Germany in 1918–1919* (1955) criticizes the Social Democrats, for whom see also R. N. Hunt, *German Social Democracy, 1918–1933* (1970) and W. L. Guttsman, *The German Social Democratic Party, 1875–1933* (1981). E. J. Hobsbawm, 'Confronting Defeat: The German Communist Party' in *Revolutionaries* (1977) looks at the KPD. For the working class as a whole, see S. Salter 'Germany' in S. Salter and J. Stevenson (eds.), *The Working Class and Politics in Europe and North America, 1929–45* (1990) and 'The Object Lesson: the Division of the Germans and the Triumph of National Socialism', in H. Graham and P. Preston (eds.), *The Popular Front in Europe* (1987). Two leading characters in the Republic are discussed in H. A. Turner, *Stresemann and the Politics of the Weimar Republic* (1963), H. W. Gatzke, *Stresemann and the Rearmament of Germany* (1954) and A. Dorpalen, *Hindenburg and the Weimar Republic* (1964).

J. W. Wheeler-Bennett, *The Nemesis of Power: the German Army in Politics, 1918–45* (1980 ed.) is critical of the military under Weimar; the same theme is covered by F. L. Carsten, *The Reichswehr and German Politics, 1918–33* (1966) and G. Craig, *The Politics of the Prussian Army, 1640–1945* (1955). The rise of the Nazis at 'grass roots' level can be traced in M. Kater, *The Nazi Party, 1919–45* (1984). W. S. Allen, *The Nazi Seizure of Power* (1966) and J. Noakes, *The Nazi Party in Lower Saxony* (1971). There is a useful set of essays in E. Matthias and A. J. Nicholls (eds.) *German Democracy and the Triumph of Hitler* (1971) and P. D. Stachura (ed.), *The Nazi Machtergreifung* (1983). Of the biographies of Hitler, A. Bullock, *Hitler* (1962) remains a readable, but full account; J. C. Fest, *Hitler* (1974) and J. Toland, *Adolf Hitler* (1976) are long and detailed, whilst N. Stone, *Hitler* (1980) is short but stimulating. J. C. Fest, *The Face of the Third Reich* (1970) looks at Hitler's deputies, one of whom receives full coverage in E. K. Bramstedt, *Goebbels and National Socialist Propaganda* (1965). Two interesting attempts at 'psycho-history' can be found in W. Langer, *The Mind of Adolf Hitler* (1972) and W. Carr, *Hitler: A Study in Personality and Politics* (1978). A good general history of the Nazi rise and impact is K. Bracher, *The German Dictatorship* (1973), itself written by a German; see too, I. Kershaw, *The Nazi Dictatorship* (1985) and K. Hilderbrand, *The Third Reich* (1984). D. Orlow, *A History of the Nazi Party, 1933–45* (1973), R. Gruenberger, *A Social History of the Third Reich* (1974) and J. P. Stern, *The Führer and the People* (1975) cover various aspects of the Third Reich, while J. Hiden and J. Farquharson, *Explaining Hitler's Germany* (1983) looks at historical views of the Nazi regime. J. Noakes (ed.), *Government, Party and People in Nazi Germany* (1980) has several good essays and a bibliography of recent writing. On other aspects of German society, see A. Schweitzer, *Big Business in the Third Reich* (1964), D. Guerin, *Fascism and Big Business* (1979), R. J. O'Neill, *The German Army and the Nazi Party, 1933–1939* (1966), Z. A .B. Zeman, *Nazi Propaganda* (1964), E. K. Bramsted, *Goebbels and Nationalist Socialist Propaganda, 1925–1945* (1965), J. S. Conway, *The Nazi Persecution of the Churches* (1968), and G. Lewy, *The Catholic Church and Nazi Germany* (1964).

Hitler's opponents are considered in H. Graml et al., *The German Resistance to Hitler* (1970) and I. Kershaw, *Popular Opinion and Political Dissent in the Third Reich: Bavaria, 1933–1945* (1986). Hitler's anti-Semitism is considered in Kershaw, *Nazi Dictatorship*, ch. 5 and H. Krausnich, 'The Persecution of the Jews' in H. Krausnich *et al, Anatomy of the SS State* (1968) but see also L. Dawidowicz, *The War*

Against the Jews, 1933–45 (1975), H. Hohne, *The Order of the Death's Head* (1970) and K. Schleunes, *The Twisted Road to Auschwitz* (1970).

Foreign policy is considered in G. I. Weinberg, *The Foreign Policy of Hitler's Germany: diplomatic revolution in Europe, 1933–1936* (1970) and *The Foreign Policy of Hitler's Germany: starting World War II* (1980). K. Hildebrand *The Foreign Policy of the Third Reich* (1973) stresses Hitler's pragmatism, while W. Carr, *Arms, Autarky and Aggression: a study in German foreign policy, 1933–1939* (1972) relates economic policy to foreign policy. On Hitler's economic policies, see W. Carr, *Arms, Autarky and Aggression*, B. A. Carroll, *Design for Total War: arms and economics in the Third Reich* (1968), and B. H. Klein, *Germany's Economic Preparations for War* (1959). T. Mason, 'The Primacy of Politics: Politics and Economics in National Socialist Germany' in S. J. Woolf (ed.), *The Nature of Fascism* (1968) discusses the Nazi attitude to economics, a view taken up by A. Milward in W. Laqueur (ed.), *Fascism: A Readers' Guide* (1979). For the German economy at war, see A. Milward, *The German Economy at War* (1965) and his wider *War, Economy and Society, 1939–1945* (1977).

The Second World War

For documents see H. Jacobsen and A. Smith (eds.), *World War II* (1980) on military policy and strategy; there are also numerous collections of memoirs of which W. S. Churchill, *The Second World War* (6 vols., 1948–54) and C. de Gaulle, *War Memoirs* (3 vols., 1955–9) are perhaps the best from European statesmen, and, from the generals, D. Eisenhower, *Crusade in Europe* (1948) and Montgomery of Alamein, *Memoirs* (1958); A. Speer, *Inside the Third Reich* (1970) remains a telling account of the resilience of the German war machine. On the civilian side, O. Frank, *The Diary of Ann Frank* (1947) is a moving classic, while O. Lengyel, *Five Chimneys* (1959) is a powerful evocation of the concentration camps. The German civilian experience is recorded in C. Bielenberg, *The Past is Myself* (1985). For accounts of the war see R. A .C. Parker, *Struggle For Survival: the history of the Second World War* (1989), J. Keegan, *The Second World War* (1989), and M. Gilbert, *The Second World War* (1989). G. Wright, *The Ordeal of Total War* (1968), B. Liddell Hart, *The Second World War* (1970), P. Calvocoressi and G. Wint, *Total War* (1974) and A. J. P. Taylor, *The Second World War: an illustrated history* (1976) are all useful, whilst A. Marwick, *War and Social Change in the Twentieth Century* (1974) concentrates on the social effects. D. Irving, *Hitler's War* (2 vols., 1983) gives a controversial account from the German side. On Russia, see A. Werth, *Russia at War* (1965) and on Britain, A. Calder, *The People's War* (1969). A. S. Milward, *War, Economy and Society, 1939–1945* (1977) is a brilliant synthesis of the economic ramifications of 'total war'; see also his *The German Economy at War* (1965) and *The New Order and the French Economy* (1970).

The opening phase of the war is covered by B. Collier, *1940: The World in Flames* (1980) and *1941: Armageddon* (1982). The controversy over the effectiveness and morality of the bombing offensive against Germany is considered in N. Frankland, *The Bombing Offensive Against Germany* (1965) and M. Hastings, *Bomber Command* (1979). For the German side of the air war, see D. Irving, *The Rise and Fall of the Luftwaffe* (1973). For the war at sea, see D. Macintyre, *The Battle of the Atlantic* (1961), J. Costello and T. Hughes, *The Battle of the Atlantic* (1977), and W. Frank, *The Sea Wolves* (1955). The decisive struggle on the Eastern Front is considered in A. Clark, *Barbarossa* (1965) and J. Erickson, *The Road to Stalingrad: Stalin's War with Germany* (1975). For the final phase of the war see E. Belfield and H. Essame, *The Battle for Normandy* (1965) and J. Erickson, *The Road to Berlin* (1983). Specifically on the new form of mobile warfare, see H. Guderian, *Panzer Leader* (1952) and F. W. von Mellenthin, *Panzer Battles* (1955). Technical developments affecting the conduct of the war are discussed in R. V. Jones, *Most Secret War* (1978) and B. Johnson, *The Secret War* (1978).

The fate of areas conquered by the Germans is considered in W. Warmbrunn, *The Dutch under German Occupation* (1963), A. Dallin, *German Rule in Russia, 1941–5* (1957) and R. O. Paxton, *Vichy France* (1973), whilst the resistance movements are analysed in H. Michel, *The Shadow War: resistance in Europe, 1939–45* (1972) and M. R. D. Foot, *Resistance* (1976).

On diplomacy during the war see H. Feis, *Churchill, Roosevelt, Stalin* (1957), W. H. McNeill, *America, Britain and Russia* (1953) and G. Kolko, *The Politics of War* (1968).

The Cold War

There is a good introduction in J. Smith, *The Cold War, 1945–65* (1989), while more detailed are J. W. Spanier, *American Foreign Policy since the Second World War* (1980), S. E. Ambrose, *Rise to Globalism* (1983), W. Lafeber, *America, Russia and the Cold War* (1982), and L. J. Halle, *The Cold War as History* (1967). On Britain see W. N. Medlicott, *British Foreign Policy since Versailles* (1940); Soviet policy is the subject of A. B. Ulam, *Expansion and Coexistence* (1968) and T. W. Wolfe, *Soviet Power and Europe, 1945–70* (1970). The early years of the Cold War have received most coverage. There are conservative accounts, such as G. F. Hudson, *The Hard and Bitter Peace* (1966) and H. L. Feis, *From Trust to Terror* (1970), criticisms of America in G. and J. Kolko, *The Limits of Power* (1972) and D. Yergin, *Shattered Peace* (1977). J. L. Gaddis, *The United States and the Origins of the Cold War* (1973) is good, and on the British see V. Rothwell, *Britain and the Cold War, 1941–7* (1983). For coverage of the continental states see G. de Carmoy, *The Foreign Policies of France* (1970) and E. Furniss, *France, Troubled Ally* (1960). See also M. J. Hogan, *The Marshall Plan: America, Britain and the Reconstruction of Western Europe, 1947–1952* (1988).

Western Europe since 1945

For general coverage of events see W. Laqueur, *Europe since Hitler*

(1970), D. Urwin, *Western Europe since 1945* (1981), and P. Calvocoressi, *World Politics since 1945* (1982 edn.). Also good are R. Mayne, *The Recovery of Europe* (1970), M. Crouzet, *The European Renaissance since 1945* (1970), R. Morgan, *West European Politics since 1945* (1972) and S. Smith, *Politics in Western Europe* (1976). Rather narrower in interest is F. R. Willis, *France, Germany and the New Europe, 1945–67* (1969), whilst F. Fry and G. Raymond, *The Other Western Europe* (1980) looks at the smaller democracies. The post-war economic recovery of Europe is examined in A. S. Milward, *The Reconstruction of Western Europe, 1945–51* (1984) and M. J. Hogan (above). On France in this period see P. M. Williams, *Crisis and Compromise: Politics in the Fourth Republic* (1964 edn.); P. M. Williams and M. Harrison, *Politics and Compromise: politics and society in de Gaulle's Republic* (1971); J. Ardagh, *The New France* (1978), and M. Anderson, *Conservative Politics in France* (1974). See also the important recent study by D. S. Bell and B. Criddle, *The French Socialist Party* (2nd edn., 1988) and M. Larkin, *France since the Popular Front: government and people, 1936–86* (1988). On de Gaulle, see D. Cook, *Charles de Gaulle* (1984). For Germany, see A. Grosser, *Germany in Our Time* (1971), T. Prittie, *The Velvet Chancellors* (1979) and *Adenauer* (1971). On Italy, see M. Clark, *Modern Italy, 1871–1982* (1984) and S. Tarrow, *Democracy and Disorder: Protest and Politics in Italy, 1965–75* (1989). For Spain see R. Carr, *A History of Spain, 1808–1975* (rev. edn., 1982), R. Carr and J. P. Fusi, *Spain: Dictatorship to Democracy* (1979) and D. Gilmour, *The Transformation of Spain* (1985).

There are general discussions of the European unity movement in W. Laqueur, *Europe since Hitler* (1970) and D. Urwin, *Western Europe since 1945* (1981). The fullest account of the early years of the unity movement can be found in W. Lipgens, *A History of European Integration, 1945–7* (1982), though this is very detailed. J. W. Young, *Britain, France and the Unity of Europe, 1945–51* (1984) is shorter and more analytical, whilst on the early 1950s see E. Fursden, *The European Defence Community* (1981), on the vain bid to create a 'European Army'. On the Common Market itself see R. Pryce, *The Politics of the European Community* (1973), J. Galtung, *The European Community – a Superpower in the Making* (1973), J. Herman and J. Lodge, *The European Parliament and the European Community* (1978), S. Holland, *Uncommon Market* (1980), L. Tsoukalis (ed.), *The European Community Past, Present and Future* (1983) and F. R. Willis, *France, Germany and the New Europe* (1968). On particular themes see D. Swann, *Economics of the Common Market* (4th edn., 1978), R. B. Talbot, *The European Communities Regional Fund* (1977), M. Shanks, *European Social Policy* (1977), and R. Fennell, *The Common Agricultural Policy of the European Community*. American relations with the European unity movement are discussed by M. Beloff, *The United States and the Unity of Europe* (1963) and R. Manderson-Jones, *Special Relationship* (1972). British relations are discussed in M. Camps, *Britain and the European Community, 1955–63* (1964), U. Kitzinger, *Diplomacy and Persuasion* (1974), W. Wallace, *Britain and Europe* (1980), and F. E. C. Gregory, *Dilemmas of Government – Britain and the EC* (1983).

Eastern Europe since 1945

The essential background can be found in F. Fejto, *A History of the People's Democracies* (1971), R. Okey, *Eastern Europe, 1740–1985* (2nd edn., 1986) and H. Seton-Watson, *The East European Revolution* (1985). On the early background to post-war eastern Europe see M. McCauley (ed.), *Communist Power in Europe, 1944–49* (1977) and on the general decay of Soviet influence see G. Ionescu, *The Break-up of the Soviet Empire in Eastern Europe* (1965), Z. Brzezinski, *The Soviet Bloc* (1974), L. Labedz (ed.), *Revisionism* (1962) and H. Seton-Watson, *Nationalism and Communism, Essays, 1946–63* (1964); the impact of Gorbachev is considered in K. Dawisha, *Eastern Europe, Gorbachev and Reform: The Great Challenge* (1988). For individual countries see M. McCauley, *The German Democratic Republic* (1983), J. P. Nettl, *The Eastern Zone and Soviet Policy in Germany, 1945–50* (1951), and J. Stele, *Socialism with a German Face* (1977); on Yugoslavia, see D. Rusinow, *Yugoslav Experiment, 1948–1974* (1977), P. Auty, *Tito* (1974) and, more generally, F. Singleton, *Twentieth Century Yugoslavia* (1976); on Hungary, see F. Vali, *Rift and Revolt in Hungary* (1961) and M. Molnar, *Budapest 1956: a history of the Hungarian Revolution* (1971); on Czechoslovakia, see V. V. Kusin, *Intellectual Origins of the Prague Spring* (1971), G. Golan, *Reform Rule in Czechoslovakia* (1973), H. G. Skilling, *Czechoslovakia: the interrupted revolution* (1976); for Poland, see generally R. F. Leslie (ed.), *A History of Poland since 1863* (1983), N. Bethell, *Gomulka* (1969), N. Ascherson, *The Polish August* (1981) and T. G. Ash, *Polish Revolution: Solidarity 1980–82* (1983).

Imperialism and decolonization

V. Kiernan, *European Empires from Conquest to Collapse; 1815–1960* (1982) and M. A. Chamberlain, *The New Imperialism* (Historical Association Pamphlet, 1967) are good overviews on the imperial question; see too D. K. Fieldhouse, *The Colonial Empires* (1966) and *Colonialism, 1870–1945* (1983). See also R. Koebner, *Empire* (1961) and R. Koebner and H. D. Schmitt, *Imperialism . . . a political word, 1840–1966* (1964). B. Porter, *The Lion's Share: a short history of British imperialism, 1850–1970* (1975) provides a comprehensive account of the British imperial experience, see too R. Hyam, *Britain's Imperial Century, 1815–1914: a study of empire and expansion* (1976) and J. Bowle, *The Imperial Achievement: the rise and transformation of the British Empire* (1971). For France, see C. M. Andrew and A. S. Kanya-Forstner, *The Climax of French Imperial Expansion* (1981) and D. B. Marshall, *The French Colonial Myth and Constitution – Making in the Fourth Republic* (1973). The Portuguese Empire is considered in M. Newett, *Portugal in Africa* (1981) and G. Clarence-Smith, *The Third Portuguese Empire, 1825–1975* (1985). The Pacific is considered in W. P. Morrell, *The Great Powers in the Pacific* (1965).

Many of the debates about the economic dimension to imperial expansion relate to the period before 1914, but are relevant to the last phase after 1914. See D. C. M. Platt, *Finance, Trade and Politics in British Foreign Policy, 1815–1914* (1968), H. Feis, *Europe, the World's Banker 1870–1914* (1930), A. R. Hall (ed.), *The Export of Capital from*

Britain, 1870–1914 (1968), A. K. Cairncross, *Home and Foreign Investment, 1870–1913* (1953), S. B. Saul, *Studies in British Overseas Trade, 1870–1914* (1960), D. K. Fieldhouse, *Economics and Empire, 1830–1914* (1976), and L. David and R. Huttenback, *Mammon and the Pursuit of Empire: the political economy of British imperialism* (1986).

On decolonization see M. E. Chamberlain, *Decolonization: The Fall of the European Empires* (1985), R. F. Holland, *European Decolonization, 1918–1981* (1985) and R. von Albertini, *Decolonization: the Administration and Future of the Colonies, 1919–60* (1960, Eng. trans., 1971). Specifically on British decolonization see J. Gallagher, *The Decline, Revival and Fall of the British Empire* (1982), C. Cross, *The Fall of the British Empire, 1918–1968* (1968), J. Darwin, *Britain and Decolonization: the retreat from Empire in the Post-War World* (1987) and D. Judd and P. Slinn, *The Evolution of the Modern Commonwealth* (1982). The specific military strains upon the major colonial empire are discussed in P. M. Kennedy, *The Rise and Fall of British Naval Mastery* (1976) and *The Realities behind Diplomacy* (1981), A. Clayton, *The British Empire as a Superpower* (1986), C. J. Bartlett, *The Long Retreat: a short history of British defence policy, 1945–70* (1972) and P. Darby, *British Defence Policy East of Suez, 1947–1968* (1973). See also D. Dilks, *Retreat from Power* (2 vols., 1981), R. Douglas, *World Crisis and British Decline, 1929–56* (1986), A. N. Porter and A. J. Stockwell, *British Imperial Policy and Decolonization, 1938–64: vol. 1*, (1987), and N. Mansergh, *The Commonwealth Experience: volume 2, from British to Multiracial Commonwealth* (2nd edn., 1982). French decolonization is discussed in R. Betts, *France and Decolonization* (1982). The role of the League of Nations is considered in S. R. Gibbons and P. Monican, *The League of Nations and UNO* (1970) and of the UN in E. Luard, *The History of the United Nations: Vol. 2: The age of decolonization, 1955–1965* (1988). J. M. Lee, *Colonial Development and Good Government: a study of the ideas expressed by the British official class in planning decolonization* (1967) and W. H. Morris-Jones and G. Fischer, *Decolonization and After: the British and French experience* (1980) examine the attitudes of the colonial powers, while the external pressures on them are the subject of W. R. Louis, *Imperialism at Bay 1941–5: the United States and the decolonization of the British Empire* (1977); see also M. Kahler, *Decolonization in Britain and France: the domestic consequences of international relations* (1984). For the history of colonialism and independence movements in particular countries, see the separate geographical sections below; leaders of decolonization movements can be found in H. Tinker, *Men who Overturned Empires* (1987).

iii   The Middle East

For introductory reading on the Middle East see I. Asad and R. Owen, *The Middle East* (1983), A. Hourani, *The Emergence of the Modern Middle East* (1980), S. N. Fisher, *The Middle East. A History* (1979), G. Lenczowski, *The Middle East in World Affairs* (4th edn., 1980), N. Bethell, *The Palestine Triangle* (1979), A. Goldschmidt, *A concise*

History of the Middle East (1979), P. Mansfield, *The Arabs* (1976) and
W. R. Polk, *The Arab World* (1980). The broad sweep of Middle
Eastern history is considered in the latter part of G. E. Perry, *The
Middle East, Fourteen Islamic Centuries* (1983). Particular themes can
be explored through M. Halpern, *The Politics of Social Change in the
Middle East* (1963) and P. Mansfield, *The Middle East: a political and
economic survey* (4th edn., 1973); B. Schwodran, *The Middle East, Oil
and the Great Powers* (1973) and Y. Porath, *In Search of Arab Unity,
1930–1945* (1986). T. G. Fraser, *The Middle East, 1914–1979* (1980) is a
helpful collection of documents.

The Turkish Revolution

S. J. and E. K. Shaw, *History of the Ottoman Empire and Modern
Turkey, vol. II* (1977), W. Yale, *The Near East. A Modern History*
(1958) and B. Lewis, *The Emergence of Modern Turkey* (1973) are
good starting points. For Kemal Ataturk, see Lord Kinross, *Attaturk –
The Rebirth of a Nation* (1964), while contemporary accounts of
relations between Greece and Turkey can be found in A. Toynbee,
The Western Question in Greece and Turkey (1922) and H. Edils, *The
Turkish Ordeal* (1928).

The mandates in Iraq, Syria and Lebanon

Initially see J. C. Hurewitz, *The Middle East and North Africa in World
Politics: Vol II* (1979); E. Munroe; *Britain's Moment in the Middle East,
1914–1971* (2nd edn., 1980) is a classic account of British involvement;
see also P. Mansfield, *The Ottoman Empire and its Successors* (1973).
On Iraq see Sir A. T. Wilson, *Mesopotamia 1917–20: a Clash of
Loyalties* (1931), S. H. Longrigg, *Iraq, 1900 to 1950* (1953) and P. Marr,
The Modern History of Iraq (1985). For Syria and Lebanon see A. H.
Hourani, *Syria and Lebanon* (1946), S. H. Longrigg, *Syria and
Lebanon under French Mandate* (1958), N. A. Ziadeh, *Syria and
Lebanon* (1957).

Egypt

General accounts can be found in P. J. Vatikiotis, *The History of Egypt
from Muhammad Ali to Sadat* (2nd edn., 1980), J. Berque, *Egypt:
Imperialism and Revolution* (1972), A. Sattin, *Lifting the Veil: the
British in Egypt, 1800–1956* (1988), and J. C. B. Richmond, *Egypt,
1798–1952* (1977). For the early period see Monroe, *Britain's Moment,*
Lord Lloyd, *Egypt Since Cromer* (1933–4) J. Darwin, *Britain, Egypt and
the Middle East: imperial policy in the aftermath of war, 1918–22*
(1980), Mahmud Zayid, *Egypt's Struggle for Independence* (1965), and
A. Hourani, *Arabic Thought in the Liberal Age, 1789–1939* (1962). For
the post-1945 period, see R. Stephens, *Nasser. A Political Biography*
(1971), R. Ovendale, *The Origins of the Arab-Israeli Wars* (1984), R.
Mabro, *The Egyptian Economy; 1952–1972* (1974) and I. Beeson,
Sadat (1981). On the Suez crisis, see W. Roger Louis and R. Owen
(eds.), *Suez 1956: The Crisis and its Consequences* (1989). An
important view of social change is contained in J. Neinin and Z.

Lockman, *Workers on the Nile; Nationalism, Communism, Islam and the Egyptian Working Class, 1881–1954* (1988).

The creation of Israel and the Arab-Israeli conflict

J. C. Hurewitz, *The Middle East and North Africa in World Politics: Vol. II* (1979), E. Monroe, *Britain's Moment*, W. R. Louis, *The British Empire in the Middle East, 1945–1951* (1984), and N. Bethell, *The Palestine Triangle* (1979) are essential works. Some useful first-hand evidence can be found in R. Storrs, *Orientations* (1937), R. H. S. Crossman, *Palestine Mission: A Personal Record* (1947) and M. Begin, *The Revolt* (1951). The history of the Zionist movement is covered in the three volumes by D. Vital, *The Origins of Zionism* (1980); *Zionism: the formative years* (1982), and *Zionism: the crucial phase* (1987). On the origins see L. Stein, *The Balfour Declaration* (1961) while H. W. Sachar, *History of Israel: from the rise of Zionism to our time* (1985) and *From the Aftermath of the Yom Kippur War* (1989) is a comprehensive history of Israel. M. J. Cohen, *Palestine: Retreat from the Mandate: the making of British policy, 1936–45* (1989) and *Palestine and the Great Powers, 1945–1948* (1982) deals in detail with the British period. G. Antonius, *The Arab Awakening* (1938) and R. Ovendale, *The Origins of the Arab-Israeli Wars* (1984) examine the growth of conflict, see also E. W. Said, *The Question of Palestine* (1980). A. Shlaim, *Collusion Across the Jordan: King Abdullah, the Zionist Movement and the Partition of Palestine* (1988) and I. Pappe, *Britain and the Arab-Israeli Conflict, 1948–51* (1988) discuss the early years, while the American involvement is considered in Z. Ganin, *Truman, American Jewry and Israel, 1945–1948* (1979). C. D. Smith, *Palestine and the Arab-Israeli Conflict* (1989) is a recent introductory work while Cohen's work (see above) has received a fresh format as M. J. Cohen's *Palestine to Israel: from Mandate to Independence* (1988). On the later years of the Israeli state see A. Sella and Y. Yishai (eds.), *Israel: the peaceful belligerent, 1967–79* (1986).

Arab nationalism and the Islamic Revolution

Y. Porath, *In Search of Arab Unity, 1930–1945* (1986) discusses the attempt to weld the Arab world into a larger whole. The important non-Arab power of great influence since the 1960s is considered in H. Amirsedeglu and R. W. Ferrier, *Twentieth Century Iran* (1977) and N. R. Keddie, *Roots of Revolution: An Interpretative History of Modern Iran* (1981), while the Islamic dimension is examined in S. A. Arjomand, *The Turban for the Crown: the Islamic Revolution in Iran* (1988). P. Marr, *The Modern History of Iraq* (1985), D. Hopwood, *Syria, 1945–1986: Politics and Society* (1988), and U. Dann, *King Hussein and the Challenge of Arab Radicalism: Jordan, 1955–1967* (1989) examine other states since 1945. M. Shemesh, *The Palestinian Entity, 1959–1974* (1988) and H. Cobban, *The Making of Modern Lebanon* (1985) examine two major sources of conflict. R. B. Betts, *The Druze* (1988) examines one of the major factions in the Lebanese conflict. On the Iraq-Iran war see D. Hiro, *The Longest War: the Iran-Iraq conflict* (1989); also Z. Schiff and E. Ya'ari, *Intifada* (1990).

iv   Africa

There are useful introductions in P. J. M. McEwan and R. B. Sutcliffe (eds.), *The Study of Africa* (1965), B. Freund, *The Making of Contemporary Africa* (1984), J. Hatch, *Africa Today and Tomorrow* (1965) and *Africa Emergent: Africa's Problems Since Independence* (1974), B. Davidson, *Africa in Modern History* (1978), H. S. Wilson, *The Imperial Experience in Sub-Saharan Africa since 1870* (1977) and M. Crowder, *Historical Atlas of Africa* (1985).

For the colonial period and decolonization, see J. D. Hargreaves, *Decolonization in Africa, 1945–64* (1988), L. H. Gann and P. Duignan (eds.), *The History and Politics of Colonialism, 1870–1960* (4 vols., 1969–75), P. Gifford and W. R. Louis, *The Transfer of Power in Africa: Decolonization, 1940–1960* (1982), P. Gifford and W. R. Louis, (eds.), *Decolonization and African Independence* (1988), and W. H. Morris-Jones and G. Fischer, *Decolonization and After: the British and French Experience* (1980). The post-colonial period is considered broadly in D. Fieldhouse, *Black Africa, 1945–1980* (1986), J. Jackson and C. Rosberg, *Political Rule in Black Africa* (1982), S. Decalo, *Coups and Army Rule in Africa* (1976), W. F. Gutteridge, *Military Regimes in Africa* (1975), G. Hunter, *The New Societies of Tropical Africa: a selective study* (1962), R. I. Rotberg and A. A. Mazrui (eds.), *Protest and Power in Black Africa* (1970), P. C. Lloyd, *Africa in Social Change* (1971), A. A. Mazrui, *Political Values and the Educated Class in Africa* (1977), C. Rosberg and T. M. Callaghy, *Socialism in Sub-Saharan Africa* (1977), T. M. Shaw and K.A. Heard, *The Politics of Africa: dependence and development* (1979), and W. Tordoff, *Government and Politics in Africa* (1984).

External influences on Africa other than from the colonial powers are discussed in P. Duignan and L. H. Gann, *The United States and Africa: a history* (1984) and R. D. Mahoney, *JFK: ordeal in Africa* (1984). The issue of Pan-Africanism and African Nationalism is discussed in C. Legum, *Pan-Africanism* (1962) and I. Geiss, *Pan-Africanism* (1974); see also G. Padmore (ed.), *Colonial and Coloured Unity: history of the Pan-African Congress* (2nd edn., 1963) and T. L. Hodgkin, *Nationalism in Colonial Africa* (1956). Two important sets of documents are J. A. Langley, *Ideologies of Liberation in Black Africa, 1956–1970: Documents on Modern African Political Thought from Colonial Times to the Present* (1979) and J. Minogue and J. Molloy, *African Aims and Attitudes: selected documents* (1974). Some reference data can be found in W. M. Hailey, *An African Survey* (rev. edn., 1956) and B. R. Mitchell, *International Historical Statistics: Africa and Asia* (1982).

Colonial policy

The phasing of African developments can be traced in M. E. Page (ed.), *Africa and the First World War* (1987), R. D. Pearce, *The Turning Point in Africa: British colonial policy, 1938–1948* (1982), A. Cohen, *British Policy in Changing Africa* (1959), L. H. Gann and P. Duignan,

African Proconsuls (1978), J. M. Lee and M. Petter, *The Colonial Office, War and Development Policy* (1982) and S. Constantine, *The Making of British Colonial Development Policy, 1914–40* (1984). The effects of the Second World War are discussed in D. Killingray and R. Rathbone (eds.), *Africa and the Second World War* (1986) and for post-war see Y. Baugura, *Britain and Commonwealth Africa* (1983), D. Fieldhouse, 'The Labour Governments and the Empire-Commonwealth' in R. Ovendale (ed.) *The Foreign Policy of the British Labour Governments, 1945–51* (1984), E. Mortimer, *France and the Africans, 1944–60* (1969), and G. Clarence-Smith, *The Third Portuguese Empire, 1825–1975* (1985).

North Africa

For North Africa see J. Berque, *French North Africa: the Maghrib between two World Wars* (1967), M. Bennoune, *The Making of Contemporary Algeria, 1830–1987* (1988), D. C. Gordon, *The Passing of French Algeria* (1966), P. Bourdieu, *The Algerians* (1962), E. O'Balance, *The Algerian Insurrection, 1954–62* (1967) and A. Horne, *A Savage War of Peace* (rev. edn., 1988). The essay in J. Dunn, *Modern Revolutions* (2nd edn., 1989) has an excellent analysis of the Algerian Revolution, while F. Fanon, *Studies in a Dying Colonialism* (1955) and *The Wretched of the Earth* (1965) are two important studies of the causes of the Algerian revolt. For the post-revolutionary situation see S. Amin, *The Maghreb in the Modern World* (1970). On other parts of North Africa, see W. D. Swearington, *Moroccan Mirages: agrarian dreams and deceptions, 1912–1986* (1988). A valuable recent study of North and West Africa is D. B. C. O'Brien and C. Coulou (eds.) *Charisma and Brotherhood in African Islam* (1988).

West Africa

For West Africa, see M. Crowder, *West Africa under Colonial Rule* (1968), J. D. Hargreaves, *The End of Colonial Rule in West Africa: essays in contemporary history* (1979) and *West Africa Partitioned: Volume 2: the elephants and the grass* (1985), C. Harrison, *French Policy Towards Islam in West Africa, 1860–1960* (1988), S. Dunn, *West African States* (1978), and R. Schachter-Morgenthau, *Political Parties in French-Speaking West Africa* (1964); see also J. Suret-Canale, below. Particular countries are discussed in D. Austin, *Politics in Ghana, 1946–60* (1964) and C. L. R. James, *Nkrumah and the Ghana Revolution* (1977), J. Coleman, *Nigeria: Background to Nationalism* (1958), K. Ezera, *Constitutional Developments in Nigeria* (1960), K. W. J. Post and G. D. Jenkins, *The Price of Liberty: personality and politics in colonial Nigeria* (1973), B. Dudley, *An Introduction to Nigerian Government and Politics* (1982), and S. Egite Oyovbaire, *Federation in Nigeria: a study in the development of the Nigerian state* (1983).

Tropical and Equatorial Africa

See J. Suret-Canale, *French Colonialism in Tropical Africa, 1900–1945* (1971), C. Young, *Politics in the Congo, Decolonization and*

Independence (1965), H. F. Weiss, *Political Protest in the Congo* (1967), R. Slade, *The Belgian Congo* (1960), R. Anstey, *King Leopold's Legacy: the Congo under Belgian rule, 1908–60* (1966), J. Gerard-Libois, *Katanga Secession* (1966) and R. Lemarchand, *Political Awakening in the Congo* (1964). M. Njeuma (ed.), *Introduction to the History of Cameroon* (1989), R. A. Joseph, *Radical Nationalism in Cameroon* (1977) and D. A. Low, *Buganda in Modern History* (1971) examine other states.

East and Central Africa

For introduction see V. Harlow, E. M. Chilver and A. Smith (eds.), *History of East Africa, Vol. II* (1965) and D. A. Low and A. Smith (eds.), *Vol. III* (1976), J. Saul, *State and Revolution in East Africa* (1979), and K. Ingham, *A History of East Africa* (3rd. edn., 1975). E. A. Brett, *Colonialism and Underdevelopment in East Africa* (1973) and P. H. Gulliver (ed.), *Tradition and Transition in East Africa* raise general issues. On the Sudan, see R. O. Collins and F. M. Deng (eds.), *The British in the Sudan, 1898–1956* (1984) and D. F. Gordon, *Decolonization and the State in Kenya* (1986) on Kenya. Kenya's Mau Mau movement is discussed in C. G. Rosberg and J. Nottingham, *The Myth of Mau Mau* (1966) and in W. R. Ochieng and K. K. Janmohamed (eds.), *Some Perspectives on the Mau Mau Movement* (Special edition of the *Kenya Historical Review*, Nairobi, 1977); see also on Kenya, G. Wasserman, *Politics of Decolonization: Kenya Europeans and the Land Issue, 1960–1965* (1976), C. J. Gertzel, *The Politics of Independent Kenya, 1963–69* (1970) and D. Goldsworthy, *Tom Mboya* (1982). J. Iliffe, *A Modern History of Tanganyika* (1979), C. Pratt, *The Critical Phase in Tanzania, 1945–1968: Nyerere and the emergence of a socialist strategy* (1976) and G. Hyden, *Beyond Ujaama in Tanzania* (1980) cover one of the other major east African states, while Uganda is examined in J. J. Jorgensen, *Uganda: a modern history* (1981) and G. A. Ginyera-Pincwa, *Apolo Milton Obote and His Times* (1977). A combined economic history of Kenya and Uganda is R. M. A. Van Zwanenberg and A. King, *An Economic History of Kenya and Uganda, 1800–1970* (1975). The Central African Federation is discussed in R. Gray, *The Two Nations* (1960) and P. Mason, *Year of Decision* (1960); see also A. J. Wills, *An Introduction to the History of Central Africa* (3rd. edn., 1973), while the rise of opposition to white rule in the region is considered in R. Rotberg, *The Rise of Nationalism in Central Africa* (1965). R. Blake, *A History of Rhodesia* (1977) is a broad survey, but T. O. Ranger, *Peasant Consciousness and Guerrilla War in Zimbabwe* (1985), R. Hodder-Williams, *White Farmers in Rhodesia, 1890–1965* (1984) and R. Palmer, *Land and Racial Domination in Rhodesia* (1977) examine the rural situation, while the general economic background is discussed in I. Phimister, *An Economic and Social History of Zimbabwe, 1890–1948* (1988). For the White declaration of UDI and the subsequent war see M. Loney, *White Racism and Imperial Response* (1974) and D. Martin and P. Johnson, *The Struggle for Zimbabwe* (1981). Two useful groups of studies are C. Stoneman (ed.), *Zimbabwe's Inheritance* (1982) and G. Peele and T. O. Ranger (eds.), *Past and Present in Zimbabwe* (1983). For Zambia, see A. Roberts, *A History of Zambia* (1976), E. L. Bergen,

Labour, Race and Colonial Rule: the copperbelt from 1924 to independence (1974), C. J. Gertzel *et al.*, *The dynamics of the one-party State in Zambia* (1984), and W. Tordoff (ed.), *Administration in Zambia* (1980).

Southern Africa

For Angola see J. Marcum, *The Angolan Revolution, Vol. I, 1950–62* (1969), B. Davidson, *In the Eye of the Storm: Angola's people* (1974) and G. J. Bender, *Angola under the Portuguese: the myth and the reality* (1978). The other Portuguese colony, Mozambique, is discussed in A. and B. Issacman, *Mozambique: from colonialism to revolution* (1983), E. Mondlane, *The Struggle for Mozambique* (1969), and T. W. Henriksen, *Revolution and Counter-Revolution: Mozambique's war of independence, 1964–74* (1983). For South Africa see M. Wilson and L. Thompson (eds.), *The Oxford History of South Africa, Vol. II, 1870–1966* (1971) and T. R. H. Davenport, *South Africa: a modern history* (3rd. edn., 1987). S. Dubow, *Racial Segregation and the Origins of Apartheid in South Africa, 1919–36* (1988) deals with the development of the character of the South African regime, while B. Davidson, J. Slovo, and A. R. Wilkinson, *Southern Africa: the new politics of revolution* (1976) examines the movements and responses in the whole of southern Africa. T. G. Karis and G. Carter (eds.), *From Protest to Challenge. A Documentary History of African Politics in South Africa, 1882–1964* (4 vols, 1972–77) provides source material. L. Marquand, *The Peoples and Policies of South Africa* (4th edn., 1969), G. Carter, *The Politics of Inequality: South Africa since 1948* (1958), J. Hoagland, *South Africa, Civilisations in Conflict* (1973) and T. D. Moodie, *The Rise of Afrikanerdom: power, apartheid and the Afrikaner civil religion* (1975) are all useful studies. The opposition to the dominant apartheid policy is considered in J. Robertson, *Liberalism in South Africa, 1948–1963* (1971) and P. Walshe, *The Rise of African Nationalism in South Africa: the African National Congress, 1912–1952* (1970).

v Asia

The Indian Subcontinent

The historiography is dominated by the theme of empire and decolonization, in spite of more than forty years of independent politics for the new states of India, Pakistan, and Sri Lanka. For imperial policy in general and decolonization see earlier (pp. 483–4), but specifically on India, see S. Wolpert, *A New History of India* (1977), P. Heehs, *India's Freedom Struggle, 1857–1947: A Short History* (1988), W. T. De Bary, *The Sources of Indian Tradition* (1958), S. Sarkar, *Modern India, 1885–1947* (1988), R. J. Moore, *The Crisis of Indian Unity, 1917–1940* (1974), B. R. Tomlinson, *The Political Economy of the Raj, 1914–1947* (1979) and D. A. Low, *Congress and the Raj: Facets of the Indian Struggle* (1977). The role of Gandhi has received short introductory treatment in A. Copley, *Gandhi* (1987), but much more substantially in J. M. Brown, *Gandhi: prisoner of hope*

(1989), while M. K. Ghandhi, *Autobiography* (1966) is an important source. P. Moon, *Gandhi and the Making of Modern India* (1968) and B. R. Nanda, *Mahatma Gandhi* (1958) are also available.

The early phase in the movement for independence is considered in P. G. Robb, *The Government of India and Reform: policies towards politics and constitution, 1916–1921* (1976), S. R. Mehrotra, *India and the Commonwealth, 1885–1929* (1965) and Gandhi's role in J. M. Brown, *Gandhi's Rise to Power: Indian Politics, 1915–1922* (1972) and J. M. Brown, *Gandhi and Civil Disobedience: the Mahatma in Indian politics, 1928–1934* (1977). The growing power of the Congress in the localities is considered in C. A. Bayly, *The Local Roots of Indian Politics: Allahabad, 1880–1920* (1975), C. J. Baker, *The Politics of South India, 1920–1937* (1974), while specifically Muslim nationalism is considered in P. Hardy, *The Muslims of British India* (1972), whose leader Jinnah, is examined in S. Wolpert, *Jinnah of Pakistan* (1984), and A. Jalal, *The Sole Spokesman: Jinnah, the Muslim League and the Demand for Pakistan* (1985); see also I. Talbot, *Provincial Politics and the Pakistan Movement, 1937–47* (1989). The run-up to Partition is in F. G. Hutchins, *India's Revolution. Gandhi and the Quit India Movement* (1973), B. N. Pandey, *The Break Up of British India* (1969), R. J. Moore, *Churchill, Cripps and India, 1939–1945* (1979) and *Escape from Empire. The Attlee Government and the Indian Problem* (1983), H. V. Hodson, *The Great Divide. Britain-India-Pakistan* (1969) and C. H. Philips and D. Wainwright, *Partition of India: politics and perspectives, 1935–1947* (1970). Mountbatten's role is discussed in P. Ziegler, *Mountbatten* (1987). Post-partition India is discussed in S. Gopal, *Jawaharlal Nehru* (1970), M. Brecher, *Nehru: a Political Biography* (1959) and M. Edwardes, *Nehru: a political biography* (1971). See P. J. Nehru's, *Glimpses of World History* (1989) and, on the earlier phase of the independence movement, his *An Autobiography* (1942). Indira Gandhi has been the subject of a recent biography, I. Malhotra, *Indira Gandhi: a personal and political biography* (1989). India's relations with other states after 1947 is considered in C. Heimsath and S. Mansingh, *A Diplomatic History of Modern India* (1971), W. J. Barnds, *India, Pakistan and the Great Powers* (1972) and A. Stein, *India and the Soviet Union: the Nehru era* (1969). India's agricultural development is considered in B. M Bhatia, *Famine in India, 1860–1965* (2nd edn., 1967) and F. R. Frankel, *India's Green Revolution: economic gains and costs* (1971).

On the background to the emergence of Pakistan, see the works cited above on Jinnah, see also the essay on Jinnah in H. Tinker, *Men who Overturned Empires: Fighters, Dreamers and Schemers* (1987) and K. B. Sayeed, *Pakistan: the formative phase, 1857–1948* (rev. edn., 1968). Pakistan's development is considered in L. Binder, *Religion and Politics in Pakistan* (1963) and E. I. Rosenthal, *Islam in the Modern National State* (1965), see also the essay by Halliday in F. Halliday and H. Alavi (eds.), *State and Ideology in the Middle East and Pakistan* (1988). The break-up of Pakistan and the emergence of Bangladesh is considered in K. Siddiqui, *Conflict, Crisis and War in Pakistan* (1972), R. Jahan, *Pakistan: failure in national integration* (1972) and W. Wilcox, *The Emergence of Bangladesh* (1973). Pakistan's foreign policy is examined in S. M. Burke, *Pakistan's Foreign Policy: an historical analysis* (1973). The Bhutto years are considered in S. J. Burki, *Pakistan under Bhutto, 1971–1977* (2nd edn., 1988). On Sri Lanka see S. Arasarátnam, *Ceylon* (1964) and A. J. Wilson, *Politics in Sri Lanka, 1947–1979* (2nd. edn., 1979).

South-East Asia

D. G. Hall, *A History of South-East Asia* (4th edn., 1981) and J. F. Cady, *The History of Post-War Southeast Asia* (1974) are useful introductions; see also D. J. Steinberg, *In Search of South-East Asia: a modern history* (1971), J. M. Phivier, *South-East Asia from Colonialism to Independence* (1974).

The histories of individual south-east Asian countries are considered in J. F. Cady, *A History of Modern Burma* (1958) and D. E. Smith, *Religion and Politics in Burma* (1965), see also F. R. Von der Mehden, *Religion and Nationalism in Southeast Asia: Burma, Indonesia, the Philippines* (1963), and D. K. Wyatt, *The Politics of Reform in Thailand: education in the reign of King Chulalongkorn* (1969).

The Indonesian nationalist movement is considered in G. M. Kahin, *Nationalism and Revolution in Indonesia* (1953), B. Dahm, *History of Indonesia in the Twentieth Century* (1971) and *Sukarno and the Struggle for Indonesian Independence* (1969); see also J. D. Legge, *Indonesia* (1964). H. J. Benda, *The Crescent and the Rising Sun: Indonesian Islam under the Japanese Occupation, 1942–1945* (1958), L. H. Palmier, *Indonesia and the Dutch* (1962), and M. Ricklefs, *A History of Modern Indonesia* (1981) are helpful studies. The role of Sukarno is considered in the essay in H. Tinker, *Men who Overturned Empires: Fighters, Dreamers and Schemers* (1987) and J. D. Legge, *Sukarno: a political biography* (1972). The communist role in Indonesia is discussed in L. Palmier, *Communists in Indonesia: power pursued in vain* (1973), A. Brackman, *Indonesian Communism* (1963), and R. T. McVey (ed.), *Indonesia* (1963). The Army's role is considered in H. Crouch, *The Army and Politics in Indonesia* (1978). On Malaya see J. G. Butcher, *The British in Malaya, 1880–1941* (1979). Malayan independence receives some attention in R. Jeffrey, *Asia: The Winning of Independence* (1981), but see B. W. Andaya and L. Y. Andaya, *A History of Malaysia* (1982) for a more substantial account. The communist attempt at a seizure of power is considered in A. Short, *The Communist Insurrection in Malaya, 1948–1960* (1975); see also J. M. Gullick, *Malaysia* (1969), W. R. Roff, *The Origins of Malay Nationalism* (1967), M. E. Osborne, *Region of Revolt: focus on Southeast Asia* (1971) and A. C. Brackman, *South-East Asia's Second Front: the Power Struggle in the Malay Archipelago* (1966).

For the Philippines see T. A. Agoncillo, *A Short History of the Philippines* (1969), O. D. Corpuz, *The Philippines* (1965) and the essays in F. R. Von der Mehden, *Religion and Nationalism in Southeast Asia: Burma, Indonesia, the Philippines* (1963) and M. E. Osborne, *Region of Revolt: focus on Southeast Asia* (1971). See also A. Jorgenson-Dahl, *Regional Organisation and Order in South-East Asia* (1982).

Indochina, and especially Vietnam, has attracted huge attention. For the earlier part of its history see D. G. Marr, *Vietnamese Anti-Colonialism, 1885–1925* (1971), M. E. Osborne, *The French Presence in Cochin China and Cambodia* (1969), W. J. Duiker *The Rise of Nationalism in Vietnam, 1900–1941* (1976) and E. J. Hammer, *The Struggle for Indochina*, 1940–55 (1966). J. Buttinger, *Vietnam: a dragon embattled: Vol. I, From Colonialism to the Vietminh; Vol. II, Vietnam at War* (1967) is a major narrative history, while R. B. Smith, *An International History of the Vietnam War: Vol. I, Revolution versus Containment, Vol. II, The Struggle for South East Asia, 1961–65* (1983–5) are the first two volumes of four placing the war in an international context; for a crucial episode, see J. Cable, *The Geneva Conference of 1954 on Indochina* (1986). A. Short, *The Origins of the Vietnam War* (1989) is a useful modern summary, see also the chapter in J. Dunn, *Modern Revolutions* (2nd edn., 1988). The dynamics of the communist insurrection are discussed in R. Smith, *Vietnam and the West* (1968), P. J. Honey, *Genesis of Tragedy: the historical background to the Vietnam War* (1968), J. M. McAlister, *Vietnam: the origins of revolution* (1969), and D. J. Duncanson, *Government and Revolution in Vietnam* (1968). The peasant origins of the war against the colonial powers is exemplified in J. Race, *War Comes to Long An: revolutionary conflict in a Vietnamese province* (1972). For Ho Chi-minh, see J. Lacouture, *Ho Chi-minh: a political biography* (1968) and H. Tinkner, *Men who Overturned Empires: Fighters, Dreamers and Schemers* (1987). North Vietnam's relations with other power are considered in P. J. Honey, *Communism in North Vietnam: its role in the Sino-Soviet Dispute* (1963). The history of Cambodia has been less well treated than Vietnam, but see M. Leifer, *Cambodia: the search for security* (1967).

China

L. Bianco, *Origins of the Chinese Revolution, 1915–49* (1972), C. P. Fitzgerald, *The Birth of Communist China* (1964), J. E. Shendan, *China in Disintegration: the republic era in Chinese History, 1912–1949* (1976) and J. Chesnaux, C. Barbier and M. C. Bergere, *China from the 1911 Revolution to Liberation* (1978) deal with the pre-Communist regime. J. Chesnaux, *Peasant Revolts in China, 1840–1949* (1973) and C. A. Johnson, *Peasant Nationalism and Communist Power: the emergence of revolutionary China, 1937–1945* (1962) look at the dynamics of peasant protests; see also R. H. Myers, *The Chinese Peasant Economy: Agricultural Development in Hopei and Shantung, 1890–1949* (1970). Chow Tse-tung, *The May Fourth Movement: intellectual revolution in modern China* (1960) looks at the earlier reform movement, and H. Z. Schiffrin, *Sun Yat-sen and the Origins of the Chinese Revolution* (1970) and C. M. Wilbur, *Sun Yat-sen: frustrated patriot* (1976) discuss its most famous leader. See also on the origins of the communists J. Chesnaux, *The Chinese Labor Movement, 1919–27* (1968) and A. Dirlik, *The Origins of the Communist Party of China* (1989). The ideologies contending for power in China are considered in J. B. Grieder, *Hu Shih and the Chinese Renaissance: liberalism in the Chinese Revolution, 1917–37*

(1970) and M. Meisner, *Li Ta-chao and the Origins of Chinese Marxism* (1967). For Mao, see S. R. Schram, *Mao Tse-tung* (1966) and *The Political Thought of Mao Tse-tung* (1969), B. J. Schwartz, *Chinese Communism and the Rise of Mao* (1967), H. H. Salisbury, *The Long March* (1985), P. Carter, *Mao* (1976), S. Uhalley, *Mao Tse-tung: a critical biography* (1975), H. Suyin, *Wind in the Tower: Mao Tse-tung and Chinese Revolution, 1949–1975* (1976), and L. W. Pye, *Mao Tse-tung: the man in the leader* (1976). W. Hinton, *Fanshen: a documentary of revolution in a Chinese village* (2nd edn., 1972), J. Chen, *A Year in Upper Felicity: life in a Chinese village during the Cultural Revolution* (1973) and, Ch'ing K'un Yang, *A Chinese Village in early Communist Transition* (1959) are good studies 'on the ground' of village life at different phases after the revolution. A. Eckstein, *China's Economic Revolution* (1977), N. R. Chen and W. Galenson, *The Chinese Economy under Communism* (1969) and D. H. Perkins (ed.), *China's Economy in Historical Perspective* (1975) examine the economy, while the workings of the regime are considered in D. J. Waller, *The Government and Politics of Communist China* (1973) and J. Domes, *The Internal Politics of China, 1949–72* (1973). The People's Army is considered in J. Gettings, *The Role of the Chinese Army* (1967), while J. W. Lewis, *Party Leadership and Revolutionary Power in China* (1970) and J. M. H. Lindbeck (ed.), *China: Management of a Revolutionary Society* (1971) give some insight into the dynamics of party leadership. J. Myrdal and G. Kessle, *China: the Revolution Continued* (1971) give some insight into the cultural revolution. For China's foreign relations see M. B. Jansen, *Japan and China: from war to peace, 1894–1972* (1975), W. Gungwu, *China and the World since 1949* (1977), and J. Gittings, *The World and China, 1922–1972* (1974). Russia's relationship with China is examined in O. E. Clubb, *China and Russia: the 'Great Game'* (1971), W. E. Griffith, *The Sino-Soviet Rift* (1964), D. Zagoria, *The Sino-Soviet Conflict, 1956–61* (1961) and D. Floyd, *Mao against Kruschev: a short history of the Sino-Soviet Conflict* (1964). For relations with the United States, see J. K. Fairbank, *The United States and China* (1971). The impact of the Korean involvement is discussed in A. L. George, *The Chinese Communist Army in Action: the Korean War and its aftermath* (1967) and see also P. Van Ness, *Revolution and Chinese Foreign Policy: Peking's Support for Wars of National Liberation* (1970).

Japan

There is a good modern survey in J. E. Hunter, *The Emergence of Modern Japan: an introductory history since 1853* (1989), but see also W. G. Beasley, *The Modern History of Japan* (1963) and R. S. Storry, *A History of Modern Japan* (1960). On the economic development of modern Japan see G. C. Allen, *A Short Economic History of Japan, 1867–1937; with a supplementary chapter on economic recovery and expansion, 1945–1970* (3rd edn., 1972), W. W. Lockwood, (ed.), *The State and economic Enterprise in Modern Japan* (1965) and on the earlier history, *The Economic Development of Japan: growth and structural change, 1868–1938* (1954), B. K. Marshall, *Capitalism and Nationalism in Prewar Japan: the ideology of the business elite, 1868–1941* (1967) and J. W. Morley (ed.), *Dilemmas of Growth in*

Prewar Japan (1971). A critical view of Japanese economic impact in
Asia is contained in J. Halliday and G. McCormack, *Japanese
Imperialism Today: 'Co-prosperity in Greater East Asia'* (1973). C.
Nakane, *Japanese Society* (1970) has some useful themes, see also S.
Watanabe, *The Peasant Soul of Japan* (1988), P. Lehmann, *The Roots
of Modern Japan* (1982), and on the particular forms Japanese society
took in the first half of this century see R. J. Smethurst, *A Social
Basis for Prewar Japanese Militarism: the army and the rural
community* (1974), T. C. Smith, *The Agrarian Origins of Modern Japan*
(1959), T. R. H. Havens, *Farm and Nation in Modern Japan: agrarian
nationalism, 1870–1940* (1974) and R. Storry, *The Double Patriots: a
study of Japanese Nationalism* (2nd edn., 1973). R. A. Scalapino,
*Democracy and the Party Movement in Japan: the failure of the first
attempt* (1953) examines political development, see also R. A.
Scalapino and J. Masumi, *Parties and Politics in Contemporary Japan*
(1962). Two recent studies examine the life of the emperor, E. Behr,
Hirohito (1989) and E. P. Hoyt, *Hirohito* (1989). Japanese foreign
relations are examined in I. Nish, *Japanese Foreign Policy, 1860–1942*
(1977) and M. B. Jansen, *Japan and China: From War to Peace,
1894–1972* (1975). A. Iriye, *After Imperialism: the search for a new
order in the Far East, 1921–1931* (1955) and *Across the Pacific: an
inner history of American-East Asian Relations* (1967), and J. B.
Crowley, *Japan's Quest for Autonomy, 1930–1938* (1966) examine the
inter-war, years. Japan's search for a secure area of economic control
and its disastrous consequences are examined in F. C. Jones, *Japan's
New Order in East Asia: its rise and fall, 1937–1945* (1954). D. Borg
and S. Okamoto (eds.), *Pearl Harbour as History: Japanese-American
relations, 1931–41* (1973) examines the background to the pivotal
event. The study by A. Iriye, *The Origins of the Second World War in
Asia and the Pacific* (1987) now provides a good overview of the
origins of the war. M. E. Weinstein, *Japan's Post-War Defence Policy,
1947–1968* (1971) examines the peaceful role of Japan in the post-war
world, while E. O. Reischauer, *The United States and Japan* (3rd edn.,
1965) and A. Iriye and W. I. Cohen (eds.), *The United States and
Japan in the Post-War World* (1989) deal with the post-war character
of Japanese-American relations. K. Van Wolferen, *The Enigma of
Japanese Power* (1989) poses some questions about Japan's role as
an economic superpower with little military power.

vi Australasia

C. Hartley Grattan, *The South-West Pacific since 1900* (1963) offers a
comprehensive history of the region. On the Pacific islands, see W. P.
Morrell, *The Great Powers in the Pacific* (1965) and M. R. Peattie,
Nanyo: the Rise and Fall of the Japanese in Micronesia, 1883–1945
(1988). For Australia itself, see F. K. Crowley (ed.), *A New History of
Australia* (1974), F. K. Crowley, *Modern Australia in Documents,
1901–1970* (2 vols, 1973) and R. Ward, *The History of Australia: The
Twentieth Century, 1901–1975* (1978). Though somewhat older, G.
Greenwood (ed.), *Australia: A Social and Political History* (1955) is still
helpful, as on the early twentieth century are W. K. Hancock, *Australia.*
(1930) and W. F. Whyte, *William Morris Hughes: His Life and Times*

(1956). R. Ward, *Australia* (1965) and D. Pike, *Australia: the quiet continent* (1962) are also helpful one-volume studies.

On inter-war Australia, see J. Mackinolty (ed.), *The Wasted Years: Australia's Great Depression* (1982), while the impact of the Second World War is discussed in P. Hasluck, *The Government and the People, 1942–1945* (1970). Post-war developments are considered in D. Horner, *The Lucky Country: Australia in the Sixties* (2nd edn., 1966) and J. D. B. Miller, *Australia* (1966). Australia's involvement in the region is considered in D. M. Horner, *High Command: Australia and Allied Strategy, 1939–1945* (1983) and P. King (ed.), *Australia's Vietnam: Australia in the Second Indo-China War* (1983).

For New Zealand, see K. Sinclair, *A History of New Zealand* (1959) and J. Rowe and M. Rowe, *New Zealand* (1967). Also useful are W. H. Oliver, *The Story of New Zealand* (1960), W. P. Morrell and D. O. W. Hall, *A History of New Zealand Life* (1957) and H. G. Miller, *New Zealand* (1950). Particular aspects of New Zealand's history are considered in P. Baker, *King and Country Call: New Zealanders, Conscription and the Great War* (1989), J. B. Condliffe, *New Zealand in the Making* (2nd edn., 1959), mainly dealing with economic and social history, and his *The Welfare State in New Zealand* (1959). On the Second World War see F. L. W. Wood, *The New Zealand People at War* (1958).

vii   The Americas

There are numerous histories of the United States, but amongst the most helpful introductions are H. Brogan, *The Longman History of the United States of America* (1986) and M. A. Jones, *The Limits of Liberty: American History, 1607–1980* (1983). See also A. Nevins and H. S. Commager, *America: The Story of a Free People* (1976), S. E. Morrison, H. S. Commager and W. Leuchtenburg, *A Concise History of the American Republic* (1969) and Carl Degler, *Out of the Past* (3rd edn., 1984). For the twentieth century, R. Hofstadter, *The Age of Reform: Bryan to F. D. R.* (1955) covers the period from the end of the nineteenth century to the Second World War, while on the inter-war years, see W. E. Leuchtenburg, *The Perils of Prosperity* (1958) and *Franklin Roosevelt and the New Deal* (1963). For the period after the Second World War see A. L. Hamby, *The Imperial Years: the United States since 1939* (1976).

On particular themes and topics in North American history see. C. Vann Woodward, *The Strange Career of Jim Crow* (3rd edn., 1974) on the history of racial segregation, and on the growth of the cities C. N. Glaab and A. T. Brown, *A History of Urban America* (1976); M. A. Jones, *American Immigration* (1960) deals with one of the major themes of the early years of twentieth century America. H. Pelling, *American Labour* (1960) examines the organized working class, while for American social history in general see W. Issel, *Social Change in the United States, 1945–1983* (1985). The broad sweep of America's foreign relations is discussed in R. D. Schulzinger, *American*

Diplomacy in the Twentieth Century (1984), S. Ambrose, *Rise to Globalism: American Foreign Policy, 1938–80* (2nd edn., 1981) and L. C. Gardner, *Covenant with Power: America and the world order from Wilson to Reagan* (1984).

For the West Indies and Caribbean region, see J. H. Parry and P. M. Sherlock, *A Short History of the West Indies* (3rd: edn., 1960) and J. R. Ward, *Poverty and Progress in the Caribbean, 1800–1960* (1985). On Latin America, see, T. Skidmore and P. Smith, *Modern Latin America* (2nd edn., 1989); L. Bethell, *The Cambridge History of Latin America* (1986), and G. Pendle, *A History of Latin America* (1967) for general histories. Books which examine some of the themes dominating Latin American history are P. Calvert, *Latin America: internal conflict and international peace* (1969), S. and B. Stein, *The Colonial Heritage of Latin America: essays on economic dependence in perspective* (1970) and C. Furtado, *Economic Development of Latin America: historical background and contemporary problems* (2nd edn., 1976). The recent collection by E. P. Archetti, P. Cammack, and B. Roberts (eds.), *Latin America* (1987) surveys some major common elements in the history of the continent. Also useful are J. Cockcroft, et al, *Dependence and Underdevelopment: Latin America's political economy* (1972), I. L. Horowitz, *Radicalism in Latin America* (1969), and J. J. Johnson, *Latin America in Caricature* (1980).
Specific issues are considered in J. J. Johnson, *The Military and Society in Latin America* (1964) and A. Stepan, *The Military in Politics* (1971), W. S. Stokes, *Latin American Politics* (1959), J. L. Mecham, *Church and State in Latin America: a history of politico-ecclesiastical relations* (rev. edn., 1966), H. A. Landsberger (ed.) *The Church and Social Change in Latin America* (1970), F. C. Turner, *Catholicism and Political Development in Latin America* (1971), H. A. Landsberger (ed.), *Latin American Peasant Movements* (1969), A. Pearce, *The Latin American Peasant* (1975), L. E. Aguilar (ed.), *Marxism in Latin America* (1969), J. Kohl and J. Litt, *Urban Guerrilla Warfare in Latin America* (1973). The relations of Latin America with its northern neighbour are the subject of S. P. Bemis, *The Latin American Policy of the United States: an historical interpretation* (1943), G. Connell-Smith, *The Inter-American System* (1966) and C. Blasier, *The Hovering Giant* (1976).

The Mexican Revolution

On the social and economic background see O. Lewis, *Pedro Martinez: a Mexican peasant and his family* (1967), F. Chevalier, *Land and Society in Colonial Mexico: the Great Hacienda* (2nd edn., 1970), and P. Friedrich, *Agrarian Revolt in a Mexican Village* (2nd edn., 1970). C. C. Cumberland, *Mexico: the struggle for modernity* (2nd edn., 1968) is also useful as introduction, but see the modern study by A. Knight, *The Mexican Revolution* (1987) and J. Womack Jr., *Zapata and the Mexican Revolution* (1969). James. D. Cockcroft, *Intellectual Precursors of the Mexican Revolution, 1900–13* (1968) and E. R. Wolf, *Peasant Wars of the Twentieth Century* (1969) provide context. The other personalities involved are examined in S. R. Ross, *F. I. Madero, Apostle of Mexican Democracy* (1955), C. Beals, *Porfirio*

Diaz: Dictator of Mexico (1932), and C. C. Cumberland, *Mexican Revolution: Genesis under Madero* (1974). The effects of the Revolution are discussed in C. W. Reynolds, *The Mexican Economy: twentieth century structure and growth* (1970), F. Tannenbaum, *Peace by Revolution: Mexico after 1910* (2nd edn., 1966), H. F. Cline, *Mexico: revolution to evolution, 1940–1960* (1962), S. R. Ross, *Is the Mexican Revolution Dead?* (2nd edn., 1966); P. G. Casanova, *Democracy in Mexico* (2nd edn., 1970), F. Chevalier, 'The *Ejido* and Political Stability in Mexico', in Claudio Veliz (ed.), *The Politics of Conformity in Latin America* (1967), R. Carr, 'Mexican Agrarian Reform, 1910–60' in E. L. Jones and S. J. Woolf (eds.), *Agrarian Change and Economic Development: the Historical Problems* (1969), and R. Vernon, *The Dilemma of Mexico's Development* (1963).

The United States and the First World War

See for introduction, L. C. Gardner, *Imperial America: United States foreign policy since 1898* (1984) and F. R. Dulles, *America's Rise to World Power (1955)*. A. S. Link, *Woodrow Wilson and the Progressive Era* (1954) is a multi-volume work, but a shorter treatment can be found in R. H. Farrell, *Woodrow Wilson and World War I, 1917–1921* (1985). A. S. Link, *Wilson the Diplomatist: a look at his major foreign policies* (1957) summarizes his views and has been revised recently as *Woodrow Wilson: revolution, war and peace* (1979), also available is A. S. Link, *Woodrow Wilson: a brief biography* (1963) and A. S. Link (ed.), *Woodrow Wilson and a Revolutionary World: 1913–1921* (1982). T. A. Bailey, *Wilson and the Lost Peace* (1944) is critical, while P. Birdsall, *Versailles Twenty Years After* (1941) is more sympathetic to the problems of peace-making. On the crucial rejection of the League by the Senate, see also R. J. Bartlett, *The League to Enforce Peace* (1944) and T. A. Bailey, *Woodrow Wilson and the Great Betrayal* (1945). The effect of the war on American society is considered in D.M. Kennedy, *Over Here: the First World War and American Society* (1980).

The Republican era

See J. D. Hicks, *Republican Ascendency: 1921–1933* (1960), F. Allen, *Only Yesterday: an informal history of the 1920s* (1931), A. M. Schlesinger, *The Crisis of the Old Order* (1957) and D. H. Burner, *The Politics of Provincialism: the Democrats in transition, 1918–1932* (1968). See also W. E. Leuchtenburg, *The Perils of Prosperity: 1914–32* (1958) and D. M. Smith, *The Great Departure: The United States and the Search for a Modern Order: A history of the American people and their institutions, 1917–1933* (1979). The overall drift of foreign policy is considered in J. B. Duroselle, *From Wilson to Roosevelt: foreign policy of the United States* (1963).
Important social issues are considered in A. Sinclair, *Prohibition* (1962) and K. Allsopp, *The Bootleggers* (1967). The black migration from the south is considered in J. Hope Franklin, *From Slavery to Freedom: the history of American Negroes* (5th edn., 1980) and on particular cities see G. Osofsky, *Harlem: the making of ghetto* (1966) and A. Spear, *Black Chicago* (1967); see also G. Myrdal, *An American*

Dilemma (1962), H. Cayton and St. Clair Drake, *Black Metropolis* (1962), and N. I. Huggins, M. Kilson, and A. Fox, *Key Issues in the Afro-American Experience, Vol. 2* (1971). The reaction is considered in D. Chalmers, *Hooded Americanism* (1965) and K. T. Jackson, *The Ku Klux Klan in the City, 1915–1925* (1967). Organized labour is considered in H. Pelling, *American Labour* (1960), J. G. Rayback, *History of American Labour* (1966), J. Wienstein, *The Decline of Socialism in America* (1967). P. Taft, *Organised Labour in American History* (1964), *The AF of L in the Time of Gompers* (1959) and *The AF of L From the Death of Gompers Till the Merger* (1959).

For the politics of the era up to the Great Crash see W. A. White, *A Puritan in Babylon* (1938), on Coolidge and on Hoover the essay in R. Hofstadter, *The American Political Tradition* (1967) and M. L. Fausold *The Presidency of Herbert C. Hoover* (1985). On the crash itself, see J. K. Galbraith, *The Great Crash, 1929* (1955), but on the economy in general see J. Potter, *The American Economy between the World Wars* (rev. edn., 1985).

Roosevelt and the New Deal

A. J. Badger, *The New Deal* (1987), P. Conkin, *The New Deal* (1968) and M. Simpson, *Franklin D. Roosevelt* (1989) are useful for introduction; see also W. E. Leuchtenburg, *Franklin Roosevelt and the New Deal* (1963) and A. M. Schlesinger, *The Age of Roosevelt* (1956–60). Other political figures of the New Deal era are considered in T. H. Williams, *Huey Long* (1969) and D. H. Bennet, *Demagogues in the Depression* (1969). Important sources are R. Moley, *After Seven Years* (1939) an autobiography by one of Roosevelt's advisers, G. Rexford Tugwell, *The Battle for Democracy* (1935), from another aide, and F. Perking, *The Roosevelt I Knew* (1947). The atmosphere of the era is captured brilliantly in the oral history volume of Studs Terkel, *Hard Times* (1970) and J. Steinbeck's *The Grapes of Wrath* (1939). For the institutions and effects of the New Deal see R. Jackson, *The Struggle for Judicial Supremacy* (1938), Harold Ickes, *Back to Work: the story of the PWA* (1935) and D. Lilienthal, *TVA: democracy on the march* (1944). Organized labour is considered in the essay on the United States by P. Renshaw in S. Salter and J. Stevenson (eds.), *The Working Class and Politics in Europe and America, 1929–1945* (1990), see also M. Derber and E. Young (eds.), *Labor and the New Deal* (1961), W. Galenson, *The CIO Challenge to the AFL* (1960), and W. R. Brock, *Welfare, Democracy and the New Deal* (1989). Amongst collections there is a useful essay on FDR in R. Hofstadter, *The American Political Tradition* (1967) and E. C. Rozwene, *The New Deal: Revolution or Evolution* (1959) and A. H. Cope and F. Krinsky (eds.), *Franklin Roosevelt and the Supreme Court* (1964).

On foreign policy, see H. Feis, *The Road to Pearl Harbour* (1953), the relevant chapter in L. C. Gardner, *Imperial America* (1973), R. Dallek, *Franklin D. Roosevelt and American Foreign Policy, 1932–1945* (1972), R. A. Divine, *The Reluctant Belligerent: American entry into World War II* (1968), S. Adler, *The Uncertain Giant, American Foreign Policy, 1921–41* (1965), D. Borg and S. Okameto, *Pearl Harbour as History: Japanese-American relations, 1931–1941* (1973), and A. Iriye, *The Origins of the Second World War in Asia and the Pacific* (1987).

The Second World War and the Cold War

S. E. Ambrose, *Rise to Globalism: American foreign policy, 1938–1980* (rev.edn., 1980) takes the story through from the pre-war phase, while H. Feis, *Churchill, Roosevelt and Stalin* (1967) examines the Grand Alliance. D. B. Rees, *The Age of Containment: the Cold War, 1945–1965* (1967), H. Feis, *From Trust to Terror, the onset of the Cold War, 1945–1950* (1970), M. Sherwin, *A World Destroyed: the atomic bomb and the Grand Alliance* (1975), G. Alperoritz, *Atomic Diplomacy: Hiroshima and Potsdam* (2nd edn., 1985) and L. B. Davis, *The Cold War Begins: Soviet-American conflict in East Europe* (1974) deal with the early phases of the dispute between the Alliance partners. W. LaFeber, *America in the Cold War: twenty years of revolutions and response, 1947–1967* (1969) and *America, Russia and the Cold War, 1945–1971* (3rd edn., 1976), D. Horowitz, *From Yalta to Vietnam: American foreign policy in the Cold War* (rev. edn., 1969) and R. Douglas, *From War to Cold War, 1942–48* (1981) are all useful. M. McCauley, *The Origins of the Cold War* (1983) and J. Smith, *The Cold War, 1945–65* (1989) are two guides to the increasingly complex debate, now highlighted in D. Carlton and H. M. Levine, *The Cold War Debated* (1988). The impact of anti-communism in America is discussed in D. Caute, *The Great Fear: the anti-communist purge under Truman and Eisenhower* (1978) and R. Divide, *Eisenhower and the Cold War* (1981). America's policy towards Europe is considered in J. Gimble, *The Origins of the Marshall Plan* (1976), M. J. Hogan, *The Marshall Plan: America, Britain and the reconstruction of Western Europe, 1947–1952* (1988), A. Grosser, *The Western Alliance: European-American relations since 1945* (1980), R. Morgan, *The United States and West Germany* (1974), R. Osgood, *NATO: the entangling Alliance* (1962), and H. Jones, *A New Kind Of War: America's global strategy and the Truman Doctrine in Greece* (1989). The later phase of the Cold War is considered in L. Freedman, *The Evolution of Nuclear Strategy* (1981), F. Halliday, *The Making of the New Cold War (1983)*, and H. M. Levine and D. Carlton, *The Nuclear Arms Race Debated (1986)*.

Particular areas are considered in E. J. Hammer, *The Struggle for Indo-China, 1940–1955* (1966), D. F. Fleming, *America's Role in Asia* (1969), S. Klebanoff, *Middle East Oil and US Foreign Policy: with special reference to the US energy crisis* (1974), G. Lenczowski, *Russia and the West in Iran, 1918–1948: a study in big power rivalry* (1968), W. R. Polk, *The United States and The Arab World* (rev.edn., 1969), J. Cotler and R. Fagan, *Latin America and the United States; the changing political realities* (1974), F. Parkinson, *Latin America, the Cold War and the World Powers, 1945–1973: a study in diplomatic history* (1974), R. Emerson, *Africa and United States Policy* (1967), J. Mayall, *Africa: the Cold War and After* (1971), E. O. Reischauer, *The United States and Japan* (3rd edn., 1965), and N. Safran, *The United States and Israel* (1963).

On particular crises, see on Korea, C. A. MacDonald, *Korea: the war before Vietnam* (1986), D. Rees, *Korea: the limited war* (1970) and P. Lowe, *The Origins of the Korean War* (1986). The American relationship with Cuba is considered in L. D. Langley, *Cuban Policy of*

the United States: a brief history (1968), R. F. Smith, The United
States and Cuba: business and diplomacy, 1917–1960 (1961), H. M.
Pachter, Collision Course: the Cuban Missile Crisis and coexistence
(1963), E. Abel, The Missiles of October: the story of the Cuban
Missile Crisis (1966), and G. Allison, Essence of Decision: explaining
the Cuban Missile Crisis (1971). For a recent overview of the
Cuban-US relationship, see M. H. Morley, Imperial State and
Revolution: the United States and Cuba, 1952–1986 (1987).

America and the Vietnam War

R. B. Smith, An International History of the Vietnam War, vol. I,
1955–61 Vol. II, 1961–5 (1983–5) is a major treatment of the war in
global context. See also A. Short, The Origins of the Vietnam War
(1989). A. Buhite, The Dynamics of World Power: a documentary
history of US foreign policy, 1945–73, vol. 4 (1973) has documents,
see also D. Ellsberg, The Pentagon Papers (1972) and M. E. Gettleman
(ed.), Vietnam and America: a documentary history (1985). The best
general treatments are G. C. Herruig, America's Longest War (1979)
and S. Karnow, Vietnam. A History (1984). The history of American
involvement is also viewed in Ambrose, Rise to Globalism (see
above), J. W. Spanier, American Foreign Policy since World War II
(10th rev. edn., 1985) and M. Berkowitz, et al., The US Foreign Policy
Process and Context; from the Marshall Plan to Vietnam (1985), and
A. F. Krepinevich, The Army and Vietnam (1986). F. Fitzgerald, Fire in
the Lake, the Vietnamese and the Americans in Vietnam (1972)
discusses the American role in Vietnam. G. Kahin and J. W. Lewis,
The United States in Vietnam (2nd edn., 1975) and J. L. Horowitz,
Ideology and Utopia in the United States, 1956–76 (1977) discusses
the implications of the war for America, as does A. Schlesinger, The
Bitter Heritage; Vietnam and American democracy (1966) and G.
Kolko, Anatomy of a War: Vietnam, the US and modern historical
experience (1986). The most prominent casualty of the war is
discussed in H. Y. Schandler, The Unmaking of a President: Lyndon
Johnson and Vietnam (1977), while the repercussions on the
campuses is considered in James A. Michener, Kent State: what
happened and why (1971), J. Axelrod et al., Search for Relevance: the
campus in crisis (1969), J. and S. Erlich (eds.), Student Power,
Participation and Revolution (1970), and Foster and D. Long (eds.),
Protest! Student Activism in America (1970).

American domestic politics since 1945

Some of the broad themes are considered in M. Marable, Race,
Reform and Rebellion: the second reconstruction in Black America,
1945–1982 (1984), R. Gatlin, American Women since 1945 (1987), W.
Issel, Social Change in the United States, 1945–1983 (1985), and K.
Fox, Metropolitan America: urban life and urban policy in the United
States, 1940–80 (1985).
On the Truman era, see D. R. McCloy, The Presidency of Harry S.
Truman (1986) and on McCarthyism, D. Caute, The Great Fear: the
anti-communist purge under Truman and Eisenhower (1978); R. M.
Freeland, The Truman Doctrine and the Origins of McCarthyism (2nd

edn., 1985) and R. M. Freid, *Men Against McCarthy* (1976). On the
Senator himself, see R. Rovere, *Senator Joe McCarthy* (1959). The
Truman and Eisenhower years are considered together in W. O'Neill,
American High: the years of confidence, 1945–60 (1987). On
Eisenhower, see E. Richardson, *The Presidency of Dwight Eisenhower*:
(1979) and R. F. Burk, *Dwight D. Eisenhower: hero and politician*
(1987). On Civil Rights, see T. Branch, *Parting the Waters* (1989) and
D. Garrow, *Bearing the Cross* (1987).
The Kennedy period is examined in T. C. Sorensen, *Kennedy* (1965)
and *The Kennedy Legacy* (1969), and C. M. Brauer, *John F. Kennedy
and the Second Reconstruction* (1977); see also J. Schlesinger, *Robert
Kennedy and His Times* (1978).
On Lyndon Johnson, see H. Y. Schandler, *The Unmaking of a
President* (1977) and P. K. Conkin, *Big Daddy from the Pedernales,
Lyndon Baines Johnson* (1987). The Ford and Nixon Presidencies are
discussed in A. J. Reichley, *Conservatives in an Age of Change*
(1987); see also R. Nixon, *The Memoirs of Richard Nixon* (1978). Two
books which examine changes in American political organization and
thought are A. Ware, *The Breakdown of Democratic Party
Organisation, 1940–80* (1988) and G. Peele, *Revival and Reaction: the
Right in contemporary America* (1984).

Canada

K. McNaught, *The Pelican History of Canada* (rev. edn., 1982) is an
up-to-date introduction. D. Creighton, *Dominion of the North* (1958),
G. S. Graham, *A Concise History of Canada* (1968) and J. M. Bliss
(ed.), *Canadian History in Documents, 1763–1966* are also useful.
J. M. S. Careless and R. Craig-Brown (eds.), *The Canadians,
1867–1967* (1967) is a collaborative work dealing with Canadian history
decade by decade and with a series of thematic chapters, to conclude.
The development of the once separate province of Newfoundland is
considered in R. A. Mackay (ed.), *Newfoundland: economic,
diplomatic and strategic studies* (1946) and St. J. Chadwick,
Newfoundland: island into Province (1967). M. Wade, *The French
Canadians, 1760–1967* (rev. edn., 1968) examines the background to
the tension between French Canada and the rest of the country. See
also M. Rioux and Y. Martin (eds.), *French Canadian Society* (1964),
R. Cook, *Canada and the French-Canadian Question* (1966), E. M.
Corbett, *Quebec confronts Canada* (1967), R. Jonas, *Community in
Crisis: French Canadian nationalism in perspective* (1967), T. Sloan,
Quebec: the not-so-quiet revolution (1965), and P. E. Trudeau,
Federalism and the French Canadians (1968).
On the economy see R. E. Caves and R. M. Holton, *The Canadian
Economy: prospect and retrospect* (1959), H. G. Johnson, *The
Canadian quandary: economic problems and policies* (1963), and
H. G. J. Aitken, *American Capital and Canadian Resources* (1961).
The relationship of Canada with the United States and her place in
world affairs is considered in J. S. Dickey (ed.), *The United States and
Canada* (1964), J. K. Gordon (ed.), *Canada's role as a middle power*
(1966), W. L. Gordon, *A Choice for Canada: independence or colonial
status* (1966), P. V. Lyon, *The Policy Question: a critical appraisal of
Canada's role in world affairs* (1963) and L. T. Marchant, *Neighbours
taken for granted: Canada and the United States* (1966).

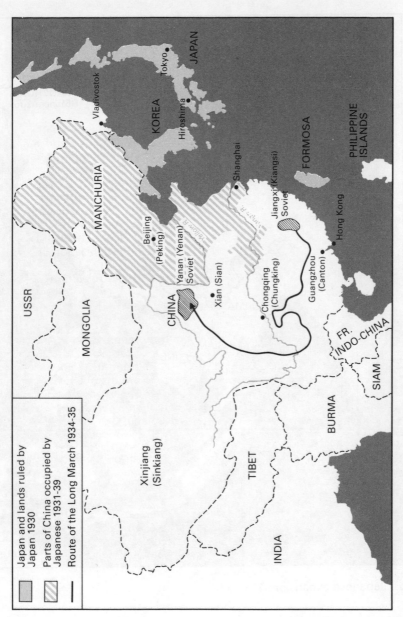

4   China and the Chinese Revolution

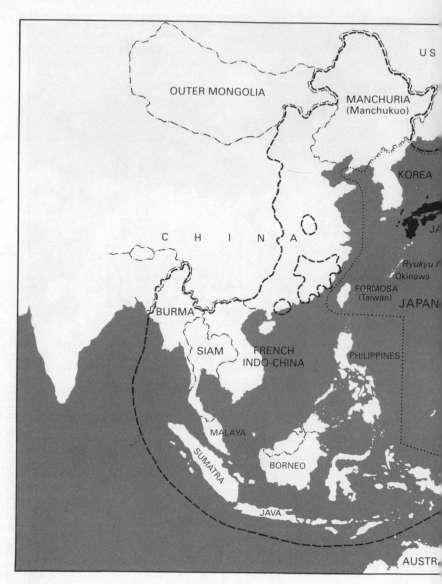

5   Japanese expansion, 1931–45

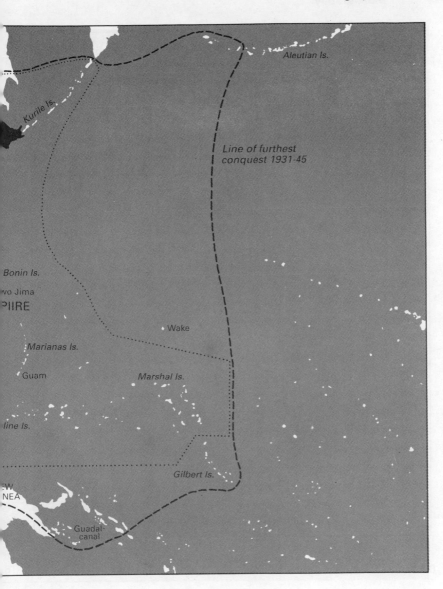

Aleutian Is.

Kurile Is.

Line of furthest
conquest 1931-45

Bonin Is.

wo Jima

PIIRE

Wake

Marianas Is.

Guam

Marshal Is.

line Is.

Gilbert Is.

EW
NEA

Guadal-
canal

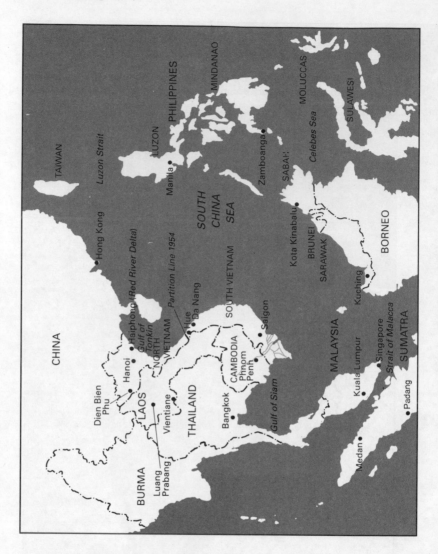

6   South East Asia in the 1960s

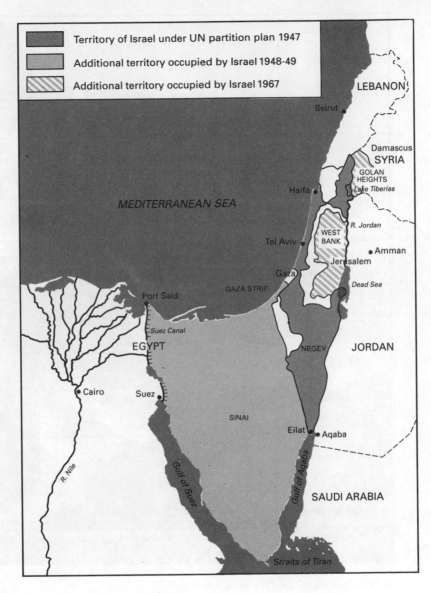

Territory of Israel under UN partition plan 1947

Additional territory occupied by Israel 1948-49

Additional territory occupied by Israel 1967

LEBANON

Beirut

Damascus
SYRIA
GOLAN
HEIGHTS
Lake Tiberias

Haifa

MEDITERRANEAN SEA

R. Jordan
WEST
BANK

Tel Aviv

Amman

Jerusalem

Gaza

Dead Sea

GAZA STRIP

Port Said

Suez Canal

NEGEV   JORDAN

EGYPT

Cairo

Suez

SINAI

R. Nile

Gulf of Suez

Eilat   Aqaba

Gulf of Aqaba

SAUDI ARABIA

Straits of Tiran

7   Israel and her neighbours

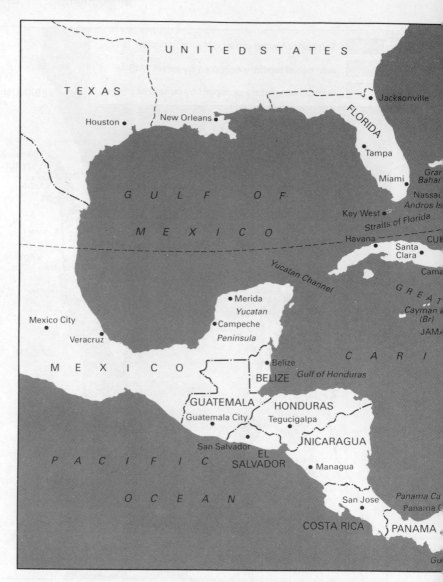

8 The Caribbean and Central America

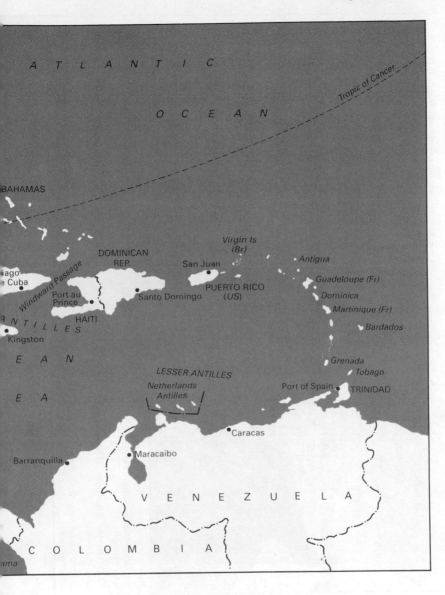

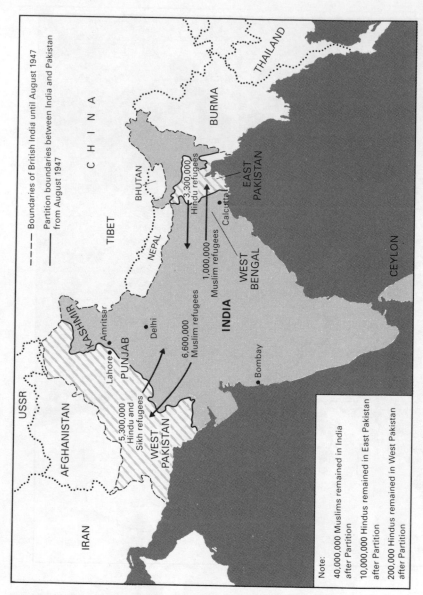

Boundaries of British India until August 1947

Partition boundaries between India and Pakistan from August 1947

CHINA

TIBET

BHUTAN

NEPAL

BURMA

THAILAND

3,300,000 Hindu refugees

EAST PAKISTAN

Calcutta

1,000,000 Muslim refugees

WEST BENGAL

KASHMIR

Amritsar

Lahore

PUNJAB

Delhi

INDIA

6,600,000 Muslim refugees

5,300,000 Hindu and Sikh refugees

WEST PAKISTAN

Bombay

CEYLON

USSR

AFGHANISTAN

IRAN

Note:
40,000,000 Muslims remained in India after Partition

10,000,000 Hindus remained in East Pakistan after Partition

200,000 Hindus remained in West Pakistan after Partition

9 India and Pakistan after Partition, 1947

Territory annexed by USSR 1939-40, and reincorporated in USSR in 1945

Former German and Czechoslovak territory annexed by USSR IN 1945

States in which Communist regimes came to power between 1945 and 1948

The 'Iron Curtain' in 1955

FINLAND

Vyborg

Tallinn • Leningrad

ESTONIA

Pskov

SWEDEN

Riga

LATVIA

LITHUANIA

Königsberg • Stettin   Kaunas • Vilnius

GDR since 1949   Minsk

Bremen   Berlin   SOVIET UNION

annexed by Poland from Germany   Bialystok

Poznan   Warsaw   Pinsk

Bonn   SILESIA

Erfurt   Dresden   POLAND

GFR

Nuremburg   Breslau   Cracow   Przemysl

Prague   Lvov   GALICIA

FRANCE   CZECHOSLOVAKIA

Munich   Uzhgorod   Chernovtsy

Vienna   BESSARABIA   Kishinyov

SWITZ.   AUSTRIA   Budapest   Jassy

Trieste   HUNGARY   ROMANIA

Belgrade   Bucharest

YUGOSLAVIA   BULGARIA

ITALY   Sofia

ALBANIA

GREECE   TURKEY

GFR: German Federal Republic (West Germany)
GDR: German Democratic Republic (East Germany)

10 The Soviet Union in Eastern Europe

Index